THE
CHURCHILL
DOCUMENTS

THE
CHURCHILL
DOCUMENTS
RANDOLPH S. CHURCHILL

VOLUME 1
YOUTH 1874–1896

Hillsdale College Press, Hillsdale, Michigan

Hillsdale College Press
33 East College Street
Hillsdale, Michigan 49242
www.hillsdale.edu

Originally published in 1967 by William Heinemann Ltd. in Great Britain and by Houghton Mifflin in the United States.

Printed in the United States of America

Printed and bound by Edwards Brothers, Ann Arbor, Michigan

Cover design by Hesseltine & DeMason, Ann Arbor, Michigan

THE CHURCHILL DOCUMENTS
Volume 1: *Youth, 1874–1896*

Library of Congress Control Number: 2006934101

ISBN 10: 0-916308-09-X
ISBN 13: 978-0-916308-09-4

First printing 2006

Contents

Note
to the New Edition

Winston Churchill's personal papers are among the most comprehensive ever assembled relating to the life and times of one man. They are so extensive that it was only possible to include in the narrative volumes of his biography a part of the relevant documents.

The Companion Volumes, now titled *The Churchill Documents*, were planned to run parallel with the narrative volumes, and with them to form a whole. When an extract or quotation appears in a narrative volume, the complete document appears in an accompanying volume of *The Churchill Documents*. Where space prevented the inclusion of a contemporary letter in the narrative volume, it is included in the document volume.

Here in the first two volumes of *The Churchill Documents*, Volume 1: *Youth, 1874–1896* and Volume 2: *Young Soldier, 1896–1901*, are set out all the documents relevant to *Winston S. Churchill—* Volume I: *Youth, 1874–1900*. Mention in this text of "Main Volume" refers to this first volume of the biography.

The chapter and page numbers for Volumes 1 and 2 of *The Churchill Documents* run consecutively through the two volumes. The index to both volumes appears in Volume 2.

Preface

AS I EXPLAINED in the Preface to Volume I of *Winston S. Churchill* this book served as the brief on which Volume I was written: it is also its companion. The two volumes into which this book is divided contain nearly all the letters which my father wrote during the first twenty-six years of his life which have been available to me: the vast majority of these are contained in his own papers, but others have been sent to me or tracked down and obtained from other sources. These volumes also contain the bulk of the relevant letters he received: also some correspondence concerning him which passed between other correspondents. Except where indicated, it should be assumed that the papers come from the Chartwell Trust.

I hope that these bulky companions have been presented in a way which will be serviceable to the reader and in particular to historians. They may perhaps be irritated that in many cases important letters lack an answer. The reader may rest assured that this has also been a matter of irritation to me. Every effort has been made to track down the missing links. It is hoped that the publication of these documents may prompt readers to search their files and supply me with missing details. I would then hope to include additional material that comes to light as an extra appendix in the succeeding Companion Volumes.

Very little material which has been published before has been included. Among this, though, are extracts of some important articles and speeches which it would be difficult for the reader to track down. The material is printed in sections with explanatory headings: the chapters or pages of the main book which they supplement and fortify are printed at the beginning of each section.

Short biographies similar to those in the main volume will be found at the beginning; other characters are explained in the footnotes. Styles of dates and addresses have been standardised: where they are not in the original, but can be ascertained, they are placed in square brackets, and where there is a doubt a question mark is added. As in the Main Volume, spelling and punctuation have for the most part been corrected, but in the case of Winston S. Churchill's the original spelling and punctuation are preserved until he comes to manhood at the age of 20, on the death of his father.

I wish once again to acknowledge my indebtedness to Her Majesty the Queen who graciously gave permission for me to have access to the Royal Archives and to use documents which are her copyright. I desire also to express my thanks to all who have made the papers in their charge available to me, and to all who have granted copyright permission. In some cases it has unfortunately not been possible to trace the holders of copyright, and I again beg them to accept my apologies.

The chief credit for editing these Companion Volumes goes to Mr Michael Wolff, who has been in charge of all the research of the Companion as well as the Main Volume. He has been helped in what has been an intricate as well as a laborious task by Mr Andrew Kerr and also by Mr Martin Mauthner. My thanks are also due to Miss Eileen Harryman, Archivist, Mrs Trevor Adams, Miss Alice Golding, Mrs Richard von Goetz, Mrs Martin Mauthner and Mrs Bettye Verran for their secretarial assistance.

Stour   RANDOLPH S. CHURCHILL
East Bergholt, Suffolk
31 March 1967

Short Biographies

of the

PRINCIPAL CHARACTERS

to be brought before the reader in this volume

AYLESFORD Heneage, 7th Earl of (1849–85); succeeded his father two days after his marriage to Edith (1844–97), third daughter of Colonel Thomas Peers Williams. They had two daughters. A son born to Lady Aylesford in Paris in 1881 was reputed to be the child of the Marquess of Blandford (qv). Aylesford, popularly known as Sporting Joe, was renowned for his lack of success on the Turf and for his violent disposition. He settled in Texas, where he was said to be popular with the cowboys and where he died of heart failure.

BALFOUR Arthur James (1848–1930); eldest son of James Maitland Balfour and Lady Blanche Cecil, second daughter of 2nd Marquess of Salisbury. Succeeded his uncle, 3rd Marquess of Salisbury (qv), as Prime Minister 1902–5 and leader of the Tory Party 1902–11. Conservative MP for Hertford 1874–85, for Manchester East 1885–1906, for City of London 1906–22. For a time a member with Lord Randolph Churchill of the Fourth Party. President of Local Government Board 1885–6; Secretary for Scotland 1886–7; Chief Secretary for Ireland 1887–91; Leader of the House and First Lord of the Treasury 1891–2, 1895–1905. Succeeded WSC as First Lord of the Admiralty 1915; Foreign Secretary 1916–19; Lord President of the Council 1919–22, 1925–9. Earl 1922.

BARING Hugo (1876–1949); sixth son of 1st Baron Revelstoke. Lieutenant 4th Hussars until his resignation 1898. Rejoined Army to serve in Boer War (severely wounded), and in First World War (wounded). Married 1905 Evelyn Harriet, widow of 2nd Baron Magheramorne, second daughter of 8th Earl of Shaftesbury.

BARNES Reginald Walter Ralph (1871–1946); son of Prebendary R. H. Barnes of Stoke Canon, near Exeter. Joined 4th Hussars 1890, adjutant

1896–1900. Served with Imperial Yeomanry in Boer War (wounded, DSO). Commanded 10th Hussars 1911. Major-General and KCB 1919.

BEACONSFIELD 1st Earl of—see DISRAELI.

BLANDFORD Albertha Frances Anne (Bertha), Marchioness of (1847–1932); sixth daughter of 1st Duke of Abercorn and Louisa Jane, daughter of 6th Duke of Bedford. She had seven brothers, and was one of seven sisters, all of whom married into the peerage. She married in 1869 George, Marquess of Blandford (qv), eldest son of 7th Duke of Marlborough (qv). This marriage was dissolved in 1883; the decree nisi was awarded five months before her husband succeeded to the dukedom, but was not made absolute until four months after. However, she preferred to retain the style of Marchioness of Blandford, though by 1896 she was one of five ladies then living who were or had been entitled to the style of Duchess of Marlborough. The others were Jane, widow of 6th Duke; Fanny, widow of 7th Duke; Lily, widow of 8th Duke; and Consuelo, wife of 9th Duke.

BLANDFORD George Charles, Marquess of (1844–92); eldest son of 7th Duke of Marlborough (qv) and brother of Lord Randolph Churchill (qv). He married (1) 1869, Albertha (qv above), daughter of 1st Duke of Abercorn; (2) at the Tabernacle Baptist Church, New York, Lilian Warren (Duchess Lily), widow of Louis Hammersley and daughter of Cicero Price, Commodore, U S Navy. He succeeded as 8th Duke in 1883.

BLOOD General Sir Bindon (1842–1940); son of W. B. Blood of Co Clare, and a descendant of the famous Colonel Thomas Blood, who attempted to steal the Crown Jewels from the Tower of London in 1671. Major-General commanding Malakand Field Force 1897. KCB 1896, GCB 1909. Retired as General 1907.

BRABAZON John Palmer (1843–1922); son of Major H. Brabazon of Co Mayo and Eleanor Ambrosia, daughter of Sir W. H. Palmer, 3rd Bart. Served in Grenadier Guards and 10th Hussars; appointed to command 4th Hussars 1893. He was thus WSC's first commanding officer. Later he commanded 2nd Cavalry Brigade in South Africa. Major-General and KCB in 1911.

BRODRICK William St John (1856–1942); eldest son of William Brodrick, 8th Viscount Midleton, and Augusta Mary, daughter of Sir Thomas Francis Fremantle. Married (1) 1880, Hilda Charteris, daughter of Lord

Elcho, later 10th Earl of Wemyss. She died in 1900, and he married (2) 1903, Madeleine Cecilia Carlyle, daughter of Col John Constantine and his wife Mary, later Lady Jeune (St Helier) (qv). Conservative MP 1880–5 (West Surrey); 1885–1906 (Guildford). Secretary of State for War, 1900–3, where he helped create, in 1902, the Committee of Imperial Defence. Secretary of State for India, 1903–5. Succeeded as 9th Viscount 1907; created Earl 1920.

BULLER Redvers Henry (1839–1908); second son of James Wentworth Buller of Downes and Charlotte, daughter of Lord Henry Thomas Howard-Molyneux-Howard, brother of 12th Duke of Norfolk. Commissioned in King's Royal Rifle Corps 1858. Served in Zulu War 1879: awarded VC. In October 1899 sailed out to South Africa, as Commander-in-Chief. Succeeded by Lord Roberts (qv) December 1899. After indiscreet speech removed from command of 1st Army Corps 1901. General 1896. KCMG 1882, KCB 1885, GCB 1894, GCMG 1900.

CAMBRIDGE George William Charles, 2nd Duke of (1819–1904); cousin of Queen Victoria. Commander-in-Chief of the British Army 1856–95. Colonel 1837, General 1856, Field Marshal 1862.

CAMDEN Clementina Augusta, Marchioness of (1848–86); youngest daughter of 6th Duke of Marlborough by his second wife, Charlotte, daughter of 4th Viscount Ashbrook. She was thus a half-sister of 7th Duke of Marlborough and an aunt of Lord Randolph's. In 1866 she married John Charles, Earl of Brecknock, just 25 days before he succeeded as 3rd Marquess of Camden. He died 1872 leaving four children; she married again, in December 1876, Captain Philip Green (1844–1904). She was present at the birth of WSC and was his godmother.

CASSEL Ernest Joseph (1852–1921); born at Cologne, youngest son of Jacob Cassel, a small banker. In 1869 he came to England, where he amassed a vast fortune. He became an intimate friend of the Prince of Wales, later King Edward VII, and of Lord Randolph. Knighted 1899.

CHAMBERLAIN Joseph (1836–1914); eldest son of Joseph Chamberlain, a boot and shoe manufacturer, and Caroline, daughter of Harry Harben, a provision merchant. Made a substantial fortune as screw manufacturer in Birmingham; three times Mayor of Birmingham 1873–5, MP 1876–1914. President of the Board of Trade under Gladstone 1880–5, and President of Local Government Board 1886, when he left the Liberal party on the issue of Home Rule and allied himself with Tories as Liberal Unionist. Secretary of State for Colonies 1895–1903, when he left the Tory government to campaign for imperial preference. Three times married; one son (Austen) became Chancellor of the Exchequer and Foreign Secretary, the other (Neville) Chancellor of the Exchequer and Prime Minister.

CHURCHILL John Strange Spencer- ('Jack') (1880–1947); younger brother of WSC. Born in Dublin 4 February 1880; educated at Harrow; served in the South African War 1889–1900, where he was wounded and mentioned in despatches and in First World War at Gallipoli. By profession a stockbroker. He married in 1908 Lady Gwendeline 'Goonie' Bertie (1885–1941), daughter of 7th Earl of Abingdon.

CHURCHILL Lady Randolph Spencer- ('Jennie') (1854–1921); mother of WSC and Jack Churchill. She was born 10 January 1854 in Brooklyn, New York, second daughter of Leonard Jerome (qv), and married (1) Lord Randolph Churchill (qv below); (2) on 28 July 1900, George Cornwallis-West (1874–1951), whom she divorced in 1913; (3) in 1919, Montagu Porch (1877–1964).

CHURCHILL Lord Randolph Henry Spencer- (1849–95); father of WSC and Jack Churchill. Born in London 13 February 1849, third but second surviving son of 7th Duke of Marlborough. Educated Eton and Merton College, Oxford. He married 15 April 1874 Jennie Jerome. MP for Woodstock 1874–85, and for South Paddington 1885–95; Secretary of State for India, 1885–6; Chancellor of the Exchequer and Leader of the House of Commons, July–December 1886. He died in London 24 January 1895.

COCKRAN William Bourke (1854–1923); American lawyer and politician noted for his oratory. Born in Co Sligo, he went to America in 1871. Democratic Member of Congress for New York 1891–5, 1904–9, 1920–3.

CURZON George Nathaniel (1859–1925); eldest son of Reverend Alfred Curzon, 4th Baron Scarsdale, and Blanche, daughter of Joseph Senhouse of Netherhall. Viceroy of India 1899–1905. Earlier, Tory MP for Southport 1886–98; Under-Secretary of State for India 1891–2; Under-Secretary of State for Foreign Affairs 1895–8. Later, Lord Privy Seal 1915–16; Lord President of the Council 1916–19; Foreign Secretary 1919–24. Married (1) 1895 Mary, daughter of Levi Leiter of Washington, DC, who died in 1906; (2) 1917 Grace, daughter of J. Monroe Hinds of the United States and widow of Alfred Duggan of Buenos Aires. Created Baron Curzon of Kedleston (Irish Peerage) 1898; Earl Curzon of Kedleston, Viscount Scarsdale and Baron Ravensdale 1911; Marquess Curzon and KG 1921.

DEVONSHIRE Spencer Compton, 8th Duke of (1833–1908); eldest son of 7th Duke of Devonshire, whom he succeeded 1891. As Marquess of Hartington, Liberal MP for North Lancashire 1857–68, for Radnor Boroughs 1869. Under-Secretary for War under Palmerston 1863, Secretary of State for War under Lord John Russell 1866; under Gladstone successively Postmaster-General, Chief Secretary for Ireland (1870–4) Secretary of State for India (1880–2) and, again, for War (1882–5). Broke with Gladstone over Home Rule, 1885 and eventually became a Liberal Unionist. Lord President under Salisbury and Balfour 1895–1903: resigned over tariff reform. Married 1892 Louise, daughter of Count von Alten of Hanover and widow of the 7th Duke of Manchester, for many years his inseparable companion and a noted hostess.

DE RAMSEY Lady Rosamond (1851–1920); second daughter of 7th Duke of Marlborough, sister of Lord Randolph and aunt of WSC. She married in 1877 William Henry Fellowes (1848–1925) who succeeded his father as 2nd Baron de Ramsey in 1887.

DISRAELI Benjamin (1804–81); son of Isaac D'Israeli, author and literary critic. Twice Prime Minister, 1868, 1874–80. Entered Parliament 1837; Tory MP for Maidstone, for Shrewsbury and for Buckinghamshire 1847–76. Became leader of the party in the Commons 1848. Wrote more than a dozen novels, the last, *Endymion*, published in 1880. Created Earl of Beaconsfield 1876; KG 1878.

EVEREST Elizabeth Ann (1833–95); born in Kent. Children's nurse, first with Rev Thompson Phillips of Carlisle, then with Lord Randolph Churchill 1875–93. Nicknamed by Winston and Jack 'Woom' or 'Woomany'.

FINCASTLE Alexander Edward, Viscount (1871–1962); eldest son of 7th Earl of Dunmore. Commissioned in 16th Lancers; served with Sudan Field Force 1896; ADC to Viceroy of India 1895–7; served with Malakand Field Force and ADC to Sir Bindon Blood 1897 (VC, despatches three times). Published *A Frontier Campaign* 1898. In Boer War he raised and commanded Fincastle's Horse (despatches); and in World War I (DSO, despatches four times) was wounded twice. Succeeded as 8th Earl of Dunmore 1907.

FREWEN Clara (1850–1935); eldest daughter of Leonard Jerome (qv). Married 1881 Moreton Frewen (qv below); they had two sons, and a daughter, Clare, who married William Sheridan, a descendant of Richard Brinsley Sheridan, 18th-century playwright and politician. Clare Sheridan achieved fame as a sculptress and as a traveller in North Africa.

FREWEN Moreton (1853–1924); son of Thomas Frewen MP, of Northiam, Sussex, and Helen Louisa, daughter of Frederick Homan of Co. Kildare. Married 1881 Clara (qv above), eldest daughter of Leonard Jerome. A knowledgeable if unlucky student of economic affairs (he was nicknamed 'Mortal Ruin'), the author of a number of works on bi-metallism. MP for North-East Cork, 1910–11.

GLADSTONE William Ewart (1809–98); fourth son of Sir John Gladstone, 1st Bart, and Anne, daughter of Andrew Robertson, Provost of Dingwall. Three times Chancellor of the Exchequer and four times Prime Minister 1868–74, 1880–5, 1886, 1892–4. Liberal MP for Newark, Oxford University, South Lancashire, Greenwich (1868–80) and Midlothian (1880–95). Author of numerous works on religious and philosophical topics.

GUEST—see WIMBORNE.

HALDANE (James) Aylmer Lowthorpe (1862–1950); eldest son of Daniel Rutherford Haldane and Charlotte, daughter of James Lowthorpe of Welton Hall, Yorks. Joined Gordon Highlanders 1882; served in India and South Africa with WSC. He was in command of the Chieveley armoured train when he and WSC were captured and imprisoned in Pretoria. KCB 1918; retired as General 1925.

HAMILTON Ian Standish Monteith (1853–1947); born in Corfu, the son of Col Christian Hamilton and Corinna, daughter of 3rd Viscount Gort; he married 1887 Jean, daughter of Sir John Muir, 1st Bart. Commanded 3rd Brigade, Tirah Campaign, 1897–8. Served in South Africa, 1899–1901, where he took part in the defence of Ladysmith, and later commanded one of the mobile columns described by WSC in *Ian Hamilton's March*. At the battle of Majuba Hill 1881 he received a wound in his wrist which affected his left arm for the rest of his life. Commanded Mediterranean Expeditionary Force 1915, which attempted to capture the Gallipoli Peninsula. KCB 1900; General 1905.

HARTINGTON—see DEVONSHIRE.

HICKS-BEACH Michael (1837–1916); eldest son of 8th Bart, whom he succeeded 1854. Conservative MP for East Gloucestershire, 1864–85, for Bristol West 1885–1906. Twice Chief Secretary for Ireland 1874–8 and 1886–7, twice Chancellor of the Exchequer 1885–6 and 1895–1902. Created Viscount St Aldwyn 1905, Earl 1914.

HIRSCH Baron Maurice (1831–96); born in Munich the son of a prominent Bavarian banker, made a fortune from the building of the Vienna-Constantinople railway. Noted for his philanthropic efforts to help East European Jews settle in North and South America. A friend of Lord and Lady Randolph, whom he entertained on his estates in Slovakia. In 1892 his filly La Fleche won the One Thousand Guineas, the Oaks, and the St Leger and came second in the Derby and in the Gold Cup in 1894.

JAMES Henry (1828–1911); lawyer and politician, befriended Lord and Lady Randolph and later WSC. Liberal MP for Taunton 1869–85, for Bury 1885–6. Twice Attorney-General under Gladstone 1873–4, 1880–5. With Chamberlain and Hartington left Liberal party and became Liberal Unionist (MP for Bury 1886–95). Chancellor of Duchy of Lancaster 1895–1902. Knighted 1873; created Baron James of Hereford 1895.

JEROME Clara (1825–95); wife of Leonard Jerome (qv below) whom she married in 1849 and mother of Clara (Frewen), Jennie (Spencer-Churchill) and Leonie (Leslie) qv. Youngest daughter of Ambrose Hall, a member of New York State Assembly, and Clarissa daughter of David Willcox whose father and grandfather had been blacksmiths in Dartmouth, Massachusetts. Lived for many years in Paris with her three daughters. After they were married she settled in England and died at Tunbridge Wells.

JEROME Leonard Walter (1817–91); husband of Clara Jerome (qv), fifth son of Isaac Jerome of Pompey, New York, and Aurora, daughter of Reuben Murray of Connecticut. First a lawyer and small-town newspaper proprietor, he came to New York in 1855 and became a successful stock-broker and financier, and for a period principal proprietor of the *New York Times*. American Consul in Trieste 1851–2. A keen yachtsman, founder of the American Jockey Club and a patron of the opera.

JEUNE Mary Susan Elizabeth (1845–1931); daughter of Keith Stewart Mackenzie of Seaforth and Hannah, eldest daughter of James Hope-Vere of Craigie Hall. Married (1) 1871 John, second son of 2nd Baron Stanley of Alderley (d. 1878); and (2) 1881 Sir Francis Jeune 1st Bart, later 1st and last Baron St Helier, President of the Probate Divorce and Admiralty Division of the High Court. Celebrated London hostess who befriended WSC.

KINSKY Count Charles (1858–1919); son of Ferdinand, seventh Prince Kinsky, and Marie, Princess Liechtenstein. Friend and admirer of Lady Randolph. Served in Austro-Hungarian diplomatic service, first in London and later at Brussels and Paris. A great sportsman and rider to hounds, he rode his own horse Zoedone to victory in the Grand National of 1883. Married 17 January 1895 Elisabeth, Countess Wolff Metternich, and succeeded as Prince 1904.

KITCHENER Horatio Herbert (1850–1916); second son of Lieutenant-Colonel Henry Horatio Kitchener of Cossington, Leicestershire and his first wife Anne Frances, daughter of the Rev John Chevallier, vicar of Aspall, Suffolk, who kept a lunatic asylum there and became a noted agriculturist. Commissioned in the Royal Engineers, he was Sirdar of the Egyptian Army 1892–9, planning and executing the campaign that ended in the Battle of Omdurman 1898 and led to the reconquest of the Sudan. Chief of Staff to Lord Roberts (qv) in South Africa, 1899–1900; Commander-in-Chief 1900–2; Commander-in-Chief India 1902–9; British Agent and Consul-General, Egypt 1911–14; Secretary of State for War 1914–15. Drowned in HMS *Hampshire* on way to Russia. KCMG 1894, KCB 1896, Baron 1898, Viscount and OM 1902, Earl (Kitchener of Khartoum) 1914, KG 1915.

KNOLLYS Francis (1837–1924); second son of General Sir William Knollys, and Elizabeth, daughter of Sir Edward St Aubyn, 1st Bart. Private Secretary to the Prince of Wales from 1870. He continued to serve in that capacity on the Prince's accession as Edward VII 1901, and to King George V until 1913. KCMG 1886, Baron 1902, Viscount 1911.

LANSDOWNE Henry Charles Keith, 5th Marquess of (1845–1927); elder son of Henry, 4th Marquess of Lansdowne and Emily Jane Mercer, Baroness Nairne in her own right. Under-Secretary for War 1872–4; Under-Secretary for India 1880; Governor-General of Canada 1883–8; Viceroy of India 1888–94; Secretary of State for War 1895–1900; Foreign Secretary 1900–5. Married 1869 Maud Evelyn Hamilton, daughter of 1st Duke of Abercorn and sister of Albertha, Marchioness of Blandford (qv).

LESLIE Leonie Blanche (1859–1943); youngest daughter of Leonard and Clara Jerome (qqv), favourite aunt of WSC. Educated in France, she married 1884 John, only son of Sir John Leslie, 1st Bart, of Glaslough, County Monaghan. Their son, John Randolph Shane (born 1885), was a godson of Lord Randolph.

LITTLE John David George (1868–   ); tutor for WSC and his brother Jack. Entered Merton College Oxford 1889 but did not take his degree. Taught briefly at Eton.

MARJORIBANKS Edward (1849–1909); eldest son of Dudley, 1st Baron Tweedmouth, whom he succeeded 1894. Married 1873 Lady Fanny Spencer-Churchill, third daughter of 7th Duke of Marlborough. Liberal MP for Berwick 1880–94, Chief Whip 1892–4; Lord Privy Seal and Chancellor of Duchy of Lancaster 1894–5, First Lord of the Admiralty 1905–8, Lord President of the Council 1908. His son Dudley (1874–1935) was at Harrow with WSC, joined Royal Horse Guards 1895; married 1901 Muriel, eldest daughter of W. St John Brodrick (qv).

MARLBOROUGH Charles, 9th Duke—see SUNDERLAND.

MARLBOROUGH Frances Anne Emily ('Fanny'), Duchess of (1822–99); first daughter of Charles, 3rd Marquess of Londonderry, by his second wife, Frances, daughter and heiress of Sir Henry Vane-Tempest Bart. She married John Winston, Marquess of Blandford (later 7th Duke of Marlborough), in 1843, and had five sons and six daughters. Only two of the sons (Lord Blandford, the eldest, and Lord Randolph, the third) survived their early childhood.

MARLBOROUGH John Winston, 7th Duke of (1822–83); eldest son of George, 6th Duke of Marlborough and Jane, eldest daughter of 8th Earl of Galloway. Father of Lord Randolph Churchill and grandfather of WSC.

Tory MP for Woodstock 1840–5 and 1847–57, when he succeeded to the dukedom. Lord President of the Council 1867–8; Viceroy of Ireland 1876–80. Married 1843 Frances Anne, daughter of 3rd Marquess of Londonderry (qv above).

MAYO Charles Harry Powell (1859–1929); Mathematics master at Harrow 1892–1919.

PLOWDEN Pamela Frances Audrey (born April 1874); daughter of Sir Trevor John Chichele Chichele-Plowden and Millicent Frances, daughter of General Sir C. J. Foster. As a young girl accompanied her father to Hyderabad, where he was the Resident. Married 1902 Victor, 2nd Earl of Lytton.

RHODES Cecil John (1853–1902); fifth of nine sons of Rev Francis William Rhodes, vicar of Bishop Stortford. Sent out to Natal at 17 to help his brother grow cotton, he staked one of the earliest claims on the diamond fields at Kimberley. Became principal shareholder of De Beers and later Kimberley mines. Pioneered settlements to the North, establishing Rhodesia. Prime Minister of Cape Province 1890–6, but his position was irretrievably damaged by his involvement in the Jameson raid (1895–6). A munificent benefactor to Oxford University and many charities, he left £6 million for public benefactions.

ROBERTS Frederick Sleigh, 1st Earl (1832–1914); born at Cawnpore, son of General Sir Abraham Roberts and Isabella, widow of Major Hamilton Maxwell. Commanded Brigade of Native Levies, Kabul 1852; Staff Officer to Sir Neville Chamberlain during Mutiny; Battery Officer of Delhi 1858, where he gained the VC. Lord Randolph Churchill, as Secretary for State for India, was instrumental in his appointment as C-in-C India 1885–93. Field-Marshal and C-in-C Ireland 1885–99; supreme command South Africa 1899. For the skill and rapidity with which he improved the fortunes of the war, he received the Garter and an Earldom.

ROOSE Robson (1848–1905); 3rd son of Francis Finley Roose. An eminent and well-connected physician who practised in London and Brighton. Attended Lord Randolph and his family.

ROSEBERY Archibald Philip Primrose, 5th Earl of (1847–1929); son of Lord Dalmeny and Catherine, daughter of 4th Earl Stanhope. Succeeded his grandfather 1868. Married 1878 Hannah, only daughter of Baron Mayer Amschel de Rothschild. Friend of Lord Randolph at Oxford and later of WSC. Secretary of State for Foreign Affairs 1886 and 1892–4; Leader of Liberal Party, Prime Minister 1894–5.

ROTHSCHILD Nathan Mayer, 1st Baron (1840–1915); eldest son of Lionel de Rothschild, the first Jewish MP, and Charlotte, daughter of Baron Charles de Rothschild of Naples. Besides being head of the family banking house, he was a noted breeder of cattle and sheep and a keen horticulturist. Married 1867 his cousin, Emma Louisa, daughter of Baron Charles de Rothschild of Frankfurt. They entertained generously at Tring. Created Baron 1885, the first professing Jew to be raised to the peerage.

ROXBURGHE Anne Emily Duchess of (1854–1923); 4th daughter of 7th Duke of Marlborough and an aunt of WSC. She married on 11 June 1874 James Henry Robert Innes-Ker, Marquess of Bowmont (1839–92), eldest son of 6th Duke of Roxburghe, whom he succeeded in 1879. She was Mistress of the Robes 1883–85, an extra Lady of the Bedchamber 1895–7, and Lady of the Bedchamber 1897–1901.

SALISBURY Robert Arthur Talbot, 3rd Marquess of (1830–1903); three times Prime Minister 1885–6, 1886–92, 1895–1902. Second son of 2nd Marquess of Salisbury and of Frances Mary, only daughter of Bamber Gascoyne MP. Conservative MP for Stamford 1853–68; Secretary of State for India 1866–7 (resigned in protest against Disraeli's reform bill). Succeeded his father 1868. Secretary of State for India 1874–8, Foreign Secretary 1878–80, 1885–6,1887–92 and 1895–1900.

SNEYD-KYNNERSLEY Herbert William (1848–86), educated at Trinity College, Cambridge, ordained 1874, founded and became first head-master of St. George's School, Ascot, 1877.

SUNDERLAND Charles Richard John, Earl of ('Sunny') (1871–1934); courtesy title of eldest son of Marquess of Blandford (qv) whom he succeeded 1892 as 9th Duke of Marlborough. Became close friend of his cousin WSC. Served with Queen's Own Oxfordshire Hussars, staff captain with Imperial Yeomanry in South Africa. Paymaster-General of the Forces 1899–1902, Under-Secretary of State for the Colonies 1903–5; Joint Parliamentary Secretary to the Board of Agriculture and Fisheries 1917–18. Married (1) 1895 Consuelo, daughter of Commodore William

Vanderbilt of New York (marriage dissolved 1921), (2) 1921 Gladys, daughter of Edward Parke Deacon of Boston.

THOMSON Charlotte (1843–1901), with her sister Catherine Amelia (1845–1906) founded and directed the preparatory school at Brunswick Terrace, Brighton.

TWEEDMOUTH—see MARJORIBANKS.

WALES Albert Edward, Prince of (1841–1910); eldest son of Queen Victoria, whom he succeeded as King Edward VII 22 January 1901. Married 1863 Princess Alexandra (1844–1925), daughter of King Christian IX of Denmark.

WELLDON James Edward Cowell (1854–1937); son of Rev Edward Welldon. Educated Eton and King's College, Cambridge. Headmaster of Harrow, at the age of thirty-one, 1885–98. Chaplain in Ordinary to the Queen 1892–8. Bishop of Calcutta and Metropolitan of India 1898–1902; Canon of Westminster 1902–6; Dean of Manchester 1906–18; Dean of Durham 1918–33.

WILSON Lady Sarah Isabella Augusta (1864–1929); eleventh and youngest child of 7th Duke of Marlborough. Married 1891 Gordon Chesney Wilson (1865–1914), Royal Horse Guards, eldest son of Sir Samuel Wilson MP, and was besieged with him in Mafeking.

WILTON Laura Caroline, Countess of (1842–1916); youngest daughter of William Russell, Accountant-General of the Court of Chancery, who was a great-grandson of 4th Duke of Bedford. Married (1) 1862 Seymour John Grey Egerton (1839–98), younger son of Thomas 2nd Earl of Wilton, who succeeded 1885 his elder brother Arthur as 4th Earl. She married (2) 1899 Sir Frederick John William Johnstone (1841–1913), 8th Bart. Befriended Winston when he was at Harrow, and called herself his 'Deputy Mother'.

WIMBORNE Cornelia Henrietta Maria, Lady (1847–1927); eldest daughter of 7th Duke of Marlborough, aunt of WSC. Married 1868 Ivor Bertie Guest (1835–1914), 2nd Bart, who was created 1880 1st Baron Wimborne. When young, WSC frequently stayed with the Wimbornes at their house near Bournemouth with his first cousin Ivor (1873–1939) who succeeded as 2nd Baron 1914 and was created Viscount 1918.

WOLFF Henry Drummond Charles (1830–1908); born in Malta, only child of the Rev Joseph Wolff and Lady Georgiana, daughter of Horatio Walpole, 2nd Earl of Orford. Married 1852, Adeline, daughter of Walter Sholto Douglas. Conservative MP Christchurch, Hants 1874–8; Portsmouth 1880–5. With Lord Randolph Churchill, John Gorst and Arthur Balfour, formed the 'Fourth Party'. Founder, with Lord Randolph, of the Primrose League. Ambassador at Madrid 1892–1900. GCMG 1878, PC 1885, GCB 1889.

WOLSELEY Joseph Garnet (1833–1913); distinguished himself in various military campaigns in the Empire and elsewhere, including Nile campaign for relief of General Gordon. Commander-in-Chief 1895–9: responsible for radical changes in British Army. Viscount 1885. Field Marshal 1894.

WOOD Henry Evelyn (1838–1919); son of Rev Sir John Page Wood, 2nd Bart, rector of St Peter's Cornhill, London, and Caroline, daughter of Admiral Sampson Michell. Midshipman 1852. Served in Crimean War, in trenches before Sebastopol. Transferred to Army 1855; served Indian Mutiny 1857; VC 1859. Adjutant-General 1897–1901. KCB 1879, GCMG 1882, GCB 1891. Field Marshal 1903.

1

Birth

(See Main Volume Chapter 1)

O N the 30th Nov, at Blenheim Palace, the Lady R ANDOLPH
C HURCHILL, prematurely, of a son.

The Times 3 December 1874

Birth Certificate

REGISTRATION DISTRICT WOODSTOCK									
1874 Birth in the Sub-district of Woodstock in the County of Oxford									
No	When and where born	Name, if any	Sex	Name, and surname of father	Name, surname, and maiden name of mother	Occu-pation of father	Signature, description, and residence of informant	When registered	Signature of Registrar
388	Thirtieth November 1874 Blenheim	Winston Leonard	Boy	Randolph Henry Spencer Churchill	Jennie Churchill formerly Jerome	MP for Wood-stock	Randolph S. Churchill Father Blenheim	Twenty third December 1874	George Foster Registrar

Lord Randolph Churchill to Mrs Leonard Jerome[1]

Monday 30 [November 1874]   Blenheim Palace
12.30 p.m.   Woodstock

Dear Mrs Jerome,

I have just time to write a line, to send by the London Dr[2] to tell you that
all has up to now thank God gone off very well with my darling Jennie. She
had a fall on Tuesday walking with the shooters, & a rather imprudent &

---

[1] Mrs J EROME was living at this time in Paris at 5 Avenue du Roi de Rome.
[2] William Hope MRCS (1837–93) of Bolton Row, Mayfair, a fellow of the Obstetrical
Society and Senior Physician at Queen Charlotte's Lying-in Hospital.

rough drive in a pony carriage brought on the pains on Saturday night. We tried to stop them, but it was no use. They went on all Sunday. Of course the Oxford physician cld not come. We telegraphed for the London man Dr Hope but he did not arrive till this morning. The country Dr[1] is however a clever man, & the baby was safely born at 1.30 this morning after about 8 hrs labour. She suffered a good deal poor darling, but was vy plucky & had no chloroform. The boy is wonderfully pretty so everybody says dark eyes and hair & vy healthy considering its prematureness. My mother & Clementine[2] have been everything to Jennie, & she cld not be more comfortable. We have just got a most excellent nurse & wet nurse coming down this afternoon, & please God all will go vy well with both. I telegraphed to Mr Jerome; I thought he wld like to hear. I am sure you will be delighted at this good news and dear Clara[3] also I will write again tonight. Love to Clara.

Yrs affty
RANDOLPH S. C.

I hope the baby things will come with all speed. We have to borrow some from the Woodstock Solicitor's wife.[4]

Duchess of Marlborough to Mrs Leonard Jerome

30 November [1874]   Blenheim

My dear Mrs Jerome,

Randolph's Telegram will already have informed you of dear Jennie's safe confinement & of the Birth of her Boy. I am most thankful to confirm the good news & to assure you of her satisfactory Progress. So far indeed she could not be doing better. She was in some degree of Pain Saturday night & all Sunday & towards evg of that day we began to see that all the remedies for warding off the Event were useless. Abt 6 of P.M. the Pains began in earnest.

We failed in getting an accoucheur from Oxford so she only had the Woodstock Doctor; we telegraphed to London but of course on Sunday ev there were no trains.

Dr Hope only arrived at 9 of this Morg to find dear Jennie comfortably

---

[1] Dr Frederic Taylor (1831–1909), physician and surgeon to the Woodstock Police, the Queen's Own Oxfordshire Yeomanry Cavalry, the Duchess of Marlborough's Almshouses &c. He was a JP and Coroner for Woodstock until he left the district for Lavender Hill, London, in 1887.

[2] The Marchioness CAMDEN.

[3] Clara Jerome, later Mrs Moreton FREWEN.

[4] Elizabeth Ann Brown, whose husband, Thomas Brown, had recently joined the local firm of solicitors, Thos White & Sons. She was expecting the birth of her first child, which was duly delivered on 28 January 1875. It was a boy, christened Thomas Stephen, who practised as a solicitor in Burford until shortly before his death in 1927.

settled in bed & the baby washed and dressed! She could not have been more skilfully treated though had he been here than she was by our little local doctor. She had a somewhat tedious but perfectly safe & satisfactory Time. She is very thankful to have it over & indeed nothing could be more prosperous.

We had neither cradle nor baby linen nor any thing ready but fortunately *every* thing went well & all difficulties were overcome. Lady Camden, Lady Blandford & I were with her by turns & I really think she could not have had more care. She has had an anxious Time and dear Randolph and I are much thankful it is over. I will be sure to see you receive a Bulletin every day.

We expect today a 1st Rate Nurse. Best love to Clara & Believe me,

Yrs sincerely
F. MARLBOROUGH

Lord Randolph to Mrs Leonard Jerome

Tuesday [1 December 1874]   Blenheim

Dear Mrs Jerome,

Jennie I believe dictated an account of herself to you today, but I just add a few lines by a succeeding post to tell you that she is going on wonderfully well. She is most comfortable & excellently looked after. Yr promise of coming over with Clara the 1st week in January gave her great delight & we shall both look forward to it vy much. We can make you both most comfortable, & perhaps if all goes well we shall be able to accompany you back to Paris for a short time. Jennie is awfully good and patient & takes great care of herself. Clementine is quite devoted to her & does all her correspondence & business. I am rather glad I was not all alone in Charles Street when it took place. I don't know what I shld have done. I was quite enough worried as it was. I telegraphed to Mr Jerome yesterday, & rather expected he wld have answered, but he has not yet. I wrote to him today. We want him to be godfather. I suppose we shall be here till the end of the month. She will be able to have very nice drives when she gets stronger and it will be much nicer for her than in London. Give my best love to dear Clara, Aunt Clara I *shld* say.

Yrs affty
RANDOLPH S. C.

Mrs Leonard Jerome to Duchess of Marlborough

2 December [1874]   Paris

Dear Duchess,

I was so thankful to receive yr kind letter which relieved me from the great anxiety I had felt since receiving Randolph's telegram. I was so dreadfully disappointed not to have been with my dear Child during her trial but she has told me of yr goodness and kindness to her that I feel sure she could not have been more comfortable in her own home.

I hope Jennie's confinement has not given you too much trouble and inconvenience. I can't say how thankful I am that it is all safely over. Hoping Randolph will not fail to give me daily news of dearest Jennie and the little boy, pray believe me, With love from Clara

Yrs most sincerely
C. H. JEROME

Lord Randolph to Mrs Leonard Jerome

Wednesday [2 December 1874]   Blenheim

Dear Mrs Jerome,

I have very little to report; but must thank you vy much for your letters which were a great delight to Jennie. You must write regularly if you have time to her as she looks forward to yr letters much. Please thank dear Clara for her letter to me & for all her kind wishes. Many thanks also for the cheque which has reached me safely. Jennie had a quiet good night & is going on wonderfully well. She is vy good & quiet & does everything she is told. We shall be quite alone here next week, Jennie & I, everybody is going away. The weather has turned vy cold again. Goodbye. I wonder Mr Jerome has not answered my telegram. Do write to Jennie every day.

Yrs affty
RANDOLPH S. C.

Duchess of Marlborough to Mrs Leonard Jerome

3 December [1874]   Blenheim

Dear Mrs Jerome,

I am happy to send you a most favourable report of dear Jennie and her little Baby. She is progressing steadily towards Convalescence. She has no Fever, the Milk is subsiding satisfactorily. Her appetite is fairly good & her strength keeps up well. The little Boy is a very healthy pretty little Child & I think will be a large Child in time. We are most fortunate in the Nurse & Wet Nurse & now that dear Jennie's troubles are over I really think she will get on much faster than if she were in London. She is of such a placid & patient disposition that she is not restless in Bed as some people are & this is greatly in her Favour. You may depend she is having all the Care & affection which is possible for we are all very fond of her. Nothing can progress better than she does.

Please give Clara my love & excuse a short letter for I have a house full of Children and Grandchildren.

Believe me, Yrs most sincerely
F. MARLBOROUGH

Lord Randolph to Mrs Leonard Jerome

Friday [4 December 1874]   Blenheim

Dear Mrs Jerome,

I did not write yesterday because my mother wrote. I am happy to say I have only good news to report. Jennie goes on wonderfully well & so does the boy. She slept all the night, last night without any sleeping draught, her appetite is very fair & she has no fever of any sort, and all the little troubles with milk etc are disappearing. The weather is vy cold. I expect it will be a long time before we can allow her to go out. I think Mr Jerome might have answered my telegram I sent him. It is so unsatisfactory when people dont appreciate one's news. Jennie sends her best love to you and Clara. I have really no news.

Yrs affty
RANDOLPH S. C.

Lord Randolph to Mrs Leonard Jerome

[6 December 1874]   Blenheim

Dear Mrs Jerome,

You will be glad to hear that Jennie is going on vy well. She wanted to get up today on the sofa, but that was rather too soon. She has been going on so well that she is apt to fancy herself stronger than she is. She is a little difficult to keep quiet & one does not like to cross her about anything because she worries & frets so. However she is really doing vy well and so is the baby. The layette has not turned up yet, but she hopes it will tomorrow, as the poor child is rather badly off for all sorts of things. She was much pleased with dear Clara's letter this morning; she says that now that she & Helen are out of the way Clara seems to have it all her own way with Dunhoff.[1] Madame de

---

[1] Probably August Karl, Graf von Dönhoff (1845–1920). He eventually married, in 1896, Maria von Lepel.

Hatzfeldt[1] wrote to her a day or two ago, who also mentioned that Prussian as having paid her a visit. Jennie sends you all her very best love. You must not make any prepations for a nursery or anything in Paris, we *shld* not take the baby all that way while he is so young. He *cd* not be in better hands than with his present nurse. Mind we expect you and Clara the first week in January & if you dont come we shan't come to you.

Perhaps you wont hear from me tomorrow as I am going to London for the day.

Goodbye & best love to Clara. Yours afftly
RANDOLPH S. C.

Lord Randolph to Mrs Leonard Jerome

Tuesday [8 December 1874]   Blenheim

Dear Mrs Jerome,

I cld not write to you yesterday as I was up in town all day making preparations for the nursery furniture. Jennie got on the sofa today for the 1st time. She is wonderfully well. She sleeps so well which I think helps her on very much. She never requires a sleeping draught. We are quite alone here except Bertha Blandford. My father will be back tomorrow, as he has put off his voyage to Gibraltar till the 17th on account of the bad weather. My mother is gone away for a fortnight with Rosamond,[2] on visits. Jennie thinks she will get a cloak or *pelisse* for the baby in London, so you need not trouble about it. The layette has given great satisfaction, but the little shawls with *capuchons* have not arrived. Jennie says they are much wanted also the pillow cases have not come. Jennie and I are much '*intrigués*' about Dunhoff, & we doubt his going to Russia vy much. Jennie says the violets look like business.

Best love to Clara. Yrs affty
RANDOLPH

---

[1] Helen, wife of Paul, Graf von Hatzfeldt–Wildenburg (1831–1901), who was a frequenter of Mrs Jerome's *salon* in Paris before the Franco-Prussian War, when he was Secretary of German Legation there. He became German Ambassador in Madrid in 1874, in Constantinople in 1881, and from 1885 in London where he died. He had for many years enjoyed the confidence of Bismarck, having served as Secretary of State at the Foreign Office in Berlin. His wife was the daughter of Charles Moulton, of Paris.

[2] Lady Rosamond Spencer-Churchill, later Lady DE RAMSEY.

Baptismal Certificate[1]

BAPTISM solemnised in the Chapel of Blenheim Palace in the Parish of Woodstock in the County of Oxford in the year 1874								
No	Alleged Date of Birth	When Baptized	Child's Christian Name	Parents' Names		Abode	Quality Trade or Profession	By whom the Ceremony was performed
				Christian	Surname			
20963	*Nov 30th 1874*	*Dec 27th*	*Winston Leonard*	*Randolph Henry and Jennie*	*Spencer-Churchill*	*Blenheim Palace*	*Second son of the Duke of Marlborough KG Member of Parliament for the Borough of Woodstock*	*Henry Wm Yule MA BCL Chaplain of Blenheim*

Lord Randolph to Dr Frederic Taylor[2]

Estates Office
Blenheim

28 December 1874

Dear Mr Taylor,

I enclose a cheque for 25 gs to you for yr kind services, & wish to say that I appreciate highly yr skilful management of & careful attention to her Ladyship during her confinement. We go to town today.

Believe me Yrs truly
RANDOLPH S. CHURCHILL

*   *   *   *

Early in August 1873 an invitation had arrived at Rosetta Cottage, Cowes, where Mrs Jerome was spending the season with her elder daughters Clara and Jennie:

[1] Two of the Godparents were Mr Leonard Jerome and the Marchioness Camden. The Christening Cup presented by Lady Camden is still preserved.
[2] This letter is in the possession of Dr Taylor's grandson, Mr J. C. P. Taylor.

To meet

Their Royal Highnesses the Prince and Princess of Wales

and

Their Imperial Russian Highnesses the

Grand Duke Cesarewitch and Grand Duchess Cesarevna[1]

Captain Carpenter and the officers of H.M.S. 'Ariadne'[2]

request the honour of the Company of

MRS & MISSES JEROME

On board, on Thursday, August 12th, from 3.30 to 7.30 p.m.

DANCING

Boats will be in attendance at the R.Y.C. Landing Place.

R.S.V.P.

Afterwards, Jennie wrote in her own hand immediately below the words 'To meet', 'Randolph'.

Leonard Jerome to Miss Jennie Jerome

Union Club[3]

Sunday August 8th   1 West 21st Street

[? 8 September 1873][4]   [New York]

My dear Jennie,

You quite startle me. I shall feel very anxious about you till I hear more. If it has come to that – that *he* only 'waits to consult his family' you are pretty

---

[1] Later Tsar Alexander III (1845–94) and Empress Maria Feodorovna.

[2] The cruiser then lying as guard-ship in the Roads.

[3] Founded in 1836, the Union was one of the oldest and most fashionable of New York clubs. It has been described as the mother of clubs there because so many other clubs were later started by discontented members or by those who had failed to gain admission to the Union.

[4] From internal evidence it appears that this letter was written around Monday 8 *September* 1873. The envelope which almost certainly contained it is addressed 'via England' to 'Miss Jennie Jerome – care of Messrs Monroe the Bankers – 7 Rue Scribe Paris.' The original date stamp has, with the postage stamps, been cut out. But the red New York Transit stamp, which usually seems to be dated at least one day after the original date stamp and up to two days after the date of the letter (cf letters and envelopes 27 August 1872, 11/13 September 1873) shows the date as September 10. The receipt stamp in London is Sp 24 73 and in Paris 25 Sept 73. It is probable therefore that the letter was written between Sunday the 7th and Tuesday 9 September 1873. If this is correct the explanation for Mr Jerome's mis-dating (and it can only be a guess) may lie in the emotional stress under which he was writing.

far gone. You must like him well enough to accept for yourself which for you is a great deal. I fear if anything goes wrong you will make a dreadful shipwreck of your affections. I always thought if you ever did fall in love it would be a very dangerous affair. You were never born to love lightly. It must be *way down* or nothing. Something like your mother. Not so Clara – happily not so. Such natures if they happen to secure the right one are very happy but if disappointed they suffer untold misery.

You give no idea of who it is and but for a letter from Clara some week or two ago I should be utterly in the dark. Clara mentioned among other gentlemen on a certain yachting party one – 'son of the' – etc 'who is a charming young man and has taken a great fancy to Jenny' so you see I have an idea. I fear he is too swell according to English ideas to gain the consent of his family, though he will have to look a good while among his countrywomen to find one equal to you. I hope I will not be kept long waiting for the news.

I am glad you had Johnnie Heck to dinner. I have a letter from him written a few days previous to yours in which he says, 'When I was here about a week ago I did myself the honor of calling on your family & fortunately found them at home. They were all dressed for the great yacht ball and I assure you they did honor to their country. Two handsomer girls I never saw, such style & grace can not be surpassed – especially Miss Jennie who is about the handsomest girl I ever saw. They are great belles here' etc. So whatever poor Johnnie's faults may be you see he has most excellent taste – excellent.

I am spending most of my time preparing for the races. The weather favorable we shall have a splendid meeting. The park[1] is looking beautifully – the programme is the best we have ever had and the fashion is all preparing to come to town in time.

From present appearances it is quite likely I may join you as early as November. Do you intend to hunt at Pau[2] this winter? Now that you are engaged it may not be worth while to risk your precious neck. If I go to Pau I hunt, Mama may as well make up her mind to that. She thinks I am too old but I will show her to the contrary.

Do you apprehend any serious opposition from me supposing it comes to that? Hardly. You know my views. I have great confidence in you & still greater in your mother and any one you would accept and your mother

---

[1] Jerome Park, the racecourse built by Leonard Jerome, with his brother Lawrence and August Belmont, the banker, at Fordham, New York. It was leased by Jerome to the Jockey Club of America, which held its first meeting there in September 1866.

[2] A fashionable resort in the French Pyrenees where Mr Jerome liked to stay in the winter. The discovery of its amiable climate during the months of December, January and February in 1816 led to a great influx of English visitors, and it was on their presence that the prosperity of the town mainly depended for the next 125 years. Pau is the birthplace of Henry of Navarre, later Henry IV of France.

approves I could not object to Provided always he is not a Frenchman or any other of those continental cusses.

You are no doubt now in Paris. I hope you got your old appartment & found your renter all right. I drove Lawrence's[1] trotting horse to Jerome Park today. Last night I went to see the *Fille de Mme Angot*.[2] It is pretty well got up – of course not equal to Paris. Thursday evening I drove with Tom Foote[3] from Jerome Park to Irvington 12 miles – returning Friday morning, charming roads and beautiful moonlight. Last week I spent three days at Long Branch with the Holys [? or Hoeys]. Thus I have been lazing about all the summer. Headquarters here at Lawrences & 'taking trips' almost daily. Kate[4] is at Lebanon still. Lawrence living about as I do. Maggie Middleton with the Hunts at Bennington. Gertrude spent ten days with Mrs Heckscher at Newport. She had a great success, was very much admired in fact was said to be the prettiest girl in Newport. 'All the Jerome girls are pretty' I heard several times. Kate is living with Julia. She will probably stay with her permanently. Julia has invited her to do so. Why did you not give me a description of the balls that is – how you & Clara got on. I suppose you danced to your hearts content. Was *he* there? I am glad you saw Jennett Bennett & liked her. I was sure she would turn out a nice girl. James[5] is making great preparations for next

[1] Lawrence Roscoe Jerome (1820–88), sixth of the eight sons of Isaac Jerome and Aurora Murray of Syracuse, New York, early became the sporting companion and business partner of his slightly older brother Leonard. He was known as Genial Larry, and Lady Randolph records that he was remembered as one of the wittiest men of his day and 'kept us in transports of laughter'. In 1844 he married Catherine (Kate) Hall, whose sister, Clara, Leonard was to marry four years later. Their son, William Travers Jerome, became the great reforming District Attorney of New York who was once a Democratic candidate for nomination for the Presidency of the United States.

[2] *La Fille de Madame Angot: opéra-comique* by A. C. Lecocq (1832–1918). His greatest success, it was performed for 400 nights consecutively. It was first produced in Paris 21 February 1873 and in New York and London later in the same year. The first New York performance took place on August 25.

[3] A Jerome New York lawyer.

[4] Catherine Jerome, wife of Lawrence.

[5] James Gordon Bennett Jnr (1841–1918) was the son of the millionaire founder of the *New York Herald*, which he took over at his father's death. He had sailed his yacht *Henrietta* to victory (with Leonard & Lawrence Jerome on board) in the first transatlantic race in December 1866. He also took a leading part in the running of the *Herald*: he first sent out Stanley to search for Livingstone, and in 1887 he established the paper's Paris edition. 'Always eccentric, temperamental and irascible', as his biographer Allan Nevins describes him, he had virtually exiled himself from America in 1877 after he had been attacked with a horsewhip outside the Union Club by the brother of a girl to whom Bennett had been engaged. 'Apparently a confirmed bachelor,' writes Nevins, 'he made little attempt to avoid scandal.' But at the age of seventy-three he married the widow of Baron George de Reuter, chairman of Reuter's. At his death Bennett left the greater part of his fortune to found a home for indigent New York newspapermen.

winter. He intends entertaining on a grand scale. Good night my dear Jennie. Best love to Mama & Clara.

As ever your affectionate

POP

Where is that photo on horseback?

Lord Blandford to Lord Randolph
(*Blenheim Papers*)

EXTRACT

25 August 1873   Arisaig
                                                    N.B.

My dear Old Man,

I got your letter on Saturday when I arrived but as there is only a post twice a week I could not write before today. I must say that I am not in the least surprised at the contents of your letter as I know you so well that I could easily judge of the effect that impressions such as you describe have on you. You will say when you read this that you expected as much from me. This will be partly because you know my general opinion & partly because you really feel doubtful of yourself & your hasty judgement. I myself am a specimen of the latter class, & I would therefore place before you my own example as one to be avoided. Had you been five and thirty or forty I could have pitied you but five and twenty with life before you instead of behind you I tell you that you are mad simply mad. I don't care if *la demoiselle* was the incarnation of all moral excellences & physical beauties on God's earth. My opinion is the same. Had you told me it was a married woman you wanted to go off with I should say if you can't live happily without her go fate calls you. Had it been a woman for whom you were ruining yourself, I should say fatality. But my friend *le mariage*! It is a delusion and a snare like all the rest, and in this disagreeable addition, that it is irrevocable.

Will no one believe me!

Have you any . . . end in view in this affair

No!

Do you marry for her fortune? No!

Do you marry to get children? No!

Do you marry because you have loved a woman for years? No!

Do you marry because you feel you are getting old & played out? No!

You really only want to marry because you are in love with *an idea 'une phantasie de . . . .'*

Damnation! Here you are a sensible man no longer a child positively trifling in this manner & here am I a born ass trying to argue the matter seriously with you. My dear Randolph for God's sake listen to me (though of course you won't) you are bored ... though in fact *'vous êtes à la recherche des emotions et vous avez touché mal'*. *Très mal!* ...

Duke of Marlborough to Lord Randolph
(Blenheim Papers)

31 August [1873]   Guisachan[1]

My dearest Randolph,

It is not likely that at present you can look at anything but from your own point of view but persons from the outside cannot but be struck with the unwisdom of your proceedings, and the uncontrolled state of your feelings, which completely paralyses your judgement; never was there such an illustration of adage *'love is blind'* for you seem blind to all consequences in order that you may pursue your passion; blind to the relative consequences as regards your family & blind to trouble you are heaping on Mamma and me by the anxieties this act of yours has produced: I do not write the expression of my constant thoughts when I say this, that you must not think me unkind for telling it to you.

Now as regards your letter I can't say that what you have told me is reassuring. I shall know more before long but from what you told me & what I have heard this Mr J. seems to be a sporting, and I thould think vulgar kind of man. I hear he drives about 6 and 8 horses in N.Y. (one may take this as a kind of indication of what the man is). I hear he and his two brothers are stock brokers, one of them bears a *bad* character in commercial judgement in *this* country, but which of them it is, I do not know, but it is evident he is of the class of speculators he has been bankrupt once; and may be so again: and when we come to think of N.Y. speculators & their deeds look at Fisk[2] and *hoc genus omne.*

Everything that you say about the mother and daughters is perfectly compatible with all that I am apprehensive of about the father and his belongings. And however great the attractions of the former they can be no set off against a connection should it so appear which no man in his senses could think respectable. I can say no more at present til I have seen you, & get

---

[1] The home of Lord Tweedmouth.
[2] James Fisk (1834–72), the flamboyant Wall Street financier, who was murdered by a former business associate.

some further replies to enquiries I have set on foot. I am deeply sorry that your feelings are so much engaged; and only for your own sake wish most heartily that you had checked the current before it became so overpowering.

May God bless and keep you straight is my earnest prayer.

Ever your affectionate father
MARLBOROUGH

Lord Randolph to Miss Jennie Jerome

Thursday 4 [September 1873]   Blenheim

Dearest Jeanette,

I had hoped so to have had a line from you ere this. Do try & persuade your mother to let you write darling. I am sure there is no harm in it and your letters are perfectly *safe* with me. Just a short line every now & then, it is such a comfort to me and I do so love your little notes. I came back from London yesterday. I had a long talk with the Prince [of Wales] on Tuesday afternoon; he spoke much of you & your sister, & said the Princess liked you both so very much. He said I was a very lucky fellow in which I quite agree with him for when I am alone here I keep wondering often why you shld like me, as you do, I know, I suppose it is partly because you feel I am so very fond of you & wld do anything or sacrifice anything for you. I am sure you must be very dull now at Cowes as most of your friends have I suppose left now. I shall hope to be able to come down the end of next week, only you *must* write & tell me whether your mother will mind, & what she says of me & whether you think of me sometimes. I keep counting the days till yr father's answer can arrive, I get so low & nervous about it sometimes, I feel it depends so much on how your mother has written to him. I went & got photographed the other day in London & shall send you the proofs when they come. I have got your photograph & your little curl in a locket now & am always looking at it. My father comes home tomorrow from the N. Of course we shall have a lot of talk about you my darling, tho I have written to him volumes. I shall write to you again soon. This is a bit of my best writing paper[1], on which I hardly ever write to anybody. Please remember me to your sister & your mother.

Yrs ever truly & devotedly
RANDOLPH S. CHURCHILL

[1] With a picture of Blenheim embossed in gold at the head.

Leonard Jerome to Miss Jennie Jerome

Thursday 11 September [1873]   Union Club

My dear Jennie,

I found your long letter & one from Mama at the Club this morning on my return from Newport. I must say I have been very happy all day. I have thought of nothing else. I telegraphed your mother immediately that I was 'delighted' and that I would arrange £2,000 a year for you which she says in her letter will do.

The letter I recd from you the other day only filled me with anxiety. I feared nothing would come of it and that you would be left shipwrecked. The situation as related by you today leaves no reasonable doubt of the accomplishment of your hopes. The consent of his paternal I should say must follow when he learns that moderate provision can be made for you and that our family is entirely respectable – which is all that can be said for any American family.

However I shall say nothing about it until it is announced by you & the people there.

I cannot imagine any engagement that would please me more. I am as confident that all you say of him is true as though I knew him. Young, ambitious uncorrupted. And best of all you think and I believe he loves you. He must. You are no heiress and it must have taken heaps of love to overcome an Englishmans prejudice against 'those horrid Americans'. I like it in every way. He is English. You will live in England. I shall see much of him & you. And my dear Jennie the very best of it is – *a love match*. Like your mother & me. Did you ever know a couple to get on better than we do? There is nothing that compensates for love rank wealth all the honors that all the world can heap upon you are nothing compared with genuine love.

You give all your sweethearts but no likeness. He cannot be very bad looking or you would not propose to send me his photograph. Is he big? I hope so. However it will do *for you* if he is not. You are a light weight yourself. Does he ride? Dear me if he does I shall expect you to break your neck before you are a year married.

Poor Clara! How does she like the idea of your going first? It is extraordinary the blindness & folly of some young men. I know how it happened *she wouldn't let her hair down*. If Monsieur Randolph had ever seen that – good bye Miss Jinks. Well my good amiable dear darling Clara never mind. Remember about the fishes & all that – we wont despair of you yet. I have spent the day at Jerome Park directing the improvements going on there & right glad I was to get away from the city. I wanted to be away alone.

Yesterday I was at Newport. Marina Grevy [?] is divorced – incompatibility of temper. She takes her name of Travers – 'Mrs W. M. Travers' she will spend the winter in Baltimore. I saw all the young ladies in Newport though I was there but one day. Mimi Stevens[1] Consuelo Mrs Joe Stove Miss Heckscher etc etc. Newport has been excessively dull this season.

Best love to Mama & Clara, Ever your affectionate

PAPA

Lord Randolph to Mrs Leonard Jerome

Tuesday 30 September [1873]   Blenheim

Dear Madame Jerome,

I can never sufficiently thank you for your kind, too kind letter to me, & I cannot tell you with what glad feelings I received it. I am more relieved and happy than I can say at hearing that Mr Jerome consents to his daughter's marriage with me. It has been a great source of anxiety to me to know what he wld say, & I cannot but feel that it must be principally owing to you having been so very good as to form a good opinion of me & to write to him favourably about me. I cannot ever be sufficiently grateful to you for doing so, as I know well how great a treasure you are giving into my care, and all I can say is that with God's help you will never regret having done so for I do feel an intense conviction of my power & will to render Madlle Jeanette's life a happy one, free from care & trouble. When I told you at Cowes that I was sure there wld be no opposition from my parents to my marriage with her, I told you no more than the truth; there is no opposition to it & there has been none. Of course as you will understand my father & mother have been very much taken by surprise & find it difficult to convince themselves of the reality & probable permanence of our feelings for each other. Tho I deprecate I cannot but acknowledge that those doubts are to a certain degree intelligible. Till quite lately I have never asked my father formally for his consent; but I did so the other day & he then told me that even if he wished to or had the power to, he wld never take upon himself the responsibility of opposing what I had most strongly represented to him had become my only chance of future happiness; but that taking into consideration the suddenness & rapidity of the attachment formed he said he wld give his consent if we were of the same mind in a year hence. In this I regret to say he rather agrees with you.

But he added & on this point I questioned him closely that he did not wish

[1] Mary 'Mimi' Stevens (?1854–1919) was the daughter of Paran Stevens and Marietta Reed. She married in 1878 Major Arthur Paget, a grandson of 1st Marquess of Anglesey; as General Sir Arthur Paget, he commanded the troops in Ireland 1911–17.

for a moment that we shld not be engaged to each other & have many opportunities of knowing each other better & proving to him by a longer acquaintance & the lapse of a certain period the strength & durability of our attachment & that when he was convinced of that, he wld no longer interpose any
obstacles but wld gladly receive your daughter Madlle Jeanette with all the
affection & love that she wd have a right to as my wife & that she has such
high claims to herself. This I shall bring you in his own writing when I come
to Paris. Of course he & my mother act as one in the matter & I need scarcely
assure you that you need have no doubts as to your dear daughter finding
here a second home & a family ready to become as fond of her as her own.
You know her well enough to feel certain she wld easily & at once win the
hearts & affections of all with whom she comes into close contact. Of my own
feelings for her it is unnecessary for me to speak, & I feel the impossibility of
thoroughly describing them to you. I think you know them, they are so
strong that if I was not quite *sure & confident* of the reception & affectionate love
of her by my own family, I shld hesitate if I did not even prevent myself from
asking her to share her life with me. Thank God, I do feel with every right
perfect confidence on that point. You my dear Madame Jerome are fortunate
& much to be envied in having the happiness of having a daughter like her
and another like her sister Madlle Clara and I cannot tell you how fortunate
I consider myself in having secured the love of the one & I think I may add
the sisterly affection of the other more than all fortunate in having been able
to win your confidence and esteem. I have forwarded your letter to my father
& shall receive an answer from him tomorrow. I shall go to town on Thursday
& arrive in Paris Friday evening; if you wld be kind enough to write a line to
the Hotel France et de Bath, Rue St Honore & say what time you wld allow
me to call on you I shld be much obliged. I cannot tell you how much I look
forward to seeing you all again.

Tho perhaps not a very long it has been a weary anxious time for me, & it
is with unspeakable relief that I feel now that all the uncertainty is removed &
that my marriage with Madlle Jeanette has become merely a question of time.
I think I shall be able to explain to you that unless you insist on a long delay,
my parents will not insist on a whole year, of this I am sure. Still even if it was
so, it can make no difference to us. Time can only strengthen our attachment
for each other. I can quite however understand both you and Mr Jerome
wishing for a certain delay & my parents doing the same, & tho I may regret
it, still I am sure both Madlle Jeanette & I will cheerfully acquiesce. From the
beginning you have treated me with the greatest kindness, & I shall endeavour
to prove my gratitude to you by striving at all times to fall in with your wishes.

Believe me my dear Madame Jerome, yrs ever most sincerely

RANDOLPH S. CHURCHILL

Lord Randolph to Mrs Leonard Jerome

Thursday 2 October [1873]   Blenheim

Dear Madame Jerome,

I read with some surprise and good deal of pain in a letter I received from
your daughter that you did not *'believe'* all that I had told her & written to
you about my father's wishes. I am afraid you must have a very bad opinion
of me if you think, that in a matter like this, I shld be likely to lead you to
believe anything that was not strictly the case or state anything that was not
actually, fact. I am not in the habit of doing it at any time, & I fail to understand why you shld think me capable of it.

I beg to enclose you a letter I received from my father which bears out
entirely every word I told you, but I regret to find that such guarantee of what
I state shld be thought necessary by you. I shall be in Paris on Friday evening
& shall hope to have the honour of waiting on you on the following day &
making any more explanations you may wish for. I wld merely finally observe
that this want of confidence in, and distrust of anything I may tell you cannot
but lead to an unpleasant state of affairs, & that if you are unable to place any
confidence in me, I cannot but wonder you have permitted me to attempt to
win your daughter.

Believe me my dear Madame, yrs very sincerely
RANDOLPH S. CHURCHILL

Leonard Jerome to Miss Jennie Jerome

7 October 1873   Union Club

My dear Jennie,

I have just recd your two letters – one written at Cowes, the other at Paris.
I feel quite reassured now. I did not like the situation at all as I understood it
from your mother. Your name was even in the papers & all over the world
coupled with his as engaged while his father had not given his consent. I know
the great prejudices the English have against Americans socially and I feared
you might be left in a very disagreeable position. The extract you send me is
very gratifying because it explains why his father hesitates. His reasons are
perfectly natural & proper. It is precisely the same thing that I wrote you. I
feared a reaction it was all so hasty. I did not fear it for you but for him.

You all seem to expect a formal letter from me. Do you mean that you want
anything more than what I have written? I have said *whom you choose* and
your mother approves is certain of my consent. That is if he is English or American.

If Lord Randolph writes to me I shall answer at once & will send my letter to you. I shall be perfectly frank as I do not believe in any reserve in such a matter.

Between you & I and the post – and your mother etc. *I am delighted* more than I can tell. It is magnificent. The greatest match any American has made since the Duchess of Leeds.[1]

I dont want you to sell your horse. I intend to buy another when I come out. She will ride every day. I want you to have all the dresses &c that you wish. You ought to have a box at the opera occasionally. You should give parties and live handsomely. You will be more swell than ever now and you will be certain to have a great influence on Clara's future.

I havent finished this or written half what I want to but I am obliged to stop abruptly for the mail.

POP

*　　*　　*　　*

THE MARRIAGE SETTLEMENT

(*Source: Blenheim Papers*)

The Duke of Marlborough settled on Lord Randolph £20,000 'or rather, as you will see, by and by it must be something less, which I have power to devise by will as a charge on the Blenheim Estates and the interest in this at 5% will produce you £1,000 per annum which I will undertake to pay you'. [*Undated letter ? February 1874 to Lord Randolph.*]

Mr Jerome proposed a settlement of £40,000 to yield £2,000 per annum. The property from which the income was to be derived was the house on the corner of Madison Avenue and 26th Street in New York. [*Letter dated 23 January 1873 from Shipmond, Barlow, Sarocque, Macfarland, lawyers of New York.*]

---

[1] Louisa Catherine, Duchess of Leeds (1789–1874), third daughter and co-heiress of Richard Caton, a merchant of Baltimore, and his wife Mary, daughter of Charles Carroll, of Carrollton, Maryland. She married, 1) 1817, Sir Felton Elwell Hervey-Bathurst, 1st Baronet, who died in 1819; 2) in 1828, Francis, Marquess of Carmarthen, eldest son of 6th Duke of Leeds, whom he succeeded in 1838. He was six years younger than his American bride and, with the Marquess of Clanricarde, was described in 1852 by Mrs Edward Twistleton as 'about as ugly men, each in his own style, as one is likely to meet'. He died of diphtheria in 1859, but his widow survived until 8 April 1874. Her two elder sisters and co-heiresses also made splendid marriages.

The capital sum was increased to £50,000 because the Duke's solicitors objected that 'it is not usual to give trustees power to make investments which yield 5%'. [*Letter dated 19 February 1874 from Frederick L. Capon.*]

Mr Jerome intended that the income from his settlement should be paid to his daughter. The Duke's solicitors wrote to Lord Randolph objecting that 'such a settlement as far as you are concerned [cannot be] considered as any settlement at all, for . . . Miss Jerome is made quite independent of you in a pecuniary point of view, which in my experience is most unusual, & I think I might add in such a case as the present without precedent. And His Grace desires it to be distinctly understood that in accepting Mr Jerome's proposal you have done so in direct opposition to his views & wishes and solely upon your own responsibility.' [*Letter dated 25 Februray 1874 from Frederick L. Capon.*]

As a compromise it was suggested that Lady Randolph should be given 'pin money' first £300, then £500, then £600 and that the residue of the £2,000 should be paid to Lord Randolph. In the end Mr Jerome agreed [*letter dated 7 April 1874*] that half the allowance of £2,000 a year should be paid to his daughter and half to Lord Randolph. 'My daughter although not a *Russian* Princess is an American and ranks precisely the same and you have doubtless seen that the Russian settlement recently published claimed *everything* for the bride.'[1]

Originally, Mr Jerome wanted to leave the disposal of the capital sum of £50,000 to be entirely at the discretion of Lady Randolph should she die before Lord Randolph. Now [*letter dated 7 April 1874*] it was agreed that the apportionment of the £50,000 should be decided between Lord Randolph & Lady Randolph in the event of there being children or if no apportionment was made, for the sum to be divided equally. If there were no children and Lady Randolph died before Lord Randolph, half the £50,000 was to be paid to Lord Randolph and the other £25,000 to be paid to Lady Randolph's family.

---

[1] When the Grand Duchess Marie Alexandrovna, only daughter of Tsar Alexander II, married Queen Victoria's second son, the Duke of Edinburgh, on 23 January 1874, she was given a marriage portion of 2 million roubles (£250,000) which was considered her property, and the income from which was to be 'for her separate and exclusive use and enjoyment.'

Leonard Jerome to Duke of Marlborough
(*Blenheim Papers*)

9 April [1874]   Paris

Dear Duke,

Your very kind letter of the 7th reached me this morning. I learned on my arrival on Wednesday that you and the Duchess had paid a visit to Paris and I am extremely gratified to know that the impression you formed of my daughter was so favourable. The assurances you give me of the kindly manner in which she will be received into your family afford me much pleasure. I have every confidence in Randolph and while I would entrust my daughter to his sole care alone in the world still I can but feel reassured of her happiness when I am told that in entering your family she will be met at once with 'new and affectionate friends and relatives.'

I am very sorry you are not able to come over to the wedding. We had all hoped to have had the pleasure of seeing both yourself and the Duchess. Under the circumstances however, we must of course excuse you – and we do this the more readily as we know the occasion has your best wishes and the young people your blessing.

In regard to the settlement – as it has finally, I am happy to say, been definitely arranged – little more need be said. In explanation of my own action in respect to it I beg to assure you that I have been governed purely by what I conceived to be in the best interests of *both* parties. It is quite wrong to suppose I entertain any distrust of Randolph. On the contrary I firmly believe there is no young man in the world safer, still I can but think your English custom of making the wife so utterly dependant upon the husband most unwise.

In the settlement as is finally arranged I have ignored American custom and waived all my American prejudices. I have conceded to your views and English custom in every point save one. That is simply a – somewhat unusual allowance of pin money to the wife. Possibly the principle may be wrong but you may be very certain my action upon it in this instance by no means arises from any distrust of Randolph.

With kind regards, Believe me dear Duke, Yours most sincerely

LEONARD JEROME

Lord Randolph to Duchess of Marlborough

Tuesday 14 [April 1874]   Hotel d'Albe
                                                                                          [Paris]

Dearest Mama,

It is very good of you finding time to write to me such long and frequent letters; I write today to wish you very many happy returns indeed of your birthday to-morrow; and I am sure you think it is being well kept in Paris, for to-morrow I ensure myself a happy home and future. Please Mama dear dont allow yourself to get too angry with Mr Jerome. I have quite forgiven him, as he is evidently very sorry for himself & for his bad behaviour & will I think make amends. Things are all going now as merrily as a marriage bell. I expect the settlements over to-night and they will be signed to-morrow. The weather is vy unpromising but as it is your birthday to-morrow, it shld be a fine day. F. Knollys made his appearance last night. He brought over to Jennie a very pretty locket of pearls and turquoises from the Prince and Princess, & a very kind letter from H R H to her. They certainly are awfully good hearted people with all their little faults and weaknesses. The Standishes have presented a very handsome old Dresden soup tureen very valuable. There are some other presents coming in to-day but I dont know what. We have not many but they are all vy good. A little American of the name of Rice gave Jennie a beautiful bracelet with a watch like a little gold ball hanging from it.

The Guests stupidly came by the tidal train, & did not arrive till late, so I have not seen them but am just going. The dresses are not all home yet; there are 25 in the trousseau. Where they are going to stow them away in Curzon Street[1] I can't imagine. The house linen I have sent over by *petite vitesse*. Very kind of Bowmont[2] offering to come over; he has written me a vy nice letter. I am sure Annie is *very* fortunate, but she deserves to be. Do thank dear Rosamond for her long letter. She said she cld excuse my answering it, as I have so much to do today. I really must protest against you continuing to be low, & to say that you are losing us all. I shall be you know, as near you and as much with you as ever, & shall be able perhaps to be of more assistance and use than before. Annie and Bowmont will I think be a little tiresome at times vy proper stuck up & reserved but you know I am not in the least like that & never shall be. I dont like to bother Papa any more about it, but I do so wish that 2000 £ cld be paid. There are several bills that I shld like to get paid before I get back to London, and as I have them with me here it wld be a nice occupation at Petitval. Please give him my very best love; I am sure when I think of the way you and he have behaved all along since this affair began I really am vy grateful to you and I am afraid you found me very cross and disagreeable at times. But really I do think you have both been awfully good and kind.

Goodbye dearest Mama, Believe me ever, Yr most affte son
RANDOLPH

Blandford arrives tonight.

[1] No 1 Curzon Street, the furnished house which Lord Randolph had rented from Captain and Mrs Bristowe until the end of July for £250, and into which he moved with his bride on their return from the honeymoon.

[2] Marquess of Bowmont, later 7th Duke of ROXBURGHE. He had become engaged to Lord Randolph's sister, Lady Anne Emily, on 26 March 1874, and their marriage took place in June.

Duke of Marlborough to Lord Randolph
(*Blenheim Papers*)

14 April [1874]   London

My dearest Randolph,

I must send you a few lines to reach you tomorrow, one of the most important days of your life, & which I sincerely pray will be blessed to you & be the commencement of a united existence of happiness for you & for your wife. She is one whom you have chosen with less than usual deliberation but you adhered to your love with unwavering constancy & I *cannot* doubt the truth & ? power of your affection: & now I hope that as time goes on, your two natures will prove to have been brought, *not* accidentally, together may you both be 'lovely & pleasant in your lives' is my earnest prayer. I am very glad that harmony is again restored, & that no cloud obscures the day of sunshine but what has happened will show that the sweetest path is not without its thorns, & I must say ought not to be without its lesson to you. Your dear mother would have loved to have been with you tomorrow; but though she is getting on very well she could not have exerted herself again. We shall think of you at your Petit Val where I hope you will enjoy yourselves & have some fine weather: we shall look forward shortly to seeing you & Jeanette here, whom I need not say we shall welcome into her *new family*. Give her my love & with the same to yourself.

Ever your affectionate father
MARLBOROUGH

The marriage between Lord Randolph and Miss Jennie Jerome was solemnized at the British Embassy, Paris, by the Reverend Dr Edward Forbes on 15 April 1874.

2
Ireland

(See Main Volume Chapter 2, pp. 24–34)

O n 11 October 1875 the Prince of Wales set out on a visit to
India. Among those who accompanied him were Lord
Aylesford and Lady Aylesford's brother, Colonel Owen Williams.[1]

Lord Aylesford to Lady Aylesford
(Phillips Papers)

30 December [1875]
Government House
Calcutta

Copy

My darling,

I have nothing in the world to tell you out of the common we have done
here the same as we have done in all the other places as you may already know
Sutherland[2], Probyn[3], Knollys and self are left here to take care of HRH

---

[1] Owen Lewis Cope Williams (1836–1904), eldest son of Thomas Peers Williams MP and
Emily Bacon, became Lieut-Colonel of the Royal Horse Guards at the age of 30 and Colonel
in 1871. He sat in Parliament for the family seat of Great Marlow 1880–5, was promoted
Maj-General in 1882 and Lieut-General in 1887. He married 1) Fanny Florence, youngest
daughter of St George Francis Caulfeild, who died 28 July 1876; and 2) Nina Mary Adelaide,
daughter of Sir John Tollemache Sinclair, 3rd Bart. Lady Aylesford (Edith) was the third
of his six sisters, all of whom married into the peerage with the exception of the eldest,
Margaret, who married Sir Richard Williams-Bulkeley, 11th Bart, and is the grandmother
of Mrs Edward Phillips, in whose possession are many of the Aylesford papers.

[2] George Granville William Sutherland Leveson-Gower, 3rd Duke of Sutherland (1828–92)
spent £500,000 on opening up and developing the Highlands. A keen sportsman and traveller,
he was said to be fond of riding on locomotive engines and of watching the fire brigade at work.
His first wife Anne was Mistress of the Robes to Queen Victoria, a post also held by his
mother for a total of 17 years.

[3] Dighton Macnaghten Probyn (1833–1924), Colonel of Probyn's Horse (later 11th King
Edward's Own Lancers) was Equerry to the Prince of Wales 1872 to 1877, when he became
Comptroller and Treasurer of the Prince's Household and then during the reign of King
Edward VII Keeper of the Privy Purse. Won VC in India 1857; knighted 1876.

as all the others have gone off for two days pigsticking. Today we have been on board the *Serapis*[1] to lunch. We had a party of about twenty five the object of the lunch was to see the embarkation of a lot of animals. Two little Elephants dogs without tails like Manx cats parrots and others. This morning two dead niggers were found in the paddle wheel of the *Osbourne*[2] they had thrown themselves into the Ganges so as to be sure of going to heaven. All this week the *Serapis* has been thrown open to the public and of course there are many amusing stories connected with the visits. One is about a Rajah who visited the ship who was anxious to take away a recollection of his visit. He looked everywhere but could find nothing but at last as good luck would have it he went into HRH's WC and there found a packet of five hundred Curl papers which he put in his pocket and walked off in great delight. Two nights ago Charlie Carrington[3] and self went to dine at the Club. We got a trap and drove off at a walk which continued till we got close to the Club where the driver whipped his horse into a canter and turned into the Club garden but he did not give enough room to the gate post – so over we went and broke the carriage into little bits. Since this accident Matches have become much cheaper in Calcutta. We walked into the Club having ordered dinner before and we found that it had not been ordered so we made a great row about it and at last got it. In the middle of a first rate dinner we by accident found that we had come to the wrong Club. But as usual always calm on such occasions we said nothing and finished our dinner in peace.

We then asked the head waiter who was a native to get us a fresh trap to take us to the theatre. He replied 'You go to theatre, I go too.' Upon which he ordered a carriage put a rug over him took all the keys with him (cellar keys included) and came with us leaving at least forty people dining at the Club without saying a word to any of them. We reached the theatre and found the house quite empty with the exception of the steward of the *Serapis* and a Rajah in the stalls. After a long time we got them to begin to act and I must say I do not think I have laughed so much before for a very long time 4 ballet

1 *Serapis* (6,211 tons) was one of HM Indian troopships.
2 *Osborne* (1,536 tons), the Royal Yacht.
3 Charles Robert, 3rd Baron Carrington, (1843–1928) was the eldest son of Robert John, 2nd Baron by his second marriage to Charlotte Willoughby de Eresby through whom he became co-heir to the hereditary office of Lord Great Chamberlain. He had been Captain in the Royal Horse Guards, and MP for High Wycombe 1865–8. He was Captain of the Royal Bodyguard 1881–5, Governor of New South Wales 1885–90, Lord Chamberlain of the Household 1892–5; he was created Viscount Wendover in this last year. He was President of the Board of Agriculture 1905–11 (his grandfather held the same office 1800–3) and Lord Privy Seal 1911–12; he was created Marquess of Lincolnshire in 1912. When he married in 1878 Cecilia, eldest daughter of 5th Baron Suffield (q.v. below), no fewer than ten members of the Royal Family, including the Prince and Princess of Wales, were present at the ceremony in the Chapel Royal, Whitehall.

dancers with red spotty faces which could only walk across the stage and did not pretend to dance as they were so fat on account of family reason and others. The curtain fell when it should not have done so and left two girls on one side and two on the other. I laughed so much I was nearly turned out. I never was so amused in my life as in the cast of the play nobody knew their parts I must tell you, to see this great performance we had to pay £4 for our box and it was well worth it.

We have had one crowded ball and there is one tomorrow night. I have nothing more to tell you except that I have had to send Myson my servant away and have paid his passage back. Tell James not to let him into the house as I have since found that £150 worth of sapphires, two guns and lot of clothes besides other things have gone and I am sure he has stolen them he has turned out very badly as he took to drink and I could do nothing with him and I had to call the guard out to get him out of the ship. Happy New Year to you my darling and all the rest and believe me yr most

affecate
JOE

Lord Aylesford to Lady Aylesford
(Phillips Papers)

15 February [1876]   Prince of Wales' Camp

My darling,

Here we are in camp in the middle of the jungle many many miles from any town. We have only a small shooting camp which consists of 3,000 persons, 600 camels, 130 elephants, 100 horses, 100 bullocks. We change our camping ground every day and while we are out shooting the camp is moved ten miles per diem and on our return in the evening we find everything as if it had been there for a year. Up to Monday 14th we have not had very much sport as during the whole of last week we only saw one tiger which we did not get. Yesterday we began the new week in better form by killing two very large bears one fell to HRH's rifle the other to mine. Today one of the party killed a bear and when we went to pick her up we found she had got two cubs on her back which she was carrying away out of danger. When we had nearly finished our days sport we chose a pet place of Sir H. Macready which as good luck would have it held a she tiger which broke covert close to Charlie Carrington he shot at it but it missed fire he had another one which he held straight and which proved deadly and so killed his first tiger which also had young ones which escaped. When the tiger got up Suffield[1] saw her make a spring at a deer which she killed with one blow and which we also got. We have had lots of small game shooting in the way of deer and Black partidges but everything here is in young or have just had young ones it is really very odd to have such things in the winter time. By the way we have got the young bears in camp.

I think I prefer riding horses to elephants it is most awfully trying to the nerves going in and out of these awful nullas some of them look impossible places it is also very hard to shoot off the elephants back which is the only way you can shoot here as the grass is 8 and ten feet high. So I hear dear old Charlie has gone to South America with Affie. I do hope they will enjoy themselves and return home all safe and sound. Poor old Owen I am sorry to say leaves us tomorrow but I trust he will find poor Fanny[2] better than he expects on his arrival. The poor old boy is awful cut up and shaken. I have not had a letter from you for a very long time in fact I should hardly know your hand writing HRH says that I am the only one that hardly ever has any letters when the bag is opened which is true as I have had two or three from my mother and about five from you in five months. There is a heavy storm tonight the first rain we have had since we left Ceylon. With best love to all. Only a month more before we leave India which I shall regret in many ways.

Believe me, Yr most affecate

JOE

When Lord Aylesford went to India Lady Aylesford went to reside with her two daughters at Packington Hall. 'During her residence at that place,' Mr Charles Russell QC subsequently told a Committee of Privileges of the House of Lords on 1 July 1885, 'the Marquis of Blandford visited the hall not in an ordinary way, but surreptitiously. He was living at the time in the neighbourhood, and it would appear that in some way he had obtained possession of a private key, by which he was able to gain access to a portion of Packington Hall, which was not frequently used by the family, and thence to other parts of the house. It would be shown that Lord Blandford had obtained

---

[1] Charles Harbord, 5th Baron Suffield (1830–1914), was Chief of Staff to the Prince of Wales' expedition. Formerly a Lord-in-Waiting to Queen Victoria, he became Lord of the Bedchamber to the Prince in 1872 until the accession in 1901, when he was made a Lord-in-Waiting. He married in 1854 Cecilia Annetta, daughter of Henry Baring and sister of Edward Charles, 1st Baron Revelstoke.

[2] Owen Williams' wife. She died in July.

possession of this private key with the knowledge and sanction of Lady Aylesford, with whom he passed many nights. The fact came to the knowledge of the servants, who spoke to Lady Aylesford on the subject. So matters went on from the autumn of 1875 until the beginning of 1876 when Lady Aylesford eloped with Lord Blandford. . . .'

On 13 February 1876 Lord Lansdowne, Lady Blandford's brother-in-law and trustee, wrote to the Duke of Marlborough from Bowood that Blandford had asked him to draw up a deed of judicial separation and acquiesce in certain financial arrangements on the grounds that 'there are circumstances which made it imperative for him to take action at once'.

Lord Aylesford to Dowager Countess of Aylesford
(*Minutes of Evidence, House of Lords:* 1 *July* 1885)

[? 16 February 1876]   India
Copy

TELEGRAM

Send for the children and keep them till my return. A great misfortune has happened. Am writing by the mail.

Lady Aylesford to Dowager Countess of Aylesford
(*Minutes of Evidence, House of Lords*)

Friday night [? 25 February 1876]   [Packington Hall]
Copy

Dear Lady Aylesford,

By the time this letter reaches you I shall have left my home for ever. Guernsey[1] knows of this, which will account for his telegram to you. I do not attempt to say a word in self defence, but you can imagine I must have suffered much before I could have taken such a step; *how* much it would be impossible to tell you, but it is the only reparation I can make to Guernsey, and he will now have the opportunity of getting rid of one who he has long ceased to care for. You do not know, you never can know, how hard I have tried to win his love, and without success, and I cannot live uncared for. I do not ask you to think kindly of me; I know you could not do it, but for God's sake be kind to the children, and do not teach them to hate their wretched mother, let them think

---

[1] The courtesy title by which her husband had been known until he succeeded, two days after their marriage, to the earldom of Aylesford.

I am dead, it will be the best. I heard from Minna[1] the other day, but never answered her letter; she will know why.

You have always been most kind to me, and it is the last word I shall ever say to you; do not be offended if I thank you for all your kindness and tell you how very wretched it makes me feel to think that I should have brought such sorrow and disgrace upon you all. Oh! Lady Aylesford, if it is possible, try and forgive me, as you hope for forgiveness. I know that Guernsey does not care for me, therefore, I do not think he will feel my loss, and perhaps may be glad to be free; but what it costs me to leave my children I cannot tell you, and I cannot bear to think; that they will be cared for I know, as you will be a mother to them, but my God I shall *never* see them again, it is like being dead and yet alive. I could not give orders about the children; they, therefore, know nothing, so please give the necessary orders yourself. I have left the diamonds with James, and as regards the things belonging to me, I have written to him to send them, and they will be forwarded to me. I wrote to Madge[2] to come to me today. I have told her all as I have told you; she has just returned to town, and I am left alone completely broken-hearted. I bring this letter to town myself. I would have seen you, but feel that perhaps you would rather not see me. God bless you, dear Lady Aylesford, and for the last time farewell, and try not to think too hardly of

EDITH

Edward Marjoribanks to Duke of Marlborough
(*Blenheim Papers*)

1 March 1876   134 Piccadilly

My dear Duke,

I write in fulfillment of my promise in the telegram I sent to Zante to explain to you the circumstances which led to it.

I hope you will forgive what may seem presumption on my part when I said that I think that any steps that you may take to influence Blandford to give up Lady Aylesford would be for the present at any rate entirely thrown away.

The only thing we can hope for at present is to postpone his final departure for as long as possible. Any suggestion of the possibility of parting them only serves to increase his obstinate determination. The one argument that seems

[1] Anne Francesca Wilhelmina (1853–1933), Lord Aylesford's sister who had married in 1875 Charles James Murray, eldest son of Sir Charles Augustus Murray who was second son of 5th Earl of Dunmore and a former Master of the Queen's Household and Minister in Portugal.

[2] Margaret Elizabeth (1839–1909), eldest daughter of Colonel Thomas Peers Williams and sister of Lady Aylesford. She married in 1866, as his second wife, Richard Lewis Mostyn Williams-Bulkeley (1833–1884), who in August 1875 had succeeded his father as 11th Bart.

to move him is the wretched position that Lady Aylesford will be placed in if she goes off with him, more particularly should anything happen to him.

When I first became aware for certain that Blandford intended to go away with Lady Aylesford the position was as follows.

Lady Aylesford had written to Aylesford informing him that she had been untrue to him and asking Aylesford to telegraph whether they were to leave at once or to wait till he arrived in England at the same time saying that should he still wish it she was ready to live as his wife before the world but no more. Blandford at the same time wrote Col Williams telling him of his intentions, expressing his readiness to meet Aylesford & promising that if a meeting was Aylesford's wish he would not go away with Lady Aylesford till after it had taken place. . . .

. . . On Friday Feb 25 Sir R. Bulkeley and Mr Hwfa Williams and other members of the family consulted at Linners Hotel. Mr H. Williams expressed his intention of calling Blandford out and also stated that should Blandford refuse to meet him he would shoot him down sooner than see him go off with his sister.

Randolph went into Linners during the evening of Friday 25 Febr and said to Sir R. Bulkeley and Mr H. Williams and Lord Hartington (who had been called in by them for advice) that Blandford would meet no one but Aylesford and that he (Randolph) would take measures to prevent a breach of peace.

On Saturday morning Feb 26 Randolph received a letter from Lord Hartington strongly urging him to induce Blandford if possible to postpone his departure till Col Williams' return.

Randolph and I at once went to Blandford and persuaded him after much difficulty to consent to allow matters to remain absolutely in *status quo* until Col Williams' return. He also pledged himself not to have any interview with Lady Aylesford during that period.

Mr Hwfa Williams still seeming bent on serious mischief Randolph thought it advisable to take steps to prevent the possibility of anything occurring and accordingly had detectives placed to watch Blandford and Mr H. Williams. These detectives were withdrawn on Monday 28th, Randolph having received an assurance from Mr Williams that he would hold his hand till his brother's return.

On Sunday morning Feb 27 Randolph & I were with Blandford all morning and after much argument he expressed himself willing to concede to proposals of the following nature viz that Aylesford should consent to be merely separated from his wife and not divorced.

That an establishment and position should be provided for her.

That she should be allowed to retain her children.

That these objects being attained he (Blandford) would absent himself from England for a year. This is the position until Col Williams' return.

It is proposed that Lady Aylesford shall go down for the present to Aylesford with the Dowager Lady Aylesford who has been very kind and seems to impute some at any rate of the blame to her son. I think it may be considered that she will either do this or go down to Wales tomorrow.

Whatever happens Blandford seems now inclined to take no decisive steps till Aylesford obtains a divorce.

Every pressure has been put upon the Prince to induce Aylesford to reconsider his determination and we now hear that Aylesford is to proceed home at once. I hope you will think that I have put the whole case sufficiently intelligibly before you. I don't think anything is very generally known as yet only the following people are aware of everything The Duchess of Manchester, The Princess of Wales, the Charles Kers and Bulkeley Hartington and Lord Alington and Lansdowne. Cornelia and Ivor [Guest] know nothing and Rosamond and Clemmie don't even know of Blandford's interview with Bertha. I showed the main portion of the letter to Lansdowne and he thinks that it adequately represents the state of affairs.

I think there is just a hope that it will eventually be arranged but I cannot speak sanguinely about it. Randolph is doing and has done all he can to influence Blandford but he is very difficult to move.

Believe me my dear Duke very affectionately yours
E. MARJORIBANKS

General Henry Ponsonby[1] to Francis Knollys
(Royal Archives)

Lord Blandford ran away with Lady Aylesford. Alington[2] interfering – asked the Pss of Wales to see Lady A. to try & make it up. Alington much taken to

[1] Henry Frederick Ponsonby (1825–95) had been Private Secretary to the Queen since 1870. Before that he had served through the Crimean War with the Grenadier Guards, and acted as equerry to the Prince Consort. In 1868 he was promoted Maj-General and retired from the Army as General in 1881. In 1878 he took on the additional post of keeper of the Privy Purse, was made KCB in 1879 and promoted GCB in 1887. 'He stood between the Queen and the whole of her household,' records the *Annual Register*. 'There was scarcely a matter of private moment on which the Queen did not take his advice'.

[2] Henry Gerard Sturt, 1st Baron Alington of Crichel (1825–1904), a grandson on his mother's side of 6th Earl of Cardigan, was MP for Dorchester and later for Dorset 1847–76. He married first his first cousin Augusta, eldest daughter of 3rd Earl of Lucan. In January 1876 his was one of eight new creations in the Peerage. Two years before Disraeli had written of the Sturts: 'She is ever pleasing, and his wondrous rattle is as good as champaign.' In his will, proved at above £43,000, Lord Alington left a set of waistcoat buttons to King Edward VII and £100 to Queen Alexandra. His new name was often mis-spelled Allington in contemporary letters: the spelling has been standardised throughout.

task for this and apologised. Lord R. Churchill who had been a very intimate friend of the P. of Wales and Pss also spoke to Her R. H'ss about it – and afterwards threatened to publish letters from the P. of Wales to Lady A. if HRH did not prevent Aylesford bringing an action for divorce.

The letters are said to be innocent but containing chaff which might be misinterpreted.

Hence the row.

Lord Alington to Benjamin Disraeli
(Royal Archives)

4 March 1876   Crichel
                                                              Wimborne

My dear Mr Disraeli,

I have deeply considered over our interview of this morning & I can come to no other conclusion but that I have been guilty not only of an injudicious but a wrong act. I will not for a moment attempt to justify it.

You and my other friends know how impulsive I am on all occasions and if I had only given myself time to reflect upon what I was about to do, I might have saved myself what I now know to have been a fearful mistake and of which I shall repent all my life. There is only one palliation for my conduct. I was actuated by kind motives. I cannot express how deeply I regret having been guilty of conduct so inexcusable – I feel that I owe a humble apology to the Princess of Wales.

I lament also that I have brought trouble upon you my dear Chief, one of my sincerest of friends and from whom I have received so many kindnesses.[1]

Believe me dear Mr Disraeli to be your very sincerely attached

ALINGTON

Queen Victoria to Prince of Wales
(Royal Archives)

10 March 1876   Windsor Castle

EXTRACT

. . . What a dreadful disgraceful business about Lady Aylesford and Lord Blandford!

And how unpardonable of Lord Alington to draw dear Alix into it! Her dear name shd never have been mixed up with such people. Poor Lord Aylesford shd not have left her. I *knew* last summer that this was going on. Those Williamses are a bad family. . . .

---

[1] He had been ennobled as recently as 15 January 1876.

Lady Ely[1] to Benjamin Disraeli
(*Royal Archives*)

EXTRACT

11 March 1876   Windsor Castle

My dear Mr Disraeli,

The Queen desires me to tell you how much annoyed Her Majesty is, at Lord Alington's having gone to HRH the Princess of Wales, about this unfortunate story of Lord & Lady Aylesford. Her Majesty thinks, perhaps you could give him a hint, that The Queen felt so sorry The Princess of Wales's name, should be mixed up in this matter, being so young & The Prince being absent, & that The Queen regrets, Her Royal Highness's name is mentioned in it. The Queen says you are so kind, so full of tact & judgment, Her Majesty feels you will manage this perfectly. . . .

Edward Marjoribanks to Duke of Marlborough
(*Blenheim Papers*)

EXTRACT

22 March [1876]   134 Piccadilly

My dear Duke,

. . . I have not written before this because really I have nothing to tell you. Owen Williams returned and will do all he can to prevent Aylesford applying for divorce. He says very truly that Aylesford is already so unsavoury that it will not do for him to appear in the Divorce Court. In any case I think it is very unlikely that Aylesford will apply for anything more than a separation. Great pressure can be applied to prevent him doing more than this.

Aylesford will not come to England at all so O.W. says. I do not know for what reason but I expect his money affairs will not allow of his doing so. I know he had not at the time of going to India paid one penny of his succession duty. There is not now the least question of a duel but if there were steps have already been taken to make it impossible.

Lady Aylesford is now at Eastbourne with her sister Mrs Seaton Montgomery. I am sorry to say the whole affair is now known to everybody even details are pretty accurately known. I attribute this to the Williams family who chose it to be known at Kimbolton and Crichel. Blandford is wildly infatuated.

[1] Jane, Marchioness of Ely (1821–90) was Lady of the Bedchamber 1851–89, and then an Extra Lady until her death. She married John Henry Loftus, later 3rd Marquess of Ely. On her death the Court Circular stated: 'Among the many devoted friends and servants whose loss the Queen has in the last years had to deplore there is no one more truly regretted than Lady Ely.'

I feel the only chance of a favourable issue is that he is prevented from actually going away with her or marrying her. Time will possibly work a change in his feelings towards her. I fear it is not likely.

I think you ought to know that Randolph has been most active in doing all he can to influence Blandford and his arguments have great force with him. In fact it is mainly if not entirely due to Randolph that Blandford has not yet taken any entirely irrevocable step. . . .

General Ponsonby to Prince of Wales
(Royal Archives)[1]

4 April [1876]

[Copy]

Hardwicke[2] conveyed the Prince of Wales' just indignation to Alington and Lord Randolph Churchill at their conduct in calling on the Princess of Wales. Alington expressed his sincere regret at the unwarrantable step. Acted on the spur of the moment hoping to avert an elopement. As an excitable man worked on by the sisters of Lady A. who he was fond of he hoped to save her from a terrible future. Lord R. has been very active in trying to prevent a liaison between Blandford and Lady A. He said he had seen her after Lord Alington, Lady Aylesford and Blandford had seen the Princess, and 'being aware of peculiar and most grave matters affecting the case he was anxious that YRH should give such advice to Lord Aylesford as would induce him not to proceed against his wife, that he was determined by every means in his power to prevent the case coming before the Public and that he had these means at his disposal. There were letters from YRH to Lady Aylesford written some years ago [which] had been found, copies of which he was determined to use to prevent the case coming into Court. They were of the

[1] Mr Robert Mackworth-Young, Librarian at Windsor Castle notes: 'This account, though in General Ponsonby's hand, may have been composed by Knollys. The first 3½ of the 4 pages are evidently the rough copy of a narrative composed for the Prince of Wales. The last half page is presumably the rough copy of additional details sent to Queen Victoria.'

[2] Charles Philip Yorke, 5th Earl of Hardwicke (1836–97). Master of the Buckhounds 1874–80. As Viscount Royston he had been MP for Cambridge 1865–73, Comptroller of the Household 1866–8, Privy Councillor 1866. Constance, Lady Battersea (1843–1931), remembered him as 'an easy-going, happy-go-lucky, brilliant member of the social world in the sixties and seventies, known for a time as "Champagne Charlie", [who] was not slow in dissipating the fortune that his father had been at such pains to build up for him. He was an entertaining talker and an agreeable companion, not devoid of talent and with much kindliness of heart. I can see him now in faultless attire, with his carefully arranged black satin tie, his beautiful pearl pin, his lustrous hat balanced at a certain angle on his well-brushed hair, his coatsleeves always showing precisely the same amount of white cuff, his pleased-with-himself-and-the-world expression.' Of Hardwicke's two daughters the elder was to marry the son of Lord Alington and the younger the stepson of Lady Aylesford's sister, Lady Williams-Bulkeley.

c

most compromising character – he had shown them to his Solicitor – they had been submitted to the Solicitor General[1] for his opinion & that opinion was that if they ever came before the public YRH would never sit on the throne of England – if A. went into Court YRH wd be put into the witness box.' These letters have been seen by O. Williams & I fear truth is undoubted. Lady A. had given these to Blandford – and he to Randolph. He would also tell Aylesford – Lord R. says that YRH has been main cause of Lady A.'s step, thro' your influence A. left his wife, you knew of Blandford's intimacy & had spoken to him on the subject. You rejected imploring letter from Lady A – in fact there was collusion between YRH and Aylesford to throw Lady A. into arms of Blandford. O. Williams thought Aylesford should call out Blandford. But preferred taking advice of Hardwicke and Hartington who agree that they do not think A. should call out B. A. told Hardwicke he had instructed his lawyer to take steps for divorce – he said S. Farquharson said at Pratts that B. had compromising letter from YRH. H. said I know something that should deter you from divorcing her and A. consented to delay for a week. Alington has seen Disraeli who knows all. My duty is to prevent divorce. Churchill's party are making this known.

Letter to Hardwicke from Lord R. Churchill

I can only understand HRH letter to you as a demand for an apology or a meeting. If I have acted indiscreetly or been guilty of the slightest disrespect to Her RH the Pss of W. by approaching her on so painful a subject I must unreservedly offer thro' HRH the Prince of W to Her R.H. the Princess my most humble & sincere apologies. This is the only apology which circumstances warrant my offering. With regard to a meeting no one knows better than HRH the P. of Wales that a meeting between himself and Ld R.C. is definitely out of the question. Please convey this to HRH.

R. S. CHURCHILL

R. Churchill had telegraphed to ask P. of W. to advise A. not to divorce. Said he could not interfere. He knew of the outrageous conduct and insult offered to the Pss. Wrote to Hardwicke – as one of those A. consulted. P. of

[1] Sir Hardinge Stanley Giffard (1823–1921), subsequently, as Lord Halsbury, Lord Chancellor in the three Conservative administrations 1885–6, 1886–92 and 1895–1905 and when out of office, at the age of 87, one of the leaders of the Conservative opposition to the Parliament Bill in the House of Lords. 'This somewhat indolent lawyer,' as the obituary notice in *The Times* described him, enjoyed 'a wonderful career, the very opposite of the story of the industrious apprentice; the story of an advocate who did not always read his briefs, one who might sometimes be seen coming to the Temple about 12 with a novel under his arm, reaching the top of his profession.'

Wales in most solemn way denies that he ever wrote any compromising letter to Lady A. and has told Hardwicke to ask R.C. to send copies of the letters to the Queen and Princess of Wales.

Lord Blandford to Lord Randolph [in Lady Randolph's writing]

5 April 1876   [? Rotterdam]

[Copy]

My dear R,

I got here today. I stopped in Brussels the night as I found the train inconvenient. I wired L on arrival so you will have heard from him of my movements. I shall stay here till I hear anything from you. If A. [Aylesford] were to take it into his head to tramp after me, I shall return to town via Harwich as I am not going in for being chased, but clearing out for a time to adjust matters & avoid a row if possible. I shall be very anxious to hear how you get on & what turn things take. Now I am gone A. is quite capable of saying that all he wished was to get her off & that now he shall do nothing & have his affairs to stay as they are. I know him very well – this cannot do for me & unless he at once either sets about a deed of separation, or files his petition, I shall return upon the scene very shortly, i.e. as soon as HRH comes back! and then the matter would all begin again. If he sets about settling the matter I shall stay away but be careful to let it be known that my object in going was to render this possible, but not to avoid meeting A. for if it is a question of having it out with him someday, I would 1000 times sooner it was now when HRH can be nicely compromised than later when he has managed to slip out of it. When this question is settled I shall go to Paris for a time and then away somewhere for a bit till all this row is over, but if there is a hitch anywhere the object for my being away ceases, & I shall certainly not stay away. Mind you let the other side know this. On the other hand if he is anxious to follow me here I shall come back forthwith & we will dispose of the matter in England – so I *depend upon you* to telegraph to me how matters stand. I talked to Edward [Marjoribanks] about the Nice journey & I really think for many reasons it is very important & it is very good of him to travel off there. Write to me 'S. Seymour Esq', Poste Restante *here* & tell me how matters stand & mind you tell me everything or I *would be mad* with you afterwards. I hope you have not got into any more bother – to a certain extent you know you are responsible for a good deal, as *you* will insist on preventing A.'s divorce & this was certain under present circumstances of making a row, & I do not know does not anyway perhaps ensure one for future, when I do come back!! Poor little E [Edith]. I telegraphed to her from Brussels, I enclose you a letter for

her. Please post it at once. When do you think you would leave town? I cd.
meet you here or at the Hague close by – the easiest journey if fine weather
will be from Harwich, the journey from Brussels here is filthy. Mind you
write to me & tell me all that takes place & particularly remember that if A.
thinks he is going to put off settling anything, so soon as HRH turns up, I
come back without fail. Good-bye old boy, many thanks to you for all the
bother you have – I must say though with Edith that it is not worth all the
trouble to avoid the Divorce Court.

Your affec brother
BD

PS One thing strikes me. If A. leaves matters as they are between him &
Edith I shall only wait till HRH comes back to appear on the scene and then
if A. tries to lick me I shall do my damndest to defend myself & afterwards
if I am all right, I shall lick HRH within an inch of his life for his conduct
generally, and we will have the whole thing up in the Police Court!!

General Ponsonby to Queen Victoria[1]
(Royal Archives)

17 April [1876]

[Copy]

General Ponsonby humble duty and regrets having to trouble your
Majesty with this painful subject but as it so seriously affects the Prince of
Wales he thinks it right to lose no time in submitting these papers. They will
explain why Lord Aylesford has not moved for a divorce and will exhibit
Lord Blandford and his brother in the most odious character by endeavouring
to drag in the Prince of Wales by a threat of publishing letters said to have been
written by HRH but which the Prince of Wales most strongly declares are
harmless.

Have telegraphed to Knollys.

General Ponsonby humble duty without the advantage of thinking the
matter over he scarcely feels competent to write on Mr Knollys' letter.

Lord R. Churchill's accusations are so revolting that they bear their own
contradiction. But the letters exist. Col W considers them compromising and
Solicitor General it is said has formed a bad opinion of them. The Prince
of Wales had evidently no evil intention in writing them and maintains they
are harmless. That is quite sufficient and proves that in reality they are so.
But if the Prince of Wales were placed in the witness box and if the letters

---

[1] This and that following, to Knollys, are presented in the form of notes in Ponsonby's
handwriting. For the sake of clarity the words abbreviated by Ponsonby are rendered in full.

were read and passages written in thoughtless haste were coloured by an unscrupulous counsellor the most serious interpretation might be put upon them. It is therefore desirable that no notice should take place. But it is equally desirable that this should not be prevented by the Prince of Wales – lest it should be supposed he feared an exposure. The telegram to Lord Hardwicke is therefore judiciously worded and it may be hoped that nothing now will be done. Mr Disraeli is in full possession of all the facts of the case and it would therefore be probably reasonable that your Majesty would hear from him.

The Prince of Wales is naturally much distressed and probably would be gratified and relieved by a short telegram from your Majesty expressing confidence in him. General Ponsonby cannot say how sorry he is for all the annoyance this must cause your Majesty.

General H. Ponsonby to Francis Knollys
(Royal Archives)

[Copy]

Gave your letter to the Queen. She has not the slightest doubt that the letters are not compromising from the minute she read that the Prince of Wales said so – that was sufficient. At the same time it was unfortunate there were any letters at all – added smiling that writing letters was a family failing. It would be so easy to twist sentences hurriedly written into something they did not mean. But Her Majesty is of course most anxious that the matter should be kept out of Court. At the same time not by desire of the Prince of Wales and she therefore thinks that HRH's telegram to Hardwicke – who has behaved very well – a judicious act. Conduct of Churchill's outrageous and as the Queen said accusations so extraordinary as to be impossible. The Queen telegraphed at once to Prince of Wales and really feels for his distress of mind – quite apart from the serious nature of the plot – will I think speak to Disraeli about it.

General Ponsonby to Francis Knollys
(Royal Archives)

18 April 1876

My dr K.

The messenger was going yesterday soon after I recd yr letter so that I had little time to do more than ackge it. I gave it as I told you to the Queen, and the P. of Wales will have recd a telm from HM about it. It is unnecessary to dwell on the outrageous conduct of the two individuals who are unscrupulous and daring it is lamentable that they shd have the power of making the threats they do.

The Q. has such perfect confidence in the P. of W. that HRH's disclaimer of any evil intentions are sufficient to convince HM that the letters are perfectly innocent. But the publication of any letter of this nature wd be very undesirable, as a colouring might be easily given & injurious inference deduced from hasty expressions. The Q. therefore regrets that such a correspondence harmless as it is, shd be in existence. But HM thinks it quite right that HRH shd not interfere in Ld Aylesford's affairs, in consequence of this threat, and considers that the P. of Wales is acting in the most proper manner in refusing to do so. The Q. knows nothing of what has been done as regards Ld and Ly Aylesford but reports have reached HM that he does not intend to apply for a divorce. If so it may be hoped that the matter will drop. The Q. thinks that Ld Hardwicke in writing so openly & frankly has behaved very well.

The Q. feels deeply the pain this matter has caused the P. of W. and had there been any probability of a public scandal in which his name cd be dragged by these villains, wd have agreed in thinking it advisable that he shd not return till a frank explanation had been publicly made, but as it could be hoped there is no prospect of any such misfortune HM hopes that conscious in his innocence he will discard all thoughts on the subject & enjoy the welcome which he will find on his return to England, where she hopes he will take as much rest & quiet as he can.

H.P.

Lord Randolph to Lady Randolph

EXTRACT

17 April [1876]   [The Hague]

. . . What do you think of my father's last dispatch? Blandford's eternal lectures and harangues always about himself are awfully wearying. *Dieu! comme il m'ennuie* I shall be so glad to get back to you darling as I am always thinking of you and the baby and wondering what you are doing. . . .

Lady Randolph to Lord Randolph

EXTRACT

19 April [1876]   London

. . . The Duke it seems is in a fright for fear you shd show his letter to Blandford he received B's lengthy epistle & was much disgusted E. said nothing but

ravings & appealing to him as a friend to help him to get a divorce from
Bertha. At first the Duke thought of not answering it but he has changed
his mind. . . .

Lady Randolph to Lord Randolph

EXTRACT

20 April [1876]   [London]

My dearest darling R,

I have just received your letter of yesterday. You ask me what I think of
yr father's 2nd epistle I think it very bad. He is quite willing that you shd
do all in your power to prevent Blandford from disgracing himself & his family
– but is not at all willing to take upon himself any of the responsibility or any
of the share of the *désagrément* which must arise from being at open war with
HRH. But my dearest there are few as generous as you & not many brothers
wld risk what you are risking for one so worthless as B tho he is yr only brother.
A letter came for you tonight from Hardwicke. I do not send it to you – as
you might miss it – besides you told me not to forward any letters. I can
hardly bring myself to write calmly about it so nasty & *disgusting* it is. It is
just a repetition of what he said to you in yr last conversation together – the
only important part being that he has heard from the Prince who wishes him
to acquaint you that the HRH has sent yr letter to the Queen. Hardwicke
adds that he was very much annoyed at the tone of yr letter & that he (H) is
not astonished. The letter will keep till yr return I shd think but it made me
boil with rage. If you want it immediately telegraph. I have it locked up
safely. *Au premier* moment I thought of writing to him telling him that you
had asked me not to forward any letters – but that if *he* thought his letter
important enough or worth sending on to you to let me know – However I
thought better of it *'le silence est d'or'* nasty hateful creature! Oh! I'm so angry
that a man of that kind shd *dare* to write to you in the way he has! *C'est trop
fort* – my own darling dear Randolph I shd give anything to have you here
tonight I feel so wretchedly – if we are to have all these worries – do for
Heaven's sake lets go through them together. As long as I have you I don't
care what happens. . . .

Lord Randolph to Lady Randolph

EXTRACT

20 April [1876]   The Hague

. . . I shall be awfully glad to get back to you, first because I love you and don't
like to be away from you and 2nd because Bd is a horrid bore. He came raving

to me just now because Lady Ad had been told by Bircham[1] that she had much better make it up with her husband. I told him to go to the devil, so he is rather angry. Really the heartless selfish way in which he talks is too much for me. He really is very bad. I am glad you wrote to my mother. I hope she don't intend to make herself disagreeable and give herself airs when she comes back. . . .

Lady Randolph to Lord Randolph

21 April [1876]   London

Dearest,

I half regret my letter of last night I wrote it on the spur of the moment & I was dreadfully angry – I hope it won't influence you in any way. If you answer H.'s letter I am sure it ought to be in the most calm & dignified manner. Don't be angry with me for offering my advice it is really very presumptuous of me particularly as you are such a capital writer but notwithstanding I am glad you will have a day or 2 to think over it – for if you answered it immediately you might write something rash. Do you think the Queen will have an interview with Disraeli? if so perhaps you will have one with him in which case he wld be sure to see the clever way you have managed the whole thing – & you may get him on yr side (in a way) before HRH returns. Am I talking nonsense? Yr letter to H. which the Prince has sent to the Queen – if I remember rightly was a very dignified firm one – & she certainly cant find fault with it if she is enlightened as to the whole matter – & if she shld – *après*! What harm can she do? That does not prevent my feeling horribly anxious – & I feel so restless & worried. I cant sit 2 mts *de suite* in a chair & I have done nothing but read that nasty hateful letter all day. I am glad I am not going to spend the evening by myself I'm to dine with Fanny & Edward [Marjoribanks] & go to the opera afterwards. I have had such a '*démangeaison*' all day to send word to Hardwicke to come & see me & then *délivré* myself of a *pièce 'à la Bd'* but discretion is the better part of valour I am only afraid I shall never have the opportunity. The idea of his talking about yr animosity to the Prince when his to you is a 1000 times stronger. I shall be so happy when you return darling. I daresay after all, things will turn out for the best *mais c'est une mauvaise cause* – & not worth all the energy & brain you have spent on it.

Mrs Hird tiresome woman has just been up to tell me that she is very angry with Cook because he has not had the upper part of the house painted – &

---

[1] Francis Thomas Bircham, senior partner in the firm of solicitors, Bircham & Co.

she says she intends having it done Monday – so you will have the benefit of it – unless you stop it on Sunday when you arrive. Remember I expect you –

Ever yrs

J.

On 11 May 1876 the Prince of Wales returned to England.

The Queen to General Ponsonby
(*Royal Archives*)

[?11 May 1876]   Windsor Castle

The Queen recd this somewhat angry letter from the P. of W. respecting Ld Aylesford. She feared as much – but after his appeal to the Queen to stand by him wh she promised, she said that he must help her – in giving up the Society he lived in – *so* constantly & said *tho* SHE *never* believed it – that people said it was Ldy A. the Pce admired – as Ld A. was too gt a *fool* to be really agreeable to the P. of W. – Hence the *most* improper *observation* in the letter. But that will pass – & as for the *others* being *asked* – how can he believe it. The Queen thinks Ld A. shd also be excluded! But that remains to be seen. Going to the opera the 1st night is a gt mistake. Show the letter to Sir Thomas[1].

The Times

ROYAL ITALIAN OPERA

12 May 1876

As it had become pretty generally known that the Royal Party could not reach Victoria Station so soon as originally expected, there was no unusual rush to the theatre at the hour appointed for the commencement of the performance. Signor Vianesi, the conductor, took his place in the orchestra at the usual time, and after the short prelude the curtain was raised with as much punctuality as on ordinary occasions. The opera was Verdi's *Un Ballo in Maschera*. The first act – in which Mdlle Bianchi (Oscar), Signors Bolis, Graziani, Tagliafico, and Scolara (the Duke, Renato, and the chief conspirators) took part – was somewhat tame, the audience coming in by driblets to stalls and boxes, although the gallery was speedily tenanted. When the second act, which possesses much more varied attraction, had begun, the house got gradually full, and more attention was paid to what went on.

[1] General Sir Thomas Myddelton-Biddulph (1809–78), Keeper of the Privy Purse 1867–78, and before that for nearly ten years Master of the Household. 'For twenty-seven years one of the Queen's most valued and confidential servants,' it was stated in the Court Circular on his death.

Occasion was even found for applauding a good deal of the music and for encoring the dramatic concerted piece, with chorus, '*E scherz' od e follia,*' the leading parts in which were most effectively given by the chief singers, strengthened by the addition of Madame Scalchi, as Ulrica. In fact, the whole passed off with spirit, and there was a good deal of applause at the end. From that moment but one idea prevailed among the vast assembly. The house now presented a really splendid appearance. To compliment the ladies on their toilettes (the great majority wore high dresses) would be supererogatory; but there can be no impropriety in saying that a more profuse display of diamonds has rarely been witnessed, even on such exceptional occasions. All thoughts were now concentred on the one looked-for event, all eyes were bent towards one direction – that of the Royal box. A rumour spread about to the purport that the illustrious party had already reached their destination, but declined to interrupt the performance of the second act by coming forward in the middle.

Rumour, however, not for the first time by many, seems to have been ill-founded. At all events, more than half an hour elapsed, amid whisperings and exclamations, 'They are coming now,' before they actually came. But when they did make their appearance – the Prince of Wales, with the Princess to his left, the Dukes of Edinburgh and Connaught to his right, and the young Princess in front – the shouts, the cheers, the 'bravos!' were as vociferous and long-continued as they were hearty and spontaneous. The whole assembly rose; and it seemed as if the demonstrations of welcome would never cease. The Prince bowed and bowed repeatedly, till he must have been fatigued with bowing; but the cheering went on. At last the curtain was lifted, the chorus filling the stage, with Mdlle Albani, as solo singer, in their midst; and Signor Vianesi raising his bâton, 'God bless the Prince of Wales,' to the stirring tune of Bronley Richards, was sung and played with a vigour and unanimity that led to a renewal of the manifestations in the form of reiterated cheering. The National Anthem followed, as a matter of course, Mdlle Albani giving the first solo with admirably marked emphasis. While all this went on the *Coup d'oeil* was really magnificent, such, perhaps, as could not be surpassed in any European theatre.

Lord Hardwicke to General Ponsonby
(*Royal Archives*)

12 May 1876   17 Arlington Street

My dear General,

I am happy to say to you that it is all settled. When I got back from the Drawing Room, I found a note from Lord Aylesford, asking me to come to see him at 5 o'clock. I went immediately. He asked my advice on these matters wh have caused anxiety. and said he wd abide by it. The result is that no Public Scandal will take place. He will arrange his matters privately and will separate from his wife making proper Provision for her etc. I went to Marlboro' House late to get to see the Prince of Wales by appointment at 7 o'clock. I saw HRH ½ an hour after that time & told him the result of my interview with Ld Aylesford.

I was & am very glad that I could state to HRH that the matter wh has caused so much anxiety was settled – if I had not been able to spare him on that point, I think complications might have arisen from the causes that I stated to you in previous conversation.

Thank God it is over & I am most thankful.

Yr sincere
HARDWICKE

General Ponsonby to Lord Hardwicke
(*Royal Archives*)

13 May 1876

My dear Hardwicke,
    The Queen is much relieved and thinks you deserve the highest credit for the manner in which you have conducted this difficult transaction and for the frank and honest way you have spoken to the P. of Wales about it.

P.

Lord Hardwicke to General Ponsonby
(*Royal Archives*)

14 May 1876   17 Arlington Street

My dear General,
    I was very glad to receive yr note yesterday.
    The Queen's gracious approval of the course I thought right to adopt is indeed a great reward, & I am most glad that my humble efforts in preventing a Public Scandal have been in some small way successful. I have advised Aylesford to keep quiet & out of the way & not to put himself forward in the Prince of Wales's society more than he is obliged to do – & certainly not to attend the Levée or the State reception.

    The Prince of Wales's opinions quite coincide with mine about *those Letters* & I hope it may be clear to him for the future what a real scoundrel Blandford is – it is quite inconceivable that a man brought up in his position shd be so lost to all feelings of self-respect & honour.

Yr sincere
HARDWICKE

The Queen to General Ponsonby [?]
(*Royal Archives*)

EXTRACT

[? 21 May 1876]   Balmoral

. . . Would he express the Queen's satisfaction at what has been done about Ld Blandford and her earnest hope that as a true friend of the Pce of Wales he [Hardwicke] will not lose this opportunity of urging him to keep clear of *all* doubtful people and especially not to let himself be mixed up in their private affairs. . . .

Lord Randolph to Lady Randolph

EXTRACT

29 June [1876]   [London]

. . . My father was to go and see HRH today at 3.30. I have not yet heard the result. . . .

Duke & Duchess of Marlborough to Lord Randolph

[?29 June 1876]   [? London]

Dearest Randolph,

Your father has written such an ample Memorandum of 'the Interview' that I have begged him to allow me to write the rest to you. He begs me to say that as he has done his best to smooth matters while at the same time avoid compromising your Position as a Gentleman & a man of honour he is sure you will now do your part in making an ample & proper apology *gracefully* worded for indiscreet language. He is sending you what he has undertaken you should say, and we think there is nothing you can object to. You will put it in your own language & no doubt express it well. The Prince was much more peacefully disposed and will not be unwilling we think to make it up. Nobody can write a letter better than you can when you take pains. The Prince seems to have gone into the whole matter fully & your Father has I am sure explained the position you are in & your objects & motives in the most favourable light to yourself. F.K. was present but I fancy he is not inclined to war and I believe that everybody in the Set are sick of the whole Fight and the unpleasantness it makes in society generally. Do not write in an antagonistic spirit and acknowledge nicely the Prince's kindness to you and Jennie last year as your ingratitude seems to rankle in his mind and disclaim any intention to make any unworthy use of those Letters. You will not suppose *I* ask you to do anything abject or humiliating but though you can truly say you have been wronged and misrepresented still you were not cautious or prudent enough. I feel so strongly that Jennie's & your future comfort is concerned in this being satisfactorily closed up, and then when you come back to England you can enter on a new *phase* and all this will be forgotten. I enclose Lord H's reply to me which I shall not answer further. It is better to let him alone. I will now admit to you that *I* wrote myself to HRH. I did not tell your Father but the Prince told him he had heard from me. As I do not wish to conceal anything from you I enclose a copy of my Letter. I have reason to think it has had a good effect. And now my dearest Boy write as your good heart and head dictate – you have no idea how all this has worried me and how I have schemed and worried to get it right. As to your dear Father his Name and reputation & advocacy with the Prince has been a Tower of strength. If it convinces you of our Love & desire for your good and makes you prudent for the future we shall not [feel] we have done it all in vain.

Yr most affec
MOTHER

[Postscript from Duke of Marlborough]

Your letter should be to the Prince, and I will look over & consider it well for you before sending it: remember 'a soft answer turneth away wrath.'

Your most affectionate Father
M.

Lord Randolph to Lady Randolph

EXTRACT

30 June [1876]
8 Clifford Street
Bond Street
London

. . . The interview between my father and HRH came off yesterday evening. It led to no satisfactory result. The Prince seems to have expressed the greatest animosity agnst me, but I believe my father stuck up to him well, and told him that if he intended to remain so highly displeased with me, he had better extend his displeasure to himself and my mother.

Hardwicke's account of his interview with me written to the Prince was read to my father. Hardwicke appears to have exaggerated much and invented more, and altogether done his best to embitter the quarrel. I have written my father an account of what really passed between Hardwicke and myself, a copy of which I will show you when you return. It is a very good letter, and my father will send it to HRH.

I have no particular news. HRH has declined Ivor's [Guest] ball. Fancy Ivor going a 2nd time to see F.K. [Francis Knollys] and ask if he was coming. F.K. shewed him all the correspondence relating to late events and also the letters and Ivor seems to have quite chimed in with F.K. He had the impudence last night to tell me that he thought I had been completely wrong all thro and when I said that whatever he thought I hoped he wld keep his opinion to himself, he replied that he *shld* do nothing of the kind. He must be mad.

Blandford has been going on in an extraordinary manner but it is much too long to write. He has been expelled from the Blues mess[1] by the committee, don't tell this to your people. . . .

Lord Randolph to Lady Randolph

EXTRACT

5 July [1876]   8 Clifford Street

. . . I think we have *remporté* a victory over Hardwicke. I met him the other day. I was in a cab in a block in Bond Street, and 'fixed' him from a long way off. I gave him such a prolonged look one of my worst scowls right at him. I fully expected a row, and indeed hoped for one, but he turned down his eyes after a second or two. He told Rosamond [Spencer-Churchill, later de Ramsey] last night that he had been very badly treated that the family distrusted him, and that he had seen my letter to my father, which was most unfair and unkind to him. What a snake!! Knollys has written to my father that HRH wishes to see him to-morrow. I think it looks like peace. . . .

Duchess of Marlborough to Montagu Corry[2]
(Royal Archives)

15 July [1876]

Private

Dear Mr Corry,
    I enclose Randolph's Letter or rather the copy of it as corrected by his Father. I should like Mr Disraeli to see it as he was so kind to me about him.

---

[1] He had served as Lieutenant, Royal Horse Guards.

[2] Montagu William Lowry-Corry (1838–1903) was private secretary to Disraeli 1866–80. The second son of Henry Thomas, 2nd son of 2nd Earl Belmore, and Harriet Anne, 2nd daughter of 6th Earl of Shaftesbury, Corry was created Baron Rowton when Disraeli retired. After his old master's death he played an influential role at Court. 'The Queen loves him,' a contemporary wrote, 'and is constantly sending for him.' It was he who had built and maintained the London lodging houses for homeless men that bear his name. Rowton died unmarried, and the title became extinct.

It was sent on Tuesday but no answer has been sent to it as yet. The letter was written at the Duke's suggestion & is a full apology for anything Randolph has done. It appears to me due to *us* that HRH should at least cause it to be acknowledged! Let me know what Mr Disraeli thinks. I have not the courage to take up his time myself on such personal matters.

Believe me, Yrs most sincerely

F. MARLBOROUGH

Benjamin Disraeli to Duke of Marlborough
(*Marlborough Papers*)

21 July 1876   10 Downing Street
Whitehall

Confidential

Dear Duke of Marlboro',

The Duke of Abercorn[1] has tendered his resignation of the Vice-Royalty of Ireland, which I shall advise the Queen to accept.

If agreeable to you, I will have the honour of submitting your name to Her Majesty as his successor.

I am much engaged tomorrow, and Mr Corry informs me, that Yr Grace is about to leave town for a few days. The matter does not press, as the Duke of Abercorn is prepared to remain in Ireland till the autumn, but when you return to London, I shall be happy to see you, and receive your decision on what is, doubtless, an affair of much moment.

Believe me, my dear Duke, Sincerely yours

B. DISRAELI

Duke of Marlborough to Benjamin Disraeli
(*Marlborough Papers*)

22 July 1876   St James's Square

[Copy]

My dear Mr Disraeli,

I have to thank you for your letter of last evening. You have again been good enough to renew to me the offer of submitting my name to the Queen for

---

[1] James, 2nd Marquess and 1st Duke of Abercorn (1811–85). Twice Viceroy of Ireland 1866–8 and 1874–6, succeeded his grandfather as Marquess at the age of 7, and was created Duke in 1868. He married in 1832 Lady Louisa Jane Russell, 2nd daughter of John, 6th Duke of Bedford, who in the course of 24 years bore him 7 sons and 7 daughters. One of the daughters was Bertha, wife of the Marquess of BLANDFORD (later 8th Duke of Marlborough). Another married the Duke of Buccleuch, a third the Marquess of LANSDOWNE and the remaining four married the Earls of Lichfield, Durham and Mount Edgcumbe and Earl Winterton.

the Viceroyalty of Ireland, when it becomes vacant by the resignation of the Duke of Abercorn. I am thankful to say that I have benefitted very much in health by passing the two last winters in the Mediterranean, and I am therefore enabled to view your proposal now more advantageously than I could have done before. The acceptance of such a high office, is as you say a matter of much moment, and the change, I may almost say the sacrifice of one's ordinary habits and engagements in England is not an insignificant one, but as you have again done me the honour to repeat the offer, you previously made, I should not feel it my duty on the present occasion to stand aloof, and I shall be therefore happy to place myself at the disposal of the Queen's service. I am leaving town for a few days, but if you can see me Thursday or Friday next I should have much pleasure in calling on you and perhaps you will let Mr Corry send me a line to Cowes to say which day will suit you best. Believe me my dear Mr Disraeli,

Yrs sincerely
[no signature]

Montagu Corry to Duchess of Marlborough
(*Marlborough Papers*)

24 July 1876   10 Downing Street

Private

My dear Duchess,

You will have seen or heard of, the announcement in today's *Daily Telegraph*![1]

I cannot imagine from what source it comes, for it is the object of all the few who are in the secret, that I know of, to keep the matter, for a time, *strictly secret*.

To Mr Disraeli the paragraph is most embarrassing! – and it is of very great importance that the fact should not yet be recognised.

He has not yet, *formally*, approached even the Queen on the subject! – for the very good reason that the Duke of Abercorn has not yet formally resigned his post!

Believe me, Yours very truly
MONTAGU CORRY

---

[1] 'It is stated that the Duke of Marlborough is to succeed the Duke of Abercorn as Lord-Lieutenant of Ireland.' The short announcement appeared on page 5, almost at the foot of column five.

Lord Cairns[1] to B. Disraeli
(*Royal Archives*)

26 July 1876   5 Cromwell Houses

Private

My dear Disraeli,

I send you fair copy of the Memo for your signature at p.5 & initials at p.8.

I also send a note I had from Ld Hartington, & (under flying seal)[2] my answer to him. Please return me *his* letter & close & forward mine to him, with the Mem.

When I get it back will you transmit it to the P. of W. or shall I?

Ever yours
CAIRNS

[*Note from Mr Disraeli: attached*]
Re Lord Randolph Churchill & the Prince of Wales, in the matter of Lady Aylesford and Lord Blandford, enclosing copy of opinion on the case, and form of adequate apology, as framed by the Lord C., Mr D. & Ld Hartington.

Statement by [?] *Lord Blandford*[3]
(*Royal Archives*)

27 July 1876

'Copies of these letters – for I absolutely refused to allow my Brother to have the originals – were placed by my Brother before your own Solicitor, Mr W. Freshfield[4], who took the Solicitor General's opinion on the matter, in conjunction with a line of defence for Lady Aylesford, charging her husband with gross misconduct, conducive to the events which had occurred, and the bearing of the letters on the case was as follows –

'These letters clearly bear the interpretation of containing improper proposals to the person to whom they were addressed, and moreover they had been shown to Lord Aylesford by Lady Aylesford *when* she received them, but had been taken no notice of by her husband.'

[1] Hugh MacCalmont, 1st Baron Cairns (1819–85), created 1st Earl Cairns 1878, was Lord Chancellor 1868 and 1874–80. The second son of Captain William Cairns of County Antrim, he rose via the offices of Attorney-General and Lord Justice of Appeal to be Lord Chancellor in the space of 19 months. His eldest son and heir, Arthur, Viscount Garmoyle, then aged 22, paid £10,000 damages in an action for breach of promise brought in 1884 by Emmy May Finney (Miss Fortescue), an actress.

[2] With a seal attached but not closed, so that the letter may be read by the person who is requested to forward it to its destination.

[3] Copied in Mr Disraeli's handwriting and forwarded to the Queen.

[4] A partner in the firm of Freshfield & Williams, solicitors to the Bank of England.

Duke of Marlborough to Francis Knollys
(Royal Archives)

6 August 1876   Blenheim

Dear Mr Knollys,

I have the honour to acknowledge your letter of the 20th ulto with its enclosure.

My son has now left on a trip to America tho' of course I can communicate
with him.

HRH the Pr of Wales however having referred my sons' letter to him of
the 17th ulto with the subject matter of his interview with HRH to high
political personage it has assumed, in one sense, an entirely new complexion.

I have returned home & must beg leave to ask time for further consideration.

I think you may wish me to return the enclosure of which I have a copy.

I beg to remain Yours faithfully
MARLBOROUGH

Montagu Corry to Duke of Marlborough
(Marlborough Papers)

12 August 1876   Osborne

Confidential

My dear Duke,

Your letter reached me, as the special train was leaving London this
morning, and I have taken the opportunity of speaking to Mr Disraeli thereon,
on the way here.

It is true, as I ventured to point out to you when you mentioned your
feelings on this subject to me, that his policy has not been to give the Chief
Secretary of the Lord Lieutenant a seat in the Cabinet, and this is proved by
the evidence of three Sessions. But Mr Disraeli thinks it right to say, frankly,
that Sir Michael Beach is the person whom he would feel bound to recommend
to the Queen as having, from his commanding position in the House of
Commons, the first claim to such advancement in the event of its becoming
necessary to strengthen the representation of the Cabinet in that assembly.
And his own elevation to the Peerage[1] cannot but render such a change probable. In that case, I am able to say, should Mr Disraeli see his way to making
some arrangement, which would give to Sir Michael Beach another suitable
post, he would avail himself of it, nor would he resign this intention in the

[1] It was announced on August 12 that the Queen intended to create Mr Disraeli 1st Earl
of Beaconsfield.

event of its fulfilment not proving immediately possible. As to the paragraph to which you refer, it is *entirely* unauthorized.

In haste – as I am anxious to catch a departing messenger.

I am yrs very truly
MONTAGU CORRY

I leave England – and part from Mr Disraeli on Monday night.

Duke of Marlborough to Lord Beaconsfield
(Marlborough Papers)

14 August 1876   Blenheim

[Copy]

Confidential

My dear Lord Beaconsfield,

The first purpose of my pen must be to congratulate you sincerely on the dignity which you have just accepted from the Crown, and which will reflect not only credit upon, but contribute so largely to the importance of our assembly. Let me say that there is I trust, a lengthened period before us for all these accruing advantages. There is another subject upon which I must now touch, and on which I hear from Mr Corry that he spoke to you the other day. I mean the change contemplated by raising the Chief Secretary to the Lord Lieutenant of Ireland to the Cabinet. Mr Corry will have informed you, that I mentioned this subject to him in a conversation some weeks ago, and in a letter from him yesterday he has given me your views regarding it. Your own change of office, will doubtless involve some other changes in the Government, but whatever these may be, I feel bound to state to you frankly what occurs to me respecting the one to which I have alluded. If, after a different arrangement continuing during three sessions, under the Duke of Abercorn's regime, the Chief Secretary's Office were now to be held by a Cabinet Minister, I think it could not but have the appearance of, and be construed to imply a want of confidence on your part in the qualifications of the succeeding Lord Lieutenant for the administrative part of his office. It would also virtually consign him to those functions of representation only, which though an unavoidable incident of his court, have to my mind, at least, always appeared the most onerous, and perhaps least attractive part of the office itself. In my own case I should feel the significance of such a change, all the more, from having had the honour of a seat in the Cabinet myself.[1] I should deeply regret complicating your arrangements with any needless difficulties, but

[1] He had been Lord President of the Council 1867–8 in Lord Derby's third and Disraeli's first Cabinet.

I do not doubt you will recognize the force of the points I have noted, to which individually I must own, I am rather keenly alive.

Believe me, Yours sincerely
MARLBOROUGH

Lord Beaconsfield to Duke of Marlborough
(*Marlborough Papers*)

31 August 1876   Hughenden Manor

Confidential

Dear Duke of Marlboro',

I have given the greatest attention to your letter of the 14th inst with the utmost desire to meet Yr Grace's wishes.

There is, at the first blush, no doubt, some little degree of anomaly in the Secretary of the Lord Lieutenant being in the Cabinet, and not himself – but it has been the frequent practice of late years. The late Ld Derby was in the Cabinet, as Mr Stanley, when he was Secretary to the Ld Lt, so, I think, his successor, Mr Littleton – certainly Lord Morpeth, and very recently, both Lord Mayo and Mr Fortescue.[1] There has been no fixed rule, but inclusion has been quite as frequent, as the reverse.

The relations betw the Lord Lt and his Secy in the Cabinet ought not to be more embarrassing than the relations between the Governor General of India, and the Secy of India, who is always in the Cabinet.

At present, there is no wish whatever to put the Irish Secy in the Cabinet, but there is a necessity to put Sir Michael Beach there, as the Cabinet requires that its numbers, rather scanty at the best, (only six), shd be maintained in the House of Commons. The promotion is due to Beach's advance in Parliamentary life.

I would prefer his sitting in the Cabinet with some other office but, at present, I fail to find the means of accomplishing that result.

I trust that Your Grace will at once recognise, that there is nothing personal to yourself in this arrangement, if it occur, and if Sir Michael Beach is promoted to another office, I do not contemplate, at present, that his successor shd be a Cabinet Minister.

I hope the Duchess is quite well, and I am, ever, dear Duke of Marlboro',

Yours sincerely
BEACONSFIELD

[1] Lord Beaconsfield was wrong about Littleton, who was chief secretary to the Lord Lieutenant 1833–4 but was *not* a member of Lord Grey's Cabinet. He was, however, correct about E. E. Stanley 1831–3, Lord Morpeth 1839–41, Lord Mayo 1866–8 and Chichester Fortescue 1868–70.

Duke of Marlborough to Lord Beaconsfield
(*Marlborough Papers*)

10 September 1876   Auchnashellach
                                                    Ross-shire

[Copy]

Confidential

My dear Lord Beaconsfield,

I have to thank you for your letter of the 31st ult.

I could easily understand when Mr Corry called upon me some weeks ago by your wish, that, as I had previously declined the offer of the Vice Royalty of Ireland, you wd be desirous before renewing that offer to know what might be my views in regard to an acceptance of the post were it again placed before me, but as the result of that interview with Mr Corry I entertained no doubt that the offer you were prepared to make to me, and which I intimated my willingness to accept, was an offer to succeed the Duke of Abercorn in the Vice Royalty of Ireland on the same terms and arrangements under which he himself had held the office.

It would be superfluous to repeat the views I have already laid before you, and I am sincerely obliged to you for the desire you express to give effect to my wishes.

I will only say that if, since my acceptance of the office you did me the honour to make me, any change has occurred in your views with regard to the arrangements with which that offer should be accompanied and which you may consider to be advantageous to yr Govt I will on hearing from you, what you definitely propose, give my best consideration to your wishes with, of course, due regard to the position I have already had the honour to occupy in a former Government.

Believe me my dear Lord Beaconsfield, Yours sincerely

MARLBOROUGH

The Duchess begs me to remember her kindly to you. I hope to be at Blenheim by the 28th.

Lord Beaconsfield to Duke of Marlborough
(*Marlborough Papers*)

13 September 1876   Hughenden Manor

Confidential

Dear Duke of Marlboro',

I had the honour of receiving your letter of the 10th inst.

I have heard recently from the Duke of Abercorn, and it is necessary that our Irish matters shd be arranged.

When the Cabinet meets in November Sir Michael Beach will be summoned to it, not because he is Irish Secretary, but because he is personally required in the Cabinet. If the Duke of Abercorn remained, or if he remains, it will be the same. Sir M. Beach will be a Cabinet Minister, and if he do not fill some other office, of which I regret to say I see, now, no immediate probability, he will be a Cabinet Minister with the department he now occupies. I write with this precision to prevent future misapprehension.

I earnestly hope that these arrangements may be consistent with Yr Grace's decision to accept the high office of the Queen's Representative in Ireland.

Yours sincerely
BEACONSFIELD

Duke of Marlborough to Lord Beaconsfield
(*Marlborough Papers*)

16 September 1876   Tobermory
                                                                Island of Mull

[Copy]

My dear Lord Beaconsfield,

I am obliged to you for your prompt reply to my last letter.

I need scarcely assure you that I have looked at the question as it is now presented from every point of view, and with every desire if possible to have waived, for the convenience of your Government, whatever objections I might personally have entertained, to the arrangement which you now intend to make with regard to the Chief Secretary's position in the Government. I have the pleasure of some slight acquaintance with Sir M. Beach for whom I entertain the sincerest respect and esteem and I cannot fail to recognize those parliamentary abilities which have earned for him a seat in the Cabinet and which must conduce generally to the advantage of the Government in whatever office he fills: further than this I wish to say that I am not insensible to the force of your remark that in practice there need not necessarily arise inconvenience from the fact of the Chief Secretary to the Lord Lieutenant being in the Cabinet, that practice having been various in former administrations, and much of course depending on the understanding arrived at between the Chief of the Gvt and the Ld Lieutenant at the time of his taking office.

And from this point of view I am brought to say that had the change you now propose been effected at any time during the Duke of Abercorn's administration, the objections I might have entertained in principle, might have been over-ruled by my succumbing to a state of things then in existence and of the purport of which there could be no doubt.

Weighing now your statements and thanking you for the assurance you have been kind enough to give me that in the change you find it necessary to make no personal reflexion is intended upon myself, I am still forcibly brought to the conclusion, that the change in the office of Chief Secretary occurring simultaneously with the acceptance of office by a new Lord Lieutenant, would be open to misconstruction, on the part of the public, in respect of the very point you are good enough to disclaim.

While my own acceptance under such circumstances might equally be liable to an invidious aspect. With these views therefore should you feel it necessary to press for an immediate decision I must say with great regret that they must operate against my accepting this office, but as I hope to be home on or before the 25th inst I shall be happy to consult some of my political friends with whom I cannot now confer, and also, if you like, to have an interview with you to bring the matter to a conclusion.

> Believe me, Yours sincerely
> MARLBOROUGH

Lord Cairns to Lord Beaconsfield
(*Royal Archives*)

20 September 1876   Millden
                                                        Brechin
                                                        N.B.
Confidential

My dear Beaconsfield,

The Pr of W. has, thro Mr Knollys, communicated to me Ld Randolph Churchill's last amende, & has begged me to inform you of it. The P. of W. intends to accept it, but thinks that it is very 'unsatisfactory,' especially the Postscript. It comes thro' the Duke of M. & I have made a copy of his letter, which I enclose. The 'amende' itself is in the words we suggested: but there is appended a PS, of wh I also enclose a copy: & the result seems to be that the Father & Son have managed, while making a submission to make it in the most ungracious & undignified way that was possible.

> Ever sincerely yours
> C.

Copy Postscript to Lord R. Churchill's letter (The letter is in the form approved by Lord B. Lord H. & the Lord Chr)

Lord R. Churchill having already tendered an apology to HRH the Pr of W. for the part taken by him in recent events, feels that, as a Gentleman, he is bound to accept the words of the Lord Chancellor for that apology.

> (Sd) RANDOLPH S. CHURCHILL, Aug 26, 1876
> Saratoga U.S.

Duke of Marlborough to Francis Knollys
(*Royal Archives*)

Copy [in Cairns' writing]

13 September 1876   Auchnashellach
                                                     Ross-shire

Dear Mr Knollys,

I have communicated with Lord Randolph on the subject of your letter of
July 30th & have now received his reply.

My son has already frankly tendered to HRH the Pr of W. his own apology
for the part taken by him in recent events. As however HRH has
submitted the matter to the consideration of so high an authority as the Ld
Chr & as the terms proposed by him have received the approval of the Queen,
Lord Randolph has no course open but to sign the apology so formed, &
such I beg to enclose.

I shall be obliged to your letting me know that the enclosure has reached
you.

                                        I beg to remain, Yrs faithfully
                                                     MARLBOROUGH

Duke of Marlborough to Lord Beaconsfield
(*Marlborough Papers*)

24 September [1876]   Highclere[1]

[Copy]

Confidential

My dear Lord Beaconsfield,

With reference to my letter to you of the 17th I now beg to say that I have
since my return to town on Friday last confidentially placed before some of my
friends the subject matter of our correspondence on which I regret that some
difference of opinion between us should have subsisted, and I have the
pleasure of saying that I am prepared to acquiesce in the arrangements you
propose for your Cabinet so far as they relate to the office, of which you have
done me the honour to ask my acceptance.

It would be satisfactory if when any announcement is made of Sir M. Beach's
promotion to the Cabinet it could appear as being independent of and prior
to the change in the Vice Regal Office. I return to Blenheim tomorrow.

                                        Believe me, Yours sincerely
                                                     MARLBOROUGH

1 The seat of the Earl of Carnarvon.

Lord Beaconsfield to Duke of Marlborough
(*Marlborough Papers*)

30 September 1876   Hughenden Manor

Dear Duke of Marlbro',

I was glad to learn that all difficulties are removed respecting yr assumption of the Vice-Royalty. You will be prepared to repair to your post about the middle, or towards the end, of November. I have informed the Duke of Abercorn who will be his successor, and you will arrange with him, for your mutual convenience.

I could not clearly understand your solution, the other day, of the Eastern question. Irrespective of the millions of Turks you would have to encounter in your proposed Kingdom, the Roumanians, Bosnians, Servians and Bulgarians are all of different races and religions, even different christian religions. The only result would be constant civil war.

Faithfully yours
BEACONSFIELD

Prince of Wales to Lord Beaconsfield
(*Royal Archives*)

27 October 1876   Euston Hall[1]
                                           Thetford

Private

My dear Lord Beaconsfield,

Many thanks for your kind letter which I received this morning.

I am delighted to hear that you had so satisfactory a conversation with the Solicitor General. I felt convinced that the statements made by Ld B. and Ld R.C. concerning him were as false as all their other statements have been found to be – but it is most satisfactory to hear the truth from the S.G. It is a pity that there is no desert island to which these two young gentlemen (?) could be banished to.

Hoping to have the pleasure of seeing you on Sunday evening next.

Believe me, Yours very sincerely
ALBERT EDWARD

[1] Home of the Duke of Grafton.

Lord Blandford to Duke of Marlborough
(*Blenheim Papers*)

9 November 1867 [1876]   Bayham Abbey[1]
                                               Lamberhurst

My dearest Father,

Although by your letters you relegate our future correspondence to the direction of our respective solicitors, I take upon myself to write to you one last letter, as an honest exposition of my views and opinions of those letters in which I am grieved to observe that you have treated me with the most *marked* want of confidence, and that in direct opposition to the trust I have throughout placed in you. Between my mother and I although there may be no further communications, there shall *never* be any discussions. To her I will never write or say an unkind word, whatever happens; but between yourself and I explanations are possible, and I am only grieved that they should take the present form.

I have behaved to you throughout these sad affairs in a *thoroughly* straightforward spirit, and have never concealed either my wishes or my actions in any single way. For the last 3 months, I have restrained every high feeling, every personal object, so as to conform my conduct to the interests of my family & your own wishes.[2] This course I have loyally followed, at the most terrible sacrifice of one I most care for, and at the expense of *severe* condemnation by others! And the only thanks I get from you is your last letter. So long as things go as you wish, so long you favour me with what you consider sympathy and affection. But no sooner is it shewn by events[3] that your ulterior objects are unattainable, then you cast aside any scruples and are ready to sacrifice your son's life and entire happiness to the exigencies of 'Position' & 'Family importance'!

You have displayed to me an untold cruelty of intention.[4]

What can it affect you who I marry and who my children may be?

In what manner do they come into the circle of your life? What matters it in the future of our things?

For what considerations of a worldly character have you thought fit to step in to sacrifice my whole life?

[1] The seat in Kent of the Marquess CAMDEN. Blandford's aunt Clementine, the widowed Marchioness Camden was shortly (on December 28) to marry Captain Philip Green.

[2] The Duke of Marlborough made a number of comments on various passages in this letter on a separate sheet of paper. Here he notes: 'I entreated him to go abroad to give up Lady A. Further than providing for her actual requirements and to allow time for friends to intervene and settle the actions either between her and her husband, or him and his wife. Instead of which he has continued in England seeing and hearing from Lady A.'

[3] 'The event alluded to is a shameful letter to his wife determining her to commence divorce proceedings.'

[4] 'Quite incomprehensible.'

Have I not clearly shewn you what these things are to me and what issues they lead to and how dare you entail upon me such persistent misery?

You accuse me of initiating Lady Blandford into a Divorce. I have done no such thing! I wrote to her plainly the truth 'that I would not under existing circumstances desert Lady Aylesford'. (And no more I will I have always told you so). And I retorted to certain passages and *allusions* she thought fit to make in a letter to my mother which letter she clearly intended for my eye.[1]

Do you think I will allow myself to be raked without making any reply? Her sentiments were hostile, and my letter was a defence and as they had to war, I accept the conclusion.

I am fully aware of the secret agency that has influenced your conduct towards myself.

My brother Randolph . . . for the most sordid motives induced me to repose in him my confidence and *without that confidence he would have been powerless.* Against this rests the whole strength of my indictment against him. From the matter of the Prince of Wales's letters to the substance of his private enquiries the understanding was *one of honour* from one brother to another! And when you took over his case from Mr Freshfield you were *honour* bound by those conditions.[2]

Since the other day in London when you preferred to retain a set of copies of the Prince of Wales's letters notwithstanding the fact of Randolph's declaration on honour that he had returned his (though heaven knows what use they were to you)[3] and later still only the other day when you were so anxious not to write to Mr Freshfield yourself because he was 'Randolph's solicitor' and you did not wish to be mixed in the matter, I have seen that you were really concealing from me the conduct you wished to pursue, and that after having paid a large sum for these researches after evidence of a private nature

[1] 'The only allusion can be to Lord Aylesford's not obtaining his divorce and his not marrying Lady A. My only communications with him on this subject latterly have been on the ground of repeated declarations that he was willing to give up Lady A. if a proper arrangement could be made.'

[2] 'It is an absurd statement no case has been ever taken over by me from Mr Freshfield to whom I have never given an instruction. Lord Blandford applied to me to authorise Mr. F. to hand over to him and for his own use certain facts which had been ascertained with his own knowledge and connivance repecting Lord Aylesford. He called on Mr Freshfield himself in order to obtain this information by which he intended to prevent Lord A from obtaining his divorce and feeling the important bearings of the case in many ways I had a private interview with Mr F.'

[3] 'This is an absolute falsehood. Copies of these letters existed in a case for council which had been sent on to me when I was abroad and which had been looked up with other papers as soon as I was aware that the said letters and copies had been returned. I returned the case to the solicitor by whom it had been prepared, and I have reason to know that the copies were destroyed at the same time. A few days after this Lord B wrote to me hoping that I would retain the copies.'

you were determined to countenance Randolph's conduct towards myself!

Lord Aylesford most naturally considers, as most people would that it is preferable '*to wash one's dirty linen at home*' and not to deluge the law courts with defended trials of a scandalous character.

I am determined however not to be misrepresented in these affairs. Had you and my brother taken an independent line of your own from the outset you had a perfect right to do so; but I should like to know what right *you and he* had anyway, to those letters of the Prince of Wales'??!!¹

Does this fact in itself not clearly show, that you and my brother were acting in conjunction with myself?

How could *you* alone have used these letters which were *solely* the property of Lady Aylesford! Were you prepared to take this poor lady's letters and use them against her *interest*????²

I take this as a single ... of the case! What right morally have you got then for you to direct Mr Freshfield to take an independent line to my own solicitor and against Lady Aylesford?³

I have drawn up a succint statement of my "conduct" and I shall place it before all those who are concerned in this matter beginning from the beginning when E. Marjoribanks at Randolph's request took you our copies of various documents to him, and also copies of HRH's letters, down to the present time!!

I am determined to bear *my share* and *only my share* of the odium of these 'secret and mysterious family manoeuvres'.

Moreover supposing that there were the least probability of a reconciliation being effected do you think that your threats through Mr Freshfield to the other side⁴, are likely to enduce them to carry out your wishes. If it is true what you say that Lord Ad could not get his case, why did you not tell your solicitor to withdraw and let him consider what was best for him to do himself?⁵ As matters now stand everyone is perfectly aware of the state of these affairs, and there is the *very strongest* feeling generally about the line the family has adopted, from the matter of the Prince of Wales' letters downwards. And my brother's conduct is universally condemned as being inspired by the meanest and most sordid motives of self interest, and I do not think that

¹ 'This is almost amusing were it not too serious and painful. Lord B. originally handed the copies of these letters to his brother and threatened if necessary to use them himself against a certain person and it was in consequence of this threat on his part that his brother incautiously became mixed up with the possession of copies of these letters, and the part then taken by him in that affair he has frequently heard from me my disapproval and at my instance has apologised to the Prince. It is well known that I have said how I came to the copies of the letters.'

² 'Simple ravings.'

³ 'Idem. I had given no instructions whatever to Mr Freshfield.'

⁴ 'Already answered.'

⁵ 'Already answered.'

this opinion will fade as time goes on. In fact I should be very sorry to change places with him!!

There is only one course before you in refutation of the severe line of hostilities that has been credited to you, which is to instruct *your* solicitor Mr Freshfield to withdraw *honestly* and *entirely* from this matter. Whether there be a real case or not no man will stand being bullyraged by private enquiries about his life in open court & Lord Aylesford is perfectly right not to submit himself to such an ordeal.[1] Whether things could be proved against him or not or whether a defence were instituted by me or others.

So long as it was clearly detrimental to Lady Aylesford to be divorced by her husband, I was persuaded to try and check the other side by threatening to defend the case,[2] but after Lady Blandford has stated her intention of going into court, it no longer becomes necessary for me to follow this line of opposition, and as both you and my brother from the beginning associated yourselves in *honour* with my line of action, you have no sort of right to depart from it, without being accused of utter breach of confidence towards myself.

Regarding Oak Dene I am much obliged to you for your offers generally, but as it is my intention to reside there sooner or later, it will be unnecessary for me to discuss them with Mr Milward.[3]

The copy of this letter I keep as the last I shall write you on this most painful subject, and as a testimony of the line of conduct I have pursued *throughout* in the matter, and I hold myself at liberty if necessary to show it to all my friends in this affair.

I can only say in conclusion that though I have been for some considerable time prepared for Randolph's treachery *you* certainly were the very last person I should have believed would have countenanced it, after it had been put plainly before you and was patent to *every* member of the family and the whole world besides!!!

Herewith I close this letter which is indeed the last you will ever receive from me unless you give me the opportunity of withdrawing the statements therein contained by a *free* and *frank* assurance of yours and my brother's entire withdrawal from the whole of these affairs so far as they concern myself and Lady Aylesford.

Your affectionate son
BLANDFORD

---

[1] 'Lord B's application to Mr Freshfield will be remembered.'

[2] 'These threats have probably brought about what Lord B. is now so angry at.'

[3] Robert Harding Milward (1838–1902), solicitor, Justice of the Peace. In 1902 having been declared bankrupt for £97,000 and struck off the rolls, he was sentenced by the Lord Chief Justice to six years penal servitude on conviction of fraudulently converting to his own use moneys entrusted to him. He died in prison a few months later.

Duke of Marlborough to Lord Calthorpe[1]
(Blenheim Papers)

14 November 1876   Blenheim

Copy [in Lord Randolph's writing]

My dear Calthorpe,

I think it best to write to you a few lines at once, as I hear from Mr Milward that you have had an interview with him, with reference to some statement which it appears Blandford has placed in your hands.

What the contents of that statement may be, I am of course unaware, and do not trouble myself for a moment to know, and I am equally indifferent as to any use that Blandford may choose to make of it. All I have to remark on this subject is (and it may be as well, as he has put himself into communication with you, that I should state it unequivocally) that I have received from him a scandalous letter of misrepresentations, and assertions without a shadow of fact; and that though it is wholly beneath me to notice them with any reply, this must necessarily break off all correspondence between him and me for the future, and except so far as family interests may necessitate, any interference on my part with his affairs.

Of the honourable and friendly intentions which have led you hitherto to interest yourself in Blandford's matters I have no doubt, but as I have now unhappily had to acquaint you with the setting on which Blandford by his letter to his wife and his subsequent one to me, has now placed himself with his family I leave it to you to judge whether further interference can do any good.

Believe me (tho I write this with much pain)

Yours sincerely
signed
M.

Lord Calthorpe to Duke of Marlborough
(Blenheim Papers)

15 November 1876   Willey Park[2]

Private

Dear Duke,

I wrote to Randolph at Blandford's particular request and not because I had any wish to be mixed up in these unhappy matters. Last week at Henham

[1] Frederick Henry William, 5th Baron Calthorpe (1826–93). Formerly MP for East Worcestershire. Died unmarried.
[2] Seat of Lord Forester in Shropshire.

I received a letter asking me to call on Saturday and read a letter which Blandford had written to you. On hearing it read on Saturday I said it was a most improper one and ought not to be sent. And then I heard for the first time that it had gone by Thursday's post. I repeated that to Blandford on Sunday morning and he then said he would not have sent it, if I had been against so doing. He then read me a statement which I locked up and got him to promise that he would not show it to friends as he had intended. He said that he had been accused of conniving at difficulties placed in Aylesford's way of sueing for a divorce. I told him that one of the penalties he must pay for his great faults, was to bear evil reports and even false ones, but that replying in the way he intended was of no use. Blandford suffers from *cacoethes scribendi* and he has a liking for what the Yankees call tall writing which leads him to use language which is stronger than which he perhaps fancies at the time and which I am sure, he must regret in quieter moments. I do not say this [as] an apology for his letter to you which nothing can excuse, the only palliation to be offered is that he is half mad with worry, anxiety and suspense. He broods over his wretched affairs till he hardly knows what he is saying and writing. It is all very melancholy and I confess I do not see a way out of them at present. I happened to call at Milward's on Monday, and there I found Blandford's unmistakeable volumes on his table. I did not go to Milward's to consult him on that subject but naturally asked him about Lady Blandford's divorce and how soon it could take place and about evidence with reference to Aylesford etc. I should not have thought of seeing Blandford on these matters had I not been asked to do so. He came to breakfast on Sunday as I left for Birmingham in the afternoon. Please to thank Randolph for his letter.

Yours very truly
CALTHORPE

In great haste

Lord Blandford to Duke of Marlborough
(Blenheim Papers)

[?] November 1876   Bayham Abbey

My dearest Father,
    I address you the following letter feeling convinced that I was totally and entirely in the wrong, in writing to you the letter I did the other day and I offer you my entire apology and retract all the statements therein contained which were hurtful to you ... I have asked Calthorpe to be so kind as to forward you this letter on my behalf and I beg you to consider the excessive mental

pressure produced, by *months* and *months* of perpetual anxiety, driven in the end to the verge of despair, as the cause of my writing to you as I did.

I am prepared to surrender myself to your decisions unconditionally, and I shall offer no opposition to the course you pursue and I shall also refrain from making any intrusions of opinion on the subject in any way whatever. From the beginning of these disasters I have tried my utmost to consider the interest of my family and preserve their friendship and affection, and I am only sorry that at a time of the most fearful apprehensions of my own extinction I was so carried away as to address you in the manner in which I did.

It is for this reason that I now write to you this letter, as a free withdrawal of my sentiments, as expressed in my last letters and *from no other* motive.

I can truly assure you that so far as in me lays, I most firmly wish, under these most difficult and trying circumstances, to act in a proper way to you as regards my family and for myself as a gentleman.

Once more then: forgive me if, borne down by care and anxiety, I have so far succumbed as to have temporarily departed from that course, and accept my assurances that I write you this letter solely from the wish to withdraw myself from an improper position as regards yourself & that whatever be your line of conduct, I have fully and entirely divested my mind of all ill feeling in the matter.

With regard to my brother Randolph I have endeavoured in my life to act as a kind brother to him, in proof of which I can only refer him to his own conscience, and if I have unjustly suspected his feelings towards me, or in any way misrepresented his actions, I am truly sorry for it.

With these words I conclude and can only hope, that whatever be the future, you will extend to me those generous feelings of forgiveness, which if uncommon in the world in which we live, are surely not out of place between a father and his son.

Your most affectionate son
BLANDFORD

Sir Michael Hicks Beach to Duke of Marlborough
(*Marlborough Papers*)

20 November 1876   Chief Secretary's Lodge
Phoenix Park

My dear Lord Duke,

When we met in London you mentioned to me your intention of appointing a Roman Catholic to a place in your Household – and as you rather consulted me on the subject, I venture to write a line to you upon it. The enclosed paragraph appeared in Saturday's *Evening Mail* the Orange Tory Dublin organ, which has, however, supported us very steadily. The point in it worth notice is, I think, that an English Roman Catholic nobleman would not be a popular appointment: and in this, I quite concur with the paragraph. I dare say I failed to express this view in our conversation: but I had the precedent of Lord Gormanston[1] in my mind, and it did not occur to me that you would be likely to think of an Englishman. Very likely you have never done so, & the whole story is an invention: but I think you will excuse me for calling your attention to it. The place in question is, I presume, the Chamberlain; and I think you would want in that office some one who knows something of Irish (& Dublin) society. I do not know whether you propose to have any R.C. ADC – but that is a minor office, & would not be considered by the R.C.'s as of any particular consequence.

You mention that you understand that Lord Randolph, if appointed your Private Secretary, would not have to vacate his seat. If I might advise, I think you should obtain the opinion of the highest authority on this, to avoid the possibility of trouble. I hardly see how the appointment of private secretary to the Lord Lieutenant differs *technically* from that of Chief Secretary to the Lord Lieutenant, which certainly vacates the seat. The Law offices might be consulted: but Sir Erskine May's[2] opinion would probably be the best.

I expect to be back in London on Thursday morning for the Cabinet. If it were convenient to you to meet me either in St James's Square or at the Irish Office at any time not later than 2 p.m. on that day (the Cabinet is at 3) we might talk about these and many other matters. Or if not, could you name some subsequent day which would suit you?

The Duke of Abercorn leaves on the 6th: so I dare say you will come on 7th or 8th, instead of in the following week, as I think you had intended.

Your Grace's very truly

M. E. HICKS BEACH

Duke of Marlborough to Lord Blandford
(*Blenheim Papers*)

26 November 1876   Blenheim

Copy [in Lord Randolph's writing]

My dear Blandford,

I am sure you must be unhappy, and I truly pity anyone who has so much cause for it. If any remedy is possible it will not be found in writing letters which can only do harm and render your case more desperate.

---

[1] Jenico, 14th Viscount Gormanston and premier viscount of Ireland (1837–1907), had been (as Hon J. Preston) Chamberlain to the Duke of Abercorn in Ireland 1866-8.

[2] Thomas Erskine May (1815–86); constitutional lawyer, Clerk of the House of Commons 1871–86. Author of standard work on parliamentary procedure. KCB 1866, created Baron Farnborough 1886.

D

It can only be by looking at and recognising your own acts, seeing yourself as the agent and not attributing to others the results of yr proceedings.

Yr last letter is a full retraction of yr former one and I accept it in the freest manner in the spirit in which it is meant; but when you say 'You resign yourself to my decisions unconditionally and that I have no opposition to the course I pursue' you are still under a misconception. I have come to no decision, I have pursued no course, I have given no instructions; Mr Freshfield is not my agent, neither am I his client, and if you wish to be convinced of this Mr Milward can let you know what he Freshfield has written him. It is absolutely necessary he should see and answer the statements you made in your letter of the 9th.

There is not much more that I can say. I can tell you truly that I am no more implicated in any relationship to your unhappy affairs, than I ever have been since its commencement, and my only desire is and has been, in any interposition in your affairs to save you from the discredit of a public lawsuit with Bertha and from the consequences of a future which would annihilate every hope of your retrieval or restoration.

Believe me, yours affectionately

MARLBOROUGH

Sir Michael Hicks Beach to Duke of Marlborough
(*Marlborough Papers*)

23 November 1876   Irish Office
Great Queen Street

My dear Lord Duke,

After I had written to you the other day, the Duke of Abercorn told me that it had been arranged that your patent should date from the 10th. I did not know this before – of course under these circumstances, the day originally fixed (the 12th) would be the best for taking the oaths. I shall therefore expect you & Lord Randolph on that morning – and will send my carriage to meet the mail train at Westland Row station.

The paragraph about the Chamberlain's appointment is certainly not worth contradiction – I doubt if Lord Gormanston would take office now, even if this office could be held by a Peer: his father was alive, & he was a younger man by some years when he was in the Duke of Abercorn's household.

I really fear there is something in the point about Lord Randolph's vacating his seat. *I* certainly had to do so – the point is, that the Lord Lieutenant is the Crown in Ireland, and therefore his private secretary may be taken to hold office from the Crown, which of course the private secretary of no Minister does. In fact your private secretary is, I imagine, in the same position as her

Majesty's. I believe that Dyke[1] thinks that the seat would have to be vacated, and he ought to know. But I will make further enquiries, and let you know. I would suggest that you might postpone *formally* making the appointment until you can arrive at some certainty on the matter.

I should have much liked to have gone down to Blenheim for a night or two, as you kindly propose. But today and tomorrow, the Cabinets do not begin till 3 p.m. and by the time they are over, I could not catch any but a late train.

From Saturday to Monday I am engaged to go into Hampshire. However, except this matter of Lord Randolph, I don't think there is anything that requires discussion, & that might keep. You will I believe have to make a fresh application through the Home Office for a Queen's letter authorising you to appoint Lords Justices on the 12th, without which you could not leave Ireland. I will get the form in a day or two, and send it to you for signature: and the Queen's letter will then be sent to you, so that you can bring it over when you come. This is rather irregular – but otherwise you would have to remain in Ireland for a week, while the forms of applying for and obtaining the Queen's letter were gone through.

Believe me, Your Grace's very sincerely
M. E. HICKS BEACH

Lord Beaconsfield to Duke of Marlborough
(*Marlborough Papers*)

1 December 1876   2 Whitehall Gardens

Confidential

Dear Duke of Marlborough,

The Queen mentioned to me, that her Majesty intended to have the pleasure of receiving the Duchess and yourself, at Windsor, and begged me to take an opportunity of intimating to you, that it would be highly agreeable to Her Majesty, if no references were made to domestic circumstances, wh have occasioned the Queen anxiety and deep regret.

Your Grace will, therefore, I am sure, excuse me for writing to you thus frankly.

I trust I shall have the pleasure of seeing you before you leave England.

I leave town on Monday for a week; after that, I shall be found here for some time: at least to Xmas.

With my complimts to yr Duchess, Yours sincerely
BEACONSFIELD

[1] Sir William Hart Dyke, 7th Bart (1837–1931), a Conservative Whip since 1868, was patronage secretary to the Treasury 1874–80 and himself chief secretary to the Lord Lieutenant of Ireland (Lord Carnarvon) 1885–6.

Duke of Marlborough to Lord Beaconsfield
(*Royal Archives*)

2 December 1876   Blenheim

Confidential

[Copy]

My dear Lord Beaconsfield,

In reply to your letter; the Queen has done the Duchess and myself the honour of inviting us to Windsor on Monday next and I need hardly say that under any circumstances I should have considered it quite out of place on such an occasion to have made any allusion to her Majesty without her Permission to recent domestic events which have been a source of anxiety and regret to the Queen and are still an occasion of the severest pain to ourselves. I may say to your Lordsp, and I trust when you are able you will have the kindness to express it to her Majesty, that in the course of these events which have been entirely beyond our control, the opinion which her Majesty may have formed over such of the facts as have come within her knowledge has been a matter of deep concern to me and that in the painful position it has occasionally been my lot to occupy, whatever may have been my individual feelings the advice I have tendered has been influenced by my Duty to the Queen and when given, it has been, I must say, unhesitatingly accepted.

I propose going to Dublin on the 11th and hope to have the pleasure of calling on you on my return through town.

Believe me, Yrs Sincerely
MARLBOROUGH

Duchess of Marlborough to Lady Cornelia Guest
(*Wimborne Papers*)

EXTRACT

[?2 December 1876]

. . . We got on Friday a telegram from Sir J. Cowell[1] inviting us to Windsor Monday with Rosd. I suppose this is mere civility, but it would be horrid going there & today your father got a letter from Dizzy saying that the Q. hoped no allusion would be made to certain domestic events which had given HM "the greatest concern & anxiety". Its all most unpleasant & humiliating. Oh dear – when will all this annoyance be at an end? . . .

[1] Sir John Clayton Cowell (1832–94), Master of the Household 1866–94. Before that, as a Major in the Royal Engineers, he had been tutor to Prince Alfred and Prince Leopold 1856–66. His wife, Georgina Elizabeth Pulleine (1846–1927), was a first cousin of Edward Marjoribanks, later 2nd Baron TWEEDMOUTH.

The Queen to Lord Beaconsfield
(*Royal Archives*)

5 December 1876   Windsor Castle

In returning the Duke of Marlborough's letter, the Queen wishes to say that she was much grieved to see the alteration in both of them since she saw them at Osborne a year & 4 months ago. They looked so *distressed, wretched* & the poor Dss especially, who cd scarcely restrain her tears. They avoided any allusion but spoke to the Dss of Roxburghe[1] & she described their *agony* of *anxiety* about the *Divorce* as most distressing. She told them of the advice the Queen *had* given the Abercorns, but they are very much hurt at the Abercorns not having consulted them about it. Could not Lord Beaconsfield *write* to the Duke saying he hoped he wd follow (for the position of his children & gd children) the advice wh. he knows the Queen had on consulting the Chancellor given him? The Queen does not feel sure whether he showed this last letter to Lord Beaconsfield, & the Dss is ill in bed, & the Duke in thanking the Queen for the 2nd Vol of the Prince's life *never* alluded to the subject. The Marlboroughs are vy sore abt Lord Randolph the Dss of Roxburghe said.

Duchess of Marlborough to Lady Cornelia Guest
(*Wimborne Papers*)

EXTRACT

7 December 1876   Blenheim

. . . The Visit went off very well. The Queen *wonderfully* civil in fact I never saw her more gracious. She talked a long time to me, complimented me on Rosd's appearance made all sorts of little jokes abt the Ladies kissing the Duke & she joked about Clemmy[2] marrying a Green in short she was in wonderful spirits. . . .

The Times

13 December 1876

DUBLIN, Tuesday night

His Grace the Duke of Marlborough arrived at Kingstown this morning from Holyhead by the mail steamer Connaught. Although the weather was

---

[1] Susanna Stephania, only daughter and heiress of Lt-General Sir James Charles Dalbiac, married John, 6th Duke of Roxburghe, in 1836. Born in 1814, she was a Lady of the Bedchamber from Queen Victoria's accession (1837) to her death 7 May 1895. Lady Anne Spencer-Churchill, a younger (b. 1854) sister of Lord Randolph, had married the Duchess of Roxburghe's eldest son, the Marquess of Bowmont, on 11 June 1874. He became Duke of Roxburghe on his father's death 23 April 1879.

[2] Lady CAMDEN.

bitterly cold, and there was no shelter on the landing pier from a piercing wind, blowing from the north-west, a number of people assembled to see the new Viceroy, and awaited his arrival with exemplary patience. The steamer was three-quarters of an hour late, having been detained at Holyhead by a delay of the mail train. His Grace, who was accompanied by Lord Randolph Churchill, was received on landing by Lord Caulfield, Controller of the Household,[1] Captain St Leger, Harbour Master[2], Captain Byng, ADC[3], Mr Bernard, ADC,[4] and other members of the Viceregal Staff, and was conducted to the carriage prepared for his accommodation in the special train which was waiting. At Westland-row other members of the Household awaited the arrival of his Grace, and a carriage was in readiness to convey him to the Chief Secretary's Lodge. At 4 o'clock he drove to Dublin Castle, where he was received by the Lords Justices and Privy Council, and having delivered the Letters Patent of the Queen appointing him to the office of Lord-Lieutenant, took the usual oaths, and was invested with the Collars and Insignia of the Order of St. Patrick. His Grace then took his seat at the Council, and at a given signal a salute of 15 guns was fired from the ordnance in the park. His Grace then proceeded with the members of the Privy Council and officers of State to the Presence Chamber, where he took his seat on the throne, and a salute of 21 guns was fired. The principal officials were afterwards presented, and his Grace, at the conclusion of the ceremonial, drove to the Chief Secretary's Lodge.

Lord Randolph to Lady Randolph

13 December [1876]   Vice Regal Lodge
                                                              Dublin

My dearest,

    I have just time to write you a few lines. We have had a vy interesting time over here & everything has passed off in a most satisfactory manner.

    [1] James Caulfeild (1830–1913) was not entitled to a courtesy title, being heir to the Irish Viscountcy of Charlemont and to an Irish Barony as Lord Caulfeild, of Charlemont, to which he succeeded in 1892 on his cousin's death, but not to the Irish Earldom of Charlemont or to the United Kingdom Barony of Charlemont which became extinct in that year. Caulfeild, who had served as Captain, Coldstream Guards, throughout the Crimean War, was Comptroller to the Viceregal Household 1868–95, and Usher of the Black Rod of the Order of St Patrick 1879–1913.
    [2] James Aldworth St Leger (1814–77), Captain, Royal Navy, retired. He was the fourth son of Colonel Richard St Leger, younger son of the 1st Viscount Doneraile.
    [3] George Stanley Byng (1841–89); Captain, Rifle Brigade, ADC to the Lord Lieutenant of Ireland 1876–82. Succeeded his uncle as 8th Viscount Torrington, 1884.
    [4] Percy Brodrick Bernard (1844–1912) had previously been private secretary to the Duke of Abercorn. He was the eldest son of the Rt Rev Charles Brodrick Bernard, Bishop of Tuam, who was the second son of 2nd Earl of Bandon. At the time of his death Percy Bernard, who was twice a widower and three times married, was heir presumptive to the earldom.

We are just starting for the boat on our way home & have every prospect of a most rough passage. I am to act as my father's private secretary without any salary which obviates any difficulty abt the seat & still allows of my making myself useful. Percy Bernard will be gazetted P.S. I can live in the house, which I have been to see & which is charming in every way, but I cant write it all.

I hope you have been happy & enjoying yourself. Please give my best love to Aunt Mary & Uncle Vane[1]; & tell them how sorry I was to leave Wynyard. I shall expect you at Blenheim Saturday night.

Goodbye darling, Yours ever
RANDOLPH

Duke of Marlborough to Lord Beaconsfield
(*Royal Archives*)

17 December 1876　　　　　　　　　　　　　　　　　　　　　Blenheim

Most Confidential

My dear Lord Beaconsfield,

I was interrupted in the few things I wanted to say to you respecting the enclosed correspondence, which is the sequel of, and must also be taken as concluding the matter of the 'Memorandum and Apology'.

Although Randolph may have been indiscreet in his share of these transactions, not to say intemperate, it could not escape observation that the Memorandum bore somewhat of an '*ex parte*' character and which became equally imparted to the apology as well.

However, as in all such circumstances the disparities of position are so great and the issues so disproportionate, it was better that an error where it had been committed should be acknowledged in terms which admitted those disparities and withdrew from those issues.

Nothing can now be gained by keeping these questions alive; for my own part I consider them settled, by the correspondence which I enclose: but as the facts may not as yet have been put before you, I am desirous that *you* should know that an acceptance of a certain apology was promised; and that that apology has been tendered, and its receipt has been acknowledged.

Believe me, Yours sincerely
MARLBOROUGH

[1] The Marchioness of Londonderry (1826–1906) and her husband, George 5th Marquess (1821–84), brother of the Duchess of Marlborough. He had succeeded his father as 2nd Earl Vane in 1854 before succeeding his step-brother, 4th Marquess, to the Londonderry title in 1872. Lady Londonderry was Mary Cornelia, only daughter and heiress of Sir John Edwards, 1st and last Bart.

Francis Knollys to General Ponsonby
(*Royal Archives*)

17 December 1876   Marlborough House

My dear Ponsonby,

Lord Blandford and Lord Randolph Churchill laid so much stress upon what they stated was fact, viz, that the Prince of Wales in spite of all that Lady Aylesford could say to the contrary, insisted on taking Lord Aylesford to India with him, that his Royal Highness thinks the Queen ought to see the two accompanying copies of letters which he received from Lady Aylesford, and which he has only just accidentally found.

You will see by letter No 2 that Lady Aylesford gave up her opposition, and that she thought with the Prince of Wales, that it would be greatly to Lord Aylesford's advantage that he should accompany His Royal Highness on the occasion in question.

I shall be obliged to go to Windsor on some private business either tomorrow or next day, and I shall try and find you.

Yours sincerely
FRANCIS KNOLLYS

The Queen to General H. Ponsonby
(*Royal Archives*)

[?25 December 1876]

The Queen considers that the P of W understands that the Queen *cannot entirely* exclude Ld Randolph from *Court Festivities* after the *Apology*? She wd like to have this letter back. The Queen is in no hurry to see the letters & only *asked* as the P of W *originally said he* had desired copies to be sent to the Queen.

General H. Ponsonby to Francis Knollys
(*Royal Archives*)

25 December 1876

My dear Knollys,

I gave yr letter to the Q. HM commands me to observe that she concludes that the P. of Wales understands the Q. cannot entirely exclude Ld R.C. from Court festivities now that the apology has been accepted.

I think yr remarks that the P of Wales will bow but not speak to him, shows that HRH takes the same view.

The Q. agrees with the P of W in looking over the letters with him.

P.

Francis Knollys to General H. Ponsonby
(*Royal Archives*)

EXTRACT

27 December 1876   Sandringham

My dear Ponsonby,
   I think it will be desirable that no formal intimation respecting R. Churchill's apology should be sent to the D. of Marlborough, but I see no reason why if an opportunity presents itself, he should not be informed through some mutual friend, the reason why no regular acceptance was returned by the Prince. . . .

Duchess of Roxburghe to General H. Ponsonby
(*Royal Archives*)

Thursday [?28 December 1876]   Windsor Castle

My dear Gen Ponsonby,
   Before sending this in – please say if you approve – as I quote you freely!
                                                         Yours [? very sincerely]
                                                         S. ROXBURGHE

Attached:

From General H. Ponsonby

MEMORANDUM

The P. of Wales thro' Knollys agreed to accept Ld R's apology if couched in language dictated by Ld Chancellor, Hartington & Beaconsfield. It was acd [acknowledged] (Sept) But not yet accepted. However ungraciously done it *was done* by Ld Randolph & he performed his part of the agreement he is entitled to have it accepted.
   If utterly unworthy of being noticed no apology shd have been suggested. G.P. agrees that the P shd (privately) consult Ld Ch who is his *friend* – & *proposer* of the document
F. Knollys said in the July letter
If he writes an apology according to the exact terms & wording of the appendix HRH will accept it.
I spoke to Knollys who said that his acknowledgement of the letter was meant as an acceptance

———

Knollys wrote to me Dec 23. The P of W did not conceive it was necessary or was expected that he should write formally and say the apology was accepted. The Duke of Marlbro' having been previously told by me that it would be admitted if so worded. This was done and it was thought that nothing more was requisite than accept it

Francis Knollys to Lord Beaconsfield
(Royal Archives)

10 January 1877   Sandringham

Private

Dear Lord Beaconsfield,

I have the honor to enclose you by the Prince of Wales' desire a letter which he proposes should be sent to the Duke of Marlborough.

If you approve of it, HRH would beg of you kindly to transmit it to the Duke, should you have no objection to do so.

I have the honor to be dear Lord Beaconsfield, Your faithful servant

FRANCIS KNOLLYS

Francis Knollys to Lord Beaconsfield
(Royal Archives)

10 January 1877   Sandringham

Confidential

Dear Lord Beaconsfield,

In the draft letter to the Duke of Marlborough which I submitted to the Prince, I said at the end of the last paragraph 'he' (the Prince) 'has accepted your son's apology and retractation'. HRH would not however hear of the word 'accepted' and I was obliged to therefore substitute the word 'received' for it, but I do not know whether this will satisfy the Duke as well.

I have the honor to be dear Lord Beaconsfield your faithful servant

FRANCIS KNOLLYS

The Times

11 January 1877

DUBLIN, Jan 10. Evening.

The Duke of Marlborough, accompanied by the Duchess and members of his family, made his public entry today into Dublin, and received a loyal and hearty welcome from the citizens of all classes and denominations. Few noblemen have come to the Irish capital to assume the high and responsible office of Viceroy in more auspicious circumstances. He finds the country peaceable and prosperous, and the people as ready as ever to give a respectful and cordial reception to the Queen's representative. . . .

Their Graces the Duke and Duchess of Marlborough left London yesterday morning in a special saloon carriage attached to the Irish Limited Mail. They were accompanied by Lord and Lady Randolph Spencer Churchill, Sir Ivor and Lady Cornelia Guest, Lady Rosamond Spencer Churchill, Lady Georgiana and Lady Sarah, and Lord Winston Spencer Churchill, their children.[1]

After arriving at Holyhead they left by the Connaught steamer at 7 o'clock yesterday evening, and, after a fine passage, occupying little more than three hours, arrived at Kingstown, and anchored last night in the Man-of-War Roads.

Francis Knollys to Duke of Marlborough
(Marlborough Papers)

10 January 1877   Sandringham

Dear Duke of Marlborough,

The Prince of Wales desires me to say that as he received and retained your son's 'apology and retractation' he thought you would understand he had accepted it, His Royal Highness having previously intimated to you his intention of doing so should your son send to him an 'apology and retractation' framed according to the terms laid down by the Lord Chancellor, Lord Beaconsfield and Lord Hartington.

The Prince having lately heard, however, that some uncertainty and misapprehension exists in your mind on the subject, directs me to let you know that in accordance with the above named condition, he has received your son's 'apology and retraction.'

Believe me to be, dear Duke of Marlborough, Yours very truly
FRANCIS KNOLLYS

---

[1] This was unworthy of *The Times* newspaper's usually high standard of sub-editing. Master Winston Churchill had no right to the courtesy title bestowed upon him, and of course Lady Cornelia, Lady Rosamond, Lady Georgiana and Lady Sarah were his aunts not his sisters.

Lord Beaconsfield to Duke of Marlborough
(*Marlborough Papers*)

17 January 1877   2 Whitehall Gardens

Private

My dear Duke,

I enclose you a letter from Sandringham. I have kept it by me some days, that I might not precipitately decide upon its character. But, on the whole, I shd recommend you to accept it, and I trust that neither of us may hear anything again about a painful business.

I hope all is going on to the satisfaction of yourself, and every member of yr family.

Yrs very faithfully
BEACONSFIELD

It was six years before the first steps were taken to bring about a reconciliation between the Prince of Wales and Lord Randolph.

Dowager Duchess of Roxburghe to Duchess of Marlborough

25 February 1883   Windsor Castle

It gives me sincere pleasure dearest Duchess to tell you that The Queen hopes Lord Randolph will go to the Levee & Lady Randolph to the Drawing room. I feel you may rely on a courteous reception. I did not filter this enquiry thro anyone but spoke to The Queen – whose kindness and feeling are always to be relied on. There is a Levee on the 12th and certainly a Drawing room the week after next abt the 14. Dearest Duchess yrs very aff
S. ROXBURGHE

There *may* be a Drawing room next week – but doubtless Ly Randolph will prefer giving precedence to the Levee!

The Times of 15 March 1883 recorded that among those at the Drawing Room the day before was Lady Randolph. But there is no record of Lord Randolph having attended the Levee.

Another year was to elapse before the reconciliation was finally effected.

Vanity Fair

15 March 1884

A full and formal reconciliation has been effected between HRH the Prince of Wales and Lord Randolph Churchill, MP., who have for some years been strangers, on account of differences arising through the attitude respectively taken by them in relation to private matters. The reconciliation was effected last week at a dinner given for the purpose by Sir Henry James, MP. It is understood, however, that while Lord Randolph feels much satisfaction at being again on friendly terms with the Heir-Apparent, he does not propose to become intimate with all the Prince's friends.

Francis Knollys to Sir Henry James
(*Lord Randolph Papers*)

15 March 1884

Marlborough House
Pall Mall, S.W.

My dear Sir Henry,

I have shown your letter of this day's date to the Prince of Wales, and perhaps you will be so good as to assure Randolph Churchill that HRH never for one moment entertained the idea that he was in any way responsible for the words that appeared in *Vanity Fair* in connection with the subject to which you refer.

Yours sincerely
FRANCIS KNOLLYS

I was delighted to hear that your dinner was in all respects most successful, & that R. Churchill's manner was *just* what it ought to have been

3
Childhood

(See Main Volume Chapter 3)

IN JANUARY 1882 Lady Randolph wrote in her diary:

Wednesday January 4. Fine. Randolph arrived from Ireland – had a long talk and then went out and breakfasted with Blanche Hozier[1] – only Emily Yznaga[2] – took a little walk then went home. The Star[3] and Cornelia[4] turned up. Sir H. Wolff and Gorst[5] came to luncheon – took the 5.30 train to Oakham. Went to bed very early – had a long talk with Custance[6] before going.

Winston to Lady Randolph

[Postmark 4 January 1882]   [Postmark Blenheim]

My dear Mamma,
I hope you are quite well. I thank you very much for the beautiful presents those Soldiers and Flags and Castle they are so nice it was so kind of you and dear Papa I send you my love and a great many kisses

Your loving
WINSTON

[1] Lady Blanche Hozier (1852–1924), eldest daughter of David, 7th Earl of Airlie, and Henrietta, daughter of 2nd Baron Stanley of Alderley. She had married 1873 Colonel Sir Henry Hozier, and their third daughter, Clementine, born in 1885, married WSC in 1908.

[2] The youngest daughter of Don Antonio Yznaga del Valle, sister of Consuelo (later Duchess of Manchester) and Natica (Lady Lister-Kaye). She was unmarried.

[3] Evelyn Edward Thomas Boscawen (1847–1918); eldest son of 6th Viscount Falmouth, whom he succeeded in 1889, and of Mary, Baroness de Despencer in her own right, to whose title he succeeded in 1891. He was assistant Military Secretary to the Duke of Marlborough in Ireland; commanded the Coldstream Guards in action in Egypt; retired as Major-General 1902.

[4] Lady Cornelia WIMBORNE.

[5] John Eldon Gorst (1835–1916), one of Lord Randolph's colleagues in the 'Fourth Party'. When Lord Randolph took office in 1885 he became Solicitor-General and was knighted.

[6] Harry Custance, jockey to the Duke of Hamilton.

Winston to Lady Randolph

Monday [? March 1882]   [? Blenheim]

My dear Mamma,

I am quite well and getting on very nicely with my lessons. Baby[1] is quite well. I am enjoying myself very much. With love and kisses

your affectionate
W. S. CHURCHILL

Winston to Lord Randolph

20 March [1882]   Blenheim

My dear Papa,

I hope you are getting better.[2] I am enjoying myself very much. I find a lot of primroses every day. I bought a basket to put them in. I saw three little Indian children on Saturday, who came to see the house. Best love to you and dear Mamma.

I am, Yr loving son
WINSTON

Winston to Lord Randolph

28 March [1882]   Blenheim

My dear Papa,

I was so delighted to get your letter and thank you very much for it. I do lessons every morning with Grandmama she is going to London to day and says she will see you to-morrow so I wish I was with her that I might give you a kiss. Please give Mama my love. I will write to her soon. And with many kisses to you.

Your loving son
WINSTON

Winston to Lady Randolph

1 April [1882]   Blenheim

Dearest Mama,

It was such a lovely day yesterday that we went for a drive. I am enjoying myself here very much it is so nice being in the country. The gardens and the park are so much nicer to walk in than the Green Park or Hyde Park.

---

[1] Winston's brother Jack was two.
[2] Lord Randolph was taken ill on February 26, and remained seriously ill until the middle of March.

Baby is very well and sends you his love I have been playing out of doors at making encampments which is great fun. I pretend I pretend to pitch a tent and make the umbrella do for it.

With best love to you and Papa, Ever your loving son
WINSTON

Winston to Lord Randolph

10 April [1882]   Blenheim

Dearest Papa,

I am so glad you are better Baby and I went to the Lince[1] Thursday and gathered a lot of wild hyacinthes. When we were out on Friday near the cascade we saw a snake crawling about in the grass. I wanted to kill it but Everest would not let me.

With best love and kisses to you and Mama

Ever your loving son
WINSTON

Winston to Lady Randolph

? [April 1882]   [? Ventnor]

Dearest Mamma,

I do want you come down so much. We are going out now.

your loving
WINSTON

Winston to Lady Randolph

? [April 1882]   2 Handborough Road
Ventnor

Dearest Mamma,

I thank you very much for the beautiful Easter Egg. Jack and I like them so much. We had a Picnic we went to Sandown took our dinner on the Beach and we went to see the Forts & Guns at Sandown there were some enormous 18 ton Guns. We went for an hours drive yesterday to St Lawsen.

Winston to Lady Randolph

? [May 1882]   Blenheim

My dear Mamma,

I got your letter today a I am so glad to hear dear Papa is better. Grandmama has just come. I have been out riding Robroy to day in the park – he

---

[1] A wooded area on the Blenheim estate.

was very fresh so Chapman had to ride him first 20 times round the school and led me in the Park. There are a great many violets in the gardens. Jack does like gathering the daises so much we went down to see Grandpapa at breakfast this morning with many kisses & love from

WINSTON

Winston to Lady Randolph

? [May 1882]   Blenheim

My dear Mama,

    I hope you are quite well. When are you coming to Blenheim again Jack and I both want you very much please do come soon. I rode Robroy to day round the Park and rode him all by myself in the school.

With love and kisses, from your loving
WINSTON

Winston to Lord Randolph

21 August 1882   Beech Lodge
                                          [Wimbledon][1]

My dear Papa,

    Thank you very much for your nice letter, which I received this morning.

    I am very pleased to hear that you are better, and hope that you will soon be quite well.

    Baby is very well, and sends you his love and a kiss.

    Tell Sunny that I send him my love, and I hope that he enjoyed being at school.

With love and kisses, Believe me, Your loving son
WINSTON

On 3 November 1882 Winston, then aged nearly eight, went to school. He was sent to the Rev H. W. Sneyd-Kynnersley's establishment recently opened at Sunningdale House, and known as St George's School, Ascot.

---

[1] The house Lord and Lady Randolph took during the summer. They had given up 29 St James' Place when they went to America in May, and they did not move into their new home at 2 Connaught Place until the autumn.

Winston to Lord Randolph

? [3 December 1882]   Ascot

My dear Papa,

I am very happy at chool. You will be very plesed to hear I spent a very happy birthday. Mrs Kynersley gave me a little bracket. I am going to send a Gazette wich I wish you to read.

With love and kisses, I remain your loving son
WINSTON

Winston to Lady Randolph

? [3 December 1882]   Ascot

My dear Mamma,

I hope you are quite well. I am very happy at school.

You will be very glad to hear I spent a very happy birthday. I must now thank you for your loveley present you sent me. Do not forget to come down on the 9th Dec^{er}.

With love and kisses I remain your loveing son.

WINSTON   kisses

Winston to Lady Randolph

[Postmark 6 February 1883]   2 Connaught Place[1]

My dear Mamma,

I hope you arc well. I am longing for another Feudal Castle. Aunty is having my Banjo mended. I mst not much for my eyes are wake.

With love and kisses
WINSTON

Winston to Lady Randolph

[? 9 June 1883]   [? Ascot]

My dear Mamma,

I hope you are quite well. I want to know if in the Holidays I shall see Everest or what are our plans. I cannot say more as I am in a hurry.

With love and kisses, I am your loving son
WINSTON

[1] The home of Lord and Lady Randolph 1882-92.

Winston to Lady Randolph

? [17 June 1883]   Ascot

My dear Mamma,

    I hope you will come and see me soon. Did Everest give you my flour I sent you. Give my love to my ants, and tell not to forget to come down.

I am comeinge home

In a month.

... W ... I ... T ...H

love & kisses

I

Remain

your

loveing

Son

W.L.S. CHURCHILL

Winston to Lady Randolph[1]

[? June 1883]   Ascot

My dear Mama,

    I hope you are quite well. Please do let Everest and Jack come down to see the athletics and come down your self dear. I shall expect to see you and Jack & Everest down on SATURDAY.

With love & kisses I am your loving son

WINSTON

---

[1] On the back of this letter are two lists of names, one may assume of dinner parties, written in pencil in Lady Randolph's writing.

Cadogans	2	Selves	2
Selves	2	Hornes	2
Wharncliffe's	2	Gerards	2
Gladys	1	Bochim	
Bochim	1	Ld Marcus	1
Sir R. Peel	1	Duke of Portland	1
Leighton		Consuelo	1
Millais	1	Sir R. Peel	
Escotts		Fife	1

Winston to Lady Randolph

[? 2 July 1883]   Ascot

My dear Mamma,

It was so kind of you to let Everest come down here. I think she enjoyed her-self very much. Only 18 more days.

Now I will say Good bye.

> With love & kisses I remain, Your affet
> WINSTON

Winston to Lady Randolph

15 September 1883

My dear Mamma,

I hope you are quite well. I went out fishing to day & caught my first fish by my self. Jack & I are quite well. With love & kisses.

> I am your loving
> WINSTON

Winston to Lady Randolph

[? September 1883]   Ascot

My dear Mama,

I hope you are quite well. I thank you very much for that nice bag. It ought to have gone yesterday but oweing to my lazyness it did not. I hope you will forgive me. As now I have sent the bag. My love to Jack & Everest & anty Clary & anty leoney.

> With love & kisses I remain your loveing son
> WINSTON

Winston to Lady Randolph

[? October 1883]   Ascot

My dear mamma,

I hope you are quite well. We went to hampton cort palace, & looked over the maze. & then we had diner, but it was not quite so good as the diner at the *Buffet*. after diner we went to see the picture gallry & then we went to the station. I went on a station to far.

> With love & kisses, I remain yours affect
> WINSTON

Winston to Lady Randolph

[? November 1883]   Ascot

My dear Mama,

I hope you are quite well. The firworks have been put off till next week. There are tow guys messers Bradlaugh[1] & O'Donavan Rossa[2]. I am in the singing class there is Hmpty Dumpty, The lion & four wolves, Euclid, Softly falls the moonlight, The voice of the bell, Wilow the king, old daddy long legs.

With love & kisses I remain yours affec
WINSTON

Winston to Lady Randolph

2 December 1883   Ascot

My dear Mamma,

I hope you are quite well. I thank you very much for your nice books. I hope your quite well. I have just been out to dinner with Lady Alfred Churchill,[3] and she wants to know if you mind it, do you?

Whith love & kisses I remain yours affet
WINSTON

Winston to Lord Randolph

9 December 1883   Ascot

My dear Papa,

I hope you are quite well. We had gymnastic trials yesterday. I got 39 marks out of 90. I beat some of the boys in two classes above me. The play room is getting ready for concert we are learning to sing for it. It is about 75 feet long

[1] Charles Bradlaugh (1833–91), freethinker. Elected for Northampton as a radical in 1880, he was attacked by the Fourth Party and did not succeed in sitting unmolested in the House of Commons until 1886. In 1883 he had presented himself for the fourth time at the bar of the House but was excluded by a resolution of the House. His pamphlets include 'John Churchill, Duke of Marlborough' (London 1884).

[2] O'Donovan Rossa (1831–1915) or Jeremiah O'Donovan; a Fenian leader who was elected to Parliament while serving a sentence of life imprisonment. He was amnestied and released and went to America, where he died. His funeral in Dublin became the occasion of a great Irish nationalist demonstration which immediately preceded the Easter Rising of 1916.

[3] Harriet (1832–1901), daughter of 4th Baron Calthorpe, who was married to Lord Randolph's uncle, Lord Alfred Churchill (1824–93).

& 20 broad and lighted by 920 cp lamps it will show a very bright light wont it.

With love and kisses I remain yours affet

WINSTON

X one big kiss

and a lot of little ones.

Winston to Lady Randolph

[? December 1883]   Ascot

My dear Mamma,

I hope you are quite well. I had a nice letter from Jack, but I think Everest held his hand. I will try to be a good boy. Aunty Leonie has been staying here at Ascot. I want you to come here for the concert on the 14th of dec Aunty is coming to see the concert.

With love and kisses I remain yours affect

son

WINSTON

good by

Winston to Lady Randolph

3 January 1884

My dear mamma,

I hope you are quite well. My cough is nearly well now. I went out to dinner today with Lady Alfred Churchill. And had great fun. I hope to see you soon again. Give my love to Aunty Leonie & Clara. Come & see me soon dear Mamma.

With love & kisses I remain your affet

WINSTON

Winston to Lady Randolph

2 February 1884   Ascot

My dear Mamma,

You will be very glad to hear that I am doing well and have got a chance for the prize if I work hard. Give my love to Aunty Leonie. I am sending you the Gazette. And I hope you will like it. Now it is time to say Good by.

With love & kisses I remain yours affet

WINSTON

Winston to Lady Randolph

10 February 1883 [1884] [Ascot]

My dear Mamma,

I hope you are quite well. Did jack get my owl & did he like it. *You must let Everest come & see me on* saterday. how many presents did Jack get[1] mind do not forget to let Everest come.

Wilove & kisses I remain yours affet
WINSTON

Winston to Lord Randolph[2]

17 February 1884

My dear Papa,

I hope you are quite well. It was so kind of you to send me that nice book. I am very happy indeed.

With love and kisses I remain your loving son
WINSTON

Winston to Lady Randolph

24 February 1884 Ascot

My dear Mamma,

I hope you are quite well. I am wondering when you are coming to see me? I hope you are coming to see me soon, dear. How is Jack. You must send somebody to see me.

I went out to diner last sunday with the Alfred Churchills.

With love & kisses, I remain, Yours affet
WINSTON

[1] Jack's birthday was February 4, but members of the family (including Jack) were often vague as to the precise date, and the birthday was not necessarily celebrated on the correct day.
[2] This and a number of the ensuing letters had childish drawings of faces and people added to the end.

Winston to Lady Randolph

9 March 1884   Ascot

My dear Mamma,
    I hope you are quite well. We had lots of on wednesday. And we all went by train *to Bagshot* & walked back. Now you must tell me about the pony. Has he been chasing any body lately. 30 day more and the *Holidays* will be *Here*.
                                With love and kisses I remain your loving son
                                                        WINSTON

Winston to Lady Randolph

16 March 1883 [1884]   Ascot

My dear Mama,
    I hope you are quite well. Mrs Kynnersly went to Birmingham this week. And she heard that they were betting two to one that Papa would get in for Birmingham.[1] We all went too a sand pit the other day and playd a very exciting game. As the sides are about 24 feet high, and a great strugle, those who got out first kept a fierce strugle with the rest.
                                With love & kisses I remain your affec
                                                        WINSTON

Winston to Lady Randolph

8 June 1884   Ascot

My dear Mama,
    I hope you are quite well. It is very unkind of you not to write to me before this, I have only had one letter from you this term. Now though; I will have my point you must come down and see me on June 24th as it is a grand day with us we have a whole Holliday and I want you to come down and see me, let Everest come and Jack.
                                With love and kisses, I remain your loving son
                                                        WINSTON

[1] Lord Randolph agreed to contest Central Birmingham in January 1884. The election took place in November 1885, when John Bright (Liberal) held the seat by 4989 to 4216, a majority of 773.

Winston to Lady Randolph

[13 July 1884] Ascot

My dear Mama,

I hope you are quite well. In ten more days I shall be home. Write to me soon dear. Has Papa got in I hope he has.[1]

You must let me no if he does.

With love & kisses I remain, Yours affet
WINSTON

Winston to Lady Randolph

?[July 1884] Ascot

My dear Mama,

I must ask you to send me a little money. 10 bob would do as I want to give a little to the chaple fund every-one gives some, so send me a little.

With love & kisses I remain yours affet
WINSTON

Winston to Lady Randolph

[? July 1884] Ascot

My dear Mamma,

I hope you are quite well, you will be glad to hear I have a chance of a prize. I am all wright and well. I have been allowed to go back into my own room.

With love & kisses I remain, Your loving son
WINSTON

* * * *

Winston's letters gave no indication of how he was getting on in school; his parents had to rely on the reports of his schoolmasters.

[1] This probably refers to Lord Randolph's candidature for election to the committee of the National Union of Conservative Associations. As a challenge to the Conservative Party leadership, Lord Randolph had resigned from the chairmanship of the Committee on May 2; but he was re-elected by an overwhelming vote when the National Union met at Sheffield on July 23.

S. GEORGE'S SCHOOL
ASCOT

Report from Nov 3rd to December 9th, 1882

Place in 4th Division of 11 boys for ½ term – 11th

Division Master's Classical Report

Composition

Translation

Grammar   Has made a start

Diligence   He will do well, but must treat his work in general, more seriously next term

---

Set Master's Report

Place in 3rd Set of 14 boys for ½ Term – 14th

Mathematics very elementary

French   Knows a few sentences, but knowledge of Grammar is very slight

---

Scripture   f

History ⎫

Geography ⎭ fair

Writing and
 Spelling   Writing good but so slow – spelling weak

H. MARTIN COOKE

General
 Conduct   Very truthful, but a regular 'pickle' in many ways at present – has not fallen into school ways yet – but this could hardly be expected.

H. W. SNEYD-KYNNERSLEY
Head Master

Total place for Term 11th Times late 4

S. GEORGE'S SCHOOL
ASCOT

Report from June 8th to July 20th 1883

Place in School Order 7th		½ Term 9th
Place in 4th Division of 9 Boys for Term		9th

Divisional Master's Classical Report

Composition	Very feeble
Translation	Good
Grammar	Improving
Diligence	Does not quite understand the meaning of hard work – must make up his mind to do so next term

Set Master's Report

Place in 3rd Set of 13 boys for ½ Term		13th
	Term	13th
Mathematics	Could do better than he does	
French	fair	
German		

Scripture	f
History	very good
Geography	very fair
Writing and Spelling	Writing good but so terribly slow – Spelling about as bad as it well can be.
Music	—
Drawing	—

H. MARTIN COOKE

General Conduct	improved

H. W. SNEYD-KYNNERSLEY
Head Master

Total times late 19

S. GEORGE'S SCHOOL
ASCOT

Report from September 20th to November 3rd 1883

Place in School Order   5th

Place in 4th Division of 11 Boys for ½ Term   8th

Division Master's Classical Report

Composition	very variable
Translation	
Grammar	fair
Diligence	Began term well, but latterly has been very naughty! – on the whole he has made progress

Set Master's Report

Place in 4th Set of 10 boys for ½ Term – 7th

Mathematics	Greatly improved, but very uncertain
French	Not very good
German	—

Scripture	v.f.
History ⎫	weak in Geography
Geography ⎭	good in History
Writing and Spelling	improved
Music	—
Drawing	very elementary

H. MARTIN COOKE

General Conduct	on the whole he has improved – though at times he is still troublesome

H. W. SNEYD-KYNNERSLEY
Head Master

Times late – 6

S. GEORGE'S SCHOOL
ASCOT

Report from Jan 24th to Feb 29th 1884

Place in School Order in Division at the end of last Term. 5th	Present place for 5th

Place in 4th Division for 10 boys for ½ term – 5th

Division Master's Classical Report.

Composition	Improved
Translation	Good
Grammar	Good at *viva voce*, but fails on paper
Diligence	I am more satisfied with him than I have ever been but there is still room for improvement
No of times late	7

Set Master's Report
Place in 4th Set of 11 boys for ½ Term – 7th

Mathematics	Shews decided signs of being very good
French	Fair – does not learn the Grammar with sufficient care
German	—

Scripture	Good
History } Geography }	very erratic – sometimes exceedingly good
Writing and Spelling	Both very much improved
Music	will do well
Drawing	fair H. MARTIN COOKE

General Conduct	much better
Headmaster's Remarks	he is, I hope, *beginning* to realize that school means work and discipline. He is rather greedy at meals.

H.W.S.K.
Head Master

S. GEORGE'S SCHOOL
ASCOT

Report from March 1st to April 9th 1884

Place in School Order in Division at the end of last Term.	5th	Present place in new School order for Term	6th

Division Master's Classical Report.
Place in 4 Division of 11 Boys for Term.　　6th

Composition	Improved
Translation	Improved
Grammar	Improved
Diligence	Conduct has been exceedingly bad. He is not to be trusted to do any one thing. He has however notwithstanding made decided progress.
No of times late	20.　very disgraceful.　　　　Very bad. HWSK.

Set Master's Report.
Place in 4th Set of 11 Boys for Term　　6th

Mathematics	Improved
French	Improved
German	

Scripture Paper	60 out of 120. f
History Geography }	very good, especially history
Writing and Spelling	Both very much improved
Music	Promising.
Drawing	fair, considering.

H. MARTIN COOKE

General Conduct	very bad – is a constant trouble to everybody and is always in some scrape or other.
Headmaster's Remarks	He cannot be trusted to behave himself anywhere. He has very good abilities.

H. W. SNEYD-KYNNERSLEY
Head Master

S. GEORGE'S SCHOOL
ASCOT

Report from May 8th to June 20th 1884

Place in School Order in Division at the end of last Term.	3rd	Present place for ½ Term	3rd

Division Master's Classical Report.
Place in 4th Division of 9 Boys for ½ Term

Composition	wants more care
Translation	very fair
Grammar	good
Diligence	Better on the whole but still far from satisfactory
No of times late	2. a great improvement

Set Master's Report.
Place in 4th Set of 8 Boys for ½ Term   3rd

Mathematics	ought to be better – careless
French	good
German	—

Scripture	f
History ⎫ Geography ⎭	very good
Writing and Spelling	Spelling improved. Writing full of corrections & untidy.
Music	good
Drawing	fair

H. MARTIN COOKE

General Conduct	better – but still troublesome
Headmaster's Remarks	He has no ambition – if he were really to exert himself he might yet be first at the end of the Term.

H. W. SNEYD-KYNNERSLEY
Head Master

S. GEORGE'S SCHOOL
ASCOT

Report from June 20th to July 21st

Place in School Order in Division at the end of last Term. 3rd	Present place for . . .

Divisional Master's Classical Report.
Place in 4th Division of 9 Boys for Term 3rd

Composition	Good
Translation	very fair
Grammar	good
Diligence	Fair on the whole. Occasionally gives a great deal of trouble.
No of times late	4

Set Master's Report.
Place in 4 Set of 8 Boys for Term 3rd

Mathematics	not satisfactory
French	very fair
German	—

Scripture	v.f.
History Geography	very good
Writing and Spelling	both improved
Music	should be better, does not practise carefully enough.
Drawing	fair

H. Martin Cooke

General Conduct	improved a little
Headmaster's Remarks	He will be promoted into Div 3, and will I hope make a good start. He might always do well if he chose.

H. W. Sneyd-Kynnersley
Head Master

4

Brighton

(See Main Volume Chapter 4)

━━━━

A T the end of the Summer Term of 1884 Winston was removed
from St George's and in September he went to the little
school run by the Misses Thomson at 29 and 30 Brunswick Road,
Brighton. Only the reports of his first three terms survive; but
they, like the letters to his mother, show quick progress in
Winston's development.

29 & 30 BRUNSWICK ROAD

Lower School – Class 4th

REPORT

for

Term beginning September 16th – ending December 19th '84

	Marks gained	Highest gained	Position in class	No in class
Scripture Knowledge	270	755	8th	9
English Subjects	1341	6031	11th	11
Mathematics	363	1550	7th	7
Classics	1932	3635	5th	11
French	273	1780	7th	7
German				
Music				
Drawing	300	675	6th	11
Conduct	135	704	26th	32

REMARKS

Showed decided improvement in attention to work towards the latter part of the term.

Figures of the report almost valueless as frequent absence from the school-room made competition with other boys very difficult.

C. THOMSON

29 & 30 BRUNSWICK ROAD

Lower School – Class 4th

REPORT

for

Term beginning January 20th – ending April 2nd '85

	Marks gained	Highest gained	Position in class	No in class
Scripture Knowledge	495	730	5	8
English Subjects	2864	4093	4	10
Mathematics	647	1472	7	10
Classics	1488	2010	4	10
French	1270	1855	4	10
German				
Music				
Drawing	11	55	8	18
Conduct	135	582	29	29

REMARKS

Very satisfactory progress made during the term.

C. T.

29 & 30 BRUNSWICK ROAD

Lower School – Class 4th

REPORT

for

Term beginning April 22nd – ending July 28th '85

	Marks gained	Highest gained	Position in Class	No in Class
Scripture Knowledge	665	920	6	12
English Subjects	4418	6110	4	9
Mathematics	1432	2501	5	9
Classics	2904	2904	1	9
French	1810	1890	3	9
German				
Music				
Drawing	73	468	11	12
Conduct	292	782	30	30

REMARKS

Very marked progress made during the term. If he continues to improve in steadiness and application, as during this term, he will do very well indeed.

C. T.

Winston to Lady Randolph

[Postmark 26 October 1884]   [29 & 30 Brunswick Road
                                                              Brighton]

My dear Mamma,

I am very happy here.

Will you kindly ask Mr Thomas[1] if, when has any good stamps he will send them on to me.

I must now say good bye, your loving son
WINSTON

[1] Robert D'Oyly Freeman Thomas (1866–1911) was acting as Lord Randolph's secretary. Both he and his wife are buried near Lord Randolph's grave in Bladon Churchyard.

Winston to Lady Randolph

28 October 1884   Brighton

My dear Mamma,

I hope you are quite well. I am quite happy here. I have been very extravagant, I have bought a lovely stamp-book and stamps, will you please
send a little more money. Good-bye dear Mumy.

With Love and kisses, I remain your loving son
WINSTON

Winston to Lady Randolph

6 December 1884   Brighton

My Dear Mamma,

I hope you are quite well. I wrote to Papa yesterday. The Holidays begin
on the 19th so there are not many more days before I shall come home. Will
you send me Everest's address. The examinations have begun. Now I must
say good-bye with love and kisses.

I remain your loving son
WINSTON

Winston to Lord Randolph

1 January 1885   2 Connaught Place

My dear Papa,

I hope you are quite well. Jack had such a beautiful box of soldiers sent him,
from Lady De Clifford, called The Nile Expedition, by Cremor. I have been
out to tea to Aunt Bertha's this evening and enjoyed myself very much indeed.
We had a Christmas Tree and party here this year, which went off very well.
My Stamp Book is gradually getting filled. I am very glad to hear you arrived
safely.[1] Will you write and tell me all about your voyage, was it rough at all?
I wrote to you once when the ship stopped at Gibralter. How nice for sailing
all over the sea. Jack is quite well & so am I.

I hope you had a happy Christmas, and a Glad New Year (Jackey is
quite well). Clow is very fat indeed, I give her a run every day to take her fat
down.

With love and kisses I remain, yours affect
WINNY

---

[1] Lord Randolph arrived at Bombay in the *Nizam* on 30 December 1884. He had sailed
for India in the *Rohilla*, December 3, and returned 7 April 1885.

Lady Randolph to Lord Randolph

2 January 1885   2 Connaught Place

EXTRACT

. . . Winston brought me down the enclosed[1], which he wrote last night –
the handwriting is moderate – but the spelling is not bad. They both went to
tea with Sunny yesterday – they all met in the Park and Bertha wrote & asked
if they might come – so I let them. . . .

Winston to Lady Randolph

21 January 1885   Brighton

My dear Mamma,
    I hope you are well. I am getting on pretty well. The Play is on the 11th of
February 1885. You must be happy without me, no screams from Jack or
complaints. It must be heaven upon earth. Will you try and find out for me
what day Dr Rouse[2] is going to take me to see Dr Woaks[3] write and tell me.
Will you tell me what day the mail goes to India, because I want to write to
him.
    Now I must say Good-bye.
                              With love and kisses I remain, Your Loving son
                                                            WINSTON

Winston to Lady Randolph

24 January [1885]   Brighton

My dear Mamma,
    I hope you are quite well. The weather is very cold one day, wet another,
and hot the next. I have been out riding to day and rode without the leading
rein and we cantered. When are you coming to see me?
                              With love and kisses, I remain yours aff^{te}
                                                            WINSTON

---

[1] The letter from Winston dated 1 January 1885, above.
[2] Dr Robson ROOSE.
[3] Edward Woakes (1837–1912) of 78 Harley Street; Senior Aural Surgeon, London
Hospital; Surgeon, London Throat Hospital; author of *On Deafness, Giddiness and Noises in
the Head.*

Winston to Lady Randolph

27 January 1885   Brighton

My dear Mamma,

I hope you are quite well. I am sorry to hear of the death of Col Burnaby.[1]
I went to see Dr Roose to-day. He is going to Sweden for a fort-night I believe,
when he comes back he is going to take me to see Dr Woakes. There is a
ripping good Pantomime down here. I have got a Glass with two Gold-fish.
Will you send me some postage stamps.

                              With love and kisses I remain Yours affectly
                                                                  WINSTON

Winston to Lady Randolph

28 January [1885]   Brighton

My dear Mamma,

I hope you are quite well. I ride three times a week, I have one hour on
Tuesday, an hour and a half on Wednesday, and an hour on Friday. Do
you think Papa will stay long in India? Have you heard from him lately?
Is Jacky quite well and happy? does he cry at all now? I am quite well and,
very happy. How is old Chloe, has she been shaved yet? I make my pony
canter when I go out riding. I will send you a list of the work we have. A master
here is going to give a lecture on Chemistry, is it not wonderful to think that
water is made of two gases namely hydrogdgen and nitrodgen I like it, only
it seems so funny that two gases should make water. With love and kisses.
                                         I remain, Your loving son
                                                                  WINSTON

[1] Lt-Colonel Frederick Gustavus Burnaby (1842–85), Royal Horse Guards, was killed on
January 17, 'sword in hand, while resisting the desperate charge of the Arabs at the battle of
Abu Klea'. A soldier of astonishing daring and enterprise, he roused the imagination of the
public in 1875 with his ride from London to Khiva, and only the protests of the Russian
Government and the personal intervention of the Duke of Cambridge prevented him from
riding on into Central Asia to Samarkand. His enterprises included a ride through Asia Minor
to Persia, service as a war correspondent for *The Times*, a solo balloon flight from Dover to
Normandy. In 1880 he stood unsuccessfully as a Conservative candidate for Birmingham, but
early in 1884 he arranged to contest Birmingham again, this time with Lord Randolph as
his fellow candidate.

Winston to Lady Randolph

30 January 1885   Brighton

My dear Mama,

I hope you are quite well. The Play is on the 12th of February 1885, do not forget too come and see the Play and bring Aunt Leonie and Aunt Clara, I shall expect to see you and shall be very disappointed indeed if I do not see you, so do come. How is Jack? I hope he is well. Thank you very much indeed for your news-paper.

With love and Kisses.

I remain, Yours affect
WINSTON

Winston to Lord Randolph

Friday
[13] February 1885   Brighton

My dear Papa,

I hope you are enjoying yourself in India. Mamma came to see me on the 12th of February. Is it not bad about poor Col Burnaby? I hear you have been out shooting at Calcutta and shot some animals. When are you coming home again. I hope it will not be long. I am at shcool now and am getting on pretty well. Will you write and tell me about India what it's like. It must be very nice and warm out there now, while we are so cold in England. Will you go out on a tiger Hunt while you are there?[1] Are the Indians very funny? I hope you are quite well, and will keep so till you come home again. I hope Mr Thomas is quite well. Try and get me a few stamps for my stamp album, Papa. Are there many *ants* in India if so, you will have a nice time, what with *ants mosquitos*. Every body wants to get your signature will you send me a few to give away? I am longing to see you so much.

I think you will be glad to know I am well and happy. We had a play here on the 12th Feb and a grand party. We went on dancing till ten oclock and I enjoyed myself very much indeed it was so nice. I am learning dancing now and like it very much indeed. I am afraid it will boor you very much to read my scribble so I will not write much more. I went out riding this morning and cantered. Now I must say good-bye.

With love and kisses
I remain, Your loving son
WINSTON CHURCHILL

[1] He did – and shot one. See Lord Randolph's letter to his mother in WSC's *Lord Randolph Churchill* Appendix iv.

Winston to Lady Randolph

6 March [1885]   Brighton

My dear Mamma,

I hope you are quite well. You have forgotten your promise in sending me a hamper. The lecture went off Capitally. I have not got anything to say so goodbye.

                    With love and kisses I remain Yours affte
                                                    WINSTON

Winston to Lady Randolph

10 March [1885]   Brighton

My dear Mama,

I hope you are quite well. I am very well. There are only three more weeks of this term I am glad to say. Tell Everest that I am quite well and will write to her when I have time.

                    With Love & Kisses I remain, Your loving son
                                                    WINSTON

Winston to Lady Randolph

17 March [1885]   Brighton

Dearest Mamma,

I hope you are quite well. The weather is very nice indeed. We are going to have the Play over again to-morrow. The holidays begin on the 2nd and we are coming back on the 21st of April. We do not have any any work at all on Tuesday evening, with a few exceptions.

                    With love and kisses I remain, Your loving son
                                                    WINSTON

Winston to Lady Randolph

20 March 1885   Brighton

My dear Mamma,

I hope you will not mind my asking for a Postal Order of ten shillings. I have not got a single farthing. I shall be coming home soon and will tell you what I should like instead of a hamper. Of course I have not got anything to say that would interest you only that I am quite well and am looking forward to the Holidays very much indeed. Is Jackey quite well and happy. I am in a hurry as I have got a French Exercise to do, so you must excuse bad writing if you want a long letter.

Did you enjoy yourself at Derby races the other day. The Play was acted over again on Wednesday and went off capitally with no hitches at all. We go off by the 9.45 train on Thursday. We are going to have a half holiday on Tuesday if the weather permits. There has been a Bazaar here this week and some of the boys went I had no money so I could not go. We have 19 days holiday at Easter. I hope you will send some one to meet me at the station if Dr Roose takes me up as I have no wish to go on his rounds with him.

Dont forget to have the maid turned out of my room. I must close this scribble now and believe me to be for ever—

Your loving son
WINSTON

Winston to Lady Randolph

24 March [1885] Brighton

My dear Mamma,

I hope you are quite well. I should like you to send me a Postal Order as I said in my last letter. The Examinations commence on the 25th the first paper is Latin. There was a heavy fall of snow on Sunday

With Love and kisses I remain, Your loving son
WINSTON

PS Give my best Love to Everest and Jack. I am quite well, send some one to meet me at the station on Thursday.

Winston to Lady Randolph

31 March [1885] Brighton

My dear Mamma,

I have not got anything particular to say only to remind you that I want you to meet me at the station on Thursday. I shall be glad when Thursday comes. I am quite well. We went for a Paper Chase on Saturday it was about nine miles long.

With love and kisses I remain, Yours affect
WINSTON

Winston to Lord Randolph

24 April [1885]   Brighton

Dearest Papa,

I got here all right on Tuesday. I hope you are quite well. Will you write and tell me where Mamma is staying, what is her address? The weather is lovely and we have begun Cricket. I am in the 1st Eleven as extra man. I should be very proud if you would write to me Papa. With love and kisses

I remain Your loving son
WINSTON

Winston to Lady Randolph

29 April [1885]   Brighton

My dear Mamma,

I have received a letter from Everest telling me that you have arrived. You must write and tell me all about the races. We went to the baths this morning and I enjoyed it immensely. We had a game of cricket this afternoon. The School Colours are red and white alternately and very pretty. I want you to come down and see me and we will go on the Electric car. I am very happy and well. It continues very fine indeed.

With love and kisses
I remain, Your loving son
WINSTON

Winston to Lord Randolph

5 April [May] 1885   Brighton

My darling Papa,

I hope you are quite well. The weather continues very fine though there has been a little rain lately. I have been out riding with a gentleman who thinks that Gladstone is a brute and thinks that 'the one with the curly moustache ought to be Premier' The driver of the Electric Railway said 'that Lord R. Churchill would be Prime Minister' Cricket has become the foremost thought now. Every body wants your Autograph but I can only say I will try, and I should like you to sign your name in full at the end of your letter. I only want a scribble as I know that you are very busy indeed. With love and kisses.

I remain your loving son
WINSTON

Winston to Lady Randolph

9 May 1885   Brighton

My dear Mamma,

I hope you are quite well. Have you recovered your good health again as I expect you were rather frightened when the shaft went into your leg.

I am looking for another letter from you. I recd a nice letter from Papa this morning, he sent me half a dozen autographs I have been bussy distributing them to-day every body wanted one, but I should like you to send me a few of yours too. I must now say Good-bye.

I remain your loving son
WINSTON

Winston to Lady Randolph

27 May [1885]   Brighton

My dear Mamma,

I hope you quite well. There was a Cricket Match on today at the County Ground between Sussex and Hampshire.[1] The weather is very wet and damp. I have been to see Dr Roose to day and he ordered me some medicin, but gives me permission to go to the Baths. I have been taking that Fer Bravaé but Dr Roose has made me leave it off. Will you allow me to have a nice riding suit as my trousers always ruck up to my knees which looks anything but pretty. With love and kisses.

I remain Ever your loving son
WINSTON

Winston to Lady Randolph

30 May 1885   Brighton

My dear Mamma,

I hope you are quite well. The parade is perfectly crammed. I received a 'Pictorial world' this morning and I guessed from which quarter of the globe it came from. The first Cricket Match came of on Wednesday, we were beaten as the weather did not permit us to practise sufficiently. But there has been a change for the better lately in the weather and we have been able to practise regularly for the match on Saturday. I am learning to swim and getting on capitally. Do write to me and tell me if Chloe is better as I should be very sorry if she were to die. Thank Everest for her letter and give her my best love.

[1] Sussex v Hampshire, May 25–27. Sussex won by an innings and 64 runs.

Will you tell me if Jack is well? Do you miss me much? I go out riding very often now. Will you send me the paper with Victor Hugo's funeral in it.[1]

I am getting on with my French and Latin but am rather backward with Greek, but I suppose I must know it to get into Winchester so I will try and work it up.

Do you mind me having a riding suit as I am getting on very well. I am quite well and very happy. I am learning a piece of Poetry called Edinburgh after Flodden. There are no new boys this term except a very little one. The matches are comming in very quick succession.

With love and kisses, I remain Your loving son
WINSTON

Winston to Lady Randolph

2 June 1885   Brighton

My dear Mamma,

I hope you are quite as well as I am. I am enjoying my rides so very much that I hope you will allow me to continue them. I am quite well and excessively happy. We are going to Bramber on Thursday. We have had two Cricket Matches as yet, but we have been beaten in both. If you come to Brighton I shall be most delighted to see you. The Extra Supplement to the Graphic is very good indeed, it is of Papa in the library with all the Photographs and the ink-stand. Will you write and tell me about poor Chloe! There is another match on to-morrow.

With love and kisses, I remain, Your loving son
WINSTON

Winston to Lady Randolph

9 June 1885   Brighton

My dear Mamma,

I hope you will accept my scribble. The weather is doubtful, and there has been a sharp wind to day. I like riding better than anything else so I know you will allow me to continue it.

---

[1] The funeral on June 1 'was one of the grandest and most imposing in the annals of Paris, and was described as an apotheosis not only of Victor Hugo but of democracy itself'. A description of it filled three and a half columns in *The Times*. The ceremonies began at the Arc de Triomphe at 11 a.m. and ended at 6.45 p.m. The Government had decided to give Hugo a state funeral in the Panthéon, but as Hugo lived and died a freethinker it was first necessary to secularise the Panthéon. The decree making this possible roused strong political passions, being vigorously opposed by the Right and the Church; this in turn incurred the fury of the anarchists, revolutionists, socialists and communists.

You know that Postal Order you sent me, I could not get it cashed at the Post Office because it was crossed out, so I am going to send it back to you. There is a grand Agricultural show on, this week.[1] I hope you will come and see me, the time is slipping away and if you do not come quickly it will not be worth coming at all. I want you to write your name in the Birthday Book I am sending you, and ask Papa to do the same, and then send it back to me again. Give my love to all my Aunts and Everest. I write this hoping you are well, and flourishing.

With love and kisses

> I remain, Your loving son
> WINSTON

Winston to Lady Randolph

12 June 1885   Brighton

My dear Mamma,

I hope you are quite ready to receive another scribble from me. I hope you will not mind me asking you to send me the long promised hamper as I should like one so much. I am sure it would not do me any harm. How is Jack and your self? Give my love to my aunts and Everest.

> With love and kisses I remain, Your loving son
> WINSTON

Winston to Lady Randolph

19 June 1885   Brighton

My dear Mamma,

I hope you are quite as well as I am. Could you send me another Postal Order as the other one you sent me was no good at all as it was scratched out. I am going to write to Everest so I hope you will excuse my writing. I have not rec__ed my hamper yet. With love and kisses

> I remain, Your loving son
> WINSTON

Winston to Lady Randolph

30 June 1885   Brighton

Dearest Mamma,

I am quite well, and hope you are the same. I have been to the dentist today. I have received the long promised Hamper.

[1] Meeting of the Bath and West of England and Southern Counties Agricultural Associations was held at Preston Park June 8–13: 'Mr Skinner's General Gordon is head of the yearling bulls, and Mr Walters' Prince of Wales the Reserve and highly commended'.

We are going for a picnic on the 11th of July. There are only 28 more days before the end of the term.

> With love and kisses I remain, Your loving son
> WINSTON

Winston to Lady Randolph

5 July 1885   Brighton

My dear Mamma,

I hope you are quite as well as I am. We went to Bramber on Thursday it was most enjoyable. Do please let me go on with my riding as I am getting on so nicely I like it more than anything else. We won our first match on Wednesday by 15 runs.

> With love and kisses I remain, Your loving son
> WINSTON

PS Thank you very much indeed for that Postal order.

Winston to Lady Randolph

16 August 1885   Tuckers Hotel
                                                                              Cromer

My dear Mama,

I hope you are quite well. Do come and see us soon. The weather is very nice indeed. I cannot walk or bathe or paddle at all because I have got Irrisipelas in my legs in a very mild form. The Regatta takes place to-morrow. I hope you will excuse me for not writing to you. I am very happy on the whole, for I drive myself about in a little donkey carriage. With love and kisses

> I remain your loving son
> WINSTON

Winston to Lady Randolph

20 August 1885   Tuckers Hotel

My dear Mamma,

I have not been enjoying myself badly, lately:– The weather has been very rainy lately. I am working a Text for you in wool. Will you allow me write once a week instead of twice. I am quite well and happy.

> With love and kisses I remain, Your loving son
> WINSTON

PS Please excuse the writing as I have * to get out between the showers. Jack sends love.   * = want

Winston to Lady Randolph

22 August 1885 Chesterfield Lodge
Cromer

My dear Mama,

I hope you are as I am, quite well:– The weather is very fine:– Will you come and see me.

We have left Tucker's Hotel and have gone to a place, called, "Chesterfield Lodge". We went out for a long walk yesterday. I write this hoping you are well.

With love and kisses I remain, Your loving son
WINSTON

Winston to Lady Randolph

25 August 1885 Chesterfield Lodge

My dear Mama,

I hope you are quite well.

The weather is very fine. We have been to the Roman Camp today.

We bathe at 7 o'clock, Then we have Breakfast, then we go on to the rocks and hunt for Sea Anennomies. I have got a hundred of them. I can't be as happy as I might be as I can't see you. I am not enjoying myself much as the lessons always tie me down.

With love and kisses I remain, Your loving son
WINSTON

Winston to Lady Randolph

2 September [1885] Chesterfield Lodge

My dear Mama,

I have recd your letter this morning. The weather is very fine, But, I am not enjoying myself very much. The governess is very unkind, so strict and stiff, I can't enjoy myself at all. I am counting the days till Saturday. Then I shall be able to tell you all my troubles. I shall have ten whole days with you. I like the stamps very much indeed. My temper is not of the most amiable, but I think it is due to the liver as I have had a billious attack which thoroughly upset me, my temperature was 100 once instead of 98 & $\frac{2}{5}$ which is normal.

With love and kisses I remain your loving son
W. CHURCHILL

Winston to Lady Randolph

17 September 1885   Brighton

My dear Mama,

I arrived at school safely on Tuesday. I have had a ride today. The weather
is rather dismal. Will you write and tell me who won the leger ?[1] How are you
enjoying yourself. The weather is not very nice for races I suppose. Come and
see me as soon as you can. The Brighton Regatta came off on Tuesday.

With love & kisses I Remain Your loving son
WINSTON

Winston to Lady Randolph

29 September 1885   Brighton

Dearest Mamma,

I write you a line to thank you for your letter. When do you think Papa will
come & and see me. One of the boys has got a Camera and takes Photos very
well, you must be taken when you come down.

With love & kisses I remain, Your loving son
WINSTON

Winston to Lady Randolph

6 October 1885   Brighton

Dearest Mamma,

I write to tell you that I am quite well, and hope you are the same. I got your
letter this morning, and so I must proceed to answer your questions, and also
to give you some information. The weather was fine in the morning, but about
one o'clock it began to rain, so we were not able to go to the field and play
football. We have been to the baths this morning and I managed to swim
across for the first time. We have got a pretty good eleven and we are going
to play a Match to-morrow. With love & kisses

I remain, Your loving
WINNY

[1] The winner of the St Leger, run at Doncaster on September 16, was the favourite, Lord
Hastings' Melton, ridden by F. Archer. He won by six lengths.

Winston to Lady Randolph

10 October 1885 Brighton

Mama dear,

I have got leave to write a private letter. And so you will excuse writing.
I enclose a photo of myself, and ask if you will be so kind as to send me the sum
half a quid or 10 bob if you know what that is. I want to get 2 doz more and
I will send you some. I am flourishing.

With love and kisses I remain, Your loving son
WINNY

PS This was taken by a boy who is at this school.

Winston to Lord Randolph

20 October 1885 Brighton

Dearest Papa,

I cannot think why you did not come to see me, while you were in Brighton,
I was very disappointed but I suppose you were too busy to come.

I have got 708 stamps from foreign parts and I want to get a stamp Album,
I reckon, guess, and calculate that the volume would come to about 17/6, it
may be 17/6¾ for all I know but I think I could manage without the ¾, I hope
you will grant my mild request. The weather is very bracing here. Will you
give my love to Mamma. With love & kisses

I remain Your loving son
W. CHURCHILL

PS Look out for post-scripts.

Winston to Lady Randolph

10 November 1885 Brighton

Dearest Mamma,

I hope you are quite as well as I am. We have had our display of Fireworks,
they came off on Saturday, there were some 3/6 Rockets, things that go up with
a whiz and a lot of coloured stars came out. The weather is rather Gloomy
down here, but we were able to go the Field and play Football all the same.
There is a portrait of you in the Graphic. I wonder when you are coming down
to see me. Give my best love to Everest and tell her that I have recd her letter,

With love and kisses Your loving son
WINSTON

Winston to Lady Randolph

[?17 November 1885]   [Brighton]

My dear Mama,

I am not very happy. But quite well. I want you to come and see me when the Elections are over.

I recd 2/6 many thanks. Tell Oom[1] I got my coat. Give my best love to Oom and Jack. I want two more Pencils. With Love

I remain
Your loving son
WINNY

Winston to Lord Randolph

28 [?24] November 1885[2]   Brighton

Dearest Papa,

I hope most sincerely that you will get in for Birmingham,[2] though when you receive this the Election will be over. There is another whole holiday to-morrow. There is a boy here whose Pater is going to put up for Winchester he is a Conservative, his name is Col Tottenham.[3] If he gets in for Winchester and you get in for Birmingham I Believe we are going to have a supper.

With much love I remain, Ever your loving son
WINSTON CHURCHILL

Winston to Lady Randolph

26 January 1886   Brighton

My darling Mama,

I hope you will forgive me for not writing to you. I am in a higher form. The weather is cold. Will you write to me as soon as you can. We are going to a Concert on Tuesday, I ought to have said Thursday.

Give my best love to Jack.

Tell Womany that I am quite well, and give her my love.

With best love I remain, Your loving son
WINNY

---

[1] Mrs EVEREST.

[2] Lord Randolph was defeated on November 24 for the Central Division by 773 (the voting was John Bright 4989, Lord Randolph 4216), but elected the next day at Paddington South.

[3] Colonel A. L. Tottenham was elected November 25 by 171 votes: Col Tottenham 1153, Viscount Baring 982.

Winston to Jack

[?10 February 1886]   Brighton

Dear Jack,

Thank you so much for your nice letter it was very good – Vous avez fait
beaucoup de progrès dans votre écriture.

Quant a le combat en Trafalgar Square[1] voici une petite illustration (pen
and ink drawing)

I have tried to imitate your drawings as much as I can [picture of cannon
firing] your writing is much improved – you are now making great progress
in every way. Try and make a difference between the up strokes and the
down ones as =

Dearest Jack Remember me

Try also to get on in your work.

Because if Mama sees that you are getting on you will not have to go to school
next year.

When I come home I must try and teach you the rudiments of Latin.

Winston to Lady Randolph

14 February 1886   [Brighton]

My darling Mummy,

I trust you will not be the object of any malice at the hands of the London
Mobs. I have a little plan to ask, namely:– to let Oom and Jack stay a little
longer at Brighton. It makes me feel so happy to think that my Oom and Jack
are down here, so will you let them stay here, wont you?

                          With much love I remain, your loving son
                                          W. CHURCHILL

Winston to Lady Randolph

23 February 1886   Brighton

My dear Mamma,

I expect you are very busy now. The weather is very dull and gloomy, and
we had a small hail-storm, or rather sleet.

[1] A meeting of unemployed organised by the 'Revolutionary Social Democrats' took place
in Trafalgar Square on 8 February 1886. At the end of it a huge rioting mob moved down
Pall Mall, St James's, Piccadilly, Half Moon Street, and South and North Audley Street,
breaking the windows of clubs, entering and pillaging shops, and causing considerable
destruction of property generally.

We are going to have a concert on Thursday, we were going to have it to-day but it was postponed. I hope you are quite well.

When is that Bazaar for the Working-Men's Club going to take place? I have been out to dinner to-day to see Everest and Jack, and enjoyed myself very much.

> With love & kisses I remain, Your loving son
> WINSTON S. CHURCHILL

Three weeks later Winston went down with pneumonia.

Lord Randolph to Lady Randolph[1]

13 March 1886   [London]

TELEGRAM

Will arrive at Brighton at nine ten.

> RANDOLPH

Dr Robson Roose to Lord Randolph

Sunday 10.15 p.m.   29 & 30 Brunswick Road
[14 March 1886]   Brighton

Memo: W. Churchill

Temp: 104.3 right lung generally involved – left lung of course feeling its extra work but, as yet, free from disease! Respirations more frequent. Pulse increased!

NB This report may appear grave yet it merely indicates the approach of the crisis which, please God, will result in an improved condition should the left lung remain free.

I am in the next room and shall watch the patient during the night – for I am anxious.

> ROBSON ROOSE

[1] Lady Randolph was staying in Brighton at the Bedford Hotel.

Dr Robson Roose to Lord Randolph

6 a.m.   Bedford Hotel
[15 March 1886]   Brighton

Dear Lord Randolph Churchill,
   The high temp indicating exhaustion I used stimulants, by the mouth and
rectum, with the result that at 2.15 a.m. the temp had fallen to 101, and now
to 100, thank God. I shall give up my London work and stay by the boy today.
                                                                    R.R.

Dr Robson Roose to Lord Randolph

1 p.m.   Brunswick Road
[15 March 1886]

Dear Lord Randolph Churchill,
   We are still fighting the battle for your boy. His temp is 103 now but he is
taking his nourishment *better* and there is no increase of lung mischief. As
long as I can fight the temp and keep it under 105 I shall not feel anxious,
and by Wednesday the fever ought to have subsided and the crisis be past.
Nourishment, stimulants and close watching will save your boy. I am sanguine
of this. I shall remain here until 3.30 when I will walk to the Orleans[1] and leave
a report but I shall not leave the house for more than an hour.
                                              Yours faithfully and gratefully
                                                       ROBSON ROOSE
Pardon this shaky writing. I am a little tired. R.R.

Dr Robson Roose to Lord Randolph

11 p.m.   Brunswick Road
15 March 1886

Dear Lord Randolph Churchill,
   Your boy, in my opinion, on his perilous path is holding his own well,
right well! The temp is 103.5 at which I am satisfied, as I had anticipated

---

[1] The Orleans was a residential club at 64 King's Road, Brighton, founded in 1883. Lord
Randolph became a member in the following year, along with his friend and colleague, Sir
Henry Drummond WOLFF. His brother, BLANDFORD (8th Duke of Marlborough), was a
founder-member and Lady Randolph's brother-in-law, Major John LESLIE, became a
member in 1890. Other members included friends of the Prince of Wales such as John Delacour
and Christopher Sykes, newspaper proprietors and journalists such as Algernon Borthwick
(*Morning Post*), Edward Levy-Lawson (*Daily Telegraph*) and George Augustus Sala; Alfred
de Rothschild, Arthur Sassoon; and Captain W. H. O'Shea, who was elected in 1891, the
year in which his former wife married Charles Stewart Parnell.

104! There can *now* be no cause for anxiety for some hours (12 at least) so *please* have a good night, as we are armed at all points.

Ys faithfully
ROBSON ROOSE

Lord Randolph to Lady Randolph

Monday [15 March 1886]   [Brighton]

My dearest,
 The return of the fever is most distressing: I think you do much good by remaining with him. I send the sandwiches & sherry. Tell Roose he will find me here and not at the Orleans. I enclose a telegram which I have answered. Give dear Winny my love when he is himself.

Every yours
RANDOLPH S.C.

Dr Robson Roose to Lord Randolph

16 March 1886   Brunswick Road

Dear Lord Randolph Churchill,
 We have had a very anxious night but have managed to hold our own the temp. now is 101, the left lung still uninvolved, the pulse shews still good power and the delirium I hope may soon cease and natural sleep occur, when one might hope he would awake free from the disease – on the other hand we have to realize that we may have another 24 hours of this critical condition to be combatted with all our vigilant energy. I have telegraphed that I remain here today.

Ys gratefully
ROBSON ROOSE

I have given you a statement of fact, your boy is making a wonderful fight and I do feel please God he will recover.

Sir Henry James to Lady Randolph

Tuesday [16 March 1886]   28 Wilton Place
                                                 Belgrave Square

My dear Lady Randolph,
 I do hope you will believe how much sympathy is felt for you & your husband in this anxious time. I most sincerely hope that the prospect is brightening.

With love Yours most truly
HENRY JAMES

Lord Salisbury to Lord Randolph

EXTRACT

16 March 1886   Monte Carlo

... [PS] I am very sorry indeed to have just heard that you have had anxiety about one of your sons at Brighton. I earnestly hope it is entirely removed by this time.

Dr Robson Roose to Lord Randolph

Wed. 7 a.m.   Brunswick Road
[17 March 1886]

Dear Lord Randolph Churchill,

I have a very good report to make. Winston has had 6 *hours quiet sleep*. Delirium has now ceased. Temp: 99, P.92, respiration 28. He sends you and her ladyship his love.

I will call in on my road to the station, and I meet Rutter[1] in consultation at 8.45 so that I will bring his report too. I shall not return tonight as now the case will I hope not relapse and nourishment the *avoidance* of *chill*, *rest* and quiet are the essential factors. I will however come down tomorrow night or Friday as the lung will I hope begin to be clearing up and must be carefully examined. I leave the case in Rutter's hands in whom I have every confidence.

Yours faithfully
ROBSON ROOSE

Dr Robson Roose to Lady Randolph

Wed   The Station
[17 March 1886]   [Brighton]

Dear Lady Randolph Churchill,

Forgive my troubling you with these lines to impress upon you the absolute necessity of quiet and sleep for Winston and that Mrs Everest should not be allowed in the sick room today – even the excitement of pleasure at seeing her might do harm! and I am so fearful of relapse knowing that we are not quite out of the wood yet.

Yrs faithfully and obliged
ROBSON ROOSE

---

[1] Dr Joseph Rutter (1834–1913), MD (London 1862), a Brighton physician who practised at Codrington House, 141 Western Road. He was at this time consulting physician at the Brighton and Hove Provident Dispensary and assistant physician at the Sussex County Hospital.

Sir Michael Hicks Beach to Lord Randolph
(*Lord Randolph Papers*)

EXTRACT

17 March 1886   House of Commons

My dear Churchill,

I was very glad to hear at Connaught Place this morning that your boy was
better. You must have had a very anxious time – but I hope all will go well
now. . . .

Moreton Frewen to Lady Randolph

17 March 1886   18 Chapel Street
                                                     Park Lane

My dear Jennie,

It is such a relief to us all to hear that you regard the crisis as past; I am so
glad you dear thing. Poor dear Winny, & I hope it will leave no troublesome
after effects, but even if it leaves him delicate for a long time to come you will
make the more of him after being given back to you from the very threshold
of the unknown.

Everyone has been so anxious about it; The Prince stopped the whole line
at the levée to ask after him, & seemed so glad to hear (on Monday) that he
was a little better.

Bless you both; when do you come back.

Yours ever
M

Duchess of Marlborough to Lady Randolph

17 March 1886   46 Grosvenor Square

Dearest Jennie,

I do indeed congratulate you and pray that now all will go on well. You
must have had a most anxious time.

Such Hours make one years older and one feels how one's Happiness in
this world hangs on a thread. I hope and trust you will come to town and
have a little change. I move for the day. I saw dear R and thought him
pretty well and he dines here tomorrow.

The accounts of Cannes are much the same, no worse.

The weather is beastly, no real change. I am sure you will insist on a grand
cure and *quiet* after such an illness. I hope Everest will be sensible and not
gushing so as to excite him. This certainly is not wise.

God bless you. I am so thankful for God's Goodness for preserving your dear Child.

Yours most affectionately
F.M.

In haste – dining out.

Lord Randolph to Lady Randolph

18 March [1886]

My darling,

I hope things are going well. Everyone of our friends here are so glad to hear the good news of Winny. Things political in which I was interested have gone rather kriss-kross since I was away.

I saw Joe this evening. I think he is determined to go.[1] Dont repeat this.

I dine at the Turf tonight with Castlereagh.[2]

Ever yours
RANDOLPH

When Dr Rutter ceases his attendance you should send him a cheque. Remember his fee is 2£ 2s. each visit.

Mrs Leonard Jerome to Lady Randolph

[?18 March 1886]   [London]

Dear darling Jennie,

I have just received yr dear little note so kind of you to think of me in the midst of all yr trouble. I can't tell you how anxious we have all been about poor little Winston. And how delighted & thankful now that he is better. And what a relief for you my dear child. Yr whole life has been one of good fortune & this the crowning blessing that little Winston has been spared to you. You can't be too *grateful* dear Jennie. Papa has been so ill with a dreadful cold but hopes to be well enough to sail for America next Thursday. Perhaps Winston will be so much better that you will be able to come up for a day to say goodby to him. I would have offered my services to go to Brighton but I also have been

---

[1] Joseph Chamberlain resigned from Gladstone's third Cabinet, in which he was President of the Local Government Board, on March 26.

[2] Charles Stewart, 6th Marquess of Londonderry (1852–1915), Lord Randolph's first cousin, who had in fact succeeded to the title in 1884. Became Viceroy of Ireland 1886–9, Postmaster-General 1900–2, President of the Board of Education 1902–5, and Lord President of the Council 1903–5. He was later a leading Ulster Unionist campaigner against Home Rule. KG 1888.

ill ever since my arrival here. We are dying to see you again so take good care of yourself. Leonie says she can't come as Jack has just come from Aldershot for the night. Best love from us all. God bless you.

Affectionately
MAMMA

Lord Randolph to Lady Randolph

[?18 March 1886]   Carlton Club

My dearest,

I am going down to Brighton tomorrow morning by 10.45. Castlereagh is coming with me. I shall remain the night. Roose is also going down to-morrow. It is so pleasant to continue to receive good accounts. The change in the weather is delightful. I have no particular news. I went to Covent Garden this morning & bought the grapes.

Ever yours
RANDOLPH S. CHURCHILL

Lord Randolph to Lady Randolph

17 April 1886   2 Connaught Place

EXTRACT

. . . Winston is going on well & is attended by Dr Gordon.[1] He cannot go out yet as the weather is raw with a N.E. wind. He is in great delight over a Locomotive steam engine I got for him yesterday. . . .

Winston to Lady Randolph

[?6 July 1886]   Brighton

My darling Mummy,

I hope you are well. Has Everest gone for her holiday yet? I should like you to come and see me very much. I am very glad Papa got in for South Padding-ton by so great a majority. I think that was a victory![2] I hope the Conservatives will get in, do you think they will? Give my love to Jack and Everest.

With love and kisses I remain, Your loving son
WINSTON S. CHURCHILL

[1] *Sic.* But more likely Dr Clement Godson (1845–1913), a leading pediatrician.
[2] Lord Randolph was elected on July 2 by 1807 votes: Lord Randolph 2576, Rev J. Page Hopps 769.

Winston to Lady Randolph

13 July [1886]   Brighton

My dear Mama,

I am sorry I have not written to you before. Has Everest gone for her holiday yet? I want to know if I may learn the Violincello or if not The Violin instead of the Piano, I feel that I shall never get on much in learning to Play the piano, but I want to learn the violincello very much indeed and as several of the other boys are going to learn I should like to very much, so I hope you will give sanction I would be delighted. I hope you are quite well. I had a very nice ride this morning. The weather kept fine till Monday when it rained from dawn of day till evening without intermission. Do you think the Conservatives will get in without any of the Unionist Liberals.[1] I am very sorry to say that I am bankrupt and a little cash would be welcome.

With much love I remain, Your loving son
WINSTON

Winston to Lady Randolph

27 July [1886]   Brighton

My dear Mamma,

I received Papa's letter this morning, it was so kind of him to write to me when he was so busy. Do you think he will be Secretary of State for India, or that he will have a new post.[2] Our Examinations have begun already, and we go home on the fourth of August. Has Everest come back from Ventnor yet? If she has, will you ask her to write to me. The weather has been very wet, but to-day it was fine. Have you made any plans for the holidays I should like to go to Jersey very much. We had a lecture on Science and Astronomy by Mr Woodman. Give my best love to Jack and Everest and tell Jack that I shall soon be home and then we will have some fine barricades.

Are you quite well I received the P.O.O. [Post Office Order] which you sent me and am very thankful for it. You have not said anything about the Violincello, in your letter. One of our boys passed into Clifton Colledge.

With best love I remain, Your loving son
WINSTON S. CHURCHILL

[1] As a result of the election, the Conservatives formed a Government with Unionist support. Final figures: Conservatives 316, Liberals 191, Unionist 78, Irish 85.

[2] On July 29 Lord Randolph was appointed Chancellor of the Exchequer and Leader of the House in Lord Salisbury's second administration.

Winston to Lady Randolph

7 September 1886,

My dear Mamma,

I am enjoying myself very much. I have caught a good many Butterflies and Dragon-Fly. I had a beautiful ride to day. Jack send you his love and a 6,666,666,666,666,666,666,666 kisses. And I send you double.

With much love I remain, Your loving son
WINSTON S. CHURCHILL

Winston to Lady Randolph

28 September 1886   Brighton

Dearest Mama,

I am well and hope you are the same. I have received 3 letters from Everest and answered two. The weather was warm to such an extent that we were enabled to go to the Swimming Baths, I managed to swim across, easily to-day. The parade is being greatly enlarged. I think it is a great waste of money 19000£ it cost. I am not in want of any warm day clothing though I should not object to a rug for my bed and a thicker great coat for the winter. With much love

I remain, Your loving son
WINNY

Winston to Lady Randolph

5 October 1886   Brighton

My dear Mama,

I have much joy in writing "Ye sealed Epistle" unto thee. I will begin by informing you the state of the weather after that, I will touch on various other equally important facts. I received your letter and intend to correspond in the best language which my small vocabulary can muster. The weather is fearfully hot. We went to the Swimming Baths to-day, I nearly swam the length which is about 60 feet. We are going to Play a Football Match to-morrow. Last night we had a certain Mr Beaumont to give a lecture on Shakspeare's play of Julius Caesar. He was an old man, but read magnificently.

I am in very good health and am getting on pretty well. Love to all.

I remain, Your loving son
WINSTON S. CHURCHILL

Winston to Lord Randolph

19 October 1886   Brighton

My darling Papa,

I received your kind letter, and the Autographs and stamps. I heard about the fire at Connaught place, It is very unfortunate, Is it not? We have had a tremendous gale here, several seats on the parade were smashed, and some twenty feet of wall destroyed.[1]

We are learning Paradise Lost for Elocution, it is very nice. I am getting on very well indeed in my work. We are going to be Photographed tomorrow. I will try and send you a copy. I am very well indeed and trust you are the same.

I am trying for the Classical Prize and hope I shall get it. I am also getting on well in my swimming. The weather is graually settling down. I hope you will [be] as successful in your speech at Bradford as you were at Dartford, and regularly "cut the ground from under the feet of the Liberals", I trust that you will have a pleasant crossing.[2] I too find how quickly time flies, especially the holidays. I cannot give you any more information, for the simple reason that there is no more to tell you.

With much love I remain, Your loving son
WINSTON S. CHURCHILL

Winston to Lady Randolph

19 October 1886   Brighton

My dear Mama,

I have received a letter from Papa and am going to write him another this evening. I want some of your autographs. Come and see me as soon as you can. I am getting on very well indeed. How is Everest? give her my love, and tell her that I will write soon. With best love

I remain, Your loving son
WINNY

[1] *The Times* reported: 'At Brighton the tide was at high water about midday, and the heavy south-west wind threw the waves over the esplanade, doing great damage to the band-stand and grounds erected near the West pier, and the railway between the Aquarium ticket office and the Chain pier was undermined at points, and at others was embedded with shingle.'

[2] On October 2 Lord Randolph made what WSC later called probably the most important speech of his life at Oakfield Park, Dartford. He pledged himself to a reduction in public expenditure, and called for closer links with the Central Powers against the Turks. The speech was a great sensation, and Lord Randolph left immediately, 'secretly and silently', for a short continental holiday.

Winston to Lady Randolph

24 October 1886   Brighton

My darling Mummy,

I received your kind letter on Friday, and hope you will not meditate long. I want to ask you a great favour and I hope you will grant it, it is a follows:–
There is going to be a Concert at the Pavilion, on the *18th of Nov.* Miss Kate is going to get it up, They are going to act the Finale of the First Scene of the Mikado,[1] and various other things, now the highest ticket price is 5/- and Miss Kate says That if you would come and play, she would double the prices at once and make it 10/- instead of 5/-. It would give me tremendous pleasure, do come please.

With best love I remain
WINSTON

Winston to Lady Randolph

26 October 1886   Brighton

My darling Mama,

I am expecting an answer to my letter, I hope it will be in the affirmative. We are going to play a match tomorrow.

I have an idea that they are, in addition to the Mikado, going to act the "goodnight" scene from Ermine.[2] I am quite well and very busy.

With much love, I remain, Your loving son
WINNY

Winston to Lady Randolph

2 November 1886   Brighton

My dearest Mummy,

I am looking for the promised visit from you. The weather is beautifully warm, though showery.

When you come to see me bring Jack and Everest with you. I am getting on splendidly, and am very happy. What are you going to allow me to have

---

[1] *The Mikado* by W. S. Gilbert and Sir Arthur Sullivan had been first performed at the Savoy Theatre, 14 March 1885.
[2] *Erminie* – a comic opera by C. Bellamy and Harry Paulton, music by Edward Jakobowski; first produced at the Comedy Theatre, 9 November 1885. Contemporary critics described it as well-dressed and sumptuously mounted; it was said to be the first musical comedy using revolving scenery.

for Christmas? I propose that we have a Christmas party, and tree, and have about 18 of my juvenile friends. We will have another Conjuror etc etc.

We are going to have a play at the end of this term and I hope you will come and see it.

Love to all I remain, Your loving son
WINSTON S. CHURCHILL

Winston to Lord Randolph

10 November [1886]   Brighton

My dear Papa,

I hope you are quite well. The weather is very wet today. You never came to see me on Sunday when you were in Brighton. We went to the Museum on Saturday. I was very much interested in the Curiosities, there were several Mummies, also some curious fish. And there were some curious Instruments of Torture used about two centuries ago in the Holy Spanish Inquisition, which one of the masters kindly explained to us.

I require another half dozen Autographs if you please. Give my love to Mama and tell her I will write to her soon.

With much love I remain, Your loving son
WINSTON S. CHURCHILL

Winston to Lady Randolph

23 November 1886   Brighton

My dear Mama,

I hope you are quite well.

Whatever you do do not forget to write to Miss Thomson, to ask her to allow me to come home on Saturday 27th of the 11th month of 1886.

You may imagine what a treat it will be to me. We had a Gymnastic Examination on Monday, I find that in Addition to having gained back my strength, I have gained more than I possessed before, I will give you an Illustration "Last Christmas term I beat Bertie Roose by 1 mark, Last term he beat me by 10 marks. This term I beat him by 3 marks getting top of the school by a majority of 1 mark, I got 60 out of 64.

I am in good health. It is superfluous to add that I am happy.

With much Love, I remain, Your loving son
WINSTON S. CHURCHILL

Winston to Lady Randolph

7 December 1886   Brighton

My dear Mamma,

I am working very hard at the Play, which is getting on admirably. There is to be a Rehearsal this evening. Mind and Come down to distribute the prizes. You had better spend the Saturday night and Sunday in Brighton. I am quite well and hope you are the same. There was a heavy hailstorm to-day. We are going to have a concert tomorrow. I am quite happy.

With much love, I remain, Your loving son
WINSTON CHURCHILL

Winston to Lady Randolph

14 December [1886]   Brighton

My darling Mama,

I hope you will not think my demand unreasonable or exorbitant, but nevertheless I shall make it all the same. Now you know that you canot be watching a juvenile Amateur Play in the borough of Brighton, and at the same time be conducting a dinner party at,

2 Connaught Place
London.

If you go up to town in time for the dinner party you will not be able to see the Plays, but simply distribute the prizes and *go*.

Now you know I was always your darling and you can't find it in your heart to give me a denial, "I want you to put off the dinner party and take rooms in Brighton and go back on Monday morning. . . ." "and perhaps take me with you *No II is* more moderate, *"not bring Jack if inconvenient, but come alone and go back by about the* 10.30 *p.m. train, bring Jack if you* can. I am quite well and hope you are the same. You know that mice are not caught without cheese:

Programme is as near as I can guess as follows:-

English Play
French play
Latin & Greek
Recitations
Supper
Dancing

commencing 4.30 p.m. ending *12* p.m.

This petition I hope you will grant.

Love to all. I remain Your loving son
WINSTON S. CHURCHILL

Winston to Lady Randolph

Sunday 23 [January 1887]   [Brighton]

My dear Mamma,

I got back to school allright and without any mishap. I am quite settled down again. I expect I shall be in the first eleven of Football this term.

The weather is very moderate. We are going to church in about half an hour.

We have a new master whom, I like very much indeed. He was a master a Winchester before he came here, and is now working up for his Exam after passing which he will be a BA I suppose.

Will you tell me what is in my report.

I remain, Your loving son
WINSTON S. CHURCHILL

Winston to Lady Randolph

25 January 1887   Brighton

My dear Mamma,

I am in good health and hope you are the same. I am also getting on very well in Conduct. My marks are as follows:– 10,9,7,7,10 not bad for me.

Little Kim[1] seems to like school very much indeed, and gets on very well indeed.

I am in the first eleven in football. Give my love to all.

With much love, I remain, Your loving son
WINSTON S. CHURCHILL

Winston to Lady Randolph

1 February 1887   Brighton

My dear Mama,

If you are as well as I am, you will do no harm. I should like to see Ruddy-Gore[2] acted, you must take me to see it when I come home, however there is plenty of time to look forward to it. Do not forget to get the set of chess for me. I should like the board to be red and white and not black and white. In our singing classes, we are now learning an Operetta entitled "The merry men of Sherwood forest." I am Robin Hood and Bertie Roose is Meg Marian the

---

[1] William Angus Drogo Montague, Baron Kimbolton (1877–1947). Only son of William, Viscount Manderville (who became in 1890 8th Duke of Manchester) and Consuelo, daughter of Señor Antonio Yznaga del Valle of New York and Cuba, and a friend of the Jeromes. "Little Kim" succeeded as 9th Duke of Manchester in 1892.

[2] *Ruddygore*, first performed at the Savoy Theatre 22 January 1887.

remaining characters are Little John, Much the Miller's son, Friar Tuck and Will Scarlett.

Give my love to to all. I remain, Your loving son
WINSTON S. CHURCHILL

Winston to Lady Randolph

23 February 1887   Brighton

My dear Mamma,

I write, or rather I try to write, this small epistle unto you, hoping you are in good health. The weather to-day has been that of May, the warm sun, the cool breezes, the —— in fact it has been very nice indeed. As we went for a walk on the "marine Parade" this afternoon we saw – this may need some explanation, for you must know, that for some time past 3 men in a costume, resembling an ulster with a hood, have been performing on a cottage piano on the Parade, well, as we were out this afternoon we saw them, and about 50 yards off an other troupe exactly the same, I expect there is a good deal of rivalry between them.

We are going to attend divine service tomorrow at 9 a.m.

Do not forget my request for more money.

Love to all. I remain Your loving son
WINNY

Winston to Lady Randolph

7 March 1887   Brighton

My dear Mamma,

I am quite well and hope you are the same after your crossing. The weather is very changeable indeed. You did not answer me when you were down here about my riding for two hours you know. Miss Thomson is not quite well to-day. We had a Euclid Examination to-day, and an Arithmetic Examination on Saturday. No more news. Love to all.

I remain, Ever your loving son
WINSTON S. CHURCHILL

Winston to Lady Randolph

15 March 1887   Brighton

Dear Mamma,

I am hoping you are quite well, & none the worse for your crossing. Did you have a good crossing, a nice berth, and a bad sickness? There was a very heavy fall of snow this morning at about 9.30.

I am looking forward to the Easter holidays very much, and also to going to Birmingham & Paris. Only 21 more days before I do come home. I have learnt the Latin days of the month to day would be "Ante diem Pridie Idus Martias." Love to all.

> I remain Your loving son
> WINSTON S. CHURCHILL

Winston to Lady Randolph

23 March 1887   Brighton

Dear Mamma,

I write this epistle, hoping it will reach you, finding you as well as I am myself.

We go home on the 6th day of the 4th month of 1887. *Weather*, changeable in the extreme, warm in sunshine, moderate wind, causing a running sea, but on the whole fine. We went for a walk on the Parade, I should say sea-wall, and had a game. Miss Thomson has had a dear little fox-terrier puppy given to her.

The Examinations begin on Monday. I am looking forward to going to Birmingham.

Now there is nothing more to tell you. Love to All.

> Good-bye
> I remain, Your loving son
> WINSTON S. CHURCHILL

Winston to Lady Randolph

3 May 1887   Brighton

My dearest Mama,

I hope you are quite well; I, at present, am blessed with that inestimable treasure, i.e. "Good Health" which I trust will not be withdrawn from me, for a long time.

I received your letter this morning. I am quickly settling down, though I have not got into full swing quite yet. The weather, though showery, is fine and rather hot. We had a game of Cricket this afternoon, I hit a *twoer*, as the expression goes, my first runs this year.

I hope to improve this year in Cricket as well as in my studies.

As we were out this morning on the Parade, we saw a wreck which had been run down by a steamer, about 3 miles out at sea & was being towed in by tugs bit by bit.

Now I must close this scrawl with the usual amount of love.

Give my love to Everest and thank Jack for his letter tell him I will write Friday.

> I remain Your loving son
> WINNY

Winston to Lady Randolph

10 May 1887   Brighton

My dear Mama,

I am writing to tell you, that I have had a bad cough, but, it is much better now.

I am sorry to hear that Jack & Everest are not well.

I have not been out since Saturday so I am no judge of the weather.

Let me know about Everest & Jack.

We are going to play our first Cricket match, on the first Wednesday in June. When are you coming down to see me? Come soon! Give my best love to All.

> With best love I remain, Your loving son
> WINNY

PS Write to me soon. WSC

Winston to Lady Randolph

17 May 1887   Brighton

My dear Mama,

I had the pleasure yesterday morning of receiving an Epistle from thee, and in return intend to gladden thy heart with one from me. I am quite well. Rather a blunt sentence but you will think it very satisfactory, I have no doubt.

I saw grandmama on Sunday. I am going out tomorrow with Aunt Wimborne.

Mind & come down on 21st.

> Love to all I remain, Your loving son
> WINNY

Winston to Lady Randolph

[Postmark 20 May 1887]   [Brighton]

Dear Mama,

It is impossible for you to come on Monday it is not a half holiday and we I am are going to have a concert and it would not amuse you or I to stay at the school all day.

I am chief feature in it. I am very disappointed indeed, but couldn't you come Sunday & stay till Monday. I should like it so much. I would not mind kicking the Concert off, I have so many things to tell you. Whatever you do come Monday please. I shall be miserable if you don't.

Love & kisses, I remain, Your loving son
WINNY

Winston to Lady Randolph

24 May 1887   Brighton

My dearest Mother,

Will you soon oblige me, by a line or two to let me know if you arrived safely. I did not feel a bit dull after you left yesterday. About a dozen boys have joined the Primrose League[1] since yesterday, I am among the number & intend to join the one down here, and also the one which you have in London. Would you send me a nice badge as well as a paper of Diploma, for I want to belong to yours most tremendously. The ices and the bath did not have any effect upon my constitution. I again visited the baths today and got on capitally.

I am, stop! I must not be too egotistical, getting on well in Cricket and slowly improving. I wish the Jubilee[2] was here very much. I also hope that you will think my little letter more sensible.

I remain Your loving son
WINNY

Winston to Lady Randolph

31 May 1887   Brighton

Dear Mamma,

I hope that you have not been looking for a letter, from me, long. I try and think of sensible sentences for my letter, but they are very hard to think of. There is a grand Match in Cricket at the County ground between Gloucestershire and Sussex; W. G. Grace who is playing for Gloucester made 53 runs, his side was 230 and 3 more wickets to go down yesterday afternoon, but as it is a

[1] Founded by Lord Randolph and Sir Henry Drummond Wolff in 1883 to preserve the memory of Disraeli. But when the Electoral Reform Laws of 1884 made the employment of paid canvassers illlegal the Primrose League took on the more practical object of providing voluntary constituency workers for the Tory Party at a time when the constituency organisations tended to be weak. The League's motto is *Imperium et Libertas*; at one time it had more than 2,000,000 members.

[2] The fiftieth anniversary of the accession of Queen Victoria to the throne was celebrated during the summer. The Jubilee festivities began with a Service of Thanksgiving held in Westminster Abbey on 21 June 1887.

three-days-match the result is uncertain, as yet.[1] I am, at present quite well, and hope I shall continue so for a long time.

The weather is very fine & hot. We are going to play our first match of the season tomorrow afternoon. Give my best love to all. With love to yourself

I remain Your loving son
WINNY

PS Remember the "Jubilee."

Winston to Lady Randolph

7 June 1887   Brighton

My dear Mamma,

I hope you are as well as I am. The weather is very foggy and damp. I went to the baths yesterday and got on all right. We are going to play a match today, but I expect the weather will stop that. Will you send me a few autographs.

Love to all I remain, Your loving son
WINNY

Winston to Lady Randolph

[Postmark 11 June 1887]   [Brighton]

My dear Mamma,

Miss Thomson does'nt want me to go home for the Jubilee and because she says that I shall have no place in Westminster Abbey and so it is not worth going. Also that you will be very busy and unable to be with me much.

Now you know that this is not the case. I want to see Buffalo Bill & the Play as you promised me.[2] I shall be very disappointed, disappointed is not the word I shall be miserable, after you have promised me, and all, I shall never trust your promises again. But I know that Mummy loves her Winny much too much for that.

Write to Miss Thomson and say that you have promised me and you want to have me home. Jack entreats you daily I know to let me come and there are 7 weeks after the Jubilee before I come home. Don't disappoint me. If you write

---

[1] Sussex eventually beat Gloucestershire by four wickets. Gloucestershire 240 and 190, Sussex 253 and 180 for 6. For Gloucestershire Dr Grace, besides scoring 51 runs in the first innings and 47 in the second, bowled 99 overs in the match to take 5 wickets for 150.

[2] At the American Exhibition at Earl's Court. He was advertised in *The Times*: '*Three* p.m. to 4.30 p.m. – BUFFALO BILL'S WILD WEST – Rain or shine (Colonel W. F. Cody.) Grand stand for 20,000 people. Bands of Sioux, Araphoes, Shoshones, Cheyennes, and other Indians, Cowboys, Scouts and Mexican Vacqueros. Riding, shooting, lassoing and Hunting. Attacks on Stage Coach and Settler's Cabin. 200 Native Mustang, Indian fighting. Riding Bucking Horses, Frontier Girl Riders and Cowboy bands.'

to Miss Thomson she will not resist you, I could come home on Saturday to stay till Wednesday. I have got a lot of things, pleasant and unpleasant to tell you. Remember for my sake. I am quite well but in a torment about coming home it would upset me entirely if you were to stop me.

Love & kisses

I remain Yours as ever, Loving son

WINNY

(Remember)

Winston to Lady Randolph

Sunday [? 12 June 1887]　　　　　　　　　　　　　　　　　　Brighton

My dear Mamma,

I hope you are as well as I am. I am writing this letter to back up my last. I hope you will not disappoint me. I can think of nothing else but Jubilee. Uncertainty is at all times perplexing write to me by return post please!!! I love you so much dear Mummy and I know you love me too much to disappoint me. Do write to tell me what you intend to do. I must come home, I feel I must. Write to Miss Thomson a letter after this principle so:— "My dear——

Could you allow Winston to come up to London, on Saturday the 18th for the Jubilee. I should like him to see the procession very much, and I also promised him that he should come up for the Jubilee.

I remain

Yours

JSC

I think that the above will hit its mark, anyhow you can try. I know you will be successful.

I am looking forward to seeing Buffalow Bill, yourself, Jack, Everest, and *home*.

I would sooner come home for the Jubilee and have no amusement at all than stay down here and have tremendous fun.

The weather is fine.

Please, as you love me, do as I have begged you.

Love to All

I remain as ever, Your loving son

WINNY

For Heavens sake Remember!!!

[*Pen and ink sketch of cannon firing and soldiers.*]

Winston to Lady Randolph

[15 June 1887]   [Brighton]

Dear Mamma,

I am nearly mad with suspense. Miss Thomson says that she will let me go if you write to ask for me. For my sake write before it is too late. Write to Miss Thomson by return post please!!!

I remain Your loving son
WINNY

Winston to Lady Randolph

[?19 June 1887]   [Brighton]

My dear Mamma,

I am much better now though not very happy I am so dull and want to come home so badly. I have not got much time.

Thanks for your letter. Won't forget the 21st. I shall have a lot of news good & bad to tell you. Weather cold, & changeable.

Am going to write to Everest. Just a line on Sunday to tell you how I am.

Good Bye, Much love I remain your loving son
WINNY

Winston to Lady Randolph

24 June 1887   Brighton

My dear Mamma,

I arrived hear alright yesterday, and took a cab to the school, at which I arrived at 7.15. I am settling down alright now, though rather dull at first. The weather is beautifully fine. We went to the baths to day they were fine.

I hope you will soon forget my bad behaviour while at home, and not to make it alter any pleasure in my summer Holidays. I telegraphed to Everest as soon as I arrived at the station. All serene.

Kim came back to day, another boy will come back tomorrow, so I was not the latest back.

I am getting on capitally in Euclid. I and another boy are top of the school in it we have got up to the XXX Proposition. Will you send me a book to read I have got nothing at all to read now. I should like "She" or "Jess"[1] very much indeed – I am quite well.

Please be quick and send me the autographs 6 of yours & 6 of Papa's.

With much love, I remain as ever, Your loving son
WINNY

W. S. Churchill

[1] *She* by Rider Haggard was first published on 1 January 1887. *Jess,* by the same author, appeared in March of that year.

Winston to Lady Randolph

28 June 1887   Brighton

My dear Mamma,

I am getting on capitally in everything especially Euclid which I like tremendously now, also in Greek & Latin.

We went to the baths this morning, I am getting on in swimming very well, I jumped off the top spring board. Weather beautiful, not too hot, & not to warm. We break up on the 28th of July. I want to collect Butterflies in the Holidays so much, I enjoy it immensely.

I should so much like to have "Jess" by Haggard I want something to read very much. Will you send it to me soon.

My Money will last a long time yet, I think. Please write soon to me, I rather want a letter.

Please send me the autographs 6 of yours & 6 of Papa's.

Love to All, I remain As Ever, Your loving son
WINNY

Winston to Lady Randolph

5 July 1887   Brighton

My Dear Mamma,

I received your letter this morning, it gave me a good deal of pleasure. The weather on Monday was so intensely hot that we kept our whites on all day for coolness. But to-day the oppressive heat was relieved in the morning by a refreshing shower which cooled the whole day, and gave a beautiful freshness to all things.

Tomorrow we are going to Bramber for our annual treat, we start about 10 a.m. and return at about 8 p.m. I will tell you all about it next letter. I am looking forward to the book, autographs, & holidays. The latter commence on the 28th of this month. We were unable to go to the Baths today, owing to the repainting of the same. I have now got a piece of good news for you, viz. I am told by Mr Best[1] that I am getting on much better in my Greek. Now Greek is my weak point & I cannot get into Winchester without it, so I am very glad I have made a start. We have got up to the end of the Passive voice of the verb "λυω". I believe I am beginning to like Greek now. In Euclid, too, we have got up to the XXXIV Proposition.

It was Miss Kate's Birthday on Monday & it is for that we have our treat, we *do* enjoy ourselves. I am getting on allright in the character of "Robin Hood" we have learnt to the end of it.

---

[1] James Theodore Best (1864–1925); educated at Harrow (Scholar) and at Trinity College, Dublin (Scholar). Senior Mathematical master at Queen Elizabeth School, Kingston, 1887–97; Principal, St John's College, Rangoon, 1897–1923.

Do you think there will be a chance of my going to Paris in the Holidays or somewhere on the continent. I should like 5/– as I am absolutely bankrupt.

Give my best love to all at home.

I hope you will be, when this reaches you as well as I am when it leaves me.

With much love, I remain As ever, your loving son
WINNY

Winston to Lady Randolph

[?8 July 1887]   [Brighton]

Dear Mamma,

I am in want of 5/– because Miss Kates Birthday Present has taken 5/– out of my Exchequer. I want "Jess" or "She" soon. Autographs for goodness sake. My darling I hope you don't intend to make my Holidays miserable by having a Tutor.

Love & Kisses, I remain, Your loving son
WINNY

Winston to Lady Randolph

12 July 1887   Brighton

My dear Mamma,

I am looking forward to the Holidays tremendously now. I hope to have very happy ones. Do you think Bertie Roose could come too? It would be double pleasure for me. The weather is nice and fine. Please be quick with the "Autographs" "Book" & "5/–". I should like them at once. I was tremendously surprised by the news I received on Sunday.

We *did* enjoy ourselves at Bramber. Do you think you could come down to see me on Saturday I want to tell you so many things. We went to the Swimming-Baths this morning.

I am quite well.

With Love & Kisses I remain, Your loving son
WINNY

Winston to Lady Randolph

[July 1887]   [Brighton]

My dear Mamma,

I am told that "Mr Pest" is going to be my tutor in the Holidays. Now as he is a Master here and I like him pretty well I shall not mind him at all, on one condition v.i.z. "Not to do any work" I give up all other conditions except this one I never have done work in my holidays and I will not begin now. I will be very good if this is not forced upon me and I am not bothered about it. When I am doing nothing I don't mind working a little, but to feel that I am forced to do it is against my principles. Without this I might have very happy holidays.

Hoping you will grant this.

I remain Your loving son
WINNY

Winston to Lady Randolph

[? 14 July 1887]   [Brighton]

My dear darling Mummy,

I received your letter yesterday evening & I was very pleased to get the Autographs + 5/- but I did not enjoy the letter quite so much, nevertheless I deserved it, I know. I promise you I will be a very good boy indeed in the Holidays. Only *do* let me off the work because I am working hard this term & I shall find quite enough to do in the Holidays.

I am never at a loss for anything to do while I am in the country for I shall be occupied with "Butterflying" all day (I was last year). Do let me try it for a week & then if it becomes a burden let me off it. (I ask this as a favour.)

For even if it is only 1 hour a day I shall feel that I have got to be back at a certain time and it would hang like a dark shadow over my pleasure.

Do you think you could possibly come down to see me Saturday. It is 3 weeks to day since I came back & I want to see you very, very much.

Do come if you can, I have got so many things to talk to you about, more than would fill a quire of Paper.

You may have thought me unaffectionate
but I always was
& always will be

Your loving son
WINNY

Winston to Lady Randolph

19 July 1887   Brighton

My dear Mamma,

I am getting on all right in my Examinations. We have had "Euclid" "Algebra" "French" And Greek. The weather is beautifully warm. We went to the baths this morning.

The Gymnastics Examination comes off on Thursday.

I am well & hope you are the same.

With love and kisses I remain, Your loving son
WINNY

Winston to Lady Randolph

Saturday 11 a.m. [?August 1887]   7 South Grove Terrace
                                                   Ventnor Isle of Wight[1]
Dear Mamma,
    We arrived safe and had a comfortable journey, although it was rather
rough crossing. We have got very nice rooms. I enclose address. I am just going
out walking So I guess I'll remain Your loving son
                                        WINSTON S. CHURCHILL

Winston to Lady Randolph

21 September 1887   [Brighton]

My dear Mamma,
    I have arrived safely and am settling down all right.
    Auntie Clara took us to the Dyke when you had gone.
    I hope you arrived allright. I can find nothing else to tell you so
                            With love and kisses I remain, Your loving son
                                                        WINSTON

Winston to Lady Randolph

?[September 1887]   [Brighton]

My dear Mummy,
    I hope you will excuse my writing, as I am in rather a hurry. I am very
interested in the picking up or getting together of the first eleven at football.
The weather is rather cold. I have not had a letter from you yet do write to me.
                            With love & kisses I remain, Your loving son
                                                        WINNY

Reverend J. E. C. Welldon to Edward Marjoribanks
                    (*Blenheim Papers*)

24 September 1887   Harrow

My dear Mr Marjoribanks,
    I hope you will have felt that my long delay in replying to your letter of
August 6 was simply due to my being beyond the reach of correspondence. I
have been travelling through America so rapidly that it was not safe to have
any letters sent after me; and I returned to Harrow only this evening.

---

[1] The address is written in Mrs Everest's writing.

If Lord Randolph Churchill is good enough to wish to send his son to Harrow it will be a pleasure to me to find room for him somewhere.

It is difficult to speak positively about vacancies; and my own house is terribly full. But with Lord Randolph's leave I will make an arrangement by which his son may go temporarily into a Small House and may then pass from it into my own house or, at the worst, into some other Large House.

With many thanks for your letter

Believe me very faithfully yours
J. E. C. WELLDON

PS Will Lord Randolph kindly fill up the enclosed form? I think his son had better come to Harrow next Easter at the same time as your own boy.

Winston to Lady Randolph

25 September 1887　　　　　　　　　　　　　　　　　　Brighton

My dear Mother,

I recd your letter this morning before going to the baths.

Thank you for sending me Papa's speech,[1] I read a little of it. I am very glad that I am going to Dr Wildon's house it is very kind – of him indeed. The weather, though cold, is fine and nice. I am getting on all right in work. We had an Examination in Ancient History on Monday, and not withstanding, that the results are not yet known, I do not think that I am so very far from the top.

We have only had 2 Exams this term v.i.z. History 50 marks & Algebra 18, in both I was top.

With love I remain, Your loving son
WINSTON

PS I will write again on Friday. wsc

Winston to Lady Randolph

27 September 1887　　　　　　　　　　　　　　　　　　Brighton

Dear Mama,

I received your letter yesterday. I read Papa's speech, or rather part of it on Sunday. My breeches have not turned out badly. I have not begun boxing yet. I am afraid you have forgotten all about "She" please remember as I am longing to read it.

My Conduct Marks are at present 10,10,8,9,7,10 the best I have ever had.

With love & kisses I remain Your loving son
WINSTON

[1] Lord Randolph's speech at Whitby on 23 September 1887.

Winston to Lady Randolph

1 October 1887 Brighton

Dearest Mother,

Can you tell me where Papa is? I shall write to him on Tuesday. Everest left Brighton this morning.

It was a pity that you sent me the P.O. for 5/- as I have plenty of money just now, Uncle Ivor[1] having given me 10/- when I went to see him. The weather is most unpleasant, that is to say, it pours with rain & when it does not, it blows so hard that all the windows rattle.

Owing to the weather which has just been described we have been unable to go out at all today.

"I want you to come down on some fine day and see me."

I am getting on all right in swimming. I can now shoot the breadth of the swimming baths which is 30 ft, by shooting it, I mean that I dive off the bank and keep my body perfectly straight until I reach the other side keeping under water the whole time.

In Euclid I have got up to the XLII Proposition. There are XLVII in the first book so I have nearly finished it.

We have played 2 football matches.

With Love I remain, Your loving son
WINSTON

Winston to Lady Randolph

4 October 1887 Brighton

Dearest Mother,

It was a great pity you could not come down Sunday week, but as Aunt Clara went up to town it would not have been any good Auntie went to the Gymnasium on Monday, it was very nice.

I have not yet begun my Boxing lessons. The weather is nice and not too cold. The riding-breeches have turned out very well indeed. I am afraid that you have forgotten all about "She". If you know how I am longing for "Her" I am sure you would send her to me.

I am thinking of trying to write a little Play, and as you proposed, we might act it at Christmas.

It would employ my "Leisure Hour" with an at once amusing and useful occupation. If you think it is practicable, say so, and I'll try my hand on a "Comedy".

[1] Lord WIMBORNE.

We had a "Concert" last night, I recited, and the Boys sang the "Operetta", it went off very well. I hope this letter will find you as well as it leaves me.

With much love I remain, Your loving son
WINSTON S. CHURCHILL

Reverend J. E. C. Welldon to Lord Randolph
(Blenheim Papers)

4 October 1887   Harrow

My dear Lord,

I wish to thank you for your letter respecting the admission of your son to Harrow School.

I shall look forward with much pleasure to his coming, & I hope I may be useful to him, when he is here.

You may rely upon my placing him in a House where his health will be carefully watched, if I cannot find room for him immediately in my own.

Believe me very faithfully yours
J. E. C. WELLDON

Winston to Lord Randolph

8 October 1887   Brighton

Dearest Father,

I am very glad to hear that I am going to Harrow & not to Winchester. I think I shall pass the Entrance Examination, which is not so hard as Winchester. I shall know by the time I go there the 1st 2nd and part of the 3rd books of Euclid. In Arithmetic we are doing "Square Root" and have quite mastered Decimal fractions & Rule of three. Greek, however is my weakest subject as I have yet to learn the Verbs in "$\mu\iota$" which are very hard. Will you send me some of your autographs? We are, at the end of the term, going to act Molière's "Médecin Malgré lui". I take the part of "Martine".[1]

We are getting up a Greek Play too, in which, there are only 2 characters one of whom is myself. The Play is called "The Knights" by "Aristophanes". Of course we are only doing one extract but I think it will prove very amusing to all. I wish you would come to the distribution of prizes at the end of this term, but I suppose it is impossible. The weather, today is moderately fine, but we have had some severe storms. I went to see Grandmamma a fortnight ago & she read me your speech on the Distribution of Prizes at the school of

---

[1] His grand-daughter, Arabella Spencer Churchill, at the age of eleven, was to play the same role at her school – Ladymede, near Princes Risborough – in 1961.

Art, it was just the sort of speech for school boys. You had great luck in Salmon fishing, I wish I had been with you I should have liked to have seen you catch them. Did you go to Harrow or Eton? I should like to know.

Please do not forget the autographs.

With Love & Kisses
I remain, Your loving son
WINSTON S. CHURCHILL

Winston to Lady Randolph

11 October 1887   Brighton

My dear Mama,

I received your letter yesterday morning, I was very much astonished at the news about Harrow. I no longer want "She" as my time is sufficiently filled up now. I am most backward in Greek I have yet to learn the verbs in "$\mu\iota$" which are very hard.

In Euclid however I am not at all backward on the contrary I am pretty forward. I am told that I could get in well with 1 book, I shall know 1.2. and part of the 3rd books when I go. In Latin I shall need a little work.

Let Jack & Everest stay down here a little longer.

With much love I remain, Your loving son
WINSTON

Winston to Lady Randolph

19 October 1887   Brighton

Dearest Mother,

Feeling that I should like to know something about Harrow, I wrote to a boy who was formerly here, but went in for the Entrance Examination & passed very well indeed & he wrote back & told me all about it. What house am I going to, I hear Crookshanks is the best & I should like to go there because I know a boy there & he would show me my way (figuratively) about, & it is nice to to know somebody especially as he is a very nice boy, very weak however his spine is weak.

There is a swimming bath $\frac{1}{4}$ of a mile long & in the open air and made to look like a river. He says "I am sure you will be learned enough to pass the Examination" also that I ought to know some Greek Translation Herodotus or something of the sort. Unfortunately there will be in all probability no Euclid.

We went to the baths this morning I fished up some shells from a depth of 6 feet.

It is rather fine you have to open your eyes under water and then you see the bottom and the shells looking like a blotch of luminous paint and sometimes just as you are rising to the surface with it, it slips through your fingers, which is very irritating. I brought one of the shells away with me.

Will you send me 5/- as I have only 2/10 left: The weather is very nice, and we had a good game of Football this afternoon. On Wednesday we went to a Concert at the Town Hall given by Mr G. P. Hawtrey,[1] he gave us all seats *gratis* for which we were very *grateful*.

G. Grossmith & W. Grossmith[2] were there.

G. Grossmith gave a Musical Sketch entitled "Homburg" which I should have liked you to have heard. He said that wherever he went he was always haunted by the Mikado. I must now say Good bye.

With love & kisses I remain, Your loving son
WINSTON

Winston to Lady Randolph

22 October 1887   Brighton

Dearest Mother,

I am quite well – quite happy – in fact all that could possibly be wished. Please try and get Father to come down to the Distribution of Prizes as well as yourself. You ought to take a room at Mr Johnson's and stay the night so as not to have to hurry off to catch the train. I should like to come home for my birthday but then I should sacrifice any chance of a prize. I finished the 1st Book of Euclid to-day.

I suppose you are coming down for my birthday, I also suppose that we are going to have a party; are we not?!!!!!

I will not forget to get the addresses of all those boys whom I want to invite. I think that there will be about a dozen.

"The Examinations are drawing very near" I am glad of that as there is always some excitement then & I am hoping to have the success that is due to a long term of hard work. I can conscientiously say that I have learnt more in this term than I had learnt in the 2 preceeding ones. I have got a large manuscript book in which I am writing all my Recitations. I am sure you will be much amused by the "Greek Play".

I saw Lady Kaye[3] on Sunday & also Mr & Mrs Thomas.

---

[1] George Procter Hawtrey (1846–1910), actor, producer and manager; an elder brother of Sir Charles Hawtrey (1858–1923), the actor-manager.

[2] George (1847–1912) and Weedon (1851–1919) Grossmith, actors, authors and theatrical producers. Their best known work is *The Diary of a Nobody*.

[3] The wife of Sir John Pepys Lister-Kaye, 3rd Bart; she was Natica, second daughter of Señor Antonio Yznaga del Valle and sister of Consuelo, later Duchess of Manchester.

Thank Father from me for his letter & autographs. Will you send me some of yours not merely the initials but the full name "J. S. Churchill" as there is rather a demand for them here. I must now end this epistle as I shall not have time to do some Latin Prose. Love to all

I remain Ever your loving son
WINSTON S. CHURCHILL

Winston to Lady Randolph

[Postmark 28 October 1887]　　　　　　　　　　　　[Brighton]

My dear Mama,

I recd the P.O. last night, many thanks. I went out to Grandmamma's yesterday (Thurs).

I have only done that which you asked me about a very little and lately I have left it off all together. I am working hard and am top in every Examination except one where I was 1 mark behind.

My marks are –

Eng History	– 50	1st
Algebra	– 18	1st
Ancient History	– 80	1st
Bible History	– 30	1st
Geography	– 17	2nd

TOTAL 195

I am quite well and see plenty of Everest and Jack.

I am sorry they are going away next week as I shall not see them after that.

With Love I remain, Your loving son
WINNY

Come and see me soon

Winston to Lady Randolph

15 November 1887　　　　　　　　　　　　　　　Brighton

Dearest Mother,

I received your letter yesterday. I have at last begun the verbs in "$\mu\iota$" of which the first is "$\H{\iota}\sigma\tau\eta\mu\iota$".

We had an Examination in Arithmetic yesterday in which I was second with *33* marks.

The "Grand Finale" Examinations are coming off in about 3 weeks. The weather is cold & we were unable to go to the baths to-day.

On Saturday I went out with Aunt Wimborne, and saw, or rather heard, Ch Brandram[1] recite "Twelfth night".

I have not yet had any boxing lessons. Perhaps you would not mind me hinting That *my Birthday* is drawing near. I am looking forward to a visit from you on that day. I should rather like "Gen Grant's History of the American War. (*Illustrated*)

Give my best love to Papa, & try and get him to come down at the end of the term.

With Love & kisses I remain, Your loving son
WINSTON

Winston to Lady Randolph

29 November 1887   Brighton

Dearest Mother,

I recd your letter this morning. I have found that my Birthday falls on Wednesday not Thursday but no matter.

I am writing to Father to night. Am about to have a rehearsal of the greek Play so I must conclude,

With Love & Kisses I remain, Your loving son
WINSTON S. CHURCHILL

Winston to Lady Randolph

6 December 1887   Brighton

Dearest Mother,

I saw Papa on Sunday, we went to the Orleans Club for tea. He asked Miss Thomson to let us have a half-holiday on Monday. We have had two Examinations as yet Algebra and Greek and we are going to have Latin to-morrow. Mr Best has gone to Dublin for his Examination it is his last before he is a BA.

I have not much news to tell you, I know.

With love & kisses I remain, Your loving son
WINSTON S. CHURCHILL

PS I have only read 1 book and ½ of another. I have still 2 fresh ones. w c

---

[1] Probably Samuel Brandram (1824–92), a noted Shakespearian reciter from about 1870.

Winston to Jack

[? 6 December 1887]   [Brighton]

My dear Jack,

I have not had a letter from you for a long time. I am afraid you are rather lazy. Papa gave me 10/- when he came down on Sunday. I have played 6 football matches this term and have won 5 of them.

Mr Best is in Dublin doing his examinations. Dearest, mind and be a good boy and dont use any naughty words. I am writing to ask you to write me a little English letter.

I cant write more now but will write again soon.

With love and kisses I remain, Your loving Brother
WINSTON S. CHURCHILL

Winston to Lady Randolph

[? 13 December 1887]   [Brighton]

Dearest Mother,

I have not written to you lately but I will try to write now.

I am very hard at work what with Play and Examinations. You said you would not mind a "scribble" if I wrote to you 1 decent letter a week.

When Papa came down he asked Miss Thomson to let us have a half-holiday and she let us have one.

We will not have a Christmas tree this year, But I think a good 3 guinea Conjuror and a Tea and amusements and games after tea would answer better. You see the Conjurer for 3 guineas gives "ventriloquisim" and an hours good conjuring which always causes some amusement. I will get a lot of addresses this time. We might have

Vince
Finch
Beauville
Horne
Roper
Wroughton
Rusle
and a lot of others

I must now say good bye

With love and kisses I remain, Your loving son
WINSTON S. CHURCHILL

Winston to Lady Randolph

14 December 1887   Brighton

Dearest Mother,

Miss Thomson told me your plans before your letter arrived.[1] I am very disappointed at hearing that I must spend my holidays without you. But I am trying to make the "Best of a bad job". We shall not be Able to have a party of course. Try and get Mr Best to stay with me and Jack in the holidays. Jack will not want a governess if Mr Best comes. I shall see you on Saturday and I have no doubt you will try your best to make me happy.

I remain, Your loving son
WINSTON

Winston to Lady Randolph

26 December 1887   [2 Connaught Place]

Dearest Mother,

I did not know your address or how to send it (the letter). I have got two prizes one for English Subjects & one for Scripture.

I must tell you all about Christmas Day.

Auntie Clara was too ill to come so Auntie Leonie & Uncle Jack were our only visitors. We drank the Queens health Your health & Papa's. Then Everest's and Auntie Clara and Uncle Moreton. In the Evening I went to Stratford Place[2] and played games till 6.30.

I get on all right with Mademoiselle. Auntie Leonie & Auntie Clara both gave me 10/- which I was to spend on a theatre. Auntie Leonie also gave 20/- from Papa so I am well up in '[?Jam]'.

Grandmama wrote to me from Blenheim and wanted me to go to Blenheim but I told Auntie Leonie and she is arranging it. I don't want to go at all.

I am so glad you arrived safely.

Bertie Roose came to luncheon to day. My darling Mummy I do wish you were at home it would be so nice. But you must come and see me when you come back. In fact you might have me back from school for a day or two. Please thank my dear Papa for the 20/-.

Excuse my writing but I will write very often now I know what to do.

With much love I remain, Your loving son
WINSTON S. CHURCHILL

It is very dull without you. But after all we are very happy. Jack sends His love to you & Papa and is going to write.

[1] Lord and Lady Randolph were going on a visit to Russia. They left on December 19 and returned, via Berlin, on 3 February 1888.

[2] 11 Stratford Place, the London house of Sir John Leslie.

Duchess of Marlborough to Lord Randolph
(*Blenheim Papers*)

EXTRACT

26 December [1887]   Blenheim

. . . I hope you & Jennie will not be angry with me, I have asked Winston
to come to stay *a week* with me. I would be responsible for him. He wrote me
such a nice little letter & I *never* see him. B was very pleased & I will take great
care of him. I expect him tomorrow & send to Oxford for him . . . .

. . . Just got a Tel from Leonie that Winston is not to be allowed to come
& see me! I feel much aggrieved & shall trouble no more about my Gd-
Children I should have thought I was able to take care of him as Leonie
& Clara. . . .

Winston to Lady Randolph

[? 30 December 1887]   45 Hill Street,
                                                       Berkeley Square

Dearest Mother,

I suppose you have heard about Everest's illness. I & Jack at present (Sat
30)[1] are staying at Dr Roose's. It is very hard to bear – we feel so destitute. Dr
Gordon says that Everest has 2 patches down her throat but that it is more
Quinzy than Diphtheria.

Darling I hope you will come down to see me when you come home and
bring Everest.

I feel very dull – worse than school. I must now end. Thank you for your
letter.

Good bye my dear
I remain, Your loving son
WINSTON S. CHURCHILL

Lord Randolph to Duchess of Marlborough
(*Lord Randolph Papers*)

EXTRACT

2 January [1888]   Hotel de France
Copy   St Petersburg

Dearest Mama,

We were troubled yesterday by receiving a telegram from Roose saying that
Everest had got bad diptheria and that he had moved the two boys into his own

[1] 30 December 1887 was in fact a Friday.

house. This was a very disquieting message for New Years day. We got another message last night to say that the boys were perfectly well and that Everest was doing well. We have telegraphed to Clara to take the boys into her house for a time, which I hope she may be able to do. . . .

Duchess of Marlborough to Lord Randolph
(*Blenheim Papers*)

EXTRACT

3 January [1888]   Blenheim

. . . I fear you will have been bothered about this Misfortune of Everest having diptheria but she appears to be recovering & the 2 children are here safe & well with their nice gov. Such a contrast to Bertha's X scowling gov. They will go to 46 on Monday when all leave this place & I can keep them there till you return. Poor Leonie was much perplexed abt them & glad to telegraph to me in her difficulty so that I am appeased as regards Winston not having been allowed to come here. . . .

Lord Randolph to Duchess of Marlborough
(*Lord Randolph Papers*)

EXTRACT

8 January 1888   Slavianski Bazaar

. . . . I had a telegram from Roose yesterday, in reply to one of mine, saying that the boys had gone to Blenheim. It is very good indeed of you and Blandford taking care of them for us. Please tell B. I am very grateful to him. . . .

Duchess of Marlborough to Lord Randolph
(*Blenheim Papers*)

EXTRACT

8 January 1888   Blenheim

. . . The boys are very well. The gov is a nice sensible person & seems to be quite happy about them. They leave here & go to Grovr Sq tomorrow so you might write (or Jennie might in your name) a line to B for having had them here. It has done them good & I keep Winston in good order as I know you like it. He is a clever Boy & really not naughty but he wants a firm hand. Jack requires *no* keeping in order. They will stay at 46 till you return. . . .

Winston to Lady Randolph

12 January 1887 [1888]   46 Grosvenor Square

Dearest Mother,

Grandmamma has kindly allowed us to sleep here until you come back. I do long to kiss you my darling Mummy. I got your kind letter yesterday. How I wish I was with you, in the land of the "Pink, green, & blue roofs."

We have been staying at Blenheim lately – it was very nice. Everest is much better – thanks to Dr Roose. My holidays have chopped about a good deal but as I expect an exeat in the term I do not wish to complain. It might have been so much worse if Woomany had died. You will let me come up for a week to see you & Woomany I am sure.

I am going to a Play called "Pinafore"[1] tonight (Thursday) with Olive Leslie.[2]

Tomorrow I am go to Dr Godson's Party. Sat Sir G. Womwell[3] is going to take me to Drury Lane[4] so I am making up for other inconveniences. Auntie Leonie & Auntie Clara gave me together a beautiful theatre which is a source of unparelleled amusement.

I must perform before you when you come back. Have you heard that uncle Jack has resigned the army? Having told you all the news.

I remain With Love & Kisses, Your loving son
WINSTON S. CHURCHILL

PS Give my best love to Papa.

Duchess of Marlborough to Lord Randolph
(*Blenheim Papers*)

EXTRACT

15 January [1888]   46 Grosvenor Square

. . . I hope you neither of you worry about the Children. They are here all right & I will look after them. But do not mind if you hear I am strict & discourage going out & keep Winston in order. I only do as if they were my

[1] *Pinafore* by Gilbert and Sullivan had its first performance at the Savoy on 12 November 1887.

[2] Olive Leslie (1872–1945) was the youngest daughter of Sir John Leslie, 1st Baronet, and so the sister-in-law of Leonie LESLIE. She married first Walter Murray Guthrie.

[3] George Orby Wombwell (1832–1913), 4th Baronet, a prominent Yorkshire landowner and Master of Foxhounds and friend of Lord and Lady Randolph. He took part in the charge of the Light Brigade at Balaclava, where he was ADC to Lord Cardigan.

[4] At Drury Lane Augustus Harris was presenting his ninth annual pantomime – *Puss in Boots*.

own. I do not like Winston going out except Leonie & Clara take him & are responsible. I gave them the room downstairs to sit in & do not let them rampage. I make Sped a sot of *usher* or tutor to look after them at breakfast & the Gov is very nice & sensible & she now comes at 10 & goes away at 7 o'clock. I have got little Francis Curzon[1] as their house is painting & I expect Kelso[2] on his way back to school so that I consider this is the real Churchill home! I only tell you this that Jennie & you should not worry. Sir George Wombwell took both boys to the pantomime last night, it was very good-natured of him, & I expect it is to pander to you. . . .

Duchess of Marlborough to Lord Randolph
(Blenheim Papers)

EXTRACT

19 January [1888]   46 Grosvenor Square

. . . I am glad to report well of the Children. I fear Winston thinks me very strict, but I really think he goes out too much & I do object to late parties for him. He is so excitable. But he goes back to school on Monday. Meantime he is affectionate & not naughty & Jack is not a bit of trouble. I feel unhappy about your house. Roose has been making investigations there. I certainly do not advise anything being done till you can consider the matter & you can always use this house if you choose. . . .

Winston to Duchess of Marlborough

[19 January 1888]   Brighton

Dearest Grandmama,

Please forgive me for not writing before, but as pens were not given out till last night, I could not do it before.

I arrived all right and quite well. I hope Mama will soon be home. The weather is rather foggy but not unpleasant. Give my best love to Aunt Sarah and Jack. I have settled down to work again. I must now end.

With best Love I remain, Your affectionate Grandson
WINSTON S. CHURCHILL

[1] Francis Richard Henry Penn Curzon (1886–1964), son of George, Viscount Curzon and Winston's Aunt Georgiana, fifth daughter of 7th Duke of Marlborough. He succeeded his father as 5th Earl Howe in 1929.

[2] Henry John Innes-Ker, Earl of Kelso (1876–1932), eldest son of 7th Duke of Roxburghe and Winston's aunt Anne, fourth daughter of 7th Duke of Marlborough. He succeeded his father as 8th Duke in 1892, when still a boy at Eton.

Duchess of Marlborough to Lord Randolph
(Blenheim Papers)

EXTRACT

23 January [1888]   46 Grosvenor Square

. . . Winston is going back to school today. Entre nous I do not feel very sorry
for he is certainly a handful. Not that he does anything seriously naughty
except to use bad language which is bad for Jack. I am sure Harrow will do
wonders for him for I fancy he was too clever & too much the Boss at that
Brighton School. He seems quite well & strong & very happy – Jack is a good
little boy & not a bit of trouble. . . .

Winston to Lady Randolph

31 January 1888   Brighton

Dearest Mother,

I have not heard until to-day how long it would be before you came home,
but I suppose you will be home before the end of the week. Please come & see
me as soon as you come home. I think you might come & stay at a Hotel for a
night or so. I am very hard at work, *as usual*. I want a good Latin-English & a
good English-Latin dictionary. I had rather dull holidays but I am sure you
will make them up to me. We are not coming home at Easter but on the 12th
of April, so, if I get into Harrow and they have their holidays early I shall get
about 8 days and then another long term.

Hoping you are well I remain, Your loving son
WINSTON S. CHURCHILL

PS Love to Papa. W C

Winston to Lady Randolph

7 February 1888   Brighton

Dearest Mother,

I received your letter this morning, it was so nice to see it without a Russian
Stamp on it. I am longing so, to see you & Papa, it is such a long time since I
saw you. I hope it has been arranged which house I am to go to; I want to go to
"Crookshank's" as I know a boy there & I should like to be with him. I am
working hard – very hard to get in – I only hope that my efforts will be rewarded. Mr Best says that I am certain to pass the Entrance – but he wants me
to try & pass the "Farther" as it is called – meaning an Exam which would give
me a good place. He wants me to try and get in at the Shell about the middle,

he says that I have a pretty fair chance. I have been moved into the VIth Form & have begun "Virgil", which I like and also "Herodotus in Greek".

I hear that Algebra is an Extra Subject and so I hope to score in that as I am very fond of it.

At the end of this term I shall know the first Book of Euclid perfectly, which will be more than I shall want. They only require in Arithmetic, Vulgar Fractions, & Decimal Fractions & Simple & Compound Interest, which I know. I have already this term made some progress. I have learnt some Greek irregular Verbs & a lot of French. I do so want to get in. I want you to get me a good Latin-English Dictionary also good English-Latin an English French & a Greek Lexicon and one or two others – which I will ask you to get me when I come up on Saturday.

I am very anxious to look at the wonderful Box you have brought. I have not begun my boxing lessons yet.

Love to All
I remain, Your loving son
WINSTON S. CHURCHILL

Winston to Lady Randolph

14 February 1888   Brighton

Dearest Mother,

I am writing very soon you will think, but as it is "writing letter night" I think I may as well take advantage. I came down by Pullman Car and had a comfortable journey. Mr Best met me at the Station and told me that the Theatre Rage is very great. I must have mine sent down at once.

Please ask Everest to send down all the things and Scenes connected with the Play "Aladdin" & the stage as soon as the 5 trap doors are made.

Also please send me a bottle of Sperm oil for the 8 footlights. I am very ambitious to beat the others. Ask Auntie Leonie to be quick with Britannia & Fairies.

With Love & Kisses I remain, Your loving son
WINSTON S. CHURCHILL

Winston to Lady Randolph

21 February 1888   Brighton

Dearest Mother,

I received your letter on Sunday morning. I am looking forward to the arrival of my theatre.

I shall have a hard job to beat the others but if I get all the requisites I think

I can make a pretty good attempt. Everest says that "Sperm oil" is rather expensive but I think you can manage to stand me a bottle, also a small bottle of "Spirits of Camphor" as that is the best thing to burn in the footlights.

You know when you went to Russia I came up to see you & not having got a ticket I had to pay 5/-.

You must understand that I had had a ticket taken but Mr Best forgot to give it to me & so I had to pay.

You remember that you said you would give me either 5/- on the day I lost it or 10/- on the day you went away – so you did. The lost money for the ticket has been recovered and I want to know if I shall have it. Will you tell me when you write?

Please be quick with the promised 10/-

I can tell you some of the stages are splendid things. There are 10 or 11 different ones – though of course they are not all good ones.

Bertie Roose is getting up a very nice theatre with the Play of "Jack & the Beanstalk". You may send me any comic pictures or anything that you think would be of use in a small theatre. I hope you will allow Everest to have those Programmes printed. Will you ask Auntie Leonie to be quick in finishing "Britannia & the Fairies".

We have had a lot of snow down here lately. Give my best love to Jack, Papa, Aunties Clara & Leonie & every body else.

Miss Thomson says that she has received the cheque so it is all right.

I have nothing more to say so

I remain, Your loving son
WINSTON S. CHURCHILL

Winston to Lady Randolph

[? February 1888]   [Brighton]

Darling Mother,

I have rec^d my theatre. Will you tell Everest so?

Please send me the 10/- Friday or I shall not be able to buy one or two little things in the way of cardboard till next week.

Your loving son
WINSTON S. CHURCHILL

Winston to Lady Randolph

28 February 1888   Brighton

My dear Mother,

I am working hard for Harrow. I hear Miss Thomson is going to take me up for my Exam. I sincerely hope I shall pass well. I am not very good at Latin

Verse but it is of very little importance, Prose being the chief thing in which I am rapidly improving. I am going through the first book of Euclid again & although I have not done more than 27 Propositions I can safely say that I should not make *many* mistakes in them. We are doing L.C.M's [Lowest Common Multiples] in Algebra & Simple Interest in Arithmetic.

You will be pleased to hear that we are learning the Geography of the U.S. When I come home you must question me. Many days will not elapse I hope before I receive a Postal Ordre.

With Love & Kisses I remain, Your loving son
W. CHURCHILL

Winston to Lord Randolph

6 March 1888   Brighton

Dearest Father,

I am working hard for my Examination which is a very Elementary one, so there is all the more reason to be careful & not to miss in the easy things. We are getting through the 2nd Book of Virgil's Aeneid all-right, I like that better than anything else. I have done the 1st 30 Propositions in Euclid & I should not be very afraid of missing in them. In Greek we have finished the Verbs in "$\mu\iota$" & are now revising the Elementary work. In Arithmetic we have finished Simple & Compound Interest – Rule of three – Double Rule of three & are now simply working up the Fractions, Vulgars & Decimals.

In Algebra we are doing L.C.M.'s. In English History the Saxon Period. In Ancient History the 2nd Persian Invasion & in Geography the Continents of North & South America. I hope I shall pass – I think I shall –

Will you come down & see me after the Exam & I will tell you all about it.

I will take your advice about doing the most paying questions first & then the others.

Please come down & see me afterwards. Give my love to Mamma.

Miss Thomson has got the Dictionaries but I have not seen them yet.

Write to me & let me know if you will come down or not.

Hoping you are well, I remain, Your loving son
WINSTON S. CHURCHILL

Miss Charlotte Thomson to Lord Randolph
(*Blenheim Papers*)

16 March [1888]   Brighton

My Lord,

I hear from Mr Welldon today that Winston passed the examination yesterday.

My worst fears were realised with regard to the effect the nervous excitement would produce on his work: and he has only scraped through.

He was terribly upset after his mornings work and assured me over and over again that he had never translated Latin into English so of couse he could not do the piece of prose set on the paper.

As I knew that he had for more than a year been translating Virgil and for much longer Caesar, I was rather surprised by the assertion but of course I did not contradict him.

I am glad to find Winston today much more composed, and I think he will soon recover from the excitement.

He had a severe attack of sickness after we left Harrow and we only reached Victoria in time for the 7.5 o'clock train.

If Mr Welldon would allow him to try again on the 18th April, I believe that Winston would do himself more justice; but I think the permission would be difficult to obtain.

Believe me very truly yours
CHARLOTTE THOMSON

Winston to Lady Randolph

16 March 1888   Brighton

Dearest Mother,

I have passed, but it was far harder than I expected. I had 12 or 13 lines of very, very, hard Latin Translation & also Greek Translation No Grammer in which I had hoped to score no French – no History no Geography the only things were Latin & Greek Trans. Latin Prose – 1 or 2 questions in Algebra & Euclid. And a very easy Arithmetic paper in which I scored I think. However I am through, which is the great thing.

I was afraid that I had not passed after the Examination it was so much harder than I expected in every way. We had luncheon with the Head Master Mr Weldon, who is very nice. One of the boys fainted in the morning as he was dressing.

The roads were in a horrible condition mud & water & in some places the road was covered with water which reached up to the carriage step and extended for over 200 yrd.

Well, I saw Papa as he may have told you and he told me that I was coming home on the 6th of April. I was not excited before the Examination but felt very (uncomfortable in every way & sick) afterwards. I am very tired now but that does not matter now I know that I have passed. I am longing to go to

Harrow it is such a nice place – beautiful view – beautiful situation – good swimming bath – a good Gymnasium – & a Carpentering shop & many other attractions.

You will often be able to come & see me in the summer it is so near to London you can drive from Victoria in an hour & 15 minutes or so. They say that the subscription in the summer term amount to 30/- or more & that every boy is supposed to have 2/- a week pocket money.

Mr Weldon's sisters are very nice. I like them very much we talked to them after the Exam.

If my writing is bad you must excuse it as I am telling you a good deal of news.

"*My funds are in rather a low condition the Exchequer would bear replenishing.*"
I am very tired so I must conclude.

With love & kisses I remain, Your loving son
WINSTON S. CHURCHILL

PS please show this letter to Everest as I am to tired to write anymore tonight.

WINSTON

Winston to Lady Randolph

23 March 1888   [Brighton]
Evening

Dearest Mother,

I have, by begging, procured a sheet of writing paper & am writing to ask you to excuse my bad writing in my former letter.

I have bad mumps but *I do hope* that I shall be able to come home on the 29th and have Easter at home. I shall be well enough myself but I suppose Dr Roose will say some nonsense about "fearful danger of infection" but as I am at present down with the other boys and doing my work I don't think you have much to fear. I am so longing to see you my mummy. I do hope I shall see you on the 29th. It would be nice to have Easter with you. I am sure I shall come home so you had better tell Kate to set about making Hot Cross Buns at once as I'll eat as many as she can make.

Could you send me a little money to send some theatrical thing home and to do other little things. I am so glad I passed it was such a relief it was fearfully hard.

Is it not a pity about Jacky's sight?

I am going to give a grand performance when I come home. You must let me get a few friends and you must come & see it your self darling.

My mumps are getting smaller every day the very thought of going home is enough to draw them away.

With Love & Kisses I remain, Your loving son
WINSTON S. CHURCHILL

Winston to Lady Randolph

27 March 1888   Brighton

Dearest Mother,

Please write soon and say whether I shall be able to come home on Thursday or not. I am looking forward immensely to seeing you.

As you will not be able to extend my holidays at the other end & the Harrow term is 16 weeks, I hope you will try & let me come home, Anyhow please write & tell me. I want to have Easter with you, tremendously.

Hoping soon to be with you.

I remain, Your loving son
WINSTON S. CHURCHILL

Winston to Lady Randolph

?[4 April 1888)   ?[2 Connaught Place]

Dearest Mother,

I rec^d your letter this morning. All is going well – Jack is all right – he slept in your bed last night. Do come home soon. The boys from Brighton come home on Thursday and I wish that I could go and meet them. Bertie Roose is going to & wants me to go with him. And I should like to go, but I want to go alone because I don't think Bertie would like Everest – he would think it so babyish.

Will you write me a line – or send a "telegram" to say if I may? Everest says she thinks it would be all right. The train comes in at 2 minutes past 11 so I am afraid a letter would not reach me in time. I must begin to go out by myself someday.

Hoping to see you on Thursday
I remain, Your ever loving son
WINSTON S. CHURCHILL

5

Harrow

(*See Main Volume Chapter 5*)

HAVING passed his entrance examination on 14 March 1888 Winston entered Harrow on April 17 as a member of H.O.D. Davidson's Small House. He was placed in the bottom form of the school, the third Remove of the Fourth Form.

Winston to Lady Randolph

[Postmark 20 April 1888] [Harrow]

My dear Mamma,

I am writing according to promise. I like everything immensly. I bought a 'frouster' the cheapest I could find it was only 3/6 a sort of deck chair canvass bottom. It is perfectly true that I shall have to have 30/- for subscriptions. Boys generally bring back hampers. I shall not have to find my breakfast. They only do that in large houses. At tea a boy had a chicken and jam and those sort of things. If you will send me a

1 Chicken
3 pots jam
1 plum cake

I think that will be all. I am afraid I shall want more money.

I want to learn Gymnastics [*and carpentering. You make what you like with the assistance of the car*] Gymnastics is all I want.[1]

Dudley [Marjoribanks] is here and Luke White,[2] Sterling[3] 2 boys from Brighton.

[1] The italicized passage in square brackets is crossed through in the original.

[2] Francis William White (1873–1931), youngest son of Luke, 2nd Baron Annaly. He left Harrow after only five terms; lived in Argentine and South Africa. He was Major, superintendent Remount Services 1915–18.

[3] Henry Francis Stirling (1874–1914), son of Major Gilbert Stirling and Lady Randolph's friend Norah, daughter of 3rd Baron Rossmore. Served in Coldstream Guards 1896–1909; fought in Boer War.

I will write tomorrow evening to say what form I'm in. It is going to be read out in the speech room tomorrow.

With love & kisses I remain Your loving son
WINSTON S. CHURCHILL

Winston to Lady Randolph

[? 21 April 1888]   [Harrow]

My dear Mamma,

Please send me some more money. This evening I had to give 10/- to the Cricket subscription. Which doesn't leave me much.

Most boys, at least those I have questioned, about 5 in number say they usually bring back £3 and write for more. I shall be asked for more subscriptions tomorrow or perhaps to night amounting to 10/- more. So I do not know what to do. Please send me the money as soon as possible you promised me I should not be different to others.

I have some more pleasing intelligence to come. Though I am in the 3rd 4th just above Harry Sterling I have gained in Arith a place in the 1st div of the 4th very high indeed.

The master said my Entrance paper in arith was *the best*.

With love & kisses I remain, Your loving son
WINSTON

Winston to Lady Randolph

[Postmark 4 May 1888]   [Harrow]

Darling Mummy,

Please bring Jack & although I may not go to the station as it is out of bounds I am allowed to wait outside for you. Mind & come by the Metropolitan. Come about 2.30 if not sooner.

We will go round the Vaughan Library – the 4th Form Room which is panelled from head to foot with names among which is Byrons – the Chapel – The speech room – Ducker[1] which is not open – Racquet Courts – The Gymnasium – The Grub Shops etc etc.

I have to go to bill[2] every 2 hours so we shall not be able to go far but I can get 'signed' for bill if you like.

I remain Your loving son
WINSTON

---

[1] The Harrow School swimming pool.
[2] Harrow roll-call.

Winston to Lady Randolph

[? 14 May 1888]   [Harrow]

My own Mummy,

I have been so naughty in not writing to you, but really the days simply fly & I have had a good deal of work out of school. However I have some news. I joined the Corps as you know & attended my drills punctually. On Saturday I went with the corps to Rickmansworth & we fought Haileybury it was very exciting. The plan of battle was (as far as I could make out) like this. [*sketch*]

As I had not got a uniform I only carried cartridges. I carried 100 rounds to give away in the thick of the fight consequently my business enabled me to get a good view of the field. It was most exciting you could see through the smoke the enemy getting nearer & nearer.

We were beaten & forced to retire.[1] There is a whole holiday on Saturday – try & come down it is such a little way.

Ask Papa to come on Saturday as there is a very good Cricket Match[2] & I want to show him all over the school.

With love and kisses, I remain Your loving son
WINSTON S. CHURCHILL

Winston to Lady Randolph

[? 16 May 1888]   [Harrow]

Darling Mummy,

Saturday is a whole holiday. Please come down it would be such a good opportunity. I have got another heavy subscription of 10/- to pay and I have not got enough money to pay it with. You see I shall have to pay hardly anything next term but their are an awful lot of subscriptions to pay. Write & let me know if you can come. I am longing to see you. Come early 10.30 train if you can.

Your loving son
WINNY

[1] 'The action,' reported the *Harrovian*, 'began about three o'clock. The manœuvres were simple. The Haileybury Corps, regardless of life, advanced gallantly over a large open space, and would, without doubt, have been annihilated, if it had not been for an unfortunate mistake made by the right flank of Harrow, who mistook a flag supposed to represent a company of 100 for a detachment of four men. They were obliged to retire in ignominious haste.'

[2] The School v. E. E. Bowen's XI. The School Eleven included two future Test cricketers, A. C. MacLaren and F. S. Jackson.

Essay

"Palestine"
In the time of John the Baptist

26 May 1888

At the time of John the Baptist Palestine's physical features were the same as they are now – The even coast line with its only projection of any importance, Mt Carmel, forms the Eastern boundary of the Levant. A range of mountains running parrallel to the coast, East of which the country slopes down to a depth of several hundred feet below the level of the sea – The river Jordan which passes through the Lake of Gennesareth & the Dead Sea. So shall they be till hoary Time be merged in boundless Eternity.

In the time of John the Baptist Palestone lay at the feet of the Roman, who was then at the apex of his glory.

In the N & N.W. were a class of people, always ready for a rebellion, ready to risk their lives, their homes, their all for their country's freedom. These were called "Patriots" a word so familiar in France but used in a different sense. Rebellion after Rebellion broke out, but the stern and splendidly organized legions of Rome crushed & stamped these outbreaks into nothing.

The Sadduces were a class of people whose *god* was "money" & whose plan was "Let it be – things are just as well as they are – There is no Resurrection – There is no Hereafter – We will try to make the short span of life that we have as happy for *us* as possible; no matter what happens to our country – our people – & our religion. "Money is the vital principal of the world it is the key of happiness & power, there are no heights however great to which it cannot carry you – there is no gulf however deep it cannot bridge you.

With this as a Creed, we may now wonder at the state of the country. They had gained a great deal of money by letting money changer stalls in the temple & also to the sellers of doves.

We have briefly considered two of the important classes which existed in Palestine BC 25–AD 1. The third is by far the most familiar of the three – it was not the worst, but it was not the best – it was termed the "Pharisees" – it embraced the aristocracy of Palestine – Its Creed may have been as follows – "We have sinned – the Messiah is angry – the Law is not properly kept – We believe that one day the Messiah will come. We will sweep away our Roman oppressors, we will then drive into everlasting ever-living fire all those cursed & sinners who do not keep the Law – He will then reign in glory at his City of Jerusalem & subduing to his sway the powers of this earth will preach from the minarets of the Temple of Zion the "Keeping of the Law". That is the Future – For the Present – The Law – The Law – The Law – before man – wife – child – house – limb & life & all will be well. That is the most favourable view of the Pharisees, others, worse than this might be taken – but we must remember that the greatest Apostle "Paul" declared that "He was a Pharisee & the son of a Pharisee" without shame.

Their faults were many. Whose faults are few? For let him with all the advantages of Christianity avouch that they are more wicked than himself, *he* commits the same crime of which he is just denouncing *them*. To sum up their faults *briefly* yes *briefly* – (we do not wish to dwell upon the failings of others for that is not Christian) we may set the chief down as follows:—

    Their hypocrisy
    Their idea that all, who were not *as good* as themselves, were cursed for ever more.
    Their self-pride & self-Justification. These formed their principle faults.

Now *I* think that having mentioned peoples faults we ought to mention their excuses. When we think that for nearly 800 years their had been no prophet & consequently they attributed this absence of a protector to the "not keeping of the Law". Thereafter they enforced it all the more rigorously, adding & enlarging on it every year until the Public were hemmed in a Perfect network of sinister (?) & worthless laws which to the poorer classes became at once onerous & impossible to obey. Those who did not obey the law were "outcasts" & "sinners" & they were excluded from the pale of religion & Eternal life. We have considered the three classes of people inhabiting Palestine at this period viz.

Pharissees
Sadduces
Patriots

Both our Lord & John the Baptist seem to denounce the former class the most. Why? Because they hindered poor from coming to the Door of Heaven.

To the creed of the Sadduces there is one answer. Written by a well known American Poet. It runs as follows:—

> "Tell me not in mournful numbers
> Life is but an empty dream
> And the soul is dead that slumbers
> And things are not what they seem.

> "Life is real, Life is joyous,[1]
> And the Grave is not its goal
> Dust thou art to dust returneth
> Was not spoken of the soul."

Winston S. Churchill

[1] Longfellow wrote 'earnest', not joyous.

Winston to Lord Randolph

3 June 1888　　　　　　　　　　　　　　　　　　　　[Harrow]

Dearest Papa,

Please forgive me for not writing to you before, but I have had a good deal of work to do, and kept putting it off day after day.

I have been working rather hard this week to secure a good place in my form, for if you are first or second at the end of the term you generally get a double Remove. I am getting on very successfully in the corps especially in the Shooting. We use the full sized Martini-Henry Rifle and cartridges, the same as the Army. The rifles kick a good deal, it is awfully jolly.

We are going to camp out the first 3 days of the holiday, Government supplied the tents and cooking apparatus. There will be cricket and swimming – and as we are going to go into canvass with three other Public Schools it will be an awful joke. I suppose that there will be about 50 from each school.

I am learning 1000 lines of Macaulay for a prize I know 600 at present.

Anyone who likes to take the trouble to learn them can get one, as there is no limit to the prizes.

Next term I am going in for Shakespere but I think I shall begin this term as you have about 4 plays to work up thoroughly and may be asked questions on several others.

Will you get me a nice Shakespere as I have not got one? When are you coming to see me? Please come soon and let me know by what train to meet you.

With love & kisses, I remain Your loving son
WINSTON S. CHURCHILL

PS I am called, and written Spencer Churchill here and sorted under the S's. I never write myself Spencer Churchill but always Winston S. Churchill. Is it your wish that I should be so called? It is too late to alter it this term but next term I may assume my **Proper** name. Thank you so much for your Letter & the 'Sov'. WLSC

Winston to Lady Randolph

[? 15 June 1888]　　　　　　　　　　　　　　　　　　[Harrow]

My dear Mamma,

I am very lazy – very well & quite happy and I hope you are the same. Please come down on Saturday. I have such a lot to tell you. We (the Corps) had a whole Holiday on Wednesday. There is another whole holiday on Saturday.

I hope you will take advantage of it. I hope also that you are enjoying *yourself* at *Ascot* as much as I am enjoying *myself* at *Harrow*.

With love & kisses I remain, Your loving son
WINSTON S. CHURCHILL

Winston to Lady Randolph

[Postmark 24 June 1888]   [Harrow]

Dearest Mother,

Thank you so much for sending Jack & Everest down to see me on Saty.

Please come down one Sat. I am coming home in 3 weeks for the Lord's Exeat.

My Essay is getting on all right tho not yet finished.

With love & kisses I remain, Your loving son
WINSTON S. CHURCHILL

Winston to Lady Randolph

[Postmark 27 June 1888]   [Harrow]

Dearest Mother,

I recd your letter the other day. My Reports for this week are
Mathematics.
'Churchill has done decidedly better in the last week'
Form Report.
Conduct decidedly improved.

Work irregular.

I think I shall be higher this week 2nd or 1st. I did try and work before only I fell behind at the beginning and it was too late to make it up afterward. I got 3rd one week not having done half the work that the others had done.

This week I have done everything & so I expect to be pretty high.

Don't be cross with me any more. I will try and work, but you were so cross to me you made me feel quite dull.

I have kept my room pretty tidy, since you came.

Please don't scold Everest for giving me 5/-.

I will try to work harder. Do come down Mamma on Saturday – I am not lazy & untidy but careless & forgetful.

Good Bye My Mummy

I remain, your loving son
WINSTON S. CHURCHILL

Winston to Lady Randolph

Sunday [1 July 1888]   [Harrow]

Dearest Mamma,

I was very sorry to hear you could not come down yesterday. But as you are coming down for Speech Day which is on Thursday the 5th I do not mind so much having such a short time to wait.[1]

Last night there was a Rehearsal of the speeches. On Thursday Speeches begin at 12 o clock. House Singing at 5 o clock.

At the 'House singing' you will hear 150 of the best voices trebles & tenors – bases etc. in the school.

I rank as one of the most prominent trebles & am in what is called the nucleus of the choir. I am also in the school 20 and the small house choir of 12. Out of 98 boys.

Of course I am so young that my voice has not yet broke and as trebles are rare I am one of the few.

I must now end begging that you will let Everest bring over some money on Tuesday & that you will come early enough on speech day.

                                          I remain Your Loving son
                                          WINSTON S. CHURCHILL

PS I am going to learn 300 lines of an 1000. w.s.c.

H.O.D. Davidson[2] to Lady Randolph

12 July 1888   Harrow

Dear Lady Randolph Churchill,

After a good deal of hesitation and discussion with his form-master I have decided to allow Winston to have his exeat; but I must own that he has not deserved it. I do not think, nor does Mr Somervell,[3] that he is in any way *wilfully* troublesome; but his forgetfulness, carelessness, unpunctuality, and irregularity in every way, have really been so serious, that I write to ask you, when he is at home to speak very gravely to him on the subject.

When a boy first comes to a public school, one always expects a certain amount of helplessness, owing to being left to himself so much more in regard to preparation of work &c. But a week or two is generally enough for a boy to get used to the ways of the place. Winston, I am sorry to say, has, if anything

---

[1] She did not come; but Lady Fanny MARJORIBANKS, Dudley's mother and Winston's aunt, did.
[2] Henry Oliver Duncan Davidson (1854–1914), assistant master at Harrow 1878–1913. A noted weight-putter at Oxford.
[6] Robert Somervell (1851–1933), English and History master at Harrow 1887–1911; WSC's first form master.

got worse as the term passed. Constantly late for school, losing his books, and papers and various other things into which I need not enter – he is so regular in his irregularity that I really don't know what to do; and sometimes think he cannot help it. But if he is unable to conquer this slovenliness (for I think all the complaints I have to make of him can be grouped under this head, though it takes various forms), he will never make a success of a public school. I hope you will take the opportunity to impress upon him very strongly the necessity of putting a check on himself in these matters, and trying to be more businesslike. As far as ability goes he ought to be at the top of his form, whereas he is at the bottom. Yet I do not think he is idle; only his energy is fitful, and when he gets to his work it is generally too late for him to do it well. I thought it wd do him good to spend a day with you, and have therefore let him go; but unless he mends his ways, he will really have to be heavily punished and I cannot help thinking he does not deserve any special treat during the exeat! I have written very plainly to you, as I do think it very serious that he should have acquired such phenomenal slovenliness. At his age, very great improvement is possible if he seriously gives his mind to conquering his tendencies but I am sure that unless a very determined effort is made it will grow upon him. He is a remarkable boy in many ways, and it would be a thousand pities if such good abilities were made useless by habitual negligence.

I ought not to close without telling you that I am very much pleased with some history work he has done for me.

I am afraid this is a very long letter, but my excuse must be my interest in the boy.

Believe me yours sincerely
H. O. D. DAVIDSON

Winston to Lady Randolph

[? July 1888]   [Harrow]

Darling Mummy,

I want you to come down to see me on Saturday – "Please come". You will be glad to hear that I have passed in my Recruit Drill
Manual Drill
And in Shooting – I made 22 out of a possible 25.

My dearest Mummy I beg your pardon for the scribbling in side but I did not know it was there untill I turned over. However Jack may be pleased with it.

Hoping to see you Saturday.

I remain, Your loving Son
WINSTON S. CHURCHILL

Winston to Lady Randolph

My dearest Mama,

I am sure you are very cross with me for not writing to you before, but I have really and truly been very busy. I have had a lot of work to do, but still I might have found time to write if I had not been so lazy. Please forgive me dearest Mamma. I have learnt 1000 lines but I find that I have got to 200 more of Macauley. I shall soon be able to speak to you in London. I believe, though I am not certain that I have got a "copy". That is to say a prize not given in Speech Room but by the tutor for English History.

Good Bye,
With love & kisses, I remain your loving son
WINSTON S. CHURCHILL

PS I have got rather a nice J nib it writes so smoothly and is very good for flourishes.

Winston to Lady Randolph

[29 July 1888]   [Harrow]

Dearest Mamma,

I have got a plan which I sincerely hope will meet with your approval. I am going up to get my prize in speech-Room on Monday night at about 6 o'clock – Now I want my best trousers & jacket & waistcoat, because I cannot go up untidily.

Could you let Everest come down bring my clothes + 10/- for "journey money" & she could help me pack up and take my big portmanteau home so I should not have the anxiety about it on Tuesday morning. I am sure I shall lose it amongst 500 others' portmanteaus.

Do let Everest come, because my ideas of packing are very limited. I know you will do this as it is the only way in which I can get my "journey money" & trousers. It only costs 1/6 for Everest to come 2nd Class return – do let her come. I should have written before – I did only I forgot to post the letter & so it would now be impossible for anything to be sent to-day being Sunday.

You will get this 1st Post tomorrow morning – if you will let Everest come please telegraph by what train *she will arrive* at once or I shall not know what to do. I think I am 3rd in Terms order & so I shall probably get my remove. I shall be able to bring my Essay back with me on Tuesday. and 1 copy & 1 prize.

> Good Bye my dearest Mummy
> I remain, Your loving son
> WINSTON S. CHURCHILL

PS Don't forget to telegraph *at once* Monday is a whole holiday anytime after dinner will do for Everest to come.

Winston to Lady Randolph

Thursday [Postmark 2 August 1888]   [2 Verona Cottages
                                                                   Ventnor]

Dearest Mother,

We are enjoying ourselves very much indeed – I went in the sea this morning – and for a long walk over the downs this afternoon. We are staying at Woomany's sister's[1] House & are very comfortable: Address

> 2 Verona Cottages
> Ventnor I.W.

Jackey is very happy & said as he got into bed to-night 'Well I think this *has* been a successful day'. I enjoyed my self tremendously, we (that is I & Jack) eat about a ton a day.

It was raining in the morning, but it came over so warm & fine that we have had a jolly walk.

We had a good 'go' at some raspberries and gooseberries which we picked ourselves & eat.

> Everything is very Jolly & nice, Hoping you are quite well
> I remain, Your loving son
> WINSTON S. CHURCHILL

Winston to Lady Randolph

[? October 1888]   [Harrow]

Dearest Mother,

Thank very much for letting Jack & Everest come down.

Please try to come on Saturday & not to put it off. Come by train arriving at 2.30. Do try to come early because it spoils my afternoon to wait at the Railway Station.

---

[1] Mary, wife of John Balaam, a principal warder at Parkhurst Prison.

Let me have a line to say whether you can come or not.

I want you to bring me a nice hamper *the other boys have them*. Not so much for tea as for supper. Send me a nice

Ham

or something of that sort.

I remain, Your Loving son
WINNY

Winston to Lady Randolph

[? October 1888]   [Harrow]

My dearest Mother,

I have just read your letter & am delighted to hear you are coming. I will be specially got up for the occasion. 'Nails, teeth, clothes, hair, boots, & person well brushed.' My room looks very nice but I want some ornaments.

I suppose Everest has told you about 'King & the box of ornaments.' Would you let me have a line to say by what train you could come? Come if it is convenient by the 2.37 arriving here at 3.7. Do let me know because it is rather 'stale' waiting.

With love & kisses I remain Your brushed & affectionate son
WINSTON S. CHURCHILL

Winston to Lady Randolph

[Postmark 23 October 1888]   [Harrow]

My dear Mummy,

Please do not be cross with me for having been so forgetful. But I have been working up for the 'Shakespere Prizes' very hard and I am so sorry I did not write. I won't borrow any more from any boy, but I found that my debts were rather more than 5/- & so my money soon decreased.

I don't want you to think that I only write to you when I want anything. I have not been lazy either but I have been working up very hard. The Exam comes off tomorrow. I do not 'spec' on the prize as there are boys of 17 going in for it.

Good Bye My darling Mummy
I remain, As ever your loving son
WINSTON S. CHURCHILL

Winston to Lady Randolph

POSTCARD

[Postmark 26 October 1888]   [Harrow]

Dearest Mother,

Will you come tomorrow morning as early as possible. Do come, you can take me out to luncheon & we can be very happy. I have a lot to tell you but as I am expecting you tomorrow I shall wait.

It is a whole holiday and I shall not have another for some time.

> Good bye My darling
> With much love, I remain your loving son
> WINSTON S. CHURCHILL

Winston to Lord Randolph

[28 October 1888]   [Harrow]

My dear Papa,

I am quite well & I hope that you are the same. I am getting on all right & I hope to get another Remove at the end of the term. Mamma came to see me yesterday. I enjoyed her visit very much. My Form Master says I have improved very much since the Summer.

Mamma said I could come home for my 'Absit' on Saturday next. Did you enjoy yourself at 'Monte Carlo'? I went to see Jack some time ago, he was in great spirits, though he did not show much surprise on seeing us. He did not think I was coming. But he simply said 'Hullo Winny'. He looked very well, But it was too cold to talk much. Do you think there is any chance of your coming to see me this term??

The Rifle Corps had a grand Sham fight yesterday which Mamma saw. Harrow versus Haileybury & Cambridge. Harrow won – we defended the town successfully for 2 hours. I am going to learn 1000 lines of Shakespeare this term for the Prize. I hope I shall get it.

The weather is very changeable. But yesterday it was very fine.

I hope you will come down and see me sometime this term.

> Hoping to see you on Saturday, I remain, Your Loving Son
> WINSTON S. CHURCHILL

Winston to Lady Randolph

[29 October 1888]   [Harrow]

Darling Mummy,

I am so sorry I have not written before. I am getting on all right. I lost the Shakespeare Prize' for the Lower School by 27 marks. I was rather astonished as I beat some twenty boys who were much older than I. Dear Mummy I am very naughty – I am so 'put-off-ified'. I am very glad of the ten shillings although I feel that [I] don't deserve them. I am very sorry. I will write again after Everest has gone because she is going to take this.

> Good bye, My darling Mummy
> I remain, Your forgetful son
> WINSTON S. CHURCHILL

Winston to Lady Randolph

7 November 1888   [Harrow]

Dearest Mamma,

I am going to write you a proper epistle, hoping you will forgive my former negligence. On Saturday we had a lecture on the

'Phonograph'

By 'Col Gouraud'. It was very amusing he astonished all sober-minded People by singing into the Phonograph

> 'John Brown Body lies – Mouldy in the grave'
> And is soul goes marching on
> Glory, glory, glory Halleluja'

And the Phonograph spoke it back in a voice that was clearly audible in the 'Speech Room'

He shewed us it in private on Monday. We went in 3 or 4 at a time.

His boys are at Harrow

He fought at Gettysburg

His wife was at school with you.

Papa gave him letter of introduction to India

He told me to ask Papa if he remembered the 'tall Yankee'.

I want to be allowed to join the Harrow work shop for they then supply you wood and I want to make some scenery for the nursery if we have any Party. 3 or 4 scenes cost about ½ a sovereign and the man who is in charge thoroughly understands scenery making.

> With love & kisses, I remain
> WINSTON S. CHURCHILL

PS Will you write to say whether I may join as I have no imployment for odd half hours. W C

Winston to Lord Randolph
(*Blenheim Papers*)

7 November 1888   Harrow

My dear Papa,

I hope you will forgive me for not writing to you before. I have got a lot to tell you about. On Saturday we had a Lecture in the Speech-Room on the 'Phonograph' by Col Gouraud who asked me, afterwards, to ask you, if you remembered the 'tall Yankee' to whom you gave the letters of recommendation, when you were Secretary of State for India. It was very interesting – we heard a tune on the Orange Band played in America. I entered into one of the competitive examinations for knowledge of Shakespeare. We had to learn & work up the notes in 'Merchant of Venice'

Henry VIII

Midsummer Night's Dream

I came out 4th for the Lower School among some 25 boys – some of whom were not less than 7 forms above me. I got 100 marks & the boy who got the prize got 127.

When do you think you will be able to come & see me?

With love, I remain, Your loving son

WINSTON S. CHURCHILL

Winston to Lady Randolph

[Postmark 11 December 1888]   [Harrow]

My darling Mummy,

My 'Remove' I think is pretty certain. I have got a 'Copy' for History like last term & hope to get another one for Arithmetic. I am all right and working very hard. I am going to write to Papa tomorrow and try and persuade him to come down for 'Cock House Match.'[1] I am working up my Bible for the Examination tomorrow morning.

I hope to come out 'top'. I have come out 'top' in my other Roman History Paper.

I expect to come out first in

Roman Hist

English Hist

Scripture Hist

Repetition   }   1st

French

---

[1] The Harrow football champion house match, 'one of the most exciting and interesting on record' (*Harrovian*, p. 143), in which Mr Welldon's beat Mr Hutton's by three goals to two.

and to come out among the 1st 6 in

Greek Construe
Latin Construe
Anglice Reddenda
        Construe
Latin Grammar
Euclid

I feel in 'working trim' & expect many rises in my position.

With love My darling Mummy
I remain, Your loving son
WINSTON S. CHURCHILL

Winston to Lady Randolph

Wednesday 2 January 1889   ? [2 Connaught Place]

My darling Mamma,

I have just recd your nice letter, it was quite dis-ennuyé-ing

My throat it still painful & swelled – I get very hot in the night – & have very little appetite to speak of. I am not allowed to go to the Circus by Doctor Gordon. But he says that there is no reason why Jacky may not go.

I asked Dr Gordon to ask Bertie Roose to come & sit with me.

How slow the time goes – I am horribly bored – & slightly irritable – no wonder as my liver is still bad – Medecin 6 times a day is a horrible nuisance. I am looking forward to your return with 'feelings, better imagined than described'.

It is awful 'rot' spending ones holidays in bed or one room.

I am going to sit in your room part of to-day & have luncheon in the dining-room. Monday night we had a telegram from Lady Mandeville saying 'If Kimbolton is with Winston keep him as the fog is dense.'

He was not with us & so I concluded he must have lost his way & that she was telegraphing to all the likely places.

Poor little Kim I do not know if he is found yet or not.

Give my best love to Papa & tell him I will write to him to-morrow.

Will you let me have 5 shillings to get some scenes to paint.

Jack is writing too, so with Love & Kisses

I remain As ever, Your loving son
WINSTON S. CHURCHILL

PS B. Roose has just arrived and says Kim was found Oxford Street.

Winston to Lady Randolph

[? January 1889]   ? [2 Connaught Place]

My darling Mummy,

Rash nearly gone. Get up tomorrow, – tired of bed and slops. – Magic
Lantern won't work – am looking forward to the sea – It is unfortunate because
immediately I get well the Dr says I ought to go to the seaside, & then *I shan't
see you at all.* My holidays are utterly spoilt, a week in one room that leaves a
little more than a fortnight. 2 or 3 days about the park & 1 week a the seaside
leaves 1 week & that 1 week you will be away. It is an awful pity. I don't know
what to do. I think I ought to have it made up to me and go back a week late,
they would average me & a week would make no difference to any one but you
& me.

Hoping to see you soon

WINNY

Lord Randolph to Fanny, Duchess of Marlborough

EXTRACT

5 January 1889   Turf Club
                                                    Piccadilly

. . . The boys go to Ventnor on Monday: they have been seedy and look
pale. . . .

Winston to Lady Randolph

[Postmark 25 January 1889]   [Harrow]

My dear Mamma,

I arrived safely and my portmanteau came a few hours afterwards.

I am in Davidson's still – but I am very comfortable.

There is every probability of my Remove. Mr Davidson says that he thinks I
shall get it.

I am not at all dull.

I hope Everest is all-right & has not fretted much about Jack.

Good Bye Mummy

With love & kisses I remain, Your loving son

WINSTON S. CHURCHILL

Winston to Mrs Everest

25 January 1889   Harrow

TELEGRAM

Am quite well have got my remove into higher class

CHURCHILL

Winston to Lady Randolph

[? 3 February 1889]   [Harrow]

My darling Mummy,

How long is it since I have written to you? I am ashamed to say! But I will try and write a nice letter to you now.

To begin with I told you how I got my remove. I am getting on very well in that form & the master says I have much improved since the Summer Term.

I came out 2nd in Holiday Task getting 71 marks.

I am very happy & am getting on very well indeed in my house as I am on very good terms with the boys. One night we had a 'Sale by Auction' & I did not sell any of the things which I had brought from home but only a few things I had bought down here. What I sold were probably worth 2/- but I made 5/9 off it. One Boy got 13/6. But then he sold a Racket & an Electric Battery.

I am very interested in my work & am getting on in a way. Which quite satisfies me, that *if* I only keep it up I shall get my remove again & that would be 'awfully decent' because then I might get another and change on to the Modern side.

Saturday is Jack's Birthday. Everest is going to see him. Tomorrow we are going for a Paper Chase, & hope to have great fun. I & another boy are hares & all the rest of the house are hounds. The weather is fair & cold & snowy & dry & then warm and bright and sunny & dull about 3 times a day.

I am keeping my Room in much better order than in any preceding term. By the way I have been steadily advancing in Arithmetic ever since I went to Miss Thomsons & now, you will be pleased to hear, I have begun 'Stocks' It (is not) or rather (they) are not at all easy they require a good 'Stock' of knowledge but still they are very interesting.

One of them reads like this

'when Cash Price is £300 & Quotation £90 find the nominal value of stock of consuls.'

It is rather a 'swot'.

I hope you (& the bonnets) are well & enjoying your 'spree on the Continong'. I wrote an order for a 'Squash Racket' to-day and have had several good games.

We (the rifle Corps) are going to have a sham fight with Haileybury in the football field this term.[1] If you are in London you must try & come down to it.

Forgive me, my Mummy, for not writing.

Hoping you will be as lenient as you can.

I remain, As ever your loving son
WINSTON S. CHURCHILL

Winston to Lady Randolph[2]

[Postmark 23 February 1889]   [Harrow]

My dear Mamma,

I am so sorry I have not written before. I am an awful boy for correspondence I know. I am getting on very well and I am told I shall get a good report.

Do forgive my dilatoriness but I am very sorry.

I cannot write much now. As I have a lot of work to do.

My darling Mum I am so glad to hear that you are soon coming back to me.

Good Bye my darling
With love, I remain Your loving son
WINSTON S. CHURCHILL

Winston to Lady Randolph

[? March 1889]   [Harrow]

My darling Mummy,

I am so delighted to hear that you have come home. I had been feeling quite dull at your protracted delay. However I am now sure that you're once again in '*Merry England*'. Do try and come & see me soon. I am looking forward to a visit very much. I am rather, or rather my funds are rather low. However, I do hope you will not go off to Ireland without seeing me.

Good Bye Mummy, With love & kisses I remain, Your loving son
WINSTON S. CHURCHILL

PS Getting on very well in class.

Winston to Lady Randolph

[? February/March 1889]   [Harrow]

My dear Mamma,

I am much better to-day but I am still far from well & am in bed because I can hardly stand. I am so weak as I have had very [little] food for 4 days. I am

---

[1] It took place on March 9. A company of the Cambridge University corps joined forces with Haileybury against the Harrow school corps.

[2] Lady Randolph was staying in Paris at 9 Rue Marbeuf.

very glad you sent me the book for which I thank you. Also for enclosing Woomany in the Frontispiece. Mrs Davidson who has been in 3 times today says that she hopes you will let Woomany come tomorrow, because she says that the companionship does me good. I do not know how the day would have passed but for Woomany. I have had another big poultice on my liver to-day to make it worse. I hope you will allow Woomany to come tomorrow as I shall certainly be very disappointed if she does not turn up.

Goodbye my darling Mummy, With love and kisses
I remain, Your loving son
WINNY

For 'Mamma.'

Winston to Lady Randolph

? [February/March 1889]   [Harrow]

My darling Mamma,

I am writing you a line to thank you for letting Woom come down today. I was very sick but feel decidedly better now. I think that Mr Davidson was rather glad that she came, because I gave the Matron & head housemaid a lot of extra work when I was sick. I have been sick 4 times. Mr Davidson says he hopes you will let Woomany come tomorrow & I second that motion.

Do let her come as I have nothing to do, and nobody to speak to, it is awfully dull. I have seen the doctor & I have to take beastly powders every 4 hours.

Good Bye, With love & kisses, I remain
WINNY

Winston to Lord Randolph

[? 27 March 1889]   [Harrow]

My dear Papa,

I am so sorry to hear of the cold you have had, I hope it is much better now. The weather here is very warm & damp. I have got rather a cold myself.

Will you write to Mr Welldon & ask him to take me in next term. He promised to take me in long ago. I am looking forward to a big house. I have heard several people speak of my going in, but I was advised to write to you & make certain.

We, that is the Corps, went to Aldershot on Monday and had a great sham fight with some 1300 boys of other Public Schools & about 11,000 regulars. Harrow, Eton, Charterhouse, Clifton, Cheltenham, Rugby, Winchester, Haileybury & Dulwich were there and several other which I can't remember.

It was great fun. The noise was tremendous. There were 4 Batteries of Guns on the Field & a Maxim, & several Nordenfeldts.

We were defeated because we were inferior in numbers & not from any want of courage. I have bought a Book on Drill as I intend going in for the corporal Examination next term. I went down to the Range on Tuesday & fired away 20 rounds.

I am working hard this fortnight. You will be glad to hear that I have got a fair chance [of] a Remove at the beginning of next term. I am looking forward to the holidays tremendously, could you send me one or two autographs. Do try and come down to see me.

> With much love I remain, Your loving son
> WINSTON S. CHURCHILL

Winston to Lady Randolph

[Postmark 28 March 1889]   [Harrow]

My darling Mamma,

I am so sorry I have not written to you before. I went to Aldershot on Monday with the Rifle Corps. We had a grand Sham fight in the Long Valley with about 12,000 regular troops. All the Public School Corps were there. Eton, Charterhouse, Clifton, Winchester & Rugby, Haileybury, Dulwich. We were defeated, our army only consisted of 3,500 men and two batteries of guns & Regiment of Cavalry. While the attacking force was considerably over 8000 strong.

I furnish a small plan[1] of the fight at its climax as far as I could see. I enjoyed myself very much. I *am* looking forward to the holidays. I am swotting very hard. Hope to get a good report. In fact feel sure I shall get one.

> Good Bye I will try & write more
> With love & Kisses, I remain, Your loving son
> WINSTON S. CHURCHILL

Reverend J. E. C. Welldon to Lord Randolph
(<i>Blenheim Papers</i>)</center>

2 April 1889   Harrow School

Dear Lord Randolph,

I can have no hesitation in saying that I will take Winston into my House next term. If I have left him so long as I have in a Small House, the reason is only that in Davidson's opinion, and, I may add, in my own it seemed to be best for him, as he was very much of a child, when he first came, to be under more personal care than can well be given to a boy who is one of a large number.

---

1 This plan was attached to the letter.

However, as it happens, I told Davidson a fortnight ago that I should like to take him into my own House next Term. He has some great gifts and is, I think making progress in his work.

It has occurred to me that as you are naturally occupied through the week it would perhaps not be disagreeable to Lady Randolph and yourself to come here from Saturday to Monday some time when Winston is in the House and the weather is warm enough to make life enjoyable. Is there any time in May or June you could come? You would have, if nothing else, at least the oppor- tunity of seeing what Winston's school life is like.

With kind regards, very faithfully yours
J. E. C. WELLDON

Winston to Lady Randolph

[Postmark 2 May 1889]   [The Head Master's
                                                              Harrow]
My dear Mamma,

I arrived safe & am now comfortably lodged in Welldon's new house No 4.

I have got into a 2 Room, that is a Room with only 2 boys in it. I am one, & as the other does not come back yet I have it all to myself. I have bought a Mantle-Board and a big fan. It is an awfully nice room, it has two windows and is much bigger than Davidsons Rooms. Will you tell Woom that I want

1. a pair of Blue Rugs
2. The Vases she gave me
3. My table cloth
4. My Draw-cover
5. and all my fans

Will you buy me a nice Rocking Chair as there is lots of Room for one.

I also want my curtains.

Good bye my dear Mummy
Am getting on very well and Remaining Your loving son
WINSTON S. CHURCHILL

Winston to Lady Randolph

[Postmark 3 May 1889]   [Harrow]

Dearest Mummy,

I am vy happy & quite well I have not time to write any more now. Will you give Everest leave to buy a few things for my room as it is a vy nice one.

Tell her to bring down that big cabinet I wanted last Term.

Good Bye, Love & Kisses from
WINSTON S. CHURCHILL

Winston to Lord Randolph

[15 May 1889]   [Harrow]

My dear Papa,

I am writing to thank you for the money to buy the Bicycle – It is so kind of you. I should have written long ago only I wanted to wait until I could write and say that I could ride it. I can now, on Saturday I rode 8 miles with it, it is a beautiful little machine. 2 days ago I had written the letter, but that evening the money came so I am writing a different letter. I would also have written yesterday but I was part of a Guard of Honour *all* the afternoon, for the Princess Louise.[1]

I am very well I like Welldon's awfully.

Good Bye dear Papa once more thanking you

I remain Your loving son
WINSTON S. CHURCHILL

PS *Do come & see me soon.*

Winston to Lady Randolph

[15 May 1889]   [Harrow]

My dear Mamma,

I am very sorry I have not written to you before. I have written to Papa to thank him for sending me £7. 2. 6. for my Bicycle. I am getting on very well in Welldon's. All the boys are so kind & nice. I want a few more pictures and some white curtains. I have had to pay for my breakfast and I have a 10/6 subscription to pay so I would not mind a little cash.

Do try and come down soon I believe Saturday is a whole holiday. If you and Papa could manage to come then it would be grand. You could come down at about 11 o'clock and take me to luncheon at the Kings Head Hotel.

With much love I remain
Your loving son
WINSTON S. CHURCHILL

[1] Princess Louise, Marchioness of Lorne (1848–1939), had come to open an exhibition and a sale of work at the Public Hall in connection with the local Technical School. The Harrow School Rifle Corps, with a detachment of the Town Volunteers, the 9th Middlesex, acted as a guard of honour.

Winston to Lady Randolph

[Postmark 7 June 1889]   [Harrow]

My dear Mamma,

I am so sorry I have not written before, I have no excuse. I am very well and happy. Do do do come down tomorrow. I would be disappointed if you did not come.

I am looking forward to tomorrow tremendously

Good Bye my darling
With love and kisses I remain, Your loving son
WINSTON S. CHURCHILL

Winston to Lady Randolph

[? 11 June 1889]   [Harrow]

Darling Mummy,

I was sorry you did not come yesterday, as I had given up going to a sham fight and had little or nothing to do in the afternoon. I am awfully sorry to hear you are not well, but I hope you will be all right by tomorrow. Please do do do do do come by the 12.59 from London arriving at 1.29. Try and stay till the 5.37 or 6.7 train.

Please wire *immediately* you receive this – don't wait till 12 or 1 before you let me know as I have to make arrangements. I hope you will come my darling Mummy if you are well enough. Please come alone, when you come I like to have you all to myself. Please do do do do do do do do do come to to

Your Loving Son
WINSTON S. CHURCHILL

Winston to Lady Randolph

[? 14 June 1889]   [Harrow]

My darling Mummy,

I am quite well and very happy. I came out 11th on Sunday in my form that is 3 places higher. I went down to the rifle range yesterday – I fired 30 rounds. 4 4 3 4 4 4 0 3 2 3 = 31. 200 yards.

Please come down on Sat (tomorrow). Wire by what train you will come.

Good bye My darling –
I send you my best love And Remain, Your loving son
WINSTON S. CHURCHILL

Reverend J. E. C. Welldon to Lady Randolph
(*Blenheim Papers*)

20 June 1889   Harrow School

Dear Lady Randolph,

I am sorry to say Winston has fallen off his bicycle and hurt himself. I do not wish you to think the hurt is serious. The Doctor expressly tells me he does not believe it to be so. But, as he has ordered him to the Sick Room, it seems to be right to tell you at once what has happened. The Doctor calls it 'slight concussion'. I will write to you again tomorrow.

Sincerely yours
J. E. C. WELLDON

Reverend J. E. C. Welldon to Lady Randolph
(*Blenheim Papers*)

21 June 1889   Harrow School

Dear Lady Randolph,

I send you the Doctor's report of Winston that you may see exactly how he is. I am so sorry for this second interruption to his work, but I am very grateful that in a week, if not sooner, he will be all right again. I will let you know at once if there is the least cause for anxiety about his condition.

Sincerely yours
J. E. C. WELLDON

21 June 1889   Harrow School

Mr Churchill had a fall from a bicycle yesterday resulting in a slight concussion of the Brain. He has been put to bed and will require careful watching for a few days – probably he will be all right again in a short time. and serious consequences are not to be anticipated. He is doing well this morning.

G. C. BRIGGS[1]

Winston to Lady Randolph

[? 22 June 1889]   [Harrow]

My darling Mummy,

Thank you so much for letting Woom come down. I do not feel very fit – but I shall soon be better, at least I hope so. Do let Woom come down tomorrow.

[1] George Chapman Briggs, medical adviser to Harrow School.

Can't you come instead – I was rather disappointed at not seeing you as I fully expected to.

It is rather dull here, and it was not at all nice being kept in bed on a whole holiday.

Good Bye my darling. If you come bring something to read.

With love, I remain, Your loving son

WINSTON S. CHURCHILL

Winston to Lady Randolph

[? 23 June 1889]   [Harrow]

My darling Mummy,

Thanks awfully for letting Woom come down today. Both Doctor & Nurse say that they think I shall need a rest. I hope, most excruciatingly that I do come home. Do come tomorrow or if you send Woom.

Good Night Much Love I remain

WINNY

PS I am very delighted a *the idea* of coming home.

Temp 97

Throat better WLSL

Winston to Lady Randolph

[? 25 June 1889]   [Harrow]

Dear Mamma,

Woomany says I am looking so fresh and well to day. I wonder when you are coming down to see me again I am looking forward to a visit. I stay up all day and do not feel a bit the worse for it. My hand gets the cramp after a few lines and aches badly. I am very tender all over my body but feel very cheery and not a bit dull the time passes very quickly. Especially when I can have visitors. I hope you will excuse my writing as I am rather shaky. I think I must get you to ask for a half holiday for the boy who were really very quiet. I knew you would like a letter or rather a scribble from me. The hospital nurse has [gone] and so I am alone with Woomany.

I have got some chalk and to day I am sitting down and endeavouring to write you a scribble

With love and kisses I remain, Your loving son

WINSTON S. CHURCHILL

Lord Randolph to Lady Randolph

[?12 July 1889]   46 Grosvenor Square

Dearest,

Send Winston with King to Fanny's carriage (block C 2nd row) at Lords. Fanny will give him luncheon & look after him & bring him home.

Yrs ever
RANDOLPH

Winston to Lord Randolph

[? 2 July 1889]   [Harrow]

My dear Papa,

I am writing to tell you all about Speech-day. If you take the 11.7 from Baker Street you will get to Harrow at 11.37. I shall meet you at the station with a fly, if I can get one.

The 'Speeches' begin at 12. But dont let the name hinder your coming. Speeches simply mean the Greek – English – French – German plays & the distribution of Prizes by Mr Welldon who makes a short speech to each of the prizemen.

I don't think that you will be asked to make a speech. In fact I should think it will be very improbable. I do hope that both you & Mamma will come as last Speech day nobody came to see me & it was vy dull.

You have never been to see me & so everything will be new to you. Ducker is reserved specially for the visitor to look at. You will see the Vaughan Library – the Gymnasium – the Racquet Courts – My room – & other places. Am going to school this morning, so I must say "Good Bye" & Love & Kisses

Remain Your loving son
WINSTON S. CHURCHILL

PS I shall be awfully disappointed if you don't come.

Winston to Lady Randolph

[? 2 July 1889]   [Harrow]

My own Mamma,

I don't feel quite so well as I did. I am looking forward to speech day. *Do* try to get Papa to come, he has never been. Do let Everest come down to-morrow. because I mayn't go to Ducker & mayn't Cycle & I don't play Cricket so I have got nothing to do. 2 of the masters have told me I ought to go home for a little rest. However hoping that I shall see both *you & Papa* on Thursday I remain

Your loving son
WINNY

PS 'Branksome Dean'?[1]

Winston to Lady Randolph

[? July 1889]   [Harrow]

My dear Mother,

I have but 1 penny left which will pay for the stamp of my letter. I am writing on this[2] because I have no other paper – will you send me 2/6 or 2/- or even 1/-. I know I am very extravagant but I am very sorry.

I remain Your loving son
WINSTON S. CHURCHILL

Winston to Lady Randolph

[? Summer 1889]   [Harrow]

Darling Mamma,

300 Boys have gone. 32 out of our house alone. I have never had the measles. But I would so like to come home. There will be about 5 boys left on Monday & we all go to Chapel on Sunday & it is in Chapel that measles spread. There is really no danger whatever, but I should have imagined that as 300 Mamas & 300 Papas like to have their 'offsprings' home You would like to have me.

Please Please do.

My own Mamma.

Wire to Welldon as follows, please,

'I have remembered that Winston has not had measles so please allow him to come this evening.'

And then I'll be home. I can sleep anywhere. Do please, as all the friends I

---

1 Lady WIMBORNE's place near Bournemouth.
2 A leaf torn from a notebook.

have made have gone, & it isn't very nice to see them all going. Milbanke[1] is leaving this for me as he goes home. I will have my portmanteau packed.

And remain
WINNY

Reverend J. E. C. Welldon to Lord Randolph
(*Blenheim Papers*)

26 August 1889   Harrow School

Dear Lord Randolph,
I meant to have written a line to you at the time of sending Winston's last report. You told me last term that you wished him to go into the Army Class but he did not know whether he is destined for Woolwich or for Sandhurst.[2] Perhaps you will let him tell me, when he comes back to Harrow, what your wish is, and I will then put him into the hands of my two colleagues who devote themselves to the interests of the Army boys.

With kind regards
J. E. C. WELLDON

Reverend J.E.C. Welldon to Lord Randolph

23 September 1889   Harrow

Dear Lord Randolph,
You asked me in the holidays to write to you about Winston's Army Examination.
I have handed him over to my Army Masters; and it is their opinion that he is not good enough in Mathematics to pass into Woolwich but that he ought to aim at passing into Sandhurst.

---

[1] John [Jack] Peniston Milbanke (1872–1915), elder son of Sir Peniston Milbanke, 9th Bart, whom he succeeded in 1899. Came to Harrow (the Head Master's House) two years before Winston, left in December 1889. Joined 10th Hussars; received the Victoria Cross during the Boer War for saving the life of a trooper in his regiment. Retired as Major 1911. Rejoined 1914; Lieutenant-Colonel, Sherwood Rangers. Killed in action on Hill 70, Gallipoli Or Mark Richard Milbanke (1875–1927), his brother. Came to the Head Master's House the term after Winston, left the same term, December 1892. An artist whose early sketches were published in the *Harrovian*; he exhibited at the Royal Academy.

[2] Woolwich, known as 'The Shop', was the military academy for cadets seeking commissions in the Royal Artillery and Royal Engineers. Sandhurst catered for the infantry, cavalry and remaining arms.

Of course I shall be better able to tell you at a later date what his chances are, but he has now a definite object for which to work.

With kind regards to Lady Randolph

Believe me, Sincerely yours
J. E. C. WELLDON

Winston to Lady Randolph[1]

[? 26 September 1889]   Harrow

My dear Mama,

I have arrived here safe and well. I have got a Room with a boy called 'Count Eric Steenbock'[2] – his father is the Swedish Ambassador.

I am not spending my money rashly, I put 1 quid in the P.O. Savings Bank to take care of it.

I hope Jack is not dull. I am writing to him.

I remain, Your loving son
WINSTON S. CHURCHILL

Winston to Lady Randolph

[Postmark 28 September 1889]   [Harrow]

My dear Mamma,

I got your letter all right, I have joined 'Army class'. It is rather a 'bore' as it spoils your half Holiday: however we do French & Geometrical drawing which are the two things which are most necessary for the army. I am working up for the Shakespeare prize. Good Bye dear Mummy.

With Love & Kisses I remain, Your loving son
WINSTON S. CHURCHILL

Winston to Lady Randolph

[Postmark 2 October 1889]   [Harrow]

My dear Mamma,

Will you please allow Everest to send my bicycle here immediately. There is a grand field day at Wimbledon on Sat.

---

[1] Written in white ink on a grey card.

[2] Count Eric Magnus Julius Stenbock (1876–1933), only son of Count Otto Stenbock, Swedish-Norwegian Minister at Lisbon and later (1900) Ambassador at Constantinople, and of his wife Clemence Maria, 2nd daughter of Baron Julius de Reuter. The Stenbocks lived chiefly in England.

Mummy, will you sign the little 'order' enclosed. Please do. I am working hard – have had a bad toothache lately but it is better now.

Please give 'order' signed to Woom to send enclosed in Bicycle pouch.

Goodbye. Much love, I remain, Your loving son
WINNY

Winston to Lady Randolph

[? 5 October 1889]   [Harrow]

My darling Mummy,

It is more than a fortnight since I heard from you. In fact I have only had one letter this term. It is not very kind my darling Mummy to forget all about me, not answer my epistles. However remiss I may have been in the past in my correspondence, you must never scold me again about it. I have many requests to make. In the first place I beg that you will give me some money. This much has been spent by me on my 2 journeys up to Town

1st Journey	7/6
2nd „	6/6
Total	14/-

My eyes have been rather painful lately & I want you to make an appointment with the oculist for Tuesday afternoon between 2.45 & 5 o'clock. He could just whether anything is wrong or not with them. I want to learn fencing. I go to the Gymnasium a great deal and I think it would be so much better for me to learn something which would be useful to me in the Army, as well as affording me exercise and amusement. I'm sure since I have been working well, you will not hesitate to sign the enclosed order and return it by post. Edney sent me four broken pheasants but the Bicycle has not yet arrived.

Please write to me soon and send me 'oof' as I want to come up to town on Tuesday.

With much love, I remain Your loving son
WINSTON S. CHURCHILL

Winston to Lady Randolph

[Postmark 9 October 1889]   [Harrow]

Dear Mamma,

So kind of you to send me the 'order'. Thank you so much. Do you think you could come down on Saturday ? It would be awfully jolly if you could it is a long time since you have been to see me. Dear Mummy please do come, I want to talk to you awfully,

Am very busy dear Mummy, So must shut epistle & Remain,

Your loving son

WINSTON S. CHURCHILL

PS You will be glad to hear that I won the 200 yrds handicap in shooting on the Rifle range. Position of Bullets out of 7 shots [diagram].

Total 25 + 8 handicap 32 out of

35

I won 6/- it was very useful

Intend to buy a 'cup'.

WSC

Winston to Lady Randolph

[Postmark 28 October 1889]   [Harrow]

Dear Mama,

I had rather rather a bad toothache & Mr Searle[1] says that I had better get you to make an appointment at the dentist for me. Can you come down on Thursday please do as I want to arrange about an early dentist appointment & a late doctors appointment, so that I can have tea with you in between. Please do try & come on Thursday as I want you to jaw Welldon about keeping me on reports for such a long time. Therefore do not forget to come.

Goodbye

With much love and many kisses I remain, Your loving son

WINSTON S. CHURCHILL

PS Milbanke is writing this for me as I am having a bath.

Lady Randolph to Winston

Monday ?[November 1889]   2 Connaught Place

Dearest Winston,

I suppose when yr exchequer is at a low ebb I shall have the pleasure of hearing from you.

Your affectionate

MOTHER

---

[1] Frederick Charles Searle (1859–1904), educated at Charterhouse and Pembroke College, Cambridge, where he obtained a first class in the Mathematical tripos and a second class in the Theological tripos. Ordained; came to Harrow as an assistant master in 1884.

Winston to Lady Randolph

?[November 1889]   [Harrow]

Dearest Mummy

Not at all my darling Mummy, my Exchequer is quite full at present. I don't want anything for a wonder (except a hamper which is always welcome). I have written to ask Papa to come down to-morrow. *Don't go to Mashonaland*[1] it is very dangerous.

Good bye my darling sceptical Mummy
Your loving son
WINSTON S. CHURCHILL

Winston to Lady Randolph

[Postmark 9 November 1889]   [Harrow]

Dearest Mamma,

I am writing to you to tell you how much I enjoyed Papa's visit.[2] It was so kind of him. I hope you are quite well & looking forward to the holidays as much as I am. I am quite well, & getting on all right in my work.

Good Bye my darling, With love & kisses
I remain, Ever your loving son
WINSTON S. CHURCHILL

PS Please give the enclosed to Grandmamma. wsc

Winston to Lady Randolph

[Postmark 11 November 1889]   [Harrow]

My dear Mamma,

You know that you spoke to Welldon, when you came down last, about taking me off reports. Well he said to you that he would do so of course the moment I got a good report. I am on still.

My reports have been as follows

Quite Satisfactory No Complaint	1 week
Satisfactory Satisfactory	another week
Quite satisfactory Quite satisfactory }	this morning

It is a most shameful thing that he should keep me on like this.

[1] Lord Randolph was to visit Mashonaland (now part of Rhodesia) during his tour of South Africa in the summer of 1891.

[2] This is Lord Randolph's first recorded visit to Winston at Harrow.

Well you know that you promised to help me when I wrote & tell you; so that's what I am doing now. I am awfully cross because now I am not able to come home for an absit on Thursday which I very much wanted to do.

I hope you don't imagine that I am happy here. It's all very well for monitors & Cricket Captains but its quite a different thing for fourth form boys. Of course what I should like best would be to leave this [hell of a][1] place but I cannot expect that at present. But what I want you to do is to come down and speak to Welldon on Tuesday. Please don't be afraid of him because he always promises fair & acts in a very different way. You must stick up for me because, if you don't nobody else will. Its no good writing to him, so Please come down yourself. Now you know Mamma that you told me to rely on you & tell you everything so I am taking your advice.

Good Bye my own Mummy, Hoping to see you on Tuesday,
I remain, Your loving son
WINSTON S. CHURCHILL

Winston to Lady Randolph

[Postmark 16 November 1889]   [Harrow]

My dear Mamma,

I can wait another week all right; but it is a great bore, one does not feel free at all. Mr Welldon says he is going to make me get my remove, this term, nevertheless I think he might give me a chance of being off reports.

I don't mind so much, so long as I am off by Sat week the 30th of November which is I believe a whole holiday so I shall be able to come home for my birthday. Please write dear Mama & sign the following order please do. I have just seen Mr Ricardo galloping past with the drag hounds; he stopped & spoke to me, he was smart. Come down dear Mummy as soon as you can.

Your loving son
WINSTON S. CHURCHILL

Winston to Lady Randolph

[? November 1889]   [Harrow]

My darling Mummy,

I was very disappointed at you not being able to come down on Tuesday, as I had got off Army Class and other things. I can come home on Saturday for my absit if you write to Welldon and 'invite me'.

Do write to him in good time as I am rather keen on coming home.

I send you very best love & remain your loving & lazy son
WINSTON S. CHURCHILL

1 Subsequently crossed out.

Winston to Lady Randolph

[Postmark 6 December 1889]   [Harrow]

Dearest Mamma,

I did not expect you to come down in all that rain. But I'll tell you what you would like & that is to see, either the 'Assault at Arms' in the gymnasium on Monday or the 'Grand Concert' in the speech Room on Saturday.

Please write & tell me which day you will come & which you think you would like best.

Good Bye

With love & kisses I remain, Your loving & kissing son

WINSTON S. CHURCHILL

Winston to Lady Randolph

[Postmark 8 December 1889]   [Harrow]

Darling Mummy,

I have not been able to write before as I have been so busy. Well, I was put 'on lines' for 2 half holidays, that was rather hard luck. Do come & see me soon. Couldn't you come Saturday. I am working very hard & I have asked Mr W. to send a Report home at the end of the term. I am sure I shall do good 'Trials'. Send me a Telegram if you will or will not come.

Good Bye darling Mummy,

With much love & many kisses I remain, Your loving son

WINNY

WINSTON S. CHURCHILL

Winston to Lady Randolph

[?15 January 1890]   [Harrow]

Dearest Mother,

I arrived here allright Last night. Was Jack at all unhappy? I think I've got my remove I will write tonight again, when I shall have more time.

With Love I remain, Your loving son

WINSTON

Winston to Lady Randolph

[Postmark 16 January 1890]   [Harrow]

Dearest Mama,

I have got my Remove, & as you will be glad to see I have become economical I am sending it in Papa's envelopes. I want you to sign this bit of paper, to show that I have had the measles, or else you see I might Have invented the measles to get off, my holiday task.

With much love and many kisses I remain, Your loving son
WINSTON S. CHURCHILL

PS Please send the signature at once, before you leave England.

Winston to Lord Randolph

[? January 1890]   [Harrow]

Dearest Papa,

I have got a Remove in to the '1st 4th'. I am awfully pleased as the next time I get a Remove it will land me in the 'Shells' which are equivalent to the Lower parts of the Remove at Eton. Only one more Remove is necessary before I go on to the modern side.

Mr Welldon comes back on Sunday; I expect he has had a rough passage especially in the bay of Biscay.

With much love, I remain, Your loving son
WINSTON S. CHURCHILL

Lady Randolph to Winston

Saturday [? 25 January 1890]   2 Connaught Place

Dearest Winston,

We were delighted to hear that you had yr remove & I do hope you will continue to work. You ought to feel much encouraged & full of ambition. We are off at 3 oc & I fear will have a fearful tossing as it is blowing a gale. Everest will go & see you next Tuesday – as she has a great deal to do today. Will you you naughty boy! explain to me where the economy comes in, of sending 2 letters in one envelope – & at the same time telegraphing next day to Everest – when a letter wld have done as well? Mind you write at least twice a week, & write to Jack. Goodbye darling – best love

Yr loving Mother
JSC

Count Kinsky to Winston

25 January 1890   [Paris]

My dear old Winny,

How nice of you to think of writing to me! –

I was *very* pleased to get your lettre. – Well I caught it off you – no doubt, but I don't mind. I am really quite right again. but the Dr wont let me go out as yet.

You know the measles are nothing when one has it as a child but it's much worse with grown up people. They say one has to be very careful not to catch cold for some time as one is apt to get all sort of diseases.

I hope *you* do feel quite right again and that you will be a good boy this term. Write to me sometimes. I shall always answer. My address is '5 Avenue Montaigne, Paris'.

Yours ever
CH KINSKY

Winston to Lady Randolph

[? January 1890]   [Harrow]

Darling Mummy,

I am getting on capitally in my new form & I think I shall come out much higher than I did in the one below it. I am going up for my 'preliminary Exam' for 'Sandhurst' in June. Mr Welldon is back, immensely pleased to find I have got my remove.

I am very anxious to learn drawing. Papa said he thought singing was a waste of time, so I left the singing class & commenced drawing. But Mr Davidson said that it was one thing to 'take drawing lessons' & another to 'Learn Drawing' I get now an hour & a half a week & if I had another hour with the army class boys who learn Drawing in the Evening I am sure I should get on, as you know I like it. Drawing count 1200 marks in the further & every mark is useful.

Also I want to go on fencing & as you will perceive am vy anxious to have my Bicycle cleaned.

I have had such a beautiful letter from Jack.

Did you have rough passage?

Thanks for the 2½ stamps. However I don't know your address, so I guess I'll send this to Connaught Place for 1d.

Please give my best love to Papa, Auntie Leonie & Grand Papa.

Good Bye
With much love and kisses I remain, Your loving son
WINSTON S. CHURCHILL

Lady Randolph to Winston

Friday 7 February 1890   Grand Hotel
                                                Monte Carlo

Dearest Winston,

I hope you have written to Jack for his birthday. I sent you back the orders you wanted signed. I have also sent you some oranges – which I hope you will like. Papa returns to London tomorrow – but stops a night in Paris. I daresay if he is not too busy with his parliamentary work, & you write & ask him, he might go to see you next Saturday. I am so pleased that you are working up – it must be a great feeling of satisfaction to you – it certainly is to me!

The weather here is cold & bracing – Aunt Leonie has gone to Cannes for a couple of days. Grandpapa is fairly well – but very weak. I think it is a very good idea of yours to do a little extra drawing. I am sure it is a good thing if you have any taste for it.

Goodbye darling – mind you write.

Yr loving

MOTHER

Mrs Everest to Winston

Friday 10.30   2 Connaught Place

My Precious darling,

Yours to hand this morning. I wrote Jackie a long letter yesterday to explain to him I should not be able to go to Elstree this wet weather it would be running a great risk of getting laid up again you forget how recently I have had a bad illness – it is not that I won't go dear it would be the greatest pleasure to me but it is no use to go & get wet or damp & get ill again it is such terrible weather perhaps next week it may be more settled. Jackie is not dying to see me why are you so keen about my going. If you like to send me the money & it happens to be a very fine day tomorrow I will go not unless.

Mamma is still in Paris have not heard when she returns. I hope you have recovered from the effects of the dental opperation deary. I have had Mr Balaam & Charlie[1] to see me Charlie is staying a week in London. I hope you wear your coat this wet weather & change your Boots when they are damp, that is what gives you tooth ache sitting in wet Boots. It is just clearing up fine sun come out now.

Good bye my angel be good – where have you procured your 7/- from since last I saw you.

Much love from Your loving

WOOM

Jack to Winston

15 February 1890   Elstree School
                                                Herts

Dear Winey,

I am quite well. It as been snowing all the morning It is thick on the ground the first week I was 3rd out of 12 and the 2nd 5th out of 12 I am working up

---

[1] Charles John Balaam (1873–1944). He later became a Civil Servant.

I come home on the 2nd of April do you come on the 14th? I have still got 3 pound at home their are a lot of game's chess and Halma I often get a game I will write some oather time

I remain
J ACK S. CHURCHILL

Winston to Lady Randolph

[Postmark 16 February 1890]   [Harrow]

My dear Mamma,

Thank you so much for those beautiful oranges. I am getting on all right & I expect to get another remove at the end of the term. I have got rather a cold. I have just had a letter from Jack.

Give my best love to Aunt Leonie and Grand Papa.

With much love, I remain Your loving son
WINSTON S. CHURCHILL

Winston to Lord Randolph

[?16 February 1890]   [Harrow]

My dear Papa,

I am getting on all right & hope to get my Remove next term. Mamma sent me some oranges from Monte Carlo, they were certainly very good. I have just had a letter from Jack, he tells me that there is a great deal of Chess & Halma at Elstree, of which he is very fond. Did you enjoy yourself at Monte Carlo? When will you come & see me? With much love.

I remain, Your loving son
WINSTON

Lord Randolph to Winston

24 February 1890   2 Connaught Place

Dearest Winston,

Very many thanks for two letters. I am delighted to hear that you are getting on so well and hope you will be able to keep the steam up till the end of the term. I expect Mama home on Thursday and I have no doubt she will soon run down and see you. The weather is vy cold and disagreeable but I have lots of work to get through at home and in the House.

You heard I suppose of poor Daisy's death. It was vy sad: we must try and find a successor to her.

I send you a P.O. for a sovereign which will I hope keep you going for a time.

Ever yr most affte father
RANDOLPH S.C.

Winston to Lord Randolph
(*Leslie Papers*)

[? 26 February 1890]   [Harrow]

My dear Papa,

Thank you so much for the "P.O.O." It has enabled me to make up my Budget. Do you think you will get your "Session Bill" through?[1] The "Harrow Local Gazette" criticized it in very favourable terms. The Conservative Club here, I believe, are very keen on your coming down to "resusitate" them so to speak as the Liberal Club is getting up so tremendously. I am quite well and have not the influenza yet, although several fellows in our house have got it.

Well good bye dear Papa. Dont trouble to write because you are so busy.

With much love I remain ever your loving son

WINSTON S. CHURCHILL

Frances, Duchess of Marlborough to Winston

27 February [1890]   50 Grosvenor Square

Dear Winston,

I was very glad to get your letter, and to find you sometimes recollect your Grand Mother!

I take the greatest interest in your welfare & progress. Am pleased to see you are beginning to be ambitious! You have a great example of industry in your dear Father & of thoroughness in work. Dudley has just been in to see me he is up for an exeat but returns tonight.

I have had a nasty chill & can hardly sit straight for rheumatism so I am scribbling under difficulties. Oh how I do sigh for a little warmer weather! I went to the Gaiety Theatre a week ago & saw Rhuy Blas.[2] Lots of dancing and comics songs & topical ones with allusions to your Father! Have you seen Punch this week with his Picture? Its easy to quiz but he is quite right to denounce intemperance & so it will prove in the end. It is the curse of England and I am glad he has taken it up.[3]

---

[1] Lord Randolph brought in his bill for amending the licensing laws on April 29.

[2] *Ruy Blas* or the Blasé Roué, a burlesque of the celebrated play by Victor Hugo, by A. C. Torr (Fred Leslie) with music by Meyer Lutz, first performed at the Gaiety Theatre 21 September 1889.

[3] On March 1, *Punch* featured a full-page cartoon entitled 'Grandolph's Latest' and commented on Lord Randolph's introduction of his temperance bill,

'Gladstone he'd beard, Corruption he would throttle
And here he stands behind the Water Bottle!'

I am sorry to hear poor Mr Frewen has been so ill & I fear Mr Jerome is no better. I hear your Mother returns home this week. Sarah is going to Ireland to stay with the Zetlands' next week after the Drawing Room to which I hope to take her if I am well enough. Good bye dear

I am – with much love, Your most affect Grand Mother
F.M.

Jack Milbanke to Winston

9 March [1890]   Eartham
                                                                 Chichester

My dear Winston,

You seem to have been getting into rather difficulties with Phipps.[2] I hear that you have entirely gone to the devil. We have been having such beastly weather here quite deep snow of course hunting was quite out of the question. How do manage now about football do you ever go down or have you still got those dreadfully dangerous ulcers. I am sorry that I have not written for so long but I have been working so hard 3 hours every day except hunting days. How was it you did not manage to catch the influensa & go home for a week, I dont think you managed that very well. Give my love to Dudley & tell him I am going to write in a few days. Have you had 3 canes broken over you as I heard that that was the punishment for the next offence. I have been gazetted to the Sussex Militia & have come up in June for the first training at the Wellington Barracks.

No more time, Yours ever
JACK MILBANKE

Winston to Lady Randolph
(Leslie Papers)

12 March 1890   [Harrow]

My dear Mamma,

How are you? How is poor Uncle Moreton How is Grandpapa? I got your letter and all the signatures quite correct. I am getting on in drawing and I like it very much. I am going to begin shading in Sepia tomorrow. I have been drawing little Landscapes and Bridges and those sort of things. The "Orange Trick" might be repeated with safety as it is warranted to work. I have got my gold watch here; she is keeping capital time and looks very well.

[1] Lawrence John Lumley Dundas, 1st Marquess of Zetland (1844–1929). Viceroy of Ireland 1889–92. Married Lillian, 3rd daughter of 9th Earl of Scarbrough.

[2] John Lewis Phipps (1872–1902), came to the Head Master's 1886, left July 1890 to go to Christ Church, Oxford. Became Master of the Savernake Stag Hounds.

I am writing to Jack today. Everest came down yesterday. We have got a Chess Tournament on in the house, I stand some chance of winning it. I believe I passed the examination for Corporals yesterday, in the Rifle Corps.

Well good bye

With much love, I remain, Ever your loving son

WINSTON S. CHURCHILL

Winston to Lord Randolph

[?1 June 1890]   [Harrow]

My dear Papa,

I have been congratulated on all quarters on account of the 'flukey filley'.[1] When I went to telegraph at the post office the man who took my telegram informed me that he had 'dropped a quid hover that there orse'. Does two hundred sovereigns of Plate mean a cup of some sort? I am so glad to hear you are going to take that place near Newmarket[2] for some time. Mamma says that there are 500 acres of shooting. Are they fens, moors, or coverts. Millbank came down here yesterday. He is at Wellington Barracks drilling as he is in the militia. I wish I could go into the army through the Militia. Much more amusing – much easier & instead of being unaquainted with drill I shall have passed the full standard required in the Army. Any way here, I shall never get through my further. 1 Percent of those boys who go up pass their further from Harrow. The Army Class loses me my remove, takes me away from all the interesting work of my form & altogether spoils my term. Still I am sure I can pass my preliminary from here but more than that is not in the bounds of possibility.

9/10 of the boys in the Army Class will go to a Crammer before their Exam. They all dislike the Army Class because it makes them come out low in their forms. Of course Mr Welldon will tell you that a Public School etc but he cannot deny that a boy who gives 2 hours a day to Army Class work has not so good a chance as a boy who gives 6 hours.

Harrow is all right for a Preliminary Examination but 6 months & James or any other crammer is more to a chap than 2 years at Harrow. I should like to go in through the militia because then you begin much earlier which is a distinct point. It is a well known thing that a fellow who goes through the

---

[1] L'Abbesse de Jouarre, Lord Randolph's four-year-old black filly, won the Manchester Cup on May 30 at 20 to 1. The Abbess, or Abscess on the Jaw as she was popularly known, had won the Oaks in the previous year. She was by Trappist out of Festive, and was bought for Lord Randolph at the Doncaster Sales on 15 September 1887 for 300 guineas. Between 1889 and 1891 she won ten races whose value totalled £10,050.

[2] Banstead Manor.

militia is always much more use than a Sandhurst Cadet. Be that as it may I have to pass my further if I go to Sandhurst and then pass out.

While I only have to pass out of the Militia. Another difference is that on one side one gets practical instruction & on the other theoretical.

Harrow is a charming place but Harrow & the Army Class don't agree. I have not heard from Jack yet.

I see that the Abbess has two other engagements – has she any chance? When does your Bill come on again? It will be sure to go up for second reading. Every body down here is excited about it one way or another "I zay zir, yor feyther goin to shut up the Pubs tip us a drink sir while we can get it" and on the other hand I hear the respectable tradesmen say that they hope it will pass especially those who live near the Public Houses. I am writing to Grandmamma, Mamma tells me she will be with us at Newmarket – Perhaps I shall see the Abbess there.

Well good Bye Papa.

> With much love & many kisses I remain, Your loving son
> WINSTON S.C.

Winston to Lady Randolph

[? May 1890] [Harrow]

My darling Mummy,

I have told all the news to Papa & Grandmamma, still it will not be 'stale' if I tell you once more that I have got my Remove. 'Modern 3rd Shell'. I began German yesterday – Ugh. Still I hope to be able to 'Sprechen ze Deutche' one of these days.

Will you please sign the enclosed 'Billy doos' with 3 autographs in your best handwriting   'Good old "Habbess" '

I got a full account from Jack of the Race and the D. of Cambridge nose, not flattering to his Royal & Military Highness.

Please come & see me 'aussi vite que possible'

> I remain, As usual Your loving and affectionate offspring
> WINSTON S. CHURCHILL

Winston to Lord Randolph

[? 8 June 1890] [Harrow]

My dear Papa,

Thanks awfully. I was quite astounded – stricken 'all of a heap in fact.' I am not going in for my Preliminary this term as I am not strong enough in Geometrical drawing.

I drank the Abbess's health in Lemon squash and we eat her luck in strawberry rash.

Goodbye,
With greatest love, I remain, Your loving son
WINSTON S. CHURCHILL

Lady Randolph to Winston

Thursday 12 June 1890   2 Connaught Place

Dearest Winston,

I am sending this by Everest, who is going to see how you are getting on. I would go down to you – but I have so many things to arrange about the Ascot party next week that I can't manage it. I have much to say to you, I'm afraid not of a pleasant nature. You know darling how I hate to find fault with you, but I can't help myself this time. In the first place your Father is very angry with you for not acknowledging the gift of the 5£ for a whole week, and then writing an offhand careless letter. Your report which I enclose is as you will see a *very* bad one. You work in such a fitful inharmonious way, that you are bound to come out last – look at your place in the form! Yr Father & I are both more disappointed than we can say, that you are not able to go up for yr preliminary Exam: I daresay you have 1000 excuses for not doing so – but there the fact remains! If only you had a better place in your form, & were a little more methodical I would *try* & find an excuse for you. Dearest Winston you make me very unhappy – I had built up such hopes about you & felt so proud of you – & now all is gone. My only consolation is that your conduct is good, & that you are an affectionate son – but your work is an insult to your intelligence. If you would only trace out a plan of action for yourself & carry it out & be *determined* to do so – I am sure you could accomplish anything you wished. It is that thoughtlessness of yours which is your greatest enemy. Your Father threatens to send you with a tutor off somewhere for the holidays – I can assure you it will take a great deal to pacify him, & I do not know how it is to be done. I must say I think you repay his kindness to you very badly. There is Jack on the other hand – who comes out at the head of his class every week – notwithstanding his bad eye.

I will say no more now – but Winston you are old enough to see how serious this is to you – & how the next year or two & the use you make of them, will affect your whole life – stop and think it out for yourself & take a good pull before it is too late. You know dearest boy that I will always help you all I can.

Your loving but distressed
MOTHER

Winston to Lady Randolph

[Postmark 19 June 1890]   [Harrow]

My darling Mummy,

I have not written till now because I can write a much longer letter. I will not try to excuse myself for not working hard, because I know that what with one thing and another I have been rather lazy. Consequently when the month ended the crash came I got a bad report & got put on reports etc. etc. That is more than 3 weeks ago, and in the coming month I am *bound* to get a good report as I have had to take daily reports to Mr Davidson twice a week and they have been very good on the whole.

And then about not answering Papa's letter – I did that very evening & I gave it to the Page to put in the Pillar box & a 1d for him at the same time.

I could not put it there myself because it was after Lock-up. He I suppose forgot & did not post it till several days had elapsed. My own Mummy I can tell you your letter cut me up very much. Still there is plenty of time to the end of term and I will Do my *very best* in what remains. I wanted to go in for my Preliminary & I will explain the whole thing to you. If in your examination you succeed in passing any 3 of the 8 subjects you need only compete in those you failed in. Now I knew that if I worked at

1   Geography
2   French
3   & English Dictation & Composition I should pass in all these 3.

I knew that work however hard at Mathematics I could not pass in that. All other boys going in were taught these things & I was not, so they said it was useless.

Good Bye, my own,
With love I remain, Your own
WINSTON S. CHURCHILL

J. W. Spedding to Winston

10 July 1890   The Primrose League
Wimborne Habitation No 410
50 Grosvenor Square

Sir,

I beg to enclose with much pleasure your diploma as a knight of the Primrose League and as a member of this Habitation and as I am resigning the Secretary-ship, I expect you will be the last member I shall make. I am proud to

have added such an illustrious name to the register. I will forward your
badge.

I have the honour to remain, Your obedient servant
J. W. Spedding

Receipt
No 177

3 July 1890   Wimborne Habitation No 410

Received from Winston Spencer Churchill Esq the sum of   Pounds
Seven Shillings Six pence– & Badge.

to April 19th 91

Entrance Fee	£ –	2. 6.
Annual Tribute to Head Office		2. 6.
do do Habitation		2. 6.
Decorations Badge		2. 0.
	£	9. 6.

J. W. Spedding
Secretary

Winston to Lady Randolph

[Postmark 17 July 1890]   [Harrow]

My darling Mamma,
  I have ordered

                    1 pair of trousers
                    1 of knickerbockers
                    1 jacket & 1 Waistcoat
                    all of the same stuff.

I enclose a pattern, it is one which will look very well when into [sketch of
kneebreeches] & also do to wear on Sunday [sketch of long trousers] with
Etons – it also looks very well when [sketch of jacket and racket] the jacket
waistcoat & trousers are worn.

They have not yet begun to make it so you can change it if you wish. They
fully understand the making of Knee Breeches. Nice & Bagsy over knee.

My darling Mummy. I want you to send me 11/6 to pay the Bill for my bicycle being painted; you told me you would 8 weeks ago & I have forgotten all about it. Now the man sends his Bill and wants me to pay him. If you will send me a P.O.O. for 11/6 I shall be much obliged.

With love I remain, Your own
WINNY

Winston to Mrs Everest

[July 1890]   [Harrow]

My darling Old Woom,

I am all right – back here well & thankful. I am much better as I had nine lots of araroot. No news except that I have ordered my clothes.

1 pair of Trousers	
1 „ „ Knicks	
1 Jacket	of the same man. [?]
1 Waistcoat	
1 Blue coat	

Good Bye darling
I hope you will enjoy yourself
With love from WINNY

Lady Randolph to Winston

Friday 19 [September 1890]   Invermark
                                                                                    Brechin N.B.

Dearest Winston,

I hope you enjoyed yr play Tuesday night – & that you got back to school all right – & are settling down to yr work. I was so sorry to have to leave in such a hurry – hardly had time to say goodbye to you & Jack. Write & tell me if you went to Elstree, & how Jack felt. I hope he was not too low. It is cold & damp up here – but very bracing. I tried to catch some fish in the loch yesterday but only succeeded in getting 1 rise. Darling Winston I hope you will try & not smoke. If you only knew how foolish & how silly you look doing it you wd give it up, at least for a few years. If you will give it up & work hard this term to pass yr preliminary I will get Papa to get you a gun & a pony – & perhaps next season there will be something to shoot at Banstead. Anyhow dear – I will do my best to get you some sport & make you enjoy yourself – but you must do something for me in return. Now mind you write a nice long

letter & tell me all you do. I want you *so* much to get on. Don't forget to brush
yr teeth! & think of me.

Your loving
MOTHER

Winston to Lady Randolph

Friday 12.45 a.m. [19 September 1890]   [Harrow]

My own dear darling Mummy,

I am so glad you caught the train and arrived safely.

I am back at Harrow and am settling down to 'swot'.

My dearest Mamma you can't think what a ripping piece 'An English
Rose' at the Adelphi is.[1] Well acted – well put on – excellently carried out –
beautiful scenery – capital songs. It was much better than A Million of Money
on tick![2]

Not any Oh ah eh

all sort of going on, Capital girl – good old hero – splendid villain. Enchanting
horse called 'Bally (Heaven knows what)' a very good sergeant of Con-
tabulary who plays a very important part very well.

Good Bye I will write when I have more to tell you. And remain
Your loving son
WINSTON S. CHURCHILL

Winston to Lady Randolph

Sunday [21 September 1890]   [Harrow]

My dear Mamma,

I have just recd your letter. Thank you very much. I will leave off smoking
at any rate for 6 mths because I think you are right. Jack was very low but
has written to Everest to tell her he is 'all write'. We drove from Elstree on to

---

[1] A drama by George R. Sims and Robert Buchanan which *The Times* described as 'a
notable achievement'. Its review continued: 'It has quite a special and realistic interest for the
Adelphi public, after the romantic nonsense which has hitherto passed as Irish drama, while in
purely emotional and sensational elements it exhibits no falling away from the accepted
standard. Mr Leonard Boyne as O'Mailly is a valiant and chivalrous hero, whom it is refreshing
to behold. . . . His talents, besides being indubitably Irish, have the true ring of passion. . . ."

[2] By Henry Pettitt and Augustus Harris, and produced at the Drury Lane. Of this drama
The Times commented: 'To Literary merit or any subtle development of character the play
holds no pretensions nor is there any novelty of plot or situation to raise the piece above the level
of ordinary melodrama. There is no abandonment of the beaten track – save that from the
beginning the lovers are married, so that no stern parent intervenes to thwart their hopes – and
no unforeseen evolution of circumstance.'

Harrow. We have bought a hearth rug – & a cushion – our room looks very nice but I have need of some 'Liber 't' art' Fabrics. Please come when you come now Good Bye my darling Mummy

With ever so much Love I remain, Your loving son
WINSTON S. CHURCHILL

I am holding myself

Lord Randolph to Winston

22 September 1890   Moulton Paddocks
                                                           Newmarket

Dearest Winston,

I was vy glad to hear from you. I expect that yr dissipation in London was the cause of the indisposition from which you say you have recovered. I have been here since Wednesday. Vy quiet & peaceful. I have occupied myself looking after the horses & yearlings. That new Irish hack of mine is a perfect creature. I go to Banstead[1] today where I expect some friends for the week's racing. Freddy Johnstone,[2] Tommy Trafford & Colonel North.[3] I do hope you will work hard for yr 'preliminary'. It will be quite a disgrace to yourself & to Harrow if you were to fail. Mama writes that she is vy well at Invermark and likes the change.

Ever yr affte father
RANDOLPH S.C.

Frances, Duchess of Marlborough to Winston

23 September [1890]   Cliveden
                                                           Maidenhead

My dear Winston,

Thanks for your letter – I am glad you are settled down & getting into harness. Here we have missed you & Jack very much & feel a little flat so

[1] Banstead Manor, Newmarket, was rented by Lord Randolph from 1890 to 1892.

[2] Frederick John William Johnstone (1841–1913), 8th Baronet, elder twin son of 7th Baronet, born posthumously. A noted and successful racehorse owner. Married 1899 Lady WILTON.

[3] Col John Sidney North (1804–94), second son of General Sir Charles Doyle, married Susan, second daughter of 9th Baron North and 3rd Earl of Guilford, and assumed the name of North in 1838. Three years later his wife became Baroness North. Col North (he held his commission in the Oxfordshire Light Infantry) was Conservative MP for Oxfordshire 1852–85, and was subsequently created a Privy Councillor.

that in spite of the beauty & grandeur of the place we shall be glad of a change
to Banstead especially as the weather is grown cold & stormy. Annie Roxburghe was here last week & brought Alastair Ker[1] who is at School at Mr
Fenn's Chalfont St Giles 7 miles from here so after Annie returned to London
she left him here & I drove him there as I knew the rector of the Parish &
his wife.

Alastair is a nice boy just the age of Jack. The Dog Cart & Pony & the Cob
are gone to Banstead where your Father is having a party this week. Spedding
is gone there to help him with it. Good bye. Sarah sends best love & wishes
often for your Company. She & I are quite alone here & have no news.

I read with great interest your Head Master's article in a Review & I quite
agree with all he says!

Believe me dear Your affect Grandmother
F. MARLBOROUGH

Take care of yourself & work well & keep out of scrapes & dont *flare* up so
easily!!!

Lady Wilton to Winston

24 September [1890]   [The Hatch]

D<u>t</u> Winston,

It is too nice of you asking me to come to Harrow – & I would like it above
all things – but just now – I fear I will have to stay here – as I have some relations
arriving & must remain on to look after them. But later on, I should so much
like to come & see you.

Have you had any news of your Father lately? I suppose your Mother will
be going to Baron Hirsch's soon.

My love, dear Winston Yr very affecte Deputy Mother
LAURA WILTON

Winston to Lady Randolph

[?25 September 1890]   [Harrow]

My dear Mamma,

I have not written because I have been waiting to hear from you. I wrote &
sent you the pattern but you have not answered. The man says if I do not let

---

[1] Alastair Robert Innes-Ker (1880–1936), second son of 7th Duke of Roxburghe and thus
a grandson of the Duchess. Served with Royal Horse Guards in South Africa and in First
World War (Lieutenant Colonel, DSO) and also with Royal Flying Corps (Squadron Commander). Equerry to King George V 1930–6.

him know about the patterns by Saturday he cannot possibly get them made. Please write. I want some oof awfully badly as I told you last time I wrote. Do send me a "quid" 25/- would be nearer the mark. You told me to write to you Mummy when I wanted money and I had to pay out 6/- of my sovereign to a Master who had given the journey money for my Dental exeats. What a pity the Abbess was beaten. I knew it – She had too much weight.[1]

I send my condolences.
Good Bye with best Love, I remain
WINNY

Winston to Lady Randolph

[? September 1890]   [Harrow]

My dear Mamma,

I am quite well & settling down all right. How are you enjoying yourself in Scotland. Please write & tell me all about yourself.

I am making my room very pretty & 'chic' with lots of silk 'draperies'. We want it to be the prettiest room in the house. You must come down & see it when you come back (& mind my darling Mummy to bring me some 'Liberty art Fabrics' & some 'Heathen Goddesses')

With 'No news but old news'
I remain, Your loving son
WINSTON S. CHURCHILL

Winston to Lady Randolph

[Postmark 13 October 1890]   [Harrow]

My dear Mamma,

I have not written before because I did not know your address.[2] I wish I were with you – Mind & bring the shooting hat home & one for Jack too. What a pity the Abbess did not win the other day.

I have had a tremendous hamper from Fortnum & Mason sent anonymously. It must have cost at least £3.10.0. I rather suspect Lady Wilton, who has answered a letter I wrote. I am working very hard & I hope to pass my Preliminary in at least 3 subjects.

[1] In the Great Eastern Railway Handicap run at Newmarket on September 24 L'Abbesse de Jouarre (carrying 9 st 7 lb, the top weight) was third, three lengths behind L'Abbé Morin (6 st 10 lb) and Bel Demonia (6 st 10 lb) who dead-heated for first place.

[2] It was St Johann sur March, Lower Austria, where Lady Randolph was staying at Baron Hirsch's place.

viz I. English Essay – & diction.
     II. Geography.
     III. French.
     IV. Euclid.

But I am afraid I shall fail in arithmetic & Algebra & Geometrical Drawing. Still if I pass in 3 I shall only have to go in, in those things which I did not pass. Most boys have two shots. Still I have a good 2 months before me and I am working 'to some purpose'.

> Good Bye my darling Mummy With much love & many kisses
> I remain, Your loving son
> WINSTON S. CHURCHILL

PS I am so awfully sorry for the Blots, but someone has been doing something to the Blotting Paper.

> W. CHURCHILL

Winston to Lord Randolph

[?23 October 1890]   [Harrow]

My dear Papa,

Thank you so much for the game; I have only eaten one of the pheasants as yet; what lovely cock! I have had a letter from Lady Wilton. How many birds did you slay? Was Alicante[1] a 'good thing'?

Jack is in want of figs. The army class master says I am sure to pass in English Essay & Spelling. It is beastly weather here.

I see Lord Calthorpe's horse was beaten yesterday.

I am quite well, but as you probably know have got to wear a truss for 12 months, an awful bore.

Jack is making some 'Rabbit nets' for Banstead. Has he been writing you long well spelt letters?

What a disagreeable Eccles Election.[2]

> Good Bye dear Papa
> With Love & Kisses I remain, Your loving son
> WINSTON S. CHURCHILL

[1] The Cambridgeshire Stakes run at Newmarket on October 22 were won by Monsieur M. Ephrussi's Alicante, the 9–2 favourite.

[2] At the Eccles by-election on October 22 the Hon A. F. Egerton (Conservative) lost the family seat previously held by his nephew to H. J. Roby (Gladstonian Liberal) by 4,901 votes to 4,696.

Lady Wilton to Winston

24 October [?1890]   Le Nid
                                                    Monte Carlo

My dear Winston,

(My fat cat just knocked my pencil out of my hand – which accounts for this awful scribbling!) How are you? – I am sending you some of the preserved fruits from here – I thought you might like them. – Herewith is £2 for pocket money. When do your Holidays begin? – & can you tell me where your mother is now?

With my love Yr affecte Deputy Mother
LAURA WILTON

Miss C. Thomson to Winston

3 November [1890]   28 Brunswick Road
                                                     Brighton

Dear Winston,

Since receiving your letter a few days ago, I have kept it on my desk with the intention of answering it. This morning your handsome present reached me, and gave my conscience so sharp a prick that I have seized my pen on the first opportunity.

Thank you very much for your useful gift to the Brunswickers. I hope they will be able to learn some of the songs before Christmas and that you will come and hear them on 18th December. Mrs Roose and Bertie have already promised to be with us. Our dramatic talent this term is not great, but we mean to do our best.

My thoughts were directed to Harrow yesterday for a wet morning kept us all at home, and I read Dr Welldon's sermon on 'All Saints Day', to the boys. I think we all enjoyed it, and wished ourselves Harrovians. We were glad to hear of Forster[1] and Gun[2]. Forster is such a great favourite of mine, I should much like to see him.

Miss Kate and I send you our love & thanks.

Yours very sincerely
CHARLOTTE THOMSON

[1] Claude William Forster (1873–1936), came to Harrow (Church Hill House) April 1887, left in December 1891 to go to New College, Oxford. Ordained 1898.

[2] William Townsend Jackson Gun (1876–1946) had gone to Harrow in April 1890. He left in December 1894, went up to Trinity College, Cambridge, was called to the Bar 1901, and later became a noted genealogist.

Winston to Lady Randolph

[? Nov 1890]   [Harrow]

My darling Mama,

I hear that you are greatly incensed against me! I am very sorry – But I am very hard at work & I am afraid some enemy hath sown tares in your mind. I told you I thought I should not pass my preliminary on account of my being put under a master whom I hated & who returned that hate. Well I complained to Mr W. & he has arranged all things beautifully. I am taught now by masters who take the greatest interest in me & who say that I have been working very well. Now I have got over 3 weeks & I may easily do it. I am working very hard & if I am not slanged too much I stand a very fair chance & I have much the best chance of knowing. I said I should pass if I had a fair chance & I have got one – now so I'll have a pretty good try at it. Arithmetic & Algebra are the dangerous subjects. I am sure of

	English
nearly sure of	Geography
	Euclid &
	French
can work up	
	Geometrical drawing.

Besides if you want to give me a chance please let me know the extent of the evil of which I am accused.

As for the rest – that can be seen to later. I am thinking only of my preliminary. If you will take my word of honour to the effect that I am working my very best, well & good, if not – I cannot do anything more than try,

Good Bye my darling Mummy, With love from
WINNY

Jack Milbanke to Winston

Sunday 16 November 1890   17 Cliveden Place
                                                  Eaton Square

My dear Winston,

I have just been to call on your mother I thought it might be some use, but unluckily I found her out, if you think I can be of any use to you in any way mind you let me know. I got back all right last night at about 12.30 I nearly missed my train in consequence of having lost my hat. I was dreadfully afraid Searle would catch some one with their candles alight, he would not stamp enough. However I dont think he did catch any one. I hope to be down next week. Give my love to my brother and Dudley.

Your affect friend
JACK M

Lady Wilton to Winston

20 November [1890]   Le Nid

Dearest Winston,

Very pleased to get your nice letter. I'm sorry you have so much hard work before you – But – if you *face* it – it will gradually appear less hard – & I'm sure you'll pass *well*. Yes – its very nice out here – tho' there are tiresome things *here* – as well as everywhere else.

Your Father is here[1] – & lunched with me yesterday. He is looking very well. He doesn't gamble at all! I heard too from your Mama, who sent me a lovely umbrella she bought for me in Vienna – wasn't that kind of her?

A little later on I'll send you a large box of those small mandarine oranges from this garden. I enclose £2 with my best love & a kiss –

Yr very affecte Deputy Mother
LAURA WILTON

Winston to Lady Randolph

[? November 1890]   [Harrow]

Darling Mamma,

I am not off Reports yet. I was so disheartened that I fell off again. I hope you will try & come to see on my birthday. I thought, that as it is a whole holiday you might come down & see me. If you could come in the morning it would be so nice.

Good Bye,
With much love, I remain Your loving son
WINSTON S. CHURCHILL

Winston to Lady Randolph
(Blenheim Papers)

[? November 1890]   Harrow

Darling Mummy,

One line to tell you I am well – working – happy tho' very tired – I am getting on alright & am learning lots each day.

---

[1] Lord Randolph stayed at Le Nid on his way to Egypt where he wintered until late January.

I have written to Lady Wilton – Papa etc.

I now send you my youthful love & remain

your loving son

WINSTON S. CHURCHILL

PS Send Everest down tomorrow because she can help me do some work (*if convenient*) WSC

Winston to Lord Randolph
(*Blenheim Papers*)

?[November 1890]   Harrow

Dear Papa,

I am working very hard & am 'specking' on passing in 3 things & hope to pass in 5. Still I shall do well if I pass in 3.

I got a good report this week – I think Mr Welldon is pleased with me. He is very keen & takes any amount of trouble about me.

I am working to the very best of my ability so I'll remain, Your loving son

WINSTON S. CHURCHILL

Lady Wilton to Winston

28 November [1890]   Le Nid

My dearest Winston,

Thank you very much for your nice letter.

I am delighted to hear you are working so hard & I expect you will *distinguish yourself* – I will rejoice in it.

Your Papa left yesterday. He looked very well. Tell me where you go for your Holidays & when – whether to Banstead – or to Connaught Place –

I will send you later on some of the oranges from this garden.

Take care of yourself – & believe me – ever your very affecte Deputy Mother

LAURA WILTON

Chester Dawson to Winston

28 November 1890   The Mount
                                                           Hampstead

My dear Churchill,

The 30th of November is a date to be remembered in the family to which I belong, it also happens to be your birthday & I write this letter to wish you 'Many Happy Returns of the Day'. Thinking it not improbable you will have a holiday I have addressed the envelope, as you will see, to Connaught Place. I dare say you have heard I have left Brighton after being there for seven years. Would it be impossible for you to take me over Harrow School? I should so like to see it, you might name a day if you will.

Remember me kindly to your brother and Mrs Everest.

With kind regards Yr affectionate Friend
CHESTER DAWSON

Reverend F. C. Searle to Winston

29 November 1890   10.5 p.m.

My dear Churchill,

One line to wish you many happy returns of tomorrow. I was [?aware] that tomorrow was your birthday before you came in just now and mentioned your presents. You start the year free from all reproach, may you end it free from all regret. May God bless and keep you throughout this and all your years.

Yours affectionately
F. C. SEARLE

Winston to Lady Randolph

[Postmark 10 December 1890]   [Harrow]

Darling Mama,

Of course I cannot judge whether or not I have passed in this day's exam. But I can tell you that I am very contented with the result.

Last night I thought I would try & see if I could learn up the right map. Therefore I threw all the maps (their names on little scraps of Paper) into my hat & drew out one with my eyes shut. New Zealand was the one and New Zealand was the very first question in the Paper. I consider that this is luck. To draw the right map out of 25 different scraps of paper. Of course I had learnt all about New Zealand. I think I can say I have passed

English
Geography

& I should [not] be at all surprised if I passed in Geometrical Drawing.

I have had a very successful day.

Of course this is only my opinion still I am very pleased.

The subjects for the essay were

i.   Rowing versus Riding
ii. Advertisements Their use & abuse
iii. The American Civil War

I did the last.
Show this to Everest as she is awfully keen.
A Remittance would not be altogether misplaced.

Tomorrow $\left\{\begin{array}{l}\text{algebra \& arithmetic} \\ \text{Euclid}\end{array}\right.$
                    French

> Wish me luck
> I remain, Your loving son
> WINSTON S. CHURCHILL

Mrs Everest to Lady Randolph
(*Blenheim Papers*)

1 January 1891   Banstead Manor
                                                 Newmarket

My Lady,
    We arrived here safely at 3 o'clock yesterday & I am very sorry but I quite
forgot to send you a telegram until we had got some way on the road here.
I hope you got Master Winston's letter he wrote last evening. They are both
so happy & delighted & in towering spirits. Mr Winston walked from Chevely
up to the house yesterday & said he left all his bad throat in the train he feels
nothing of it. They danced all evening & were out before breakfast this
morning & have been out with the keeper the whole morning, killed 5 rabbits
& frightened 50. They have just had luncheon & gone off again. They do not
need pressing to go out here. On the contrary now I have the trouble to get
them to come in to their meals. But they are so happy & well today. The house
is very comfortable & warm. The weather changed in the night & it has been
thawing today – otherwise the pond is beautiful for skating. They were looking forward to it, but if the thaw continues they will be able to ride. I should
like to keep Master Jack here untill Mr Winston returns from Canford.
Mr W could come up with Walter the boy. It is so much better for them
than London. I am desired to enclose drawings of last night with their best
love & kisses.

> Your ladyship's, obednt servant
> E. A. EVEREST

Winston to Lady Randolph

Thursday [1 January 1891]   [? Banstead]

Darling Mummy,

We have slaughtered many rabbits–About 11 brace altogether. Tomorrow we slay the rats. The Pond is frozen 8 inches – The ground is covered with 4 inches of snow. Pipes are frozen – Oil freezes in the kitchen. No wind. V-happy V. well. We are enjoying ourselves very much. We exist on onions and Rabbits & other good things. The ferrets are very well & send their love so do the guinea-pig & rabbit I have bought. If I hear the result of my Examination I will wire.

Once more kissing you
I remain, Your loving son
WINSTON S. CHURCHILL

PS I wish I had not got to have my nose destroyed.

! ! ! ! ! !

Lady Wilton to Winston

[? January 1891]   Le Nid

My dear Winston,

I was very pleased to get your amusing letter yesterday.

You will soon be going back to Harrow, I suppose? & how is Jack? My love to him – & yourself. I am sending you some oranges from this garden to Connaught Place.

Ever yr affecte Deputy Mama
LAURA WILTON

Lady Wilton to Winston

[? January 1891]

With your Deputy Mother's best love.
I hope they *are* good.

Frances, Duchess of Marlborough to Winston

17 January [1891]   Woodlands
                                                      Uxbridge

Dear Winston,

I am very pleased to hear the good news in your little notes as regards yourself.

I hope it will encourage you to continue to exert & and distinguish yourself & make us all proud of you. Your Father will be much pleased.

Give Mama my love. I was so ill with the fog in London that I am anxious not to go back while this cold weather lasts. Sarah & I hope now to return there on Wednesday I fear now I shall miss you. I hope all was going on well at Banstead. Do write and tell me what you did there & if the house was very cold. I almost think of going there in Feb^ry.

Good bye. I write this line to catch the Post. Tell Mother I have nothing to say but will write.

Your most affectionate Grand Mother
FM

Love to Jack.

The results of the Army preliminary examination held in the previous December were announced in the middle of January 1891. There were 29 candidates from Harrow. Of these, twelve, including Winston, passed in all subjects; seven, including Dudley Marjoribanks, passed in four subjects; four passed in three subjects, and six boys failed.

Reverend J. E. C. Welldon to Winston

19 January 1891   Harrow School

My dear Churchill,

It is a great pleasure to me to learn that you have passed the Preliminary Examination.

This success must encourage you to work hard for the Examination which still lies before you. You must be quiet, sensible and industrious; then I am sure you will do well.

With best wishes, Affectionately yours
J. E. C. WELLDON

Jack Milbanke to Winston

17 January 1890 [1891]   Eartham
                                                        Chichester

My dear Winston,

I am so glad you have passed your exam. After all you wont have to go to Australia or where ever you were to be sent. I suppose you ought to be allowed a weeks extra holiday on the strength of it. I hope your mother is all right again.

Probably I shall meet you on Wednesday as I am coming up some time next week.

The post is just off.

Yours ever
JACK M.

Mrs Everest to Winston

[21 January 1891] Wednesday 4.00   [2 Connaught Place]

My darling Winny,

It is such dreadful weather & I am awfully busy covering up the house & have so many commissions to do for Mamma that I really cannot come to Harrow before Saturday. I am rather knocked up too have had a great deal to do the last few days. I hope you are better dearest Boy – don't get wet mind & wear your coat when you go out it is such fearful weather. I took Jackie back to School on Monday got a letter from him next day. Mamma left for Banstead yesterday & Grandmamma & Aunt Leonie. Letter from Paice[1] this morning saying how cold it is there. Banstead belongs entirely to Mamma & Papa now The Duchess has relinquished her share of it to Mamma so that is much better for all parties concerned. I can't get out anywhere it keeps on snowing so. My little Ella[2] came to tea with me yesterday she will try & come on Saturday with me to Harrow. Papa is coming back tomorrow I don't know how long he will stay. I hope you will take care of yourself or when you come home we shan't be able to go to Banstead if you are poorly so you must try & get well old man.

Lots of love & kisses From your loving old
WOOM

I enclose Jackie's letter.

Winston to Lady Randolph

[?21 January 1891]   [Harrow]

Darling Mummy,

I skated to-day on Ducker. It is very wet a quarter of an inch of water all over, but the ice is beautiful, quite clear & very very slippery.

---

[1] Lady Randolph's maid.

[2] Eliza Sleigh Phillips (1862–1929), eldest child of the Venerable Thompson Phillips, Archdeacon of Furness. She married in 1895 Nigel Francis William Buchanan: she had no children.

I have received very many congratulations from scores of boys & many masters. Dudley has to go in for part of his Exam again & may not join the 'Special Sandhurst Div.'

I have had to buy a lot of things for my room. Do come down to-morrow, like a darling. I am very anxious to talk to you on a lot of subjects before you journey to Monte Carlo. Please come down & skate part of the time, but come alone, because I find there are several things which I want to talk to you about.

Please send me a wire very early time of arrival.

I remain, Your loving son
WINSTON S. CHURCHILL

Lady Randolph to Winston

Thursday [22 January 1891]   2 Connaught Place

Dearest Winston,

I am very sorry not to be able to go to you today, but Grandpapa is not quite so well & Grandmama has asked me to go back there this afternoon. If possible I will go & see you on Sat or Jack & Everest will go. Dear boy, I do hope you are sticking to yr work & are not spending *all* yr money. Jack is here looking over my shoulder – says he has "nothing to say". I am still trying to get Papa to sacrifice that terrible beard – but up to now without success.

With best love Yr Loving
MOTHER

Winston to Lady Randolph

[? January 1891]   [Harrow]

My dear Mamma,

I was so sorry you could not come down to see me to-day but I realize the impossibility of it.

Well I will write all that I wished to communicate. In the first place I want you to look out some ornaments, fans, & pictures & let Everest keep them on Tuesday.

I have had to spend a great deal of 'oof' on my room I give you particulars :–

2 Pictures of Steeplechasing	7/-
Draper to ornament them	3/-
2 little tiny 2nd Hand Pictures	
& 2 Brackets	1/9
2 Japanese Scrolls	2/-
1 tongue	3/-
Food	4/-
Hammer ⎫ nails ⎬ tintacks ⎭	2/-
Telegram	/9
Jam	1/-
Book	2/-

Total   £1   6   6

I have also got to pay away

Subscriptions	4/-
Money for Journey home last term	4/-
& above a little bill for repairing my bicycle some time ago	8/-

Dearest
Mummmmmmmy

I know you will say I am very extravagant but I am sure that you will send me a P.O.O. And tell Everest to arrange about my breakfast

Dudley has not spoken to me. Vive la joie!! He has not passed & is furious.

I am working now with boys in the VIth & Vth Forms. The work is very hard but I can do it if I work hard. I want you to write and ask Mr Welldon to allow me to come up early on Tuesday afternoon & see Grand Papa before I am cauterized. I am so sorry to hear that he is worse. Don't worry yourself my Mummy. Jack says you look awfully worried.

Darling Mummy. I remain
Ever your loving son
WINSTON S. CHURCHILL

Lady Randolph to Winston

Monday [26 January 1891]   2 Connaught Place

Dearest Winston,

You will be glad to hear that you will find me here tomorrow when you come – but you will be sorry for the cause. I have been obliged to give up my journey as poor Grandpapa is so much worse. Telegraph what time you are coming up.

In haste, Your loving
MOTHER

Lady Wilton to Winston

26 January [1891]   [Le Nid]

My dear Winston,

So many thanks for yours – I was pleased to see your writing again. I'm sorry to hear you have had Influenza but hope you are all right again now?

Your Father is well – but as yet, we have only had one fine day – I hope he will gain strength here.

Do give my very best love & a kiss to your pretty Mama from me & tell her I wish she were coming here to brighten us all up. I will try & send her some nice flowers.

With love to yourself Yr very affecte Deputy Mother
LAURA WILTON

Winston to Lady Randolph

[Postmark 30 January 1891]   [Harrow]

Dear Mummy,

How is poor Grandpapa? I am all right as to my work but I have caught cold. My Leg has been giving me pain where I strained it, & I am frightened. Tell Everest to make an appointment with McCormack[1] for Tuesday afternoon 3.30 or thereabouts. He told me to come & see him every 2 months or so. Give my love to Grandmama & Auntie Leonie. I have [Sketch of teeth and brush] regularly.

Give my best love to every one.
I remain With much love, Your affect son
WINSTON S. CHURCHILL

[1] Sir William MacCormac (1836–1901), specialist in hernia surgery. A native of Belfast, he became surgeon-in-chief to the Anglo-American ambulance in the Franco-Prussian war and was present at the battle of Sedan, 1870. Five times president of the Royal College of Surgeons, 1896–1900, he was created a knight in 1881 and a baronet in 1897.

Lady Randolph to Winston

Saturday [?31 January 1891]   2 Connaught Place

Dearest Winston,

Grandpapa is about the same today, tho' we had a great fright last night as he had a fainting fit. Papa arrives tomorrow night so you will see him when you come up on Tuesday. I will write you a line tomorrow as to how Grandpapa is & keep you posted. I am so tired I can't write any more.

Jack writes that I must not write *only* to you.

Goodbye darling. Best love.
Yr loving Mother
JSC

Winston to Lady Randolph

[?2 February 1891]   [Harrow]

Darling Mummy,

I am so glad Grand Papa is no worse. I was getting uneasy because Jack wrote to me & told me you had been up all night. I am looking forward to seeing Papa. Darling Mummy Dont tire yourself with sitting up, you have enough worries without getting ill. Will you write to me *by return of post* & let me know what time McCormack's appointment is for, or else I shall not know in time to get my paper made out.

Goodbye my darling Mummy
With much love I remain, Your loving son
WINSTON S. CHURCHILL

PS Love to all.

Mrs Everest to Winston

[?2 February 1891]   [2 Connaught Place]

My darling Winny,

Have just been to Sir W. McCormac to make appointment for your tomorrow Tuesday at 6.30 but he was out told them to let us know this evening – so will telegraph in morning.

Papa came home last night. Grandpapa is better should not be surprised if he gets well after all & Mamma has been 3 or 4 nights up with him expecting any minute he would draw his last breath.

Shall have you tomorrow goodbye sweet love
WOOM

Count Kinsky to Winston

5 February 1891   Austro-Hungarian Embassy
                                         18 Belgrave Square

My dear Winnie,

I am sending you all the stamps that I could scrape together for the moment. Do you want some more later on? If so say so.

How is your old head? I hope all right again. I am off to Sandringham tomorrow until Monday. If I have a good thing racing you shall be on.

I am going to lunch with Mama now so must be off.

Be a good boy and write if you have nothing better to do.

Your Grandpa is much better again. Quite as well if not better than he was 2 months ago the Dr says.

Yours ever
CK

Mrs Everest to Winston

6 February 1891   2 Connaught Place

My darling Winnie,

I am afraid you must not expect Jackie & I tomorrow – as there is a telegram from Mr Sanderson[1] to say he would arrive at St Pancras at 2.23 tomorrow so there will not be time to come down to Harrow. I am very sorry darling you will be very disappointed I know so I am sending this to prepare you for it. How are you my darling. If he has had his dinner before he leaves Elstree perhaps Mamma will let him come by the 3.30 train but it is hardly worth while just for an hour.

In haste to take the Dogs out for promenade.

Much love & kisses from your loving
WOOM

Winston to Lady Randolph

[? February/March 1891]   [Harrow]

Darling Mamma,

I do not know where you are, nor how grand papa is, nor how Jack is, nor when you return from Brighton, if you are there, nor anything. Please write to me by return of Post dear Mummy. Will you send me a P.O.O. for £1 if you please. Do write to me.

I remain, Your loving son
WINSTON S. CHURCHILL

[1] Lancelot Sanderson (1838–1904) headmaster of Jack's school, Elstree, 1869–1904. Formerly an assistant master at Harrow. In Holy Orders.

Mrs Everest to Winston

Saturday 9 p.m. [?14 February 1891]   29 Bedford Square
                                                      Brighton W.

My darling Winny,

I have been going to write to you all the week but there was no ink in the house & I kept forgetting to get some when I was out. Well dearest Boy how are you, has Mamma been down to see you yet. Jackie is much better since he came here but his cough is still troublesome in the early morning. We have had such nice sunny days since we came here but today it has changed very foggy & damp. but the Niggers came & performed outside our windows this afternoon so Jackie liked it better than being out of doors. Auntie Clara's children & nurses are here in the same house as us they came yesterday for a fortnight so it is company for Jackie. Mamma & Auntie Clara came down last Wednesday & Count Kinsky came & looked at our lodgings. Mrs Pill has given up this house retired to a cottage but John Bull keeps it now so we are living with John Bull & he is such a nice big man just like the pictures of John Bull.

Grandmama house is about a mile from us near the chain Pier. Grandpapa was brought here in an ambulance & is much better since he came here. I think we shall stay another week here if the weather is fine.

We had the 3 little pups up in the nursery last Sunday the twins came to tea they are fat merry little creatures full of fun biting everything you would like them – they are quite big.

Jackie sent you the stamps in his small Album did you get them. Do send us a few lines by return post he is anxious to know. We will come & see you before he goes to School then we can bring his Album back with us. I hope you are keeping well darling goodbye my lamb lots of love from Jackie & from loving old

WOOM

Winston to Lady Randolph

Monday [Postmark 16 February 1891]   [Harrow]

Darling Mummy,

I am so glad Grand Papa has got to Brighton safely. Please do do do do do do come down to see me tomorrow Tuesday. Please do come I have been disappointed so many times about your coming. Please do come to see me before you go to Brighton. If you *are coming* telegraph *early* the train by which *you leave* London.

Please come my own Mummy I have not seen you for so long. Do come down tomorrow.

I remain Your loving son
WINSTON S. CHURCHILL

Jack Milbanke to Winston

15 February 1891   Depot, Royal Sussex Regiment

My dear Winston,
    What an age it is since you last wrote to me. Fancy you beating Dudley in the prelim, you will soon be in the Army now, probably long before I shall, How are you getting on this term, have you got any friends now, and how is young Gray[1] treating you? I wish you were here you would enjoy this sort of life. I am getting to know such a lot of drill, you won't be in it with me soon. What a pity you did not get that hiding from Phipps after all, when he went down on purpose. I hope to be down at Harrow soon again as I am going to James's to cram. No news so I shall stop.

Yours
JACK M

Chester Dawson to Winston

19 February 1891   c/o The Rev H. P. Waller
St Catherine's School
Broxbourne

My dear Churchill,
    I was so glad to hear you had successfully passed the "Army Prelim", allow me to congratulate you. I hope this success will inspire you to work still harder in the future. You must know, or you will very soon learn, that in these days there is no chance of getting on in the world without good hard work.
    Thank you very much indeed for your interesting and cleverly illustrated letter, there is no reason whatever why you should not make some use of your sketching, certain it is, it will always be a source of amusement to you and to those who get any of your comic sketches.
    I do not think I shall start papers yet, it really takes up too much time and

---

[1] There were two brothers Gray at the Head Master's, both good footballers. Frederick William Gray (1872–1915) served with the South Wales Borderers in South Africa and at Gallipoli, where he was killed in action. Henry George Wyndham Gray (1874–1926) lived in Argentina and New Zealand, where he farmed.

the boys here have to work hard, it is a grand school for work I can assure you.

I teach very little drawing here and that only to the smaller boys. We have a visiting drawing master here.

Haileybury College is not far from here about two miles. I passed it yesterday walking to Hertford. I hear that the Harrow Volunteers come over there sometimes to have a sham fight or to shoot with them. You will let me know when you come over with your comrades in arms as I should very much like to see you all.

Don't you think you could let me have one of your photos I have not one of you excepting that which was taken by Harry Firth some years ago. A cabinet I should like the best if you could spare one. I also wish I had your pater & mater's too. I wish you would let me have Brownfield's address and Kimbolton's too, if you can.

We had a grand football match on Saturday but we were beaten, getting only one goal to our opponents' three, considering they were all men, I do not consider it was a disgraceful beating. Our boys played splendidly, our backs and halfbacks over and over again knocked the men down & were stiff the next day after such hard play. I was centre forward and did not do as much as I should have liked but hope to do better next time.

Has Jack gone to Harrow yet? Remember me kindly to him and with best wishes & kind regards to yourself.

Believe me, Yr old tutor, & affectionate Friend

CHESTER DAWSON

Lady Wilton to Winston

27 February [1891]　　　　　　　　　　　　　　　　　[Le Nid]

My dearest Boy,

I am not angry at all! – only I have been very ill – bronchitis – and my son Arthur,[1] is also laid up, ill with bad bronchitis & gout in his feet! – & we have quite a *Hospital* here as some of the servants are ill too. I am *so* sorry Jack is ill – give him my love. I hope to see you at "the Hatch" when I return to England. & I must hear from you now & then –

Enclosed £2 with best love & a kiss from yr Deputy Mother

LAURA WILTON

Please remember me to your Mama when you write to her.

---

[1] Arthur George Egerton (1863–1915), only son of 4th Earl of Wilton, whom he succeeded in 1898.

Winston to Lady Randolph

[Postmark 9 March 1891]   [Harrow]

My darling Mummy,

I am all right, with the exception of a cough which I hope will very soon pass away. I suppose you will realize that I have nothing to tell you.

So with much love I'll remain, Your ever loving son
WINSTON S. CHURCHILL

Winston to Lady Randolph

[?26 April 1891]   [Harrow]

My dear Mamma,

I have had an awful toothache ever since I got here; and so I have written to Everest to ask her to make a Dental appointment on Tuesday. I have not been able to do any work at all. And they will not let me get the Chemist to take it out as they think it would make you angry.

I have got my Remove, & am 'Head of the fags.'

So with love I remain, Your loving son
WINSTON S. CHURCHILL

PS How is Gem? WSC

Mrs Everest to Winston

Tuesday [28 April 1891]

My poor old Lamb,

I am so sorry about your toothache. Poor darling. I went off early this morning 8 O'clock but the Dentist's Man said they were full up & could not possibly give you an appointment before Thursday at 5. Poor old Man – have you tried the heroine I got you – get a bottle of Elliman's embrocation & rub your face when you go to Bed & tie your sock up over your face, after rubbing for a 1/4 of an hour, try it I am sure it will do it good. I shall be here on Thursday but so busy don't know which thing to do first – taking inventory tomorrow. Excuse this hurried scrawl darling.

Your loving
old WOOM

Winston to Lady Randolph

[? April 1891] [Harrow]

Darling Mummy,

My face is swelled up double its natural size through toothache. I have made an appointment with Pritchard[1] for Tuesday. I have got some money of my own which you gave me, but want you to send me journey money for Tuesday.

2/- 1st Return Fare.
2/- Cab There
2/- Cab Back
_____
6/-
_____

As it will play old Harry with my Finances to pay this sum. I have paid my debts & relinquished Betting. I have lost your address so I have to send this through Auntie Clara.

Please send me the "oof" in time.

Will you be in town on Tuesday? Write & let me know.

Good bye my darling

With love & kisses I remain, Your tooth tormented – but affectionate – son

WINSTON S. CHURCHILL

Lady Randolph to Winston

Wednesday [29 April 1891] Banstead

Dearest Winston,

I am *so* sorry to hear you have a toothache, & I hear from Everest that the dentist cannot see you until tomorrow. Perhaps he will pull it out. I don't want to lecture on the subject – but I am sure if you wld take a little more care of yr teeth you wd not suffer so much. Quite apart from the "pigginess" of not brushing them!! However I do hope darling that you are better. I am quite settled here & like it very much. The Curzons[2] & Lady Kaye are with me, & tho' I do not go to the races, I see people & it is pleasant. I saw all the horses yesterday. Carlina was beaten but Col Montagu[3] did not expect her to win.

[1] John Walter Pritchard practised in Grafton Street. He became a doctor of dental surgery at Philadelphia.

[2] Richard George Penn, Viscount Curzon (1861–1921), who in 1883 had married Georgiana, 5th daughter of the 7th Duke of Marlborough. He was Tory MP for High Wycombe from 1885 until he succeeded his father as 4th Earl Howe in 1900.

[3] Oliver George Paulet Montagu (1844–1893), 4th son of 7th Earl of Sandwich, formerly commanding Royal Horse Guards. His filly Carlina ran fifth in the First Spring Two-year-old Stakes at Newmarket on April 28.

Rough and Ready[1] was 2nd. I have had several telgs from Papa[2] who is well
& says everything is pleasant.

Write to me often my darling.
Yr loving Mother
JSC

So glad you have yr remove.

Jack to Winston

? [May 1891]   Elstree

Dear Winney,
    when you come I shall be in so go in at the front door and ask for Mrs
Sanderson and she will send for me and I will try and have dinner with Mrs
Sanderson *alone* for the Boys will talk about it to me and after you have gone so
if we have it with Mrs Sanderson they will no know of it
    Remember what to come in at the *front door*

I remain
JOHN S. CHURCHILL

Winston to Jack

? [May 1891]   Harrow

My darling Jack,
    I suppose you have quite settled down now: I have. I have got such a dear
little room all to my self. It is awfully nice. I have put up all my pictures, &
hangings. How are you? Are Mrs Sanderson & her only child well? I hope so –
Indeed I do. I might come over on Sat week I think but do not take any steps
till I let you know. I will send you a few stamps I find here when I have swapped
the 2 Austrians.
    Good Bye my burrd.

With love & kisses
I Remain, Your loving brother
WINSTON S. CHURCHILL

Winston to Lady Randolph

?[10 May 1891]   [Harrow]

Darling Mummy,
    I am much Better, my toothache is all gone now. How is Gem? & my
Mummy how are you. I hear poor Grandmamma Duchess is very bad indeed.

---

[1] Colonel North's Rough and Ready ran second behind St Symphorien in the Visitors'
Welter plate at Newmarket on April 28.
[2] Lord Randolph sailed for South Africa on April 24.

Will you send me my subscription money 13/- as it will make such a hole in my exchequer otherwise I am allright as regard money.

Do write to me soon my Mum. Poor Woom is ill with the influenza but is getting better.

With much love I remain, Your loving son
WINSTON S. CHURCHILL

Hurrah for Nunthorpe.[1]

Lady Randolph to Winston

Sunday [10 May 1891]   Banstead

Dearest Winston,

I am so sorry to hear that you have had such a bad time with yr teeth. I expect you will have to have one out – otherwise am glad to hear that you are well & happy.

Grandmama Marlborough has been very seriously ill with influenza & bronchitis, but she is better now. We have all been very much worried about her – you must write & tell her you are glad to hear she is better.

Everything is going on well here. I am expecting a few people for the races this week – Col Montagu etc. You will probably have heard that Nunthorpe won the Jubilee yesterday. I must say that I was astounded – the "glorious uncertainty of the Turf" once more exemplified. "Gem" is all right, I have been driving her this afternoon, & yr chickens are indefatigable in their laying!

Write to me my darling & tell me all you do. I will go and see you the first time I go to town in about a fortnight. I hope you are working hard.

Yr loving
MOTHER

I can't hear from Papa for some time – but the last letter I had was written in a very cheery mood – from Lisbon.

Jack to Winston

10 May 1891   Elstree

Dear Winney,

I hope you got back all right. I ran all the way with out stopping coming back and got back at 15 to one. I hope you were very tired after it. Our Masters

---

[1] On May 9 Colonel North's Nunthorpe won the Great Jubilee Stakes at Kempton Park by a head at 100–7. After winning his first race as a three-year-old – a match – two years before, Nunthorpe won no races as a four-year-old, losing in seven consecutive races until he won the City & Suburban Handicap in April 1891.

were licked utterly yesterday in cricket against Easher [sketch of cricket] they made 170 we made 95 a very bad beginning we are going to play Lanchastre so I hear but I am not sure do do do do do do send my stamp book if you can. I hope lady Wilton sent you £2/-

We have been back 3 weeks and our little chickens ought to be Hatched. Write to Herbert and ask him if they are all right.

I hope he will look after them well I wonder if the eggs pay

I must say good bye I remain
JOHN CHURCHILL

[Sketch of horse]
The white ponney wins by a good neck

Jack to Winston

17 May 1891   Elstree

Dear Winney,

It is very good our four little chickens and the 8 eggs where are the rest of the 73 eggs did the whole of the 73 only come to 2/-.
Fancy Nunthorpe winning again and Simonion is favourite for the Derby.
Do send me my stamp book for I have got nothing to do did you get the postcars from The Gov Mind and come on Saturday as soon as you can will you come to Diner? Let me know all about it before Friday because I can know what to do when you do come what time will be here. It is awful weather it is hailing as hard as it can.

The boy stood on the tram way line.
The conducter rung the bell
The tram went to London
and the boy went to hell.

POETERY

dont forget to send me my stamp book as soon as you can.

I remain
JOHN S. CHURCHILL

Winston to Lady Randolph

[?19 May 1891]   [Harrow]

My darling Mummy,

I wrote to you on Thursday and you did not answer. I am well & all right, but have just been in the deuce of a row for breaking some windows at a factory.

There were 5 of us & only 2 of us were discovered. I was found, with my usual luck, to be one of these 2. I've no doubt Mr Welldon has informed you of the result. I hope to go with the Rifle Corps on Friday; (D.V.).

Please come & see me on Thursday or Saturday, anyway please send me a little money to keep the exchequer solvent. Please send £1 by next post as I am absolutely '*oofless*'.

Good Bye my darling Mummy.

With much Love, I remain, Your loving son

WINSTON S. CHURCHILL

Mrs Everest to Winston

Sunday 8 p.m. [?24 May 1891]   Banstead

My darling Winny,

How are you I hear your Mamma has been to see you. I hope you are getting on well. Be careful about the Ducker the wind is still east & treacherous not safe to go into the Ducker yet especially to stay long in it. I am happy to tell you I am convalescent again & enjoying the lovely country air. Rosalie & I go for a walk every evening for an hour exploring. You would enjoy being here now. Herbet Bell brought me a large Bunch of wild flowers to day & some birds eggs for Rosalie, he is really a nice little Boy was so pleased to see me when he saw me the first time. I go to look at your chickens they look thriving there are 2 Bantam chickens & 3 or 4 others. Bell has got 2 of your Hens sitting on some Turkey's Eggs. The guinea pig died & 2 of the little Rabbits & Herbert told me he has sold all the eggs for 1/6d so I am afraid your farming will not pay the labourer's wages. Dick is grown quite a young man so tall & strong looking. Flossy has been very ill but is getting better down here. The cat has got 4 such pretty little Kittens & Edney is going to keep them all 2 in the Stables & 2 in house. The Puppies are grown very much but extremely ugly. I hear no signs of a Pony for Jackie yet. Did you go to see Jack yesterday it was a nice day – write & tell me please. Mamma is going to give me 3 weeks holiday the end of June till the last week in July so I am going to Ventnor for 10 days & then Mrs Balaam wants me to go to Oxford with her for a week. She is going with Charlie he is going for his exam which last a week 12 subjects he goes in for. I had planned in my mind to go to Carlisle for 10 days but Mrs Balaam wishes me so much to go with her so I have consented but it is a great disappointment not to go to Carlisle. I daresay the sea air will do me more good. The house here is going to be full up with visitors for the race meetings so they have no room for me to sleep here. You will not know this house when you come it is so smart – the little play room down in the hall is being done up –

papered blue & white paint & new white painted furniture. The Piano is
down in the Servants Hall. Now I have told you all the news so I hope you will
send me a letter in return & rather a longer one than the last – good bye my
dear old Pet Boy lots of love & kisses.

From your loving old
WOOM

Winston to Lady Randolph

[? 23 May 1891]   [Harrow]

Darling Mama,

I am very well & getting on capitally. I want you to send me £1.0.0. for
myself as over 10 days have passed since I told you I was all right. Darling
Mummy please send it soon as I am going to walk over to Elstree on Saturday
to see Jack and I shall want a little money to 'stand him'. Try and find out
from Sherwood what chance Simonian[1] has of the Derby.

Good Bye my darling Mummy.

I have heard that my hen has reared a brood of 4 little chickens.

With best Love I remain, Your loving son
WINSTON S. CHURCHILL

So glad to hear Papa has arrived.[2] WSC

Winston to Lord Randolph
(*Blenheim Papers*)

Wednesday 27 May [1891]   [Harrow]

Derby Day

My dear Papa,

I am so glad to hear you have arrived safely at Cape Town. You were very
lucky to have such a long rest from English weather. We have only had 2
really decent days this year. Mama came to see me yesterday and told me a
lot of news. She says that Banstead is delightful and that they had perfect
weather during the £2,000 week. Have you heard of the accident which
happened to the dog-cart? Mama was driving rather fast and Lord Elcho[3]

---

[1] Colonel North's Simonian was unplaced in the Derby on May 27. The race was won by Sir
Frederick Johnstone's Common, the odds-on favourite who had previously won the 2000
Guineas.

[2] Lord Randolph arrived at the Cape on May 14.

[3] Hugo Richard Charteris, Lord Elcho (1857–1937), fourth but eldest surviving son of 10th
Earl of Wemyss, whom he succeeded in 1914. He was Unionist MP for Ipswich 1886–95.
Despite his mishap he was in his place on May 26 to move, successfully, the adjournment of
the House of Commons for Derby day.

was sitting on the back seat when suddenly there came a jolt and the back seat and Lord Elcho were in the middle of the road, while the Dog-cart kept the "even tenor of its way" onwards. He put his shoulder out and sat in great pain for 2 hours till the Doctor could come and put it in again. Mama says the stable has been winning lately. Nunthorpe won the Jubilee, and St Simon of the Rock ran third in the Newmarket Stakes and fourth in the two thousand pounds. Today the Derby is to be run. Common, Sir Frederick Johnston's colt is first favourite at 5–4. Fitzsimon is expected to do well. But I will insert the news of the running, when I hear of it.

My hens have had one brood of four chickens and laid eighty eggs. Everest had the influenza very badly but is all right now. Grandmama is much better, Mama saw her yesterday. Jack has come out top of his form and is very well. I too am in good health and spirits.

There was rather a row about some broken windows not long ago. I, young Millbank,[1] and three others went out for a walk a week ago and discovered the ruins of a large factory, into which we climbed. Everything was in ruin and decay but some windows yet remained unbroken; we facilitated the progress of time with regard to these, with the result that the watchman complained to Welldon, who having made enquiries and discoveries, 'swished' us. However this is not a serious row, and Welldon never even mentioned it to Mama yesterday. Will you send me all the stamps you can get as I am in want of some 'Bechuanaland'.

I suppose you will not go up the Pungwer river on account of these disturbances.[2] Please don't go trying to conquer the Portugeuse. I suppose by the time this reaches you you will have slain multitudes of lions and natives. When will your first letter to the *Daily Graphic* arrive? Did you enjoy yourself at Cape Town? How are Mr Williams[3] and the others?

Please don't forget my youthful antelope. I am getting on all right and have just finished a large plan of the 4 principal battles of the Great Rebellion. The horses are all quite well, so says Mama and as everything is satisfactory,

With much love & many kisses, From me and Jack,

I remain, your loving son

WINSTON S. CHURCHILL

The order of the Derby is Common, Gouverneur, Martinhurst. WSC

[1] Mark Milbanke.

[2] Portuguese warships had stopped the progress of the Chartered Company's gunboats up the Pungwé river in Mashonaland; and in a skirmish near Fort Salisbury between a Portuguese force and men of the Company on May 14 the Portuguese lost seven killed and were forced to withdraw.

[3] Owen Gwynydd St George Williams (1865–93), eldest son of Lieutenant General Owen Williams (see p. 23). He travelled to South Africa with Lord Randolph as his assistant; two years later he was killed in the Matabele War.

Jack to Winston

[? late May 1891]   [Elstree]

Dear Winney,

I am so sorry you did not come on Sat. I was so disapointed you did not come.

You were sily to do that I thought at first that you were fooling me but when I saw the other boys I knew you were not.

V. bad Simionian coming in last in the derby and commyn 1st. I hope Lord – will send you the money if he put you on 2nd Gouveneur I hope you did not bet in a sweep stake and lost I surpose you won I hope you did not get anything else

dont write to the Gov have you done so? Gold told me that you would not be aloud to come

I remain
JSC

Please Send My Stamp book

Mrs Everest to Winston

Wednesday [? June 1891]   Banstead

My darling Winny,

You are good to write to me I was so glad to hear you are so well & quite free from tooth ache what a relief to you. Poor old Boy after suffering so much with it you were brave to go & get it taken out. Banstead is looking lovely now all the roses & flowers are out in bloom – charming.

Mamma came back on Monday – but is going away again to London this week. Aunt Leonie is still here & Grandmama Jerome. I often go to see your chickens the old Cock is a noisy old fellow he wakes me up all hours of the night crowing. I think your hens must lay plenty of eggs for they are constantly cackling. Herbert seems to keep them well supplied with corn but they never seem to have much water – I must go presently & try & see him he takes the letters to post every evening. I only see him on Sundays when he is minding the young turkeys. Mamma has got a Victoria now for Grandmama to drive out in. The Servants have had a letter from Thomas[1] he says they have had a very pleasant journey so far & have enjoyed it very much. They had a fire break out on the ship which caused a panic the Boats were man'd but they got it put out burnt the store room out & one sudden death a mate died in a few minutes while pouring out some tea.

I was sorry to hear of the Boy dying at Harrow.[2] Mind you are careful about the ducker not get a chill don't stop in too long have you commenced the ducker yet?

I have just written to Jackie.

Mamma is in despair about you spending so much money. She is greatly troubled about it she says you are always asking her for more money.

I see your Bicycle is getting knocked about badly. I told Loder to have it cleaned and put up in the loft. That Henry has been riding it & when I spoke to him about it he said you told him he might use it but he said other men had been using it that were too heavy for it. It is no use having it mended till you come because they will go & break it again if we do. That Henry is such a forward fellow.

All the Ranners[3] have had influenza lots of people in the village have had it some have died. That Sam is turned out very bad, drinks all he earns & wife & children are badly off.

Well my love I shall be off the end of next week all being well. I will write again before I go. Lots of love & kisses write soon again my angel.

Your loving
WOOM

Lady Wilton to Winston

4 June [1891]   Le Nid

My dearest Boy,

(Tho' I ought to say "young man" now!) Many thanks for yours. Yes, "Common" is indeed a splendid fellow.

I have been awfully poorly & am still obliged to keep my room & I don't know when exactly I will be able to start from here – But I'll let you know dear, directly I get to Paris. Where I propose remaining for 4 days – & then to

[1] Thomas Walden, Lord Randolph's devoted personal servant who later accompanied him on his last voyage round the world in 1894, and went to South Africa as WSCs soldier servant 1899–1900.

[2] Baptist Wriothesley Leland Noel died of influenza on June 9 at Harrow.

[3] They worked at Banstead. See page 1206.

London – till 1st July –when I go down to the Hatch – & I do hope to see you there – & I will come to Harrow if you'd like me to – with great pleasure.

My love dear – Yr affecte old friend
LAURA WILTON

Love to Jack. Enclosed £2 for pocket money.

Winston to Lord Randolph
(*Blenheim Papers*)

[?8–9–10 June 1891]   [Harrow]

My dear Papa,

When last I wrote to you the news of the Derby had just arrived, now I can tell you the result of the Oaks. *Mimi* a strange filly whose first achievement was the thousand pounds and who also carried off the Newmarket Stakes beating all the colts except Common, was first. *Corstorphine* was second and *Lady Primrose* third *Mimi* was a hot favourite and started 9–4 on.

I am not able to go out as I am tormented with toothache which has now turned to an abscess, so that my face is swelled to twice its normal size. I am going to Pritchard tomorrow so I expect he will put me right.

I have just written to grandmama who is much better.

The baccarat case[1] comes off today; I will enclose a cutting. I will tell you more news about Harrow and myself if I would by any stroke of genius alight on something of interest. But no, there is nothing that will entertain or amuse you and my daily life might be summed up in the words of Mark Twain's Diary as a schoolboy, 'got up, washed, went to bed."

However I presume you have not so completely ostracised yourself to be uninterested by the news of the day. The Archbishop of York is dead and Dr Maclagan reigns in his stead. Your telegrams were published in the *Graphic* and it also stated that 'the channel squadron would be ordered to repair to Portuguese S. Africa,' a fact the veracity of which I should deem questionable.

Jack is very well and quite happy. I am writing for him as well as for myself. Simonian came in nowhere in the Derby which I suppose will be annoying to Colonel North.

The rifle corps had a sham fight on Friday; I went and enjoyed myself

[1] On June 9 after a trial lasting seven days the jury in only ten minutes returned a verdict for the defendants in the action brought by Sir William Gordon-Cumming (1848–1930), 4th Baronet, late Colonel of the Scots Guards, against Berkeley Levett and others who had accused him of cheating at baccarat at Tranby Croft. The Prince of Wales and General Owen Williams, who had also been playing at Tranby Croft, were both called to give evidence.

immensely. I took the opera glasses you gave me and through them scrutinised the foe.

Mama is staying with Lady Mandeville – I mean the Duchess of Manchester, in town. "Gem" is very well, so are the puppies. "Turvy" who belongs to me is the best of all. I have told you all the news most of it is "stale" already and all will be old when it reaches you. Will you write to me and tell me many things. You must have lots of time, ener[g]y and material for letter writing whilst I have none of these 3.

See if you can get me some foreign stamps and send them home. How did you manage about the Uni Code? My love to Mr Gwenydd [Williams], or however he spells his name. Have you had any shooting yet? I would like to be with you. If you have time you might write to me from the land where the Rudyards cease from Kipling and the Haggards ride no more.

Goodbye dear Papa with much love and many kisses
I remain ever your loving son
WINSTON S. CHURCHILL

[Sketch of man with sabre cut] I imagine you so. [Sketch of bearded hunter with gun] Leo [and picture of lion.] Don't forget my [picture of an antelope's head.]

I had intended to put in an account of the Baccarat Case but it is too long.

The Solicitor General spoke so strongly of General Williams' conduct that he rose and appealed to the protection of the judge.

Of course Sir William lost the case and had to pay five thousand pounds costs. Though that will not make much odds as he married Miss Garner[1] next day.

Frances, Duchess of Marlborough to Winston

10 June [1891]   Brighton

My dear Winston,

I must thank you for your affect letter of enquiry after my illness. I was very ill indeed and suffered a great deal – but thank God I am well again and only feel weak. That influenza is a dreadful illness especially for old people. I do not think I ever was so ill in my life. I am going back to London in a day or two and expecting Sarah there. She is now with a party for Ascot races. This place is very empty now and nobody to see but innumerable schoolgirls.

What a dreadful end Sir William G. Cumming's cheating has brought him

---

[1] Florence Josephine (d. 1922), daughter of William Garner, Commodore of the New York Yacht Club.

to. Its quite dreadful and I only hope this trial will put an end for ever to Baccarat.

I have heard from your dear Father and he has written a long delightful account of his voyage to your Mother which she shewed me. I dare say she will read you some of it.

And now goodbye dear Winston
Yr affect Grandmother
F. MARLBOROUGH

The Headmaster has kindly asked me to the Speech Day but I fear I may not be able to go.

Mrs Everest to Winston

Thursday [11 June 1891]   Banstead

My darling Winny,

Mamma is not here she come on Saturday & Aunt Leonie & Uncle Jack – so as she was not here I took it upon myself to send you a hamper it was sent off by passenger train this morning so that you ought to get it tomorrow Friday early. Please let me know soon as you get it or I will not send you any more – you never acknowledge anything I send – if you did I should send you something oftener. Edney has got up a cricket club here on the green a regular proper club so many members who all pay & Edney is the Captain of it Loder is treasurer. Have you been to see Jackie yet I sent his Bat off yesterday. How is your poor face ache. Did you go to the Dentist? Don't eat too many of those nasty pickles they are poisonous things. I hope you will enjoy your Chicken Pie & cake they won't hurt you.

I don't think you will be able to go to Lords this year because there is no where for you to go to I hope Mamma won't have Jackie up just for the day & send him off back to school alone. I shall be away – you probably may go but Jackie can't do it all in the day.

I can't stop to say more now & don't forget that I never cease to think of you if I do not write my lamb.

Your eggs are not *cooked*.

Have you met Teddy Richmond[1] at Harrow he is on a visit there he has just passed his exam & got an appointment from the Railway compy as clerke.

Good bye dearest much love & heaps of kisses from

Your loving
WOOM

---

[1] Edmond Philip Richmond (1874–1928), Mrs Everest's nephew.

Lady Wilton to Winston

11 June [1891]   Le Nid

Many thanks for yours – my dear Winston. At present – I've hardly any foreign stamps – But I'll try & get some for you. I hope to start from here on 14th & to arrive in Paris next day. "Hotel Bristol, Place Vendôme", will find me till 19th – when I hope to get to London – "10, Mandeville Place, Manchester Square" will find me till 1st July. I'm woefully bad still. Mind you let me hear from you again 'ere long. My love to Jack.

Ever yr affecte Deputy Mother
LAURA WILTON

Winston to Lady Randolph

[?11 June 1891]   [Harrow]

My darling Mummy,
    I think I shall have my tooth taken out on Thursday. I had the abcess lanced the day before yesterday. The swelling has quite gone down. I am very well & happy. Is Gem quite well? Are the chickens joyful? Are you very healthy? Give my love to Everest, she sent me a beautiful hamper.

Hoping to see you on Thur I remain, Your loving son
WINSTON S. CHURCHILL

PS I will write again as soon as I know the date of my appointment.

Winston to Lady Randolph

[? 13 June 1891]   [Harrow]

Darling Mummy,
    I have got an appointment for 4.30 on Thursday afternoon with Doctor Braine.[1] Do come up & write & tell Welldon you will look after me & "give me Tea."
    I have had no more pain. Please do come I shall not like going alone at all.

Good Bye my darling
With love & kisses I remain, Your loving son
WINSTON S. CHURCHILL

---

[1] Charles Carter Braine and his father, Francis Woodhouse Braine, were the leading authorities on the use of anaesthetics in dental surgery.

Sir Frederic Johnstone to Winston

Sunday 14 June 1891   9 Arlington Street
                                                              Piccadilly

Dear Winston,

I am afraid I was rather indiscreet, but I suppose that does not matter when I enclose your £5. I hope you will come down to the Hatch this summer.

                                                            Yrs very truly
                                                            F. JOHNSTONE

I have got a nephew at Druries you must be nice to him.[1]

Lady Wilton to Winston

16 June [1891]   Hotel Bristol
                                                           Place Vendôme
                                                              Paris

Dear Winston,

Very many thanks for yours which I received this morning. Having a tooth out is not at all a pleasant ordeal! However, I hope to see you looking very fit 'ere long.

I shall cross over Saturday or Sunday – "10, Mandeville Place, Manchester Square" will be my abode till 1st or 2nd July – after which – the Hatch – Surly Hall, Windsor – till 1st Octr.

I sent you today a Box of Paris "Sweets". I hope you may like such things – or perhaps some of your friends will. If I am well – I will try & see "Common" run for the Eclipse Stakes on the 10th July. I do hope he'll win!

I should like to write a few lines to your father – Please tell me how direct to him.

I hope to see your mother in London.

                                                      With my best love –
                                              Your ever affect Deputy Mother
                                                        LAURA WILTON

Mrs Everest to Winston

Mamma's address is Oakley Court Windsor

Wednesday [17 June 1891]   Banstead

My Precious old Boy,

So pleased to get your 2 letters & that you liked your hamper. I hope the cake was well baked she does not do them nicely as a rule. Well my poor

---

[1] Charles John Johnstone (1877–1937), second son of Colonel George Johnstone, Sir Frederic's twin brother, and Agnes, daughter of Thomas Chamberlayne. Went to Druries House in April 1891. Joined Rifle Brigade 1900, retired 1905.

darling I am so sorry about your tooth ache – & that you have to go & have it out you remember Dr Pritchard said he would not undertake to extract a tooth he has not nerve enough now who is going to do it for you? Mamma is gone off to London for Windsor this morning. She told me she would write to Aunt Clara & ask her to see to you tomorrow. Be sure you don't attempt to get into the train after it moves off dear. I always feel uneasey about that because you stand at the Book Stall reading & forget your train do be careful there's a dear Boy. Aunt Leonie is here staying. She told me how she regaled you with Cake & Strawberries the day you came up to the Dentist. I shall try & run down to see you when I return from my holiday if I can – but you see it is so inconvenient having no place in London where I can sleep for a night. We heard from Jackie on Monday they have got the mumps there & 2 Boys have got some eye disease so you had better not go over there dear.

I leave here all being well on the 28th of this month. Do you get the *Graphic* Friday's was interesting. Let me hear how you are after having your tooth out my own old lamb heaps of love.

From WOOM

Lady Randolph to Winston

Thursday [18 June 1891]   Oakley Court
                                       Windsor

Dearest Winston,

I am so sorry I could not go up to meet you today but it was impossible.

I hope you went to Aunt Clara's. She promised she would look after you. Write here & tell me how you got on with yr tooth.

I shall try & see you one day next week – The weather at last is warmer.

Goodbye & bless you –
Yr loving Mother
JSC

Winston to Lady Randolph

[?19 June 1891]   [Harrow]

Darling Mummy,

I had my tooth taken out very successfully. I remembered nothing but went to sleep & snored throughout the whole performance. Do send me some money

as I am awfully hard up owing to journey money for dentist. I am coming up
to town on Thursday by the 3.30 to have another out, do try and come. Auntie
Clara was very kind.

Goodbye Your loving son
WINSTON S. C.

Cecil Drummond Wolff to Winston

19 June 1891   St James' Club
Piccadilly

Dear Winston,
    The Duchess of Marlborough asked me to send you extracts of a letter which
Lady Randolph has received from your father.

Your sincerely
CECIL DRUMMOND WOLFF

Mrs Everest to Winston

[? June 1891]   Banstead

Do write to poor
little Jackie
dearest.

My darling Winny,
    Don't go to Elstree Jackie has got the mumps poor darling. How are you I
hope keeping well. I am not going to Ventnor on Saturday now – Mamma
wrote this morning to say don't go till Tuesday. I got your letter but I have
not heard anything from Mamma about your coming home on the 11th July.
I think you are very much mistaken because this house will be full of People
being race week so I think you had better not depend on that & I shall be away
I expect – who told you that you were coming. Bell is going to send you some
Mushrooms he gets me some beauties. Mamma comes back from London on

Monday & brings a house full of company for the races next week. Aunt Sarah is coming.

Can't stop to write more it is post time best love my own old darling do write again.

Your loving old
WOOM

Winston to Lady Randolph

[? 21 June 1891]   [Harrow]

Darling Mummy,

Do come up & meet me on Thursday. I come by the 3 o'clock from Harrow. I am very well. I like the Dentist and think him a much more capable man than Pritchard. Please send me £1 as I have had to pay an old Bicycle debt of 10/- that I had quite forgotten.

Also I have to pay 8/- as my share of those windows we smashed. Please send it to me before Tuesday as I have to pay the 8/- then.

Goodbye my darling Mummy,

Ever your loving son
WINSTON S. CHURCHILL

Winston to Lady Randolph

[25 June 1891]   [Harrow]

Darling Mummy,

So sorry you could not come. Have got to pay some of that 'Window Smashing stupidity.' 8/-. Various other items; Will explain *ad lib* Please give me 30/- shall be awfully delighted.

Excuse Telegraphic communication as the Post leaves in 10 minutes. Will arrive on Friday do not leave till Monday morning.

Ever your loving son
WINSTON

Lord Randolph to Winston

27 June 1891   Johannesburg

Dearest Winston,

You cannot think how pleased I was to get your interesting & well written letter & to learn that you were getting on well. I understand that Mr Welldon thinks you will be able to pass your examination into the army when the time comes. I hope it may be so, as it will be a tremendous pull for you ultimately. I have been having a most agreeable travel in this very remarkable country. I expect that when you are my age you will see S Africa to be the most populous & wealthy of all our colonies. I suppose Mama has read you my letters & that you have seen my letters in the *Daily Graphic*, for I cannot tell you more than I have already written. You would have enjoyed an expedition I made last week for shooting purposes. A regular gipsy life, sleeping on a mattress in a bell tent, dressing and washing in the open air & eating round a camp fire. The sport was vy fair & wild & there was much variety of game to shoot. Here I have been examining gold mines & investing money in what I hope will be fortunate undertakings for I expect you & Jack will be a couple of expensive articles to keep as you grow older.

Tomorrow we start for our journey up country staying a few days at Pretoria on the way. My waggons have been slowly treking up through Bechuanaland with Captain Giles[1], Rayner[2] & and the others since the middle of May & ought to be now at Fort Juli in Matabele Land where I hope to join them in about 10 or 12 days. I expect that we shall be vy comfortable & jolly when we get to the waggons. I have not had any roughing it or discomfort yet, as we have always been put up by friends and have avoided the Hotels which are most dirty & uncomfortable. We have a six or seven days journey before us from Pretoria to Juli. We travel in a "spider" a sort of light framed waggonette with eight mules, and do about 50 miles in the day. The accommodation on the road for the night is said to be vy indifferent. I suppose this will just reach you as you are going home for the holidays. I hope you will have a good time at Banstead & that you and Jack will amuse yourself well. Give him my vy best love & tell him how glad I am to hear of his good place in the school. Perhaps he will write to me before long. Goodbye take care of yourself, don't give Mama any trouble.

Ever yr most affte father
RANDOLPH S. CHURCHILL

I am doubtful about being able to bring home a tame antelope. The Bechuanaland stamps I think I can obtain: I have a pointer called Charlie & a shooting pony called Charlie both excellent animals. When we travel we always have our guns ready to secure any game which may show itself.

---

[1] George Edward Giles (1855–1900), late Royal Artillery, who acted as manager of Lord Randolph's tour and had gone out to the Cape a month ahead. He had served in the Kaffir War 1878 and later commanded a troop of Cape Mounted Riflemen.
[2] Hugh Rayner (1860–1924), Surgeon-Captain, Grenadier Guards, who acted as medical officer to the expedition.

Lady Randolph to Winston

Sunday [28 June 1891]   Compton Place[1]
                                                    Eastbourne

Dearest Winston,

I shall be up by one but fear I shall just miss you – I do hope yr face is better & that the abscess has burst. Auntie Leonie promised to look after you today. I wish you were here – such a lovely place – just 15 mts from the sea. It is blowing somewhat but we are going for a long walk notwithstanding. I shall hope to see you tomorrow. If not let me know when the Eton & Harrow match takes place.

                                                Yr loving Mother
                                                        JSC

Winston to Lady Randolph

[29 June 1891]   [Harrow]

Darling Mummy,

It was a pity you could not come to see me on Sat. I did not expect you & so was not disappointed. Mr Searle says there is every chance of my being allowed to come to your concert, however we can talk it over at 'Lords'.

I have copied out Papa's letter and sent it to Jack.

                            Good Bye my darling Mummy.
                    With love & Kisses I remain, Your loving son
                                        WINSTON S. CHURCHILL

Winston to Lady Randolph

[? June 1891]   [Harrow]

Dear Mamma,

I wish you would try & get someone to come down here on Speech Day. I suppose grand mamma Duchess could not come.

Try and get Auntie Clara to come if no inconvenience to her. Do get someone as I shall be awfully 'out of it' if no one comes. Next Thursday is Speech Day.

Please try and arrange something darling Mummy. I hope to be able to spend Lord's at Banstead with you. Jack will probably be well enough by then.

                                            Good Bye Mamma
                    with Love & Kisses I remain, Your loving son
                                        WINSTON S. CHURCHILL

[1] One of the smaller houses of the Dukes of Devonshire.

Lady Wilton to Winston

30 June [1891]   10 Mandeville Place
                                                 Manchester Square

My dear Winston,

It is *so* nice of you asking me to come to Harrow – & I should like it above all things – But – I am obliged to be very busy indeed all this week – & I am not very strong; I am trying to get the Hatch into order. *Next* week I might get down to Harrow. When will you be able to come & stay at the Hatch?

Do tell me – & I will write to your Mama –

I wish, dear, you'd tell me *where* to write to your Papa –

My best love.
Yr very affecte Deputy Mother
LAURA WILTON

Lady Randolph to Winston

[? July 1891]   [?   ]

Dearest Winston,

Too sorry to have missed you – you ought to have wired. Write to me fully about next week – do you want money?

Yr loving
MOTHER

Lady Randolph to Winston

Wednesday [?] July 1891   18 Aldford Street
                                                 London

Dearest Winston,

I thought it was something about money – I send you the £1.1.0. you want & will reserve my lecture for tomorrow!

Affectly
MOTHER

Winston to Lady Randolph

[3 July 1891]   [Harrow]

My darling Mummy,

Please do all you possibly can for me. Think how unhappy I should be being left at Harrow when 90 out of every hundred boys are enjoying themselves. You promised me I should come. It is no special exeat but a regular holiday given in the Summer Term to every boy whose conduct has been such to merit it. I was terribly frightened when I got your letter this morning. The Possibility of my not being able to come being to my mind entirely out of the question. Could you not ask Grandmamma Marlborough to let me stay with her (at least).

I managed all right about Speech day (having taken the precaution of writing & of telegraphing) Mummy darling if you knew or had known how much I was looking forward to my 'Lords' I am sure you would have endeavoured to avoid that Engagement, or make some provision for my holiday.

It will be a poor time indeed for me if I have to go to Lords, Friday & Saturday as a Harrow boy & answer my name every 2 hours & not leave the ground etc (as 100 other unfortunates usually have to do.)

My darling Mummy I am sure you have not been very much troubled about me this term. I have asked for no visits & I forfeited the pleasure of seeing you on Speech Day therefore I do hope you will endeavour not to disappoint me utterly with regard to July 11th & 12th.

Please do come down in any case on Tuesday.

I have many things to talk to you about which take so much longer to write than to tell. How is poor little Jack? I have written several times & sent several newspapers & books for him to read but I have recd no answer; so I conclude he is not well enough to write. I have had Mumps so there is no danger for me.

Where is everybody?

No one has written to me to tell me any news for a long time. Where is Everest. Do try my Darling Mummy to please your

Loving Son
WINSTON S. CHURCHILL

Lady Randolph to Winston

Sunday [5 July 1891]   Banstead

Oh! dear oh! dear what an ado!! You silly old boy I did not mean that you would have to remain at Harrow only that I cld not have you here, as I am *really* obliged to go to Stowe on Saturday. But I shall see you on Friday & can arrange something for you. I shall be at Aunt Clara's. Perhaps she can put you up too. I will write & let you know. I believe Jack is all right – so Everest writes – but he has not written to me tho' I sent him some fruit. I had a long letter from Papa from Johannesburg – in very good spirits & health. He sent his best love to you both – I suppose you write to him? The mail leaves Friday night.

Goodbye my darling. Write to Aldford Street where I go tomorrow.

Your loving
MOTHER

Jack to Winston

5 July 1891   [Elstree]

Dear Winney,

I got all your papers you sent me & thank you very much for them.

I have left off my flanel round my head and am going back to work to morrow I think. I hope you are all right. It is very dull with nothing to do but to read which I do all day long. We shall just have to come away from the ex. on the 13th and the races begin on the 14th.

I can not write much more Woom came to see me on tuesday & said she would try & see you when she comes back from ventnor.

I remain
your loving brother
JSC

Lady Randolph to Winston

Monday [6 July 1891]   18 Aldford Street

Dearest Winston,

It is all right Grandmama Marlborough will put you & Jack up Friday night & I suppose you go back Saturday evening? Write & tell me. I am trying to arrange for a coach – for Lords' –

You must come here the first thing – & mind you make yrself *very* smart –

Yr loving mother
JSC

I have bought a lovely pony for Jack.

Mrs Everest to Winston

Monday 11 a.m. [6 July 1891]   2 Verona Cottages
                                                                        Ventnor

My precious Darling Winnie,

I have just this moment recd your letter the 2nd of yours I have had this morning so I am writing immediately poor old Boy I am very sorry I have neglected writing to you but have been waiting a reply to my last letter to you & was very busy before leaving Banstead. I left last Monday & went to see Jackie Tuesday morning found him looking remarkably well in spite of the mumps. He was much better & the swelling going down. There were about 16

Boys isolated in a house called the Homestead which Jack considered rather dry. However he expected to go back to school this week. He told me about the hamper & 5/- you sent him. Awfully kind of dear Winnie.

Mrs Balaam & I & Charlie go to Oxford on Saturday next. I am going to stay with Mrs Keyte. Charlie has got a very stiff exam to pass. I hope he will succeed. He will have to go up every day for a week – 4 & 6 hours each day. He is up every morning at 6 o'clock working hard for the exam very persevering.

Well my dearest the reason Mamma cannot have you home is the house is to be full of visitors for the race week which commences on the Tuesday tomorrow week. But I don't see why you could not go from Friday till Monday because you could go by yourself & I talked to Jackie about it & he said he did not care about going much & should not feel at all disappointed if I don't go. Mr Sanderson asked him if he would like to go to Lords he has got a Break to go. He is such a contented little Lamb. But I should think you could go quite well but if you do go alone please be careful & get into the right train & change at Cambridge. You see you would return to Harrow the day before the visitors go to Banstead & then perhaps Aunt Clara or some one would see you off to Harrow. Let me know the decision dear soon as you know it yourself.

Mr & Mrs B. send their love to you & Charlie – Mr B. wants to know if you have forgiven him yet. The weather is not very nice here fresh wind. Rather cold for July. I wish Mamma would go & see Jackie. He does look so solemn dear little Man. But in 3 weeks time you will both be home for a long holiday & we will enjoy our little selves will we not.

Now I must finish as I want to write to Jackie. With best love to you my sweet darling.

From your old
WOOM

Winston to Lord Randolph
(*Blenheim Papers*)

[?8 July 1891]   [Harrow]

My dear Papa,

You cannot imagine what vials of wrath you have uncorded. All the papers simply rave. Shareholders, friends of the company, and directors from Sir Donald Currie[1] to the lowest Bottle Washer are up in arms.

Truth, the *Speaker*, *Standard* and others including even the *Harrow Gazette*

---

[1] Donald Currie (1825–1909); shipowner, director of the Castle Line. MP for Perthshire and West Perthshire 1880–1900. KCMG 1881.

devote a column to "Lord Randolph's Grumbles". The *Standard* quotes the *Speaker* & is particularly offensive. It states that – but oh I will not bore you with the yapping of these curs hungry for their money bags.[1]

Speech day has come and gone. Aunt Clara and Miss Winslow[2] came down to Newmarket for the "Julys" and we had great fun – lunched at the King's Head and then I showed Aunty Clara the different objects of interest at Harrow. She was very pleased and I'm sure will send Sunny here. I went to breakfast with Mr Welldon this morning – Lord George Hamilton[3] was there and begged me to remember him to you.

Mr W also asked after you. I get your letters in the *Daily Graphic* when ever they come out. I think them charming. Grandmama sent me a copy of one of your private letters & told Mr Wolfe to copy out another.

Poor Jack has got the mumps! Not very badly though, still it is awfully bad luck. Mama says she is looking out for a pony for him. I shall ride "Gem" whom I look upon as my own. He is very well as is the other – the brown mare. Lords is in a very short time. I expect we shall win as Winchester beat Eton yesterday. Cambridge also defeated Oxford.

Have you shot a lion yet? Mind and do not forget my little antelope. Send me some foreign stamps if you can get any as I have very few of South Africa.

I am going to camp out for a week at the end of the term with about fifty of the Rifle Corps we are under strict military discipline. Eleven other schools are coming and the Battalion (500) will be inspected by Gen E. Wood.

I shall think of you when I am "under canvas".

What would you do if a General Election were to come off now? It might very easily as the Government have received several defeats and have also allowed the initiative to fall from their hands.

Goodbye my dear Papa wishing you luck, fun and health in your proceedings

I remain ever your loving son
WINSTON S. CHURCHILL

---

[1] Lord Randolph's letters concerning his African trip, published in the *Daily Graphic*, drew much unfavourable attention. The *Speaker*, 4 July 1891, said, 'they show his lordship in the light of what the French call a *mauvais coucheur*', and the *Harrow Gazette* was 'very sure that a second-rate American reporter would leave him nowhere in a competition in what is professionally known as the "descriptive line".'

[2] Kathleen Winslow was an American friend of the Jerome sisters.

[3] George Francis Hamilton (1845–1927); third son of 1st Duke of Abercorn and brother of Albertha, Lady Blandford. MP for Middlesex and Ealing 1868–1906. Lord Randolph's colleague in the first and second Salisbury administrations, in which he was First Lord of the Admiralty. Secretary of State for India 1895–1903.

Lady Wilton to Winston

7 July [1891] The Hatch

Many thanks for yours, my dear Winston,

Here I am settled down in the country; & I doubt my being able to come to Harrow for some little time. But I hope to see you here, 'ere long. How are you? & why so much "punishment work"! I go to town probably Thursday afternoon so as to get down early on Friday morning for the Eclipse Stakes where I hope to see "Common" walk in! – I will try to win for you in it. How is Jack? My love to him when you write.

Ever yr affecte Deputy Mother
LAURA WILTON

Winston to Lord Randolph
(*Blenheim Papers*)

[11 July 1891] [50 Grosvenor Square]

Dear Papa,

I am so sorry you have not recd my letters. I have written three times. I am up for the Lords exeat Harrow as usual are winning easily.[1] I am staying with grandmama at Grosvenor Square.

Last night I dined with Millbank and afterwards went on to the Naval Exhibition. I suppose Mama has told you about the Eclipse Stakes. Surefoot, Gouverneur, Common.

I am going to try and see the fireworks tonight at the Crystal Palace. They will be wonderful as the Emperor will be there. Poor Jack cannot come up for exeat on account of infection, but is consoled by Mama's having purchased a beautiful pony for him. I have got a good report so says Mama.

Do send me some stamps in your next letter.

Hoping you will have luck health and pleasure
I remain ever your loving
WINSTON S. CHURCHILL

Lady Randolph to Lord Randolph
(*Blenheim Papers*)
EXTRACT

11 July [1891] 18 Alford Street

Winston is here and is sleeping at your mothers' as there is no room here. We spent the day at Lords yesterday – very hot and tiring and Harrow is

---

[1] At the end of the first day Eton, with all their second innings wickets in hand, were 80 behind Harrow. Harrow won on the following afternoon by seven wickets.

getting much the best of it. Jack is too infectious with the remains of mumps to be allowed up. They both have good reports, but Welldon says W should have special help for the french this summer. I am going to try and find a little governess (ugly) who wants a holiday. Just to talk and read with him. . . . As you may imagine the whole town is in a ferment about the German Emperor and Empress.[1] . . . The Emperor begins his day at eight in the Park riding with half a doz ADC's in uniform and he changes his clothes about five times a day. Margot Tennant[2] sallied forth yesterday on a prancing steed determined to make his acquaintance and she did . . . .

Winston to Jack

[11 July 1891]   [Harrow]

My darling Jack,

I sit down to write you an account of the exeat from beginning to end. But first let me tell you how sorry I was you could not come.

Having eluded the Masters I escaped with the sanction of the authorities to London which I reached on Friday at 11 o'clock. I went, as Mamma had told me to Aldford Street, where I found Mamma & Count Kinsky Breakfasting. (I have been staying you know with Grandmamma at 50.) I then went on to see Grandmamma & after that I went to Lords. I lunched with Grandmamma. In the Afternoon I went again to Lords. Came back & Dined with Milbanke at the Isthmian Club. After dinner we went on to the 'Naval Exhibition'. Most beautiful models & guns of every description. Got home at 11.45.

Sat

Breakfasted with Mamma at 18 Aldford Street. Arranged with Count Kinsky that he should take me to the Crystal Palace, where the German Emperor was going. (he Drove me in his phaeton.)

The programme of what we saw (everything of course was awfully well done on account of the Emperor) is as follows.

Wild Beasts. (wonderful never seen any thing like them.)

Fire Brigade Drill before the Emperor.

This was perfectly splendid. There were nearly 2000 firemen & 100 Engines. They all marched past the Emperor to the music of a band of infantry.

[1] William II, Emperor of Germany (1859–1941), son of Emperor Frederick III and Princess Victoria, eldest daughter of Queen Victoria. Succeeded 1888, abdicated 1918. Married 1881 Princess Augusta of Schleswig-Holstein-Sonderburg-Augustenburg (1858–1921).

[2] Emma Alice Margaret Tennant (1864–1945), fifth daughter of Sir Charles Tennant 1st Baronet. She was to marry in 1894 H. H. Asquith.

Then the Engines trotted past & finally all the lot Galloped past as hard as they could go. Then we went & had dinner.

The head man said he could not possibly give us a table but Count K. spoke German to him & it had a wonderful effect. Very tolerable dinner. Lots of Champagne which pleased your loving brother very much.

Then ensued a most exciting incident.

'Row with Kaffir'.

We went to see Panorama but it was closed so we went to the Switch Back Railway. On the way however we came across a new thing called the "Aerial Car" [sketch of aerial car]. Which rushed across a wire Rope nearly 300 yards in length & awfully high. We waited about 10 minutes for our turn & then the thing went wrong, & the Gun summoning people to the fireworks went off, so Count K & I clambered over the rails in anger & wished to go. However a half breed sort of Kaffir who was in charge attempted to stop Count K. caught him by the coat tail. The Count whom you know is immensely strong grew furious and caught hold of the blackguards hand, crushing the fingers in his grasp; the Mulatto dropped the coat & took to swearing telling Count K. that He should think himself 'd – d lucky' that he did not pitch him over the banni- ters. 'By ———' said Count Kinsky 'I should like to see you touch me.' 'You go and learn manners' retorted the cad. 'But not from you' said Count K.

Then the audience & the other people made the scoundrel be quiet & we went on our way angry but triumphant.

The Fireworks were wonderful & I wished you had been there to see them.

They began with a perfect volley, rockets etc.

Then there were two great set pieces of Cornflowers & Roses (the Emperors Favourit Flowers) which afterward changed to the heads of the Emperor & Empress. [sketches of Emperor and Empress].
Then there was the Battle of the Nile.

The ships actually moved & the cannonading was terrific. Finally L'Orient blew up. Then a great mixture when everything was let off in all directions.

Then we went & got our coat & had each an American drink & then we went to our carriage. Count K. drives beautifully & we passed with our fast pair of horses everything on the road.

I must describe the Emperor's uniform. A helmet of bright Brass surmounted by a white eagle nearly 6 inches high [sketch of Emperor's helmet]. A polished steel cuirass & a perfectly white uniform with high boots [sketch of Emperor's high boots]. Of course you know Harrow won by 5 wickets.[1] I could not

---

[1] He was wrong. Harrow won by seven wickets (see page 255).

K

'smash an Eton hat' as I had to leave the ground early to go to the Crystal Palace.

I hear your pony is a regular beauty & the fastest on Newmarket heath, but I don't believe he will beat the 'Gem . . . .'.

I saw 'Touty' at the Match. Kim I saw looking dirty disreputable & ill.

The 'City Clerk' is at Staines.

I shall soon see you so will now say good bye.

Ever your loving brother
WINSTON S. CHURCHILL

Reverend J. E. C. Welldon to Lady Randolph

13 July 1891   Harrow

Dear Lady Randolph Churchill,

You will, I am sure, forgive my making a suggestion about Winston. Mr Moriarty, the master who takes charge of my Army boys, is very anxious that he should spend his holidays or a good part of his holidays in France, so as to enhance his getting more marks in French when his examination comes on. It will probably be suggested that he should spend some future holidays in Germany.

I do not know if the idea of sending him to France will fall in with your own plans, and of course, if he goes there, it will be necessary that he should go with a steady purpose of work; but I may say that I have again and again found it convenient to send many boys abroad for the holidays, and I could easily recommend a family in which he might live, if you could spare him.

I broke this painful subject to him in conversation some days ago and I do not doubt it involves some self sacrifice, but Lord Randolph has so strongly argued the importance of letting him enter the Army straight from Harrow that it seems only right to point out a means of increasing his prospect of success.

Believe me Sincerely yours
J. E. C. WELLDON

Winston to Lady Randolph

[?14 July 1891]   [Harrow]

My darling Mummy,

Mr Welldon told me last night that he had written to you about my going to spend "at least 4 weeks" in France. His ideal of course is a 'family' one of his own 'specials'. I told Papa when he came down that I ought (in Mr W's opinion) to go, but he said "utter nonsense, if you like I'll get a German scullery maid for Banstead". I'm sure you would not like me to be away the greater part of the holidays with some horrid French Family. It would be perfectly ——— well unpleasant. Besides practically there is no hurry. I have very nearly 3 years at the outside limit.

Furthermore Dudley is not going & he has 9 months less time than I. How can you expect me to work all the term & then go to a filthy den all the holidays.

How frightfully dull it would be. I shouldn't see Jack nor you, nor Everest at all. Of course it is (as says Welldon) entirely in your hands. But I am sure you will not send me to any such abominable drudgery with your free consent.

Even if the worst comes to the worst you could send me to some of your friends & not to the 'respectable creatures'. A governess would I am sure answer all the immediate colloquial requirements. As Papa absolutely veto'ed the idea & as I beg you to let me have a bit of fun.

I remain Your loving son
WINSTON S. CHURCHILL

PS Really I feel less keen about the Army every day. I think the church would suit me much better. Am well, safe, & happy. About Fire works ask Count K.

Lady Wilton to Winston
EXTRACT

16 July [1891]   The Hatch

Dearest Winston,

Tell me when your holidays are – & then we'll settle a time for you to come here if your mother doesn't object. . . .

Best love from Yr ever affecte Deputy Mother
L. WILTON

Winston to Lady Randolph

[? 19 July 1891]   [Harrow]

My darling Mummy,

I have been waiting 'depuis longtemps' for an answer. You might send me a line just to let me know what you intend. I am going to camp out till the Saturday so I will not be home till Sat week.

I have been made a Lance Corporal so I expect to have some fun. I shall just see you before you start, as you do not go away till the 2nd of Aug.

The Rifle Corps are going to 'Bisley' on Thursday. I am sorry to be so importunate but I shall need some £.s.d. Please send me some darling Mummy & above all send it in time. Do write and tell me your arrangements & where you will be on the 28.

Good Bye my darling
I remain, Ever your loving son
WINSTON S. CHURCHILL

WSC to Lord Randolph
(Blenheim Papers)

22 July 1891

My dear papa,

Thank you so much for your letter. It was so kind of you to write to me. You must have such a large amount of long letters to write that I wonder you get any time to yourself.

I have just been reading your description of the Kimberley and De Beer diamond mines. I think your letters very interesting. The papers are exceedingly spiteful & vicious, shareholders, directors etc of the Castle Line have not calmed down yet.

I never meant you to bring home a 'live' antelope. What I meant was a head for my room.

The African stamps are very good. But I suppose by now (22 July) you are out of the region of stamps, newspapers etc. What fun you must be having. I do wish I were 'out' with you. How is Mr Williams! I hope you won't stay away more than 6 months more. "Punch" has got a very stupid article in which they assumed that Capt Gwynned writes the letters & reads them to you for approval.

I spent the "Lords Exeat" with Grandmamma in London. I had tremendous fun. On the Saturday I got Count Kinsky to take me [to the] Crystal Palace, whither the German Emperor was going. There was a grand review of all the Country Fire brigades before HIM. About 3000 Firemen & 100 Engines, a fine sight. We had splendid seats & saw without any crush or struggle. The Emperor's uniform is worthy of description. A bright brass helmet coming right down the nape of his neck [Sketch] surmounted by a magnificent white eagle nearly 6 inches high. Black tin cuirass and white uniform.

Then of course there was a most splendid show of Fire-works. The German Emperor has made a great impression I believe, though there are those who denounce him as a prig.

Of course Harrow won the match, by 7 wickets. I am going to camp out at the end of the term for 5 or 6 days at Aldershot. I shall think of you, who will probably be doing the same thing, some distance away.

Jack is all right now. The mumps have left him no less 'hale and hearty' than before. He wrote me such a beautiful letter yesterday, 8 sides very well written. I am getting on all right in my work, except the German at which I . . . [?] Mr Welldon is doing his best with Mamma to get me sent abroad for the holidays. I hope she will turn a deaf ear.

I go home next week and will write again when there.

Good Bye dear Papa, With best love and kisses,

I remain Your loving son

WINSTON S. CHURCHILL

Lady Randolph to Lord Randolph
(*Blenheim Papers*)

EXTRACT

24 July [1891]   33 Hill Street
                                        Berkeley Square

I was going to have a quiet evening after the people had gone when I got a frantic message from Mary G [Gerard] imploring me to come and dine and sleep at Moulton [Street] as she had something very particular she wanted to tell me, and I could help her. I went over and found her in a dreadful state of mind and Billy too. It appears that it is quite true about his cook and that the night before he had discovered her with a valet whereupon she bolted and Billy was like a madman. The moment I arrived he took me off and burst into tears and told me the whole story how he could "worship" this woman, how he had offered her ten thousand pounds a year if she would live with him, and how she wouldn't – which I don't believe is true. Well to make a long story short I can't get out of it for he swore he would shoot himself if he did not find her – and I passed the rest of the night with Mary who was going to leave at once . . . I feel so sorry for poor Mary. She was in such a rage – and Billy fancies she knows nothing. She said "fancy he came and lived with me a fortnight ago fresh from the cook who was probably fresh from the valet". She swore she *never* would have anything to say to him again – and would have Hugh T [?] about as much as she liked. Meanwhile they have come to town and are dining out together and though a good many people know of the cook there is not much talk. . . . I had a letter from Welldon about Winston, I went to see him Thursday to discuss matters. Welldon wanted me to send the boy abroad for five weeks in a french family – as he says it is absolutely necessary for him to get on with his french if he is to pass his next exam. After talking to him

(Welldon) he thinks a good governess will do as well – and I think so too if I can find the right kind – but if I can't I shall have to send him away. Welldon gave me an excellent account of him and said his next report would be very good and he was most anxious to meet your views and get him to Sandhurst next year – "a triumph for me and for the boy". . . .

Winston to Lady Randolph

[? July 1891]   [Harrow]

Darling Mummy,

I am quite well, happy and contented. How sweet!!! I am coming home on Tuesday; Jack on Wednesday Banstead Thursday.

Do try & make arrangments about my shooting, I am awfully keen. I have been working hard at my Examinations as I hope to get a Remove.

Good Bye darling Mummy,
I remain, Your loving son
WINSTON S. CHURCHILL

Winston to Lady Randolph

[? 24 July 1891]

My darling Mummy,

I am so sorry I missed you. I did send a telegram but I thought you were staying at 18 Aldford Street. I can't tell you how happy I am to hear that I am not to go abroad for the holidays. I enjoyed myself immensely at Wimbledon yesterday. I went to the "Revolver Range" & shot 12 shots with a full sized weapon.

About the Camp.

25 – 30 Harrow Boys are going under charge of a Master who is a Lieutenant. 13 other Public Schools send detachments to form 1 Battalion of Cadets about 300 strong. Harrow & Winchester together form 1 Company.

The board & Lodging is to cost 30/- for the week, but I expect the food will be passing meagre so as I shall have to amuse myself in the afternoons, Money will be most agreeable. We do not have to take the 30/- with us it is put in the Bill. On one of the Days you must try & come down to see me at the camp. I will let you know the exact address at a later date. I am in a tent with Dudley, young Millbanke & 2 other boys. There will be lots of amusements & it will be very good fun. I shall come away on Sat.

I spent a lot yesterday at the camp at Bisley so I will 'leave it to you' how much to give me for next week. I should think 35/- would be enough.

Will you buy me a pair of 'butcher boots' to ride in at camp. Marshall & Willats have got my measure or perhaps you could get them at Newmarket. I want something to pull on quickly over uniforms as I am not allowed to appear out of uniform.

If you like you might send "Gem" & the groom to put up at a stable there so that I could ride the darling & not a 'hired screw'.

I enclose a copy of the regulations, which will show you how strict everything is. We shall be inspected by Brig-Gen Drury Lowe.[1] If you know any officers in camp at Aldershot you might give them the tip to make my acquaintance. I have recd a long letter from Papa in which he says how great was his pleasure at receiving my long & well written letter.

Ever your loving son
WINSTON S. CHURCHILL

C. J. Balaam to Winston

[? July 1891]   Verona Cottage
                                                 Ventnor
Dear Mr Winston,

I am very much obliged to you for so kindly tendering me your congratulations and good wishes. It was the Oxford Local (Senior). In return I must congratulate you on your success, please excuse me being late in doing so. I hope in the future you will always be equally successful. Believe me to remain

Yours truly
C. J. BALAAM

Jack to Winston

Sunday ? [Summer 1891]   Banstead

Dear Winney,

Woom is so buisey that she asked me to write and ask you to leave that watch which you have got at Grosvenor Square and tell some one to take it back for your old one has arrived and is waiting your arrival here.

The Den is dirty inside but has withstood the weather well Nothing is spoilt except the bag's ropes are broken and there is something rong with the lever. I dont know quite what it is, but I will find out, I will try and get the Den clean

---

[1] Drury Curzon Drury-Lowe (1830–1908), Lieutenant-General, lately Inspector-General of Cavalry, Aldershot. KCB 1882.

by the time you come It is very hard to aproach for huge thistles & stinging nettles are all round about, and the ditch is empty of water. I shall not make much noise for there are a lot of Rabbits in the gras there which has grown very high and we will have a feast.

Dodo is quite well but is shut up Jem, Pady, Brown Mare are all well

Mama is writing and sending you some money. She has got a new little dog named [?] Ponsel I do think I have told you everything of importance. Wire what train you come by, & we will meet you.

Sunny & Co are here.

best love from Mama

I remain Your loving Brother

JACK S CHURCHILL

Lady Randolph to Lord Randolph
(*Blenheim Papers*)

EXTRACT

29 July [1891]   Banstead

. . . Mama is asleep in the drawing room Jack playing with the soldiers and I are in the little hall writing – you can see us! Winston is camping out with Dudley Marjoribanks etc, I send you his letter. I am sorry it is so wet for them. I hope to goodness he won't catch cold. I am trying to arrange to get a French tutor over from Cambridge 3 or 4 times a week and the other days Winston can prepare lessons. He is quite alive to the necessity of working – he has improved very much in looks and is quite sensible now . . . Since beginning this who should turn up but Winston who arrived from Aldershot having got permission to leave. He says it was too much of a good thing camping out in this downpour – and au fond I am glad he left – as he would only have taken cold. He is very well and in tearing spirits. . . .

Winston to Lord Randolph
(*Blenheim Papers*)

[20 August 1891]   Banstead

Dear Papa,

I got your letter some time ago and immediately wrote an answer, but determined to wait till I got home before I sent it off. My Portmanteau was eight days on the road so I was unable to send it until it came since then I have no excuse whatever.

'Here I am at Banstead leading what to me is an almost ideal existence'.

Today (Aug 20) we got your telegram and rejoiced. In the afternoon we went to Boro Green to see the yearlings. Lacey seemed very enthusiastic about two colts of yours (Robert the Devil and Cymbal colts). I have been riding 'Norce' and also 'Paddy'. I and Jack have both learned to jump.

All the Horses are very well here & I believe they are all right at the 'stables'

We are all staying in doors today (Aug 21) on account of the customary English climate. [There is a drawing of rain across this sentence]

Mamma took me out to dinner at Lord Gerards. Captain Mitchell was there but no one else of interest.

Col Oliver comes here today to sleep. Count Kinsky is already staying here. We are all very well, and happy and hope that you will soon be back.

> With much love I remain ever your loving son
> WINSTON S. CHURCHILL

Lady Randolph to Lord Randolph
(*Blenheim Papers*)

EXTRACT

21 August [1891]　　　　　　　　　　　　　　　　　　Banstead

. . . I have found a rather nice young man from Cambridge. Winston will only have to have four weeks of work but it will be better than nothing. The boys are very happy. Kinsky has gone out with them to put up a target. I am going to try and borrow a gun for Winston, he must learn to shoot. I shall be very careful about it. Both boys ride very well – particularly Jack. . . .

Mark Milbanke to Winston

22 August 1891　　　　　　　　　　　　　　　　　　Eartham
　　　　　　　　　　　　　　　　　　　　　　　　　　Chichester

Dear Churchill,

I am so sorry I cannot come to stay with you, but we have got some people coming here which I am afraid I must stay for and then after they've gone away it will be September and I rather want to stay here for partridge shooting as I think there are a good lot of birds here. I am very sorry as I should like to come very much. I suppose you are riding a great deal, and having great fun. We had much better fun after you had gone, and never had another afternoon parade except once when there was an alarm. On the Sunday we all went up the Basingstoke Canal in boats which was great fun.

> I remain yrs truly
> MARK MILBANKE

Count Kinsky to Winston

2 September 1891
Freiung 4
Vienna

My dear Winnie,

I enclose a 1 fl & one 2 fl stamp. I meant to send the same to Jackie but they only brought me one specimen of each by mistake. However I will get his the moment I come back to Vienna – after the manoeuvres. I am off there now in ½ an hour. I have been very busy all day with my arrangements – & am also now in great hurry – I couldnt leave the rifle here for various reasons – one of them because it wanted mending. You couldnt have used it anyway – I got you a gun for rabbit shooting instead so this will do just as well if not better & now good bye Best love to Jack.

Remember me kindly to Mamma & Grandmamma

Yours afftly
Ch Kinsky

Lady Randolph to Lord Randolph
(*Blenheim Papers*)

EXTRACT

11 September [1891]
Banstead

... I am going to town on Tuesday, to see the last of the boys, who return to School on the 16th. They have been as happy as kings riding and shooting and lately they have had great fun building a house. We had tea there today – the Coopers came over to luncheon. Mama Clara and Leonie are here and one of Clara's children. It is a bit overpowering – but I don't mind. . . .

Winston to Lady Randolph

[19 September 1891]
[Harrow]

Darling Mummy,

Welldon wants you to write to him & 'explain' why I did not come back Thursday. 'The Doctors Certificate' says he 'accounts for Wed.' I told the animal I understood that if you telegraphed, it was sufficient. "Nay" saith he. But *I* see, & *he* says he does not want to make a row. So he proposes that you should write him a letter saying that I was unable to 'favour him with my prescence' on account of———————anything. Twiggez-vous?

Don't say anything about the Theatre or that would make him rampant. Merely say I looked tired & pale from the journey (as indeed I did) & that combined with the fact that you wanted me to see a doctor induced you to 'Keep me back'. I have got a little room to my self this term.

Do write to him by return post.

With much love & many kisses
I remain your dull homesick exiled darling
WINSTON S. CHURCHILL

Reverend J. E. C. Welldon to Lady Randolph
(*Blenheim Papers*)

21 September 1891   Harrow School

Dear Lady Randolph Churchill,

Thank you very much for your letter about Winston. I will not be hard upon him. I am anxious for him to make as much progress as possible this year. The only condition on which he can pass into Sandhurst is that he should work hard. Will you let me arrange for his Christmas holiday after carefully discussing with my army masters what is best for him? They will probably send him to Germany. I should, of course, not wish to take any step that you might disapprove, but I promised Lord Randolph that I would spare no effort to get him into the army.

With kind regards, sincerely yours
J. E. C. WELLDON

Winston to Lady Randolph

[? 22 September 1891]   [Harrow]

My Darling Mummy,

I am quite settled down & happy now. My room is very pretty & I have not bought any pictures, only 1 pr of candlesticks (second hand) a mantel board, & a curtain for my bed. These are all necessities. I have been allowed to leave off German & take up Chemistry instead. I am so glad, it means that I can safely declare that I will pass next June. In the 9 months that elapse between Sandhurst & the Army I can easily 'rechauffer' my German. Besides obviously the first thing is to get into Sandhurst. I am told that I can easily get up enough Science in the time I have got. Don't forget to write to Welldon. I want you to send me a P.O.O. for 11/- which I have got to pay for my food & necessaries at Camp, during the 2 days I was there.

With love & kisses I remain
Your loving son
WINSTON S. CHURCHILL

Lady Randolph to Lord Randolph
(*Blenheim Papers*)

EXTRACT

25 September [1891]   2 Connaught Place

Dearest R,

At last I have seen the boys safely off. Winston conveniently worked himself
into a bilious attack and had to stay on a couple of days. On the whole he has
been a very good boy – but honestly he is getting a bit too old for a woman to
manage. After all he will be 17 in 2 months and he really requires to be with a
man. I send you Welldon's letter. You will have time to answer me before I
decide anything. Of course it will be hard upon him not spending his holidays
at home – but after all I shan't know what to do with him, and it will be
impossible for him to pass his exam if he does not get a smattering of German
Young Millbank spent the last week at Banstead – but he is rather dull and
stupid. Winston will be all right the moment he gets into Sandhurst. He is
just at the "ugly" stage. – slouchy and tiresome. I managed to get a very nice
little man from Cambridge – very clever spoke 12 languages. He might be
made use of later to travel with him –. It will be all the better for Jack [?] to
be without him – the difference in their ages is beginning to tell and poor
Jack is quite worn out rushing about after Winston. . . .

Mrs George Johnstone to Winston

EXTRACT

22 September [1891]   Cranbury Park
                                                Winchester

. . . I venture to write to you about Charlie who has been very ill, but is
better; and returning to Mr Griffith's to-morrow: he likes *you* much: but I
fear he had a very unhappy half last time as it seems he was continually bullied
and kicked etc by an older boy in his room. Charlie hadn't complained, as he
did not wish to get the boy in disgrace: and I only found it out when he was ill.
I went down to Harrow last week and saw the culprit and I don't think he'll
bully again! I also saw Mr Welldon who has kindly promised to change
Charlie's house as soon as he can. My boy is only 13 & not at all strong, & I
am venturing to ask you a favour: it is to look after my boy as much as you
can and if you don't think he is well and happy kindly write me a line.

Charlie never *will* complain but perhaps he'd tell *you* more than he'd write
to me: & if you see or hear of any bullying, please speak to the "Bullies" as of
course at your age they would obey you etc. . . .

Jack to Winston

Wednesday 23 September 1891   [Elstree]

Dear Winney,

Woom wrote to me & said you wanted your £2. I have got them in my desk and am sending them to you now did you get the Books? Let me Know if you do or not I *enclose the £2.*

I remain
JACK S. CHURCHILL

R. J. Lacey to Winston

26 September 1891   Boro Green Hall
                                                        [Cambridgeshire]

Dear Mr Winston,

I ought to have replied ere this to your kind note received some little time since, but having been so very heavily engaged, I must beg of you to accept my apology for not doing so.

Your short visit to the old Hall with your brother gave me and my Father very great pleasure and when next you are over at Banstead or your brother, and can spare the time for a ride over it will give us very great pleasure to see you both.

The yearlings and greyhounds are going on splendidly.

I find the overcoat was not sent to Sherwoods, but dare say it is all right, and I will write to the House Steward or Butler at Banstead asking him to send it on to Sherwoods where I shall most likely call in the course of the next week.

Believe me, Sincerely yours
R. J. LACEY

PS Perhaps you will kindly send the Butler a line to forward the coat to The Rutland Hotel, Newmarket.

WSC to Lord Randolph
(*Blenheim Papers*)

27 September [1891]   .   Harrow

My darling Papa,

Here I am back at Harrow after a very good time at Banstead. I began shooting and had some very fine sport but I don't think I killed very many partridges. I went to stay with Grandmamma at Windsor for a day or two and we had very good fun. In the morning I rode with my future uncle

[Gordon WILSON] and on Monday I went to see the Scots Guards drill under command of Adjutant Pultney[1] sometimes pronounced Putty. I rode almost every day at Banstead for 2 or 3 hours. Twice we went over to Boro-Green to see the yearlings. They are awfully pretty. Milbanke came down to stay towards the end of the holidays and together we went there to see the Rodpers [?]. put on the colts after Doncaster sales.

Jack and I amused ourselves with building a "den" at the corner of the "Gorse." When you come home you must come and see it. It has 2 rooms and 2 storeys (the upper storey is a shelf). [Attached is a diagram marked 'Plan']. About my Further. I am going in in June as originally intended and everybody says that if I work I will get through. Algebra and Latin are my two weakest subjects, History Science and French are good for me. Marks to be got in order to get through comfortably:

Subjects	Maximum	What I ought to get
Latin	2000	700
Mathematics	2500	1000
French	2000	1300
History	2000	1500
Science	2000	1200
Essay	500	300
Geometrical drawing	1000	500
Freehand	500	250
	Total	6750

How are you? I know a Harrow boy who has been to Kimberley in the summer holidays and he told me that people out there said that you were looking ill. Mama has got a big map of S.A. on which she follows your route. I wish you had taken me. What fun I should have had. Have you shot my little "antelope" yet? When are you coming back? Give my love to Captain Gwenydd. I read your last letter (at Fort Tuli) in the D.G. and thought it much the best that you have written, especially the end. I hear the horrid Boers are incensed with you. It would have been much wiser, if you had waited till you came back, before you "slanged the beggars." Have You Found a Gold Mine? What beautiful diamonds those were you sent Mamma! Please don't forget my stamps. The Bechuanaland expecially are very rare in England. When this reaches you, you *ought* to be on your way home. Please bring home the Pointer and also the pony if you can, the Pointer would be

[1] William Pulteney Pulteney (1861–1941), who became Lieutenant-Colonel commanding Scots Guards 1904–8 and Lieutenant-General Commanding 3rd Army Corps in France, 1914–18.

very useful at Banstead. And we could I have no doubt find a good place for "Charlie." That horrid Conybeare[1] has written to say that "he considers the fare of the Grantally Castle simply unequalled" perhaps it is. The papers have not been quite so vicious lately. But I suppose Mama sends you the "Romaiques" [*Romeikes*].[2] I am working very hard this term but hope to see myself safely through in June. I hope to be able to meet you at Paddington before three months are passed and with best wishes for good luck to all and love and kisses to yourself.

I remain your loving son
WINSTON S. CHURCHILL

Jack send Best Love and will write himself. WSC

Jack to Winston

Sunday 27 September 1891   [Elstree]

Dear Winney,

I am making the hammocks but they will be very small and you will only jus be able to get into them, did you mean them to go in the sleping compartments or in the day, shall I net some bags to keep things in for the den. I can make them any size.

Write to me and send me some swaps if you can. I hope Woom is better. I am just going to write to her. I am just going to church cant write now till afterwards. I have now come back from chappel. It is very cold here. Write and tell me if you want the big book of stamps do send me some swaps for I cannot do anything as I am. I hope Woom goes to the den sometimes. Thanks for the "Daily Graphic". Have you written to Papa. We shall soon come home, I come back on the 12th [December] on Sat.

I must say good bye now with best love & kisses. By the way Lady Claud Hamilton[3] came down yesterday & asked after you, But did not give me anything.

With much love I remain Your loving brother
JACK S. CHURCHILL

---

[1] Charles Augustus Vansittart Conybeare (1853–1919). Radical MP for Camborne or North-West Cornwall. In 1888 Lord Randolph had been instrumental in securing his suspension from the House of Commons for one month for reflecting on the impartiality of the Speaker. In 1889, he was imprisoned for three months in Derry Gaol under the Coercion Act.

[2] Romeikes and Curtice, a Press cutting agency. In later years WSC subscribed to Durrants.

[3] Carolina (1857–1911), third daughter of Edward Sacheverell Chandos Pole, who married in 1878 Lord Claud Hamilton (1843–1925), second son of 1st Duke of Abercorn.

Mrs Everest to Winston

Monday 3 p.m. [28 September 1891]   Banstead

My darling Winnie,

I have just recd your nice letter & very glad I am to hear you are settling down so comfortably at school once more & fancy having a room all to yourself but my dearest Boy do let me impress it upon you to be careful of your fire & candle at night don't go to sleep & leave it burning by your Bedside.

I am very much distressed about your 2 postal orders. I put them in one of the little drawers of the looking glass in your little room I think but I remember saying to you I have put your P. orders in this drawer & I never thought of them from that day till this. Mary says she put all stray letters she found in the drawers into your writing desk so will you devote 1 hour & search very dilligently in the desk look in all the empty envelopes. Also in that blue satin box. I rather think they may be loose in the desk one of the compartments. Why ever did you never think about them all the time you were here. Mind & look through all the envelopes & write & tell me if you find them.

I had a letter from our darling Jackie this morning he does not seem to get over that drowsy feeling. I hope it is not the forerunner of an illness – it is cruel he was completely worn out up every night till 11 o'clock & all the fagging he went through each day poor child it was enough to knock him up.

Mamma & Aunt Sarah, Mr Wilson & 2 more gents came on Friday & have all gone again this morning. Telegram came from Annie this morning to say she is ill in bed at C. Place. The Doctor came to see me this morning he says I must not leave my room for another week or 10 days so I cannot visit the den. He also says I must not go to London for November so I am in a pretty strait. I expect I shall have to go to Ventnor again. Will you please write & tell me what you did with the table cloth you took to the den the day you had the tea fight there, it cannot be found anywhere. I have told Edney about the overcoat to send it. Your diamond pin is all safe here take care of the Lapis pin dear also your gold links you lost your other gold pair last term. If I were you I would buy a cheap pin for common wear before you lose those good ones. Did the Matron get my note & did they find your other shirts & things. Mamma said you would get yourself some black ties & thick stockings for foot ball. I am sending you a dozen new Handkerchiefs so do not buy any. I shall have to make them so they will not come for some days. How I do miss you both. My only consolation my 2 Boys. I hope you will try & work well dearest this term to please His Lordship on his return & your Mamma has given you every pleasure & indulgence she could these holidays so I am sure you will try & do your best to please them & disappoint some of your relations who prophecy a future of profligacy for you. I trust you may be kept from all evil & temptation.

I will pray for you & don't forget to pray hourly to be kept my sweet precious dear Boy.

> Much love from your loving
> W.

Winston to Lady Randolph

[? September 1891]   [Harrow]

Darling Mummy,

I am getting on all right but wish you would wire particulars about the 'APPOINTMENT' or write to Mr Welldon. Do come down to see me. There is no meeting on now. I hope you will arrange Tuesday for appointment not Thursday. I am very glad to hear of Papa's expected return. There is of course no news of any sort, so with love

> I remain Your ever loving
> WINSTON S. CHURCHILL

Winston to Lady Randolph

[? September 1891]   [Harrow]

My darling Mummy,

Why have you not written to me, as you said you would, in answer to my 3 letters! I think it is very unkind of you because I am very dull here, and am working very hard. I don't know whether you have made the appointment I asked you to for Tuesday or anything. If Everest did not write to me I should hardly imagine there was such a place as Banstead. Please do write or wire about the appointment. I suppose you are busy with your 'race party' & so have not time to send me a line. I have been back 10 days & you have not sent me a single word. If you have not time to write you might telegraph, that takes very little time.

> Please darling mummy do write to your Loving son
> WINSTON S. CHURCHILL

Winston to Lady Randolph

[? September 1891]   [Harrow]

Darling Mummy,

Oho! Aha! What did you say? Every letter I wrote – eh? You would answer – was it not so? And now Behold I have written 3 long epistles & not one single SOLITARY LINE have I recd. Darling Mummy please do make an appointment for me at the "surgeons" on Tuesday if you leave it later I shall have to play football. I am going to sell my bicycle for a Bull-dog. I have known him some time & he is very tame & affectionate. His Pedigree is:

Dods
     By Kingcroft   out of Dods
  Gamester – Little   Blind Turk
       Dorset   – Bismarck

He is a celebrated blood dog & worth a £10. I have never had a decent dog of my own & Papa told me he used to have a bulldog at Eton so why not I at Harrow.

My bicycle is no good to me now I am too big for it & besides While I have got Gem to Ride . . .

Remember the Lurcher Puppy I was promised? I have asked credible judges about the dog & they all say he is a very good animal. So please write my mummy & give your gracious consent & I will have the bicycle cleaned up & sent down. (The bicycle cost £7 it is now worth about £4 & if I sold it would fetch £3). I am going to exchange.

Good bye my bird
With much love I remain your ever loving son
WINSTON S. CHURCHILL

Lady Randolph to Winston

Tuesday [29 September 1891]   Banstead

Dearest Winston,

I confess that I have been very remiss about writing – but I have been too busy. Do as you like about yr bicycle but it wld be wiser I think to keep it – a dog is sometimes a nuisance. I can only write you a hurried line as the post is off, but I will do so shortly & tell you all the news. You have been very naughty about the horses – Norah has a splint etc. Papa wires that he will leave Capetown early in Dec. You never dismantled the tent! Mr Murruta rode Gem & liked her. Daisy nearly went off with me.

Goodbye my darling. Will write again.
Yr loving
MOTHER

Winston to Lady Randolph

[? September 1891]

Darling Mummy,

With your permission I will get the Bull dog. As if I choose I can get whelps from her worth 30/- each as she is a Kingcraft. Thank you very much darling Mamman for your letter. I was afraid that, by your silence, you were angry about Nora. Please do not delay to make an appointment for Sat. with some doctor as I ought to be playing football now only I am prevented by Mr Searle's kindness. Mr Welldon has been taking such a lot of trouble in arranging private lessons for me. Do write him a letter. He really takes more trouble of me than any other 10 boys. I think I can show you a little boy who would do very well for groom, when you come down here. He is very small – 15 yrs – good character – strong (very) & sensible. He is the gymnasium boy. When you come you might look at him.

Good bye darling Mummy. Please let me know about the appointment.

Ever yours
WINSTON S. CHURCHILL

Mrs Everest to Winston

Friday 4 p.m. [? 2 October 1891]   Banstead

My darling Boy,

I recd your letter this morning & hasten to reply in order to present you with my humble opinion regarding the contents of it. In the first place it will cost about 3 or 4£ to get your Bicycle repaired & in the 2nd it will cost 30/- or 2£ to send it to Harrow & then what on earth is the good of your having a Bull Dog unless it is to keep us all in terror of our lives – you will not spend your holidays here again probably – & your Bicycle as it is is quite worth the value of the dog – besides His Lordship gave you the Bicycle & he would not like you to part with it. When you make an exchange the value should be equal. You are not wise about money matters my dear Boy. I hope you will reconsider your Bargain before you decide so hastily. The Bicycle some time or other will afford you more amusement & pleasure than a dangerous dog & besides the expense of repairs & carriage of Bicycle. I am so glad Jackie found the Postal orders & you have got them safe. I told Mrs Keen about your hamper & she said she was very sorry but she had not time to make the Pie the Butcher did not send the veal in time – I told her to get 2 chickens & stuff them all, 1 duck & stuff him too & roast them also 2 or 3 pots of our own made jam fruit out of our garden. She will send them off on Monday morning – did you get your luggage alright to Harrow this time it is always best to take it with you up from the Station. Well dear I have not been out of my room yet I am much better but not well yet – I may be allowed out next week. The Doctor is coming to see me tomorrow he has not been since Monday. Fancy that naughty Sonny took Loder's little girl & Mable Bell across the plank to the island on the pond & they all fell into the pond no doubt he pushed them in as he was first & managed to scramble up on to the island without getting wet but the other two poor children were drenched & terribly frightened – poor Mable got a whipping in the bargain. He is going home tomorrow & Mrs Jerome is going too. The house will be full next week for the races. Mrs Jerome thought I might turn out of my room & go off to Connaught Place. Poor Annie there is very ill indeed in Bed not able to stand & no one to do anything for her.

I had a letter from Jackie last night he is alright bless him. I will try to remember to ask Mr Richmond for some more stamps for you – Jackie took his Album to school with him I hope he will not get it spoiled & mucked about I am afraid he will, you had better caution him. Have I sent you 3 Black Waistcoats let me know dear also if you receive a small parcel of 2 shirts &c I sent off yesterday. I am sending you 1 dozen new Handkerchiefs on Monday with the hamper. Are you always going to have the room to yourself or is it only temporary.

Old Mr Wickes sent me a lot of lovely grapes from Ventnor out of his green house. I am so glad you are well my sweet mind & try & get through the exam my precious loving darling old lamb – much love & kisses from

Your old WOOM

Mamma comes back here on Monday

Lady Randolph to Winston

Sunday [? 4 October 1891]   2 Connaught Place

Dearest Winston,

I find that Sir W. McCormack won't be back until the 14th. I will make an appointment tomorrow for you with the assistant for Tuesday or Thursday & will write & tell you. If the weather keeps fine & I stay here long enough I will come down & pay you a visit. I have written to Mr Welldon. Papa wires from Hartley Hill that he will be back the end of Dec. The horses did very badly this week. The stables seem quite out of form.

I hope you are putting yr shoulder to the wheel & working up a bit. Best love darling,

Yr loving
MOTHER

Winston to Jack

[? 4 October 1891]   [Harrow]

Darling Jack,

I got both the Books & the P.O.O's. Thank you very much. What a good correspondent you are. I have bought 3 second hand curtains very big & very cheap. They will do well for the den. Make 2 hammocks 5 ft 6 long & 3 ft Broad for us to sleep in.

I have begun 'Chemistry' which I am taking up, it is very interesting & when I come home I will show you many wonders. Well Good Bye my bird I will write again soon.

Ever Your Loving Brother
WINSTON S. CHURCHILL

Jack to Winston

Tuesday [6] October 1891   [Elstree]

My Darling Winney,

When I wrote on Sunday it was just a scrall but now I will write a long one. I have netted a hammock 5ft 6 x 4 foot wide but it is very small, I will bring back lots of string & every thing that is nessesery for netting & then net what ever you like we must Buy a nice Kennel for "Dodo" & put it in the Back yard? or by the den? shall I net a big Bag for anything. I hope "Dodo" does not bite. Is it a mongrel? Mama wrote to me & said she did not mind if it amused you I will enclose the letter. Is it true Pa Pa is coming home at the end of this month. I am sorry all the horses Bar "Eldiablo" lost. It will be fun when we get the "Den" finished. Has it been thached? or tared? Save as much money as you can I still have about 25/- do try & spend as little as possible. Did you save anything on "Dodo"? can not write anything more now

I remain Your loving brother
JACK S. CHURCHILL

C. J. Edney to Winston

7 October [1891]   Banstead

Sir,

Bell is getting all the game he can for next week as the house will be full of Company. I have however told him that you want some game and I have also told Mrs Everest who I think is having some game cooked to send to you.

Have spoken to Tom Ranner re den and he says the man has been so busy thatching corn stacks that he has not been able to thatch den but expects to do it at end of week.

Re Blue coat

It was returned to Mrs Lacy immediately after you left here.

I beg to remain your obedient servant

C. J. EDNEY

Mrs Everest to Winston

Wednesday [? 7 October 1891]   Banstead

Darling Winnie,

Was very pleased to get your letter Monday & to hear you are well & happy. Mamma left here last Friday & has not come back yet it is dull here when she is away so long. Your Bicycle is gone to be done. They said it would be about 5/- so don't you let them run up a long bill for it. Edney told me today he had got a letter from you about the Den being thatched. I heard him tell Tom Ranner to do it he has not touched it as yet not even taken down the draping I told him to take it down & bring it into me. I have told Mrs Keen to cook & stuff 2 more chickens & 4 partridges. They want to keep the game for next week the races are then, begin on Tuesday & the house will be full again. Edney goes out shooting every day.

You had better give your cloth overcoat to the Tailor to be well brushed it must be awfully dusty hanging up in your room all summer. Have you got all you want in the way of clothes. Mind you wear out the oldest first.

I am going off to Ventnor again. I am allright only rather weak & I think I shall get strong again there am leaving here on Saturday to give up my room. Mamma was so nice about it. She said I should not go if I did not feel well enough, but I do now, another week has made a great improvement in me. The weather has changed here quite stormy & cold. I suppose the game must be cooked before we send it. I told Mrs Keen to send it off on Friday so that you will get it for Sunday allright. If the weather continues so stormy I shall stay at C. [Connaught] Place till it gets calm in which case I might perhaps run down & see you if I feel well enough. Will send *wire* if I do come dear.

I have just been writing to Jackie he is allright had a letter yesterday morning. Fancy that Pony Jackie had of Calons the 1st one Mrs Calon was driving it to Newmarket slowly & the Pony crossed its legs & stumbled & fell down threw Mrs C. out & broke her arm so you must not use that again. I shall not write again this week dear – so goodbye don't get wet wear your coat to Bill when it rains.

Fondest love & kisses to my darling precious Boy. Is he working well.

Ever your loving

WOOM – alias E. A. E.

Winston to Lady Randolph

[? October 1891]   [Harrow]

Darling Mummy,

    I am going to see Jack on Saturday. Will you send me a little money 15/- will be enough. What you sent me before was what I had spent in going up to London. Please do my darling Mummy as I don't know what I shall do. I have no more time as there is House Singing now so please excuse the scrawl of your
Loving son
WINSTON S. CHURCHILL

Winston to Lady Randolph

[? October 1891]   [Harrow]

My Mamma,

    I add a post script to say that I sadly want

> 1 New Eton Jacket
> 1 Waistcoat
> 1 pr best trousers.

I ought to have these in time for 2.30 Sat, so if you will please send the enclosed back signed, as they make them Alright here.

Winston may have an Eton Jacket and waistcoat also 1 pr of trousers.
    Signed

Lady Randolph to Lord Randolph
(*Blenheim Papers*)

EXTRACT

9 October [1891]   2 Connaught Place

    . . . I had promised to go and see Winston today – and it is pouring – but he will be so disappointed I don't like to put it off. Besides I think Welldon wants to see me. . . .

    . . . I have been to Harrow since writing the above, and am delighted to be able to give you a very good account of Winston. Mr Welldon told me that since his return he has worked very hard and that he thinks he is certain to pass in June. I thought Winston looking very well he was full of enquiries as regards you, and we are both very anxious to see the *D.G.* of Monday. . . .

Winston to Lady Randolph

[? October 1891]   [Harrow]

My darling Mummy,

I went up to town to see Maddick on Tuesday. I am going again next Tuesday to see MacCormack who has returned this will be final. I saw Everest who is not nearly so ill as you think and who prepared a noble tea for me.

I hope you won't be sick but I really must send in my account for my journey up to town

"Dr to Mr W. Churchill

To 1 First Return Ticket	2/-
To Hansom used for conveyance	4/6
To 1 Peach (devoured with joy)	9d
To cheap literature	3d
Total	7/6

An early settlement will greatly oblige.

I have had 1 doz photographs of myself taken and will send you one.

Good bye my darling Mummy
Reminding you of your promises
I remain, Your loving son
WINSTON S. CHURCHILL

Jack to Winston

Saturday 24 October [1891]   [Elstree]

Dear Winney,

I was not surprised at your letter because I thought that it would rain but this morning it was so fine I thought you would come, & I did not give up all hope till I saw the other fellows & then I was very disappointed However do try & come over again I will get another order when ever you like when is the next Holl I cant write more now so good Bye

JSC

Mrs Everest to Winston

[? 26 October 1891]   [2 Connaught Place]

My darling,

Mamma went off in a hurry to Banstead yesterday where she remains till Saturday then she comes here till Monday & then off again for a fortnight. I herewith enclose 10/- which is the amount I owe you. I am going to see Jack tomorrow if fine if not on Saturday don't you get wet tomorrow. I think I will send you 15/- that will be 5/- to put down to Mamma in my Book. Good bye sweet love.

Much love from your old
WOOM

Mrs Everest to Winston

[? October 1891]   2 Connaught Place

My dearest Boy,

I have only just recd your letter came this morning 8 o'clock. You put me to great straits I have so little money & have to keep paying out for the house why don't you write to Mamma. I shall get into trouble you know. I suppose I must send you a little. Fancy a sovereign since Saturday you have spent. I left you on Saturday at 5 o'clock with £1 & on Sunday you could not possibly spend it then next day Monday you write for more. I cannot understand what you can do with your money. I can only send you 10/- as Mamma did not pay me all my Book when she went away. She is coming to London next week then you can ask her for some or write to Banstead. It is too dreadful the rate you are going on at, you give it away I expect. I will enclose in this 12/- & that is more than I can spare so you must be careful. Mind your cold if you are going out with the Rifle. I am very poorly yesterday & today – in haste.

Your loving
WOOM

Lady Randolph to Winston

28 October 1891   Banstead

Dearest Winston,

Since seeing you I have been so busy I have not had time to write. I have been very remiss I confess – but dear child your letters always have the same refrain "please send me money". You do get through it in the most rapid manner. Here is a P.O.O. for £1. Mrs Keen informs me that you have sent an "order"? for ducks etc. The house being full of people she hasn't time to cook them until the end of the week. You ought to have written to me to ask. I was horrified to hear from Everest that you had had another tooth out. It is *too* silly of you & you will regret it. Send me the address of the dentist who did it as I wish to see him & give him a piece of my mind. I don't know what Mr Welldon will say to yr coming up so often. Write & tell me how yr eyes feel. Have you to come up again for that belt – for if so – you had better do the occulist at the same time. I have just had a wire from Papa who is very well & returns by Juli & Mafeking. I will write again

Best love, Yr loving MOTHER

Winston to Lady Randolph

[? October/November 1891]   [Harrow]

My darling Mummy,

Thank you very much for the P.O. You however 'slang' me wrongfully. The money I wrote for was only in reality my expenses for two journeys up to town. As for the ducks – you have got plenty at Banstead, so why should I be without I only wrote for the duck because the pheasants that were sent me were in such bad condition. Therefore chere maman be not wrathful without a cause.

Thank you very much for the Fencing order. I am working all right and getting on well. My eyes however give me pain in the evenings. Please make an appointment for between 2.30 & 4.30 on Tuesday.

Enclose a Photo & Remain
Ever your loving son
WINSTON S. CHURCHILL

Mrs Everest to Winston

2 November [1891]   2 Connaught Place

My dear Winny,

I suppose as I have not heard from you all your wants are supplied. I think you might have had the politeness & good manners to let me know whether you recd the money I sent you alright or not. I hear Her Ladyship sent you a sov. She came up from Banstead Sunday last night & started off again this morning to Wynyard, Stockton on Tees returns home next Saturday. I could not get a word with her. Well I went to see dear little Jack on Saturday he does not look so well as he usually does at school he has never recovered the effects of the over exertion he had at Banstead in the holidays it took so much out of him late hours &c. Did you go with the Rifle Corps or not. I should like to hear all about it if you can spare a 1/4 of an hour. I hope you are quite well I am getting very unhappy not hearing anything about or of you for so long. How are the teeth, not troubling you I hope? I am very busy this week – last week I was occupied 2 whole mornings with Lady Sarah shopping buying House linens. She is not going to Banstead after the wedding[1] but to Paris direct so Banstead is closed till next year. I had a letter from Mary last week in which she tells me your Tricycle is to cost 10/- now instead of 5/- & they have not begun to do it yet. Edney comes up on Friday for good. Have you enquired if they have thatched the top of your Den yet? Have you got the instrument yet you were having made does it answer? I have no news to tell you but one request to make that is will you kindly favor me with a few lines. Out of sight out of mind with Winny.

Goodbye my Lamb best love to you.

Ever your loving old
WEAE

[sketch] My photo.

Mrs Everest to Winston

Wednesday 10 p.m. [? 4 November 1891]   [? Connaught Place]

My dear Winston,

I have just got your letter or note & hasten to reply to give you time to wire to Her Ladyship if you want money. I am extremely sorry my dear Boy I cannot oblige you this time it is utterly impossible unless you wish me to starve. Your mother will be home on Saturday then perhaps she will send you some. I cannot keep on putting it down in my Book. I got into disgrace last time for doing it.

I do think you are awfully extravagent to have spent 15/- in a week some familys of 6 or 7 people have to live upon 12/- a week. You squander it away & the more you have the more you want & spend. Poor Jack had 1£ to go back to school with & he still has 5/- left & buys something every half holiday.

It was very kind of you to lend me some dear but you were not long in asking for it back again – you really must try & spend yr money with judgement you should always keep a Friend in your pocket & the only way to teach you to do so is to keep you short & let you suffer the inconvenience of being pennyless. So sorry but it is not possible to help you this time. I am so glad to hear you are going to be confirmed. When is it to be my angel I should like to see the Confirmation but I suppose visitors are not allowed. My poor

[1] Lady Sarah Spencer-Churchill married Captain Gordon WILSON on November 21.

sweet old precious lamb how I am longing for a hug – although you are not perfect I do love you so very much & I do so want you to have more discretion & judgement about spending your money you do everything at random my Pet without thinking & it is a growing evil & unless you try & cure yourself of it you will have to suffer severely later on.

Goodbye my precious old darling fondest love,

From your loving
old WOOM

I have had such a nice kind letter from Miss Phillips offering me a Matronship at a Gentlemans School at Sedburgh as I told her I thought I should have to go from here soon so I think I shall accept it, only it is rather too far north.

Lady Randolph to Lord Randolph
(*Blenheim Papers*)

EXTRACT

6 November [1891] Wynyard Park[1]
Stockton On Tees

. . . Winston is going in for his Confirmation. Perhaps it will steady him – Welldon wrote that Winston wished to became a candidate – I am afraid only because it will get him off other work! . . .

Winston to Lady Randolph

[? November 1891] [Harrow]

My darling Mummy,

I went to see Jack yesterday. He is very well. I want you to see about our coming up for Aunt Sarah's Wedding on the 21st. I find that boys are always allowed to come up for that sort of thing. It is on a Sat – & we would stay till Monday.

I have got to go to France for the holidays, but let me beg you

No Family!

No Family!

Ugh

I won't expect you to answer this of course my ma! but apropos of the 'filthy lucre' if you are in London you might give it to Everest to send & that would save you the inconvenience of writing to your loving son.

WINSTON S. CHURCHILL

[1] Seat of the Marquess of Londonderry.

Lady Randolph to Winston

Tuesday [10 November 1891]   Iwerne Minster House
                                            Blandford

Dearest Winston,

I told Everest to send you a sovereign when I left London on holiday. I have just received yr report which is not quite as satisfactory as I cd wish. You *must* try & have a better one next term as Papa will be back & will expect glowing accounts of yr work. Well you old Puss – I will try & get you both up for the 21st. I go from here to Doveridge, Derbyshire on Saturday to stay with Ly Hindlip[1] – but I shall return to London Friday 20th. I have had a telegram from Papa saying that he leaves Capetown in the *Mexican* on the 9th of Dec, therefore he will be here about the end of the month.

I had a day's hunting yesterday – which was great fun – but at first I was so 'blown' that at the 3rd fence, I cut a lovely somersault – I shan't be able to chaff you any more about yrs.

Goodbye best love, Write here Yr loving
MOTHER

Frances, Duchess of Marlborough to Winston

11 November 1891   50 Grosvenor Square

My dear Winny,

I am very much obliged to you for your letter & Photo – I think the latter very good & am very pleased to have it –

Sarah's Wedding is on the 21st Nov at 2-30. Do you think you can get leave to come up for it. She has got some lovely presents. They go to Paris for a week & then settle at Melton – I hear your Father leaves Capetown by the *Mexican* on the 9th Decr so I hope he will be Home about Xmas.

Goodbye Dear Winny
Yr aff Gd Mother
F. MARLBOROUGH

I hope you will have a first rate report for Him.

Lady Randolph to Lord Randolph
(*Blenheim Papers*)
EXTRACT

12 November [1891]   Iwerne Minster House

. . . Winston's last report was not quite as brilliant as I had been led to expect from Welldon's praise – but he is doing well. . . .

[1] Georgiana Millicent (1845–1939), eldest daughter of Charles Rowland Palmer-Morewood, who had married 2nd Baron Hindlip in 1868.

Jack to Winston

Friday 13 November 1891   Elstree

Dear Winney,

Yesterday in arith school We were let out to see a meet of a hunt in our feild It was a moderatly big field and there was a little boy not bigger than Sunny Frewen[1] on a littel white poney with a groom by him on a horse just like "Paddy" I thought it was like the old days of the "Morengo" We saw them drive a covert but they did not get anything and then they went in to the fields so we had to turn back.

There were three whips dressed in yellow coats and caps on top boots

The pack consisted of cheifly puppies and the old ones looked asleep I wished myself in that little boys shoes. [Sketch of huntsman and puppy] Please send me a dozen squashes as I have not got any.

I am getting on very well and do nothing but draw faces. [Sketch of face] Do send the dozen squashes

I remain Your loving Brother
JACK S. CHURCHILL

Lady Randolph to Winston

Sunday 15 November [1891]   Doveridge Hall[2]
                                                            Derby

Dearest Winston,

Did you ever get the sovereign I told Everest to send you – also some pheasants from Banstead? Shall I write to Mr Welldon & ask him to let you come up Saturday till Monday? The wedding is not till 2.30. I shall go to town on Thursday after the races. Write to me here until then. I hope you are sticking to yr work & that yr next report will be a *really* good one. Have you read "The Light that Failed"? I like it. Bless you old puss.

Yr loving
MOTHER

Lady Randolph to Lord Randolph
(*Blenheim Papers*)
EXTRACT

21 November [1891]   2 Connaught Place

... Welldon wrote to me that Winston must go to a French family for Xmas, or he won't pass his Exam; Welldon makes all the arrangements. I shall have to let him go. . . .

[1] Oswald Moreton Frewen (1887–1958), his cousin.
[2] Seat of Samuel Charles Allsopp, 2nd Baron Hindlip (1842–97); formerly a Conservative MP, chairman of the family brewing company.

Winston to Lady Randolph

[? November 1891]   [Harrow]

My darling Mummy,

I got your letter this morning. I recd the £1 for which I return many thanks. They tell my Report this month is much better than last. Please write to Mr Welldon & say that you would very much like me to come up for the Wedding as I have been asked by Grandmamma etc etc. I am so glad Papa will be home by Christmas or thereabouts. I must certainly go to France during the holidays, but I beg and *Pray* that you will not send me to a vile, nasty, fusty, beastly French "Family".

Please get Jack up too. I am looking forward to Saturday. There is very little time so Please write to W. I am sure he will be only too delighted to accede to any request you may make to him about

Your loving son
WINSTON S. CHURCHILL

PS I have not recd any pheasants for 3 weeks

Winston to Lady Randolph

[? November 1891]   [Harrow]

Darling Mama,

Thursday is a whole holiday. I have asked Welldon & he says I may come up for the day for my regular absit. I promise you this is no mistake. I have just come from him. A letter from you to me saying that you "would be glad to see me" will bring me up by the 8.7 on Thursday. Now don't let anything hinder you from writing by return of post to your

Loving son
WINSTON S. CHURCHILL

Reverend J. E. C. Welldon to Lady Randolph

24 November 1891   Harrow

Dear Lady Randolph,

You will, I hope, forgive me troubling you with one more letter about Winston. It seems to me essential that he should make the best use of his coming holidays. He has worked better this term than before but he is fitful, and he will need all the marks that he can get. If you will let me, I should like to send him to a M. Elmering whose address is

> 9 Rue de la Ferme
> Rouen.

M. Elmering has had Harrow boys under his care before and has taught them well. Of course I must count upon his being willing to go and upon his working steadily when he is there; for I cannot exercise the same control over him in the holidays as in the term time, and it will be in his power to defeat the project made for his good, unless he is sensible. But I ought to say plainly that his chance of passing his examination for Sandhurst depends upon himself, and, sorry as I am to spoil the pleasure of his holidays, I cannot doubt that I am advising you in his true interest.

His cousin, Dudley Marjoribanks, is going off at the beginning of the holidays, to a family in Baden.

If arrangements are made for Winston's going to Rouen, they ought to be made as soon as possible.

Believe me, Sincerely yours
J.E.C. WELLDON

Winston to Lady Randolph

[22 November 1891]   [Harrow]

My darling Mummy,

I got to Harrow all right in good time. It was very 'bad luck' having to go just as the fun was commencing. It is still worse having to look forward to such a time as you and Welldon seem to be planning out for me next Christmas.

But to return to the affair about which I write. Please let Jack and Everest come tomorrow by the 11.29 train from Baker Street. Please arm Jack with a sov to make him all the more acceptable & present Everest with sufficient "oof" for a moderate dinner at the King's Head.

Please do this for your loving son who remains,

Your loving son
WINSTON S. CHURCHILL

PS It was awfully bad luck having to go, just as I was making an impression on the pretty Miss Weaslet. Another 10 minutes and ...!?

Mrs Everest to Winston

Thursday 12 a.m. [?26 November 1891]   2 Connaught Place

My darling Winnie,

So glad to get your letter this morning & to hear you arrived safely back to school. I must write to Jackie too. Well dearest I am sorry to tell you since your visit I do not feel very happy & cannot sleep. But I suppose there must be something to bring us to our end. At any rate to shorten our days otherwise

I am quite well. I have had a nice long letter from Miss Phillips & she enclosed one from Jim[1] very interesting. He has had a great disappointment he took out a favourite dog in pup & a negro out of sheer spite killed it with a large block of wood struck it on the head he kept it alive 5 days after feeding it with port wine & essence of Beef & then it died as he was giving it a spoon full of wine he is terribly cut up about it poor Fellow especially as Dogs are not to be got out there. We have had a heavy thunder storm & lightening this morning here. I hope you wear your coat this wet weather. I have not seen anyone since you were here & have not been outside the door so I have no news to tell you – am nearly blown away I have been hourly each night expecting to be buried beneath the ruins of this house the wind has been terrific. I quite expected the skylight to come down & the chimney pots through it. When are you coming up again. Have they made that instrument comfortable for you.

I am afraid I must wait till the weather gets more settled before I can come to see you.

Please don't tell Jackie about my going away he will be so unhappy poor darling. What a cruel world this is. My darling I must wind up now as I have nothing to tell you with much love to my precious old darling from his loving old

WOOMY

Jack to Winston

Sunday 29 November 1891   Elstree

My dear Winney,

Of course you know what this letter contains, I mean all the many happy returns of the day etc.

I sent you a littel present last night (Woom addressed it etc)

It is very cold, this is a thing I always put in my letters.

This is the 1st Sunday in Advent, that means only one more Sunday this term. I must say goodbye now.

I hope my little present will be acceptable.

I hope you enjoyed your thursday's exeat.

I must say good bye.

So with very many kisses and very much love and very many very happy happy returns of the day.

I remain your ever loving Brother
JACK S. CHURCHILL

[1] James Robert Phillips (1863–1897), the eldest son of the Venerable Archdeacon Phillips. He was Sheriff of the Gold Coast and Deputy Consul-General of Nigeria, and was killed in the Benin Massacre, January 1897, after leading a peace mission there.

L

29 November 1891

My dear Churchill,

I do not think that my memory deceives me when it assures me that tomorrow (30th) is your birthday. One line to wish you many happy returns of the day. I am sure that you are far happier now than you were a year ago and so may each succeeding year prove happier than the one before. May God bless you and keep you and help you in His Strength to conquer everything that keeps you from coming to a full knowledge of Himself. You will someday understand better than now what this means.

Yours ever affectionately
FREDERICK C. SEARLE

[? 6 December 1891]   [Harrow]

My darling Mama,

I had written a long letter to you but on second thoughts I decided not to send it. I hear Papa will be nearly a fortnight later coming back. Mr Welldon is in consequence very keen on my going to Paris straight from here. Darling Mummy, I shall think it will be very unkind and unnatural of you if you allow him to do me out of my Christmas. Out of all this school not 5 boys are going away at all and I believe Duley is the only one who goes before Christmas. Please dont *you* put pressure on me. Welldon got very angry last night when I told him I couldn't give up coming home. He said "very well then you must give up the Army." That is all nonsense. But Mummy don't be unkind and make me unhappy. I have firmly made up my mind not to go abroad till after the 27th. If you in spite of my entreaties force me to go I will do as little as I can and the holidays will be one continual battle. I am sure Papa would not turn me away from home at Christmas or indeed at any time. If you do all you possibly can to make things nice for me I will go after the 27th and return so as to have 4 days with Papa.

Please don't be unkind, Ever your loving son
WINSTON S. CHURCHILL

Tuesday [? 8 December 1891]   London

Dearest Winston,

I was beginning to wonder why you had not written. My dear boy, I feel for you in every way & can quite understand your anxiety & desire to be at home for Xmas, but quite apart other considerations, the tone of your letter is not calculated to make one over lenient. When one wants something in this world, it is not by delivering ultimatums that one is likely to get it. You are old enough not to play the fool, & for the sake of a few days pleasure, give up the chance of getting through yr exam: a thing which may affect yr whole life. You know how anxious Papa is that you shld go to Sandhurst this summer – I have received a letter from him this morning, dated 7th Nov in which he says "Please tell Mr Welldon that I gladly agree to any arrangement which he may be kind enough to make for Winston's studies during the Xmas holidays". He also says "I have such a nice letter from Winston please thank him for it & give him my best love". Of course if you don't "intend" going abroad till after the 27th & have "firmly" made up yr mind to return here for the inside of a week, I suppose that wld give you about a fortnight at Versailles. If possible I will come & see you on Thursday. Meanwhile I will think it over. You can be quite certain my darling that I will decide for what is best, but I tell you frankly that *I* am going to decide not *you*. If you have to go, I shall see if it is possible to make it up to you in another way. I *count* on you helping me & not making a useless fuss – I will let you know what train I come by Thursday – until then bless you & work so that Papa may see a good report.

Yr loving
MOTHER

Winston to Lady Randolph

[? 9 December 1891]   [Harrow]

My darling Mamma,

I received your letter this morning. I hope that you will come down tomorrow as it is so much easier to explain things. You ought not however to be so sarcastic to me since it is I not you who have to make the sacrifice. You say that "You tell me frankly" very well Mamma I only told you frankly my intentions. Not intending or wishing to overcome you

"I merely stated *frankly* that I would throw every obstacle in the way of my going abroad before the 27th.

You say it is for you to decide. I am required to give up my holidays – not you, I am forced to go to people who bore me excessively – not you. You were asked to give up a short part of the year to take me abroad – you promised – refused & I did not press the point.

I am very much surprised and pained to think that both you & Papa should treat me so, as a machine. I should like to know if Papa was asked to "give up his holidays" when he was at Eton.

It also seems to me that in your letters there is an inaccuracy. You state that
5 weeks – 5 days – 4 days — 14 days.
This is a mistake.
5 weeks – 5 days – 4 days — 26 days.

You blame me for being frank to you. You say that "if I want to gain my point" other methods than those dictated by honour & honesty should be used.

Please do come down on Thursday, if possible for lunch because if you come by the 3.30 & leave by the 4.37 it does not give very much time.

Please do have a little regard for my happiness. There are other and higher things in this world than learning, more powerful agents than the Civil Service Commissioners.

With Love & kisses, I remain, Ever your loving son
WINSTON S. CHURCHILL

Mrs Everest to Winston

7 December 1891   2 Connaught Place

My darling Lamb,

I have been looking for a letter from you all last week. I never have heard anything about you for a whole week. Are you well dear. I am so afraid you will get ill in that horrid little Den – be sure & open the window & door every time you go out. I am very anxious to hear what they are going to do with you are you coming home at all. Cannot I come & see you one day. Did you get a Pocket Book or a Memorandum Book from me I sent you one. I hope you got it. I never heard. I have been very busy all the week at Grosvenor Square. Jackie will be home on the 19th in 12 days. Do write & tell me what has been decided about you. His Lordship has postponed his arrival for a fortnight. So you will not see him till you return from France. Mamma has been away since Saturday came home for lunch today.

If you have to go to France without coming home I will send or bring your big tweed coat & some Fine Flannel Shirts for you to sleep in those you wore at Banstead. One of the Storks are dead got in the pond & couldn't get out. I expect poor little Jackie will have very dull holidays here without you. & all the Soldiers at Banstead too.

Do send me a line theres a dear Boy & tell me what you are going to do. Did Mamma bring you a Birthday present. I have no news to tell you so with fondest love to you my darling.

I am ever your loving
W.

Winston to Lady Randolph

[? 13 December 1891]   [Harrow]

My darling Mummy,

I am afraid by your not answering my letter that you are angry with me. I hope this is not so. If you want me to go to France next holidays very much I suppose I shall have to go, but I can't help feeling very unhappy about it.

You will see that that beggar won't let me go out of his clutches much.

Do please write to Mr. Welldon and ask that I may be allowed to come home on the Friday night. It would mean a great deal to me. The difference of 1 night in 3 days holidays is most noticeable.

I am awfully low about it. First feeling I won't go & then that I must.

Woomany told me that you were trying to make arrangements with Baron H. Hirsch for me. I expect this little French brute will spoil it all.

—Welldon; he is the cause of all my misfortunes but for him I should be looking forward to as nice a holidays, & as merry a Christmas as I have ever had.

Goodbye my darling Mummy,

With much love & many kisses I remain, Ever your loving son

WINSTON S. CHURCHILL

Lady Randolph to Winston

Tuesday [15 December 1891]   2 Connaught Place

Dearest Winston,

I have only read one page of yr letter and I send it back to you – as its style does not please me. I confess after our conversation the other day I did not expect you to go back on yr word, & try & make everything as disagreeable for yrself & everyone else as possible. My dear you won't gain anything by taking this line. Everything that I can do for you to make things as smooth & palatable as possible I will do – more I cannot promise. I don't think I can write to Mr Welldon again – but you can ask him to let you come Friday – & say that I shld be very glad if he wld let you.

Write to me a nice letter!

Yr loving
MOTHER

Winston to Lady Randolph[1]

[? 16 December 1891]   [Harrow]

My darling Mummy,

Never would I have believed that you would have been so unkind. I am utterly miserable. That you should refuse to read my letter is most painful

[1] At the top of this letter Winston wrote: 'PS I send the other letter back that you may peruse it.' He then crossed this out.

to me. There was nothing in it to give you grounds for rejecting it. I am glad however that I waited 3 hours before answering or I would have sent you something that would have startled you. I can't tell you how wretched you have made me feel – instead of doing everything to make me happy you go and cut the ground away from under my feet like that. Oh my Mummy!

I made up my mind I would write no letter to you of any length in future as in my letters length I can perceive [is] a [reason] for your not reading it. I expect you were too busy with your parties and arrangements for Christmas. I comfort myself by this. As to the style – it was rather good. A letter of mine to the Harrovian has recently been accepted & pronounced good.[1]

IMPORTANT

READ THIS.

I have got to tell you that the Frenchman wants to know what time he can come & see you on Friday. Please let me know by return of post, or tell Everest to if you feel very 'spiteful'.

Darling Mummy – I am so unhappy but if you don't read this letter it will be the last you'll have the trouble to send back. I think you might keep your promise to me & write to W. Likely he'd let me go isn't it? (on my own recommendation).

If you don't – I refuse to go to Paris till Tuesday though you will probably be so unkind that I shall be glad to get away.

I am more unhappy than I can possibly say. Your unkindness has relieved me however from all feelings of duty. I too can forget. Darling Mamma if you want me to do anything for you, especially so great a sacrifice don't be so cruel to

Your loving son
WINNY

Winston to Lady Randolph

[? 17 December 1891]   [Harrow]

My darling Mummy,
Please don't be so unkind. Do answer my letter and let me know about the Frenchman. I am very unhappy. I think you might keep your promise about Friday.

Do be kind to your Loving son
WINSTON S. CHURCHILL

Best Love, kisses xx

1 See page 308.

Winston to Lady Randolph

[? November 1891] [Harrow]

My darling Mummy,

Welldon whom I have just seen says "I am going to let you go home for the Sunday and that's all." He says one thing to you, but quite another to me. If he doesn't let me come home till Sat. I do hope you will let me have 2 or 3 more days. Darling Mummy. do attend to my letter. I am so wretched. Even now I weep. Please my darling Mummy be kind to your loving son. Don't let my silly letters make you angry. Let me at least think that you love me – Darling Mummy I despair. I am so wretched. I don't know what to do. Don't be angry I am so miserable.

Please don't expect me to go on Monday if he doesn't let me come till then. Oh how I wish I had not believed him. How I have been tricked. I don't know what to do. Do please write something kind to me. I am very sorry if I have 'riled' you before I did only want to explain things from my point of view.

Good Bye my darling Mummy.

With best love I remain, Ever your loving son
WINSTON

Reverend J. E. C. Welldon to Lady Randolph

18 December 1891 [Harrow]

Dear Lady Randolph,

I am afraid Winston cannot leave School until tomorrow, but he shall come to you early then. Mr Minssen[1], who has received an invitation from Winston, is anxious to see you and would like to call upon you tomorrow at 12, if that were a convenient time for you. He would prefer tomorrow to Monday as he may wish to have some conversation with me after seeing you.

I have had two conversations with Mr Minssen and I shall talk to Winston once more to-day.

The arrangement seems eminently satisfactory. I am confident that Mr Minssen will be kind, careful and considerate but much depends upon Winston himself. Mr Minssen will do everything for him, if he is docile and industrious; but he will not let him waste his time and, if he is idle, he must be sent home.

It is, I think, essential that he should not accept invitations to any family where he will speak English. I want him to make as much progress as possible in French conversation.

He tells me Baron Hirsch's sons, with whom he hopes to ride speak English fluently; but if that were so, it would be a loss to him to be much with them.

[1] Bernard Jules Minssen (1861–1924), modern languages master at Harrow 1891–1921.

Mr Minssen will probably ask you not to let him accept more than three invitations a week, and it is clearly bad for him to be out alone at night. Mr Minssen will, if you wish, supply him with such pocket money as is necessary. It is, I fear, somewhat of an intrusion for me to enter into these details; but my excuse is that I have set my heart upon his passing into Sandhurst and he has no time to lose.

I fully believe he will go in a sensible and right spirit.

Sincerely yours
J. E. C. WELLDON

PS Just as I finished writing this letter, Winston came in to say you had asked to see Mr Minssen to-day.

Lady Randolph to Lord Randolph
(*Blenheim Papers*)

EXTRACT

[?18 December 1891]   2 Connaught Place

. . . Winston comes home tomorrow and on Monday goes to Versailles. He starts with the French Master of Harrow with whose parents he is to stay. Mr Welldon has arranged all.

I can't tell you what trouble I have had with Winston this last fortnight he has bombarded me with letters, cursing his fate and everyone. Of course it is a great disappointment to him not being home for Xmas but he makes as much fuss as tho' he were going to Australia for 2 years. Welldon insisted on his going at once, otherwise he wd not have time enough there to derive any benefit from it.

I have just seen Mr Minssen the tutor in whose family he is going and I think I have arranged everything satisfactorily. . . .

Lady Wilton to Winston

[? December 1891]   Le Nid

My dear Winston,

Very many thanks for yours. So you are coming to France to study the "lingo". Well – I think you might study it here! under my maternal wing! What do you say? Its lovely nice weather here & I'm very fit just at present. Do you remember my Cockatoo? He is better-looking than ever & so nice. I take him about on my hand – only he tries to destroy all the furniture!

How is Jack? & when do you expect your Father? When next you write
to your Mama, do give her my love. & with much to yourself

> Ever your very affecte Deputy Mother
> LAURA WILTON

Winston to Lady Randolph

Tuesday evening after post   18 Rue de Provence

[22 December 1891]   [Versailles]

My darling Mummy,

I was too tired to write last night. We travelled 2nd classe but notwithstanding a horrible smell of Brandy & beer on the boat, I was not sick. Au
contraire I slept all the time.

We arrived at Dieppe où nous partook of de bon Café au lait. Le chemin de
fer etait très incommode. Pour quatres heures. I waited having nothing to do.
Nous arrivames au gare St Lazare. J'ai déclaré ma boite des cigarettes. But
they did not charge me anything nor did they open mon mal.

We reached Versailles at 9 o'clock. I telegraphed to Everest immediately.
"Arrived safe. Good passage". Apres le dejeuner we went for a walk. We saw
soldiers, nothing but soldiers – De Seine de l'artillerie, des cuirassiers et de
chasseurs a pieds. There are 6,000 hommes dans la garrison, and on Sat
week there is to be a great review. 10,0000 men march past. C'est une nation
bien militaire. We then went into the "Grand Trianon" I saw that there was
much to see. The skating is perfect. I want you to buy me a pair of skates. I
do not like parting with 15 fr and a bad pair are useless.

*   *   *   *   *   *   *

Fatigue, the passage, The strange food, The cold, home sickness, the thoughts
of what was behind & what before nearly caused me to write a letter which
would have been painful to you. Now I am better & I think that I will wait
here my month though not one day more. Today we went to the 'Bon Marché'
in Paris. We spent 3 hours there. I bought a present for you, a blotting pad
which I hope will give you as much pleasure to receive & it has me to buy;
[*sketch of blotter*] and for Jack I purchased something too, Also a 'Sachée'
for Everest.

The food is very queer. But there is plenty, & on the whole it is good. There
is wine & beer to drink. I have a room to myself but it is awfully cold. However
with rugs, overcoats, dressing gowns etc. I managed to sleep.

Tomorrow I am going to ride, in my boots.

I have already made great progress in French. I begin to think in it, in the manner in which the first part of my letter is written. M. Minssen says I know far more than he thought I did. These people are very kind. Of course I would give much to return, if you wish it I will come tomorrow – but considering all things I am prepared to stay my month.

I don't know how to get to see Baron Hirsch I am afraid you have not written. I would like very much to go and see them.

If you cannot get skates made to fit me – send me a line to the effect that you wish me to have them and are willing.

Goodbye my darling Mummy, Read this to Jack

With love I remain Your loving son

WINSTON

Love to Jack.

Jack to Winston

[23 December 1891]

Keele Hall[1]

Newcastle

Staffordshire

Dear Winney,

I hope you had a good journey and a nice crossing. You were very lucky getting out of London and away from the fogs because yesterday our train ought to have started at 12 and got to Stoke at 3.25 instead of which it did not start till 12.30 and did not arrive till 4. It was like an icicle when I got here. I played bezik and won by 120 points one game I won by 55. I had 3 Knaves ♦ and 4 Queens ♠.

Mama came very late she started at 4 I had to come [with] Pace at 12. This afternoon I am going to scate I have just got a pair of Scates from Newcastle [-under-Lyme].

It is beautiful here, The sun out etc and freezing hard. There is a lake here on which I shall skate.

At breakfast this morning the gardener found a poor frozen fish which was on the ice.

Monday night when I got back, Aunt Sarah and Uncle were at dinner and wanted to know all about you.

I hope you have a nice place to ride in. I am not sure when we go from here. There are hundred of pochers about so I am told.

Write to me and tell me all what you are doing.

I have not much more to say to you. There is a great big colley which I am sure you would not like, also a little dog just like Topsy only a bit pritier.

---

[1] The home of Ralph Sneyd (1863–1949). He was married to Mary Evelyn, eldest daughter of Major General Sir Arthur Ellis and sister of Alex Ellis.

I am trying to write you a long letter, but it is not up to much I hope you are all right.

I will see about "Dodo" going to Banstead, when I go back to London which will be about Sat I think. My Master asked me if I wanted go to him today he wired about it last night, so I had to wire back no.

I will write again on Friday and tell you how I get on at scating. Mama is afraid to Scate because of her foot which you remember last year.

I must now say goodbye so with best love and very very many Kisses

I remain your loving Brother
JACK S. CHURCHILL

Winston to Lady Randolph

'Christmas Eve' [1891]   [Versailles]
Darling Mummy,

Thanks awfully for you telegram. I appreciate it muchly. We went for a long ride of 3 hours on the 'chevaux de louage' [hired hacks] they were all right but M.M. rides very well & very hard at full gallop on the 'ard'igh road. Les chevaux ne sont pas mal. Ils sont véritablement rossés. Mme Monsieur M's mère ne dit rien que "Son progrés est marveilleux." "N'est ce pas extraordinaire" etc etc.

Write to Baron Hirsch. Do! I have not heard a word from all those 'friends' you spoke about.

With much love & kisses I remain Your loving son
WINSTON

Mrs Everest to Winston

Saturday 11. a.m. [26 December 1891]   2 Connaught Place

My darling Winny,

I recd 2 letters from you this morning & it is such a relief to hear you are comfortable. Lucky for you that you have not been here we have not seen day light since last Monday 5 days utter darkness & no electric light scarcity of gas could not make any so I have lived in this room with a candle till I am half blind. This morning there is a change for the better. Your suit of clothes have come from Nicoll's, shall be sent on Monday. No Booking Office open today Boxing Day. I see it is just like Jacks.

Your letters shall be forwarded to Mamma today if she does not come home we don't know yet whether she is coming today or Monday. Jackie says in a letter to me he is getting on with his skating. The Gardener stands on the

Bank with a cape for him. I see Baron Hersch is in Paris: Soon as you get your new clothes you must go & call on them. Winny dear do try & keep the new suit expressly for visiting, the Brown one will do for every day wear please do this to please me. I hope you will not take cold my darling take care not to get wet or damp.

I hear Papa started on the 24th so he will be here in 16 days. I expect he & Mamma will be coming to Paris to see you.

We had a very happy Xmas here. Edney made himself very agreable. We had an excellent Xmas dinner & supper & after supper they all sang songs & then we went into the kitchen & they put aside the table & danced for dear life no music Edney whistled & I played the comb with a piece of paper & comb like we used to do in our good old nursery days & they all thoroughly enjoyed themselves in a quiet way. Edney made a long toast or speech after dinner & we drank to the health & happiness of Mamma & Papa, Mr Winston & Mr Jack which of course I heartily joined in you may be sure. I have had 22 Xmas cards sent me. There were 2 letters came for you this morning so I took the envelopes off to enclose them in this because I should have had to pay 5d instead of 2½ otherwise. Pray forgive me for so doing. One only had a card in it, from one of your school fellows I think. No writing on it only on the envelope & looked like a Boy's writing.

I hope you will try & feel happy. You will be seeing people you know then you will feel more reconciled. Charlie Balaam has been summoned up to be examined by the Bank authorities next Friday so I expect he will get in.

Thank you so much dearest for getting me a present it has not yet arrived. It is very kind of you but you know my Lamb I would rather you did not spend your money on me. Have you given Monsieur Minnsen the 5£ to keep for you that will have to last you I expect so be careful don't make it fly too fast. You don't know what you may want. I will write again – soon as I receive your present. Cheer up old Boy enjoy yourself try & feel contented you have very much to be thankful for if you only consider & fancy how nice it will be to be able to parlez vous francais. Did you get my letter & cards for Xmas. I posted them last Wednesday tell me when you write again. I gave them to Susan[1] to post, she came in to see me Wednesday afternoon. Mamma gave me a large Photo screen for a Xmas present to hold 10 Photo's cabinets, now my darling old Boy I must close wishing you a very happy new year.

With loving wishes & 20 kisses
From Woom

I am quite well in spite of all the fog.
Mamma gave Jackie a travelling Bag like yours but not nearly as nice as yours though it cost as much I believe.

[1] Susan Thynne, the Frewens' nurse.

Winston to Lady Randolph

[?27 December 1891] [Versailles]

My darling Mummy,

I received your letter on Christmas day. I spent a quiet Christmas. The mother is an English woman so we had the orthodox thing Turkey and plumpudding. Also a little fun on Christmas Eve.

Last night I went to the theatre to see Michel Strigoff[1], and did not return till 1 o'clock. I am very tired to day in consequence. I also went for a long ride yesterday with M.M. for 3 hours. The horses are very good considering. I have one somewhat like Gem, only capable of being galloped on the hard high road. He has a hogged mane, & lots of pluck, & eats biscuit.

Not a word from Baron Hirsch. Not a line from M. de Breteuil.[2] Not a sound from Mr Trafford. I don't know any of their addresses so what can I do?

I would awfully like to have gone to-day to B.H. but. . . . Please try and do something. A week will have gone when you receive this.

Monday 3 weeks I come home – at least my month is up. I will remind you of the promise you made me at Harrow of an extra week [at home] if I gave up my Christmas. A promise is a promise & as I have fulfilled my part I rely on you my darling mummy to do the rest. I know you won't chuck me like that.

I am longing to return. I think if all is well I shall be home on Monday 3 weeks. I count the hours. I won't travel 2nd again by Jove. They are too funny here. Last night we arrived (I & M) at 1 o'clock & we had nearly a mile to go through wet & mud. I had on my shoes. There were plenty of cabs – we needs must walk. That sort of thing is absurd.

I am going to have a look at the palace this afternoon so I must end.

Goodbye my darling Mummy

Hoping to see you in 3 weeks 21 hours, I remain your loving

WINSTON S. CHURCHILL

Winston to Lady Randolph

Tuesday [29 December 1891], 11 o'clock. [Versailles]

My dear Mamma,

It seems to me that with you 'out of sight is out of mind' indeed. Not a line from anybody. You promised to write 3 times a week – I have recd 1 letter.

---

[1] *Michel Strogoff*, adapted as a play from the novel of that name by Jules Verne. First performed in Paris 1880, and in an English translation in London 1881.

[2] Henri Charles Joseph le Tonnelie, Marquis de Breteuil (1848–1916), conservative and monarchist member of Chamber of Deputies 1877–92.

There seems to be something wrong in the Postal arrangements between France & England as well as between Africa & London.

It is not at all kind of you and, my darling Mummy, I am very unhappy about it. This is the 3rd letter I have written you. I have also sent 2 to Jack & 3 to Everest. I wish you would try my mummy to fulfill your promise. Baron Hirsch may be in Jericho for all I know.

Please do something for Your loving son
WINSTON S. CHURCHILL

Mrs Everest to Winston

Tuesday 10 p.m. [29 December 1891]   2 Connaught Place

My darling Winny,

I have just got your welcome letter & it was written all over the envelope not known you did not write the no 2 distinctly it looked like 9 instead of 2. Well my darling. The box with your lovely presents arrived today while I was at my dinner – & what a surprise I got on seeing such a lovely *sachet* much too handsome & delicate I shall have to wrap it up in lavender till I go out visiting. You must accept my best thanks my darling it is so kind of you but another time a less expensive thing will please me quite as well because it is the kind thought that pleases me not the value of the gift & you rob yourself of pocket money my angel. I am so glad you spent a happy Xmas I am also very glad the Lady of the house is one of my country women from Kent.

I hope you have got a quiet horse to ride. Do you go alone riding tell me when you write. I must not enclose any more letters as they cost so much over weight. I must get some thinner paper. Mamma & Jackie have not come back yet & we have been expecting them since Saturday & there is no word to say when they are coming. I had a letter from Jackie yesterday he says Mr Sneed gave him a 1£ on Xmas day & they had Snap Dragons in the evening & there was money in them & he got out 7/6 out of them so he has in his purse 2 : 7 : 6. quite rich. He has been enjoying himself skating & riding & going after the hounds. Paice tells me his riding Breeches are so tight he can't wear them so he must have got stouter. How are yours allright? I am so pleased to hear you are making progress in speaking French. Papa will be home next week. He will be delighted to hear it too I know. Grandmama Jerome is in bed with acute Bronchitis. I went to see her last night had tea with Susan & the children. Do you know those 3 little things repeat German verses beautifully it is funny to hear them. I took the liberty of looking at your present to Mamma & Jackie. I think they are lovely & so useful & appropriate for each that

Blotter is beautiful & I am sure Mamma will be very pleased with it for she has not got one, is that platinum on the purse & pocket book it is pretty really.

I am surprised you have not heard from Baron Hersch. They will write to you soon I expect. How did you like the French Play? as well as English? Jackie tells me in his letter he & Mamma are going to Canford on Saturday. I think they will stay there a little while as Papa meets them there I believe. Your 3 weeks will very soon slip round is it decided for you to have a week at home? The fog & darkness is gone for the present the weather is nice now but awfully muddy under foot. How do your riding Boots answer – when you write next time tell me if you have recd. your new suit from Nicoll's it was sent off yesterday morning early. I have heard nothing about your Dog Do Do I must ask Henry. I have never seen him since Mamma left. You had better not go to that Review on Horseback it might frighten your Horse the guns going off. Mary tells me Paddy & the other Boy are both got quite well now. I am glad you had some Plum Pudding & Turkey at Xmas. I have told Mrs Keen to save you some mince meat. Now my sweet old Lamb I must draw to a conclusion. If you feel sick or feverish or stomach out of order get a Bottle of Eno fruit salt & take a tea spoon full in water. I should buy plenty of fruit eat if I were you keep you *regular you know dear.*

Goodbye my precious keep well & take plenty of exercise. Much fond love.

From your loving old
WOOM

Marquis de Breteuil to Winston

1 January 1892   33 Avenue des Champs Elysées

Mon cher Winston,

Je vous écris en français puisque vous êtes ici pour l'apprendre. Je viens d'avoir une lettre de votre mère qui me le dit et me donne votre adresse.

Venez déjeuner un de ces jours avec nous à midi. Vous nous ferez le plus grand plaisir et je serai très content de vous revoir. Le plus tôt sera le mieux. Vous me direz si je peux faire quelque chose pour vous.

Mille amitiés
BRETEUIL

Winston to Jack

[? January 1892]   [Versailles]

Darling Jack,

Just recd your letter. Many thanks. Keep the £1. J'ai assez. When I return we will have much fun & great games with the army. I have seen here such beautiful soldiers. At the 'Bon Marche' I saw a sho of soldiers. Among many other French and Russian there was a box of artillery men with 3 black cannons. They were in all positions for loading & firing. Ramming home etc. Only 7 francs = 5/-. I will, if you like to send me the money in about a week buy a few battalions of Russians for you. 2 francs the dozen. And artillery men, who have 'fascines' for myself I think I will buy a box of cannon also. The Russians are like this [picture]

So glad you like the present. Write to me. I wish I could meet Papa. Lucky boy you are! Why didn't you burn that letter?

Good Bye Much love
WINNY

NB Invitations have come. Baron Hirsch Friday last Mr Trafford Sat yesterday. Baron Hirsch Tomorrow M. de Breteuil Tuesday. wsc

Winston to Lady Randolph

Friday [?8 January 1892]   [Versailles]

Darling Mummy,

Thank you very much for your telegram, I will go with much pleasure Sunday. Have you recd my present? Is it arranged that I return Monday week? Please give Papa my best love & tell him I am so sorry not to be able to welcome him myself. If you are not too busy, you might send me a line. I have recd my new suit. It fits very well.

Good bye my darling Mummy,
With much love, I remain, Your loving son
WINSTON S.

Jack to Winston

Saturday 8 [9] January 1892   Wimborne

Dear Winney,

Papa arrived yesterday morning looking very well [picture] but with a horrid beard so raged [ragged]. He was expected to arrive on Thursday night and we started in the evening from Dorset. We had 9 miles to drive to the Sation and we missed the train by 6 minits. We had to wait 2 hours for the next train and then we had to wait ¾ of an hour at Salisbury. In the morning Mamma was fast asleep when she was woken up by Pace who said that the tender would start to meet the Scot in 15 minutes. The Glob [*Globe*] said Lady R. Churchill nimbly ran across the dock.

I remain Your loving brother
JACK S. CHURCHILL

Papa gave me Spanish notes for 2½
Thomas brought stamps.

Lady Randolph to Winston

Sunday 10 [January 1892]   Canford Manor
                                            Wimborne

Dearest Winston,

Yr letter received today was very short – you do not tell me anything either of yr visit to Mr de Breteuil or to the Hirschs. What have you been doing? I am afraid that Mr Minssen was rather vexed at my letting you go out so often – I trust it does not make you neglect yr work. Write & tell me all about yrself & whether Mr Minssen is still pleased with you. Papa arrived on Friday. Jack & I went to meet him – Jack has written to you I know & has probably told you all we did. We return to London tomorrow. Papa is very well & in great spirits but his beard is a "terror". I think I shall have to bribe [him] to shave it off. Dearest boy don't be so lazy & neglectful about writing – you only seem to do so when you want something – & then you are very prolific with yr pen! I don't know when yr time is up. You must find out. I will write again shortly.

Best love Yr
MOTHER

Winston to Lord Randolph

[?12 January 1892]   [Versailles]

My dear Papa,

Much Love and many kisses! I am so glad to hear from Mamma that you have come back safe and well. I was very sorry not to be able to go & meet you with everybody else. I have missed every thing this year. Christmas, New Years Day etc.

I went to see M. de Breteuil yesterday. I saw the M. "Tonton" he told me to tell you so. Afterwards Baron Hirsch took me to see the Morgue. There were only three.

Mamma says you are to come to Paris in 10 days. My month is up on Monday or ought to be for M. Minsen says a calendar month & I maintain a Lunar month was meant. The chief inducement Mamma held out to me to go to France was the promise of an extra week. Please do see what you can arrange for me. I have seen nothing of you or Jack or any body. I have only been home 2 days. If you would like me to wait here till you come to Paris and you would give me an extra week I would be delighted to do so. But I want to see Jack a little.

> Hoping to see you soon.
> I remain, Your loving son
> WINSTON S. CHURCHILL

Winston to Lady Randolph

[? 14 January 1892]   [Versailles]

My darling Mummy,

Il faut que je vous explique quelque choses. You addressed your letter to me a Paris. Result sent back and again forwarded by Edney. I had not recd a letter from you for a fortnight when it arrived.

I have had lots of invitations. Last Monday I went to M. de B. and B. Hirsch after. He took me to the morgue. I was much interested. Only 3 Macabres – not a good bag. It is freezing hard and I am going skating this afternoon. I make much progress and Minnsen and I get on capitally.

I want either to come home Monday and see Jack and go on to France with you and Papa or – to wait here for Papa. I don't mind much which only you might easily bring Jack here too; But I am of course counting, my Mummy, on you to fulfil your promise which was more than anything the reason of my coming here willingly.

I must remind you it was a regular promise. I am willing and happy to leave all in your hands only I do hope . . .
I have written to Papa. Please write to me by return of post.
Winston S. Churchill,
    18 Rue de Provence,
       Versailles,
          France.

> With love and kisses I remain, Your loving son
> WINNY

Lord Randolph to Winston

15 January 1892   2 Connaught Place

Dearest Winston,

I was very glad to get your letter this morning. I think I will not try and get you an extra week because really every moment is of value to you now before you go up for your examination in June. The loss of a week now may mean your not passing, which I am sure you will admit would be very discreditable & disadvantageous. After you have got into the army you will have many weeks for amusement and idleness should your inclinations go in that direction, but now I do pray you my dear boy to make the most of every hour of your time so as to render your passing a certainty.

I remember when I was going up at Oxford for "final schools" I took something of an extra week & consequently altogether neglected what was called "special subjects". The result was that I just missed the First Class degree and only took a Second, & I have often thought since what a fool I was to lose the chance of a First for a few hours or days amusement. If you return Monday as I understand you will, we shall have a few days together before you return to Harrow, and after that the Easter holidays will soon be upon us, tho I must say I hope you will work like a little dray horse right up to the summer examination, only about four months off.

Your mother and I have just come back from Penn, Lord & Lady Howe's place where there was to have been a party for the Prince of Wales. Of course he could not come on account of the illness of the Duke of Clarence, & the party was broken up by the death of the poor Duke one of the saddest events I have ever known. Our party was naturally gloomy & dull. I shall stay on in London now & not go to Paris till Saturday week at the earliest. I think you must have had a novel & not unpleasant experience staying at Versailles. Hoping to see you back all safe Monday

Believe me ever Your most affte father
RANDOLPH S.C.

Lady Randolph to Winston

15 January [1892]   2 Connaught Place

Dearest Winston,

Papa showed me his letter to you. He won't hear of yr asking for an extra week. I am very sorry – but if you come home Monday you will have nearly a fortnight at home. I have written to Mr Minssen to ask him to let you stay at Baron Hirsch's Sunday night – & to give you enough money to travel home. You had better come 1st class as you will be alone. Come by the 11 o'c train Monday morning – I will send to meet you at Victoria. Don't get into any mischief on the way! It will be very nice having you home. Papa does not go to Paris until tomorrow week so you will have a week with him. Give my love to Prince Sagan[1] & take care of yrself. Jack has had a touch of influenza, & says you only write scraps to him.

Yr loving
MOTHER

[1] Charles William, 4th Duke de Talleyrand and 3rd Duke de Sagan (1833–1910).

At this period Winston wrote a number of letters to the *Harrovian* under the pen-names of 'De Profundis', 'Junius Junior' and 'Truth'.

To the Editors of the Harrovian

THE VAUGHAN LIBRARY

8 October 1891

Dear Sirs,

Might I add a reform to the managements of the opening of the Vaughan Library? Might not it be opened on whole School days, from 6.30–8, and also on half-holidays, from 2.30–4, rather than 4–6.

Yours sincerely

DE PROFUNDIS

To the Editors of the Harrovian

[Not published]

[? November 1891]

Dear Sirs,

Since you so kindly printed my last letter, I will venture to further 'ventilate my grievances'. I will not act without precedent. In a number published two or three terms ago, you sanctioned a discussion on the advantages and defects of the Harrow "Hat". Therefore I make my complaint.

The Class rooms provided for several forms are very bad. In some the light is meagrely doled out as in the Old Music Room, The Towers of the new speech room and Mr. Welsford's Room. In others as the 'cock-loft' the wind of heaven has free access from every quarter. Something ought to be done. Either the number of the school should not exceed the number for whom proper accomodation can be provided, or new class rooms should be built. Since that conspicuous, though unsightly edifice, the Music Schools was erected with so much ease I would respectfully suggest the latter alternative.

Yours etc.

DE PROFUNDIS

To the Editors of the Harrovian

19 December 1891

Dear Sirs,

Great as the School undoubtedly is, it cannot afford to allow any of its mechanism to fall out of gear. When a public school possesses a Gymnasium, and especially such a fine one as ours, it becomes the duty of every one of us to see that it should not go to rack and ruin. I am far from asserting that the Gymnasium has gone completely down the hill, but it is no sceret that it is going that way. This being so, it is for each and all to see that it goes no further in that direction.

We have lately been startled by an imposing announcement that the "School Display" would take place in the Gymnasium on Saturday, 12th December. Whether those who went to see this "Display" were satisfied is more than I can say, but every one will assent when I state that the notice would have been much more correct, had it proclaimed that the Aldershot Staff would give a Display in the Gymnasium on Saturday, 12th December.

A School Assault-at-Arms is intended to bring out our own talent. The Aldershot Staff can be seen elsewhere, but untold gold could not purchase the services of the School. Among the performers, the *School* was conspicuous by its absence. The endeavour to prove that four equalled eight failed signally. Picture the "Display" without the assistant of the Aldershot Sergeants – it would indeed have been a "show".

Now, what I ask, and what the School ought to ask, and will ask, is – Why did so few *boys* do anything? Why was the performance watched from the gallery by two members of the School Eight? Why is it that when, within a hundred yards of the Gymnasium, there is an athlete, whose sparring has ever been the guarantee of a full house, boxing was entirely omitted from the programme? It seems that to these questions certain answers might be made. "The School," it might be said, "were asked and wouldn't, the boxer has been approached and has refused, the members of the Eight have been exhorted, but they have declined with thanks."

If that is so, there must surely be some reason for this spontaneous refusal, and to find this reason I turn to the Editors of *The Harrovian*.

There is another excuse that may be set forth. It may be urged that no one else was good enough to perform. In that case no further question is necessary. If, out of all who go to the Gymnasium, only five per annum are fit to perform before the School at the Assault, there is obviously a hitch somewhere.

All these things that I have enumerated serve to suggest that there is "something rotten in the State of Denmark." I have merely stated facts – it is not for me to offer an explanation of them. To you, sirs, as directors of public opinion, it belongs to lay bare the weakness. Could I not propose that some of your unemployed special correspondents might be set to work to unravel the mystery, and to collect material wherewith these questions may be answered.

The School itself has an ancient history; even the Gymnasium dates back to a Tudor. In those days they were not wont to "Riske" the success of the School Assault-of-Arms in the manner in which it was done on Saturday last. For three years the Assaults have been getting worse and worse. First the Midgets, then the Board School, and finally, the Aldershot Staff have been called in to supplement the scanty programme. It is time there should be a change, and I rely on your influential columns to work that change.

Yours truly
JUNIUS JUNIOR

To the Editors of the Harrovian

18 February 1892

Dear Sirs,

Your correspondent "Junius Junior," though he displays a most laudable zeal for the welfare of the Gymnasium, seems to be just a trifle too severe on its present condition. The absence of the members of the Eight was due to an unforeseen combination of accidents: one had left, one had been so weakened by a fractured wrist that he could not hope to perform with any success, a third was unable to practise because of an approaching Scholarship (now won), and, last of all, the captain himself suddenly fell ill the night before the assault. The Aldershot staff were, no doubt, splendid; but what member of the School could devote as much time to Gymnastic training as these men who live by it? Moreover, the last few years the proportion of the performances done by the School to that done by outsiders has always been rather small; there have generally been drilled squads, or professional boxers, or midgets, or bagpipers, *et hoc genus omne* – in fact this last time there were numerically far less outsiders than usual. Still, it is quite true that the School might to a great deal more that it does at present, not only in gymnastics, but in Boxing, Fencing, Singlestick, or Quarterstaff. It also strikes one as somewhat strange that your correspondent should say "the Eight have been exhorted, but they have declined with thanks." The absentees all had a very valid reason for their absence.

Yours truly
AEQUITAS JUNIOR

To the Editors of the Harrovian

THE GYMNASIUM

17 March 1892

Dear Sirs,

When fired by the lamentable failure of the Assault-at-Arms I wrote my last letter to you, I expected an answer. I had hoped to see an emphatical denial of the charges which I made. I had looked for an explanation, offered not only to one, but to all of my questions.

It seems, however, that I was mistaken. Your correspondent, "Aequitas Junior," does not answer my letter: he avoids my main statement and seeks to champion his cause from a side issue; in fact, sirs, I had to read his letter several times before I could determine whether it was intended for an answer or a confirmation of what I wrote. But since it explains the one sentence of my letter which he is good enough to quote, I have decided to consider it as an answer.

I will not pause to criticise his style nor comment on his probable motives, though I am inclined to think that both are equally poor. Beginning with his opening sentence we find that he thinks I have been "just a trifle too severe" on the conditions of the Gymnasium. I may have been. I will not dispute the point. But if the statements detailed at length in my last letter were only incorrect in one particular, and if the inferences I drew were only "just a trifle too severe," the state of things must indeed be bad.

As to the rest of the letter, it does not answer or concern me. He seems, however, to be under the impression that I compared the School Eight with the Aldershot staff. I deny it. Such a comparison, if indeed possible, would have been too odious. As a strong argument in favour of something not stated, he triumphantly asserts that "this time there were numerically far less outsiders than usual." That is true; but he should also state that there were far less *both of School and outsiders* than ever before.

I assert, then, that my questions remain unanswered and my charges unrefuted. If what I stated were false, surely it were easy to prove it so, and if true, who should object? And in the presence of this half-hearted reply, which says, I allow, all there is to be said, and in the presence of the confirmation afforded to me by "Octavus," I appeal to the readers of the *Harrovian* to decide whether in my last letter I stated fact or falsehood.

Yours sincerely

JUNIUS JUNIOR

(We have omitted a portion of our correspondent's letter, which seemed to us to exceed the limits of fair criticism – Eds *Harrovian*.)

To the Editors of the Harrovian

EXTRACT

17 March 1892

Dear Sirs,

The article of your correspondent "Junius Junior" in the last number of the *Harrovian,* has drawn the public attention to a fact which no longer can be concealed. Though there is a touch of youthful petulance about the style, and some of the strictures on the introduction of a foreign element into the Harrow School Assault-at-Arms are too severe, still it is quite true that the performance of the School itself were mainly conspicuous by their absence. The bout with the quarterstaff was very interesting, but its interest would have been far more than doubled if the combatants had been members of the School. The truth is that the School doesn't seem to care so much for the Gymnasium as it ought to be. It is hard to tell why it should be so; perhaps it is a passing fashion. . . .

Yours querulously

NORFOLK HOWARD

To the Editors of the Harrovian

TOPICS OF THE SCHOOL

17 November 1892

Sirs,

An article which appeared in the last issue of The Harrovian makes a statement which is worthy of note. The writer remarks that we have been spending "hundreds of pounds" on the beautifying of Harrow, in the last few years. If it is the case that money is so plentiful, it would surely not be a bad plan to expend a few of these "hundreds of pounds" on building two or three decent class rooms to re-place the "dens", (I use the word advisedly) – such as the "cock-loft," the Speech-room Towers, and the old Music-Room.

This genius proposes to pull down the wall near the Speech-room, just because the colour does not suit his taste. Nothing could be more absurd. To destroy a wall, newly built, when there are a thousand necessary causes for outlay to School buildings and other directions, is worthy of The Harrovian at its best.

*　　*　　*

An idea is being started for enlarging the Dressing-room of the Gymnasium. This is a reasonable ground for expenditure. As, however, some time must necessarily elapse before the alterations can be made, permit me to propose that more towels and towel-racks should be placed there without delay. The reasons are purely those suggested to the average mind by a survey of the following facts.

i.   The room possesses two towels at present.
ii. These are changed once a week.
iii. They are used during that time by over 300 boys.
iv. Gymnastics is conducive to warmth.

*   *   *

Apropos of the Gymnasium, it is rumoured that the Assault will this year surpass in interest all previous displays. No pains are being spared to make it a success. I hear, however, that the Harrow Mission intend sending a squad of boys to work. I think that a separate show might be fairly allotted to them, as the time at the assault is already too limited.

*   *   *

WHAT IT MAY COME TO. (Scene, Sixth Form Ground. Match in progress).
Excited Player: "Whose ball?"
Umpire, in the distance (as usual): "Don't know – wasn't looking."

*   *   *

The Rifle Corps had their usual treat this term. We must congratulate them on a very fine day, for a wonder. Not only those who knew their drill were allowed to go, but also those who had either forgotten, or had never learned it. They, however, enjoyed themselves immensely, and held "Plevna Fort," with "Volunteer" courage. Afterwards there was the usual "feed" at the Assembly Rooms. The members of the Corps have since proved their devotion to that institution by attending drill in such musters that there are now *three* morning drills a week, instead of *six*, as formerly.

*   *   *

Formerly the 5th of November was a great day at Harrow. The whole school used to let off fireworks, and generally enjoy themselves. This is no longer the case. It is, however, good to reflect that the School are compensated for the loss of their amusement by the knowledge that the Monitors have a dinner on that night.

*   *   *

The Debating Society had their "Revival" the other day. It is a pity that only the Fifth and Sixth Forms are allowed to be members. There are many rational beings below that standard who would enjoy an opportunity of arguing. I would propose that the Society should be public to the School, and that it should be in truth the *School Debating Society*.

*   *   *

At the Instantaneous Photography Lecture, the magic lantern, as usual, felt faint; but being invigorated by copious draughts of Oxygin and Hydrogin, it recovered its former mediocrity.

*   *   *

However absurd it may seem to speak of "lighting arrangement" and the "Harrow gas" in one breath, I must pause to draw attention to this extraordinary substance. Gas has two duties to perform – to light and to warm. Harrow gas does neither – it only smells. Surely the electric light project might be considered, with a view to its speedy adoption.

A new "fez," without a tassel, has been invented for the football eleven. This reflects great credit on the originator, a prominent member of that body.

*   *   *

Speaking of football, one cannot omit mentioning the need of a cap for "Thirders". Here is a chance for the masters, scholars, former scholars, and other friends of the School.

*   *   *

In conclusion, two or three words are necessary on the subject of "Swagger Rules." This ancient and historic code is rapidly falling into disuse and disrespect. Nowadays an old custom is too rare to be allowed to drop; and it is also obviously unfair that boys who have been waiting for their "Three Years' privileges" for so long, should find these same privileges granted to, or taken by, boys of one term standing in the School.

I am Sirs, Yours sincerely
TRUTH

To the Editors of the Harrovian

SCHOOL TOPICS

"Magna est veritas, sed rara"

17 December 1892

Dear Sirs,

Football is the chief subject of discussion at the present time, and all the attention of the School is rivetted on the issue of the "Cock" House match. The two rivals for the cup are Pink and Blue. Blue is the "favourite" – but only in a strictly technical sense.

*   *   *

In the match against Mr Greatorex's Eleven the School experienced ill fortune. The odd base gave rise to so much dispute, that the Harrow Eleven withdrew their claim for fear of further loosening their opponents' "hair."

*   *   *

In the last number of The Harrovian there is a mis-print. I do not advocate the necessity of a "cap" for Third Elevens, but of a "cup."

*   *   *

I have been asked to bring up again the question of allowing the Football Eleven to wear their football coats in the summer term. Sirs, I speak from an utterly disinterested standpoint. If the Cricket Eleven wear their coats down at Football, then the Football Eleven ought to wear *their* coats down at Cricket. This is logic, pure and simple.

*   *   *

The Gymnasium has made good progress this Term in many ways, and there is no reason why we should not be well represented at Aldershot in the Public Schools competition in Gymnastics. While the Boxing is under the charge of J.H.T., the School need have no apprehension of failure in that department.

*   *   *

The old prescription for many ills used to be a blue pill and a black draught. The Philathletic Club have adopted a new remedy. They distribute *black* pills, and it is the recipient who looks *blue*.

The organ is to be played "at all times" of the day in the near future. This will, I hope, make the Speech-Room Towers absolutely untenable. It is hardly creditable to the School that they should be used for class rooms. When the enterprising reporter or the "cute" American come to "see" the School they are not shown into such rooms as those I have alluded to. No! there is no time. They go and look at the Vaughan Library or the Museum Schools, and come away struck with the happy lot of the Harrow Boy.

A GLIMPSE INTO THE FUTURE – a Drama in Four Acts

SCENE – Interior of lofty pinnacle, recently converted into a class room. From below are heard sundry discordant noises suggestive of "Spring cleaning," and sounds of a violent altercation between the lady conducting the cleaning arrangements and her son. Above, a Master is endeavouring to instruct a Form in Algebra.

I. Above

Master (faintly): "Now, if we square both sides the equation becomes—"
1st Voice: "Please, sir, can we have a window open?"
M.: "I'm afraid you can't."
2nd Voice: "Please, sir, can we have some more light?"
M.: "I'm afraid you can't."
3rd Voice: "Please, sir, can I have a desk to write on?"
M.: "I'm afraid you can't."
Gruff voice from below: "D'you want th' book, sir?"
M.: "I am afraid we have no room for it up here."

II. Below

The Lady (fortissimo): "Come you here, and drop that row."
Her Son: "Well, ain't I a comin'?"
The Lady (louder than ever): "Daon't mike sech a noise – they've got a clarst on upstairs."
H.S. (scornfully): " 'oo's makin' a noise, I should loike to kneow?"
   (Dispute interrupted by entrance of a long-haired Mozartish boy, with an engineer.)
L.H.M. Boy: "Oh, Muggins, if you will start the blowing engine. I will play for an hour or so."
Engineer: "All right, Sir."
   (Sounds as of a steam engine getting to work, followed by the resonant tones of the organ playing a jerky chant.)

III. Above

All the Voices: "Please, Sir, can we go down and stop them playing the organ, sir?"

M.: "I am afraid you can't."

All Voices (decidedly): "Then we can't work."

M. (desperately): "I'm afraid you can't."

[Exeunt down the "stairs" to break their necks]

IV. Below

The organ continues playing.

Curtain

The following Euclid Paper has been sent to me by an Eton correspondent:

"Write all the Euclid you know – not more than two propositions from each book, or one if the book be very short – and the twelve easiest deductions you can think of. You are recommended to write out the Propositions in the order in which they occur to you."

I take this opportunity of expressing my thanks to M. R. Milbanke and G. T. Chowne, by whom the Cartoon has been designed and executed; and also to the Editor, who disregard of expense allowed this graphic appeal to be published. It is by an inadvertence that one artist's initials do not appear on the plate. – I am, Sirs,

Yours sincerely

TRUTH

(The Philistine Correspondent of the *Harrovian*.)

To the Editors of the Harrovian

15 June 1893

Sirs,

The appeals which were made last Term and the Term before to the Gymnasium authorities with regard to the Dressing Room have at last taken effect. The number of towels has been increased to *four* per week. It is reported that the outlay and *great* expense of this improvement will be met in part by a grant from the School Funds and in part by voluntary subscription from the friend of the Gymnasium.

The Superintendent of the Gymnasium has every reason to be congratulated on the new "A vest." There is now no reason why the House Belt should not be left to the discretion of the Captain of the House Four.

*   *   *

Why did not the winner of the Stewart-Brown Cup, who was a nine-stone boxer, represent the School at Aldershot? I am informed by a very high authority that if he had gone the School would most certainly have secured another prize. A plain question requires a plain answer.

*   *   *

I think I have before alluded to the luxurious accommodation of the Speech-Room Towers. "Music hath charms," and it has been decided to add these charms to the many advantages already enjoyed by the fortunate occupants of these Rooms. The next thing we shall hear is the *Binomial Theorem* set to music.

*   *   *

I notice, Sirs, that in your last number you again allude to the wall near the Speech-Room. This structure, which answers its purpose remarkably well, appears to be a source of "Temporary offences" to you. At risk of being called a "vandal" or even a "Philistine," I must advise you to adopt the practical motto of "Ease before Elegance," and to turn your attention to loftier, or rather "cock-loftier," things than the Speech-Room wall.

As soon as the last blank cartridge of the Term has been consumed the Rifle Corps is dead. But with the new Term comes the prospect of more cartridges to be fired, to say nothing of a whole holiday, and the Corps rises proudly from the ashes of the old ones, like a Phoenix on a large scale.

*   *   *

This Term, however, its attractions are phenomenal. Morning drills in the yard, evening drills in the Cricket Field, a chance of Bisley and a real live Camp. Join! all who are tired of being asked to join, or who cannot find valid excuses. Enlist! all who are patriotic or who desire a "whole." The eyes of Europe are upon you, and bread-and-cheese and pork pies will be provided free of charge on Field-days.

*   *   *

It was evening when the Boy entered the magnificent hall, hung with pink

satin (changed daily). A soft carpet deadened each footfall, and the harmon-
iously-shaded electric light shed a cosy glow on the elegant furniture. "Strawberry and Lemon!" said the Boy. The stately attendant handed him a plate.
"I asked for an ice," said the Boy. "And you have got one, sir," said the
kneeling page. As on inspection this proved to be true, the Boy paid his four-
pence, and departed – a thirstier if not wiser Boy.

* * *

Yours sincerely
TRUTH

* * * *

Winston to Lord Randolph
(Blenheim Papers)

Sunday 31 January [1892]   Harrow

My dear Papa,
    You will be glad to hear I have got my Remove. I was not very pleased as
I had hoped for a double. However Mr Welldon says if I work well for a
fortnight he will give me a Special Remove. I am working hard at my fencing
as I hope, with luck, to be champion. Mr W. congratulated me on having
enjoyed my holidays. I am in Monsieur Minssen's French Prose division. I
find that I have greatly improved in French. There is of course no news,
except that the authorities try to avert the influenza by quinine pills and by
prayers.
    Hoping you will come down and see me soon, I remain
                                        Your ever loving son
                                        WINSTON S. CHURCHILL

Mrs Everest to Winston

?[January/February 1892]   2 Sydney Villas
                                                                   Cranmer Road
                                                                   Forest Gate

My darling Winny,
    Very sorry I cannot do anything for you as I am in Bed with the Influenza
at Mrs Richmonds. I enclose a letter from the Dentist which was sent here by
Annie instead of sending it to you. Am so sorry you have got the toothache
poor dear Boy. I shall have to stay here another week – 5 of us have got it here.
                                        Ever your loving
                                        WOOM

Mrs Everest to Winston

Monday 9 a.m.   2 Sydney Villas
?[January/February 1892]

My darling Winny,

Have just recd your 2nd letter which has been to Banstead both of them &
caused the delay. I am very glad to hear you are better of the tooth ache. I
have been too ill to do or think of anything, have been in bed six days. I am
going to get up a little today. I am very short of money. I have only 2£ by
me to pay my Doctors bill & take me to Banstead when I go. I don't know
when I shall go at any rate not before next saturday. I enclose P. order for
10/- dear am sorry you did not get it in time for Saturday. I have had the
Russian epidemic it laid a firm grip on me & has left me very weak & a
Bronchial Cough.

I am so glad you went to see Jackie. I must write to him poor darling. Write
& tell me if you get the P. order safe.

                                        Ever your loving old
                                                    WOOM

Lady Wilton to Winston

6 February [1892]   [Le Nid]

My dear Winston,

So glad to hear from you & hope you are very "fit". Miss Trafford *is* a pretty
woman, don't you think?

I'm sorry to say the Roulette tables have *not* been treating me very well
lately!

When will you finally leave Harrow? I hope you'll come to the Hatch some
time this summer.

                        With best love – Yr very affecte Deputy Mother
                                                LAURA WILTON

Winston to Lady Randolph
(*Blenheim Papers*)

?[7 February 1892]   Harrow

My darling Mummy,

Thank you very much for your letter. I am working very hard for my
Special Remove. I do hope I shall get it, but some horrid master has been
saying that the army class get too many Removes. I am making much progress
in my fencing and have beaten the others.

I am getting terribly low in my finances. You say I never write for love but always for money. I think you are right but remember that you are my banker and who else have I to write to.

Please send me "une peu".

J'espère que vous êtes en bonne santé, comme votre fils devoué.

WINSTON S. CHURCHILL

Jack Milbanke to Winston

7 February 1892　　　　　　　　　　　　　　　　　Eartham
　　　　　　　　　　　　　　　　　　　　　　　　　Chichester

My dear Winston

Many thanks for your letter. How terribly bored you must have been by yourself in France. I am going to Paris at Easter for about a fortnight if I am still alive but it seems extremely doubtful at present as I am quite done up with over work. You must be having a good time at Harrow with no first school etc.[1] My exam comes off in March but I am afraid I have not much chance of passing as there are several hundred candidates & 40 commissions. We had a good days hunting yesterday but I lost a shoe & so had to come home.

Give my love to Dudley & tell him it is his turn to write.

Yours ever
JACK M.

Sir H. Drummond Wolff to Winston

11 Fevrier 1892　　　　　　　　　　　　　　　28 Cadogan Place

Mon cher Winston,

Votre aimable lettre m'est parvenue ce soir. Merci mille fois. Je suis très content d'apprendre que vous parlez le français magnifiquement et j'espère que vous apprendrez encore d'autres langues.

Je vais partir sous peu pour Madrid où un jour vous viendrez peut-être me voir.[2]

Mille amitiés Votre bien affectionné
H. DRUMMOND WOLFF

Winston to Lady Randolph

[? February 1892]　　　　　　　　　　　　　　　　　[Harrow]

Dear Mamma,

Many thanks for your kind letter and more for your kinder "2 quid".

I have recd a letter from Sir H. Wolfe in French, which I am about to answer.

---

[1] There were changes in the school time-table owing to an influenza epidemic.
[2] Sir Henry Drummond WOLFF was at this time Ambassador in Madrid.

M

Il neige! Il fait un froid de loup. Je suis en bonne santé. Les armes marchent très bien.

I have a little sore throat for which I am staying away from Chapel.

With much love I remain, Your loving son
WINNY

Winston to Lord Randolph
(*Blenheim Papers*)

Sunday [?14 February 1892]   Harrow

Dear Papa,

I am sorry to tell you that I have not succeeded in obtaining my Special Remove. However I am sure to get one at the End of the term.

I am working hard, though at present I am confined to the House with a bad cold.

I am getting on with my fencing and hope, with luck, to be school champion.

The number of the "Harrovian" just issued contains an answer to my letter which you saw. I will send it to you that you may see how awfully feeble it is.

When will you come down and see me? Can you manage Sat next? If it is convenient let me know, and I will tell you about the trains.

I am so glad to hear from Everest (via Thomas) that you admired my bulldog. She is really a good creature with rather a good pedigree.

There is no news except that the whole house got into a row for having a Boxing Meeting last Sunday. More notice was taken of it because the Head of the house was Timekeeper. However I am very happy and getting on capitally.

So with much love, I remain ever your loving son
WINSTON S. CHURCHILL

Winston to Lady Randolph

[?28 February 1892]   [Harrow]

Darling Mummy,

I shall be up on Tuesday, at 2.10 punctually. I have then 20 minutes to feed in. Please arrange for the oculist to see me at about 5 o'clock or (later). Then I shall have the time between Dentist and oculist to kiss and love you. My eyes are getting very weak and I think I really ought to see a man.

I will send you the next 'Harrovian' in which I think there will be another Letter of Junius.[1]

[1] The issue of March 17. (See page 311.)

There is no news. Tell Papa I thought his speech excellent – though I am not sure that Lord R. [Rosebery] appreciated it so much.[1] I saw Lord Rothschild on Thursday. Jack writes and says he doesn't expect Papa will come to see him at all – he seems rather low.

Your loving son
WINSTON S. CHURCHILL

Winston to Lady Randolph

[?16 March 1892] [Harrow]

Darling Mamma,

I am terrified by hearing that you have been robbed of your purse.[2] C'est Dommage, because at the same moment I must put in a request for 'un peu plus d'argent.

I am quite well. I am very sick with you for going away like that. I am awfully excited about the fencing which comes off on Tuesday.

I know I shall get beaten yet . . ! I am working very hard. I have lots of news but will not write it all now. Don't go to that Casino. Invest your money in me, its safer. Darling Mummy don't slang me about the shortness of this letter. You are a bird. My letter will be in the Harrovian to-morrow. I will send it you when you get back to Connaught Place.

Good Bye my darling Mummy.
Best luck and much love, From your loving
WINSTON S. CHURCHILL

I have waited for the address which is coming (like Noel)

Tommy Trafford to Winston

18 March 1892 Buckingham Palace Hotel

My dear Winston,

Would you oblige me by giving me the name & direction of the old gentleman at Versailles, where you went in the winter time? A young connection of mine Ld Granard[3] is studying for his diplomatic examination & is desirous

[1] Lord Randolph spoke at Paddington on February 22.
[2] At the Casino in Monte Carlo.
[3] Bernard Arthur William Patrick Hastings, 8th Earl of Granard (1874–1948), had succeeded to the title in 1889. In a varied career he was to become a Deputy Speaker of the House of Lords, Assistant Postmaster-General, a member of the Senate of the Irish Free State, and for twenty-two years Master of the Horse to King Edward VII and King George V.

of passing a short time in a french family to polish up his French (& german also if possible). It struck me your old friend's house would be the very place for him to go to. I think Granard is about 18, therefore he could reside there very much under the same conditions you did. Tell me what you think – as I am anxious to let Lady Granard know as soon as possible.

I hope my good friend you are getting on well & that you will end by passing your Army Examinations with flying colors. I see poor Lady Randolph has had her pocket picked at that delightful resort Monte Carlo!!

Your good friend
TOMMY TRAFFORD

Murland Evans[1] to Winston

[? March 1892]   Tubbendens
                                                        By Orpington
                                                        Kent

Dear Churchill,

I feel I must write and ask you how the fencing has got on. I suppose you are now a first rate "Monsieur a outrance"! How did you like spending your holidays in France? If you have a spare minute I should like very much to hear how you have got on. I suppose the new alteration of work at Harrow pleases you vastly in as much as you rise so late in the morning. Do you know I am actually riding every day now! I have learnt to "stick" on a horse at last.

Always dear Churchill Yours affectly
MURLAND EVANS

Lady Wilton to Winston

22 [March 1892]   [Le Nid]

Many thanks – my dear Winston – for yrs recd yesterday. I do hope you are successful in your fencing?

I see your Mama often – & I am glad to tell you she is looking *very* well. I think she is coming to lunch here today.

---

[1] Murland de Grasse Evans (1874–1946); formerly at Elstree School, he was fencing champion at Harrow immediately before Winston. Son of Francis Henry Evans, a Liberal MP who was created a baronet in 1902 and whom Murland Evans succeeded as 2nd Bart in 1907. Like his father, Murland Evans was a partner in the shipping firm of Donald Currie & Co (see p. 253); he navigated the first British Steamship Service round Africa. In 1934 he took Holy Orders and was rector of Tittleshall from 1940 until his death.

The weather is not very fine – but I have been very fit – a mere chill. I will hope to see you this summer. Perhaps at the Hatch.

> With best love. Yr ever affecte
> DEPUTY MOTHER

I've not yet seen pretty Miss Trafford.

Tommy Trafford to Winston

23 March [1892]

My dear Winston,

I thank you for your letter – It seems to me the Minssens is just the house for young Granard to go to. I suppose your Easter holidays soon begin now.

I am to dine with your Father tomorrow on his return from Welbeck.

> Yours ever
> TOMMY TRAFFORD

Winston to Lady Randolph

[? 24 March 1892]   [Harrow]

Darling Mummy,

I have won the Fencing. A very fine cup. I was far and away first. Absolutely untouched in the finals. I have written to Papa. The oranges were luscious.

My eyes are alright, though I have to wear glasses when doing fine work.

I will write again tomorrow but it is awfully late.

> Ever your loving son
> WINNY

Lord Randolph to Winston

25 March 1892   2 Connaught Place

Dearest Winston,

I congratulate you on your success. I only hope fencing will not too much divert your attention from the army class. I enclose you £2 with which you will be able to make a present to yr fencing master. Jack came up the other day looking vy well & fit. Your mother writes that they are having lovely weather out at the Riviera. She does not yet speak of coming home.

> Ever yr most affte father
> RANDOLPH S C.

Winston to Lord Randolph
(Blenheim Papers)

Sunday [27 March 1892]   [Harrow]

Dear Papa,

Many thanks for the £2. I bought a rather nice clock for the Instructor. I want to know if you think you will be able to go to Aldershot on the 7th. I am sure you would be greatly amused. All the Boxers of the different public schools about the country will be there.

Did you ever get the frantic letter I sent you about ten days ago asking you to wire to Welldon as it was a whole holiday and I could come up. I fancy you must not have received it as you took no notice, nor did you mention it in your last letter.

I should so much like you to go to Aldershot. It is not quite settled whether it will not be in London and if you reserve the 7th you will be sure of seeing it somewhere.

I want you to sign the order enclosed as after having won a school event it is customary to be photographed in the costume and to distribute the copies among ones friends.

If you could send me a soverign for myself it would be a great service in making up my accounts. I have received several letters from Mr Trafford who wants to send a boy to stay with Monsieur Minssen at Versailles.

Ever your loving son
WINSTON S. CHURCHILL

Jack to Winston

Sunday 27 March 1892   Elstree

My dear Winney,

Woom wrote to me and told me you had won your fencing, have you? Do write to me you have not written for a fortnight. I went for an ex [exeat] on last Sat till Mond do write.

I remain
JACK S. CH

Winston to Lady Randolph

Sunday [?27 March 1892]   [Harrow]

My darling Mama,

I am quite well and working as only I can work. My fencing is now my great employment out of school as now that I represent the School it behoves me to 'sweat up'.

I have become awfully wily and am sure I shall completely settle you on your return from the sunny south.

You must come back soon as I and Jack will be home in a fortnight. I will send you some of the photos I am going to have done in my Fencing attire with one hand on the cup, (which by the way is a Challenge Cup.) I am awfully tired as we had a very long field day yesterday.

Give my love to Lady W and take for yourself all the affection that can be expressed by your loving son

WINSTON S. CHURCHILL

PS I'm 'stoney'. If you could replenish the exchequer it would indeed be Tara-ra boom-de-ay.

Chester Dawson to Winston

27 March 1892   c/o The Rev H. P. Walker
St Catherine's School
Broxbourne

My dear Churchill,

Thank you so much for your short but most welcome letter. I have been so wanting to write to you but having no colleague this term, I have been, & am, very busy.

I well remember Versailles, my two or three visits there, the beautiful palace, park & fountains, The Great & Little Trianon; you are indeed fortunate in staying in such a town. How you must have enjoyed seeing those numerous pictures of battles especially Horace Vernet's[1]; did you not wish you were already in the army holding a commission?

I am very fond of Paris & its beautiful suburbs. St Germain I like too, I only went there for the first time in /89.

I am off to Malvern for a few days these next holidays but I shall not go till after Easter. We all leave here on Wednesday the 13th of next month.

I have been very unfortunate in football this term. I have hurt my knee badly & am lame, this happened last Monday, I was equally unfortunate over a month ago when our team went over to play a match at Bishop's Stortford.

Forster wrote to me a few days ago for the first time since he left Brighton. He has left Harrow & is now with a coach near Weston Super-Mare before

---

[1] Horace Vernet (1789–1863), son of the eminent French painter Carle Vernet, is well known for his spectacular battle panoramas which he painted for the historical galleries at Versailles and elsewhere for Louis Philippe and Napoleon III.

going to New College Oxford. I must find time to write to him shortly. I saw
Robin & Harry Firth during the holidays, they telegraphed to me to meet
them at the Charing Cross Hotel, they only stayed there one night on their
way from Guernsey. Robin went to Lyons the next day en route to India &
Harry to Bedford.

I dare say some day I shall hear of your going to India. How did you get
on with your fencing at Harrow or has it not come off yet? I have heard there
are several "Brunswickers' there now. Do let me hear from you again,
perhaps we may have a chance of meeting in Town somewhere these holidays.
Are you still with Mr Welldon? I think not. I believe you have left Harrow
now. Remember me kindly to Jack & Mrs Everest too when next you see her.
Accept my best wishes & remember me always as your old & faithful friend.

CHESTER DAWSON

Lady Randolph to Winston

Monday [28 March 1892]   Grand Hotel
                                                    Monte Carlo

Dearest Winston,

I am delighted that you won the fencing prize – you must write and tell
me all about it. I am in a great hurry, as they are waiting dinner for me, but
I feel I must send you my "congrats"! You will have to teach me. Jack seems
to have had a nice exeat.

Best love – Yr loving
MOTHER

Hope to be back next week.

Lord Randolph to Winston

29 March 1892   2 Connaught Place

Dearest Winston

I send you a P.O. £1, but you are really too extravagant. Do you mean to
say you spent the £2 I sent you on the present to yr fencing master. If you were
a millionaire you could not be more extravagant. I fear I cannot possibly get to
Aldershot on the 7th[1] it is Sandown races which I must go to. I think you have
got through about £10 this term. This cannot last, & if you are not more

---

[1] For the Public Schools' gymnastic, boxing and fencing competition. Winston won the
fencing championship by beating Johnson of Bradfield College and Ticehurst of Tonbridge
School. "His success," records the *Harrovian* of May 21, "was chiefly due to his quick and
dashing attack, which quite took his opponents by surprise." This was Harrow's only success:
Winston's cousin Dudley Marjoribanks was beaten in the final of the heavyweight boxing, and
the gymnastics team, which included Leopold Amery, was fourth.

careful should you get into the army six months of it will see you in the Bankruptcy Court. Do think this all over & moderate your ways & ideas.

Ever yr most affte father
RANDOLPH S.C.

Winston to Lord Randolph
(*Blenheim Papers*)

[30 March 1892]   [Harrow]

Dear Papa,

Thank you so much for the £1. I must confess that I only spent £1 on a present for Sergt Queese the other I employed in paying off some small sums I owed to various people. You don't know how easily one's money goes here. I have to get my own teas and genrally my own breakfasts – say 2/– a day then comes another shilling on fruit, and "food". Total three shillings per diem = 18/– a week + 2/– for Sat night biscuits etc. – This comes up to pound once a week. There have been 11 weeks as yet!!!

The competition is not on the 7th but on Friday the 8th. If this should by any chance be more convenient to you – please write. If not don't trouble, as I know how busy you are.

Mr Welldon tells me that I must write and "stir you up" to come down and deliver a "jaw" on S. Africa. I can't tell you how much it would be appreciated by the Boys. Lord Wolseley's lecture on the Red River expedition would be quite eclipsed. Therefore let me beg you to come as soon as you can.

I remain every your loving son
WINSTON S. CHURCHILL

Lady Randolph to Winston

Sunday [?3 April 1892]   Paris

Dearest Winston,

I shall be home on Tuesday night, & shall hope to be able to go to Harrow on Sat & see you – You dear – How have you been going on? – Paris is very cold, snowing this morning – I feel it doubly coming from the land of oranges & lemons! Jack writes very often & says he had a nice letter from you – Goodbye.

best love – Yr loving Mother
JSC

Reverend J. E. C. Welldon to Lord Randolph
(*Blenheim Papers*)

11 April 1892   Harrow

Dear Lord Randolph,

I have arranged (subject to your approval) with a gentleman, Mr F. H. C. Marshall[1] to coach Winston during the holidays. I have not seen him and can only trust therefore that he will be a success, but he is strongly recommended to me.

Mr Marshall will write to you about beginning work, and I have told him he must settle his remuneration with you. He knows exactly what work Winston ought to do. I am going out of England as soon as I am free.

Sincerely yours
J. E. C. WELLDON

Winston to Lord Randolph
(*Blenheim Papers*)

[8 May 1892]   Harrow

My dear Papa,

I got here all safe & in good time. We had a very pleasant and comfortable journey. Captain Coombes was exceedingly kind and did not leave me until he had put me in the cab. I was awfully pleased at being allowed to see the races, expecially the Guineas. I enjoyed myself immensely.

I am going to work awfully hard, and have already begun. I feel sure I shall pass in June.

If I don't it will not be any fault of mine. I feel very well and am just in time for a "spirit".

Ever your loving son
WINSTON S. CHURCHILL

Winston to Lady Randolph

[8 May 1892]   [Harrow]

My darling Mamma,

I recd your letter. Many thanks and much love. About the birth certificate and P.E. [Preliminary Examination] certificate; I am afraid it is important that they should be sent to the Military secretary as soon as possible.

---

[1] Francis Harrie Cotton Marshall (1864–1942), scholar of Sidney Sussex College, Cambridge. He became assistant master at St Dunstan's College, Downside, and Leeds Grammar School (1908–26), where he was nicknamed 'seaweed' because his long moustaches trailed in the water when he was swimming.

On the printed form it distinctly states that no delay should take place.

I am sure you must be awfully dull? [at Newmarket]. But I suppose you play the piano a good deal.

I had a letter from Papa the other day. Was Jack allowed to go to the races after I had left?

I am working awfully hard, without rotting I have done at least 10 hrs today. I am very tired so with much love

I remain, Your loving son
WINSTON S. CHURCHILL

Winston to Lady Randolph

[? 12 May 1892]   [Harrow]

My darling Mamma,

Please send the Preliminary Certificate as soon as possible, if you cannot possibly find it let me know and I will tell Mr Welldon & he will write and advise Papa what to do. I recd your letter many thanks and much love

from your Loving son
WINSTON S. CHURCHILL

I am working like blazes.

Reverend J. E. C. Welldon to Lord Randolph
(*Blenheim Papers*)

12 May 1892   Harrow

Dear Lord Randolph,

Mr Sanderson was no doubt right in saying, that your younger boy, if he enters the School in September, will be somewhat below the usual age at which boys enter. I understand that you wish to send him then, and I have kept a place for him. I shall therefore look for him at the examination in July. Of course I cannot offer an opinion upon his fitness in point of character for public school life but of that you will judge.

Winston is working admirably so far; my army masters report to me that if his work had always been as good as it is now his passing into Sandhurst would be assured. We hope he may distinguish himself in the examination.

With kind regards, Sincerely yours
J. E. C. WELLDON

Reverend J. E. C. Welldon to Lord Randolph
(*Blenheim Papers*)

16 May 1892   Harrow

Dear Lord Randolph,

Winston says Lady Randolph knows where his certificate of having passed
the preliminary examination is and can lay her hand upon it. I have asked
him to get it from her and also to get your own signature, which is necessary
to his formal application for his present examination; then I will send all the
papers to the proper authorities.

Sincerely yours
J. E. C. WELLDON

Winston to Lord Randolph
(*Blenheim Papers*)

[May 1892]   Harrow

Dear Papa,

I have recd the P [Preliminary] certificate and have sent them all in to the
Commissioners. I am working awfully hard and really think I have a decent
chance; but if I don't get through now I shall most certainly do so in November.

Dudley is going in for this exam too. He is not working a bit. He never does
a stroke more than he is forced but still as he is really very strong in Latin and
French and not weak in German he may get through.

Will you send me some money. I explained how I had had very heavy
expenses – in fact two thirds of my capital "wrenched from my grasp", in
my last letter. Please send me some more as I really have not been extravagant
this term.

With much love I remain your loving son
WINSTON S. CHURCHILL

Lady Wilton to Winston

26 [May 1892]   [Le Nid]

My dear Winston,

Very many thanks for yours. I hope to hear of your success later on & to see
you at the Hatch. I leave here on the 31st for Hotel Bristol, Paris – and will
come over to England abt 7th & go down to the Hatch about 3rd or 4th July.

'Tis *very* hot here now, & almost too hot. I heard from C. Johnstone – who seems much attached to you.

With love – Yr ever affecte Deputy Mother
LAURA WILTON

Lady Randolph to Winston

Monday [? May 1892]   Banstead

Dearest Winston,

Here is a P.O.O. for 30/-. Yr wants are many – & you seem a perfect sieve as regard money. I shall be delighted to see [you] tomorrow – wire what time you come. No more at present, as I shall see you I hope so soon.

Yr loving Mother
JSC

Lady Randolph to Winston

18 June [1892]   Banstead

Dearest Winston,

I will give you some money when I see you tomorrow. You will find me at Lady Hindlip's.[1]

affectly
Yr MOTHER
JSC

Winston to Lord Randolph
(Blenheim Papers)

[? June 1892]   [Harrow]

My dear Papa,

Thank you so much for the £2. They were very welcome. Our examinations are on the 29th June, and our medical is on the 27th; I should like to stay in London very much if it would not inconvenience you very much; as it would do away with the railway journey each morning and evening.

I am still very sanguine. Marjoribanks continued to idle and I to "sap". If he gets in and I don't it will be a shame.

Ever your loving son
WINSTON S. CHURCHILL

[1] In London at 33 Hill Street, Berkley Square.

Winston to Lord Randolph
(*Blenheim Papers*)

?[30 June 1892]   2 Connaught Place
Time 7.10

Dear Papa,

I have waited till now in the hopes of seeing you. I must catch the 7.30 so
cannot stay any longer. Yesterday I did very well, that is considering that
Mathematics is a weak Subject. I should have got 800 marks or about $\frac{1}{3}$.
Today we had Geometrical drawing (marks 1000) out of which I probably
secured 600. And English essay (500) in which, (as I did a very good one) I
ought to get 400

This is quite satisfactory and if I do not break down in my other subjects ·
I might be successful.

Ever your loving son
WINSTON S. CHURCHILL

Lady Wilton to Winston

4 July [1892]   Brown's Hotel

My dear Winston,

Your letter was forwarded to me here – Many thanks for it. I should like
some more news of you. I am going today to "Garlogs House, Winchester,
Hants", till Friday – when I will be at "The Hatch, Surly Hall, Windsor".
Too glad to see you there later on if you can come. I will try & win you a little
coin at Stockbridge.

Ever your very affecte Deputy Mother
LAURA WILTON

Lady Wilton to Winston

12 July [1892]   [The Hatch]

My dear Winston,

So many thanks for yours. I will be delighted to have you again – but
unluckily this little house is full for some time – (10 days) as I have my daughter
& my 2 grand children coming soon for 10 days – & yr father is coming on
Saturday. If you are to come one Sunday *for the day* I should be *delighted* &
later on you must come & stay a few days. Do give my best love to your Mama
& believe me.

Ever yr affecte Deputy Mother
LAURA WILTON

Chester Dawson to Winston

22 July 1892   St Catherine's School
                                                               Broxbourne

My dear Churchill,

I write to congratulate you on your success in the fencing tournament at Harrow. I was informed of this by my new colleague who also tells me you beat a friend of his, an old boy of Haileybury Coll in the semi-final. I should very much like to have been present.

I am leaving this school, for good, tomorrow, the headmaster kindly allowing me to return home a few days earlier as I am off to Cornwall very early next week. I shall be away nearly a month then I am hoping to get on the staff of some illustrated paper. I have, with that object in view, been very busy making many sketches of my surroundings down here. I only wish I had made as many & as good of the dear old school at Brighton. I need hardly tell you if you or your father could possibly help me with your influence, it would be much appreciated. I do so want to give up tutoring & in that I am sure I have your sympathy. I do hope you are equally successful in other things as in fencing. Wishing you happy holidays

I remain Yr affectionate friend
CHESTER DAWSON

Winston to Chester Dawson
(*Longleat Papers*)

[Postmark] 14 August 1892   Banstead

Dear Mr Dawson,

I feel I am sadly in arrears as regards my correspondence with you. I received your last letter with much pleasure. I am so glad you have given up teaching – sketching is much more in your line. (No insult intended!)

I have often thought of Miss Thompson & I have arrived at the conclusion that many of the rules & most of the food were utterly damnable.

Far be it from me however to speak ill of either Miss Kate or Miss J. as I have always "cherished the most affectionate remembrances of both . . . still half a sausage – ugh!!!

I wish you every sort of luck & will not fail to send you a line on the result of my examination being known.

Ever your most affectionate friend
WINSTON S. CHURCHILL

"Brulez cette lettre, s'il vous plait."

Lady Wilton to Winston

21 August [1892]   The Hatch

Dear Winston,

So very many thanks for yours. I found it on my return from *Offord*, where I went for a few days' fishing & most excellent sport I had.

What are yr plans? – & how are yr Father & Mother? My love to them both & to Jack & of course to yourself. Enclosed £2 for yr pocket money, dear –

Yr very affecte Deputy Mother

LW

Louis Moriarty[1] to Winston

23 August 1892   [Harrow]

My dear Churchill,

I am sending you the numbers[2] as far as I have got them. I cannot vouch for their accuracy:

646 – Hilton[3]
391 – Bryce[4]
792 – Marjoribanks
574 – Gowans[5]
842 – Paine[6]
787 – Mc Taggart[7]
(?896 – Rome)[8]

That is all I have got.

[1] Louis Martin Moriarty (1855–1930), Army Class master at Harrow.

[2] By which each candidate in the Army examination is identified.

[3] Horace Anwyl Hilton (1873–   ) joined The Buffs 1896 after first going up to University College, Oxford. Transferred to Scots Guards, 1897, served in Boer War, retired 1902. Served 1914–18 as Major in Royal Army Service Corps.

[4] Charles Alexander Bryce (1875–   ) joined Coldstream Guards 1898, served in Boer War, retired 1905. Served First World War as Major in Royal Naval Division.

[5] William Gowans (1873–1915) joined Yorkshire Light Infantry 1895, served in Boer War, Captain 1901, Major 1914; killed in action May 1915.

[6] Albert Ingraham Paine (1874–1949) joined King's Royal Rifle Corps 1895, served in Boer War (DSO 1902), retired as Captain 1907. Lieut-Colonel commanding 12th Battalion KRRC 1914–16 (CMG 1916, despatches twice).

[7] Maxwell Fielding McTaggart (1874–1936), an outstanding gymnast both at Harrow and at Sandhurst, joined 5th Lancers 1895, served in Tirah Expedition 1897 and in Boer War. Captain 1904, Major 1909, Lieut-Colonel, 1/5th Gordon Highlanders 1915–18 (DSO 1916, Bar to DSO 1920, twice wounded, despatches three times). Retired 1922. Author of *Hints on Horsemanship*.

[8] Claude Stuart Rome (1875–1956), a noted cricketer and athlete at Harrow; joined 11th Hussars 1895, served in Tirah campaign, South Africa, and 1914–18 (CMG, DSO, despatches). Transferred to command Queen's Bays 1920, retired as Brig-General 1925.

I think your marks & place very creditable for your first try, and I think you will remember that I had estimated the marks at less. If you work earnestly & sensibly & above all keep it up through the term I think you will pass all right this winter. But remember that it is by no means a certainty, 1500 marks are a good deal to make in about 3 months. (The Exam is on 20th Nov I think) Lang[1] who was only about 100 places out last December, & who since then had been working all day at Wren's, has failed I see. I think he would have been more likely to pass from here, as I am sure they over-crammed him. I am glad you are going to cram up your Euclid – there are marks to be made in that and I feel sure that your history might be more accurate, but I wish you were reading a few French novels (with a dictionary, & notebook for new words. One can learn a lot of French like that, without apparent effort.

I am here for some days. I spend most of my mornings in Ducker which is divine. Next week I go to Normandy to end the holidays. Let me congratulate you very heartily on the good place you have got & wish you all success for your next try.

Yours sincerely
LOUIS MORIARTY

Reverend J. E. C. Welldon to Winston

10 September 1892 [Harrow]

My dear Churchill,

Thank you for sending me your marks, which have just reached me. I shall have something to say to you about them when we meet. But I feel it to be essential that in coming back to school you should come resolved to work not by fits & starts but with regular persistent industry.

The grammatical foundation of your languages is so uncertain that you lose marks which other boys gain. You have therefore ground to make up as well as new ground to cover.

If I did not think you would be sensible I should wire your father to take you away from Harrow now and send you to a "coach". But all depends on yourself.

Sincerely yours
J. E. C. WELLDON

---

[1] Eustace Arthur Lang (1873–1951) joined Durham Light Infantry 1894, served in Boer War, Captain 1901, transferred to Army Pay Department 1905, Lieut-Colonel Royal Army Pay Corps 1922.

Lord Randolph to Frances, Duchess of Marlborough

EXTRACT

[? September 1892]   Banstead

. . . I dont think Winston did particularly well in the army examination. He was 300 places off the successful candidates 1500 marks less than the lowest successful & 700 marks less than Dudley M. However he has had two vy kind and encouraging letters from his army class tutor & his mathematical master. His next try is on Nov 24th. If he fails again I shall think about putting him in business. I could get him something very good either through Natty[1] or Horace[2] or Cassell[3]. . . .

Lady Wilton to Winston

21 September [1892]   The Hatch

My dear Winston,

I was very pleased to get a letter from you, & I wish it were possible to have you over again for a few days? I will remain here till 10th. or 12th.

Miss Plummer is flattered at your rememberance – & sends you all sorts of messages – I had two splendid days' fishing this week, – in a new place – above Marlow – 2 largest fish weighing lb 15½ between them! What do you think of that? (Bob says he's just swallowed a worm and 2 gentiles)

Dear Boy – is there anything I can send send you? Do tell me.

With my best love Your affecte Deputy Mother
                                          LAURA WILTON

Lady Randolph to Winston

Saturday [24 September 1892]   Invermark
                                                     Brechin N.B.

Dearest Winston,

I hope that both you & Jack are settled & comfortable at Harrow.[4] Do write & tell me all about it, & what you find your room wants. I *do* hope you mean

---

[1] Nathaniel, 1st Baron ROTHSCHILD

[2] Sir Horace Brand Farquhar (1844–1923); City magnate and friend of the Royal Family. Baronet 1892, Conservative MP for Marylebone West 1895–8, Baron 1898. Master of the Household of King Edward VII (KCVO 1901, GCVO 1902), Lord Steward of the Household of King George V (GCB 1922). Treasurer of the Conservative Party until 1922. Created Earl 1922. On his retirement it was discovered that a large portion of the Conservative Party's funds had been hived off to Mr Lloyd George's Liberal Party, and another considerable portion used by Farquhar for his own purpose.

[3] Ernest CASSEL

[4] Jack entered Harrow in the Michaelmas Term, 1892.

to work hard – I was rather chaffed here as to yr having been "ploughed". I suppose I made too much fuss over you & made you out a sort of paragon. However it will be all right if you put yr shoulder to the wheel this time. I shall write a line to Mr Welldon as soon as I can.

I am so much better here you would not know me – I can walk quite briskly & can stay out in the open air all day without getting tired. Poor Banstead is empty now. What a pity we forgot to be photographed as I wanted. We are going out, Ly Hindlip & I, to see a grouse drive today. We drive as far as we can & then get on ponies & walk to the grouse boxes – little mounds of earth thrown up. We sit in the ditch, & the birds fly over – *such a pace*. I thought of you & if you cld ever get any – once you are in Sandhurst you must practise all sorts of shooting. Best of love to Jack. I hope he is all right & that you take gd care of him.

Yr loving
MOTHER

Winston to Lady Randolph

[? September 1892]   [Harrow]

Dear Mamma,

We have now quite settled down. The room is very beautiful. We purchased in London sufficiency of ornaments to make it look simply magnificent.

Papa has written to Jack & says that you are better for the change. I rejoice.

I got my remove & when you come down to Harrow you will see yours truly in 'Tails'. Jack is getting on capitally though I think he finds he has plenty of work to do & that it is rather hard.

One of our hampers was spoiled "in transitu" owing to the careless manner in which it was packed.

There is of course no more news except that we both send our love & I remain

Your loving son
WINSTON S. CHURCHILL

PS I hope you can read this & if so I hope that you will not read it out for the amusement of those staying at Invermark. WSC

Winston to Lord Randolph
(*Blenheim Papers*)

Sunday [? 25 September 1892]   Harrow

Dear Papa,

Jack has just received your letter. The room is now very nice, in fact it is universally spoken of as the best room in the House.

I have begun working now though as yet I am not quite into the swing of it. My Mathematical Master wants me to get 700 more marks in mathematics and declares that if I *can* work continuously I shall attain them.

Welldon is very nice. He makes me do Proses for him every evening and looks over them himself with me; a thing hitherto unheard of, as he of course if very much pressed for time.

Jack is going on capitally & has been put on to construe without failing. He is I believe the youngest boy in the school.

I got my remove and am now in "Tails" according to your instructions.

There is very little news except that we are both well & happy. Jack sends love while

> I remain your loving son
> WINSTON S. CHURCHILL

Lady Wilton to Winston

27 September [1892]   [The Hatch]

My dear Winston,

Very many thanks for yours. I am most anxious to have your likeness – so please, dear, send me one as soon as you can.

Mrs Johnstone is her name.

A fine day today, for a wonder! With my best love.

> Your affectionate Deputy Mother
> LAURA WILTON

Winston to Lord Randolph
(Blenheim Papers)

[?3 October 1892]   Harrow

Dear Papa,

Thank you so much for the hamper which we received on Sat night. They were just the sort of things we wanted. I enclose to you the "form of application" for signature. You will see you have to sign it at the right hand bottom corner.

Please send it back to *me* by return of post as I want to get it sent in soon, though there is really plenty of time.

Jack has been getting on very well & has come out top in Essay. He was placed 20 last week out of a form of 32 so he is not doing badly, especially as he is a year younger than any boy in his form.

I had a letter from Mamma, I think she is coming to see us on Sat. I do not feel nearly so confident as I did last time but I am working awfully hard.

I hope you will be having good sport when this letter reaches you and

I remain your loving son
WINSTON S. CHURCHILL

Lord Randolph to Winston

5 October 1892   Makerstoun House
Kelso
N.B.

Dear Winston,

Herewith yr enclosure duly signed. I am glad to hear the hamper reached you safely and contained the things you wanted. I have had no fishing yet as the river has been in flood and the water very dirty. Ivor & I hope to get at the fish well tomorrow. Best love to Jack.

Ever yr affte father
RANDOLPH S.C.

Winston to Lord Randolph
(Blenheim Papers)

?[6 October 1892]   Harrow

Dear Papa,

I received your letter this morning and have sent off the Papers to their destination. Thank you so much for the hamper, it is excellent.

Jack is awfully proud of his watch which is a beauty. He sends much love & many thanks as does also your loving & hardworking son

WINSTON S. CHURCHILL

Hoping you will have good sport. WSC

Dr Thomas Keith to Dr Robson Roose
(Blenheim Papers)

12 [?13] October 1892   42 Charles Street
Berkeley Square

Dear Dr Roose,

I found that I could only venture to make a slight examination today – the parts were all so tender and so much swollen – the result, partly of the examination under ether four days ago and partly from all the pelvic organs missing the drain that has been going on for the last three months. This has ceased since the examination under ether. There has been more pain and a new pain has started in the right groin. All this ought to pass away with rest – rest is essential in order to avoid the risk of an acute attack.

Behind and to the right of the uterus and running quite close into it is an irregular tender swelling about the size of a hen's egg. This can only be an enlarged ovary and tube or boil or both. Everything was so sensitive that it would only have caused unnecessary pain to have attempted a very accurate diagnosis – besides there can be no doubt as to the local conditions.

[?] Hitherto Lady Randolph has been [?] asking for all kinds of exercise, now for a time she must rest and do nothing to bring on pain, and in moving about she must keep within the limit of pain.

Almost certainly this condition is of very recent origin – all the more reason now to be careful in the hope that things will quiet down as they so often do.

She may thus escape the necessity for an operation at some future time – everything must be done to avoid this if possible.

Yours sincerely
THOMAS KEITH

Winston to Lady Randolph

[12 October 1892]   [Harrow]

Dear Mamma,

Will you come down to-morrow. It is Founders day and we shall have all the morning with you. If you leave Baker Street by the 11.30 you can get here at 12 and we can have luncheon at the King's Head. It is not any good your coming down on half holidays at 3.30 and arriving here at 4, because I have to go to Army Class at 4.15 and could not get off.

There will not be another chance like this for a long time so I beg you to come.

I was sorry to hear you were ill on Sat Mrs Stirling[1] was down too. She and her boy[2] and young Rothschild[3] amalgamated with us and gorged eggs etc some awful sights!

Jack is very well and gets on capitally, but has a rooted objection to writing letters.

Good Bye dear Mamma. Mind and telegraph early the time you start.

Ever your loving son
WINSTON S. CHURCHILL

[1] Norah (1850–1934), wife of Major Gilbert Stirling. She was fourth daughter of 3rd Baron Rossmore.

[2] Reginald Gilbert Stirling (1878–1946), second son of Major Gilbert Stirling, and younger brother of Henry Francis Stirling, who came to Harrow in the same term as Winston.

[3] Nathaniel Charles Rothschild (1877–1923), second son of 1st Baron Rothschild and father of Victor, 3rd Baron Rothschild.

Dr Robson Roose to Lord Randolph
(*Blenheim Papers*)

14 October 1892   50 Grosvenor Square

Private

My dear Lord Randolph,

I saw Lady Randolph yesterday: her condition is so full of serious posssibilities that I felt it my duty to advise her Ladyship to see *at once* Dr Keith, the best surgeon for female complaints. The consultation occurred at 2 p.m. yesterday and I enclose Keith's letter to me which please return. The matter is not in my province but I thank God I have been called in as I may be useful.

Yrs gratefully
ROBSON ROOSE

Dr Robson Roose to Lord Randolph
(*Blenheim Papers*)

22 October 1892   35 Hill Street
Berkeley Square

My dear Lord Randolph,

Her Ladyship is holding her own but has a great deal of suffering, chiefly thro' flatulance, which in Dr Keith's experience is much more associated withs cases of pelvic peritonitis and cellulitis like hers. There was a sharp rise of temperature yesterday due to restlessness from distension and I called in Keith but he considered it would be madness, as he put it, to examine ... [?], however he inserted a tube into the rectum which caused the flatulance to come away and so gave relief, and this tube the nurse now uses frequently, moreover we are both agreed now as the absolute necessity of controlling the pain by morphia – I am *closely* watching Lady Randolph and nothing escapes my notice, but I am, I confess, very anxious until this "Pelvic storm" shews signs of abatement and in Keith's experience rest for some weeks and closely watching the case is all that can be done at present, with a restricted diet and absolute freedom from excitement and nerve worry.

I wish I could give a cheery report but I feel sure we have to face many months of trouble and anxiety and to underrate the importance of the illness would be of absolute harm to the patient as there is no margin for mistake or carelessness. I will write on Monday or telegraph.

Yours gratefully
ROBSON ROOSE

Pardon this hurried note. My house is full of patients. RR

Lord Randolph to Winston

25 October 1892   50 Grosvenor Square

Dearest Winston & Jack,

Your dear mother was extremely ill yesterday & we were rather alarmed. But thank God today there is an improvement & the doctors are vy hopeful. I only got up to town this evening. I will keep you informed as to how yr dear mother progresses.

You will have heard of the vy sad death of your poor Uncle Roxburgh who taken vy ill last Monday had to undergo an operation Saturday to which he succumbed. You did not know him much but I was vy much attached to him & my poor sister Annie is quite heartbroken. Troubles accumulate just now. I pray you try & concentrate your thoughts on your work. Your mother would be in such good spirits if she thought you were going to do real well in yr examination. Kiss Jack for me.

Ever your affte father
RANDOLPH S.C.

Winston to Lord Randolph
(Blenheim Papers)

25 [? 26] October [1892]   [Harrow]

Dear Papa,

I received your letter this morning. I am dreadfully sorry to hear Mamma was so bad, I do hope she will soon be better and that you will let me know every day how she is.

Is it any good writing to her? I told Mr Welldon about it and he said he was awfully sorry and hoped she would be better.

I am working very hard and have got a wonderful report but I have a good deal of headache lately. Please give my best love to Mamma and the same from Jack.

I remain ever your loving son
WINSTON S. CHURCHILL

Winston to Mrs Jack Leslie
(Copy: Leslie Papers)

[27 October 1892]   [Harrow][1]

Dear Auntie Leonie,

Thank you so much for your letter. Papa had written yesterday morning, so I knew that poor Mamma was very ill; How ill of course I could not tell.

---

[1] At this time Winston was using some old writing paper headed Branstead Manor, Newmarket, when writing from Harrow.

I think Everest ought to have let us know on Sunday, but I suppose she was awfully busy. I cannot thank you sufficiently for your kindness in writing; but let me beg you to let me know if any change in her condition should occur, without delay, as Jack and I are awfully anxious.

Dear Aunty thank you so much for your kindness. Please write to us as we are awfully unhappy.

Your loving nephew
WINSTON S. CHURCHILL

Winston to Lady Randolph

3 November 1892   [Harrow]

Dear Mamma,

We got back allright and were in plenty of time for the train. I saw both Aunties Leonie and Clara 'avant partir'. I have written another letter to Papa, I hope he will not continue to be angry. Mind and make haste and get well.

Ever your loving son
WINNY

Winston to Mrs Jack Leslie

Thursday [?3 November 1892]   [Harrow]

Dear Auntie Leonie,

We arrived all safe at Harrow last night. I must really thank you for your kindness to me in London on Wednesday.

How did you like Drury Lane? I ask this question to obtain an answer from you. Jack is very happy & has got through his Mathematical examination this morning.

He begs me to send love & I do so at the same time remaining

Your affect nephew
WINSTON S. CHURCHILL

Lord Randolph to Winston

4 November 1892   50 Grosvenor Square

My dear Winston,

I was very sorry to miss you yesterday. Of course it was all an accident my not getting your letter & you need not worry about it. I should like vy much to have seen you. Your visit quite cheered up yr mother who I am happy to say goes on as well as possible.

I expect yr grandmother up tonight from Scotland & I daresay I shall remain in town for some time now.

Next time you come up in the afternoon you must arrange not to have to get back so early. Best love to Jack.

Ever yr affte father
RANDOLPH S.C.

Winston to Lord Randolph
(*Blenheim Papers*)

[5 November 1892]   [Harrow]

Dear Papa,

I have just received your letter for which many thanks. I am working awfully hard and really hope to make a very good shot this time. Jack is getting on alright and expects to come out higher this week. He has not had a single line this term, which is quite a "record".

I am so glad to hear Mama is better. I was afraid our visit would have tired her. I am quite well, and with the exception of occasional headache in the evening I get on alright.

With best love I remain ever your loving son

WINSTON S. CHURCHILL

P.S. Welldon told me he thought your letter was very mild. Bosworth Smith[1] another Harrow master is pushing himself into notoriety by his letters and speeches on Uganda. Perhaps you have noticed. WSC

Reverend J. E. C. Welldon to Lord Randolph
(*Blenheim Papers*)

8 November 1892   Harrow

Dear Lord Randolph,

I am very willing that Winston should go to see Dr Robson Roose. He has worked admirably and I think the work is beginning to tell a little upon him.

He can come on Thursday at any time between one and 4 o'clock. Perhaps you will kindly let him know the hour appointed for his seeing Dr Roose. Allow me to express my satisfaction at the good news of Lady Randolph's health.

Believe me and sincerely yours
J. E. C. WELLDON

1 Bertrand Nigel Bosworth Smith (1873–1947); the son of Reginald Bosworth Smith, Housemaster at the Knoll. After a brilliant career at Harrow (entrance scholar, 16 prizes, two leaving scholarships, Head of the School, Cricket and Football XIs) and at Magdalen College Oxford (Demy), 1st Class Moderations, Football Blue) he entered the Indian Civil Service in 1897 and retired in 1920 as Deputy Commissioner, Punjab.

Winston to Lady Randolph

Wednesday 16 November 1892   [Harrow]

Dear Mamma,

Please send a wire first thing to-morrow morning or Jackie will not be able to come at all. It is a whole holiday and he is entitled to one day's leave. Say this

"Can Winston and Jack come by 11.7 train today to see me?"

I have to come in any case as I must see Woom. But Jack is awfully depressed.

Ever your loving son
WINSTON S. CHURCHILL

Winston to Lady Randolph

[?21 November 1892]   [Harrow]

My dear Mamma,

I hope you are better and out of pain now. We arrived back last night (Sunday) and did not have to do any work for the next morning. Mr Welldon was most kind and said we might come up when you wanted us in future. He also asked after you a great deal as did also Searle.

Jack has got an account book in which he puts down various expenses. Il ne brosse pas les dents. I paid for the pins [?] to be mended they cost altogether (3 of them) 6/6. I enclose a form for your signature as it is absolutely necessary that I should have a new suit for my examinations. And as I am leaving at the end of the term I think you might sign the order for some photos. You remember you let Jack be taken a little while ago.

Well good bye dear Mamma. I do hope you will soon be well and able to get about.

I remain Ever your loving son
WINSTON S. CHURCHILL

(Enclosed are 4 kisses. Please return.)

Please sign and return to

          Banstead Manor, Newmarket

Winston may have a new suit.

He may also have photos (2 doz) taken.

Reverend J. E. C. Welldon to Lord Randolph
(*Blenheim Papers*)

28 November 1892   Harrow

Dear Lord Randolph,

Winston is anxious that I should write to your about his prospect of success in the Examinations which begins tomorrow. I do so gladly. His work this term has been excellent. He understands now the need of taking trouble, and the way to take it, and, whatever happens to him, I shall consider that in the last twelve months he has learnt a lesson of life-long value.

The two disadvantages under which he lies are that he was not well grounded, when he came here; hence he is still not safe against bad mistakes; and that he partially wasted the beginning of his public schooldays.

Still, when this is said, I am of the opinion that he is now well up to the level of passing into Sandhurst according to the standard which has been usual in past years. We are aware however that the level tends to rise and that, owing to the change which is being made in the age of admission, it is likely to be very high this time. At the next examination it will be normal again.

On the whole so far as I can judge from my own observation and the reports of his masters, I should say he has a very fair chance of passing now and is certain to pass in the summer if not now.

In giving this opinion I do not forget the perils of exercising the prophetic art; but it is due to him to say that of late he has done all that could be asked of him.

I hope Lady Randolph is recovering her health.

Believe me sincerely yours
J. E. C. WELLDON

Lady Wilton to Winston

6 December [1892]   Le Nid

My dear Winston,

Very many thanks for yours. I fear that "système" will demand a very *large capital*! Where are you going when you leave Harrow? Do let me know, & where is your Mama?

My love to Jack – & much to yourself from yr ever affecte

DEPUTY MOTHER

Lady Wilton to Winston

17 December [1892]   [Le Nid]

Dear Winston,

Very many thanks for yours. I was very glad to hear from you. I do *hope* you'll pass all right – but – if not – still one can do other things. Your Father is well & resting quietly here – I think your Uncle's death was a great shock to him.[1] I am sure he will do everything for yr future career & happiness. – &

---

[1] His brother George, 8th Duke of Marlborough ('BLANDFORD'), had died suddenly at Blenheim on November 9, aged 48.

he is *so* kind & good. I am *delighted* your Mama is so much better – I heard from her the other day – & I hope she will soon be quite strong. My love to Jack when you write to him.

Dear Winston, I enclose the small sum of £2 for your *tiny* expenses.

Ever yr affecte
LAURA WILTON

Winston to Lady Randolph

[? December 1892]   [Harrow]

Dear Mamma,

I am afraid you will be very angry with me for not writing to you before, but I have been so busy with the Assault-at-Arms and Welldon that I have really some excuse. Welldon did not punish me, but says that he will keep me back a few hours at the end of the term.

I have ordered the dress suit and overcoat and I think they will soon be ready. Jack has arranged about his suit.

I am looking forward to the holidays as I feel awfully depressed now that the Exam is over. I did the Chemistry Practical quite correctly and so shall get good marks.

You told me to write to you and give you an account of the *necessary* expenses of the term's end.

Here they are –

Tip to Butler	£1.	0.	0.
Char who does the room		10.	0.
To Boot Boy		5.	0.
To the Gymnastic instructors		10.	0. (each)
		10.	0.
Total	£3.	0.	0.

For myself as pocket money   £1. 0. 0.
For travelling up to London   10. 0.
(self and Jack)
Grand Total   £4. 10. 0.

I assure you that I have only put down such as are inevitable on leaving.

Please send it to me as soon as possible as I am in great poverty.

Good-bye dear Mamma,
I remain, Your loving son
WINSTON S. CHURCHILL

6

Pre-Sandhurst

(See Main Volume Chapter 6, pp.186–206)

The Times

11 January 1893

The eldest son of Lord and Lady Randolph Churchill, who is staying with his mother and the Dowager Duchess of Marlborough at Branksome Dene, Bournemouth, met with an accident yesterday afternoon. He was climbing a tree, when a branch on which he was standing broke, and he fell some distance to the ground. No bones were broken, but he was very much shaken and bruised. He is in his nineteenth year.

Louis Moriarty to Winston

11 January 1892 [1893]   Harrow

My dear Churchill,

Just a line to thank you for your letter. I subjoin such numbers as I know. I only hope a few will not need *numbers*.

Since getting your letter I see that you have had a serious accident. I do hope that you will only suffer temporarily from it & that by this time you are feeling much better.

My wife joins in best regards;

We went yesterday to Woolwich – saw Conolly,[1] Done,[2] Monro,[3]

---

[1] Edward Michael Conolly (1874–1956); joined Royal Artillery 1894, served in Boer War (despatches), retired 1910 as Captain. Private Secretary to Governor of Hong Kong 1912–14, served as Major, Royal Horse Artillery 1914–18 (CMG, despatches three times).

[2] Reginald John Done (1874–   ); joined Royal Engineers 1894, Nile Expedition 1899, Captain 1904, Lieut-Colonel 1916 (DSO 1917, Legion of Honour, Croix de Guerre, despatches five times).

[3] John Duncan Monro (1874–1939); joined Royal Engineers 1894, Major 1914 (severely wounded at Loos, OBE, despatches). Retired as Colonel 1927.

Wade,[1] visited the lions and took tea with Musgrave.[2] They all were very fit & I was much pleased with Woolwich.

Pray excuse haste

Ever yours sincerely
Louis Moriarty

Marjoribanks	789
Strong[3]	985
Gowans	563
Cavendish[4]	409
Hilton	626
Harrison[5]	598
(Paine?)	
?Watson[6]	1041

Reverend J. E. C. Welldon to Winston

13 January 1893   The Grand Hotel
                                                    Eastbourne

My dear Churchill,

I see you have met with an accident and are somewhat badly hurt. I am very anxious about you. Will you get your brother to write me a postcard, saying if you are going on all right? I return to Harrow today.

With all good wishes Sincerely yours
J. E. C. Welldon

[1] Harry Amyas Leigh Herschel Wade (1873–); son of Sir T. F. Wade. Joined Royal Artillery 1893, served in Nile Expedition 1898 and in Boer War, Major 1910. On staff of 1st Army Corps 1914, Military Attaché, Copenhagen 1916, Brevet Lieut-Colonel 1918. Editor of the *Army Review* 1912; Editor of the *League of Nations Union* 1919.

[2] Arthur David Musgrave (1874–1931); son of Sir Anthony Musgrave, Governor of Queensland. Joined Royal Artillery 1893, Major 1910, Brevet Colonel 1916, Brig-General 1916 (DSO 1918, despatches six times).

[3] Charles Powlett Strong (1875–1901); joined Bedfordshire Regiment 1894, served in Boer War (DSO 1901) killed in action at Graspan, June 1901.

[4] Hon Henry Cavendish (1875–1897); son of 4th Baron Waterpark. Joined Rifle Brigade 1895, died in India two years later.

[5] Arthur Patrick Bird Harrison (1874–); son of General Sir Richard Harrison. Joined Rifle Brigade after first going up to Trinity College, Cambridge. Served in Boer War, retired as Captain 1905. Served 1914–17 as Military Attaché in the Field to the Serbian Army.

[6] Ivor Wilberforce Watson (1875–); joined Argyll & Sutherland Highlanders 1896, served in Boer War, Captain 1902, Major 1915 (wounded, despatches); retired 1919.

C. H. P. Mayo[1] to Winston

14 January 1893   Robert Road
                                                      Handsworth
                                                      Staffordshire

My dear Churchill,

Many thanks for your letter which reached me yesterday. I was exceedingly sorry to see a day or two ago in the *Pall Mall Gazette*, that you had met with an accident, let me offer you my warm sympathy and express the hope that you are recovering from the effects of your fall. I was glad to see that no bones were broken and trust that effects may be very temporary.

I do not remember the Sandhurst List ever being delayed so long. I have looked with interest in the papers each day; more than a fortnight ago Dr Watson[2] told me that he had that day sent off his marks: as a general impression he mentioned that some candidates had done exceedingly well, but did not remember individual papers, and indeed had I remembered your number he would not have given me any information. I still continue full of hope, and shall be very pleased if in a day or two I can offer you my congratulations: Du Port[3] did very well.

We return to Harrow in 2 days, the holidays over far too soon, I have spent them very quietly at home. My mother progresses, if at all, very very slowly. I have stayed with her as much as I could. The very severe cold has been against her; fortunately the thaw seems really to have set in. There has been some exceedingly good skating.

Your plans will probably be in a very unsettled condition, awaiting the pleasure of the Civil Service Commissioners, if the fates should be against you, an eventuality not I hope possible, you must let me know where you decide to go.

With all good wishes for your speedy recovery and all success

Believe me, Yours sincerely

C. H. P. Mayo

---

[1] Charles Harry Powell Mayo (1859–1929), mathematics master at Harrow 1892–1919.

[2] Henry William Watson (1827–1903) FRS, D Sc, Rector of Berkswell, Warwick. A 2nd Wrangler and former Fellow of Trinity College, Cambridge, he had been mathematics master at Harrow 1857–66.

[3] Osmond Charteris Du Port (1875–1929) was in the team with Winston that won the House swimming race for The Head Master's in 1892. Joined Royal Artillery 1895, served in Boer War (wounded, despatches), Captain 1901, retired as Major 1912. Rejoined 1914, DSO 1917, Brevet Lieut-Colonel 1919, despatches five times. Minister of Agriculture and Lands, Southern Rhodesia, 1927.

Reverend J. E. C. Welldon to Lord Randolph
(*Blenheim Papers*)

20 January 1893   Harrow

Dear Lord Randolph,

It is a pleasure to me to answer your questions.

I wish that, before answering them, I could have seen Winston's marks in the recent examination. It will be a disappointment to me if it does not prove that he has so far improved his position in respect of his marks as to make it clear that he would have been successful, had the standard remained what it was a year or eighteen months ago, and that his chance of succeeding if he competes again will be excellent. Unless I am wrong, the total number of marks required for admission has in the last two examinations risen by as many as six hundred. It will clearly fall again – though nobody can say how much – at the next examination. On the other hand it is necessary to take into account the possibility of his not being well or not having reasonable good fortune in his papers.

If there were an opportunity then of getting him at once into a cavalry regiment, I should upon the whole be disposed to take advantage of it. The most successful "crammer" for the Sandhurst Examination is, I believe Capt James[1] of 18 Lexham Gardens, W.

I was very sorry to hear of Winston's accident. Jack gave a very alarming account of it.

Hoping this letter will be of some use in begging that you will write to me, if I can do more.

I am sincerely yours
J. E. C. WELLDON

Duke of Marlborough to Winston

21 January 1893   Blenheim

My dear Winston,

I have the Polit Econ book quite safe, and I fear I made against you a false accusation, which I must withdraw with apologies. I am coming to town to morrow Monday on my way to Melton and I will come and look you up in the afternoon. I am sorry to hear that you are laid up with the influenza take care you don't get a relapse as I believe it is pretty full down below and you might have to wait out in the cold a bit, before you got admission.

Ever yrs
MARLBOROUGH

[1] Walter Henry James (1847–1927); formerly Captain, Royal Engineers; founded the tutorial establishment known as 'Jimmy's'.

Jack to Lady Randolph

[? January 1893]   [Harrow]

My dear Mama,

I am quite settled down now, I have the same room, which I have made very nice etc. The want me to join the "Rifle Corps" here, but unless I find Winney's close [clothes] I dont think it is worth it because they cost such a lot.

I had a letter from Winney this morning, I suppose he is nearley well know. I will write to you a long letter in a few days but I must catch the Post.

                                    I remain your loving Son
                                        JACK S. CHURCHILL

Lady Wilton to Winston

22 January [1893]   Le Nid

My dear Winston,

It was very nice of you to write to me – I have been thinking a great deal about yr exams etc. But do not worry yourself too much; I'm sure you did your very best & I know how many clever fellows get turned away for really these Exams are too hard now. You see a feeble scrawl – for I am still very poorly – & in bed (these 9 days) & so weak from fever & bronchitis. Do write to me soon again about what you are going to do.

                        Best love from yr affecte Deputy Mother
                                        LAURA WILTON

C. H. P. Mayo to Winston

22 January 1893   Glenlyon
                                                Harrow-on-the-Hill

My dear Churchill,

Let me hasten to thank you for the telegram received this morning and for your letter of Friday. You have done really well, and have no cause whatever to feel despondent. A gain of 900 marks in so short a time is very pleasing and must make you feel very confident about the exam in June, if you then go in again: you have twice the time and not half the leeway to make up. Let me hear the details of the marks when you know them, and come and see me next Saturday. I don't know what time you are coming, but I shall have lunch at 1.45 and if you care to come and join me shall be very glad to see you: come if you have nothing better to do.

I hope you have quite recovered and feel no ill effects from your headlong rush through space.

                        With kind regards Yours very sincerely
                                        C. H. P. MAYO

Reverend J. E. C. Welldon to Winston

23 January 1893   Harrow

My dear Churchill,

I am very much obliged to you for sending me the telegram. It seems to me to bear out what I have ventured to say to your father and yourself, viz that you would have passed or would have been on the borderline of passing, if the standard of marks had remained what it was two years ago, and that, if you make the same progress in the next six months as you made in the last your passing is assured. That is in my opinion not an unsatisfactory result; only, if you are going up again, do let me beg you to begin work at once and to carry it on with the greatest energy and regularity. I wish I had got you here.

Sincerely Yours
J. E. C. WELLDON

Lieutenant-General Sir Reginald Gipps[1] to Lord Randolph
(*Blenheim Papers*)

24 January 1893   Horseguards
War Office

Dear Lord Randolph Churchill,

We are not able to ascertain at present the exact position taken by your son on the List of unsuccessful candidates, but as his name does not appear amongst the first thirty and six of these come up for Cavalry as vacancies occur, I fear that your son's chance of gaining admission to Sandhurst is not a good one, but I will bear his name in mind.

Yours faithfully
REG GIPPS
Lieutant General Mily Secy

Lieutenant-General Sir Reginald Gipps to Lord Randolph
(*Blenheim Papers*)

26 January 1893   Horse Guards

Dear Lord Randolph Churchill,

In reply to your letter of the 24th inst, I regret to acquaint you that candidates that only "qualify" at the Sandhurst entrance examination are

---

[1] Reginald Ramsay Gipps (1831–1908); Military Secretary 1892–6. Entered Scots Guards 1849, present at Alma and Inkerman. KCB 1888, General 1894, GCB 1902.

not thereby rendered eligible to receive commissions in the Household Cavalry.

Yours truly

R. W. GIPPS

If you want any further information regarding University or Militia candidates, if you will write or do not mind the trouble of coming here I shall be very pleased to do any and everything I can.

Note Attached

A candidate who passes a 'qualifying' examination at the Sandhurst examination, is excepted from further literary tests as a Militia candidate for the army.

The Prince of Wales has power to nominate to commissions in the Household Cavalry, Militia officers, who, being fully qualified as to age, Militia training, length of Militia service etc (see accompanying Regulation) obtain a qualifying number of marks at the examination in Military subjects.

M. F. McTaggart to Winston

25 January [1893]

42 Montagu Square
London W.

Dear Churchill,

I received your note after some delay as it followed me to several addresses. However I got it at last & read it with all the more pleasure, (but of course missed you on Friday). Nobody from our Crammers passed not even a Queen's cadet! There were 8 went up. One of them had 6400 the time before.

Paine & Long were the only two I knew of the successful ones. I think there must be a mistake as regards my marks or I must have gone quite mad, as in the printed paper it appears I have made 5032!!!! It looks as if a 5 instead of a 6 had been printed; if not I think I really must be a bloody fool.

I have just returned from Yorks; & today I return to my Crammers to do my usual 8 hrs per diem. I am very sorry to hear of your accident but you always were unlucky what with gunpowder etc. Do you know what Crammers you are going to? Jimmy's [Captain James's] or the Blackheath man I suppose. Poor old Marjoribanks is chucked out for good, it is bad luck isn't it. Anyhow we two will walk in next time with flying colours 1st and 2nd eh!

I haven't much news to tell so I won't tell it.

Who was cockhouse last term at Harrow? and any other news of interest would oblige.

It would be excessively lucky for you if you succeeded in getting a commission, but I somehow doubt it. My address of course will be same as usual for the next 5 months viz Cedar Court, Roehampton. Well so long old chap with best wishes for luck during the year

I remain ever yours affect
MAXWELL McTAGGART

George W. Wilson[1] to Winston

Thursday [?26 January 1893]   Bannockburn House
                                                Bannockburn

Dear Churchill,

Thanks very much for your numerous letters, it was too bad of me not to write you before. I am glad to hear that you are in a fair way to recovery now, I really had no idea you were in such a dangerous condition. I thought you had more sense than to go havering around rotten trees, I would not have been surprised if it had been our young friend Jack, but I thought that you had reached years of discretion, when I was a little boy (Fisher[2] would say I was one still) I used to go and climb trees but I have renounced all that by this time. However you have learnt a lesson now, which you won't forget for some time. Please don't be offended at these remarks, I was always very plain spoken as you know by experience.

I was sorry to see that you had not passed, if anybody deserved to do so, you did, for I know you really worked hard last term; I sometimes felt I ought not to have come so often to your room as I stopped you working, but you and Jack were such an attractive pair, I often could not resist coming to talk to you.

I had a delightful letter from Jack the other day. I was so pleased at hearing from him, it shews that I am not altogether forgotten. He says he does not expect an answer as he is only a "rat" but I certainly shall answer him. He says the house is very quiet without Forman[3] and myself, I can quite believe it. What would I not give to be back, but there is no help for it, so I must grin and bear it as best as I can.

I had a long letter from Forman last Wednesday, he seems to wish pretty much as I do, only he used some stronger language. I wish I had the same

---

[1] George Walker Wilson (1874–1937) had been at The Head Master's, and was Captain of Football 1891–2. He later went into business in Karachi.

[2] Julian Lawrence Fisher (1877–1953); joined Royal Fusiliers 1897, Captain 1901, served in Tibet Expedition 1904 (DSO 1905); Major 1915, commanded 2nd Battalion Royal Fusiliers at Gallipoli (wounded), Brevet Lieut-Colonel 1917 (CMG 1919, despatches three times), retired 1920.

[3] Thomas Bailey Forman (1873–1939); became a journalist and newspaper proprietor in Nottingham.

chances as you have of going down to Harrow, I would go down pretty often, you may be sure.

At present I am having a very bad time of it with the dentist, in fact I am in a bad way altogether, like you before your exam.

I have no exercise like at school but I have toothache and a headache nearly every day, in fact I take no interest in anything. I am going to play in a footer match on Saturday and that will wake me up. I am at present one of the great unemployed, but I hope to begin work in about a month or so.

I have really no more news, so with all good wishes for a speedy recovery.

Believe me Ever yrs
GEORGE W. WILSON

Louis Moriarty to Winston

27 January 1893   Harrow

My dear Churchill,

I seize a few moments' leisure to write and thank you for your letters and the news you were so good as to send me. The information about McTaggart is the most startling. Your brother told me of it to-day. The much maligned Army Class has not done so badly after all – but no man is a prophet in his own country.

I do hope that you are in a fair way to complete recovery from your serious mishap and that we shall see you at Harrow before long.

I suppose you have not touched much work yet. If you have not read Marbot[1] *through*, he is well worth reading. I have not read so delightful a book for a long time. We lost 8 from the Special Class, but they seem to be passing the Preliminary so successfully that we ought to do more than fill up gaps. We have heard of 9 so far: 7 passes, 1 partial p. 1 failure – Hunt[2] (H.B. an idler). I must say goodnight.

Ever Yours sincerely
LOUIS MORIARTY

[1] The Memoirs of General Jean-Baptiste-Antoine Marcellin, Baron de Marbot (1782–1854). First published in French in 1891, a two-volume translation came out in London in the following year. In the Memoirs Marbot gives an account of the major Napoleonic campaigns in which he had participated.

[2] He did not lead an idle life. Gerald Ponsonby Sneyd Hunt (1877–1918), a Home Boarder (H.B.), joined the Royal Berkshire Regiment after leaving Harrow, served in the Boer War (Queen's Medal and 3 clasps, King's Medal and 2 clasps); went to France in 1914, wounded 1915, commanded an infantry brigade as Brig-General and was appointed CMG, December 1915; was commanding his regiment (DSO) when he was killed in action near Manancourt.

Jack to Winston

[? January 1893]　　　　　　　　　　　　　　　　[Harrow]

Dear Winney,

I have a bill for 8 shillings here which Mease asked me to send you from Spencer's, also one of 3 shillings for something that you broak in the gym at the end of last term.

Mease said that he would have to written to you but that he has been ill with Reumaticks Moriarty seems very cross about Sandhurst.

Thank you for your letter I cant write more.

I remain your loving Brother
JACK S. CHURCHILL

Lady Wilton to Winston

28 January [1893]　　　　　　　　　　　　　　　　Le Nid

My dear Winston,

Very many thanks for *both* your last. I can well understand how bored you must be in this forced quiet. But soon I hope you'll be up & about. Tell me what you are going to do next. I am still very poorly – & a prisoner to the House. I went downstairs yesterday for the first time, for 16 days.

Weather here not particularly nice. Please, my love to your Mama.

Ever yr affecte Deputy Mother
L.W.

£2 for odds & ends.

Captain Walter James to Lord Randolph

28 January 1893　　　　　　　　　　　　5 Lexham Gardens
London W.

My Lord,

I shall be very happy to receive your son and should be pleased to see you at 12.30 on Monday next.

Yours faithfully
WALTER H. JAMES

J. Napier Spence to Winston

31 January 1893　　　　　　　　　　　　Cambridge Villa
Harrow

My dear Churchill,

I am not disappointed at the result you have sent me – of course I should have liked it to be higher; still 400 in 8 weeks is real good work and certainly

1229 would have secured you a good place if your other marks had been up to the same standard.

Now I hope you will write to Welldon and tell him whether you think fellows sent to me will receive proper coaching or not.

And you might say something about me to W. and M. [Wellsford and Moriarty, the Army Class tutors] if you write them.

Lascelles[1] said ha! when I told him and found he was required at the Music room (sick as could be).

Now old man if you do anything to help me on I shall be very much obliged to you as I have a lot of time to fill in this term.

Yours Vy Sincerely
J. Napier Spence

Jack to Winston

3 February 1893   Harrow

Dear Winney,

I hope you have got the note books; Moriarty would not give me an order so I paid it. Edward tells me that Woodbridge aske him to ask me to pay that 3/6 for the poles, as he did not want Welldon to get to know about it, so I paid him 3/6.

As for Spencer's it is a mistake, he forgot that you had given him an order for "foils repaired when required", so he did not put it in the bills.

Conwey said he has sent off the clothes; I dont know whether you have got them or not.

Papa wrote to me and told me you were going to Brighton for a week, do write and let me know when and where you are going; if you want any books you know I have about 30 of yours here.

Moriarty some how found out that I made some History notes, and he lets me do it in prep now.

The footer field is in progress and Monro says "It will take 2 years & £4000, and then we will play once and it will be worse than ever". Well what can become of it if [?] Colier is looking after it.

I cant write any more now. Mayo has not spoken to me. I dont think he knows me.

I remain Your loving brother
Jack S. Churchill

---

[1] Brian Piers Lascelles (1859–1922), the Science Master; also Vaughan Librarian.

Jack to Lady Randolph

[3 February 1893]   [Harrow]

Dear Mama,

I suppose you are in London? I am sure I don't know.

Tonight Harry Furnis[1] is going to come and give a lecture on something.

I am quite well, but I believe that there is something going about the house, and some are ill, but what it is I dont know, I hope I dont get it. I have just written to Winney he has a lot of books here which I dont know whether he wants them or not.

There is nothing to do here, the football field is so far away (as the other one is being repaired) the other one is to cost £4000 I can't write any more

I remain Your loving son

JACK S. CHURCHILL

Winston to Jack

3 February 1893   50 Grosvenor Square

Dear Jack,

I have just recd your long letter – for which many thanks. I am going to try and go to Brighton tomorrow: But I feel far from well enough. The doctors say I shall not be cured for 2 months yet. I pass the greater part of my time in bed. Lady Wilton sent me £2. And I expect Papa will give me some more tomorrow. If I am well enough I shall go to James's on the thirteenth, but I doubt if I shall be up to much.

Did Wilson answer your letter; he told me he was going to. Spence & McTaggart come to tea on Saturday – Mr Dawson on Sunday and Bertie [Roose] to-day.

Aunt Sarah has been blessed with a son & heir.[2] Dudley came to see me the other day – he is going to try for Sandhurst again as an Indian Cadet, but will have to go to the West Indies for 2 years if successful.

I am writing a new Chemistry Note book with full page illustrations – it is beautiful. The History period for the Sandhurst exam is slightly changed. We have gone on one reign – and drop Wm III while we take up George II. I shall have to make a few more notes.

Well I must thank you for the Note Books – which are excellent. As soon as I get my money changed I will send it you. 5/- I think. If it is fine Mamma will come to see you tomorrow (Sat).

With love Yours ever

WINSTON S. CHURCHILL

[1] Harry Furniss, of *Punch*, spoke on "Humours of Parliament". The *Harrovian* records: 'Rarely has such hearty laughter resounded through the speech-room so continually as then.'

[2] Christened Randolph.

Winston to Lord Randolph
(*Blenheim Papers*)

6 January [February] 1893   26 Brunswick Terrace
                                                              [Brighton]

Dear Papa,

I did not wire to you as the Duchess had commissioned Aunt Clara to do so. We had plenty of time at Victoria and though the journey was rather cold I am none the worse. This afternoon I went for a drive with the Duchess who is kindness personified. The care that was taken of me would I am sure astonish you "muchly".

I have been reading that book "I forbid the Banns"[1] but have only finished the first volume, which is in my room with the "Land Dweller".

Have you read a new novel called "Euthanasia".[2] I got it today at Victoria. It seems very well written and I judge from references to "tame-cats" "souls" etc that the author is a gentleman.

It turns out to be by Count "Lutzo" (I don't know how he spells his name) a great friend of Count Kinsky's.

Dinner is at 8, and I must go and dress, so "I will now remain" your affectionate son

WINSTON S. CHURCHILL

Jack to Lady Randolph

[? February 1893]   Harrow

Dear Mama,

I am all right here although there have been a few cases of Fever in other houses, I have not got it yet.

When is my birthday? I thought you said the 9th of March was it.

Winney came down here yesterday, and enjoyed him-self I think, although he did not seem to have any time here, he said he had made arrangements with people he had to see etc, he said he would come down next Saturday.

When are you coming down to see me?

I have got no news to tell you this place seems to be so very dry.

The only thing I can think of is that Lock up is at 6 & coats are not compulsory and as These things do not interest you, I will say goodbye.

I remain your loving Son
JACK S. CHURCHILL

[1] *I Forbid the Banns*, a novel in three volumes (10s 6d each, 794 pages together) by Frank Frankfort Moore, a popular novelist of the day. First published by Hutchinson in February 1893, it ran to five editions by July.

[2] *Euthanasia*, or Turf, Tent, and Tomb, a novel by an anonymous author, was published in February 1893 by Routledge, price 6s 6d (310 pages).

Jack to Winston

[? February 1893]   Harrow

(There are 4 cases of
Scarlet fever).

Rivington[1]
Old Symes
Kennaway[2]
[?] Mr Forester

Dear Winney,

Thank you very much for your letter; I was very glad to here you had a good journey and that you are none the worse for it. I was very sorry that you could not come down on Saturday. Mama never telegraphed weather she was or not coming and so I waited from 2.30 till 3.30 in great despair.

They tell me here that there was an articlet on you, when the accident happened, which said you had fallen and hurt yourself, and under neath it it put "Just like him". I asked Mugridge if he knew who had put it in, he said he thought "Billy Bray".

Poor Billy Bray has during the holydays had 14 days and now is installed as coach man to one of the Job masters here.

Thrustle asked after you and said "Eh . . . . well it is a pitty he recovered; I mean ‒ !" Meese says he is quite sick of the Colonel[3] and of this place and he thinks that he will try and go to Elstree and do Gym there; I think he is very silly.

Tichey is very unhappy one of his children is dying. We have no more "[?] inventions" this term, and Instead of the "Wholes" we are to have extra "Halves".

Somerville asks after you and asked me to send his love and millions of kisses to you; I had a letter from Wilson this morning, he said "I owe your charming brother a letter, but he will have to wait a bit."

Please sent the 5/-

With best love I remain loving brother
JACK S. CHURCHILL

PS do you hear that Uncle Wilson was nearly killed, out driving.

---

[1] Herbert Basil Rivington (1877–1962) was ordained in 1900 and was a chaplain and missionary in Egypt and the Sudan 1906–32.

[2] John Kennaway (1879–1956); son of Sir J. H. Kennaway, 3rd Bart, MP for Honiton, whom he succeeded in 1919.

[3] William Barclay Gordon Cleather (1837–1919); late Lieut-Colonel, North Lancashire Regiment, Superintendent of the Gymnasium 1888–94.

Lady Randolph to Winston

Friday [? February 1893]   50 Grosvenor Square

Dearest Winston,

Papa was so angry with you for telegraphing to him in that stupid way. *Of course* we knew all about the fever from Jack & from Mr Welldon – & in any case to write was quite enough. You take too much on yrself young man, & write in such a pompous style. I'm afraid you are becoming a prig! If possible I will come to Brighton tomorrow for the day & see for myself how you are getting on. I hope you will be able to settle to yr work soon otherwise you will have a scramble for it! Goodbye my darling – I shall hope to see you tomorrow. I am writing to the Duchess give her my love.

Yr loving
MOTHER

Lady Randolph to Winston

7 February [1893]   50 Grosvenor Square

Dearest Winston,

You *are* a lazy little wretch! I thought *of course* I wld hear from you this morning. *Write.*

I hear yr new hat is a "terror"! Aunt Clara said you looked too funny in it. Please send it back to C. & Moore[1] & tell them that it is too big. What a goose you are – *write*!

Yr loving
MOTHER

Best love to the Duchess.

J. Napier Spence to Winston

7 February 1893   Cambridge Villa
                                   Harrow

My dear Churchill,

Many thanks for the trouble you have taken on my behalf – unfortunately it has done no good. I have heard nothing from Welldon and no privates have turned up so as this state of affairs is not good enough I intend trying to make a change so if you know of anything or any one who requires an analyst you might let me know.

I hope by this time you may be able to get about again and be sure and let me know when you intend coming to Harrow.

Very Sincerely Yours
J. NAPIER SPENCE

---

[1] Chapman & Moore, Hatters, of 30 Old Bond Street.

Lily, Duchess of Marlborough to Lord Randolph
(*Blenheim Papers*)

EXTRACT

9 February 1893   26 Brunswick Terrace
                                                                  Brighton

. . . The Dr (Couling) came again this morning and reported Winston as
doing very well: not quite "fit" yet but going on nicely. Do you want him to go
up Sunday or Monday? If you do not I will be so pleased to keep him another
week – after wh I "believe" he will have nothing left of that nasty fall but its
memory. You know he fell on his right side, and I discovered the right shoulder
wasn't quite right, so I have had my masseuse rub it for him – and it is already
better. We are a good deal in the open air and I think you will say that the
boy *is* better. Can you come down Saturday for the Sunday? I will try and
make you comfortable.

Please let me know about Winston – I very much hope you will let me keep
him. I don't quite like to discharge my patient until he is *cured*! I am afraid
it is very dull for him. . . .

Dr Robson Roose to Lord Randolph
(*Blenheim Papers*)

9 February 1893

My dear Lord Randolph,
    Winston has still a little albumen so I sent on to Rose and now forward his
reply.

In haste yours gratefully
ROBSON ROOSE

Dr John Rose to Dr Robson Roose
(*Blenheim Papers*)

8 February 1893   17 Harley Street

My dear Roose,
    I certainly agree with you that young Mr Churchill should not at present
return to hard study any more than he should take vigorous exercise. It would
be better to wait and see if the albumen will entirely disappear from the brain.

Yours ever
JOHN ROSE

George W. Wilson to Winston

[? February 1893]   Bannockburn House

Dear Churchill,

I feel it is my duty to write you but I have really nothing much to tell. I wrote to Jack on Monday but I am afraid my letter was very uninteresting. I hope you are all right by this time and have quite recovered the effects of your accident. It would be an awfully good thing for you if you could get into a cavalry regiment without going to Sandhurst, what a swell you would be? Have you written to Forman yet? his address if you do not know it is Wilford House, Wilford, Notts. I heard from Peggy the other day also from "Bram", the latter seems to have been down at Harrow.

I was in Edinburgh on Saturday seeing Scotland and Wales, the former got beaten much to my disgust.[1] I would not have gone if I had known what was going to happen. Old Watkins[2] wrote me the other day and one bit of his news was that Luckcock[3] had left owing to his goings on of the 2 previous terms, a very good thing for the house at least that is my opinion. You seem to think that Fisher would not write to me, I have heard from him 3 times twice during the holidays and once from Harrow, I am going to write him to-morrow. I suppose you would not notice that Gowan's brother was playing for Scotland, I mean Jim Gowan's[4] the one who was in the cricket XI, it is a good time since an Harrovian has played in an International. Do you know what Marjoribanks is going to do? I suppose he will try to get in through the militia, I expect his father was rather wild at the result.

No more news

Yrs v truly
GEORGE W. WILSON

---

[1] Wales beat Scotland at Raeburn Place on February 4 by 1 penalty goal and three tries (12 points) to nil.

[2] Frederick Bower Watkins (1876–93) died at Harrow a few weeks later, on Easter Monday, April 3. Described by the *Harrovian* as "a boy of exceptional intellectual power and promise", his career at Harrow (he was at The Head Master's) had been frequently interrupted by ill-health.

[3] Russell Mortimer Luckock (1877–1950), son of the Very Rev H. M. Luckock, Dean of Lichfield, joined King's Own Regiment 1900, after first going up to Trinity College, Cambridge. Served in Boer War, 1914–18 War; Brevet Lieut-Colonel 1917; North Russia, India, Colonel 1922; Brigadier 1928, Maj-General 1932; retired 1938. DSO, CMG, CB, Legion of Honour, Croix de Guerre, despatches eight times.

[4] James Gowans (1872–1936) played Rugby for Cambridge and Scotland, 1892–6. In this match he played at wing three-quarter and, according to *The Times*, missed a chance of scoring. Later he served in Boer War (Captain, DSO 1902); and 1914–18, Lieut-Colonel (despatches).

Jack Milbanke to Winston

14 February [1893]   [10th Royal Hussars]
                                               Cahir[1]

My dear Winston,

I was so glad to get your letter it is such a long time since I have heard from you. Write and tell me all about your accident I read in the papers that one of you had hurt himself but it didn't say which one or how you had done it. This is such a nice place no society of any description but heaps of hunting fishing etc. Wasn't I lucky getting into the 10th it was rather difficult to manage as I did not pass – however now it is all right. I anxiously scanned the Sandhurst list the other day expecting to see your name. I am so sorry for you, having to begin cramming again tho' James's is a charming place as one can do just what one likes and work as little as one likes. There are such a nice lot of men in the regiment and altogether I am having a real good time, still there is a good deal of work to do riding school drill etc and a great many days duty as so many are on leave. What is Dudley doing now. I haven't heard from him for years, is he cramming? The worst part of Cahir is that it is such a terrible long way from London and takes days to get there, it really is not worth while coming over for less than a week. I hope however to get a fortnights leave at Easter in which case you must come and dine with me and we will do a play.

                                                Yours ever
                                        JACK MILBANKE

Hugh Wyllie[2] to Winston

14 February 1893   11 Palmeira Avenue
                                          West Brighton

Dear Churchill,

The weather was certainly too disagreeable especially if you would have to be in a bath-chair.

I am glad to hear you are none the worse for your night out, you did a good deal of walking about though.

Anyhow we lunch together on Saturday at the Metropole, and if it is convenient for you to make arrangements for any afternoon or evening before then write and let me know I have no engagements at all so choose your own time after 3.30.

I think you would enjoy the Empire there is a very fair programme on there. If you are still in Brighton on Sunday we might lunch then instead of Saturday,

---

[1] A garrison town in Tipperary.

[2] Hugh Tweed Walford Wyllie (1874–1915) joined 4th Dragoon Guards, served in Tirah Expedition 1897–8, Captain 1905, killed by a shell on the Ypres-Menin road.

it is always very gay on Sundays at the Metropole as so many people come down from town.

Hoping to have a note or a call from you soon

I remain Yours sincerely
HUGH WYLLIE

Lily, Duchess of Marlborough to Winston

8.15 a.m! [? February 1893]

Dear Winston,

I have just had a letter from Papa wh I will show you later – The part that alludes to you.

Mamma comes to Brighton today for *Luncheon* arriving at 1.7 – your train – so you must write the Miss Thompsons that you will not be able to luncheon with them & why.

Affectly
AUNT LILY

Miss Charlotte Thomson to Winston

14 February [1893]   29 Brunswick Road
Brighton

Dear Winston,

Have you remembered that tomorrow is Ash Wednesday? I shall be so much obliged if you can shift your entertainment to the boys until Thursday or Friday. I cannot understand how I forgot it last night, but suppose it must have been the intoxicating effect of that Pantomime.

Yours always truly
CHARLOTTE THOMSON

Mrs Everest to Winston

15 February 1893   8 Royal Crescent
Margate

My dear Mr Winston,

We were delighted to receive your nice letter yesterday & to hear you are having such happy times at Brighton & I am so pleased to hear you are so much stronger & better. You must take care & not do too much or over exert yourself. You must have been surprised to hear Jackie & I were at Margate. I wish they had sent us to Brighton this is such a dreary dull place. No one about

& half the shops closed nothing stirring. I was very much afraid Jackie was in for it when he came here he had some symptoms. I expect the sea air blew it away he was so languid & tired & a dry cough & cold he is better than he was but not as well as he ought to be. I think you manage the type writing very well indeed considering the short time you have tried it you will like that sort of work I know. Save you trouble. Jackie has been into every shop in Margate to try & get a type writer for 6d to cut you out, but such articles are quite unknown in this outlandish place. Jackie says it is a labour for him to write to you & it is only an amusement for you to write to him with a type writer. So you can go on writing to him. We made an excursion to Ramsgate this morning by train but such a horrid little dirty place. Yesterday we walked to Westgate on Sea. There is a sand Beach here which is the one thing to recommend the place. When do you think of returning to London. It is so very kind of the Duchess [Lily] to have you there [at Brighton] so long, it will quite set you up again – you will soon have been a fortnight at Brighton. I got your room all in such nice order for you before I came away you will be very comfortable now I have taken away the old bed & one of the wash stands & put in 2 large Basket chairs I brought from Banstead. I am glad you have been to see Miss Thomson & the little Roose's. Has Bertie sent you your Watch yet? It is very unfortunate the S. fever at Harrow try & find out if it is increasing or abating & let us know. I am so afraid of my darling Jackie getting it poor little man. He makes himself very contented here in spite of the dullness of the place. He is delighted with the Boys Own annual & by way of varying his literature he spends all his coppers on comic papers which seem to amuse him very much. I have been trying to get him to write to you today but he is very idle & so keen on reading his book he is not inclined to write. We shall be glad of another letter when you feel disposed. Jackie sends you fond love & accept the same

From your Humble servant
EVEREST

Bertrand Roose to Winston

[?16 February 1893]   89 Gracechurch Street

My dear Winston,

I have been away since Friday so have not been able to send you your watch. I am sending it off tonight so I expect you will get it first thing in the morning. Am going out tonight or I would bring it in myself.

Yrs Affecte
BERTRAND R. ROOSE

Reverend F. C. Searle to Winston

3 March 1893   Harrow

My dear Churchill,

At last! I have had a letter to you commenced for nearly a month but have never found time to finish it. One thing after another has come in the way and always hindered me when I intended to go on with it. I am so glad to hear that you have so much recovered from the effects of your accident. Jack tells me that you are able now to go to James'. I hope that you are getting on well there. You must let me speak to you plainly. If I did not do so I should myself be doing wrong and I should also be doing you a wrong. This accident has brought you face to face with death. You cannot have realised how easily it might have proved fatal. You ought so to live as to be able to look death in the face without fear &, if you will, you can do this. You know what is right & you have fully enough strength of will to carry it out if only you will decide to do so. But with you the fault lies in not deciding. You must once for all realise that to please God must be the ground work [?] of your life. Up to this time you have not set this before you. You have been content to take the world as you have found it, getting out of it as much so called amusement as you could. Such a life is not a happy one – it has no worthy aim and can give no lasting satisfaction. Then, my dear Churchill, do turn and decide once for all that you will set the pleasing of God and the service of other men before you as the object of life. The effort of making such a decision is great but once made it gives you peace & happiness.

Jack is I think very happy in his room with Lampson.[1] He (Jack) is delightful – everyone likes him as indeed no one could fail to do. I am sending you the papers about the Mission and Harrovian. If you can continue to support the Mission, do do so.

Now good bye Yours affecty
F. C. SEARLE

Jack to Lady Randolph

5 March [1893]   [Harrow]

Dear Mama,

I was so sorry you did not come down on Saturday. I have not had a single line from Winney and as he has got his Type writer & it is more an amusement to him to wrote I think he might write a little to me.

[1] Ronald Cecil Lampson (1878–1952), son of Sir G. C. Lampson, 2nd Bart. An insurance broker.

Last night we had the "Elijah" played here, a troop of people came down from London to play it. My thumb is much better although it still hurts very much.

It is getting very nice now here it is quite warm.

I saw Papa's speech the other day did you see the *Daily Graphic* it said that Papa new more about Jokey's than he did about Clergymen & that when he spoke about the Welsh church he made many mistakes.

Do make Winney write to me

I have no more time to tell you anything else

Give my best love to Papa & Winney.

I remain your loving Son
JACK S. CHURCHILL

Captain Walter James to Lord Randolph
(*Blenheim Papers*)

7 March 1893   5 Lexham Gardens
London

Dear Lord Randolph,

I have issued orders for your son to be kept at work and that in future he is to do the full hours. I had to speak to him the other day about his casual manner. I think the boy means well but he is distinctly inclined to be inattentive and to think too much of his abilities. These are certainly good and if he do as he ought he should pass very well in the summer, but he has been rather too much inclined up to the present to teach his instructors instead of endeavouring to learn from them, and this is not the frame of mind condusive to success. I may give as an instance that he suggested to me that his knowledge of history was such that he did not want any more teaching in it! I think you will agree with me that this is problematical. I have no doubt that between the two of us we can manage him well enough and I am glad to have received your letter of today.

I am sorry that I cannot see him personally as I am confined to my room with a bad cold on my chest but he will be spoken to and I shall let you know how he gets on.

The boy has very many good points in him but what he wants is very firm handling.

Yours very truly
WALTER H. JAMES

Lady Wilton to Winston

1 April [1893]   Le Nid

My dear Winston,

Tis quite true, I've been owing you a letter but – you'll forgive me when I tell you that I've been *very* ill indeed with 3 weeks of the Influenza – so bad that I could hear nothing, & hardly see & was delirious. I am now *slowly* picking up – but *too* slowly for my taste. I've not been out for full 3 weeks.

Of course I will be only *too* glad if you'll come to the Hatch, whenever you like.

How is Jack?

Love from your affecte Deputy Mother
LAURA WILTON

Lady Wilton to Winston

[? April 1893]   Le Nid

Many thanks, my dearest Winston, for yours received yesterday. I was so pleased to hear from you. I hope You're very well now? & Jack? Please give him my love. & also – my best love to your Mama – I hope dear you'll come & stay at *the Hatch* as often as you like this summer – I will get home about the 1st week in June – but I'll write to you before then. I want a photo of you – & you promised me one! Do please keep that in mind – & believe me.

Yr very affecte Deputy Mother
LAURA WILTON

Enclosed £2 for small expenses.

Winston to Lady Randolph

2 April 1893   [Brighton]

Dear Mamma,

I got here all right on Friday, and have not so far injured Myself in any way. Aunt Lily put me up in a very comfortable room & I have enjoyed myself immensely; The weather is delightful and the town is crowded with people. There are a goodly number of volunteers of all sorts here also. I have just returned from the Swimming Baths, whither I go every morning.

Last night Mr Balfour came to dinner; he is just off to Ireland to "Ulsterize".[1] Uncle Morton came back from London to talk silver with him.

[1] On April 4, A. J. Balfour addressed a rally in the Ulster Hall, Belfast, after having reviewed a procession which took several hours to pass the stand.

I met Sir George Wombwell yesterday at the Metropole; he is coming to dine to night. There is, I fear no More news to tell, so I will now stop.

Ever your loving son
WINSTON S. CHURCHILL

Mrs Everest to Winston

4 April 1893   50 Grosvenor Square

My Darling Winston,
    The enclosed letter has just arrived too late for tonight's post, so I am writing a few lines to come with it. Her Ladyship came home this morning & is very much hurt not having recd a letter from either you or Jackie – | so am I | you are a naughty little Boy to forget all your Friends soon as you get out of their sight. I have sent off your note books & notes. I hope I have selected the right ones if not I must send more. I have sent your pot hat but it is very shabby why don't you buy yourself a new one at Brighton. I have also sent your tall hat in your hat Box. I hope you are keeping well & not leaping off the Pier or any Bridges or trees or taking turkish baths or riding *kicking job horses*. You are having lovely weather it is like June in London. Jackie was delighted at going off to Canford[1] he has not written yet too busy I expect enjoying his little self the darling Boy.
    I went to my niece's wedding yesterday & enjoyed myself very much which I know you will be glad to hear as it is very little I get, please let me know if you get those 2 boxes safely,

& believe me your Devoted old
WOOM

Lily, Duchess of Marlborough to Lord Randolph
(Blenheim Papers)

EXTRACT

5 April 1893   24 Brunswick Terrace
[Brighton]

. . . I am *very* glad to have Winston with me – for I have grown really fond of the boy. He has lots of good in him – and only needs sometimes to be corrected, which he always takes so smartly and well.
    I will keep him with me till his vacation is at an end – when he goes back to

---

[1] The home of Lord and Lady WIMBORNE.

Grosvenor Square. He wired Jennie today to know if he might go and stay with a friend of his for two days – and as Jennie said by reply wire "Yes", I am letting him go. He will come back here, after two days, until his holidays are over!

I made him send for his books and I will see he does a good bit of work while he is here. . . .

Lady Randolph to Winston

Friday 7 [April 1893]   50 Grosvenor Square

Dearest Winston,

I go to Belvoir[1] today only – having been put off by Ld Granby's[2] illness. I shall be back here Monday. I hope you are comporting yrself properly – I feel a little nervous at yr visiting alone. I don't want to preach dear boy, but mind you are quiet & don't talk too much & don't drink too much. One is easily carried away at yr age. I confess I was rather sad yr not writing when I begged you to at once. I suppose I shall find yr letter at Belvoir. Papa seems to have had a great reception at Liverpool,[3] & his speech is most stirring.

Bless you – hold yrself up & behave like the gentleman you are.

Yr loving
MOTHER

Winston to Lord Randolph
(Blenheim Papers)

9 April 1893   26 Brunswick Terrace

Dear Papa,

I have been to stay with Milbanke for a couple of days; but came back here last night. I had great fun there, as the Duke of Richmond[4] gave a ball to the county, and also tableaux vivants.

I read your Liverpool speeches, which I thought awfully fine. Where did you find that letter, which was mislaid, – about the "Pure Scotchman"?

Aunt Lily is very kind to me, and has promised me that if I get into Sandhurst she will give me a really good pony. I think I will come up to London

---

[1] Belvoir Castle, Grantham – seat of the Duke of Rutland.

[2] Henry John Brinsley, Marquess of Granby (1852–1925), eldest son of 7th Duke of Rutland, whom he succeeded in 1906. Married in 1882 Violet, daughter of Colonel the Hon C. K. Lindsay; one of their three daughters became Lady Diana Cooper, wife of Alfred Duff Cooper, 1st Viscount Norwich.

[3] On April 6.

[4] Charles Henry Gordon Lennox, 6th Duke of Richmond and Lennox and 1st Duke of Gordon (1818–1903); President of the Board of Trade 1867–8, Lord President of the Council 1874–80.

on Tuesday, as James's opens on Thursday. I feel very fit, and quite ready for work.

Last night I met Mr [Sir] Henry Ponsonby and Lord and Lady Carrington[1] at the Metropole. I have also made the acquaintance of Mr Tyrrhwitt-Wilson[2] a brother, I think, of Mr Harry Tyrrwhitt.[3]

There is lots to do here and I shall be very sorry to come away. We are having the most beautiful weather and the town is simply crowded.

I have no more news to tell you, except that I hope Perth will go off as well as L'Pool.[4] So, hoping to see you in a few days time,

I remain ever your loving son
WINSTON S.C.

Lady Randolph to Winston

19 April [1893]   Paris

Dearest Winston,

I am sorry not to have been able to write to you before – but I am so "hunted" here I haven't had *one* moment to myself. I am afraid you did not get to London on Sat: but never mind. When I return we will put that right. Prince Sagan asked after you the other day. I am enjoying myself immensely, ride & skate go to the races dine and even dance! It is too unfortunate tho' that the weather which was divine – is now rather wet. Write me a line dear, I do hope that you are getting on well, & that you are fit. Bless you. Do write

Yr loving Mother
JSC

Mrs Lancelot Lowther[5] has taken one of your photos & sends her love.

[1] Lord Carrington (see page 24) had married 1878 Hon Cecilia Margaret Harbord (1856–1934), eldest daughter of 5th Baron Suffield, she became a Lady of the Bedchamber to Queen Alexandra 1911–25.

[2] Raymond Robert Tyrwhitt-Wilson (1855–1918), 2nd son of Sir Henry Thomas Tyrwhitt 3rd Bart and Emma Harriet Wilson, niece of 11th Baron Berners whom she succeeded as Baroness in her own right in 1871. He assumed the name of Wilson after that of Tyrwhitt by Royal Licence in 1892, and succeeded his father as 4th Bart in 1894 and his mother as 13th Baron Berners in 1917.

[3] Harry Tyrwhitt-Wilson (1854–1891), eldest son of Sir Henry Thomas Tyrwhitt and Baroness Berners, and elder brother of Raymond Robert Tyrwhitt-Wilson (see above). He too assumed the name of Wilson by Royal Licence in 1876. An equerry to the Prince of Wales, he was also a close friend and travelling companion of Lord Randolph's.

[4] Lord Randolph was met everywhere by enthusiastic crowds. In the evening he addressed between four and five thousand people in Hengler's Circus.

[5] Sophia Gwendoline Alice (1868–1921), eldest daughter of Sir Robert Sheffield 5th Bart. She married 1889 Hon Lancelot Edward Lowther, 4th son of 3rd Earl of Lonsdale, who in 1944 succeeded his brother Hugh (the Yellow Earl) as 6th Earl.

Captain Walter James to Lord Randolph
(*Blenheim Papers*)

29 April 1893   5 Lexham Gardens

Private

Dear Lord Randolph,

I am sure you will feel that I am only impelled by kind motives in writing to you about your son. I have no definite complaint to make about him but I do not think that his work is going on very satisfactorily. All the tutors complain that while he has good abilities he does not apply himself with sufficient earnestness to his reading. He can and will succeed if he will but give up everything to the examination before him but I doubt his passing if he do not do this. Of course I feel that at a time like the present it is difficult for him not to take an interest in current political topics, but if this be done to an extent which takes his mind away from his studies, the result is bad for the latter. I have spoken to him on the question and I hope you will give him a little paternal advice and point out, what I have done, the absolute necessity of single-minded devotion to the immediate object before him, and the extreme desirability of thoroughness and detail [sic] attention to all he attempts.

Yours very truly
WALTER H. JAMES

Lily, Duchess of Marlborough to Winston

30 April 1893   26 Brunswick Terrace

Dear Winston,

I found your very kind and thoughtful letter when I came down to Brighton last night. I am very busy getting ready to leave, early next week, and am quite myself now – although I have a few tiresome days of being laid up.

I haven't forgotten that I owe you the huge sum of £1. 12. 6! Have you? – So I think you ought to have your debt paid and as ours was a 'ready money' transaction, I am sending you *interest* on the Amount! You will be glad, I know, to have the old bit from Monte Carlo back again.

Come and see me in Town, sometimes –and *mind* you pass that Examination.

Ever yours affect
'AUNT LILY'

Captain Walter James to Lord Randolph
(*Blenheim Papers*)

1 May 1893   5 Lexham Gardens
                                                     London

Dear Lord Randolph,

I do not think I have anything to add to my last letter and can only repeat if your son really do his best he is pretty certain to pass in the summer. I enclose a receipt for your cheque with many thanks.

Yours very truly
WALTER H. JAMES

Winston to Lord Randolph
(*Blenheim Papers*)

23 May 1893   [50 Grosvenor Square]

Dear Papa,

I read your speech in *The Times* this morning and I thought it awfully good. It seems you have gone down very well indeed with the papers. If you will let me say so, I thought it better than anything you have done so far. Today I went back to Captain James's and I have done a good days work. There are now only five weeks between me and the examinations so this is practically the last "lap". I find that I have made great progress in several things and particularly in mathematics: but I have been too sanguine twice before and I am not going out again until after the Examination.

Hoping that the Bradford speech will be as great a success as the Bolton one, I remain ever your affectionate son

WINSTON S. CHURCHILL

PS Don't trouble to answer as I know how busy you are. wsc

Edward Carson[1] to Winston

30 May 1893   18 Granville Place

Dear Mr Churchill,

I have an order for Friday for House under Gallery and will be very glad if you come and dine with me then to view the scramble of a House of Commons dinner.

Yours truly
EDWARD CARSON

---

[1] Edward Henry Carson (1854–1935), later to become renowned as Ulster politician, barrister and judge, had entered the House of Commons in the previous year as MP for Dublin University.

Winston to Lord Randolph
(*Blenheim Papers*)

30 May 1893   50 Grosvenor Square

Dear Papa,

I have had a letter from Mr Carson inviting me to dine with him at the House on Friday evening. I have accepted as I have very little work on Saturday. If you would rather I would not go Please send me a line. I hope you backed Isinglass.[1] I went in for a sweepstake at Captain James's. Everyone from the Captain down took a ticket – 5/- I drew Quickly Wise so this has been "a disastrous Derby" for me.

The work has been going very well, and I hear that the Examination will be easier. I hope so – but, barring accidents, it ought to come off this time.

Uncle Edward has been here to dinner. He spent nearly half an hour after dinner in explaining to me the methods by which the Opposition of the House of Lords was going to be overcome. I wish that you had been there to answer him, as I am sure that there was an answer though I could not think of it.

Mamma went down to see Jack on Tuesday and Mr Welldon gave her excellent report of him. Grandmamma has just had a letter from you and told me that you are enjoying your holiday and that it is a very pleasant part. I am so glad.

If you don't want me to go to Mr Carson, send me a line – but don't trouble to write unless you don't wish it.

> With best love I remain ever your loving son
> WINSTON S.C.

Edward Carson to Winston

1 June 1893

Dear Mr Churchill,

When I got the order for Friday I quite forgot we adjourn on Friday at 10 minutes to 7 until 9 o'c & consequently after there is no debate on Home Rule or anything of importance. I hope therefore you will not mind my suggesting to postpone your visit to the House till someday next week, as it will be better fun and more interesting for you.

> Yrs vry truly
> EDWARD CARSON

---

[1] Mr H. McCalmont's odds-on Derby winner. The colt had also won the Two Thousand Guineas and went on to win the St Leger. In 1895 he won the Gold Cup at Ascot.

Winston to Lady Randolph

14 June 1893 50 Grosvenor Square

Dear Mamma,

Just one line to tell you that Missy has come home, recovered from her illness & accident. Papa has been very kind to me and Capt James has written to tell him that he thinks I shall pass. I am told his verdict is rarely at fault.

It is very late and I am awfully tired so will remain,

Your loving son
WINSTON S. CHURCHILL

PS Hope you are enjoying yourself at [?] St Bruno. Wish you luck. WSC

Reverend J. E. C. Welldon to Winston

15 June 1893 Harrow

My dear Churchill,

Come by all means on Saturday.

Please tell your father that I shall be very glad to see him on Sunday week. I think I must ask Bosworth Smith[1] to meet him at supper after Chapel – so that the two great defenders of the Church in Wales may put their heads together.

Affectionately Yours
J. E. C. WELLDON

Jack to Winston

[? 15 June 1893] [Harrow]

Dear Winney,

Everything has come out in the *Harrovian* all right as it ought to be their are 2 printing mistakes but they do not show much.[2]

Shall expect to see you Saturday.

I remain
JACK

[1] Reginald Bosworth Smith (1839–1908); classical master at Harrow 1864–1901. Wrote on current political, religious and educational matters in the reviews. He opposed the disestablishment of the Church of England and of the Church in Wales; a great supporter of Lord Salisbury's government.

[2] Another letter from 'Truth', the Philistine Correspondent of the *Harrovian*, appeared in the issue of June 15.

Lady Randolph to Winston

Sunday [18 June 1893]   Sunningdale

Dearest Winston,

Many thanks for yr letter – I shall be up tomorrow. I hope you have enjoyed yr Sunday at Harrow. Poor Missy is not well & we are sending her up to London by Thomas to Sewell's. I hope she will get all right. I have had a delightful week & won my money. I shall make you a pres of £2. It *is* hot! I hope you are careful not to get in the sun – one might really get a sun stroke. Papa is busy preparing his speech for Leicester.[1] I do hope yr "prognostication" will prove correct & that you will pass *à demain mon cher enfant. Travaille bien et aime moi encore plus.*

Yr loving
MOTHER

Jack to Winston

[? June 1893]

Dear Winney,

Thanks for your letter. The clock is beautiful I shall take it to Switzerland. it is a repeater & strikes like the one you've got it is very small.

The Camera is a great success

I suppose Mama comes back from Ascot on Saturday.

Are you coming up I suppose you lost over the R. Hunt C.

I will write again soon & send some Photo's.

I remain
JACK S. CHURCHILL

Captain Walter James to Winston
(*Blenheim Papers*)

19 June 1893   5 Lexham Gardens

Dear Lord Randolph,

Without saying that your son is a certainty I think he ought to pass this time. He is working well and I think doing his best to get on but, as you know, he is at times inclined to take the bit in his teeth and go his own course.

I believe, however, I have convinced him that he has got to do what you wish him to do, and I have lately had no cause to complain of him.

It would not do to let him know what I think of his chance of success as with his peculiar disposition this might lead him to slacken off again.

[1] On June 21.

I tell him that if he worked till he go up he ought to have a fair chance and though I think this is a minimum estimation still I feel it would not be advisable to say more to him.

> Yours very truly
> WALTER H. JAMES

George Brodrick[1] to Lord Randolph
(*Lord Randolph Papers*)

25 June 1893

Merton College
Oxford

Dear Lord Randolph,

I think Mr Little would be free and disposed to accept an engagement for the Vacation, but he could not get away until the end of the Eton Term – i.e. – Aug 2 or 4. I am almost sure that you would like him, and that he would get on well with your boys; he is a thorough gentleman, and anything but a Don.

His address is J. D. G. Little Esq, 45 High Street, Eton, and I would suggest your asking him to call upon you, if you can give him a choice of days, so that he may not have to put aside his present duties.

> Yrs sincerely
> GEORGE BRODRICK

J. D. G. Little to Lord Randolph
(*Lord Randolph Papers*)

Thursday [29 June 1893]

45 High Street
Eton

My Lord,

I am much obliged to you for your letter; and I should be very glad to accept your kind proposal to travel with your sons for six weeks. I shall have to remain here till August 2nd when the Eton Term ends; but as one of your sons is at Harrow, he himself would probably not be free to start much before that date.

I shall be most happy to call, as you suggest, on Saturday July 15th (the second day of the Eton & Harrow match) at 10.30 a.m.

I should consider £25 very adequate remuneration for the six weeks.

> I remain, Yrs truly
> J. LITTLE

---

[1] George Charles Brodrick (1831–1903); second son of 7th Viscount Midleton. Fellow of Merton 1855, Warden 1881–1903. Opposed Lord Randolph in the Woodstock election in 1874, standing as a Liberal; but after 1886 became 'an active and earnest member of the Liberal Unionist Party'. Uncle of W. St John BRODRICK, later 1st Earl of Midleton.

Captain Walter James to Winston

5 July 1893   5 Lexham Gardens

Dear Churchill,

I have no more Chemistry going on now but really think you know enough to do well in it.

I would recommend you to read up your testing and, above all, to pay attention to the method of putting down your results as many marks are lost by this not being properly done.

I am glad to hear that you have done well and hope you will pass as you ought to do if you have done all you knew.

Yours truly
WALTER H. JAMES

PS The Laboratory will be open on Friday from 10 to 1 if you like to come.

John E. Marshall Hall to WSC

6 July 1893   14 Bonfield Road
                                                   Lewisham S.E.

Dear Churchill,

I am glad you got on satisfactorily in the paper as appears from your letter. I cannot go up to town tomorrow, but if you care to run down here & have lunch with me, I can give you an hour or two and shall be delighted to do so. Come some time about 1.0 from Charing X by the S.E. Rly. I am close to the Lewisham Junction.

Yours very truly
JNO. E. MARSHALL HALL

John E. Marshall Hall to WSC

11 July 1893   56 Marina
                                                   St. Leonards

Dear Churchill,

Thank you for your letter and paper which I return. I daresay you have done better in the practical than you wot of. I hope (as you were *told* in the second question) that you put down the *absences* of metals & acids, as well as their presence, in your analysis. It does not appear to me very hard. Surely *Lead* and *Mercury* are characteristic enough.

I quite expect you to get over your thousand marks in the Chemistry from what I have seen, though of course *all* depends on whether you have carefully *put down all* the work you did for the practical, *results or no results.*

Yours very truly
JOHN E. MARSHALL HALL

I delivered your message to my wife – who joins me in wishing you success.

Lily, Duchess of Marlborough to Winston

3 August [1893]   Harrogate

TELEGRAM[1]

So pleased and glad you have passed. Must look out for good horse for you when you return. Am writing

AUNT LILY

Lily, Duchess of Marlborough to Winston

3 August 1893   Prospect Hotel
                                                 Harrogate

Dear Winston,

I was *so* pleased to get your wire today and to know you had "got in"!! Never mind about the Infantry: you will *love* the Cavalry, and when Papa comes back we will get the charger. Your £10 is here for you – only I fear you are a wee bit extravagant and I do not mean you to have it until you begin your Army work! Truly, my dear Boy I am very glad for you and I know you will enjoy your holiday all the more that your studies, (& you *did* work) are now crowned with the "Well done".

It is very dull here, but I am 1000 times better since I came and feel 5 years younger.

[1] This telegram was addressed to Lucerne, where Winston started on a walking tour of Switzerland with Jack and their tutor, Mr J. D. G. Little.

Write me what you see and do – and *don't* tumble down another precipice and hurt any more of your organs – for I will not be there to take care of you – nor will Mrs Abell! I wish you and Jack could get on a "wishing carpet" and come here and play Bezique with me. Give my love to Jack and if you know how, give mine also to yourself – from

Your most affect
"AUNT LILY"

I wired you at once today after receiving yours – Write me to 3 CH [Carlton House] Terrace and they will forward me.

Reverend J. E. C. Welldon to Winston

4 August 1893   Harrow

My dear Churchill,

Your telegram being sent from Dover Pier makes me think you must have been on the point of leaving England.

But, even if it is long before you get this letter, I cannot help saying how much I rejoice in your success and how keenly I feel that you have deserved it.

You have I hope learnt now what hard work is, and it will be a lesson of enduring value to you.

Sincerely yrs
J. E. C. WELLDON

Captain Walter James to Lord Randolph
(Blenheim Papers)

4 August 1893   5 Lexham Gardens

Dear Lord Randolph,

You will have learned that your son has passed 4th in the Cavalry List. He cannot be far out of the Infantry List as he is only 18 marks below the lowest and I have no doubt that if you particularly wish him to go into a foot regiment he could be transferred. The marks are lower all round this time probably due to the difficulty of some of the papers and taking this into consideration I think he has done fairly well and I am glad to see his name on the list.

Yours very truly
WALTER H. JAMES

Lord Randolph to Frances, Duchess of Marlborough
(*Wimborne Papers*)

5 July [August] 1893   Hotel Victoria
                                                             Kissingen

Dearest Mama,

We had a long & tiring journey here. The first day to Cologne was long but cool & no dust. But the day to Kissingen was very hot & little air & much dust & the last three hours terribly tedious. However on the whole this is a taking little place. We have not vy comfortable rooms. I had a great dispute with the Manager because he had given me a most pokey little bedroom & I told him I would go to another Hotel & in the evening I ostentatiously betook myself to his rival at the Kurhaus Hotel who told me he could give me good rooms. Next morning the Manager of this Hotel was most meek. He told me he had made an arrangement to let me the bedroom which I wanted just the other side of our sitting room opposite to Jennie, so that we have a complete communicating suite & Paice has the pokey room next to Jennie's. I think we get all this on vy moderate terms, £13 a month which for these places is really not exorbitant. The charges for board are also moderate 4/6 for mid-day dinner, servants 5/6 per diem. The breakfasts at 8 AM & the suppers at 8 PM are vy light meals & of course of little cost. I am afraid I shall not find Gastein as cheap as this. We took sometime to settle down & find our way about & learn what the course of the cure was. I like the doctor Gottburg. He is vy attentive careful & of a good reputation.

We took a drive yesterday for 2 hours, between 4 & 6 PM. The country is a peaceful one, pastoral agricultural & thickly wooded which gives much shade in the [?]. Shortly before getting back to Kissingen we met Prince & Princess Bismark[1] driving. He gave us a grand bow but this he does to anyone & I am sure he does not know us from Adam. I do not think I shall run after him for he is a disagreeable old gentleman & was never civil to me but I suppose ordinary respect to an old statesman requires a card which I shall leave in a day or two. We have had a providential escape. The Duke of Edinboro's[2] stay here came to an end this morning. He would have been a plague if he had stayed on as he is always worrying you to do everything which bores you. He came to see us yesterday morning & insisted on our going to supper with him, & gave us a most unwholesome meal which is dead against the rules of the cure. It was vy

[1] Prince Otto von Bismarck (1815–1898), Minister President of Prussia 1862–71 and Chancellor of the German Empire, which was virtually his creation, 1871–90, when he resigned after differences with the Emperor, William II. He married in 1847 Johanna von Puttkamer (1824–94).

[2] Alfred, Duke of Edinburgh (1844–1900), second son of Queen Victoria, who was to succeed, 22 August 1893, as reigning Duke of Saxe-Coburg and Gotha. He was married to Marie Alexandrovna (a friend of Lady Randolph's), only daughter of Tsar Alexander II.

long & dull & H R H talked great nonsense & told a lot of the oldest stories & some great silly [ones]. However I got to bed at 9.30 Last night we had a vy heavy storm which rattled the windows & howled in a most weird manner, torrents of rain. The air is much fresher today & the sky is bright. I must tell you our daily life – up at 6 AM. The band plays so loudly vy close to our hotel that there is nothing to do but get up. We take two glasses of water measured, a quarter of an hours walk between & after each, that brings us vy near eight when we have breakfast eggs & fish then two hours after we take a bath 10 mts in duration. The water is the most bubbly I ever saw. When you are sitting in the bath your skin is covered with millions of bubbles & after you come out you are much wetter than I ever was after any bath. Neither is the water disagreeable to the taste nor is the bath anything but pleasant so I think we have come to a vy salubrious place and I feel vy hopeful it will do us both good.

I got your short note about the servants. I cannot think highly of Winston's. He missed the last place in the infantry by about 18 marks which shows great slovenliness of work in the actual examination. He only made about 200 hundred marks more than last time, I think not so many even as 200. He has gone & got himself into the cavalry who are always 2nd rate performers in the examination and which will cost me £200 a year more than the infantry wld have cost. I have told you often & you never would believe me that he has little [claim] to cleverness, to knowledge or any capacity for settled work. He has great talent for show off exaggeration & make believe. In all his three examinations he has made to me statements of his performance which have never been borne out by results. Nothing has been spared on him; the best coaches every kind of amusement & kindness especially from you & more than any boy of his position is entitled to. The whole result of this has been either at Harrow or at Eton to prove his total worthlessness as a scholar or a conscientious worker. He need not expect much from me. He will go up to Sandhurst when for the first time in his life he will be kept in order & we shall see whether he can stand military discipline. If he can he may rub along respectably. I shall try & get Brabazon who has a regiment of Hussars to take him & after 2 or 3 years shall exchange him with the infantry. Now this is all truth & it is better to look facts in the face. When he is at Sandhurst I wont have any running backwards & forwards to London. He shall be kept to his work so that he may acquire the elementary principles of a military education.

I will not conceal from you it is a great disappointment to me. I never had much confidence, James's 2 or 3 revelations as to his manner of working & his attitude to the tutors stopped all confidence. But I did hope seeing the chances he had he would show a considerable improvement on his last examination but one. There was much less competition in his last and the result was much worse & much more discreditable in a relative sense for Winston. Now dearest Mama goodbye; the above is only meant for you alone & need not be communicated to any of the family. After all he has got into the army & that is a result which none of his cousins have been able to do, but still that is a vy wretched & pitiable consolation.

Ever yr affte son
RANDOLPH S.C.

Winston to Lord Randolph
(Blenheim Papers)

6 August [1893]

Schweizerhof Hotel
Lucerne

Dear Papa,

I was so glad to be able to send you good news on Thursday. I did not expect that the list would be published so soon & was starting off in the train, when Little congratulated me on getting in. I looked in the paper & found this to be true. Several boys I know very well have got in too.

At Dover I sent off a lot of telegrams, and on the boat I received one from Grandmamma telling me I had passed.

We had a very rough crossing & poor Jack was very sick. At Calais we secured an empty first class carriage & travelled very comfortably to Amiens where 5 horrid people got in & stayed with us all night – till we got to Bale. Very uncomfortable it was – 8 people in one carriage.

We changed carriages at Bale & came on here in a coupe.

This is a splendid hotel – lifts, electric light, & fireworks (every Saturday). Tomorrow we are going away to Andermatt where our address will be . . . Hotel Bellevue Andermatt. We leave here on the 9th. Lucerne is a lovely place. There are excellent swimming baths, & good food, & magnificent scenery. Yesterday we went up Pilatus, which was very interesting, & came down by the mountain Railway to Alpanack & so home by steamer.

I had a telegram from Duchess Lily saying that she was going to look out for a good horse for me when I return . . . Also a letter.

I like Mr Little very much. He is unfortunately very lame, but is getting better slowly.

Miss Welldon is here with her husband a Harrow master named Stephen.[1] She was married 3 days ago & this is the honeymoon. I talk lots of French to

---

[1] Edith Welldon had married, on August 2, Norman Kenneth Stephen (1865–1948), a classics master at Harrow.

the waiters etc. Altogether we are enjoying ourselves immensely & I should be very sorry to come back if I were not going to Sandhurst.

Hoping that you are quite well & that the waters suit you.

I remain your ever loving son
WINSTON S.C.

PS If you have time to write to us write to Hotel des Couronnes, Brigue.

J. D. G. Little to Lord Randolph
(Blenheim Papers)

7 August [1893]   Hotel Sweitzerhof
                                                  Lucerne

Dear Lord Randolph Churchill,

We arrived here alright on Friday. In the afternoon they bathed and went for a row on the Lake.

Yesterday (Saturday) we went up Pilatus. We are going up the Rigi tomorrow and then go to Andermatt at the foot of the St Gothard, where we propose to stay several days, to see the tunnel &c. After that we think of going to see the Rhône glacier and the Furka Pass to Brieg.

They are both enjoying themselves I think very much: and so far we have all got on very well together; although Winston is inclined to be extravagant.

I am so glad that he has been successful in getting into Sandhurst.

Believe me Yours truly
J. D. G. LITTLE

Lady Randolph to Winston

Monday 7 August [1893]   Kissingen

Dearest Winston,

We have just received yr letters & are very pleased to think you are enjoying yrselves – I am glad of course that you have got into Sandhurst but Papa is not very pleased at yr getting in by the skin of yr teeth & missing the Infantry by 18 marks. He is not as pleased over yr exploits as you seem to be!

I am sure you must be very happy travelling about & living in the open air. I trust you won't overdo the walking for Jack's sake.

Poor Puss! being so sick. I can sympathize tho' we had a lovely crossing. We are doing the cure most conscienciously & I think it will do Papa a lot of good. Kissingen is a very pretty place – lots of walks & drives. We get up at 6.30!! & go to bed at 9.30 – drink water – take baths & listen to music. The time passes somehow.

Prince Bismarck is here & came to see us yeterday. It was very interesting meeting him – I had forgotten that he is 78.

Give Jack my best love – I will write to him next time. Mind you write often & don't forget to write to Grandmama Marlborough. Remember me to Mr Little. I hope his leg will be soon all right. I don't write more about Sandhurst as I know Papa intends to let you know his views!

Best love – & look after yrself & Jack.

Yr loving
MOTHER

Winston to Lord Randolph
(*Blenheim Papers*)

8 August [1893]   Hotel Bellevue
                                                                  Andermatt

Dear Papa,

We arrived here today from Lucerne. All through the "corkscrew tunnels" on the St Gothard railway. At Göschenen I got several letters. One from Welldon – one from the Military Secretary – and one from the Civil Service Commissioners.

I enclose you the latter as it contains my marks. This is a very gloomy place & after Lucerne – very cold. It is 4 or 5 thousand feet above the sea level & is surrounded by enormous slips & precipices. We walked from Göschenen to here through part of the St Gothard pass & over the "Devil's Bridge". I never saw such a terrible place. It certainly bears out the name.

Jack is very well & would write too only he is so tired after our journey in the train etc. I am looking forward to going to Sandhurst very much & am very thankful I was lucky enough to get in.

Welldon wrote me such a kind letter & several people whom I know very little sent me letters too.

Tomorrow we move on & shall not stay very long anywhere until we get to Brigue Hotel des Couronnes et Poste Brigue.

I hope the baths etc are doing you good after all your work. Give my best love to Mamma. (I am writing to her tomorrow). Jack sends his love & I hope you will forgive this abominable writing & the ink is hopeless.

Ever your loving son
WINSTON S. CHURCHILL

PS If you have time to write to us write to Hotel des Couronnes Brigue.

Lord Randolph to Winston

9 August 1893   Kissingen

My dear Winston,

I am rather surprised at your tone of exultation over your inclusion in the Sandhurst list. There are two ways of winning in an examination, one creditable the other the reverse. You have unfortunately chosen the latter method, and appear to be much pleased with your success.

The first extremely discreditable feature of your performance was missing the infantry, for in that failure is demonstrated beyond refutation your slovenly happy-go-lucky harum scarum style of work for which you have always been distinguished at your different schools. Never have I received a really good report of your conduct in your work from any master or tutor you had from time to time to do with. Always behind-hand, never advancing in your class, incessant complaints of total want of application, and this character which was constant in yr reports has shown the natural results clearly in your last army examination.

With all the advantages you had, with all the abilities which you foolishly think yourself to possess & which some of your relations claim for you, with all the efforts that have been made to make your life easy & agreeable & your work neither oppressive or distasteful, this is the grand result that you come up among the 2nd rate & 3rd rate class who are only good for commissions in a cavalry regiment.

The second discreditable fact in the result of your examination is that you have not perceptibly increased as far as my memory serves me the marks you made in the examination, & perhaps even you have decreased them, inspite of there being less competition in the last than in the former examination. You frequently told me you were sure to obtain 7000 marks. Alas! your estimate of your capacity was, measured arithmetically, some seven hundred marks deficient. You say in your letter there were many candidates who succeeded whom you knew; I must remind you that you had very few below you some seven or eight. You may find some consolation in the fact that you have failed to get into the "6oth Rifles" one of the finest regiments in the army. There is also another satisfaction for you that by accomplishing the prodigious effort of getting into the Cavalry, you imposed on me an extra charge of some £200 a year. Not that I shall allow you to remain in the Cavalry. As soon as possible I shall arrange your exchange into an infantry regiment of the line.

Now it is a good thing to put this business vy plainly before you. Do not think I am going to take the trouble of writing to you long letters after every folly & failure you commit & undergo. I shall not write again on these matters & you need not trouble to write any answer to this part of my of my letter, because I no longer attach the slightest weight to anything you may say about your own acquirements & exploits. Make this position indelibly impressed on your mind, that if your conduct and action at Sandhurst is similar to what it has been in the other establishments in which it has sought vainly to impart to you some education, then that my responsibility for you is over.

I shall leave you to depend on yourself giving you merely such assistance as may be necessary to permit of a respectable life. Because I am certain that if you cannot prevent yourself from leading the idle useless unprofitable life you have had during your schooldays & later months, you will become a mere social wastrel one of the hundreds of the public school failures, and you will degenerate into a shabby unhappy & futile existence. If that is so you will have to bear all the blame for such misfortunes yourself. Your own conscience will enable you to recall and enumerate all the efforts that have been made to give you the best of chances which you were entitled to by your position to & how you have practically neglected them all.

I hope you will be the better for your trip. You must apply to Capt James for advice for us to your Sandhurst equipment. Your mother sends her love.

Your affte father
RANDOLPH S.C.

Winston to Lord Randolph
(*Blenheim Papers*)

[11 August 1893]   Hotel des Couronnes et Poste
                                                    [Brigue]

Dear Papa,

Mr Little got your telegram today at this address. We have just come through the Simplon pass – 41 miles long & very tiring. We had intended to walk all the way but we got a capital conveyance for 25 francs – which is a quarter of the usual cost – & travelled very comfortably, walking part of the way. We slept last night at a little Inn in the village of Simplon – just in the middle of the pass, & started of early this morning.

The pass was very fine. The sides of the ravine of Gougo nearly meet, 2,000 feet above. We had to go through frequent tunnels & over many bridges. It is a splendid road however – 7 yards or more in width – & goes serenely on over all obstacles. Tomorrow we go by the 6 a.m. train to Zermatt where we stay till Wednesday. *Address* Hotel Mont-Cervin, Zermatt after that our address will be Hotel Londres Chamounix.

If the Duchess Lily is in town – I might stay the night with her before going to Sandhurst. I am looking forward to it very much indeed & will try & do well there, from the first.

Hoping you are the better for Kissingen.

I remain ever your loving son
WINSTON S. CHURCHILL

PS Jack sends his love. WSC

Louis Moriarty to Winston

12 August 1893   Harrow

My dear Churchill,

I should have written ere this to congratulate you on your success, but thought that most probably you would be abroad – anyhow I have determined to risk it.

I should very much like to see your marks. I see that on the whole you have gained 163 marks since last time. Strong gained 260, but I rather feared he would not do *that*, as his work, in some respects, was getting rather stale. McTaggart seems to have pulled himself together wonderfully. Do you know what *Cavendish* (Ma) did? *Rome*, who was rather a dark horse, collapsed utterly and got just under – 5000!

I don't know when this will find you – or where but I hope it will find you well and enjoying this vale of tears as much as possible. Mrs Moriarty joins in congratulating and best regards

Yours ever
L. MORIARTY

Here are some marks that may interest you:—

	Freehand	Maths	Latin	French	Germ	Hist	Science	G.D.[1]	Essay
Strong (6568)	315	1401	1168	1126	1005	582	–	678	293
Storr[2] (6413)	229	1062	1495	1000	Grk 882	645	–	845	255
Luard[3] (6049) Woolwich	275	1301	472	747	–	1048	1143 (Geology)	808	255
Churchill (6309)	338	1236	362	1233	–	1278	825 (Chemistry)	725	312

[1] Geometrical Drawing.

[2] Henry Storr (1875–1918) joined Middlesex Regiment 1895; served in Boer War (relief of Ladysmith, Spion Kop, Tugela Heights; despatches). Lieut-Colonel 1914, DSO, died from influenza & pneumonia following wounds received in action.

[3] Charles Elmhirst Luard (1875–1914), son of Maj-General C. E. Luard. Joined Norfolk Regiment 1896, served in Ashanti 1900 (despatches, DSO 1901), Captain, 1905. Retreat from Mons, August 1914 (Major, despatches). Killed in action.

Poor Storr was frightfully ill before the end of term with pleurisy on top of inflammation of the lungs. On the last Saturday and Sunday his life was almost despaired of and he was prayed for in chapel on the Sunday. I am glad to say that he is now getting on capitally, but is awfully weak.

Winston to Lady Randolph

12 August 1893   Grand Hotel Splendide
                                                                Lugano

Dear Mamma,

We arrived here yesterday from Andermatt. This place is quite different. At Andermatt everything was cold and sterile & we had lots of energy. Here it is just the other way: Very hot – beautiful scenery etc.

Politically this is in Switzerland – but its character is wholly Italian. Everyone speaks Italian or French.

The Hotel is very comfortable.[1] Jack and I have a room together, which looks out on the lake. He is enjoying himself immensely & was very much impressed with the St Gotthard Tunnel.

We are going to stay here all to-day & move tomorrow to Milan. From Milan we go to Baveno & from Baveno to Domo D'Ossola & thence through the Simplon pass to Brigue. There we get our letters.

I am speaking lots of French & think I am making progress. I also know 25 words of Italian & so we get on excellently.

I hope you were pleased at the telegram I was able to send you. Our address till further notice is

                                    Hotel des Couronnes & Postes
                                                Brigue.

Do write to me & tell me all about Gastein & Kissingen. Now I will end as I am going to swim in the lake.

                                                Ever your loving son
PS Notice this odious [violet] ink.   WINSTON S. CHURCHILL

Winston to Lord Randolph

14 August 1893   Continental Hotel
                                                                Milan[2]

Dear Papa,

I received your letter [of August 9] this morning. It had been forwarded here from Brigue. I am very sorry indeed that you are displeased with me. As

---

[1] Patronized by English and American visitors; according to Baedeker for 1893, the charges were from 5 fr (4s) a day for room, light and heat, dinner from 5 fr, and pension from 12 fr.

[2] In the Via Alessandro Manzoni, with lifts, 'also with electric lighting'. Prices similar to those charged at Lugano.

however you tell me not to refer to the part of your letter about the Examination I will not do so, but will try to modify your opinion of me by my work & conduct at Sandhurst during the time I shall be there. My extremely low place in passing *in* will have *no* effect whatever on my chance there.

We have been here for two days & start tomorrow for Domo D'Ossola on the way to Brigue. From Brigue we go on to Zermatt & Chamounix. I am very interested in everything we have seen & so too is Jack. We have been over the Cathedral & seen the town very thoroughly. It is not very hot: not nearly so hot as at Lugano & there are lovely swimming baths (with a running board 20 feet high) to which we go every day.

Lugano was delightful but so hot that one had no energy for anything but swimming. Jack is very well and sends his best love.

All the necessary equipment & outfit are supplied at Sandhurst at a charge of £30. I have nothing to do but to be there on the 1st Sept.

Thank you very much for writing to me. I am very sorry indeed that I have done so badly,

Ever your loving son
WINSTON S. CHURCHILL

PS Excuse smudge &c as pens & blotting paper are awfully bad. w s c

Winston to Lady Randolph

14 August 1893   Hotel Continental
                                                        Milan

Dear Mamma,

I have just got your letters and one from Papa. He seems awfully displeased with me. I can tell you it was a disappointment to me to find that he was not satisfied. After slaving away at Harrow & James' for this Exam, & trying, as far as I could to make up for the time I had wasted I was only too delighted to find that I had at length got in.

After all I *am* through & my chances are as good as they were before I tried at all. I begin again on quite new subjects, in which I shall not be handicapped by past illness.

If I had failed, there would have been an end of all my chances. As it is my fate is in my own hands & I have a fresh start.

Of course I realize that I am fearfully low. Look at my marks in Latin. How absurdly out of proportion they are to my marks in French or History or Mathematics.

It is also strange that I should have lost 400 marks on Chemistry the subject at which I worked more than at any other, except Mathematics.

*   *   *   *   *

Anyway I have still got my chances of getting on uninjured.

I am afraid that Papa is very angry & dissatisfied with me. I am very sorry indeed. But I am also glad that I have a fresh chance to alter his bad opinion of me.

I will write soon & tell you about our journey, but it don't come in right here.

Ever your loving son
WINSTON S. CHURCHILL

Lady Randolph to Winston

19 August [1893]   Kissingen

Dearest Winston,

I was very glad to get yr letter from Milan – you have not written very often & Jack only once – but I daresay you have little time & probably so much travelling is tiring – you have only another week. I hope Jack is not too tired, it is rather tiring work for a boy of his age – I thought you wld do less railway & more walking.

By the time we get home you will have been a whole month at Sandhurst – quite the man! I hope you will do well there – & then there will be no question as to how you got in.

If you arrive in London on the 30th you can go straight to 53 Seymour St Grandmama Jerome is there & Uncle Jack. You will have a day in London. Our life here is unchanged – & we have stuck to the Cure religiously. I think Papa is ever so much better, & after Gastein I am sure will be quite well. The heat is very great & makes one very lazy. I suppose you see the papers some-times – they still peg away at the H.R. bill,[1] & I pity the wretched MPs in this weather. Have you written to old Everest? I hear you wrote a scrap to Grandmama Marlborough. I envy you being at Chamonix. I have never been to Switzerland.

It is too hot to write any more – so goodbye, give my love to Jack. How do yr clothes do? & have the satchels been useful. Take care of yrself & of Jack.

Ever yr loving
MOTHER

---

[1] Piloted through the House of Commons by Gladstone, the second Home Rule Bill passed its third reading on September 1. A week later it was rejected by the House of Lords by 419 votes to 41 (see page 405).

J. D. G. Little to Lord Randolph
(*Blenheim Papers*)

19 August [1893]   Hotel de Zermatt
                                                      Zermatt

Dear Lord Randolph Churchill,

Your letter dated August 9th, through some mistake, was not forwarded with Winston's letters; and so it only reached me yesterday on our arrival at Brigue. I had been very remiss, I fear, in not having kept you better informed as to our movements; but we have not ourselves known them for more than three days in advance.

Before leaving Lucerne we made two expeditions; one by boat to Kuessnacht; the other on foot up the Rigi; returning by train and steamer from Vitznau.

We then took the steamer to the top of the Lake, and travelled by the St Gothard Railway as far as Goeschenen, whence we walked up the St Gothard Pass to Andermatt. From Andermatt, we went by train through the St Gothard tunnel to Lugano; and thence to Milan. At Milan we only stayed for a couple of days. We were able however able to see the Cathedral, and the Galleries, and there were excellent Swimming Baths which we all enjoyed.

On leaving Milan we went by train to Arona, where we did not stop, but went on at once by steamer as far as Baveno. We spent a day there and made an expedition in a rowing boat round the Borromean Islands.

Jack and Winston were very anxious to go back through Simplon; and as the alternative would have been to return via the St Gothard which we had already seen pretty thoroughly, I thought I might decide on the Simplon, although you were not very strongly in favour of this plan when I saw you in London.

We got a conveyance at Domo D'Ossola, to carry the baggage and give us an occasional lift, and got as far as the village of Simplon the first day. We started early the following morning and reached Brigue at about noon yesterday. When I got your telegram we only stopped at Brigue one night, as it was very hot; and came on here by an early train this morning.

I hope this outline of our wanderings will meet with your approval. We have seen a great many interesting things, and beautiful places; and we have all of us enjoyed ourselves thoroughly.

We think of staying here till Wednesday; when we go by train as far as Martigny; and then propose to walk to Chamounix. After that we have no definite plans: but I think we shall probably go either to Geneva; or to some town on the Lake. Winston will have to leave us here, and Jack and myself, might walk by easy steps to Interlaken.

Your letter to Winston arrived while we were at Milan. I had not of course received your letter to myself. When he showed me your letter, we had a long talk and he told me a good deal about his views of man and things. He was a good deal depressed; I pointed out to him that in going to Sandhurst he began, what was practically a new page in his life; and that such opportunities [for] a completely new start occurred at most, but once or twice in a lifetime, and ought therefore to me made the most of. Whatever he did at Sandhurst would have a permanent effect on his career in the army, and he ought therefore to make a sustained effort for the next year and a half to do his best, and pass out high.

I think he intends to try hard. I should be so very sorry when he leaves us, as we have got to know each other very well during our wanderings. His weak point is that he allows the whim of the moment to obliterate his calm judgments and from this point of view I think the discipline of Sandhurst will be useful.

He tells me that the outfit is got at Sandhurst; in which case he need not get to London till August 30th. Unless I hear from you to the contrary, he will start on the 27th.

Apologising for the length of this letter, I remain, Yours very truly

J. D. G. LITTLE

Lily, Duchess of Marlborough to Winston

20 August 1893   3 Carlton House Terrace

My dear Winston,

I have your letter which was waiting for me on my return to Town last night. I am very glad you have so enjoyed your journeyings and hope you will come back ready to "buckle to".

I thought your Father would be disappointed at your not getting into the Infantry – for the Cavalry is so much more expensive. However, I know you will do your best in September.

I am obliged to be in London for a few days but I am leaving again on Friday and shall not come back again until some time in October. Had I been here I would have been very glad to put you up the end of the month, but I shall not. I fancy the only one of the family will be your Aunt Fanny, who will remain until Mr G. allows the H. of C. to disperse.

Please give my love to Jack and I remain dear Winston

Yours most affect
"AUNT LILY"

J. D. G. Little to Lord Randolph
(*Blenheim Papers*)

22 August [1893]   Mt Cervin
                                                    Zermatt

Dear Lord Randolph Churchill,

Your letter dated August 19th has just arrived; having crossed in the post mine of the same date to you. I am so sorry that we have not done more walking. But I find that Jack, though he sticks to it manfully, very soon gets tired. I thought too, as Winston's time was so short, that it would be well to see as much as possible while he was with us, by making different places our headquarters, and making expeditions of a day's duration from these. Since we have been at Zermatt, we have started each day, at 6 or 7 to avoid the heat, and walked up to one of the larger *chalets*, where we have been able to lunch and rest in the hot part of the day; and returned in time for the *table d'hôte* at 7.

Tomorrow we start for Chamonix, going by train as far as Martigny and there walking via the Col de Balme which will take us a couple of days. We shall be in Geneva by Monday in time for Winston to start for England.

If you thought well of it Jack and I might stay for a couple of days on the Lake of Geneva then go to Interlaken and walk over the Sheidegg Pass to Meiringen.

I am so sorry that we did not stick more to Switzerland; but when we started I was very much afraid of making my leg worse, and as Winston was very anxious to see Lugano and Baveno, I thought I might venture to do this, and it would enable my leg time to get right.

Jack's French improves, but not very rapidly. I have got him a book of fairy tales, which I make him translate. I think he will learn more after Winston's departure; the latter's French is so voluble, that Jack seldom finds himself absolutely forced to speak.

As to the question of funds, I think the original £200 will be quite ample: indeed I think that there will be a balance over, unless something unforeseen arises. I have at present £100; but out of this there will be our Bill here which will be about £8. This, after subtracting £27 for our return tickets from London to Lucerne, leaves £81 as the cost of our three weeks tour, leaving £92 in hand. And of course when Winston goes away our expenses will be considerably reduced.

Our address till Saturday in any case will be Hôtel de Londres Chamounix. I should be so very much obliged, if it is not giving you too much trouble if you will tell me of any places which you would wish Jack and me to go to. Jack is writing today.

Believe me to be yours very truly
J. D. G. LITTLE

PS I have told W about going to Mrs Jerome.

Winston to Lord Randolph
(*Blenheim Papers*)

23 August 1893   Hotel des Couronnes
                                                              Brigue

Dear Papa,

Mr Little read me a good deal of your last letter to him. I am sorry not to have written to you more often. I wrote to you from Milan and from Brigue. Perhaps you did not receive these letters.

We have returned here for one night on our way from Zermatt to Chamounix. Tomorrow at 9 o'clock we are "off to there" via Martigny – Tête-noire – and Col de Balme.

Zermatt was charming, as we had exceptionally fine weather. Every day we made expeditions to the surrounding glaciers. We saw on Saturday the great Gorner Glacier, which is only an hour's walk from Zermatt. I was very interested as I had never seen one before. Great hummocks of ice in every direction – filling the whole valley like a river.

We had an excellent guide who showed us everything that was interesting. On Tuesday Jack and Little stayed at home and I and a guide went up to the Hotel Lac Noir which is the starting point for ascending the Matterhorn. We had a good view of this mountain which looks very impressive and fascinating. I don't wonder that people still go up, in spite of the numerous graves in the churchyard.

I should start from Geneva for London – via Basle and Paris on Monday night. We have to be back at Sandhurst by 8 o'clock on Friday. This I learn from some "gentleman cadets" I met on a walking tour.

The only clothes I want are a dark blue serge or cloth morning suit. I have only got smart clothes for London and shooting suits. What I want is a light suit to wear for travelling or in the country. If you think this unnecessary I could manage by having a pair of trousers to match one of my *knee breeches suits*. If I don't hear to the contrary I will order the former. This will save you writing about it unless you object.

Otherwise I think that I have everything except the uniform – which they will supply to me. I am looking forward to going there very much more especially as it gives me an altogether fresh start on a course which is certainly 'paved with good resolutions.'

Mr Little tells me that you are writing to me – so till I get your letter I will wait.

                                                Your affectionate son
                                                WINSTON S. CHURCHILL

Winston to Lady Randolph

23 August 1893   Hotel Couronne & Poste
                                                  Brigue[1]
Dear Mamma,

Thank you so much for your letter, which I got yesterday at Zermatt. I have written to Papa the account of what we did there. The trip is splendid & we are having such fun. Still I am looking forward immensely to going to Sandhurst.

Jack is getting on with his French but only speaks it as a last resource. You should hear me talk – it impresses the waiters immensely. But I always tell them that I am not a Frenchman, so they have reason to be impressed.

You must be quoting when you say that I have written "a scrap" to Grandmamma. The "scrap" was four sides closely written. You can't think how hard it is to write when one is moving about so much. Also when I see so many things which I want to describe to you – I feel that it is no use beginning so huge a task. Also I am very lazy.

I am going to buckle to at Sandhurst & to try and regain Papa's opinion of me. I will send you a Photograph of myself in my uniform – which I am longing to put on.

When I have been there a day or two I will write you and Papa *a long* letter & describe everything. I have got a good deal of money in hand (£7) but I don't know at all what my expenses are likely to be on joining & I have had *no* information. You might suggest an allowance to Papa.

Thanking you once more for your letter and sending you my very best love & many kisses.

                                        I remain Ever your loving son
                                        WINSTON S.C.

J. D. G. Little to Lord Randolph
(*Blenheim Papers*)

25 August [1893]   Hotel Gibbon
                                                  Lausanne
Dear Lord Randolph Churchill,

I am writing again to let you know about change of plans. When we arrived at Martigny yesterday, we were stopped by a very severe thunderstorm. We waited at a rather dismal inn there till about four o'clock. We then heard from the people who had started earlier in the morning, and whom the storm had forced to return, that the road was impassable, and that it would probably

---

[1] Although it rated a star in Baedeker, this hotel was rather less expensive than the previous ones – room 2s 6d a day, dinner 3s 3d.

take a day to put it right. Under these circumstances, I thought it was better to come on here; as if we had waited at Martigny, Winston would have had a bare day at Chamounix. We are going this afternoon to see the Castle of Chillon. Winston will leave Geneva on Monday. Our address will be Hotel Metropole. After Winston leaves Jack and I might go to Chamounix. I should be so much obliged if you wd telegraph to Geneva, if this plan does *not* meet with your approval. We have written to Chamounix, in case there should be any letters there.

Yours very truly
J. D. G. LITTLE

Frances, Duchess of Marlborough to Winston

27 August [1893]
Ramsey Abbey[1]
Huntingdon

My dear Winston,

I received your 2nd letter yesterday & am glad to hear you are well. I think Jack is very idle not writing to me. It was no use my answering your 1st Letter as you were moving about & indeed there is very little in either of your letters & unless you have been busy keeping a *journal* of your trip I think you do not exert yourself as a correspondent. I have had very long & most interesting accts from your Father from Kissingen about his interviews especially with old Bismarck & your Mother has been good about writing. I hope the Waters have done them both good and that Gastein will complete the "cure".

Missie & the Parrot are both here & very well & its very pleasant to be here & I am happy & on the whole well & they are all very good to me. I stay here till Sept 6th ; then go to Floors Castle Kelso N.B.[2] till the 11th so you have my address. I hear your Father was indeed very much disappointed at your only *just squeezing* in after all the expense of James &c & he hoped that you would have done much better & got into the Infantry Division especially as it is 200 £ a year less expensive. I can only hope you will keep all the good Resolutions you are making & distinguish yourself at Sandhurst.

I lead a very quiet life as we are alone. Parliament is dragging on its tedious course. I pity the poor Legislators.

Remember me kindly to Mrs Jerome & Believe me

Yr affectionate Grand Mother
F. MARLBOROUGH

[1] The seat of Lord DE RAMSEY.
[2] The seat of the Duke of ROXBURGHE.

Winston to Lord Randolph
(*Blenheim Papers*)

30 August 1893   50 Grosvenor Square

Dear Papa,

I am writing to you to explain my telegram of this morning. As to the Infantry Cadetship: on arriving in London last night I called at Grosvenor Square for letters and found, among others, this enclosure [not extant] from the Military Secretary. I have no doubt that you will be pleased to find that I have got an Infantry Cadetship and shall be able, after all, to enter the 60th.

As regards the money I had when I left Geneva about 140 fr (£5.10.0). This, the expenses of the journey – viz diner – dejeuner – porters, – cabs – registration of luggage – Hotel in Paris etc etc reduced to £2.13.6 which sum I have by me at the present time.

There are sure to be some things I shall have to pay at once on joining. Others that I ought to pay – for instance, Clubs and subscriptions – as soon as I can. Then there are the expenses of today and tomorrow in London and of the ticket and cab to Sandhurst on Friday.

There are also such expenses as furnishing my room etc. If I have a room with two other boys I shall be expected to do my share. If I get a room to myself it will want some sort of decoration. I enclose a circular which I have received which will show you that this *furnishing* is not uncommon.

I hope you will not be angry with me for writing to you on this subject. I should so much like to have an annual allowance – payable quarterly. Out of it I would get my clothes, pay for my amusements – railway journeys – and sundries (cigarettes etc): in fact everything. I would then know how much I was going to have and what I had to do with it. You should also know what I was given. Whereas at present (the last 6 months particularly) you have given me money when I wanted it – (more or less). (I am afraid I don't make my meaning very clear).

As to the amount, you know, much better than I do, what I ought to have. Sandhurst, is, very much, on the same footing as the 'Varsity, except of course for the military discipline – and I should think the expenses would be about the same.

You see in 18 months I shall be in the army – and I should like very much to have a trial beforehand.

Please do not be displeased with me for writing to you on this point. I am afraid I have been very extravagant in the past and have frittered a great deal of money away. But I have had no responsibilities to bear. I should very much like a trial on the allowance system during the next 18 months.

You will see on the enclosure that you will be expected to pay £150 per annum to the College. Harrow used to cost £80 a term or £250 a year (clothes and pocket money extra). There will be no extras at Sandhurst at all. If you decide to give me an allowance I will promise to keep accounts of what I spend and send them to you regularly.

I have written a very long letter and have taken up a lot of your time. Hoping you will send me some money for my immediate needs (I don't know what to do if you don't) & you will not be angry with me for what I have written,

I remain ever your loving son
WINSTON S. CHURCHILL

Address after Friday Royal Military College Sandhurst.

Winston to Lady Randolph

30 August 1893   50 Grosvenor Square

Dear Mamma,

I got your letter this morning. You did not say anything about the absorbing topic – money. I have written a long & respectful letter to Papa to ask him to give me an allowance. Please try & persuade him. It would be much better & cheaper than the present arrangements which are

"Spend as much as I can get"

"Get as much as I can".

I have been very anxiously awaiting a letter from Papa. But have had none since the one he wrote me on my examination 3 weeks ago. I hope he will be pleased to hear that I have got into the infantry after all.

I had a very tiring journey from Geneva. I stayed 5 hours in Paris – hoping to see the Eiffel Tower but 'twas shut. I went to the Hotel de Louvre & had bath & breakfast. (I wanted both after 18 hours in train.) Then I walked about till it was time to go & so came safely here.

I do not know what I shall do unless I get some money before the 1st proximo. I would have written & asked for some only I expected by every post a letter from Papa. Good-Bye dear Mamma – I will write to you from Sandhurst on Sunday.

I remain Your Ever loving son
WINSTON S.C.

Mrs John Leslie to Winston

Thursday [?31 August 1893]   Cradock House
                                                    Eastbourne

Dear Winston,

Don't think me unkind not to have written to congratulate you – I asked for yr address several times and could not succeed in obtaining it. I am *so so*, glad it was all right. I shall hope to see you later on and hear all about Switzerland. I leave this on Monday and go to Doncaster races – for the week. I *hate* racing – so shall be miserable! I have been reading lots of good things –

Yr affectly

Hope you were pretty comfy in my house.   OLD AUNT LEONIE

Lord Randolph to Winston

TELEGRAM

31 August 1893   Badgastein

Have forwarded Sandhurst papers to you there also sent cheque for term delay not my fault.   RC

Lord Randolph to Frances, Duchess of Marlborough

EXTRACT

3 September 1893   Staubinger Hof
Gastein

. . . I am very glad that Winston has got an infantry cadetship. It will save me £200 a year. I shall see the Duke of Cambridge when I get back & remind him about the 60th Rifles. I enclose you a letter I received from Winston. I wrote telling him that I thought he was somewhat precipitate in his ideas about an allowance & that his figures were too summary. I told him I would give him £10 a month out of which he would have to pay for small articles of clothing, & for other small necessaries but that I will continue to pay his tailor & haberdasher while he was at Sandhurst. I also demurred to paying for furniture for his rooms till [I] was better informed as to what was necessary. I also told him to send me a list of the subscriptions which he considered he had to pay. I think that £10 is ample of the present. I wrote very kindly to him & did not lecture. I dont agree with you about the Duchess Lily being a useful friend to him. I think her very silly & gushing and I should be horrified if he got money from her. . . .

Frances, Duchess of Marlborough to Winston

3 September [1893]   Ramsey Abbey
Huntingdon

My dear Winston,

I am leaving this place tomorrow for Floors Castle Kelso N.B. where I stay till the 7th en route to Guisachan, Beauly, N.B. so you will know my address if you write. I was very glad to get your letter of the 30th & to hear of your wonderful Luck in getting into the Infantry after all. I think your Father will be much pleased & I feel sure you will get a letter from him in time. I fancy on his first arrival at Gastein he found a lot of letters to answer. I have only had one letter from him. I shall be very glad to hear how you get on. I am in great hopes you will keep your good resolutions & distinguish yourself there by steady work & industry. The Future now is in your own hands to make or to mar it. I have trust in you to make it a success.

Well I have had a very peaceful pleasant fortnight here & am sorry to go. The Parrot & Missie seem most flourishing. This place is a Paradise for Dogs & my "Trip" has had a great "success".

So the Home Rull Bill is gone to the Lords at last & there will be a great muster of old & young Peers to thresh it out. I hear they mean to get Lords Ebury & Grey each 90 years old to vote & I suppose Jack Camden & Marlborough took their seats for the same purpose![1]

Good bye Dear. Thanks for asking after my Health. I feel pretty well. I suppose our House will be very spick & span when we return.

Yr affect Grandmother
F.M.

[1] Ebury was 92 and died November 18; Grey was just 90 and died 9 October 1894. Of the 560 Peers, 460 voted on September 8; they defeated the Bill by 419 votes to 41.

7

Sandhurst

September 1893–December 1894

(See Main Volume I Chapter 6)

═══════

The following chapter, which deals with Winston's time at Sandhurst, covers also the period of Lord Randolph's severe and progressive illness which culminated in his death. The first two letters are pre-Sandhurst but are inserted here for convenience. The Buzzard papers which concern Lord Randolph's illness were not available to the author until after the main volume had gone to press.

Lord Randolph to Dr Thomas Buzzard[1]
(Buzzard Papers)

8 July 1893   50 Grosvenor Square

Dear Mr Buzzard,

There is a group of interfering people by no means all friends who are scattering the most absurd rumours about my bad health & worse. I was much upset & I am very indignant at learning that Lady Randolph had been to see you and Roose, but I have had an explanation with her from which I find that what she said to you though in my opinion needless was of different character than I had been led to believe.

1. I would be glad to know if Dr Roose showed you a letter I wrote him which I told him to show you.[2]

2. My speeches are nearly over, I have one on next Wednesday & one on the

---

[1] Thomas Buzzard (1831–1919), specialist in diseases of the nervous system; consulting physician to the National Hospital for the Paralysed and Epileptic, London. Served on the Medical Staff with the Turkish Army during the Crimean War. His eldest son, Sir Farquhar Buzzard, became Regius Professor of Medicine at Oxford and Physician in Ordinary to King George V.

[2] This letter does not survive.

Wednesday after. Then once more on the 31st July I take my departure for Kissingen & Gastein of which places I had been told you approved. Now if I am in vy bad health I assure you I have no knowledge of it. I have never felt the slightest bad effect from a speech. I have hardly ever had that numbness or difficulty of articulation, which you yrself assured me was of small importance. My appetite is good, my sleep is good, & as to alcohol I have conformed to your directions & greatly moderated my use of it.

3. Now I would be glad to see you either on Monday or Tuesday alone so that you can decide whether I have not got through my programme we laid down yesterday fairly well. That is my belief though of course I should attend to & obey any advice from you, with the exception of the two meetings which I must attend.

The only thing which has really troubled me & really might have made me ill is all this stupid gossip & fuss about my health. But I have learnt a good deal of philosophy in recent years about my health & have not paid attention to the talk.

But still as far as my mother & my wife are concerned, I should like yr opinion. If this does not find you out of town could you give me an answer tonight as I go to Brighton the first thing tomorrow morning. I shall be in town tomorrow at the latest by 11.15. On Tuesday I am free after 10.45. Excuse my troubling you &

Believe me to be, Very truly yours
RANDOLPH S. CHURCHILL

Enclosed is prescription I have been taking as a tonic & a prescription of a pill which I take regularly.

Dr Thomas Buzzard to Lord Randolph
(Buzzard Papers)

9 July 1893   74 Grosvenor Street

Copy

Dear Lord Randolph Churchill,

I have just returned from North Derbyshire, whither I went on Friday last, and regret that, in consequence of this, Your Lordship's letter should have been left so long unanswered.

It will give me much pleasure to see you again in consultation with Dr Roose on any day next week that may prove convenient to you and him. I am sorry that I am obliged to decline acceding to your request that I should see you alone. But let me say, for your satisfaction, that even if professional usage did not preclude my doing what you wish, it would be very disadvantageous to you that any Consultant in your case should be deprived of the valuable help that can be given to him by one so long acquainted with his patient as your usual Medical attendant.

In reply to your enquiry, Dr Roose, when I was meeting him in another case on Friday, read to me a letter which he had received from you.

Believe me to be, yours very truly

TB

Mem: I returned his two prescriptions.
On envelope "Private" & sealed yr letter.

Winston to Lord Randolph
(*Blenheim Papers*)

3 September [1893]   Royal Military College
                                                     Sandhurst
                                                     Camberley[1]

Dear Papa,

I am very glad to be able to write to you on this extremely smart paper.[2]

On Friday I left London by the 12.30 and got down here in time for lunch. Since then I have had little or nothing to do. Yesterday there was a drill at 10 o'clock for an hour and today there has been a parade and Church.

The first 3 days are devoted chiefly to being measured for the uniform and finding one's way about – the latter no easy task in so huge a building. To-morrow (Monday) however, work begins in earnest. At 6.30 Revelly sounds and you have to be dressed by 7 o'clock.

I am very contented and like the place very much – though it is freely said that it "combines the evils of the life of a private schoolboy with those of a private soldier." The room I have with 2 others is very large and divided into cubicles like stalls in a stable [diagram]. I had first choice and so have the best of the 3.

Of course it is very uncomfortable. No carpet or curtains – No ornamentation or adornments of any kind – No hot water and very little cold (as far as I can make out) but the motto of the college is *"Nec aspera terrent."*

[1] The Royal Military College, otherwise known as Sandhurst, was founded at High Wycombe in 1799 by the Duke of York (1763–1827). He was King George IV's brother and Commander-in-Chief 1798–1809. It was he who 'had ten thousand men, he marched them up to the top of the hill, and he marched them down again'. The College was moved to Great Marlow in 1802 and settled at its present position in 1810. Situated two miles from the small village of the same name, Sandhurst is also near the station of Camberley and the village of Yorktown.

[2] It bears the Royal Arms surrounded by Colours surmounted by the Crown with the motto *Vires Acquirit Eundo*. The whole device is in gold red and blue.

The Discipline is extremely strict – Far stricter than Harrow. Hardly any law is given to juniors on joining. No excuse is ever taken – not even with a plea of "didn't know" after the first few hours: and of course no such thing as unpunctuality or untidiness is tolerated. Still there is something very exhilerating in the military manner in which everything works; and I think that I shall like my life here during the next 18 months very much.

I am in E. Company the "crack" Company of the battalion, and next term I shall have a room to myself. In addition to your own room – each cadet can go and sit in the Company *ante-room* – which is furnished very comfortably as a smoking room and where are *all* the daily and weekly papers. Besides this there are 2 billiard rooms to each Company and a capital Library and reading room with chess and card tables.

The food here is not very good but you can add to it by ordering extras e.g. jam – coffee – wine – fruit etc. Smoking is allowed everywhere and cigarettes are handed round after dinner – I should say "mess".

This is the great meal of the day and counts as a parade. As our mess uniforms are not finished we have to wear the ordinary dressclothes and in these we assemble in the ante room. Then the Company butler solemnly anounnces dinner and you walk down a quarter of a mile of stone passage till you reach the dining hall. The dinner is very grand – and the names of the dishes are written in French on the menu. There is nothing else French about them. After dinner there is no work and billiards and whist finish the day.

"My Servant" sounds very nice – but this part of College machinery is rather out of gear and requires frequent oiling. He will however black boots – pipe clay belt and clean rifle – clear away slops and on occasion (when he has been tipped) do odd jobs for you.

Altogether, I like the life. I am interested in the drill and in the military education I shall receive; and now that the army *is* to be my trade I feel as keen as I did before I went in for any of the Examinations. At any rate I am sure that I shall be mentally, morally, and physically better for my course here. Hoping you will write to me and send me some money for myself

I remain, ever your loving son
WINSTON S. CHURCHILL

Winston to Lady Randolph

4 September [1893]   [Royal Military College]

Dear Mamma,

I have just got your letter and I hasten to reply – though I cannot do so at length as parade is going to begin in a few minutes. Grandmamma Jerome did not give me £10 – so I had to borrow a little money – or I do not know what I should have done. As it is of course I am very anxious to pay back what I borrowed.

10,000 thanks for your kind letter – you darling. I am so pleased papa likes the Infantry. When I have more time I will write to you again – but now I really must go.

Your loving son
WINSTON S. CHURCHILL

Mrs Leonard Jerome to Winston

4 September [1893]   53 Seymour Street
Portman Square[1]

My dear Winston,

I was so pleased to get your letter this morning. You remember the conversation we had about the watch, how easily one could borrow money on it. So I was afraid you might have done so. It is all right. "All is well that ends Well." You had hardly left this house when I received the enclosed letter from your mother. I will send the cheque to the tailor so that will settle the matter according to your father's wishes, I am sure. In fact he need never know that you borrowed it.

I hope you like Sandhurst, and will be very happy there. I shall be anxious to know how you are getting on dear Winston. We are all very proud of your success so far, and take the greatest interest in your future. Good bye my *dear dear* Winston

Your affectionate
GRANDMAMAN

Winston to Lord Randolph
(*Blenheim Papers*)

4 September [1893]   Sandhurst

Dear Papa,

Thank you very much for your letter, which arrived this evening. £10 per month will be ample and I can easily pay my expenses on it. My only reason for making out a rough list of my probable expenses was to get you to send me some money to go to Sandhurst with. I have to pay my *extra mess bill*! on the 10th of each month (probably about £4 altogether with canteen account). But what I have will last me through the month with ease.

---

[1] Mr and Mrs John Leslie's house, where Mrs Jerome stayed with her son-in-law and daughter Leonie when in London.

On Wednesday afternoon I shall have time to write to you a long and very concise account of the time-table – work and meals. The work is very heavy for the first 6 weeks & there are many extra parades for juniors.

Of course for the present I have very little time. Reveille is at 6.30. 1st study at 7. Breakfast 8 – parade at 9.10. Study from 10.20 to 1.50. 2 o'clock luncheon – 3 o'clock afternoon parade (¾ hour); 5 o'clock to 6 Gymnastics. 8 o'clock Mess. So you see there is hardly any time for writing or idling. The only five subjects they teach here are

1 Fortification (with geometrical drawing)
2 Tactics
3 Topography
4 Military law
5   „   administration

I like the work – but the physical exertion of one day is so severe that at the end of one day I feel regularly fatigued.

I began this letter last night and hoped to get it done before "lights out" sounded. As I could not do this I have lengthened it a little.

My position in the College is that of a junior. That is to say one who has passed the last exam. In four months I shall become an "intermediate" and my last term here a "senior". Everyone is technically equal except the corporals and under-officers – but it is more usual for juniors to associate mainly with cadets of their own standing. I am sure I shall get on here with the boys – as I know a good many and have of course been with many at James's. Do you know he passed 20 this time. Thank you very much for your very generous allowance. I must stop now as I have to dress for parade – it was so good of you to write to me.

Ever your loving son
WINSTON S. CHURCHILL

Winston to Lord Randolph
(*Blenheim Papers*)

10 September [1893]   [53 Seymour Street]

Dear Papa,

I have received the £10 alright; thank you very much for that. My Company Officer Major Ball[1] says he prefers that instead of a list of relations etc parents

[1] Oswald James Henry Ball (1854–1936); Welsh Regiment. Educated at Trinity College, Cambridge, he joined the 69th (South Lincolnshire) Regiment in 1874, but saw no active service until the South African War 1899–1902. Retired as Colonel 1904; re-employed 1914–19, serving as Brigadier-General in Flanders.

should send a signature to say 'Please place no restrictions on my son's leave.'

He is an awfully good sort – though fearfully strict on parade – and says he likes to feel he can trust his Company.

I have now been ten days at Sandhurst and like it more than ever. Major Ball told me he would give me leave for yesterday and today as he always gives one leave without waiting for the home list, or permission so I am staying with Grandmama Jerome. Tonight I go back to RMC.

The work is very interesting and extremely practical. Shot and shell of all kinds – bridges, guns, field and siege, mapping, keeping regimental savings bank accounts – inspecting meat etc form the "study" work. Then there are all the parades and drills.

It is not a bit of good turning up for parade or study *punctually*. You are bound to be *in your place* when the bugle sounds. So far I have been ten minutes too early for everything. Public opinion of the College is tremendously against unpunctuality.

I want your leave to ride, also, as there are excellent horses in the village. Please send me the two signatures as I want to ride very much.

There does not seem to be much fury against the House of Lords for throwing out the HR [Home Rule] Bill.

Thanking you very much for your letter

> I remain ever your loving son
> WINSTON S. CHURCHILL

Winston to Frances, Duchess of Marlborough
(*Blenheim Papers*)

10 September [1893]   [53 Seymour Street]

Dear Grandmama,

Thank you very much for your letter. I have now been a full week at Sandhurst and I like it very much indeed. There is a great deal of *drill* which is awfully fatiguing and I have a very uncomfortable room with 2 other boys – but the work is very interesting – the food is good – and I have lots of my friends to associate with.

Papa is very pleased that I had got into "*Infantry*", and wrote me two very kind letters. I have also heard from Mama several times.

As I have not been [? misunderstood] or "insubordinate" so far I was allowed to come up for Sunday – and I am writing this letter from 53 Seymour Street where I am staying with Grandmama Jerome.

The House of Lords seem to have rejected the HR Bill in grand style. I wonder what Mr G [Gladstone] will do now. Grosvenor Square seems awfully clean and the alterations are going on briskly. Hoping that you are feeling well and that the change has been beneficial,

I remain ever your loving grandson
WINSTON S. CHURCHILL

Frances, Duchess of Marlborough to Lord Randolph
(*Blenheim Papers*)

EXTRACT

12 September [1893]   Guisachan

... As regards Winston I will keep for you his Letter which is a good one. He cannot fail to get on at Sandhurst it will do him a lot of good. He seems to think you have been liberal to him in which I quite agree with him. ...

Lord Randolph to Frances, Duchess of Marlborough

EXTRACT

15 September 1893   Gastein

... I send you a letter from Winston. I have demurred to "unrestricted leave", & have told him he can come to town when his mother is there. I have declined paying for horses. I do not see what an infantry cadet wants with a horse. Winston's letters are generally full of requests for unnecessary things and articles. ...

Winston to Lady Randolph

17 September [1893]   50 Grosvenor Square[1]
[Sandhurst]

My dear Mamma,

Your letter arrived last night, and made me feel rather unhappy. I am awfully sorry that Papa does not approve of my letters. I take a great deal of pains over them & often re-write entire pages. If I write a descriptive account of my life here, I receive a hint from you that my style is too sententious & stilted. If on the other hand I write a plain and excessively simple letter – it is put down as slovenly. I never can do anything right.

Thank you very much for your letter. I am afraid that you have reason to be cross with me for not writing to *you*. I will not give you cause again. Do come back as soon as you can as I am longing to see you.

I find that you do not have to obtain permission from home to ride – but

1 Winston often used writing paper headed with this address, even when out of London.

only to play polo – so the Infantry cadet will be allowed to ride for amusement until next term when *all* are taught together. As to the leave – it is very hard that Papa cannot grant me the same liberty that other boys in my position are granted. It is only a case of trusting *me*. As my company officer said he "liked to know the boys whom their parents could trust" – and therefore recommended me to get the permission I asked for. However it is no use my trying to explain to Papa, & I suppose I shall go on being treated as "that boy" till I am 50 years old.

It is a great pleasure to me to write to you unreservedly instead of having to pick & choose my words and information. So far I have been extremely *good*. Neither late nor lazy, & have had always 5 minutes to wait before each parade or study. Yesterday I went out riding with a charming Eton boy (he is 19½) whose acquaintance I have made. We got to Aldershot & were having a stiff gallop when his saddle slipped round & he fell on his head. Of course he was stunned & has now got concussion of the brain. I revived him as well as I could – with brandy & water & then had to hire a cab to drive all the way back to Sandhurst. I took him to see a doctor on the road who said he had had a marvellous escape of breaking his neck. The whole thing was a great responsibility & rather expensive.

When I got to the college they treated it most coolly: were not the least disturbed or put out. He was taken to the casualty ward & attended by a gorgeously clothed surgeon. Today he is quite sensible & I have had a long talk with him.

Well I have told you all about my life. I am cursed with so feeble a body, that I can hardly support the fatigues of the day; but I suppose I shall get stronger during my stay here.

The drill is progressing and my shoulders are greatly improved.

Goodbye dear darling Mama.

Ever so much love & more kisses from your ever loving son
WINSTON S. CHURCHILL

PS You see I have tried to spoil my handwriting for your sake. Is it any better?

Frances, Duchess of Marlborough to Lord Randolph
(Blenheim Papers)

EXTRACT

20 September [1893]   Guisachan

... I quite agree with you about Winston's letter which I keep for you. It is the nature of all Boys at his age especially sharp ones to be rather scratching to get all they can in order to compare favourably with their fellows & I think you are right to turn a deaf ear & to make your favours in proportion to his merits. Still I prefer his open requests & there is one advantage he is very frank and open in his pertinacity. I think the *no restriction* permission is most objectionable & the request for a Horse unnecessary. You give him such a liberal Allowance that it would seem he could easily hire one occasionally. But the great thing is for him to feel he is not the son of a rich man and also that he is at Sandhurst not for amusement but to distinguish himself. I know how easy it is to preach and yet how difficult to guide a Boy! I begin to think a *strict* training is the best. . . .

Winston to Lord Randolph
(*Blenheim Papers*)

20 September [1893]   [Sandhurst]

Dear Papa,

This letter ought to reach you before you start to come home: but after this I will write to Grosvenor Square. Jack is coming down to see me on Saturday; he seems to have enjoyed the end of the tour very much.

There is not much news from the College – now that I have settled down here. There is a regular routine to be gone through which takes up nearly all one's time. I have so far been successful in being punctual and have always had 3 minutes to spare. The work is very interesting: today we learnt to make all kinds of nuts and to lash beams together. We have also been out making or learning to make sketch maps. On Monday we have to go and fire with a new 12 pounder gun, which has just been issued to the Artillery.

As far as exercise goes there is plenty to do and I do not amuse myself very much. I manage however to shoot with the Revolver and the Magazine Rifle nearly every day and I am also taking lessons in the new Italian sword exercise – a kind of combination of fencing and single stick and which is greatly recommended by the authorities. In the evenings I play whist or pool, at both of which I am slowly improving, and get to bed exceedingly tired.

Hoping that you are much the better for your change, & with best love

I remain ever your loving son
WINSTON S.C.

Winston to Lady Randolph

20 September [1893]   50 Grosvenor Square
                                                          [Sandhurst]

Dear Mamma,

I have written to Papa a letter which I hope will please him. I was very unhappy at the letter I received from you – more especially as I was very tired

& worried. If therefore I wrote anything which you did not like – Please excuse it. Jack was coming down yesterday but missed his train so will come Saturday instead. Next month I will be photographed & send you one – you don't know how magnificient I look – perfectly immense I assure you.

I am very well but have a horrid boil or abcess on my left cheek – which gives me great pain & has swollen my face to an abnormal size. This will however go away in a few days. I have told Papa all the news I could think of.

I am looking forward to see you – but shall have to continue looking for some time yet. I want you to explain to Papa that on the 6th of October I have to pay the Canteen bill & extra messing account: probably over £4. They only give 24 hours notice & anyone not producing the money is posted on a blackboard. Of course it will come out of my £10 per month. Only I want you to remind Papa – so that he should not send it late – as a day would make all the difference. I hope in future months to have a balance – but the expenses of coming here – of carpet & chairs etc. have swallowed that. I have however sufficient to keep me going till the 3rd or 4th of October.

Goodbye my dearest Mamma – I have tried my best to write larger & to do all the many things you have told me to do. I am very happy here & like the place more & more.

Ever your loving son
WINSTON S. CHURCHILL

Winston to Lady Randolph

28 [?27] September [1893]   50 Grosvenor Square
                                                   [Sandhurst]
Dear Mamma,

Your letter has just arrived and, as this is Wednesday[1] afternoon, I have got plenty of time to answer it in. My face is now quite well. I went to see the surgeon about it . . . a sallow complexioned man clothed in all manner of gold & scarlet trappings. He said that boys were very subject to such things – esp at my age & that they were a sign of good health. As for "horrors" the food is so excessively plain that there is not much danger of my being ill from it. Bread, butter, jam & cold beef, almost the entire articles.

Today we had an adjutants parade of almost the whole battalion & did the new physical drill to music. A very pretty sight. You really must come down some day and see it. We appear to have got on very well & the commandant said that E. Company marched past the best.

Jack came down on Saturday & I think was really impressed – esp with the uniform. I took him into to luncheon & all round. He seems to have enjoyed

_____
[1] September 28 was a Thursday.

himself very much in London. Mr Higgins[1] took him to "A Life of Pleasure" at Drury Lane[2] & the Palace Theatre & he was very full of both. When in Paris he went to the Morgue, Louvre & Eiffel. Today he goes back to Harrow.

I am sure I really don't know what sort of Sandhurst news would interest you, therefore I will only write personal. There is going to be a smoking concert tonight which will be good fun. Meanwhile we have been here now a whole month & so far I have not been late for anything (& there are at least 6 engagements per diem) nor have I been before my Company Officer. As for my back, it is now bent the other way & I am getting slowly accustomed to the hard exercise.

I am very glad to hear from you that Papa has sent me a cheque & letter – They will probably arrive tomorrow, & I will write to him to acknowledge receipt.

Dear Mamma please remember that this letter is written to you & don't show it to anyone else. Thank you very much indeed for writing to me.

Longing to see you, I remain, Ever your loving son
WINSTON S.C.

Mrs Everest to Winston

Sunday [? October 1893]   5 Cranmer Road
                                                Forest Gate
                                                Essex

My Darling Winny,

You promised to let me know how you got home the other night. I hope you got home safe & well. Do send me a line there's a dear Boy for I feel doubly anxious about you now you are left alone. Don't expose yourself to the hot sun this hot weather dear. I have just recd my money from the London & Westminster Bank £6. 6s & have just written an acknowledgement of same. How are you this hot weather. Have you heard from your Papa how he is or

---

[1] Henry Vincent Higgins (1855–1928), a fashionable solicitor to, amongst others, the Leslie family, and a friend of Lady Randolph's. The eldest son of Matthew James Higgins ('Jacob Omnium' of *The Times*) and Emily Blanche, seventh and youngest daughter of Sir Henry Tichborne, 8th Bart. Educated at Merton College, Oxford; Lieutenant 1st Life Guards 1876–83. Director of the Carlton and Ritz Hotels, London, and the Ritz, Paris. A considerable patron of opera at Covent Garden, he was Chairman of the Grand Opera Syndicate. Married 1) 1877 Hilda, youngest daughter of 11th Earl of Winchilsea and Nottingham, who died 8 February 1893; and 2) Marie Louise, daughter of George Parsons of Columbus, Ohio, and widow of W. L. Breese of New York. Created CVO 1905.

[2] A 'melodramatic variety entertainment' staged by Augustus Harris. Of its first performance on September 21 *The Times* said: 'The Drury Lane public were thoroughly delighted with the fare set before them.'

Mamma. I have not heard from Jackie yet. Am just going to write to him. It is awfully hot out here – how is it with you. Surely you don't have to do much drill or running this weather drink Ginger Beer & Lemonade when you are thirsty. I found all your Photos at G. Square in one of the Drawers of your Cupboard after you had gone. Let me know if you would like them sent on dear & I will write & ask Hussey to send them to you or Margaret.

I am quite well hope you are the same. I have had such a nice letter from Miss Phillips she says I am to tell you when you want to get rid of me you are to send me back to her.

Be sure & send me a line my own dearest precious Boy & don't run into debt or keep bad company.

With fondest love from Your loving old
WOOM E.A.E.

Winston to Lord Randolph
(*Blenheim Papers*)

[?5 October 1893]   Sandhurst

Dear Papa,

I was so glad to see by your speech in the papers, that you were back, all the better for your rest at Kissingen. I liked it very much especially the part about the "grand act". I am getting on all right here and have not been late or otherwise irregular so far. But they are terribly strict here. For instance only today, there was a boy, who joined when I did, put under arrest, for talking after being told to keep silent. Very unpleasant, meals in his room – no visitors except officer of the day and doctor – no exercise – or amusements until his case has been disposed of.

Yesterday we went out and felled trees, which was very amusing. I like Sandhurst better than ever and the work gets more interesting every day. I would so much like you to come down and see the place – if you have got a spare Sat Sunday or Wednesday. But I suppose you have got a good many meetings this month and next. If you would like to come – I would let you know all about the trains and lunch etc then if it was not suitable you could put it off. There is going to be a ball here on the 27th. If Mama is home I shall ask her to come.

Hoping to see you soon with best love

I remain ever your loving son
WINSTON S. CHURCHILL

Lord Randolph to Lady Randolph

EXTRACT

6 October 1893

. . . . Stalybridge was a great success; *Times* had leading article but mutilated report. Buzzard & Roose sat on me for ½ an hour & were so satisfied they did not even consult. I speak at Huddersfield on Monday & go to Newmarket Tuesday. . . .

. . . . Dearest I am very sorry but I have no money at the present moment & balance overdrawn at bank. I am selling deep levels but it is vy difficult to get 4½ for them now & I must not sell more than £500. I will try & send you £105 to Paris to Hotel Scribe. . . .

Winston to Lord Randolph
(Blenheim Papers)

8 October [1893]   Sandhurst

Dear Papa,

I am so sorry I did not know, that you would be at the Hatch today, before. If I had I could have ridden over – it is only twelve miles. But as it was impossible to obtain a telegram from you – owing to the 10 o'clock closing of the offices – I thought I had better wait.

Thank you so much for your letter. It is true that the journey down here is very tiring and slow. Such a bad service of trains on this abominable south-eastern line.

We have 2 months leave at Christmas beginning about the 20th December. The great event of each term is the "Duke's Day" when the Duke of Cambridge comes down and inspects the Battalion. After he has been down the College breaks up.

At length we have finished our preliminary Drill and so shall have no more afternoon parades. Such a relief – it was awfully unpleasant to have to hurry on to parade immediately after luncheon.

Wishing you a successful meeting at Huddersfield tomorrow

I remain ever your loving son
WINSTON S. CHURCHILL

PS I have been photographed in my uniform and will send you one when I write next. WSC

Lord Randolph to Frances, Duchess of Marlborough

EXTRACT

12 October 1893   Jockey Club Rooms
                                                   Newmarket

. . . I also settled with the Duke about Winston going into the 60th Rifles
after leaving Sandhurst. . . .

Lord Randolph to Lady Randolph

EXTRACT

12 October 1893   Jockey Club Rooms

. . . Winston is flourishing at Sandhurst, the Duke of Cambridge promised
to get him in the 60th Rifles. . . .

Duke of Cambridge to Lord Randolph
(Lord Randolph Papers)

15 October 1893   Gloucester House
                                                 Park Lane, W.

My dear Randolph Churchill,
    Herewith the Office note with reference to your son's name being down
for 60th Rifles. You will observe it is all as you wish it.
                                    I remain, Yours most sincerely
                                                   GEORGE

Winston to Lady Randolph

13 October [1893]   [Sandhurst]

Dear Mamma,
    I had such a nice letter from Papa, in answer to one I wrote him about his
Stalybridge meeting. Will you be in London on Sunday week? If so, I will
come up & if you can find me a bed – can stay until Sunday. It has been rather
a bore, not being able to go up to town on Saturdays, as all my friends go &
have grand fun at the London Pavilion. However I hope to have a little more
liberty when you come home. As I have not got a permission from home to
have leave when entitled to it you will have to send me a letter explicitly

inviting me to come. Such a bore being different from everyone else. You see I am not even able to go and stay with Welldon.

Well, I have no news to tell you except that we had to run ¾ mile with Rifles & accoutrements the other day & I had to be helped off parade by a couple of sergeants at the end of it & have been bad ever since. Just the same as when I took the Turkish bath. I have been to see the doctor & he says there is nothing wrong except that my heart does not seem very strong. So he has given me a tonic & lighter work for a few days.

Otherwise I have got on exellently, No punishments or extra drills or being late. I am in an awful hurry so do excuse this horrid scrawl as I must change for Gymnastics.

Goodbye my darling Mummy. Longing to see you.

I remain, Ever your loving son
WINSTON S.C.

Winston to Lord Randolph
(*Blenheim Papers*)

18 October [1893]   Sandhurst

Dear Papa,

I should so much like to come up on Saturday to see Mama and yourself. I have not been away from this place for more than 7 weeks and the majority of boys go two out of every three Saturdays. It is fearfully dull here on Sundays – nothing whatever to do.

I am getting on all right and have not been late yet. Please excuse so hurried a note as I have left it rather late and the post is just going.

Wishing you luck at Bedford – I am looking forward to reading your speech.

I remain your affectionate son
WINSTON S. CHURCHILL

Lord Randolph to Frances, Duchess of Marlborough

EXTRACT

20 October 1893   Turf Club
Piccadilly

... I go to Tring tomorrow & take Winston who has not had a Sunday out for weeks. I think he is getting on vy well, but the work is vy hard. ...

Winston to Lady Randolph

21 October [1893]   Tring Park
                                                       Tring[1]

My dear Mamma,

I am so disappointed at not having seen you. What a pity it was. I arrived at Waterloo at 12 o'clock and you left at 11.

Papa was very pleased to see me and talked to me for quite a long time about his speeches & my prospects. He seemed very interested in the R.M.C. intelligence [i.e. news of Sandhurst] & gave me a cheque for £6 to pay my mess bill with.

I went to see Grandmamma, who was so sorry you had not been able to see me. From what she said I hear you are going to "visit" for some time to come. I do hope I shall be able to see you soon.

What a comfortable house this is – such a change after the untidy – delapidated & tobacco-smelling rooms of the R.M.C.

Thank you so much for that beautiful cigarette holder – the prettiest one I have ever seen – and so uncommon. I suppose you cannot come to the R.M.C. Ball on Friday. I think I shall come up to town for the night instead of waiting there. Saturday next I go to stay with Mr Little at Eton. I have persuaded Papa to give me permission to have leave when I want it, so that is satisfactory.

Lady Rothschild asked after you & I gave her your message. Mr Asquith *was* coming down but could not owing to speech elsewhere. Papa says he is going to pitch into him at Yarmouth.[2] Mr Schomberg Macdonald[3] is here and two or three other people whose names I have not yet mastered.

I think Papa seems much better for his rest & far less nervous.

Hoping to see you *soon*.

                              I remain Your loving son
                              WINSTON S. CHURCHILL

PS I will send you a photograph. wsc

---

[1] The home of Nathaniel, 1st Baron ROTHSCHILD.

[2] He did, on October 25. Lord Randolph described Asquith's speeches as "a labyrinth of nonsense".

[3] Schomberg Kerr McDonnell (1861–1915), 5th son of 5th Earl of Antrim. Through his great-grandmother Anne, Countess of Antrim, who first married Sir Henry Vane Tempest, he was a half second cousin of Lord Randolph, and through his grandfather, Admiral Lord Mark Robert Kerr, he was descended from Frederick, Duke of Schomberg, who fell at the Battle of the Boyne in 1690. He was principal private secretary to Lord Salisbury 1888–1902; KCB 1902; died from wounds received in action.

Lord Randolph to Frances, Duchess of Marlborough

EXTRACT

24 October 1893

. . . I took Winston to Tring on Saturday. He had to leave at 4.30 afternoon to get back to Sandhurst. He has much smartened up. He holds himself quite upright and he has got steadier. The people at Tring took a great deal of notice of him but [he] was very quiet & nice-mannered. Sandhurst has done wonders for him. Up to now he has had no bad mark for conduct & I trust that it will continue to the end of the term. I paid his mess bill for him £6 so that his next allowance might not be *"empiété"* upon. I think he deserved it. . . .

Winston to Lord Randolph
(Blenheim Papers)

27 October [1893]   Sandhurst

Dear Papa,

Many congratulations on your Yarmouth speech and on "Molly Morgan". I hope you backed her well – I won two pounds myself. I read the "Brewers speech" and I was so glad to see your protest against *The Times* leader on it.

The Yarmouth speech was very good. Even *The Times* was friendly while I read several very nice leaders in the other papers.

If you will allow me I will go tomorrow (Friday) to sleep the night with Mr Little. Saturday morning I will come up to town and go to the Duchess Lily – who has asked me to spend Saturday and Sunday with her. I can thus see Mama and perhaps run down to Harrow in the afternoon. If you would like me to lunch at 23, Brook Street on Saturday I can come there direct from Eton and go on to Carlton House Terrace later.

The reason why I am able to come away on Friday is that the half-yearly ball is coming off on that night.

Thank you so much for sending two boxes of your best cigarettes. I keep them for after lessons and smoke commoner ones in the daytime.

My address after 2 p.m. tomorrow until 9 a.m. Saturday will be 30, High Street, Eton.

With best love ever your affectionate son
WINSTON S. CHURCHILL

Lord Randolph to Frances, Duchess of Marlborough

EXTRACT

28 October 1893

... Winston has gone to Eton to spend a day & night with Mr Little. He comes back here on tomorrow. He wanted to go & stay with Dss of Lily but I told him he had seen nothing of his mother & ought to devote himself to her. For some reason or other also I do not care about his being with the Duchess Lily. A dinner or lunch *"ça se passe"* but staying in her house is not vy good for him. You never know what state she may be in. . . .

Winston to Lady Randolph

29 October [1893]   [Sandhurst]

My dear Mamma,

I have felt very uncomfortable since I got here about Everest. I fear that at the time you told me – I was so occupied with Jack & Harrow that I did not think about it seriously. Now however – I have a very uneasy conscience on the subject. It is quite easy, dear Mamma, for you to say that it is not my business or for you to refuse to read what I have got to say – but nevertheless I feel I ought in common decency to write to you at length on the subject.

In the first place if I allowed Everest to be cut adrift without protest in the manner which is proposed I should be extremely ungrateful – besides I should be very sorry not to have her at Grosvenor Square – because she is in my mind associated – more than anything else with *home*.

She is an old woman – who has been your devoted servant for nearly 20 years – she is more fond of Jack and I than of any other people in the world & to be packed off in the way the Duchess suggests would possibly, if not probably break her down altogether.

Look too at the manner in which it would be done. She is sent away – nominally for a holiday as there is no room at Grosvenor Square for her. Then her board wages are refused her – quite an unusual thing. Finally she is to be given her *congé* by letter – without having properly made up her mind where to go or what to do.

At her age she is invited to find a new place & practically begin over again. Of course I am extremely fond of Everest & it [is] perhaps from this reason that I think such proceedings cruel & rather mean.

I know you have no choice in the matter & that the Duchess has every right to discharge a servant for whom she has "no further use." But I do think that you ought *to arrange that she remains at Grosvenor Square – until I go* back to Sandhurst & Jack to school.

In the meantime she will have ample time to make up her mind where to go – to find a place & to resign herself to a change.

Then when a *good* place *has been* secured for her she could leave and be given a pension – which would be sufficient to keep her from want – & which should continue during her life.

This is what I should call a fair and generous method of treating her. It is in your power to explain to the Duchess that she *cannot* be sent away until she has got a good place.

She has for 3 months been boarding herself out of her own money and I have no doubt is not at all well off. Dearest Mamma – I know you are angry with me for writing – I am very sorry but I cannot bear to think of Everest not coming back much less being got rid of in such a manner. If you can arrange with the Duchess & persuade her to let Everest stay till after Christmas – I should feel extremely relieved. If you can't, I will write and explain things to Papa, who will I am sure forgive me troubling him.

About Finance . . . . the dinner was	15/-
diner à prix fixé	10/6
Hock	2/9
coffee	9d
attendance	1/-
	15/-

You also said you would send me the other 13/- for Harrow expenses. I am not in any immediate need.

With best love and many kisses – and apologising for having to write so tedious a letter.

I remain Every your loving son
WINSTON S.C.

Winston to Lord Randolph
(*Blenheim Papers*)

3 November [1893]   Sandhurst

Dear Papa,

Thank you so much for your letter and for sending me the £10. I shall come up to town but shall not arrive before 3 o'clock, as I have to shoot in the Company Matches in both Rifle and Revolver.

Hoping to see you tomorrow . . .

I remain ever your loving son
WINSTON S. CHURCHILL

Winston to Lord Randolph
(*Blenheim Papers*)

13 November [1893]   Sandhurst

Dear Papa,

I have just read the report of your speech in the *Scotsman* – which grand-mama sent me last night. What a splendid meeting! I find your speech, very, very interesting more especially with regard to the Navy – what was most interesting was the history of the beginning of the P [Primrose] League. It was indeed a pity that *The Times* had not got a better report.

I went down to Harrow on Saturday – but spent the night at Aunt Leonie's and returned to Harrow early on Sunday. Welldon was very kind and said that Jack was sure to get his remove this term. He is very anxious to see you as he wants to know what Jack is going to be. I told him that you were very busy with political work.

I saw Mama on Thursday as she came through London on her way to Chatsworth. She has written to me to tell me that you do not like my smoking cigars. I will not do so anymore, I am not fond enough of them in having any difficulty in leaving them off.

In three weeks the examinations begin, and so I am working rather hard. If you are in town on Sunday I should like to come up and see you as I believe you are going to Le Nid almost immediately. Things are going on very smoothly here and I hope great things from the exam.

With best love I remain ever your loving son
WINSTON S. CHURCHILL

Winston to Lord Randolph
(*Blenheim Papers*)

20 November [1893]   Sandhurst

Dear Papa,

When I got back here last night I found your letter waiting for me. I will take your advice about the cigars – and I don't think I shall often smoke more than one or two a day – and very rarely that. You sent me my November allowance in a cheque dated second which got here on the 4th. I think I wrote and acknowledged the receipt.

I went, with about 200 Sandhurst cadets, to Woolwich on Saturday, as the College was playing them at Football. It is a terrible place and I am very glad I did not go there. Aunt Leonie gave me Mama's room and, I went on Sunday to see grandmama – who was staying with the Duchess Lily. I stayed there all day – as I had not seen grandmama for more than 3 months – and got back here at 10 o'clock.

Next Saturday and Sunday I shall stay here, as it is my turn to remain for parade: but the Sunday after I should like to come up to town and see you, before you start.

Thanking you so much for writing to me and wishing you a successful week at Bradford,

I remain ever your loving son
WINSTON S. CHURCHILL

Winston to Lady Randolph

20 November [1893]   [Sandhurst]

Dear Mamma,

I got the £2 all right though I had a long walk to get them. Thank you very much. I went up to stay with Aunt Leonie and saw Count Kinsky; who was all right on Sat. night but – was down with fever on Sunday. Colonel Brabazon was there too. How I wish I was going into his regiment.[1] Sunday I went to see the Duchess Lily and found Grandmamma there. I stayed and lunched.

Papa has written me such a kind letter. Why don't you suggest taking me to "Le Nid".

I have got another of those horrid boils, & my face is very painful. Well good-bye dear Mamma, with best love

I remain Ever your loving son
WINSTON S.

Winston to Lord Randolph
(*Blenheim Papers*)

26 November [1893]   Sandhurst

Dear Papa,

If you will be in town next Saturday I can come up and see you before you go away; or if Wednesday would be more convenient I could get leave to come for the afternoon and evening – there is a train as far as Camberley at 11:55.

I am very well and the spot I had on my face has now gone away. Everything is going on very well here.

Mama wrote and told me what a successful campaign you had in Bradford. You are sure to be returned, but I suppose you will not be content unless the Western and Eastern Divisions are converted also. I thought your remarks on the termination of the Coal Strike, splendid.

[1] The 4th Hussars, of which he had taken command in 1891.

Yesterday I went over to Eton and saw Kim and Lord Londonderry's boy. In a fortnight or so the term is over and I have a couple of months leave. It is not quite certain what day we go away, as the Duke has not made up his mind which day will suit him to come down, and of course we cannot go until after he has been – so I may be 2 or 3 days late in coming home.

With best love I remain ever your loving son
WINSTON S. CHURCHILL

PS Could you send me my allowance on the 30th Nov instead of the 1st Dec as I have to pay my Fencing Bill on that day.

WINSTON

Winston to Lord Randolph
(*Blenheim Papers*)

1 December [1893]   Sandhurst

Dear Papa,

Just a line to thank you for your kind telegram. I also received one from Mamma. I shall come up tomorrow for my leave, as it is one of my days off – and it is a pity to waste it. After that I don't think I shall come up again as I want to revise my notes for the Examination.

I hope you will enjoy yourself at "Le Nid". After all your work I should think you were looking forward to a rest. Wishing you a comfortable journey, and the best of love,

I remain ever your loving son
WINSTON S. CHURCHILL

Winston to Lady Randolph

10 December [1893]   [Sandhurst]

Dearest Mamma,

Thank you so much for your kindness – v.i.z. £3. I have been working very hard and today have done an Exam in Tactics. I will refrain from prophesying having been wrong so many times before. Do come down on Friday. The Duke has changed his mind and will come on Friday. Write and ask if you can come down by the special train – If it does not rain it will be very pretty. We can go back together.

Ever your loving son
WINSTON CHURCHILL

PS I missed the post with this letter last night – and have been to-day very busy with examinations (6 hours). I think I have done well. I have had a horrid toothache on both sides which worries me very much. Do make an appointment for me for Monday. If it does not get better I will wire to you.

The Duke has again changed his mind and will not come down until Saturday. Please come if you can I am sure you will not be bored.

Ever your loving son
WINSTON S.C.

Lord Randolph to Lady Randolph

EXTRACT

12 December 1893   Le Nid

. . . I hope Lady Leslie will ask Winston. He really has more right to go than Jack because he is more grown up. But I should think she would ask the two. . . .

Winston to Lord Randolph
(Blenheim Papers)

13 December [1893]   Sandhurst

Dear Papa,

I am very sorry not to have written to you before but I have been working hard during the Examination. The result will not be known for a fortnight or three weeks – and I will write as soon as I know. I am quite happy about my papers – but I won't attempt to prophecy as I have been so often wrong before.

It is very cold & cheerless & these long stone passages are terribly draughty. I have caught a cold in my teeth on both sides & have got a very bad toothache – which has made me lose a few marks in the examination.

Otherwise everything is most satisfactory & I feel very well. The Duke comes down on Saturday 16th – & as soon as he has gone we go home. Jack comes up the Tuesday after.

I should very much like to have a few lessons in Military Riding in the holidays if you could arrange it. It would help me a good deal next term to have had a little practice.

How is your cold? I suppose that the warm weather & change of climate have taken it away. Give my love to Lady Wilton – I hope she is better now.

With best love, I remain, ever your loving son
WINSTON S. CHURCHILL

Lord Randolph to Lady Randolph

EXTRACT

18 December 1893   [Le Nid]

. . . I am not quite sure it was wise throwing over Lady C Leslie[1] after she had offered to take both the boys. I think Charles Allsopp[2] a detestable companion for Winston and I wish he had gone to Glaslough & come back in January to London when he could have had some riding school down at Knightsbridge or Regents Park. . . .

Winston to Lord Randolph

24 December [1893]   Blenheim

Dear Papa,

I arrived here last night after rather a cold journey. Sunny and Lady Blandford[3] are very kind to me and want me to stay here till Tuesday week. If you think fit I shall stay here until I go to Hindlip as you can go straight from here without the necessity of going to London.

Colonel Ferguson[4] has sent me the enclosed postcard. He has found out my marks in 3 out of the 5 subjects. The other two are not yet known. The maximum is for each subject 300. To pass you have to get 100 in each subject and 750 on the whole 5 subjects.

If the other two subjects are anything like the 3 I send you – I shall probably come out very high in the list as I have made on these 3 sufficient marks to pass without the other two. I will let you know where I come out as soon as I hear the result. I have great hopes of being in the first 10 unless the other subjects are very bad. I am very sorry to have taken so many words to explain.

I am very happy here and everybody is most kind. Hoping you are quite well and wishing you a Pleasant Christmas.

I remain Ever Your loving son
WINSTON S.C.

PS Best love to Mamma.

[1] Constance Wilhelmina Frances (18 –1925), youngest sister of 4th Earl of Portarlington. She had married in 1856 John LESLIE (1822–1916) of Glaslough, Co Monaghan, who was created Baronet 1876.

[2] Charles Allsopp (1877–1931), only surviving son of 2nd Baron Hindlip was still at Eton. He succeeded to the peerage in 1897; served in South Africa 1900–01 with 8th Hussars, and in 1914–18 war as a General Staff Officer. In 1921 he announced that he would have to give up living at Hindlip Hall, near Worcester.

[3] Charles, 9th Duke of Marlborough (*see* SUNDERLAND), who had succeeded in November 1892, and his mother, Bertha, Marchioness of BLANDFORD, the first wife of the 8th Duke.

[4] John Adam Fergusson (1845–1920), Lieutenant Colonel, Rifle Brigade; became Professor of Tactics, Military Administration & Law at the Royal Military College in September 1893. He retired as Colonel 1902. He was a younger brother of Sir James Fergusson, 6th Bart.

Winston to Lady Randolph

25 December [1893]   Blenheim

My dear Mamma,

I am enjoying myself here very much – though there is plenty of divine service. Every one is very kind and civil to me & Lady Blandford has really gone out of her way to make me comfortable. I suggested going on Tuesday but she would not hear of it & told me that she expected me to stay until the following Monday. It would be very convenient if I were to go direct from here to Hindlip as it is only an hour and a quarter – by train.

There is no sort of party & I am quite alone with Sunny. He is very good company and we have sat talking till 1.30 every night since I have been here.

I have also had long talks with Lady Blandford or "Aunt Bertha" as I am getting to call her. She really is most kind. Altogether I am quite content at the prospect of staying a week here & am in no hurry to get back to town.

On my way back from Hindlip I think I shall go – with your permission – and stay with the Dillons at Ditchley[1] . . . but that can be arranged later.

Hoping you were not bored to death in town – that Papa looked well – and that you had a "Happy Christmas".

I remain, Ever your loving son
WINSTON S. CHURCHILL

Lord Randolph to Frances, Duchess of Marlborough

EXTRACT

26 December 1893   50 Grosvenor Square

. . . Winston seems to have done well in the Sandhurst examinations. I send you a letter from him. I dont mind his going to Blenheim as long as I dont go there myself. They seem to make a fuss with him & of course he knows nothing of the past. Jennie is here & remains till Saturday when she goes with the boys to Hindlip. . . .

Winston to Mrs John Leslie
(Copy: Leslie Papers)

26 December [1893]   Blenheim

[Superscription missing]

Just a line to wish you a "Merry Christmas". I was so sorry not to come to Ireland as I was looking forward to it so much. Perhaps you are astonished at the paper. Sunny very kindly asked me down here for the Christmas week. He

[1] Ditchley Park, Oxfordshire, was at that time the home of 17th Viscount Dillon. His son, Harry Lee-Dillon (1874–1923), was at Sandhurst with Winston.

is such an interesting companion and anything but the idiot I was taught to believe him to be.

I went out hunting to day for the first time and succeeded in getting the brush. Nothing but personal news must bore you. So thanking you for being so kind to me while I was at Sandhurst and wishing you everything amiable

I remain your affectionate nephew
WINSTON S. CHURCHILL

Winston to Lady Randolph

30 December [1893]   Blenheim

Dear Mamma,

I shall come to Hindlip by some early train on Monday and will wire what time I arrive. They want me to stay here to go to Mr Brassey's[1] Party on Monday night but I think on the whole that it would be better to come away before they have too much of me.

Thank you so much for having the brush mounted – I forgot to ask you in my letter. Today I have been out again. There was however very little scent and we had very short runs. I had several jumps for all that. Lord Valentia[2] was there and I told him you had sent messages. He wished to be remembered to you.

Sunny has been very kind and we have had very lengthy conversations. It is most untrue to say he is stupid. He is very sensible & I think clever – extremely industrious and attentive to business and he seems to have made himself very popular among the tenantry and neighbours.

Yesterday he sent me out shooting & *detailed* half a dozen keepers to drive one of the biggest covers. I had real sport and shot about 25 Rabbits and a dozen pheasants. There were lots who got away.

I shall be extremely sorry to leave on Monday and nothing but the thought of the beautiful Polly Hacket[3] consoles me. Lilian & Nora[4] are very amusing and rather pretty. Lady B [Blandford] is charming.

---

[1] Albert Brassey (1844–1918), of Heythrop; married Matilda Bingham, daughter of 4th Baron Clanmorris; MP for the Banbury Division, 1895–1906.

[2] Arthur Annesley, 11th Viscount Valentia (1843–1927), of Bletchington Park, Oxon, succeeded his grandfather in the Irish Peerage 1863. He was Conservative MP for Oxford 1895–1917 when he was created Baron Annesley (in the United Kingdom peerage). Lieut-Colonel commanding Oxfordshire Imperial Yeomanry. Served in South African War.

[3] Adela Mary (1875–1946), nicknamed Polly and Molly, only daughter of George Hacket, of Moor Hall, Warwickshire, and Adela Mary, second daughter of Charles Rowland Palmer-Morewood. She was ten weeks younger than Winston. On 27 June 1895 she married Edward Kenneth Wilson, second son of Arthur Wilson, of Tranby Croft, and brother of Muriel Wilson. Her mother's sister, Georgina Millicent, married 2nd Baron Hindlip.

[4] Winston's first cousins, the youngest daughters of 'Blandford', 8th Duke of Marlborough, and Bertha, Lady Blandford. Lilian was born 1873 and died 1951, Norah was born 1875 and died 1946.

Altogether I have had a very pleasant week and am particularly glad to have made Sunny's acquaintance.

Well dear Mamma as I shall see you on Monday I don't think I need go on with this now. Grand M. has written me a very kind letter in which she talks of "distinguished careers" etc so altogether we are going "very strong".

With best love (and don't again say I don't write)

I remain, Ever your loving son
WINSTON S. CHURCHILL

PS Mind you don't show this letter to anybody.

Lord Randolph to Lady Randolph

EXTRACT

3 January 1894   50 Grosvenor Square

. . . I send Winston his Sandhurst examination marks which perhaps he may not have received. He may be quite pleased with coming out eighth. But how about the want of punctuality[1]. . . .

Winston to Lady Randolph

11 January [1894]   Hindlip Hall
near   Worcester

My dearest Mamma,

I have written to Colonel Brabazon and have stated my various arguments in favour of cavalry regiment. I have asked him to say whether or no they are correct – when he writes to you – but in case he should not state this clearly I will put them down for you.

1. Promotions much quicker in Cavalry than in Infantry. (60th Rifles slowest regiment in the army.)

2. Obtain your commission (3 or 4 months) in Cav much sooner than in Infantry.

3. 4th Hussars are going to India shortly. If I join before "Augmentation" I should have 6 or 7 subalterns below me in a very short time.

4. Cavalry regiments are always given good stations in India and generally taken great care of by the Government – while Infantry have to take what they can get.

---

[1] His marks for the first Probationary Examination held in December 1893 were as follows: (Maximum 300) Military Administration 230, Military Law 276, Tactics 278, Fortification 215, Military Topography 199 – total (maximum 1500) 1198. His conduct was described as 'Good but unpunctual'.

5.   If you want to keep a horse you can do it much cheaper in the cavalry than in infantry – government will provide stabling – forage – and labour.

---

6.   Sentimental advantages grouped under heading of
   a. uniform
   b. increased interest of a "life among horses" etc
   c. advantages of riding over walk
   d. advantages of joining a regiment some of whose officers you know. i.e. 4th Hussars.

The first 5 of these reasons I wrote to Col Brabazon the last I write to you.

There you are – now don't ever say I did not give you any reasons. There are 5 good solid arguments.

Now to other matters. I try hard to write large enough to please you but it looks unsightly especially when you like a great deal written on one page. However if you like it I will continue the practice.

What did the doctors say last night? Do send me a line sometime. Sunny is coming here on Monday – and I should like very much to stop until Wednesday. The ball being Thursday.

With best love and kisses I remain, Ever your loving son
WINSTON

PS Don't pay any attention to the Duchess she doesn't mean it – and even if she did————————————————————————

C. S. Rome to Winston

Sunday [? 21 January 1894]   Near Cheltenham

My dear Churchill,

Many thanks for your letter. I fear there is no chance of my being let in to Sandhurst. I made just over 6200 which would have got me in nicely in June for the Cavalry. How do you like being at Sandhurst? I suppose you will enjoy the pleasures(?) of the riding school this term. I heard from Mug Davidson[1] the other day – he tells me he made 6450, just a few places out for infantry. I am going into the Militia and have already been promised a place in the Worcestershire Regiment; I know two or three fellows in it and ought to have good fun.

---

[1] John Humphrey Davidson (1876–1954), joined King's Royal Rifle Corps 1896; served in Boer War (DSO, despatches), Captain 1901; served in 1914–18 war, became Director of Military Operations (Maj-General, CB, despatches eleven times). Unionist MP for Fareham 1918–31. KCMG 1919.

My governor went to Australia last September (in the same vessel, I believe as your aunt Lady Sarah), so I am at present the boss of the family.

Please remember me to all the old Harrow fellows at Sandhurst, especially Charlie Strong.

Ever yours
CLAUDE S. ROME

Jack to Winston

Saturday 27 January [1894]   Harrow

Dear Winny,

Thanks for yours.

Do come on Wednesday and bring the £1 and I could do with having my subs. paid if Mama feels inclined. I have had to buy a new Picture to go in place of the CK's [Count Kinsky's] Picture.

I must have an umbrella and I can't buy one, so when you come on Tuesday bring these things required.

I remain Your loving Brother
JACK S. CHURCHILL

Mrs Everest to Winston

Tuesday [? 30 January 1894]   5 Cranmer Road

My darling,

Thanks very much for your letter I hope you enjoyed your short visit to Brighton & arrived home safe & sound & I also hope you are all the better for the change. I had a letter from dear Jackie he is so afraid you & everyone will not think of his little birthday 9th of next month. Do try & think of it dear & send him something & also remind Her Ladyship for He does not like to be forgotten poor Boy, he says no one thought of him last year but me. I have been busy making my room comfortable it is frightfully cold here. I hope you will keep your promise & come & see me on Sunday. Have you been to the riding school. I hope you will keep well dear – do you miss me a little bit. I hope you do not sit up half the night reading. I have got my little room nice & comfortable now. I hope you will come & see me before you go.

Goodbye my Darling best love to you

From your affecte old
WOOM

Please burn this do not leave my letters about.

Please give Margaret the enclosed white Wool she will know what it is for don't forget to give it her as it is of great importance.

Miss Molly Hacket to Winston

Wednesday [31 January 1894]   33 Hill Street

My dear Winston,

Did you really mean to leave all those lovely sweets for me it was *too too* kind of you; if I had not been obliged to go and change we could have had a "stuff". The wedding was a great success and Nellie[1] a wonder, *so* composed.

Alex's[2] address is

Mothecombe

Ivy Bridge

S. Devon.

I saw the Duke at Chesterfield Street. No chance of staying for the ball alas.

In great haste, hope we may meet again soon. Again *many* thanks for sugar plums.

Yrs v: sincerely

MOLLY HACKET

Winston to Jack

31 January [1894]   50 Grosvenor Square

My dear Jack,

I went with Mamma today to get you a cash box for the 9th. Such a nice one – with yr name & two Chubb keys. Polly Hacket came for a walk this morning & we went and strolled Bond Street way.

Leaving there I met Sunny who had come up to see Nellie Bass married. He took me to Luncheon at Whites Club & was most amicable.

I think that the reported resignation of Mr Gladstone will probably prove false after all – however it is to be hoped that it is true.

I shall come down I think on Saturday & hope to see you then.

Your affectionate brother

WINSTON S.C.

[1] Nellie Lisa (1873–1962), only child of Michael Arthur Bass, 1st Baron Burton, of the great brewing family, married James Evan Bruce Baillie of Dochfour on 31 January 1894. She succeeded her father in 1909 as Baroness in her own right. Her parents lived at Rangemore, near Burton-on-Trent, and at 6 Grosvenor Square.

[2] Alexandra Mina Ellis (–1949), 3rd daughter of Major-General Sir Arthur Ellis for 40 years Equerry to the Prince of Wales (later King Edward VII). In 1899 she married Arthur Hardinge, later ambassador in Teheran, Brussels, Lisbon and Madrid.

Winston to Lord Randolph
(*Blenheim Papers*)

31 January [1894]   50 Grosvenor Square

My dear Papa,

I am sorry not to have written to you before but I have been waiting for something to tell you. The Influenza has quite gone away and I am now quite well. It was a great pity that it should come to interrupt my riding lessons just as I was hoping to steal a march on the other Cadets. However I have now begun my riding again and I am getting on alright – tho' the want of stirrups gives me many "tumbles". I think I shall be able to arrange with Capt Burt[1] to ride in the afternoon occasionally – as well as in the mornings and so I may make up for some of the fortnight I was absent. So far I have always had a quarter of an hour to spare.

Brighton was very pleasant and I enjoyed myself immensely. *Mamma's concert* was a great success – all the speakers said very gushing and complimentary things about her – while you were re-elected "with acclamation".

I am so sorry that you think that Lord Dudley's Amendment being adopted will imperil your Bradford seat: all the same I can't imagine Shaw Lefevre being successful against you.[2]

Yesterday I went down to Harrow to see Jack who was beginning Army Class work and looked very well. Welldon said such nice things about you and asked after you most particularly.

Today I met *Sunny* in Hill Street – up for the Bass wedding. He was very amiable and took me to luncheon at Whites – where I met several people I had been at Harrow with.

I wonder if when you come back to town [Lord Randolph was staying with Lady Wilton at Monte Carlo] – you would put my name down for a good club. You see in three years I shall be going out to India and – if I don't get in to some club soon it will not be much good to me.

I am so sorry to hear that you have a cough and hope that the Riviera will do it good. Please give my best love to Lady Wilton, who wrote me such a kind letter.

With best love, ever your loving son
WINSTON S.C.

---

[1] Charles Henry Burt (1852–1904), riding master of the 2nd Life Guards (Hyde Park); Hon Captain 1891, Hon Major 1903. Retired in 1904, when senior riding master in the army.

[2] George John Shaw-Lefevre (1831–1928) was Liberal MP for Central Bradford, the seat Lord Randolph had been invited to contest. At this time he was in the Cabinet as President of the Local Government Board, having previously served under Gladstone as Postmaster-General and First Commissioner of Works. Created Baron Eversley 1906.

Jack to Winston

Friday 2 February 1894   Harrow

Dear Winney,

Thanks for yours received.

I am looking forward to the cash box arriving send it so that it will not arrive a day too late, and put what jewellery there is of mine in it. Meanwhile dont forget the Poor of Japan. You seem to be having rather a good time in London

As you were down here the other day. I have got nothing to tell you

So I remain Your loving Brother

JACK S. CHURCHILL

PS Bring Meana [? Alex Mina Ellis] down some day

Lord Randolph to Lady Randolph

EXTRACT

3 February 1894   [Le Nid]

. . . I saw the old Duke of Cambridge yesterday as I was breakfasting at the Grand Hotel. I shall go over to Cannes some day as I must speak to him about Jack & the 60th Rifles. Bye the way when is Jack's birthday? I forget whether I have sent Winston his February cheque but I rather think I left £15 with you to administer judiciously. Will you thank him for his letter. . . .

Winston to Lord Randolph
(Blenheim Papers)

5 February [1894]   50 Grosvenor Square

My dear Papa,

I hope your cough is much better – and will be quite gone by the time you get this. The Riding is going on very satisfactorily – but I am afraid that my having lost a fortnight will prevent my getting a certificate – as I have only been at it 10 mornings so far. However I am doing all I can to make up for lost time and am going to ride again at 4 o'clock this afternoon.

Yesterday I went to see Everest. She is very comfortable and has got a cosy room. She begged me to thank you for the present you gave her.

I feel very well and I am looking forward to going back to the R.M.C. as there is not much to do in town. You must try and come down one day this term as I shall have a room to myself, and so be able to have visitors.

With a short break at Easter we go on for 6 months which is really a good dose.

What a pity you are having bad weather. Yesterday here was beautiful but not today it has turned very damp and is raining.

With best love I remain your loving son
WINSTON S. CHURCHILL

Lord Randolph to Winston[1]

10 February 1894   Le Nid

Dear Winston,

Many thanks for your letter. Even if you don't get a certificate the riding will have done good. That influenza was most unlucky. Well now I do hope you will do better this quarter even than you did last. They say a good beginning makes a good ending. But you must keep the standard up & keep raising. This is the critical time at Sandhurst which is now commencing for you. If you get through this time well, the rest will follow more easily. Mind if you do well at Sandhurst & get good reports good positions in the classes & even the good conduct medal you would go to your regiment so much higher in credit & more thought of. So if you feel at time like giving way or falling off "Don't". Pull yourself together & keep yourself well abreast & even ahead of those you are competing with. I rather advise you not to come up to London too often. Your mother & I can run down. It does not seem such an awful journey. Lastly take care of your health. Keep down the smoking, keep down the drink & go to bed as early as you can. Well I have written you a regular lecture but it is all sound. The better you do the more I shall be inclined to help you. I return to London on the 20th leaving this on the 18th staying in Paris 19th & leaving 11.30 A.M. on 20. The weather is not bad, but it does not quite settle down into hot weather.

Well Goodbye take care of yourself. Jack has written me two letters since I have been here & seems to be prospering.

Yr affte father
RANDOLPH S.C.

By the way I think you may substitute "Father" for "Papa". Grandmama is different.

---

[1] Lord Randolph wrote to Lady Randolph from Le Nid on 12 February 1894: 'I wrote Winston to Sandhurst a letter more of advice than anything else to keep him up to the mark.'

Lady Randolph to Winston

11 February [1894]   [?50 Grosvenor Square]

Dearest Winston,

I hope you are none the worse for yr journey. Let me know how you are getting on. I felt so sorry to have you go – you poor thing – particularly when you are not feeling well. I don't know what I shld have done in G. Square without you. Make a little list of the things you want for your room & I will see if I have them.

Goodbye – take care of yrself & write often.

Yr loving
MOTHER

Winston to Lord Randolph
(*Blenheim Papers*)

13 February [1894]   Sandhurst

My dear Papa,

Thank you so much for your letter – which arrived last night. My boils which have hitherto been very troublesome are much better – but it will be a week before I can ride.

I have got a very decent room to myself this term. It is at present very bare but I think that when I get a carpet and some curtains etc it will be quite comfortable. There are many alterations this term which do not tend to make this place very pleasant. Besides the crusade against extravagance – they have stopped hunting – polo – and owning horses. Extra work has been added in the evenings and lights out is a ½ hour earlier. Also everybody has more drill riding and gymnastics than formerly. These changes which are very unpopular among the officers as well as the cadets – are the result of the report of the Committee headed by Lord Hamilton of Dalzell[1] and Sir Arthur Hayter[2] – whose knowledge of the place *is* gathered in a one day's visit.

There is a rumour that the first twenty cadets of the junior division of last term will be allowed to pass out 6 months earlier officers being wanted badly. This will affect me – and it will probably prove too good to be true.

I have had many congratulations on my place which I think I ought to keep at the end of the present term – and perhaps even improve upon it a

[1] John Clencairn Carter Hamilton, Baron Hamilton (1829–1900). Lord-in-Waiting to the Queen 1892–4. MP Falkirk Burghs 1857–9; for South Lanarkshire 1868–74, 1880–6. Created Baron 1886.

[2] Arthur Divett Hayter (1835–1917). Visitor of the RMC Sandhurst. MP Bath and Wells 1865–8, Bath 1873–85, Walsall 1893–5, 1900–05. Financial Secretary to the War Office 1882–5. Created Baronet 1858; Baron Haversham 1906.

little. For the present I am only doing indoor work as I am rather weak from the boils.

The smoking is at present almost entirely given up and strong drink at Sandhurst is practically unknown – so I hope to get right soon.

I am so glad to hear that yr cough is better and that the weather is improving. Give my love to Lady Wilton. I will write again to Grosvenor Square.

Ever your loving son
WINSTON S. CHURCHILL

Winston to Lady Randolph

13 February [1894]   Sandhurst

My dear Mamma,

I am much better to-day all round. The boils are healing up and I do not think that they will have to be lanced again. My tooth is still very troublesome but I think it will get better gradually.

I wrote to Papa & Capt Burt this morning and generally cleared off a lot of correspondences, which had been postponed from day to day.

I am sending you a list of the things I should like for my room. Please let me have what you can – as soon as possible as it is very uncomfortable at present.

There is really no news of any kind since yesterday, except that I caught my train and got back in good time.

Please excuse so short a letter.

Ever your loving son
WINSTON S. CHURCHILL

PS I found such a kind letter from Papa (6 pages) waiting for me when I got back. WSC

Miss Molly Hacket to Winston

13 February 1894   Hindlip Hall

My dear Winston,

Many thanks for yr letter. Quite proper. Aunt M.[1] knew you had written.

How are you, have you any news? I have none. I was *so* sorry not to be at the dance, it must have been fun, did you dance with the 2nd Mrs H's[2] niece? Please give my love to Lady Randolph. How is dear Jack. When I am in London again & if you are too, we will go down & see him. Aunt M. & Uncle C.

---

[1] Lady Hindlip.
[2] Probably Mrs Hungerford (see p. 460).

are at Rangemore. Ask Frances [Guest] some more about *me*! I am so glad you think her "young man" an "*angel-man*". Quite cold here. We went into the Assizes last week, *so* amusing.

Believe me Yrs very sincerely
MOLLY

George Wilson to Winston

Wednesday [? 14 February 1894]   Bannockburn House

Dear Churchill,

You are quite right in your remarks in your last letter, it would be rather a pity if we should cease writing as we were such good friends at school. I had better give you Forman's address before I forget about it, it is Wilford House, Wilford, Nottingham. I owe him several letters in fact I have written to no one for several months. I have had rather a poor winter, one of my sisters has been ill, so we have been very quiet, as we have had no one staying with us. I am still devoted to football, and play almost every Saturday. How is Jack getting on at Harrow! I expect he will be one of the swells of the house by this time. Remember me to him when next you write him. What is Marjoribanks doing! I have heard nothing of him for ever so long. What a fool he was to fail for Sandhurst. How long do you remain at Sandhurst and in to what regiment are you going! Cavalry I suppose.

I must shut up now, as I have several other letters to write including one to Fisher.

Ever yours
G. W. WILSON

Mrs Everest to Winston

[14 February 1894]   5 Cranmer Road

My darling Winny,

I meant to have written to you yesterday but I was busy cleaning my room. Poor old Boy I am so sorry you are troubled with tooth ache do get some spirits of camphor & rub some on your gums & also on your cheek frequently nothing so good for it I got Froggy some yesterday & it has cured her she was in great pain with tooth ache yesterday. I hope the Boils are dying away & that you are feeling better dear Boy. I hope there are no fresh ones coming are there.

Take some Eno it will purify the Blood. Did you write to your Papa to wish him many happy returns of the day it was his birthday yesterday.[1]

I had such a nice letter & a present of a toilet case she made herself embroidered with silk. She wants me to postpone my visit till April as she is going away on a visit to Devonshire & she thinks it will be warmer & pleasanter for me then than now. She is quite delighted that I am going so I shall wait till after your Easter holidays are over before I go. Well my darling what about your Box Cover will you measure the box length & width & height or depth & I will soon make it. I don't think red twill will do it wants something stiffer not so flimsy some thick cretonne will be best I can get it here mind you measure it correctly. I will enclose my yard measure you can see how many inches it is. I do hope you are better dearest please let me hear as I shall feel very anxious to know how you are. I heard from Jackie on Monday he is alright. So am I. Goodbye my sweet old love.

Ever your Fond old
WOOM

Winston to Lady Randolph

15 February [1894]　　　　　　　　　　　　　　　　　Sandhurst

My dear Mamma,

I shall be coming up on Saturday – but only for the day. Perhaps you will leave my £3 – with Healy. I shall keep out of Grandmamma's sight and get some luncheon on my own account.

My spots are much better and I shall be able to ride on Monday. In the meantime I am able to go to Parades and out door work & feel generally much better.

What truth is there in the *Morning Post's* announcement of the Sebright engagement being "orf"?[2] Thank you very much for sending me letters etc which had arrived. I was disappointed at not finding a line from you inside such a large envelope.

Please Don't forget about my room – which is remarkably bare – or about the £3.

With best love Ever your loving son
WINSTON S. CHURCHILL

[1] And also Mrs Everest's birthday.

[2] 'We are authorised to state that the marriage arranged between Sir Egbert Sebright, Bart, and the Hon Frances Guest will not take place.' Sir Egbert Sebright (1871–97) was the 10th Baronet, and died unmarried. Miss Guest was married within six months to Frederick John Thesiger, eldest son of 2nd Baron Chelmsford.

Miss Molly Hacket to Winston

[? February 1894]   Hindlip Hall

Dear Winston,

  Do write & tell me *all* about F. Guest's engagement being broken off. Write me a real nice amusing letterkins!

Yours very sincerely

MOLLY

Captain C. H. Burt to Winston

16 February 1894

Dear Sir,

  Many thanks for your letter, and should have liked very much for you to have rode up till Saturday.

  I think you had 12 lessons which you pay 1 shilling a day for grooming, as regards myself I will leave it to you, or would you like to leave the matter until your Father returns and I will pay the grooming, hope you will find the few lessons useful.

Yours very Sincerely

C. H. BURT

Lady Randolph to Lord Randolph
(Blenheim Papers)

EXTRACT

17 February [1894]   50 Grosvenor Square

. . . Winston has been up for the day – he looks much better. He has been riding and was put at the head of the class. He is delighted with his progress and the pull he has over the others. Your letter pleased him much. . . .

Winston to Lady Randolph

19 February [1894]   [Sandhurst]

Dearest Mamma,

  I had a fearful night on Saturday. The most awful toothache I have ever had. Not a wink of sleep – though I took two Sulphonels. Now however the nerve is dead & will give no more pain I hope.

I looked up Morris' bill—: it is as I thought £2.4.7. I will go and see him next Saturday when I come up and explain to him. Please send the things for the room. I do hope you will be able to *lend* me that chest of drawers. It would be so useful and convenient.

Do tell Healy to send the cigarettes – which I stupidly left in the brougham – also ask him to tell the laundress I am in want of linen & she must send that basket at once.

Now no more as I am going to get ready for riding.

With best love – you darling.

Ever your loving son
WINSTON S. CHURCHILL

PS How about Col Brabazon.

1 armchair
1 pr curtains.
1 carpet (room 15′ by 12′)
Chest of drawers & washing stand (combined)
pictures (as many as you can spare)
1 spring mattress (Everest wd understand it costs 8/-)
6 pillow cases (Their pillows are made of straw & I have got a good one of
                 my own but no pillow cases. Having been used for 6 months
                 it is now too dirty for further use – without a pillowcase).[1]
Anything else you can spare.

Winston to Lord Randolph
(Blenheim Papers)

19 February 1894   [Sandhurst]

My dear Papa,

I have had a very bad time of it for the last week, especially during the latter part with my tooth. But now the nerve has been killed and so I am alright and shall I hope have no more trouble. The riding here is most interesting and I got great "kudos" from the instructors and have been put at the head of the ride. It was quite worth while getting up early and taking those lessons.

I have had a letter from Capt Burt – in answer to one I wrote him about the charges of the riding. You will see that he does not "fix" any charge for himself. I find however in the Queen's Regulations the fee for a course of riding wd be 2 guineas – but this course would last 6 weeks. The grooming is 12/- and the man who used to get me my breakfast ought to have 10/- too.

---

[1] Throughout his adult life he took his own pillow with him when travelling.

Work is now in full swing and there is lots to do. The evening study is very tiresome as it keeps you hanging about the whole afternoon. I hear however that it is just possible that it will be discontinued.

Saturday and Sunday are terrible days here. Nothing whatever to do – but to live. I am coming up next Saturday and I hope to see you then.

With best love, I remain your ever loving son

WINSTON S. CHURCHILL

Lady Randolph to Winston

Tuesday [20 February 1894]   50 Grosvenor Square

Dearest Winston,

I will send on the furniture tomorrow – but I fear I cannot manage the washing stand as it is wanted here. Pictures ? & a pair of curtains. Grandmama has got some more pictures she can spare – if you want any more. I am so sorry you had such a bad time with yr tooth but it is all right now I hope. I feel too stupid for words with neuralgia – so forgive this uninteresting letter. Papa arrives this evening. I will write & tell you how he is.

I believe Mr Gladstone will resign before the end of next week.[1] He is nearly blind.

Goodbye for the moment. I will see about yr cigarettes & linen.

Yr loving
MOTHER

Jack to Winston

Tuesday 20 February 1894   Harrow

Dear Winston,

I received your letter. Thank you very much for it, letters are very scarce now. I wrote to Papa eight sides on his birthday and I have not had an answer but as he comes home today, and perhaps he will come down and see me then.

I have only had one from Mama, the whole time this term, I wish she would write a little.

Fancy the Francisiariun marriage being broken off. I wonder why. I am in great form here. I came out 4th, 3rd & 4th. Welldon was delighted. We had a lecture on the Matterhorn, by the man who first went up to the top. It was awfully interesting he had a Lantern and he explained how, out of the 6 who

---

[1] He resigned March 3.

went up only 2 came down and how the Rope broke and they fell 4000 ft in one jump, he and a guide alone got down.[1]

> I remain Your loving Brother
> JACK S. CHURCHILL

Winston to Jack

21 February [1894]   Sandhurst

Dear Jack,

   Thanks so much for your letter. I am so sorry nobody has written to you – but Papa has been, I expect, very busy. I shall be coming down to Harrow next Saturday and will wire my train.

   I forget whether I told you that Rome had got into the same Company.

> Your ever loving brother
> WINSTON S. CHURCHILL

PS Such a good letter you wrote me – & I am very sorry to have so little to say.

> WSC

Lord Randolph to Winston

21 February 1894   50 Grosvenor Square

Dear Winny,

   I am glad to hear your riding has been so successful at Knightsbridge. It just gave you about 10 p.c. pull over the others. When you come up on Saturday – I will give the 2 gs fee for the Captn Burt, 1 sov for the groom & a sov for the man who got yr breakfast. If they object to you giving those sums to the 2 last men you can say I sent it specially on account of yr success at Sandhurst & the benefit you received from only a few & interrupted lessons. I am glad that your tooth has been at last summarily dealt with. I strongly advise you to go to my old friend Pritchard 9 Albemarle Street. You don't want to be having your teeth pulled out or having nerves killed & he will not do the one & if he does the other he will do it painlessly but as he likes me very much he will probably do anything for you & I will make an appointment with him for the first Saturday

---

[1] Edward Whymper (1840–1911), whose party – four British climbers, 2 Swiss guides and a porter – conquered the peak on 14 July 1865. Whymper's three companions and one guide lost their lives during the descent.

after the next on which you can get leave. Why don't you read books on
Saturday & Sunday. I will send you some – anyhow you are coming up next
Saturday.

Yours ever
RANDOLPH S.C.

Your mother & I were taken [to] the "Gaiety Girl" at the Prince of Wales
(very good).[1]

Mrs Everest to Winston

21 February 1894   5 Cranmer Road

My darling Winston,

I have not yet made your Box cover the measurement you sent me I am sure
was not correct that Box is more than 18 inches long I know. So I have sent you
a piece of tape to measure it accurately put a stroke across it with pen & ink for
length of box & width & depth. Am very sorry to trouble you but I feel sure
you did not measure it correctly dear & it would be useless if it did not fit. I am
glad you have got a little room to yourself. I hope you have not taken Jackie's
furniture away.

I don't seem to have anything to tell you have not seen anyone or been to
London since I saw you. When do you come home again to stay, & When is
Jackie coming. I have postponed my visit to Miss Phillips till April as Jim will
be home from Africa then.

Well my darling old Boy I hope you have quite recovered from the Boils &
that you are feeling stronger & better in health altogether. Take care of your
health & don't tamper yourself with physic take plenty of open air exercise &
you will not require Medicine. It will ruin your constitution also your interior
such a mistake. Be a good Gentleman upright honest just kind & altogether
lovely. My sweet old darling how I do love you so be good for my sake much
love from

Your loving old
WOOM

---

[1] 'A comic opera of a somewhat advanced type', wrote *The Times* of its first performance on
14 October 1893. 'Licence is pushed further than has ever been attempted in our day. . . . In
the second act the scene is transferred to a plage on the Riviera, where all the ladies appear in
bathing costume and where the Judge and the Chaplain carry on an ardent flirtation with
Lady Virginia Forest in her bathing machine.'

Winston to Lord Randolph
(*Blenheim Papers*)

22 February [1894]   Sandhurst

My dear Papa,

I got your letter this morning. Thank you so much for writing to me – it is so good of you when you have so many things to do and think about. I read about your meeting in Paddington last night – in the *Standard*. It seems to have been very successful, and they seem to quite fall in with your intention of going to Bradford.

You are very generous in giving £1 to each of the men who looked after me at the barracks. I feel the benefit of my lessons – more every time I ride and hope to keep my 10% lead of the majority with whom I ride. Of course there are one or two who have ridden before so I am not so far behind as the remainder – but I am still the most advanced. We are going to ride in half an hour.

Everything is going on very well indeed here – I have got lots of friends and have no row with anyone – and in spite of the new alterations I like Sandhurst more than ever . . . (all the same I am always glad to get away on Saturdays). I shall go down and see Jack on Saturday afternoon he has written to ask me to come.

> With best love, I remain ever your loving son
> WINSTON S. CHURCHILL

Lady Randolph to Winston

TELEGRAM

23 February 1894

Plans for tomorrow night have fallen through do not give up your bachelor dinner write.

MOTHER

Winston to Lord Randolph
(*Blenheim Papers*)

27 February [1894]   Sandhurst

My dear Papa,

Captain Burt was not in on Sunday morning when I called. He had gone on leave; so I gave the man who got me my breakfast £1 and sent the other three that night to Burt with a letter.

It was impossible to get tickets for the Gaiety Girl or for any of the good pieces on Saturday night so we finished by going to the Empire after all. The Tableaux Vivants are very good indeed.

I was so glad to be introduced to Lord Roberts, and wish very much that I had not been so late for luncheon.

Jack was very well on Saturday and Welldon told me that he had been coming out high every week and would get his Remove again this term.

With best love, I remain, ever your loving son
WINSTON S. CHURCHILL

Mrs Everest to Winston

Thursday [1 March 1894]   5 Cranmer Road

My darling Winny,

I recd your letter last night & was very much surprised to hear Mamma had sent me a cheque. I have never recd either a cheque or a letter from anyone at G. Square. I wrote off immediately to that effect. I hope it has not got lost or taken in by someone else. I left my address with Healy & Paice also. I thought Her Ladyship would be sure to ask them for it if she wanted to send me a cheque. I hope it will be found.

Well darling I have been waiting to hear from you. I am very sorry to trouble you but I have lost the piece of paper you sent me with measure of the Box & it would be useless to make it a bad fit. Please measure it again & send it me at once & you shall have it without fail the beginning of next week Tuesday or Wednesday mind & allow it large enough. I enclose a piece of tape to measure with will you mark it with pen so sorry to trouble you dear. I am sorry you do not feel quite strong don't physic too much dear. I am thinking it would be very tiring for you to drag all down here Sunday week if you have to return to Sandhurst same evening. Would you like me to come to see you in the afternoon Sunday week about 3 oclock I could stay then till 8 in evening then when you have more time at Easter you can come down here it is so fagging for you in so little time. I had a letter from Jackie he seems to be in a good way with himself, dear little Man. Write soon & send me the tape darling or don't trouble to write send it without just put it in an envelope & send it off.

Much love ever your loving old
WOOM

Winston to Lady Randolph

2 March 1894   Sandhurst

My darling Mamma,

I am coming up to see Mitchell to-morrow. The dentist is going to take out the nerves & as they are dead it will not hurt. This will finish the business. I have had a letter from him telling me I must come or they will decay and do lots of harm.

I am only coming to G. Square for lunch. Please tell Grandmama. I hope to see Papa. He forgot to send my allowance so I am very short. Everest says she has not received the cheque. What could have happened to it.

With lots of love, Your loving son
WINSTON S.C

Winston to Lord Randolph
(*Blenheim Papers*)

2 March [1894] Sandhurst

My dear Papa,

I am coming up to London tomorrow to see the dentist. My tooth has not given me any more pain, but the nerve is dead and if not taken out will decay. I enclose a note from him in which, he specially states that he wants to see me.

If you do not mind I should like him to finish those two teeth and then change and go to Dr Pritchard.

I shall go back to Sandhurst the same evening.

The riding is still very successful – and I find it quite easy to ride without stirrups now. I have had a very nice letter from Capt Burt in which he wishes me to thank you for thanking him through me.

I suppose it is really true about Mr Gladstone's resignation. His speech did not seem a farewell oration. The papers seem to be all accepting and appropriating your prophesy of a dissolution in June or July.

Hoping to see you tomorrow, and with best love

I remain ever your loving son
WINSTON S. CHURCHILL

Miss Molly Hacket to Winston

4 March 1894 Hindlip Hall

My dear Winston,

Many thanks for yr letter which amused me so much but if you find out the real reason why Miss Guest's engagement was broken off, *do* tell me, as I want to know very much and *you* must know sooner or later.

I am so very sorry you have had toothache but hope you are now all right. I am having a little hunting which of course I just *love* – Aunt Minnie and Uncle Charlie started for Monte Carlo yesterday, how nice! I have no news.

Please give my best love to Lady Randolph how is dear Jack? Do you often hear from Alex, she is going to London on Friday. I suppose you will go and see her, how you will talk. I wish I could join you, what fun! I shall be very jealous if you go very very often to see her – but she is a great dear and so *amusing*. Ask her *from me* to tell you the riddle *I* made up!!

Such a cold wind here. Shall you take Alex for a walk?

Best love Yrs ever
MOLLY

Albertha, Lady Blandford to Winston

5 March [1894]   Blenheim

My dear Winston,

I was very sorry to miss you in Lowndes Square, where I was only for a few days, to see my sister Lady Lansdowne. When I go up there in May, I shall always be at home Tuesdays.

This little line is to tell you, that if you like to come over for a Sunday here, we shall be very pleased to see you, and you have only to telegraph. Sunny is still at Melton.

Yrs affec ever
"ALBERTHA" BLANDFORD

Messrs M. F. Dent to Winston

6 March 1894   33 & 34 Cockspur Street
                                                        Charing Cross
                                                        London S.W.

Messrs M. F. Dent beg respectfully to inform Mr W. Churchill that they find his gold watch requires new balance staff, minute wheel, and pinion, seconds hand, glass, re-adjusting compensation, repairing case and cleaning and will cost to put in order £3.

Messrs Dent have sent a loan watch by registered post this evening, and wait Mr Churchill's commands.

Winston to Lady Randolph

8 March [1894]   Sandhurst

My dear Mamma,

I am coming up on Saturday and intend to stay until Sunday night. I do hope you will be in town when I come. It will be such a pity if I miss seeing you.

The weather here is very bad and it is too wet for parade or any out door work.

I will give you the £2.0.0. when I come. At present I have a horrid cough & cold & do not feel very fit. There is no news of any sort from here except that everything is going on smoothly.

Longing to see you,

I remain, Your loving son
WINSTON S. CHURCHILL

Please excuse writing.

Jack to Winston

9 March 1894   Harrow

Dear Winny,

Lord Bobs [Roberts] came down here on Sunday. But Papa did not, still I went and talked with him for a long time in Welldon's drawing room after supper. Welldon preached a most grogy sermon you ever heared. I come home next Friday week. When do you *go on leave.*

Did Woom get her £17 all right. I have written to her but she has not answered me yet. I hear you were in London last Saturday. Pa sent me £1. You have never told the reason of the Francis's marriage breaking off. I have no more to tell you.

I remain Your loving brother
JACK S. CHURCHILL

Mrs Everest to Winston

8 March 1894   5 Cranmer Road

My Darling,

I have just recd your note with tape enclosed. I also duly recd your letter on Monday morning with cheque enclosed. Please accept my best thanks for same. It was very kind of you to see after it for me dear. I was very glad to find it had been returned to Her Ladyship alright after it had travelled about so much. I wonder it did not get lost. I am longing for a sight of you again so I shall do myself the pleasure of paying you a visit Sunday afternoon the day being nice of course if it is wet I must defer the pleasure till another day. Shall try to be with you by 3 p.m. on Sunday next – don't forget.

I have just written to our darling Jackie. He tells me he will be coming home next Tuesday week. Your letters are not very communicative short &

sweet. I should when you write like to know how you are dearest. I will not write more hope to see you Sunday with fondest love,

> I am ever your loving old
> WOOM

Winston to Lord Randolph

9 March [1894]   Sandhurst

My dear Papa,

I am coming up to-morrow and hope to get to London about 12 o'clock. But as they have recently taken to keeping us on parade until half past ten I may not be able to come so early.

I have had a very quiet week since last Saturday and there is no news. The riding is going on very satisfactorily & I still keep my place at the head of the ride.

This new governor – General East[1] is very different to the old man. He gets up early and peers about going into the lecture Halls and generally superintending things. Such a fine looking man – tall & broad – & simply covered with medals & clasps. Still his energy is very disquieting & everybody seems to have been well stirred up.

Hoping to see you to-morrow.

> With best love I remain Ever your loving son
> WINSTON S. CHURCHILL

Lady Randolph to Winston

TELEGRAM

9 March 1894

We are both going away tomorrow better next Saturday but do as you like.

> MOTHER

Lord Randolph to Winston

TELEGRAM

10 March 1894   Mount Street

No use your coming up today your mother goes to Tring I dine out and go to Tring tomorrow.

> FATHER

---

[1] Maj-General Cecil James East (1837–1908), appointed Governor of the Royal Military College in September 1893. Present at siege of Sevastopol and severely wounded in the Indian Mutiny. Created KCB in 1897; promoted General 1902; retired 1903.

Winston to Lord Randolph
(*Blenheim Papers*)

13 March [1894]   Sandhurst

My dear Papa,

I was very sorry to have missed seeing you on Sunday morning. I particularly told them to call me in time – but they forgot and I did not wake up until you had started.

Jack was very well and had been coming out high when I saw him on Saturday. Mr Welldon asked me to tell you that he was preaching next Sunday if you could manage to go down. He seemed very anxious for you to come.

This morning I was going towards the Lecture Hall when up drove Colonel Brabazon – magnificently dressed. He had come over from Aldershot to conduct a Staff College riding examination. He has asked me to go and stay at Aldershot the first Saturday we are here after Easter.

I went to the "Zoo" on Sunday morning with a very nice fellow – Hogg by name – some connection of Lord Magheramorne[1] and a cousin of Dudley Marjoribanks. We had the gardens all to ourselves and saw everything. Mr Jim Lowther[2] came to see Grandmama on Sunday. Thank you so much for going to get the book for me.

With best love, Ever your loving son
WINSTON S. CHURCHILL

Winston to Lady Randolph

14 March [1894]   Sandhurst

My dear Mamma,

I have been asked to stay with the Spender-Clays[3] for the Sunday before Easter. They have got a party for the Lingfield Races & their son, who is here & of whom I have seen a good deal asked me if I could come.

[1] Ian Graham Hogg (1874–1914), second son of Quintin Hogg and younger brother of Douglas McGarel Hogg, later 1st Viscount Hailsham. He was a nephew of 1st Baron Magheramorne. Joined 4th Hussars 1896, served in South Africa and Southern Rhodesia (DSO); died of wounds received on the retreat from Mons while commanding his regiment, two weeks after landing in France.

[2] James William Lowther (1855–1949), Conservative MP for Penrith division of Cumberland 1886–1921. He was Speaker of the House of Commons 1905–21, when he was created Viscount Ullswater.

[3] Joseph and Elizabeth Spender-Clay of Ford Manor, Lingfield, Surrey. Their only son, Herbert Henry (1875–1937), became a Captain 2nd Life Guards 1901–2, Lieut-Colonel Reserve of Officers 1918–20, MC 1917. MP for Tonbridge 1910–37, CMG 1918, PC 1929. He married Pauline, only daughter of 1st Viscount Astor, in 1904.

I said I did not quite know what my plans were for the holidays and was not certain whether I was not going to Paris.

However as he is very pressing I think I shall go unless you object or have something better on hand. Please let me know soon as if I cannot come they will want to fill up my place. I did not bother Papa with this matter.

I wish I were coming up next Saturday – but I had better stay down here. Hoping you are well & with best love

I remain Your loving son
WINSTON S. CHURCHILL

PS I am coming home Wednesday week & my visit wd last from Sat to Tuesday. Please excuse bad writing as I am in an awful hurry. (Many kisses.) x x x WSC

Lady Randolph to Winston

15 [March 1894]   50 Grosvenor Square

Dearest Winston,

I haven't a moment until my concert is over tomorrow. Papa does not object to yr going to yr friends for Easter Sunday. The enclosed[1] is sent by Ly Hindlip for you – it is Ly Sebright & Egbert!!

I will write again.

Yr loving
MOTHER

Winston to Lord Randolph
(*Blenheim Papers*)

15 March [1894]   Sandhurst

My dear Papa,

I got the book from Bain's two days ago and very interesting it is. It makes very pleasant and easy reading. Such a beautiful copy with most magnificent plans. I read your speech on Tuesday night very carefully and thought it excellent. I notice that you were very much down on Dr Macgregor and Campbell-Bannerman.[2]

[1] A visiting card was attached to the letter.
[2] On March 13, during the debate on the Queen's Speech Lord Randolph drew attention to the fact that Sir Henry Campbell-Bannerman was drowsing on the Treasury Bench. He also retorted to a point of order raised by Dr Donald MacGregor, Liberal MP for Inverness-shire 1892–5, by advising 'the honourable gentleman, who has passed most of his life in Scotland, but very little in the House of Commons, to be careful before he lays down a rule of order to the Chair.' Campbell-Bannerman (1836–1908) was at this time Secretary of State for War. He became Prime Minister in 1905.

Mr Labouchere[1] seems to be making trouble for the Government. I suppose Lord Rosebery has thrown over Home Rule! The riding is going very well and they have taken to making me ride the difficult horses as soon as their other riders come off. So far all has been most successful and Major Hodgins[2] – the Riding Master is very civil and takes great pains with me.

I am coming home on Wednesday for a fortnight and hope you will be in London then. Hoping you are well and With best love

I remain, Your loving son
WINSTON S. CHURCHILL

Winston to Lady Randolph

16 March [1894]   Sandhurst

My dear Mamma,

I just got your letter. It will be rather pleasant going to stay with the Clays – and I am told the Lingfield meeting is very amusing. On Wednesday I hope to see you when I come up. Everything is going on very well here – the riding especially, and I hope to satisfy even Papa at the examination at the end of the summer.

I am awfully hard up and wish you would send me a sovereign, as I am reduced to almost bankruptcy – having been so often to town. Please do or I shall have to stay here all the holidays.

I hope your concert will prove a great success – and that I shall see you on Wednesday at lunch.

With best love & many kisses I remain, Every your loving son
WINSTON S. CHURCHILL

Lady Randolph to Winston

Saturday 17 [March 1894]   50 Grosvenor Square

Dearest Winston,

I am not going to read you a lecture as I have not time – but I must say you are spending too much money – & you *know it.* You owe me £2 & you want more besides. You really must not go on like this – think of all yr bills besides! I shall see you on Wed: & we can have a nice talk. Papa is very well & in good spirits. Goodbye old Puss! I am rather X all the same you fleece me!

Yr loving
MOTHER

---

[1] Henry Du Pré Labouchere (1831–1912), Radical MP for Northampton 1880–1906, founder of *Truth* 1876. A flamboyant and popular politician, feared by opponents for his relentlessness in Parliament and his exposures in *Truth.*

[2] Jacob Hodgins (1837–), Riding Master at Sandhurst 1871–95.

Winston to Lady Randolph

19 March [1894]   Sandhurst

My dear Mamma,

Thank you so much for the magnificent & generous present. It was very good of you to send it. I shall be up on Wednesday and am very glad you will be there. Everything is going on very well – and I am looking forward to coming home.

With much love Your loving son
WINSTON S. CHURCHILL

Winston to Lord Randolph
(*Blenheim Papers*)

19 March [1894]   Sandhurst

My dear Papa,

I send you an account I have received from the 2nd Life Guards Mess Secretary. If you will send it to me I can send it off to them at once. I saw your speech on the Army Estimates and thought the whole thing very good. I wish you could have managed a word for the RMC. It would probably have a good result. We are going to get up at 5.30 next term in order to do the work which has been added.

I should so much like to continue my Riding lessons this holidays if you could see your way to arranging it. If I could begin on Wednesday morning the (28th) I should just get in 8 lessons. At present I am still leader and I should like to keep so. The book is very interesting and I am reading it steadily – but one can't read it rapidly as you have to follow everything on the maps.

Hoping to see you on Wednesday and with best love

I remain, Ever your loving son
WINSTON S. CHURCHILL

Albertha, Lady Blandford to Winston

19 March [1894]   Blenheim

My dear Winston,

Sunny hopes you will come here for Easter, so do, & write & tell me if you can come next Saturday. I should add that there has been a very bad case of scarlet fever at the Stables, but there is none there now, & I trust we have taken every precaution.

Yr very affecte
BERTHA BLANDFORD

H. Spender-Clay to Winston

[? 22 March 1894]   Ford Manor
                                                     Lingfield
                                                     Surrey

Dear Churchill,

Can you stay till Wednesday as we have the 2nd day of the Lingfield races then. Bring down your riding breeches in case we have time to ride.

                                              Yours sincerely
                                              H. SPENDER-CLAY

Can you come by the 5 o'c instead of the 4 as the others come then.

Winston to Lady Randolph

26 March [1894]   Ford Manor

My dearest Mamma,

I have only just got back from Eridge[1] and there are only a few minutes before post: So this must be shorter – even than usual.

I saw my portmanteau labelled and put in the Van at Victoria, but since then I have been unable to see or hear anything of it. Fortunately the cadet here is just my size and I am living on hope and his wardrobe. I have telegraphed everywhere but without result. Perhaps you will send me a wire directing me what to do about it.

Everything here is very nice and comfortable and I intend to stay until Wednesday morning – waiting for my clothes for one thing.

I have got a very bad cough & cold but am more worried about the tooth than anything else. I saw lots of people at Eridge to-day – Jack in great form. To-morrow there are the Lingfield races – which are only a mile from the house. With love & kisses – lots of both,

                                              Ever your loving son
                                              WINSTON S. CHURCHILL
"Gentleman Cadet"

Molly Hacket to Winston

[? 28 March 1894]   Hindlip Hall

My dear Winston,

I am so sorry not to have answered yr letter before, but I have been waiting for yr photograph which you promised and I want so much.

1 Where the Eridge Hunt had been holding its National Hunt meeting.

Aunt Minnie is in London till Fri: she has been ill so went up to see a Dr.
How are you and what are you doing.

I do not expect we shall be in London till after Whitsuntide but any how
when we arrive you will come and see me won't you?

Is Jack having holidays now, give him my best love.

Mr Angus is staying at Droitwich, he has been over to see us once or twice.

No news have you? We had our Point to Point races the other day.

Write me all yr latest gossipp like an angel Winston. I hear Lady Randolph
is in Paris.

We have had Mildred Hungerford[1] here for a few days!

Do you often see Alex? Charlie[2] returns to Eton to-morrow.

Don't forget the photograph.

Best love Yrs ever
MOLLY

Miss Mabel Love[3] to Winston

[? March 1894]   169 Buckingham Palace Road
                                                [London]

Dear Mr Churchill,

I signed and addressed the photos you sent me some time ago, and have only
just come across them finding they had been mislaid instead of posted, so am
sending a line to apologize for my seeming rudeness.

Yrs v. truly
MABEL LOVE

Miss Mabel Love to Winston

[? March 1894]   169 Buckingham Palace Road

Dear Mr Churchill,

I must apologize for not having returned the photos sooner but I have been

---

[1] Youngest daughter of G. Rawson Reid who in 1885 had married as his second wife Henry
Vane Holdich-Hungerford of Maidwell Hall, Northants.

[2] Miss Hacket's cousin Charles Allsopp.

[3] Mabel Love (1874–1953) made her first appearance on the stage at Christmas 1886, and
her last in May 1938. She was noted as a dancer and singer in musical comedy, burlesque and
pantomime.

very busy lately on account of my rehearsals for the Lyric.[1] I am afraid I don't know anything funny or amusing so have just written my name. I shall look forward to seeing you when you come to town.

Yrs sincerely
MABEL LOVE

George W. Wilson to Winston

Thursday [30 March 1894 ?] Bannockburn House

Dear Churchill,

Many thanks for your letter, it was really my turn to have written you. You are lucky to be able to get down to Harrow and see all your old friends especially Julian [Fisher]. Harrow and all my old "pals" seem to have vanished into the dim distance: you see I am quite out of the world up here. I have been in an office in Glasgow for about a month, not an enviable position, I *do wish* I had gone in for the army, when I was young, but as I am the youngest of three I should have been rather hard up. How is that young scamp Jack getting on, he has never answered my last letter; I hope he will get his remove this term; he will never get on very well unless he rises in the school, I mean as regards his form. How did you manage to meet Mabel Love, I rather envy you as pretty females are few and far between down here. Remember me to Wickham[2] if you don't mind, I expect he will have forgotten me by this time.

The only amusement I have had lately is football, and a good deal of that too. I see Marjoribanks has been appointed to the Renfrew Militia [3rd Battalion, Argyll and Sutherland Highlanders]. Poor Marjorie I expect he regrets his wasted time at Harrow. As regards Glasgow I have to start at 8 in the morning and get home at 7 at night so you see I have not much time to myself so I have some excuse for not answering letters, however I keep up a regular correspondence with Julian so that is why he knows about me. Have you had your photo taken lately! Please send me one if you have, or as soon as you are taken. Now don't forget this.

I am afraid Forman will be thinking that I have got to the dogs as I have never answered his last letter.

[1] On 6 July 1894 she joined the cast of *Little Christopher Columbus*, a burlesque by George R. Sims and Cecil Raleigh, with music by Ivan Caryll, which had opened at the Lyric Theatre the previous October. In 1895 Mabel Love appeared first at the Folies Bergères in Paris and then at the Broadway Theatre in New York, where she scored a success in W. S. Gilbert's comic opera *His Excellency*.

[2] Henry Francis Wickham (1874–1931) joined 1st Dragoon Guards 1896; served in Boer War; Major 1910; served 1914–18, Lieut-Colonel (two despatches); Third Afghan War 1920, CIE; Colonel commanding 5th Cavalry Brigade 1921–5.

We have had most peculiar weather lately, first hot, then snow and now hot again, I don't know how I shall endure an office in the summer.

I have really no more news, so with kind regards to Jack (when you see him) and yourself.

Believe me Ever yrs
GEORGE W. WILSON

Mrs Everest to Winston

Saturday 9 a.m. [? 31 March 1894]   5 Cranmer Road

My darling,

Just a line to tell you the trains do not run during church service time there is a train at 11 or a few minutes before & no other till 10 minutes to 1 o'clock. I will meet you at the station if you tell me the time you will [arrive]. If you come by the 1 train you will not get here till 2 oclock or after I shall have no time with you scarcely. I hope it will be fine.

Best love in haste to catch post.

Your loving old
WOOM

Lord Randolph to Dr Thomas Buzzard
(Buzzard Papers)

31 March 1894   50 Grosvenor Square

Dear Dr Buzzard,

I hear you are in town. Roose wont be back till the end of the week & Dr Stevens his representative is not the slightest use except for minor matters. I particularly want to see you & I should not trouble you if what I desire to put before you was not rather urgent. So I will much obliged to you if you will make an appointment to see me at your house some morning next week & the earlier you can make it the better for me.

Yours vy truly
RANDOLPH S C

Mrs Everest to Winston

Sunday 8 [April 1894]   5 Cranmer Road

My darling Winny,

I hope you arrived at Sandhurst alright & that you are quite well & the cough gone my sweet old Boy. I feel I want to see you every day – but it cannot be. Therefore I must be content with thinking of you & looking at your Photo. Well dear I am going to Barrow on Thursday or Friday next all being well. I am going up to see dear Jackie tomorrow & again on Wednesday. I expect he is with you today & while I am writing this. What a lovely day it is. Have you commenced your shooting yet. Did you find all your things right when you got back to Sandhurst. I am very well & happy only want two things to complete my happiness your dear self & Jackie's. I have enjoyed your good things very much but I must beg you not to spend so much of your pocket money on me again it is too good of you my darling. I hope you will be kept from all evil & bad companions & not go to the *Empire* & stay out at night it is too awful to think of, it can only lead to wickedness & everything bad. I cannot bear to think of you being led astray like that.

Goodbye my precious God bless you much love from

Your loving old
WOOM

Winston to Lady Randolph

10 April [1894]   Sandhurst

My dear Mamma,

Just one hurried line. I am so sorry not to have written before but I have had such a busy time getting straight and started that I have put off writing from day to day. I want to come up on Saturday. I can't endure two Sundays running at this place. All my friends are going away and one cannot work the whole time. I beg you to try and explain things to Papa should he disapprove. 5½ days will I labour & do all that I have to do & extra work on my own account besides – but Saturday and Sunday I love to get away and one cannot turn to a fresh week's work with any energy if one has not had a short break.

I shall go down to Harrow on Saturday afternoon and to the Empire in the evening. Sunday morning I will do some reading & return Sunday night. So you need not put yourself out to make arrangements for me. Good bye you dear sweet Mamma. I am indeed sorry to write such a scrawl but I am in such a hurry – to catch the post.

With best love and many kisses

I remain Your loving son
WINSTON S. CHURCHILL

Winston to Lord Randolph
(*Blenheim Papers*)

10 April 1894   Sandhurst

My dear Papa,

I am sorry not to have written sooner, but I have been getting started on the work of the term and so have put off my letters. Jack came down on Sunday and enjoyed himself very much. I think that he is already looking forward to coming here "officially".

The weather is very warm and the roads and heaths are thick with dust. We have been doing a lot of sketching – maps etc out of doors and it is very hot and uncomfortable work. The riding progresses very satisfactorily – it is very mild work after the Barracks. Everyone here is training or being trained for the athletic sports and giving up smoking etc. It is extraordinary the distances they run after 3 or 4 hours tramping over the roughest ground with a sketching case to say nothing of parade, riding and gymnastics.

I read your speech last night and thought it very good. From the way it was cheered it seems to have been a great success. I am watching the fullfilment of your prediction of a Dissolution in July – everything seems to point that way.

I should like to come up on Saturday for leave and will do so unless I hear from you to the contrary. Everything is going very well and I like all the work except the Gymnastics which are very tiring and a great bore.

With best love, Ever your affectionate son
WINSTON S. CHURCHILL

Winston to Frances, Duchess of Marlborough
(*Blenheim Papers*)

12 April 1894   Sandhurst

My dear Grandmama,

I should like to come up on Saturday and stay the night if it would not be inconvenient to you. What a tremendous success Papa's Bradford meeting was. I thought his speech was so good. All the leading articles were most complimentary. He is sure to win the seat.

I hope your cold is now quite gone and that you are feeling quite well now.

With best love, Ever your affectionate grandson
WINSTON S. CHURCHILL

Winston to Lord Randolph
(*Blenheim Papers*)

12 April 1894   Sandhurst

My dear Papa,

I must write and congratulate you on the tremendous success of your Bradford meeting. Mr Balfour's speech I thought splendid and yours was just as good. All the leading articles were capital. In case you have not time to read them all I just mention that the best of all were the *Daily Telegraph* and the *Morning Post*. You are sure to get in. Hoping to see you very soon and with best love

I remain ever your loving son
WINSTON S. CHURCHILL

Lord Randolph to Winston

13 April 1894   50 Grosvenor Square

My dear Winston,

I have to thank you for two letters. The Bradford meeting in St George's Hall was very fine & crowded in every corner. Mr Balfour made a very fine speech and received an enthusiastic greeting.

Now I turn to another subject on which I must write seriously. You have written two letters, one to your grandmother, one to me, announcing your intention of coming up to town on Saturday. Now to this I particularly object. You have been just one day over a week at Sandhurst & you get restless & want to get away. Now this is your critical time at Sandhurst and you have got to work much harder than in the former term. If you are always running up to town every week on some pretext or other & your mind is distracted from your work besides being an unnecessary expenditure of money. Now I am not [going to] have you this term come to London more than once a month, and I give you credit for not coming to London without my knowledge. Now it is no use your telling me there is nothing to do on Sunday, because you can do work on Sunday instead of loitering about as I expect you do & getting through riding school & that practice placed you ahead of the other cadets.

The same result will arrive if you devote on Sunday at least 3 hours of real study. You will have that advantage of extra knowledge over those cadets who take their leave for Saturday & Sunday, or who do nothing all day. You not only gain Sunday but you gain some two hours extra on Saturday. Now all this may seem to you very hard & you may be vexed & say that "all work & no play makes Jack a dull boy". But it is no use complaining about what I tell you to do, for if you act as I advise you, you will excel at at Sandhurst and the sacrifice of your taking your leave so frequently will be amply rewarded, and I shall be ten times more pleased with you than if you resumed your habits of coming to London many times in the term.

You are 20 & in November 21[1] & you must remember always that you are a military cadet and not a Harrow schoolboy. Now is the time to work & work hard; when you are in the regiment your work may be slightly relaxed, by the performance of regimental duties. But even then if you desire to be thought smart & well trained & well informed about all the details of your profession you should still carefully keep up all your Sandhurst acquirements. Why do I write all this. Because when you go into the army I wish you to make your one aim the ambition of rising in that profession by showing to your officers superior military knowledge skill & instinct. This is all written in perfect kindness to you. If I did not care about you I should not trouble to write long letters to you. I shall always take a great interest in you & do all I can for you if I am certain you are wrapped up in your profession. You need not answer this letter. I only want you to think over it and agree with it.

[Ending missing]

Jack to Winston

14 April 1894   Harrow

Dear Winney,

So sorry you are not coming down next Saturday.

I suppose you will be going to London though. I hope you wont forget the "Poor of Japan" when I left it had £1. 0. 5½ in. I have started one here and have about 5/- in it.

Grandmama gave me 10/- to come back with

I supposed you did not read *The Times* on Pa's speech one whole Page a great many Papers did not mention it.

I come home on the 1st of August we shall only have a month together I am afraid. I got my remove all right. Gore[2] has been made a Monitor and everything is being turned up side down here.

I remain Your loving Brother
J. S. CHURCHILL

P.S. try this nib it is a new school one.

---

[1] In fact, Winston was nineteen and not twenty until November.

[2] George Pym Gore (1875–1959) was, as a boy at the Head Master's, a noted cricketer, footballer and boxer. When he left Harrow he became a land agent and surveyor. He served 1916–19 as Lieutenant, Welsh Guards.

Mrs Everest to Winston

[? 16 April 1894]   St George's Vicarage
                                   Barrow-in-Furness

My darling Winny,

I have not had time to write before – I came here on Saturday late. Had a pleasant journey down & Miss Phillips met me at the station with the carriage. They were all very pleased to see me & are all very nice & kind. I think I shall enjoy myself here but they have a house full of visitors. The youngest son is at home for his holidays goes back to Cambridge on Thursday he is not one of my Babys he is just your age but not half as nice as my Winny.[1] Miss P. sends you her love & likes to hear me talk about you. She thinks like me that you are a dear old Boy. I had a letter from Jackie this morning he is very well & tells me you are not going to see him.

I have been out with Miss P. this Place is rather funny Docks & Ship Building. I will write more next time darling write to me please & send a nice little message to my little Ella. She will be so pleased. We are going to a Picnic one day – the sea is quite close & large Ships. I was so glad to hear you are so well.

Excuse the scribble the post is just going out.

                     Much love Dearest From your loving old
                                           WOOM

Winston to Lord Randolph
(Blenheim Papers)

20 April [1894]   Sandhurst

My dear Father,

I did not answer your letter of last Saturday – because you told me in it not to do so. Of course I willingly do what you think best in the matter of leave.

The week has gone very quickly as we have had a new time-table – which is to last throughout the summer. Parade at 6.15 and from then, work, until 2.15 with a half an hour for breakfast. This 7¾ hours work at a stretch is very tiring, but we get our afternoon's free – except for riding.

The Governor came to see us ride on Thursday. We did a lot of jumping without stirrups and a great many came off. I have so far avoided this. Everything is going on smoothly and the work especially well.

On Saturday I did about 4 hours work – as you suggested and in the evening

---

[1] Edward Fergus Phillips (1874–1903), an undergraduate at Corpus Christi College, Cambridge.

I went out to dinner with Mr Derenberg – who plays the violin with Mama and who lives quite close. He gave me an excellent dinner and so I passed a very pleasant Sunday.

I enclose the new time-table which will show you that we do not have too much time to ourselves. I wish you would sign the enclosure – it will only amount to 15/-. But the new rule is that you must get permission from home – just like Harrow.

I have joined a class for signalling which takes up three hours a week – but as it is most useful and will not be expensive I thought it better to join. The course is purely voluntary but the instruction is very good.

Mama wrote to me today and tells me she is enjoying herself immensely in Paris.

Do you think you could come down on a Wednesday – or a Monday or a Friday. If you can – do let me know and I will arrange everything. Wednesday is best because there is no work after 1 p.m.

With best love, Ever your loving son
WINSTON S. CHURCHILL

[Enclosure:] G.C. [Gentleman Cadet] Churchill may have lessons in Fencing.

Lord Randolph to Winston

21 April 1894   50 Grosvenor Square

Dear Winston,

I have received your letter of yesterdays date & am glad to learn that you are getting on well in your work. But I heard something about you yesterday which annoyed & vexed me very much. I was at Mr Dent's about my watch, and he told me of the shameful way in which you had misused the very valuable watch which I gave you. He told me that you had sent it to him some time ago, having with the utmost carelessness dropped it on a stone pavement & broken it badly. The repairs of it cost £3.17s. which you will have to pay Mr Dent. He then told me he had again received the watch the other day and that you told him it had been dropped in the water. He told me that the whole of the works were horribly rusty & that every bit of the watch had had to be taken to pieces. I would not believe you could be such a young stupid. It is clear you are not to be trusted with a valuable watch & when I get it from Mr Dent I shall not give it you back. You had better buy one of those cheap watches for £2 as those are the only ones which if you smash are not very costly to replace. Jack has had the watch I gave him longer than you have had yours; the only expenses I have paid on his watch was 10/s for cleaning before he went back to

Harrow. But in all qualities of steadiness taking care of his things & never doing stupid things Jack is vastly your superior.

Your vy much worried parent
RANDOLPH S. CHURCHILL

Lord Randolph to Lady Randolph

21 April 1894　　　　　　　　　　　　　　　50 Grosvenor Square

My dearest,

I was glad to get your letter & to learn that you were having such a good time. But when are you coming back? It is lonely in this house – breakfasting alone & lunching alone. I have written a letter to Winston he wont forget. I heard from Mr Dent yesterday when I was enquiring about my own watch that some time ago Winston let his watch fall on the stone pavement of the Military College, and broke it badly. The repairs cost £3.17s. But imagine only yesterday morning Dent received the watch which had been tumbled into the water, & found the works in a horrible state of rust & every bit of that watch had to be taken to pieces. I assure [you] the old Mr Dent was quite concerned at one of best class of watches being treated in such a manner. Well I have told Winston that when the watch is thoroughly put in order again I shall not give it back again as he is evidently not to be trusted with a watch of any value & I have advised him to buy one of those cheap 2£ watches. I told him that Jack had had his watch longer than he had his and the only payment I had had to make on Jack's watch was 10/s for cleaning before he returned to Harrow the other day. And I wound up by telling him that in all qualities of steadiness taking care of thing[s] and of not doing stupid things Jack was vastly his superior. You see I was really very angry for I cannot understand anybody not taking the greatest care of a good watch, but also because he had never told me a word about it. However as I said he wont forget my letter for some time & it will be a long time before I give him anything worth having. I wanted you to know this as he may tell you a vy different story.

Well my dearest I do not want to cut short yr time in Paris but I shall be glad when you return. You say nothing about my article & whether you had heard people speak of it. But I am afraid your circle does not trouble much about articles in reviews. My mother has enjoyed herself much at Brooksby and she comes up on Monday. The wind has gone back in the East and the weather is most disagreeable & inclement. Well goodby dearest I have got to write to my mother & have also to preside tonight at a Hospital dinner in the absence of Connaught who is at Coburg. That is a good marriage &

must give great pleasure to all our Royal Family the marriage of Princess Alice of Hesse to the Cesarewitch.[1] I dined with Labouchere last night and gave [him] such a dressing down as he never had in his life. *The Times* as usual reports my speech as badly as it can.

RANDOLPH S.C.

Winston to Lord Randolph
(*Blenheim Papers*)

22 April [1894]   Sandhurst

My dear Father,

I have been very unfortunate about the watch – which I kept safely the whole time I was at James's – during our tour of Switzerland – and all last term. But about 6 weeks ago I broke it and within a fortnight of its being mended it is broken again. So really I have had it for over a year without an accident and then come 2 in a fortnight. Yet I have been no less careful of it during that fortnight than during the preceding year.

The first accident was not my fault at all. I had a leather case made for the watch – during the daytime to protect it and I was putting it into it when it was knocked out of my hand by a boy running past.

This time I am more to blame. I placed the watch (last Sunday) in my breast pocket – not having with uniform a waistcoat to put it in – and while walking along the Wish Stream I stooped down to pick up a stick and it fell out of my pocket into the only deep place for miles.

The stream was only about 5 inches deep – but the watch fell into a pool nearly 6 feet deep.

I at once took off my clothes and I dived for it but the bottom was so uneven and the water so cold that I could not stay in longer than 10 minutes and had to give it up.

The next day I had the pool dredged – but without result. On Tuesday therefore I obtained permission from the Governor to do anything I could provided I paid for having it all put straight again.

I then borrowed 23 men from the Infantry Detachment – dug a new course for the stream – obtained the fire engine and pumped the pool dry and so recovered the watch. I tell you all this to show you that I appreciated fully the value of the watch and that I did not treat the accident in a casual way. The labour of the men cost me over £3.

[1] Princess Alice (1872–1918), a grand-daughter of Queen Victoria, married on 26 November 1894 the Cesarewitch, later Emperor Nicholas II of Russia. They were murdered by the Bolsheviks during the Russian Revolution.

I would rather you had not known about it. I would have paid for its mending and said nothing. But since you know about it – I feel I ought to tell you how it happened in order to show you that I really valued the watch and did my best to make sure of it.

I quite realise that I have failed to do so and I am very very sorry that it should have happened. But it is not the case with all my things. Everything else you have ever given me is in as good repair as when you gave it first.

Please don't judge me entirely on the strength of the watch. I am very very sorry about it.

I am sorry to have written you such a long and stupid letter, but I do hope you will take it in some measure as an explanation.

With best love, I remain ever your loving son
WINSTON S. CHURCHILL

Captain A. Armstrong[1] to WSC

EXTRACT

17 August 1908   The Wiltshire Regiment
                                   Parkhouse Camp
                                   Cholderton
                                   Wiltshire

. . . By the way, I saw a picture of you helping to put a fire out,[2] it reminded me of the incident at the R.M.C. when you lost your watch & you persuaded the whole of "E" Company to assist in pumping the pond dry. I always quote that when I hear people talking about your unpopularity. . . .

Lady Randolph to Winston

Sunday [22 April 1894]   Hotel Scribe

Dearest Winston,

I am *so* sorry you have got into trouble over yr watch – Papa wrote to me all about it. I must own you are awfully careless & of course Papa is angry after giving you such a valuable thing. However he wrote very kindly about you so you must not be too unhappy. Meanwhile I'm afraid you will have to go without a watch. Oh! Winny what a harum scarum fellow you are! You really must give up being so childish. I am sending you £2 with my love. I shall scold you well when we meet.

Yr loving
MOTHER

[1] Allan Armstrong (1875–   ), retired 1910.
[2] At Burley-on-the-Hill, a house near Oakham.

Mrs Everest to Winston

My darling Winny,

You are very naughty not to send me a line. I am very unhappy not hearing from you wondering what happened to you. Do send me a few lines. Did you get the letter I sent you last week. I hope you are all right. My Jim [Phillips] has not yet arrived from Africa. I have just been for a ride in the Steam Tram. There was a ship launched here yesterday. I shall be back again next week I think. I have not heard from Jackie this week. Please do write. With much love I am ever

Your loving old
WOOM

C. J. Balaam to Winston

23 April 1894   Verona Cottage
Newport Road
Ventnor
Isle of Wight

Dear Mr Winston,

You will probably be surprised at receiving a letter from me, so I will tell you at once that I am writing to ask you a favour. I think you know that I am at present and have been for the past two years in the service of the London and County Bank, where I receive a yearly salary of £85. I have been very fortune up to the present, having started at £60 in a Country branch, receiving £10 extra on account of having passed the Oxford Local (Senr). I got a £10 rise the first Christmas, and a £15 this Xmas, being moved to a Metropolitan branch. When I tell you that I propose trying to enter Rothschild's Bank, you may think that as I have so far fared very well in my present employment, I am too ambitious. I have, however, heard such glowing accounts of the way in which the clerks are treated there, that I think it would be a very decided advantage for me to get in there. Of course I know there may be many difficulties to contend with, but if I could once obtain the favour of your interest, which, dare I hope, might lead to his Lordship's, they could I think be overcome. There is a Clerk now in the employ of the L and C Bk, who will I think get an appointment in Rothschild's, his present position having been obtained for him by Baron R. So that he might have a year or two's experience, as they prefer their clerks to do. He is the son of the Baron's agent at Waddesdon, and it was whilst staying with him, I heard such glowing accounts of the Bank. Had I not known the kindness of your disposition, I should not have presumed to trouble you with my affairs. I should be very glad, and grateful to you, if you could favour me with your opinion as to my chance of success.

I must apologise for inflicting you with so much about myself, and must not forget to congratulate you on your successes, which one seems to take for granted, should follow his Lordship's son.

Thanking you in anticipation for a reply,

permit me to remain yrs obediently
C. J. Balaam

PS I am now on leave which ends Sat next, when my address will be
London and County Bkg Co Ltd,
Shoreditch,
E

Winston to Lady Randolph

24 April [1894]   Sandhurst

My dearest Mamma,

Thank you so much for your letter – which I have just received. Papa wrote me a long letter about the watch and seems to be very cross. I wrote back at once saying how sorry I was and explaining the whole affair & got a letter by return of post – last night. I think that by his letter Papa is somewhat mollified. I hope so indeed. But how on earth could I help it. I had no waistcoat to put the watch in and so have had to wear it in the pocket of of my tunic.

Papa writes, he is sending me a Waterbury – which is rather a come down.

I am very sorry it should have happened – as you can well believe – and sorrier still that Papa should have heard of it. But I feel quite clear in my own mind that I am not to blame except for having brought so good a watch back here – where there is everything in the way of its safety.

However a Waterbury is as the regulations say "more suited to my position as a cadet" and there is not much time to lament, here now.

It is so dear of you to have written me such a kind letter & for sending me the £2. You are the best and sweetest mamma in all the world. With lots of love & kisses,

I remain Ever your loving son
WINSTON S. CHURCHILL

Winston to Lord Randolph
(Blenheim Papers)

24 April [1894]   Sandhurst

My dear Father,

I know I have been very foolish and clumsy with the watch and fully deserve to have it taken away. I am very sorry to have been so stupid and careless – but I hope that you will not be cross with me any more about it – and that you will accept what I say as to being an isolated case of not taking care of things.

I remain ever your loving son
WINSTON S. CHURCHILL

Miss Molly Hacket to Winston

Thursday 26 April 1894   Hindlip Hall

My dear Winston,

Many thanks for your letter. I was very glad to hear from you again, but please when you've time will you write & tell me what you meant by yr "PS" saying – "acknowledge receipt of a half a photo of what might have been" – also tell me what *did* you mean about Nellie B. have you heard anything do tell me does he keep her in order? Has there been a "question"? You say I am to tell you all about what I have been doing, well I have done nothing, except been on the canal for a row & when driving in Worcester got run into by a dray!! I am just longing for London, Aunt Minnie is still in Hill St but I think the Dr is going to let her come down on Sat. You never told me how Jack is, give him my love. Such storms & wind & rain here. Alex seems to be amusing herself in London, altho everyone says nothing is going on there.

What is the latest song comic & otherwise, I am so tired of the "Rickerty Rackerty Cerew." I am so sorry for writing such a dull letterkins. I should not have written so soon but I want an answer!!! Aren't I very rude? Never mind please forgive I feel rather +. *Why* I can't say. I think it must be because it is a nasty day.

Best love Yrs ever
MOLLY

C. J. Balaam to Winston

26 April 1894   Verona Cottage

Dear Mr Winston,

I am extremely obliged to you for sending me a reply so quickly, and for the favourable view you take of the matter. As you say there is not the slightest hurry, the opportunity must of course be left to your kind judgment and convenience. You mention in your letter the salary that you will receive as 2nd lieutenant, but then you see you don't take up the army as a means of gaining a livelihood, or in fact with any pecuniary idea, independence being a necessary to an officer, and the pay being very immaterial to you.

I know quite well that I am at present doing very well indeed, and if in my present position at Christmas, I think I may count on an addition of £10, or perhaps £15 to my salary. It is not the immediate future that I was looking at, so much as after years, when progress in the London and County Bk is often very slow indeed. I have got testimonials from my schoolmaster and from the Vicar, which I think would satisfy your requirements, and could I think obtain others from the managers of the branches where I have been, that would also prove satisfactory. I must once more apologize for encroaching so much on your time and again offer my sincere thanks for the interest you have already taken in my welfare.

Of course, as you advise me, I shall not build too strongly on any hopes you may have held out to me. My father and mother desire me to convey their dutiful remembrance to you. Please accept our united thanks,

and believe me to remain yours gratefully
C. J. Balaam

PS My address at my lodgings is
16 Prideaux Road, Clapham S.W.

Colonel J. P. Brabazon to Winston

Thursday 26 April [1894]   IV Hussars
Aldershot

My dear Winston,

If you like to come over here Saturday till Sunday night or if you can stop till Monday morning I shall be very glad to see you. If you can come go & see Cap: Julian Byng[1] of the 10th Hussars who is at the staff college & who is coming over also. You might come over with him. Let me know by return post or better still by wire if you can come.

Yours very sincerely
J. P. Brabazon

---

[1] Julian Hedworth Byng (1862–1935), who in 1917 was to command the Canadian Corps at the capture of Vimy Ridge. The 7th son of 2nd Earl of Strafford, Byng was in 1894 a Captain in 10th Hussars. Later, during the Boer War, WSC once acted as his galloper. Governor-General of Canada 1921–6. Created Baron Byng of Vimy 1919 and a Viscount 1928.

Mrs Everest to Winston

30 April 1894   St George's Vicarage

My Darling Winny,

I was very much relieved & glad to get your nice letter & to hear you are going on alright & keeping well. I began to think you had forgotten your poor old Woom.

Well my sweet, you will be pleased to hear I am enjoying myself very much here they are all so kind to me I am made quite an old Pet of here. The Archdeacon[1] took us all for a Picnic on Friday 7 young ladies, Mrs Phillips & me & Charlie the Parson who is a great big man. We went Ambleside & Windermre the Westmoreland lakes we went down the lake 17 miles in a little Steam Boat had luncheon in a Wood it was such a lovely day warm & nice I did enjoy it the mountains & the scenery were splendid. Miss Phillips wants me to ask you to come down here for a few days but I told her you could not leave at present. They are awfully nice. I get lots of love & kisses now. I have been to several entertainments concerts &c.

My Jimmy has not arrived yet from Africa but they had a letter yesterday to say he would be here on the 7th so I am not coming back just yet till I have seen him. Miss P. wants me to stop a long time. I am glad to hear your Mamma has returned from Paris. I hope she is quite well. I shall not be able to meet you next Sunday my darling as I shall be here. I will let you know when I decide to return to London – in mean time I hope to hear from you once a week you can spare 5 minutes once a week can't you? Am so glad you keep well – lots of love & kisses to my Darling old Boy.

Ever yours affectly
WOOM

Winston to Lady Randolph

30 April [1894]   Sandhurst

My darling Mamma,

I hope to be able to get up to town on Saturday. I have not yet been up this term. Papa has not written to me for some time and I am uncertain whether he is still angry with me or not.

Do write me a letter tell me. The post is just going out so I must stop but tomorrow I will write you a much longer letter,

With much love Your ever loving
WINSTON S.C.

[1] Thompson Phillips (1832–1909), Archdeacon of Furness, Vicar of St George's, Barrow-in-Furness.

Winston to Lord Randolph
(*Blenheim Papers*)

30 April [1894]   Sandhurst

My dear Papa,

I got the watch on Saturday morning – for which many thanks. I do hope you are not angry with me any more about it. On Sunday I stayed with Col Brabazon at Aldershot. He very kindly asked me down and I enjoyed myself very much indeed.

We are going through a course of Musketry which is very interesting and which we all like as it does not begin until half past seven and so we get a little longer in bed. The riding is going on very well and so is work etc.

This morning I had a letter from a man offering to lend me money on note of hand – I took it to Major Ball and he has forwarded it to the Governor – but I am afraid there is no chance of bringing the man to book.

I will write to you again very soon – but for the present have nothing more to say.

Hoping that you will not think any more of the watch and with best love
I remain, ever your loving son
WINSTON S. CHURCHILL

Lady Randolph to Winston

April 30 [1894]   50 Grosvenor Square

Dearest Winston,

How are you? A bird whispered to me that you did not sleep in yr own bed last night. Write to me all about it. I am not sure if Papa wld approve.

If fine I am going to Harrow tomorrow to see Jack. I came back Friday evening very sorry to leave Paris which was delightful. I find London cold & dull. Papa is pretty well. When shall I come & spend the day with you?
Yr loving
MOTHER

Winston to Lady Randolph

1 May [1894]   Sandhurst

My dearest Mamma,

I have just got your letter. I should not think that Papa would object to my having stayed with Col Brab at Aldershot. He distinctly wrote to me that he did not want me to come up to London much. I wrote yesterday to him and told him all about it.

I should like to come up on Saturday as I have not been to London once this term – and want to see Jack & yourself. I altogether protest against being perpetually immured down here.

I had great fun at Aldershot – the regiment is awfully smart – I think they did not always have a good name – but Col Brab did not take long in knocking them into shape.[1] I met Capt Bobby White[2] who asked to be remembered to you.

How I wish I were going into the 4th instead of those old Rifles. It would not cost a penny more & the regiment goes to India in 3 years which is just right for me. I hate the Infantry – in which physical weaknesses will render me nearly useless on service & the only thing I am showing an aptitude for athletically – riding – will be no good to me.

Furthermore of all regiments in the army the Rifles is slowest for promotion. However it is not much good writing down these cogent arguments – but if I pass high at the end of the term I will tackle Papa on the subject.

I hope he is not incensed about the watch anymore. I wish you would send me a line on the subject.

Also I wd be very grateful if you would draw Papa's attention to the date (May 1) as I am not particularly rich owing to the £3 I had to disburse for my watch.

You are a darling mamma – and I hope to see you on Saturday.

With lots of love,

> I remain, Ever your loving son
> WINSTON S. CHURCHILL

Lord Randolph to Winston

1 May 1894   50 Grosvenor Square

Dear Winston,

You need not trouble any more about the watch. It is quite clear that the rough work of Sandhurst is not suitable for a watch made by Dent. I daresay you had a pleasant Sunday with Colonel Brabazon. I am glad to hear the work

---

[1] 'Brabazon made little attempt to conciliate. On the contrary he displayed a masterful confidence which won not only unquestioning obedience from all, but intense admiration, at any rate from the captains and subalterns. Some of the seniors, however, were made to feel their position. "And what chemist do you get this champagne fwom?" he enquired one evening of an irascible Mess president.' [WSC: *My Early Life*.]

[2] Robert White (1861–1936) fourth son of 2nd Baron Annaly, was at the time Captain, Royal Welch Fusiliers. Retired 1918, as Hon Brig-General (CB, CMG, DSO); died unmarried.

is going on well, and the riding. I suppose your old volunteer experiences will make the course of musketry less strange to you. Never attend to moneylenders, put their letters into the waste paper basket. If you would like to come up on the 5th of May I am afraid you won't find me at dinner for I dine at the Royal Academy dinner, but your mother will be here & you might do a play.

Ever your affte father
RANDOLPH S.C.

Jack to Winston

2 May 1894   Harrow

Dear Winny,

Why hav'ent I heared all these goings on before, how silly to have broken the watch!!!! Mama said Papa was furious, she came down here yesterday.

I believe were going abroad again as Mama goes to Ex [Aix] & Papa to Carlsbad.

What has become of the type writer? It is not in London and I did not see it at Sandhurst. I hope not [drawing]

Old Woom has been enjoying herself very much so she told me.

Do write!! and let me know how the watch happened. I know *Aldershot*, and I told Mama. I did not see anything [wrong] in going over to Colonel Brab.

Ma says she has been trying to get Papa to let you come up more often but he does not like it.

Do write!!!!!

I remain
JSC

Winston to Jack

[3 May 1894]   Sandhurst

My dear Jack,

So glad to get your letter: I did not write before because I had been very busy & had had lots of letter writing to do: Also I don't think you had better talk about not writing. I amused myself very much with Col Brab at Aldershot – such a smart Regiment the 4th Hussars. I wrote and told Papa I had been. He did not mind. Why should he?

As to the watch: its a long story, which when I come down on Saturday I will tell you. Papa is now soothed and has written me a very kind letter. Meanwhile I have an excellent Waterbury which keeps far better time than the gold one.

I am rather worried about the summer holidays as they talk of bringing us back on the 14th August which would effectually stop Switzerland. However I hope this is only rumour.

Well, Saturday afternoon, expect me by the usual train arriving 4 o'clock. We will then have a long talk.

The typewriter is here and is much used printing all the company notices. It is in excellent health and asked to be remembered to you.

> With lots of love Ever Your loving brother
> WINSTON S. CHURCHILL

Winston to Lord Randolph

3 May [1894]   Sandhurst

My dear Papa,

I was so glad to get your letter of yesterday & shall be delighted to come up for Saturday. It was very pleasant staying with Colonel Brabazon at Aldershot. He has made such a smart regiment of the 4th. They used to be considered very slack – but he has worked a wonderful change. It was quite extraordinary how clean and smart the men were. It was the first time I had ever messed with a regiment – and the ceremony interested me very much. In the afternoon we went for a walk to the Mausoleum Chislehurst.

Everything is going very well here and I am getting on steadily in my work. Out of a riding class of 29 there are only about 6 who have not yet been off – but I have so far avoided a fall. Next term I hope to be in the First Ride. However that is looking ahead.

I have nearly finished Hamley.[1] It is a very solid but interesting work. I am reading a very good book I got from Bain[2] on Artillery which will take some time. This letter consists entirely of "shop" but I know you take an interest and won't mind.

Thanking you once more for writing, & with best love.

> Ever your loving son
> WINSTON S. CHURCHILL

Dr Robson Roose to Dr Thomas Buzzard
(Buzzard Papers)

4 May 1894   45 Hill Street
Private   Berkeley Square

Dear Dr Buzzard,

I have seen Lord R.C. and in accordance with your letter I again asked for a consultation with you about his case, however he will not sanction another consultn. at present. Further I have this week written to my patient and

---

[1] Sir Edward Bruce Hamley, *The Operations of War Explained and Illustrated.*
[2] Lord Randolph's bookseller in Haymarket, now of King William IV Street.

stated that I considered he ought to give up public life at least for a while as I considered his nerve symptoms required rest, in that letter I also suggested a consultation. Do you not think we ought to write and jointly sign a letter to Lord R.C. urging that he should be guided by our advice and take a prolonged rest? Let me hear your views.

Yrs very try
ROBSON ROOSE

Lord Randolph to Winston

7 May 1894   50 Grosvenor Square

My dear Winston,
    Enclosed is cheque as per yr allowance. You would have had it on Saturday if you had asked me for it or you might have written to me on the 1st of the month to remind me. However I hope you have not been inconvenienced.

Your affte father
RANDOLPH S.C.

Winston to Lord Randolph
(Blenheim Papers)

8 May [1894]   Sandhurst

My dear Papa,
    Thank you so much for the cheque which I got by second post to-day. It did not matter at all & if it had it would have been my own fault for not asking you. Everything is going on very well. I will write again tomorrow – but the post is just going out now. So with best love, I remain

Ever your loving son
WINSTON S. CHURCHILL

Winston to Lady Randolph

9 May [1894]   [Sandhurst]

My darling Mamma,
    I *do* hope you will come down on Friday. I have got a luncheon ticket in expectation and I am sure you will be much amused. Also you will not have to stand but can come into my room for tea. I am afraid this catalogue of

R

"advantages" won't produce much impression but please come & give great pleasure to

Your ever loving son
WINSTON S. CHURCHILL

PS Do get me a dress to ride and either bring it or send by parcels post. Something amusing. If you can come: wire & I will send trains & will meet you with conveyance etc. wsc

Winston to Lady Randolph

10 May [1894]   [Sandhurst]
Darling Mamma,
     So sorry and disappointed to find you can't come down. Had hoped that you would have been able to spare a day – as tomorrow is the only day in the whole year on which the place is at its best & when every arrangement is made for visitors. If you could come after all I should be *so* pleased as I am sure you would not be bored. There is an excellent train leaving London at (Waterloo) 11.45 a.m. arriving 1.17.
     If you find that it is impossible to come Please try and get me a costume and send it by the *guard* of the train at 11.45. I will meet it. Try and get a *gorilla* or something amusing. I do hope you will do so as I have payed 10/- for the entrance and if no costume then I can't ride.

With best love Ever your loving son
WINSTON

I fear I have missed post.

Winston to Lady Randolph

13 May [1894]   Sandhurst

My darling Mamma,
     Thank you so much for sending me the dress which I wore & which did very well. I am having it carefully washed and will send it back tomorrow night. It was perhaps just as well that you did not come down after all – for it poured with rain the whole day and I am sure you would have been very bored.
     I don't see why however you cannot come down Wednesday. If you were to write to me and say you would come I could make all necessary arrangements and would meet you.
     I am going to dine to-night with Mr Derrenburg (that's spelt wrong) and so shall get an excellent dinner which consoles me for spending Sunday here.

I wonder if you would like to send me a little money as I am desperately short and have had to go about the whole month with a mess bill of £7. o. o.

We are going to march over to Aldershot on Thursday as guard of honour to the queen. Begging you to be generous, and with lots of love & kisses also hoping to see you soon,

Ever your loving son
WINSTON S. CHURCHILL

Mrs Everest to Winston

Tuesday 15 [May 1894]   St George's Vicarage

My darling,

I have been anxiously looking out for a letter from you for the last week but not a word from either of my Boys for 3 weeks nearly. It spoils my enjoyment here not knowing how you both are – but it is out of sight out of mind I fear with some People. I am not going back to London just yet have not settled when they won't let me go. Jim has not arrived yet. His Ship is expected to arrive any moment now at Liverpool we expect him early tomorrow morning we are all excitement. I am thinking I shall be quite spoiled here, these 3 young Ladies make so much of me. I hope you are quite well my darling Boy. Do send me a few lines. I wrote to you last it spoils my pleasure not hearing from you. Tell how your Mamma & Papa are when you write. I am quite well & very happy here – I get lots of love & kisses here too & I send you the same but do write please do to your poor old

WOOM

Lady Randolph to Winston

17 May [1894]   50 Grosvenor Square

Dearest Winston,

I am sending enclosed a cheque for £2. I don't wish to be disagreeable but I wish to remind you that this makes £6 I have given you the last month – in fact more – 2 sent from Paris, 2 paid to Healy & 2 now. I really think that Papa gives you a very fair allowance & you *ought* to make it do. He wld be very X if he knew that I gave you money. It is yr own fault if you spend all yr money on food & then have nothing for other wants. I give you warning I shall not give you any more.

Yr loving
MOTHER

Winston to Lady Randolph

18 May [1894]   Sandhurst

My dear Mamma,

I have been waiting in vain for a letter from you. In the last fortnight I have only had one letter from Everest. On Monday I did not feel at all well and have had such bad headaches all the week that I have not known what to do with myself. Today the Doctor has made me come into hospital. It is deathly dull and there is nothing to do. Altogether I am very low.

Yesterday there was a grand review at Aldershot. I was not able to go with the battalion but drove over and saw it – a very fine sight. There is no news whatever. Please send me a letter. I know you won't be entrapped into coming down here just yet. I hope you got the dress all right.

With best love I remain, Ever your loving son
WINSTON S. CHURCHILL

Winston to Lord Randolph
(*Blenheim Papers*)

19 May [1894]   Sandhurst

My dear Father,

I am sorry not to have written for so long but we have had Athletic Sports & a Review & other things & I have put off my letters from day [to day]. Since Monday I have been troubled with most abominable headaches & so I did not go with the battalion to Aldershot on Thursday – but was allowed to drive over privately. On Friday they made me come into hospital – and here I remain up to the present.

It is very dull in here – no friends & hardly any visitors – but I am reading up a very good work I got from Bain on Tactics & making typewritten notes, which passes the time away. I hope to be out on Monday.

The Review was splendid. I never had seen so many troops in the field at once. I got a very good place & saw everything capitally. Colonel Brabazon looked the smartest officer there & the Fourth were very good.

I had a letter from Jack today. He is looking forward to going to lunch with Lord Roberts tomorrow, & to seeing you.

As there is no delivery in London Sunday morning I am sending this to Jack who will give it to you.

Hoping that you enjoyed your week's fishing, & with best love,

I remain, ever your loving son
WINSTON S. CHURCHILL

Winston to Lady Randolph

19 May [1894]   Sandhurst

Dearest Mamma,

Our letters crossed. I was very glad to get a line from you at last. Thank you very much for sending me the cheque; which was very welcome – though I think I should have preferred a more gracious letter.

I am considerably better this morning, though they will not let me out of hospital yet. I can't understand what has been the matter – but I shrewdly suspect *liver* – though with the plain food & generous allowance of exercise I fail to see why. Extraordinary headaches all the week. Such a bore.

Everything seemed very crude here but I judiciously distributed a few half crowns and am consequently looked after *"en prince"*. The other cadets are too loathsome to be described. Such creatures as one would not speak to out of hospital. There are however only two of them and as they behave themselves and do not whistle[1] or sing or spit, (much) they can be endured.

There is not much news to be gathered in hospital, so you must excuse so stupid a letter. I think a few days quiet & rest & peaceful treatment will elevate my soul & strengthen my broken spirit.

Do write me a letter and tell me some other news, than the fact I have for some time recognised V.I.Z. that I spend too much money.

Looking for a letter and with best love and lots of kisses.

I remain Ever your loving son
WINSTON S. CHURCHILL

Mrs Everest to Winston

21 May 1894   St George's Vicarage

My Darling,

I recd both your letters & am very sorry to hear you are not feeling well. What can it be – I am afraid you are not careful about your eating. Have you tried some of Eno's fruit salt – it would do you a lot of good – take a teaspoonful every morning with the juice of a lemon & a bit of sugar it will do your liver good you try it. I expect you are very billious. You have not been bathing in the lake yet I hope. I heard from Jackie on Saturday he is alright & said he was going to lunch with Lord Roberts. Your Mamma has been down to see him. Have you seen the Doctor don't neglect yourself if you don't feel well darling a stitch in time *saves 99* & let me hear how you are as I shall feel anxious now you have told me you are not well. What about your gold watch have you got it

1 He was always particularly allergic to whistling.

back yet is it alright? Tell me when next you write. My Jim arrived last Wednesday looking like an Indian so brown. He & Ella are gone off to London this morning for 10 days so I am going to stay here till they come back so I shall not get back to London till the beginning of June I expect. Fancy what a nice long stay I have had. I have enjoyed being with all my chicks again they are all so kind and nice to me. But I am longing to see my two dearest Boys again. I hope my dear Winny is not being led away & getting into disipated habits – Jackie tells me you are only allowed to go to London now once a month how is that? Jackie has had Mr Little to see him he tells me. Write & tell me how you are darling. Take care of yourself – with much love

From your Affecte old
Woom

Frances, Duchess of Marlborough to Winston

21 May 1894   50 Grosvenor Square

Dear Winston,

Thanks for your letter. I think you will be sorry to see the misfortune that happened to me on Satr last. There never was such a daring robbery and I wd not have believed it possible. I enclose my letter to the *D. Tel.* in case you have not seen it as it gives the account of it. I am much distressed as the thief has taken every ornament and bit of jewellery I possessed.

I see your Father does not like you coming up on Satr – But I will find out.

He seems so anxious for you to work hard and steadily and distinguish yourself. I cannot imagine why you are in Hospital.

Your Father returned yest morn and went to Harrow when he arrived for the day to see Jack. He lunched with Ld Roberts and heard Welldon preach and supped with him. He seems the better for his Scotch trip. I have nothing to tell you & feel rather seedy and out of spirits.

Yr Affect Gdmother
F.M.

You may send enclosed to Jack.

Frances, Duchess of Marlborough to the Daily Telegraph

20 May 1894   50 Grosvenor Square

A WARNING

Sir,

I write to inform you of a clever and ingenious robbery which has been carried out upon me, hoping that my unfortunate experience, should you kindly give place to this letter in your paper may save others from the loss I have sustained.

I travelled up yesterday from Wimborne to Waterloo Station by the 1.40 train. My brougham and footman met me at the station. There was a great crowd of people and vehicles of every description, and there appeared to be no order or regulation about them. I walked along the platform almost to the end of it, following the footman who carried my dressing box, railway bag, cloak, and other articles.

The horse was fidgety and the crowd so great that the brougham could not draw up to the platform. The footman had to go through the first row of carriages to get to it and deposit his burden. He then helped me and my little dog through the carriages, and I am certain I never lost sight of him while I hurried into the brougham.

I was rather surprised when I got in to find the further door ajar and shut it, thinking no more about it. But when I got home the dressing box was gone, and it flashed across me that the thief must have noiselessly opened the door and abstracted the box and not shut it, as the bang of the door would have betrayed him. The moral I have learnt is, get into the carriage first and then have your goods put in.

I do not expect ever to see mine again. Among the contents of the dressing-box were some trinkets, bracelets, and brooches, which were more precious from their associations than their intrinsic value. The thief will make little profit among these, and it would, perhaps, be more profitable for him to restore the box.

I am, Sir, your obedient servant
F. MARLBOROUGH

Winston to Lord Randolph
(Blenheim Papers)

21 May 1894   Sandhurst

[Typewritten]

My dear Papa,

I am afraid that the last letter I wrote to you has not yet reached you. I wrote it on Saturday night and posted it to Harrow, telling Jack to give it to you, thinking that, there being no delivery in London on Sunday morning, you would get it quicker. But apparently it did not reach Harrow until the Monday, so Jack is sending it on to you. I was so sorry to hear of the robbery of Grandmama's dispatch box. I had a letter from her this morning, telling me about it.

Perhaps you will remember my writing to you about a letter I had from a moneylender and which, according to the College orders I gave to my Company Officer. Well yesterday the Governor sent for me and told me they had taken counsel's opinion about it (Mr Gill's)[1] and were probably going to prosecute. He also said that he especially commended me for having reported the matter, and was very aimiable. I am afraid I shall have to be a witness.... I could not help it as I merely did what the "Governor's orders" say, but perhaps nothing will come of it.

I got out of hospital on Sunday and have been quite well since. Everything is going on very well here. Please excuse the Typewriter.

With best love, I remain ever your loving son
WINSTON S. CHURCHILL

Legal Opinion of Charles F. Gill

17 March 1894

Betting and Loans (Infants) Act 1892.

Re Letter addressed to Gentleman Cadet W. L. S. Churchill, signed Fred Ellis.

It is unfortunate in this case that the envelope containing the letter of 14 April signed Fred Ellis was not preserved as if it had been and was in fact addressed to Mr Churchill at the Royal Military College, there would have been a clear case capable of easy proof against the sender of committing the misdemeanour created by the 2nd Sec of 55 Vic C 4.

I do not think that the postscript would afford the sender any protection under the circumstances.

The fact of the heading of the letter bearing the address Blenheim, Woodstock, would suggest that Mr Churchill may be possibly be mistaken in supposing that the envelope was addressed to the College and not re-directed from Blenheim. If however Mr Churchill has a clear and distinct recollection of the address on the envelope and can swear positively that it was addressed to him at the R.M. College, I should advise a prosecution in this case. A proof might be taken from him as to the reasons which enable him to speak with confidence as to the address on the envelope and also as to what has become of it, and some enquiry should be made as to whether a circular of a

---

[1] Charles Frederick Gill (1851–1923), Senior Counsel to the Treasury 1892–9. Secretary to the Jockey Club 1903–22. Knighted 1921.

similar character was received at or since that date by any other student at the College.

It might be possible for Mr Churchill to say whether any letters were forwarded to him from Blenheim at or about that time, perhaps Mr Churchill showed the circular and the envelope to some person at the College who could speak to the address. In the absence of the envelope it is important if possible to get some evidence to corroborate Mr Churchill's memory.

The really material point to prove in any case of this kind is the fact of the circular being addressed to the University College School, or other place of Education. As it is that fact which raises the presumption against the sender that he knew the person addressed was an infant and it was no doubt for this reason that Sir Augustus Stephenson[1] in his letter of July 24 1893 pointed out the importance of preserving the envelope, or wrapper in which any circular was enclosed as well as the circular itself.

CHARLES F. GILL
Temple Gardens

Duke of Marlborough to Winston
(*RMA Sandhurst Archives*)

24 May 1894   18 Lowndes Square

My dear Winston,

Many thanks for your letter. The money lender's letter was forwarded on to you from Blenheim as Lilian opened it by mistake it being put among her correspondence. I am afraid that you will therefore be unable to prosecute the man, which I am sorry for as I have no doubt he deserves to be scored off.

In haste Yrs ever
MARLBOROUGH

Jack to Winston

[? 23 May 1894]   Harrow

Dear Winney,

I drove over to Luncheon (only 3½ miles) and there was shown into a very Indianfied room, he was out or something so I looked round and saw a sort of Butterfly case on the wall. I went for a nearer inspection and found them to be Medals!!!! of every discription under the sun. VC was among them. Then we went to meet Papa. Lord R. [Roberts] got in the little cart and the poney stood on its head, and he sat motionless, then it ran into a wall an smashed all

[1] Augustus Frederick William Keppel Stephenson (1827–1904), Director of Public Prosecutions 1884–94.

the back of the cart he seemed rather to like it and at last I got in and we went off alright. [Drawing] Papa missed his train I think or something he did not arrive till the end of Luncheon. Then he came to Harrow. But Ld R. did not stop to chapple.

I had supper with Welldon!!! etc and Skewd Prep this morning. Tell Rome "Spaniard" being a "Pot hunter" desires the jumping "pot" which he has kept about 3 years.

JACK

Your letter arrived Monday morning.
I saw in the *Standard* "The Cadets marched wonderfully"
I thought you were not there.

Lady Randolph to Winston

24 May [1894]   50 Grosvenor Square

Dearest Winston,

I have not felt much worried about you as Mr Derenburg told me you dined with him on Sunday & made an excellent dinner. Perhaps you will not have been surprised at my not writing, when you consider the tone of yr letter to me. Yr Father wld have been anything but pleased at it. However I did not show it to him as you know & as I don't consider it my "nature" to lecture we will say no more about it. My only way of showing my displeasure is by silence! I am glad you are all right again & that the weather is a little more decent. I think Papa looks much better since his week in Scotland. He is going to stay with Ld Rosebery for Epsom which he will like. I can come & see you one day next week if you like & we can have a nice talk. Sunny was in the park this morning & asked most affectly after you. By the way, the Duchess of Abercorn[1] gave a dance last night & asked you. If you want to be particularly civil & be asked again you might write to her thusly –

"Dear Duchess,

I am so very much obliged to you for sending me an invitation to your ball last night – & only regret that I was unable to avail myself of it. Yours sincerely
Address.   Her Grace the Duchess of Abercorn,
                    Hampden House
                    Green Street
                    London W.

[1] Mary Anna Curzon (1848–1929), fourth daughter of 1st Earl Howe, wife of James, 2nd Duke of Abercorn, whom she married in 1869. She had nine children, seven of whom died before her.

Now goodbye for the pres Write to Jack sometime. Uncle Moreton arrived from Austria yesterday looking very well.

Write.   Yr loving
MOTHER

Winston to Lady Randolph

25 May [1894]   Sandhurst

My darling Mamma,

So glad & delighted to get your letter. Am very sorry indeed you are not pleased with my last epistle but can't possibly imagine what I said to anger you. Yesterday I went over to see the Queen's Birthday Review at Aldershot. Very splendid – I saw Col Brab who took me home & gave me lunch with the mess. Do thank him when you see him.

When I returned I heard of such a horrid thing. A poor cadet had been drowned that morning in the lake – upset out of the very sailing [?boat] I had been using, not an hour before. About 6 weeks ago I got turned over there but though I had very heavy boots on & the water was cold I got out easily thanks to "Ducker." Very sad. All leave stopped Sunday as there is a Military Funeral.

I am going to dine with Mr Derenberg. On Sunday night, he has just sent me an invitation. They give excellent dinners which are thoroughly appreciated. Do come Down on Wednesday and scold me. Am writing again tomorrow – for the present lots of love & kisses.

Your loving son
WINSTON S. CHURCHILL

Winston to Lord Randolph
(Blenheim Papers)

25 May [1894]   Sandhurst

My dear Father,

How kind of you to have written me such a long account of your visit to Harrow! Jack wrote too, & told me how much he had enjoyed it. He was very much impressed by the pony & Lord Robert's medals – & also by being asked to supper with Mr Welldon. Such an honour – I cannot ever remember a Lower Boy going before.

There has been a terrible accident here. A cadet was drowned yesterday in the lake while sailing. He was an Eton boy too & a moderate swimmer but I believe he got hit on the head first with the boom. The consequence is we have a Funeral on Sunday & all leave stopped.

I always write "Dear Papa" first & have to tear up the sheet of paper before I can get it right. I read your remarks last night & thought them very scathing for Sir William [Harcourt]. You will excuse so hurried a letter as I am going to write again tomorrow.

> With best love, I remain, ever your loving son
> WINSTON S. CHURCHILL

PS So glad to hear you are so well after Scotland. I did not miss any work while in hospital as the Woolwich Sports were on Friday and Saturday is always a holiday. WSC

Winston to Lord Randolph
(Blenheim Papers)

27 May 1894   Sandhurst

[Typewritten]

My dear Father,

We have had a very sombre Sunday. All the morning was taken up with the funeral of the boy who got drowned and with the ordinary Church Parade. I was very much impressed with the ceremony. They had a gun from Aldershot and all the detachments of men here turned out. Then all the officers and many from the Staff College followed walking two by two, the junior in front and the Governor last of all. The cadets of his Company fired three volleys over the grave and then we all marched away to the liveliest of tunes. It was a very sad thing and I am very glad it is over, especially as we had to stand without helmets in the pouring rain. I wonder if you could come down sometime in the next few weeks! I am quite sure that it would interest you. Tonight I am going out to dinner with Mr Derenberg and as they have asked Prince Teck[1] it will be very pleasant. The work is going on very well and everything is going on alright. The moneylender and prosecution has fallen through, which is just as well as it would have been a great bore to have to give evidence. Please excuse the typewriter as I can write nearly as fast as by hand and it is much less laborious and much neater.

> With best Love, I remain, Ever your loving son
> WINSTON S. CHURCHILL

[1] Francis, Prince and Duke of Teck (1870–1910), a brother of the Duchess of York, later Queen Mary.

Lord Randolph to Winston

28 May 1894   50 Grosvenor Square

My dear Winston,

I have to thank you for two letters. I am very glad to hear you have got out of the hospital. Sick headaches sound much like biliousness of which Roose would have cured you in 24 hours. I went to Grove Park to lunch with Lord Roberts and Jack was there. Lord Roberts drove us over in his pony cart in rather showery weather to Harrow. He did not remain & would not get out of his cart as the pony could not be with anyone else. He is a Waler "Service" Australian pony & not quite safe in harness. I believe he had kicked up a fine row in the morning before I arrived when Ld Roberts started with Jack to meet me at the station. He stood on his hind legs & backed the cart against the coachhouse door inflicting some damage on the back panels. When I was being driven to Harrow he started quiet enough & remained quiet for he had been pacified with lumps of sugar by Miss Roberts. Well Mr Welldon insisting on Jack & I having tea in his drawing room alone, as he said he had some hard work to do. I expect thoughts on sermon, which I afterwards heard & thought a very fine one. It was Trinity Sunday which gave him a good subject I heard him much better than the last time I was there. There is going to be a great celebration of the Speech-day this year as the Prince of Wales is going down & I believe the town is to be decorated particularly all the school houses with flowers & flags and there will be great rejoicing. I shall go down probably with His Royal Highness. The Duke of Cambridge is dining here next Wednesday, & we have a party to meet him. I go to the Durdans for the Epsom week. Rosebery has his usual party & will in all probability take the Derby winner home for "Ladas"[1] will be stabled at the Durdans.

I do trust you may be able to make up for the time which must have been lost in the hospital & that you will have care in your diet & in your manner of eating. Eating fast, as you do, is a fertile source of indigestion biliousness & heated blood producing boils. Any doctor would tell you so and till you learn to chew your food properly, as I do to the great benefit of my health, you will always be subject to derangements of the digestive organ, which if they continue long may become chronic.

You oscillate between "Dear Father" and "Dear Papa". I think you had

---

[1] Lord Randolph's forecast proved correct: on June 6 Ladas II won the Derby at 9 to 2 on. Twenty-five years earlier, while still at Oxford, Lord Rosebery had bought the first Ladas. Bidden by the Dean to choose between Christ Church and Ladas, Rosebery chose the horse and was in consequence sent down; but in the Derby of 1869 Ladas, at 60 to 1, came last.

better stick to the former. Now Goodbye. Work as hard as you can, take care of yourself.

Ever y. affte father
RANDOLPH S.C.

I forgot to tell you that Jack was greatly honoured on Sunday evening. I told him Mr Welldon would ask him to supper. But he replied that he would only be asked in after supper as Mr Welldon never asked more out of the school than the two sixth form boys who read the lessons. Sure enough however Mr Welldon did tell him to come into supper & afterward to sit in the drawing room till I went away at nine o'clock.

Mrs Everest to Winston

Wednesday [30 May 1894]   St George's Vicarage

My darling

I was very glad to get your two letters & to hear you are quite well again take care of your health don't abuse it by too much smoking or gorging unwholesome diet such as cucumbers[1], Pastry &c.

Well dear I am very sorry not to be in London for Saturday to meet you as I shall not see you for another month now – but it is like this dear Miss Phillips went to London last week & does not return until Saturday & she wants me to stay here till she comes back & I promised her I would do so but had I known sooner you would be in London I would have come back this week. I intend coming next Tuesday if all's well. I have been here 2 months & I feel all the better for the nice change – the open sea is only a mile from the vicarage nice bracing air.

Well my darling I heard from our dear Jack on Monday, he has been to see Lord Roberts & His Lordship has been down to Harrow to see him. He writes in very good spirits is quite well. I shall go & see him when I get back. I suppose I shall not see much of you in your holidays you will be going abroad again most likely. How are your Mamma & Papa keeping well I hope. My quarters money is due on 1st July from 1st of April then I will get you to intercede for me. We have been having very cold weather here – you never tell me a word of news. I see the Duchess has had her dressing case stolen out of her carriage at the station lately. Write soon my precious old darling much love,

From your loving old
WOOM

---

[1] In later life they tended to give him indigestion and he always eschewed them before making a speech.

Winston to Jack

5 June 1894   Sandhurst

[Typewritten]

My dear Jack,

Here is the letter I promised to write to you about my stay in London. I went back and got a very good room at the corner of Jermyn street, had an excellent dinner at the Berkeley, and then went on [to] the Empire. On Sunday I went and lunched with Clay, and had tea with Molly Hackett. I am going to bring her down to Harrow next Saturday if Aunt Minnie will allow it. Well altogether had a very pleasant Sunday and not too expensive. I have written to Papa to ask him if he minds my going to the Derby. They have got a special from here which just gets in to Epsom in time to see the race. I suppose if it keeps dry that Ladas is a certainty, but I confess I should like to put a little on Galloping Dick. However I am not going to bet. The typewriting is getting on famously as you will see and I have only taken about as [long] over this letter as it would have taken me to write by hand. Do send me a line to let me know where you came out and how you are getting on etc etc.

I am afraid there is not much news and I have heard from nobody so cannot tell you anything. I hope to turn up next Saturday but will write early and let you know.

With best love I remain, Your loving brother
WINSTON S.C.

Winston to Lady Randolph

5 June 1894   Sandhurst

[Typewritten]

My dear Mama,

I hope you have no old fashioned prejudices against the Typewriter. I sent you a telegram to day to ask if Papa had got the letter that I wrote to him last night. I was seized with a wild desire to go and see the Derby. The other cadets are getting up a special and I could without missing my work get to Epsom in good time to see the Race. So I wrote to Papa, as I did not want to go incognito and have to pay all my own expenses etc. also thought that he might not approve of my going without asking. If you see him please make a combined assault with me. Send me a wire early as I should have to start at one. I hope to come up next Saturday and shall see you should you not see me tomorrow. What a great success the Bradford meeting was.

Ever your loving son
WINSTON S. CHURCHILL

PS Lots of love.

Dr Thomas Buzzard & Dr Robson Roose to Lord Randolph
(Buzzard Papers)

4 June 1894   74 Grosvenor Street
Copy

Dear Lord Randolph Churchill,
    In reference to your projected tour, since our meeting on Friday we have
been thinking over the matter, & it appears to us certain that 1st you should
not at present definitely arrange the extent in distance, & duration in time of
your trip. 2ndly that considering the season (June) in which you start you
must certainly not go to the United States, where, at this time of year, the heat
is more often than not extreme. 3rdly In the first instance it is our decided
opinion that you should go for a time to some near place, Norway for example,
where good fishing will be attainable, & that you should take with you a
medical man & your servant. After this visit you should return to England &
further arrangements should be dependent upon circumstances.

Yours very truly
T. BUZZARD
ROBSON ROOSE

Lord Randolph to Dr Thomas Buzzard
(Buzzard Papers)

5 June 1894   The Durdans[1]
                                               Epsom

Dear Doctor Buzzard,
    The contents of your letter filled me with surprise. Only a week ago or so I
laid my plans before you & both Roose & yourself fully approved of them. On
that approval I have made all my arrangements which cannot now be
altered. I have taken my passage I have made all arrangements for letters of
credit, & for letters of recommendation. I have ordered my outfit and done
everything that was necessary, and now you tell me to go to Norway. What
should I do in Norway, I have no fishing in Norway & should have absolutely
nothing to do. I have an opportunity of going round the world & I shall
certainly avail myself of it. It is not correct to say that it will be very hot in
New York in July. When I was in New York in 1876 the early days of July
were temperate. The great heat did not come on till August. But in any case
I cannot change my plans & on the 27th of June Lady Randolph & myself

---

[1] One of Lord Rosebery's houses.

sail in the White Star SS *Majestic* & I hope you will get me an agreeable &
clever doctor.

Yours vy truly
RANDOLPH S. CHURCHILL

Lady Randolph to Dr Thomas Buzzard
(*Buzzard Papers*)

Wednesday [6 June 1894]   50 Grosvenor Square

Dear Dr Buzzard,
    Can you tell me if you have heard from Ld Randolph in answer to your
letter of yesterday? I saw him at Epsom yesterday but he did not mention the
subject. I am afraid it will take a great deal of persuasion to make him give
up his plans. He seems in good spirits & quite himself – but he looked very ill
& was very restless. If you could let me have an answer before 12 – I would be
much obliged to you.

Yours sincerely
JENNIE SPENCER CHURCHILL

Dr Thomas Buzzard to Lady Randolph
(*Buzzard Papers*)

6 June [1894]   [74 Grosvenor Street]

    I have had a letter from Ld R C who seems to think it impossible that his
plans can be altered. Perhaps on his return to town some modification may
be arranged.

Yrs sincerely
T B

Winston to Lord Randolph
(*Blenheim Papers*)

7 June 1894   Sandhurst

[Typewritten]

My dear Father,
    Thank you so much for your telegram. I had hoped that my letter would
have reached you in time, but it was forwarded from London and I think
got delayed there. I did not like to send a telegram as I thought the letter was

rather a forlorn hope and that a wire would have to be very long to have been explicit. I wish indeed that I had. What a capital horse. I suppose you backed him even though you had to give the odds. If your Epsom Meeting is half as successful as your Bradford meeting you ought to have a very good week. Next Saturday I should like to come up to town very much, if you don't mind. Everything is going on very well especially the riding at which I am making much progress. The examination at the end of the term is going to be set by the Headquarter Examiners, instead of the old fossils here so I hope to benefit by the extra work I have done in Hamley, Mayne, and Prince Kraft [Military text-books]. Will you be going to Ascot? That is the great event of the year here. We can get over all three days but not always in time for the first race. You see that it is only 4 miles. With best love and wishing you very good luck and a pleasant meeting,

Ever your loving son
WINSTON S. CHURCHILL

Mrs Everest to Winston

7 June 1894   St George's Vicarage

My darling Winny,

Many thanks for your letter recd yesterday. Am so pleased to hear you are so well & happy – I am thankful to say so am I only longing to see my Boys again. Well dear you know I intended going back to London last Monday but they would not let me go. The Archdeacon is such a dear good kind gentleman he came upstairs & said you must not go away from us yet – we like having you here so much we really can't spare you yet you must stay with us till the winter comes. But I want to get back now to get some cooller clothes to wear & to see my Darlings. I have spent a very happy time here they are all so kind. We have had the Bishop of Carlisle[1] & his Daughter staying here – he held a visitation in the Church this morning for the Clergy & Church Wardens. I went in to see the procession. There were the Chancellor & the Chaplain in their wigs. After that we went to see a big ship launched at the Docks & saw all the ships being built they often have a ship launched here. They had a big dinner party here last night to meet the Bishop & a reception yesterday the Mayor & Mayoress &c. so it had been quite gay here in a clerical way.

Well my darling I shall not come back on Saturday as you say it is uncertain whether you will be in Town. The weather has changed here the last 2 days have been nice & warm & fine. I had a letter from Jackie this morning he said you went to see him last Saturday – he has got a Camera sent me a photo he

---

[1] John Wareing Bardsley (1835–1904), Bishop of Carlisle since 1891.

took of a shop [? of] Conway's. Miss P. desires her very kind regards to you & accept my best love my darling ever

Your fond old
WOOM

Lord Randolph to Winston

19 June 1894   50 Grosvenor Square

My dear Winston,

How stupid you are you do not stick to "my dear father" & relapse into "my dear Papa". This is idiotic. I am glad Little will go with you and Jack. You will see yr mother on Saturday but you won't see me as I am going to Paris on the morning of that day.

Yr affte father
RANDOLPH S.C.

Lord Randolph to Winston

24 June 1894   50 Grosvenor Square

My dear Winston,

I will see about the Club. You write stupidly on what you call "the subject of finance". "You said I would start a banking account for you and give you an extra ten pounds for Switzerland".

"But what disturbs me is that *supposing* I should have an exceptional month of *it* (good English) and have exceptional expenses which might *easily* ! happen I should have no one to go to.

"Since I had my allowance you have given me a little extra without which I should have been terribly hard up (elegant). If therefore (logical!) you could make a *deposit*!! *of say* (commercial & banking expression) £15 which I was to draw upon (rather frail security) without *real necessity* (very difficult to define) & which I was to account to you for as I drew it out (perhaps you would, you have to send your letter 10,000 miles) it would make things so much easier." Would it? Perhaps. I do not comment on this letter so delicately expressed about matters of money further than to observe that Jack would have cut off his fingers off rather than write such a very free-spoken letter to his father. And if I had written such a letter to my father he *wld* have sent it back to me with much stronger expressions than I have used to you. This is a letter which I shall not keep but return it to you that you may from time to time review its pedantic &

overgrown schoolboy style. Perhaps it is due to that stupid typewriter which I think an objectionable machine calculated to spoil your handwriting.

Finally if you are going to write letters to me when I am travelling, type-written & so ridiculously expressed I would rather not receive them.

RANDOLPH S. CHURCHILL
your father

Winston to Jack

24 June [1894]   Sandhurst

My dear Jack,

Thanks for a letter which I got this morning. I had a very pleasant week at Ascot and saw all the races. I backed a couple of winners and a lot of Stiff. . . . but altogether just about paid my way. Last night and the night before I went and dined with Lord Wolverton[1] at Windsor, and rode in the Queen Annes drive and back here 14 miles after dinner. I will tell you all about it when I see you which I hope will be on Tuesday. Everything is very damnable except Sandhurst. That is very satisfactory.

Best love from your loving brother will now form a fitting ending to this extremely badly Type written letter.

Yours ever
WINSTON S. crurrrrchcill
W. S. CHURCHILL

Lord Randolph Churchill to Dr Thomas Buzzard
(Buzzard Papers)

25 June 1894   50 Grosvenor Square

Dear Dr Buzzard

I am very sorry I did not keep my appointment; but it was my duty to bid farewell to the Prince & Princess of Wales & of the Duke of Cambridge who have for many years shown me the utmost kindness. This duty occupied my time till past two. I tried to give you notice by a message from Marlborough House but I am afraid I must have caused you and Dr Roose inconvenience & hope you will excuse me. Might I propose the same appointment for tomorrow.

Yours vy sincerely
RANDOLPH S. CHURCHILL

---

[1] Frederic, 4th Baron Wolverton (1864–1932), a former Lord-in-Waiting; Vice-Chamberlain of the Household 1902–5.

Francis Knollys to Dr Thomas Buzzard
(Buzzard Papers)

Marlborough House
25 June 1894   Pall Mall

Dear Sir,

Lord Randolph Churchill asks me to let you know that he had to take leave of the Prince & Princess of Wales and much to his regret was unable therefore to keep his engagement with you.

Will you kindly let him know if he can make the same appointment with you for the same hour (1.45) tomorrow.

Yrs truly
FRANCIS KNOLLYS

Dr Thomas Buzzard and Dr Robson Roose to Lady Randolph

25 June 1894   74 Grosvenor Gardens

Private

Dear Lady Randolph Churchill,

As you are aware, it is against our advice that Lord Randolph is starting for the United States, and you have doubtless seen the letter which we sent to his Lordship. Our wish was that previous to his attempting a lengthened journey he should go with a Medical man to some place near at hand by way of experiment as to the effect of change upon him. In these circumstances it appears to us advisable to repeat in writing, what we have already expressed by word of mouth, that we cannot help feeling a good deal of anxiety in regard to the future, and would earnestly counsel your Ladyship to insist upon an immediate return to England in case Lord Randolph should shew any fresh symptom pointing possibly to disturbance of the Mental faculties.

As it is necessary that Dr Keith[1] as well as your Ladyship, should be thoroughly aware of our views, we are sending him a duplicate of this letter. We have arranged to hear from him once a week by letter sent to Dr Roose for our joint perusal.

Believe us to be Yours very truly
THOMAS BUZZARD
ROBSON ROOSE

---

[1] George Elphinstone Keith (1864–1918), son of Thomas Keith (see p. 341) and like his father a gynaecologist. He had only lately returned from New York, where he was House Surgeon at the Women's Hospital. Died in Italy of influenza while on active service.

From My Early Life

I was making a road map on Chobham Common in June 1894, when a cyclist messenger brought me the college adjutant's order to proceed at once to London. My father was setting out the next day on a journey round the world. An ordinary application to the college authorities for my being granted special leave of absence had been refused as a matter of routine. He had telegraphed to the Secretary of State for War Sir Henry Campbell-Bannerman, 'My last day in England' . . . and no time had been lost in setting me on my way to London.

We drove to the station the next morning – my mother, my younger brother and I. In spite of the great beard which he had grown during his South African journey four years before, his face looked terribly haggard and worn with mental pain. He patted me on the knee in a gesture which however simple was perfectly informing.

There followed his long journey round the world. I never saw him again, except as a swiftly-fading shadow.

Lady Randolph to Winston

28 June [1894]   RMS *Majestic*
                                                 Off Queenstown
                                                 [Cork Harbour]

Dearest Winston,

One line to go by the mail. Take care of yrself & write often. Look after Jack & write to yr Grandmother Marlborough & be nice to her. She will do anything for you. I can't write any more – post off. Hope you did not forget the shoes & write to [?] Park Lane 23 if things go wrong.

                                                 Yr loving
                                                 MOTHER

Jack to Winston

1 July 1894

Dear Winney,

Dont forget to come next Saturday. It is Bloody hot I dont know what to do. I saw C. Strong yesterday here. It's too hot to write.

                                                 I remain
                                                 JACK S. CHURCHILL

Phew!!!!!!
I've had a letter from Ma – I don't know where it came from.

Frances, Duchess of Marlborough to Winston

Sunday 1 July 1894   50 Grosvenor Square

Dear Winston,

I went to the L & W [London & Westminster] Bank on Friday & told the
Manager to put £20 on the 1st of July & every month to your account from
mine & to send you a Bank Book & open an acct with you. When you receive
it you had better acknowledge it & the *only* thing you must avoid on *all*
accounts is not to overdraw the money due to you – How very hot it is! I had
a good acct of your dear Father from the Dr & a cheerful letter from your
Mother from Queenstown –

                              Much love from yr affect gd Mother
                                                    F M

Frances, Duchess of Marlborough to Winston

2 July 1894   50 Grosvenor Square

My dear Winston,

I have recd your letter & have no news except that I have received back
from the Post Office the letters I wrote to your Father to Queenstown so that
they must have missed the mail –

By the Bye you will like to know that Frances Guest is engaged to be married
to Mr Thesiger[1] the eldest son of Lord Chelmsford. He is very nice & clever, a
Barrister & a Fellow of All Souls & he was educated at Winchester & is a great
cricketer having been in the Eleven there so its a very nice marriage & we are
all very much pleased. I told your dear Father I thought it likely to come off &
so now I have only to wire to him *All right*.

Its dreadfully hot. I cannot write more.

Do be careful dear of bathing not to catch cold or otherwise come to grief.

                              Ever yr afft GrandMother
                                                    F M

---

[1] Frederic John Thesiger (1868–1933); succeeded his father as 3rd Baron Chelmsford in
1905; Viceroy of India 1916–21; elected Warden of All Souls 1932. Created Viscount in 1921.
The marriage took place on July 27.

Frances, Duchess of Marlborough to Winston

Sunday [? 8 July 1894]   50 Grosvenor Square

Dear Winston,

Your Father wires "Arrived Bar Harbour[1] remain till August 31st fine Air. Address August Belmont[2] All well." This is a great comfort to me.

Yr Aff
GRAND MOTHER

Winston to Lady Randolph

10 July [1894]   Sandhurst

My dearest Mamma,

I have not written to you before because there was not much to tell – except that we were very low at your departure. Grandmamma sent me a letter to tell me of Papa's safe arrival at Bar Harbour & I got a letter from you written "off Queenstown" which I was very glad to receive.

I do hope you are feeling well and in good spirits – and that the change has already worked wonders with Papa. There seems to be much trouble going on at Chicago. Quite a civil war in fact.[3] I hope you will keep well away from it.

I am doing a lot of work as the Examinations begin to-morrow. I feel I know my subject very thoroughly and am not nervous as to not getting through. I hope however to pass high as I shall take the opportunity of writing a long letter to papa on the subject of Cavalry. I have been piling up material for some time and have a most formidable lot of arguments.

Switzerland is arranged allright – though we have not yet decided exactly where we shall go. I met Mr Little some time ago . . . he is very anxious to start. Only 5 more days and then I go home. Jack does not arrive until 31st. My cheque book has arrived and I think I shall manage Funds all right until you come back. I never thanked you sufficiently for the Fiver.

I want to say such a lot of things that one can't put down on paper. We both miss you very much indeed. However it will be for the best and if Papa comes back all right I shall not regret your going away.

I am writing Papa an account of Harrow Speech day – which is practically all I have to tell about. Grandmamma is very kind and we carry on a most

---

[1] On the Maine coast.

[2] August Belmont (1853–1924), the famous New York banker and Turf enthusiast who was friendly with the Jeromes.

[3] On July 6 a rail strike affecting all the Western States of America became very serious; the strikers held all the Western suburbs of Chicago and martial law was declared.

animated correspondence. I think things will go on very well. Here at Sandhurst there is no trouble of any sort. I suppose you will have left England a month when this letter reaches you – but henceforth you will get one every week from me. I should so like to have a letter from you. Though I should like to hear about the things you do & see I would much rather hear about how Papa is and if you are feeling cheery.

Such a short and stupid letter. Good bye my darling dearest Mummy, excuse my composition and believe how very much I miss you. With best love and many kisses.

I remain, Ever your loving son
WINSTON S. CHURCHILL

Winston to Lady Randolph

17 July [1894] 50 Grosvenor Square

My dear Mamma,

I got a letter from you for which I thank you very much. I wrote to Papa yesterday and this letter will probably arrive about the same time. Everything is going on well except money which is a bore. I told Papa all the news I could think of – so I will not write to you of what we have done. Everything goes on fairly well here at G. Square. I do the model "son" very well. Church on Sundays and trot in evening now and again to see Grandmamma. People are very kind and I have had a lot of invitations to lunch and dinner. Mrs Adair[1] gave a ball last night to which I could have gone had I wanted. Tonight there is Stafford House. Lord Hindlip has repeated his invitation to me to come at Christmas and I shall most certainly accept no matter what happens with regard to coming out to join you.

Jack is well and happy. Of course we both miss you 'horrid'. I am very sorry to get away from Sandhurst as it was less dull than this fortnight in London. However we shall soon be off to Switzerland.

Grandmamma made a mistake about my allowance. She thought Papa said £20 a month. I was sorry to have to correct her. I am sure he meant £10 really.

Well then Mr Little told me Papa had said he would give him £50 more this year than last; and Papa himself told me and Jack also that we could have £10 and £5 respectively for Switzerland. Grandmamma does not remember him telling how much consequently unless you can get Papa to send a wire stating exact amount we shall be worse off than last year for then Papa gave me £15 and Jack £8.

Do try and get him to just wire the amount.

[1] Mrs Adair, daughter of an American general and widow of the landlord of Glenveagh Castle in Donegal, was a leading London hostess.

When you write let me know how Papa is and how you are. Goodbye my darling own Mamma. We miss you very much and long to see you back. Do keep well and cheery and we will try to do the same.

Lots of kisses and best love, Ever your loving son
WINSTON S. CHURCHILL

"I am writing in bed so that is why it is worse than usual. Forgive it."
17th Evening.

I saw both Aunt Leonie and Aunt Clara today. I was very glad as I was feeling very low. Jack sends love – so do Alex Ellis & Molly Hacket.

Your own & loving son
W

Jack to Winston

Wednesday [18 July] 1894   [Harrow]

Dear Winny,

Thanks for your letter of this morning.

It has been raining all this week as usual. Mind and come on Saturday & Bring Molly I will have Tea in room à la Xmas 92³ [third] term. You remember. But let me know whether she is going to come.

I have not heard from Mama or Papa. My Photo's are getting on very well.

I see the Type writer is in use – but still some mistakes in the letters such as Harow on the hill etc. Disgraceful.

Welldon is ill etc & has a bulletin on his door! he got Poisoned so I hear – I don't know –

I remain your loving Brother
JSC

Lord Randolph to Winston

18 July 1894   Bar Harbour Malvern Hotel
Maine

My dear Winston,

I was pleased to receive today your letter of the 4th. It took a long time on the road for your grandmother wrote me a letter dated the 7th which reached me also today. Your letter therefore took 14 days against 11 days. I trust the examination may be as good for you as you think. A cable to Churchill Victoria Vancouver will find me. You must just add after code word eighth or sixth or any other number. You need not sign it. We leave this place on the 23rd. and shall start for Vancouver at the end of the month, or before. You must not write to Vancouver. You must write care of Messrs (not "Mr") August Belmont, New York. I hope you will get some afternoon riding at the Park Barracks for the few days which you will have before Jack comes up. You will also bear in mind the six months you have promised me to spend at Dresden in mastering the German language. I think you told me you would consult Lord Rothschild. You must write to him to New Court, St Swithin's Lane and ask him what day you may go and see him. But after all this does not press for you will not go out of Sandhurst till December 1894. But as I am writing to remind you about it, I think you will have to make some formal application to the W.O. [War Office] for leave of absence & specifying the purpose of the leave. On this point they will direct you at Sandhurst. I suppose you will lock up this letter, after having shown it to your Grandmother, till you require to read it again. Well I do not think I have anything more of importance or interest to tell you now. You had better write a good long letter to your mother to the address I have given you and also stimulate Jack in the same direction & even in mine. Mr Little in writing to me about the tour had better also write to the same direction. You need not take the trouble of sending all round by Grosvenor Square. Address as I told you via Liverpool England whenever you may be writing. Well goodbye. Of course you will share it with Jack. I am delighted to hear that his camera so interesting to him. Tell him when he writes to me whether he has a chance of getting a remove. Tell him to remember me to Mr Welldon and Mr Searle. I wonder whether the Prince of Wales will remember to go and see his room. He promised me he would & Jack had better ask Mr Welldon to remind him.

Your affectionate father
RANDOLPH S.C.

Frances, Duchess of Marlborough to Lady Randolph

EXTRACT

19 July 1894   50 Grosvenor Square

... You will be glad to hear the Boys are well. Jack is pursuing his quiet course at Harrow. Winston is here & on the strength of your and R's popularity is invited abt as much and perhaps more than you could wish. But its a great thing to keep him in good society. He has been to Mrs Adair's Stafford House Devonshire House etc and today he has just asked my Leave to go to Sandown with Mrs Hwffa Williams. This I have given him on his giving me his word of Honour he will not be induced to bet. It is difficult to refuse him anything at his age. He is affectionate and pleasant but you know he is mercurial and plausible and all I can hope is that you will approve. His season will not last long for he is going to spend the last few days of the month with some friends (I think the Spender-Clays and he starts with Jack on the 31st. Meantime he is very well and happy & goes to ride at the Barracks of a morning. I fear he is thoughtless about money and I am always lecturing about economy but I fear with little success! . . .

Winston to Lady Randolph

22 July [1894]   The Hatch

My dearest Mamma,

I hope you have been receiving a constant stream of letters from Jack and I. We have now written at least 8 between us and most sincerely hope that they have all reached their destination.

I have had a very pleasant week in London. People have been very kind and I have had lots of invitations to dinner to lunch and to dances. I went to Stafford House on Tuesday – Lady Leconfield's[1] ball Wednesday, Devonshire House Thursday, Grosvenor House Friday & had I not come down here I should have gone to Lady Chetwode's[2] on Saturday night. I went down to Sandown on Friday with Mrs Hwffa Williams to see the 'Eclipse Stakes.' It was a very fine race. But Ladas was beaten more than 200 yards from the post. I thought he was ridden to the very last inch but he never got within 2 lengths of Isinglass.

I met Sir Frederick [Johnstone] and Lady W [Wilton] there and they asked me down here. I was delighted to come for the [?] Sunday as it is so expensive living in London & the funds are rather shocking.

Yesterday Molly Hacket and I made our great expedition to Harrow – quite alone. As soon as we got down there – we received three telegrams with "Congratulations" from young Clay and others.

I am going to lunch with Little to-morrow and he is going to ask young Castlereagh.[3] We have arranged our trip. It will be modified as we go by the funds and by the time we have – but it is roughly this. London – Brussels – Lucerne – Interlaken – Chamonix – Zermatt – Through the Furka pass –

[1] Constance Evelyn (1846–1939), 2nd daughter of Lord Dalmeny, married 2nd Baron Leconfield in 1867.

[2] Alice Jane (–1919), daughter of Michael Thomas Bass MP, married Sir George Chetwode, 6th Bart, in 1868.

[3] Charles, Viscount Castlereagh (1878–1949), who in 1915 succeeded his father as 7th Marquess of Londonderry. He was a second cousin of Winston's and later became a close friend of his.

Goeschenen – Milan – Venice (if not too hot) – Innsbruck – Salzburg – Vienna. At Vienna I leave and return by the Orient express to Sandhurst. Jack and Little will go back by easy stages – via Paris.

I have written Papa a long letter on the subject of the Cavalry. I do so hope he will not be angry – or take it as "freespoken" or stupid. I only wrote what I thought he ought to know – namely how keen I was to go into the Cavalry and how I could not look forward with great eagerness to going with even the best Infantry regiment in the world.

Jack showed me a very welcome letter from you. Do write to me and tell me what you do *& how Papa is*.

I do hope that you are well & not experiencing boredom. Do you get any riding. I have been riding regularly, in the row every morning & also sometimes at the barracks.

Well! good bye! my dearest Mama. You know how Jack and I miss you and how we long for you and Papa to come back. Keep well and cheerful and write often –

to your loving and affectionate son
WINSTON S. CHURCHILL

PS What do you think of Olive and Mr Guthrie?[1] I met them walking and they confided to me. I was awfully embarrassed but rose to the occasion.

They say Miss Peel[2] is going to marry Ferdy Rothschild,[3] but I don't know if it is true.

Lots of love
WINSTON

Frances, Duchess of Marlborough to Lady Randolph

EXTRACT

27 July 1894   50 Grosvenor Square

. . . Winston is gone to the Spender-Clays. He left yesterday and returns Monday. He has been out a great deal to all the smart things and he tells me he has written you all about himself. Cornelia has been very kind and lent him a horse to ride with Elaine[4] as it cost him 10/- a ride to hire one. I am fond of him

[1] Mrs Leslie's sister-in-law, Olive (see p. 152), who married Walter Murray Guthrie on August 30.

[2] Julia Beatrice (1864–1949), elder daughter of 1st Viscount Peel, who in April 1895 married James Rochfort Maguire.

[3] Baron Ferdinand James de Rothschild (1839–1898), MP for Aylesbury 1885–98, second son of Baron Anselm de Rothschild. He had married his cousin, Evelina Rothschild, in 1865. She died in 1866. Baron Ferdinand died without issue.

[4] WSC's first cousin, Elaine Augusta Guest (1871–1963).

and we get on well on the whole. But you will understand there is nobody but me to keep him in order and I am obliged to insist on punctuality and make him report himself once or twice a Day and so I have been obliged to exercise authority sometimes. You see Everybody is kind to him on your acct and R's & yet as you know he requires checking sometimes & I feel sure you will appprove.

This is *only between ourselves* dear. He really is good but you know him well enough to believe he is not like Jack & requires a firm hand. I thought you would like to hear all this. . . .

Winston to Lady Randolph

31 July [1894]   50 Grosvenor Square

My dearest Mamma,

I got yesterday a letter from Papa – dated the 8th – so I suppose you will get this letter in about a fortnight. Today Jack comes up from Harrow, and to-morrow we start for Switzerland. I have had a very pleasant fortnight. I stayed with the Clays at Lingfield from Thursday until Monday. They had a big house party – 18 people mostly rather secondrate – but some were nice. I made the acquaintance of a charming Russian – Princess Radziwille[1] – who was somewhat eccentric and afflicted with second sight.

Francis Guest is married at last – and the ceremony was successfully performed last Friday. Lady Essex[2] gave a great garden party on Friday, which rather antagonised with the wedding. She asked me but I could not go being in the country.

Altogether I have had a very gay time – and have met lots of nice people and done lots of interesting things. Tomorrow we start off on our tour. We go to Antwerp via Flushing and stay one night. On the 3rd we go on to Brussels. At Antwerp we see the Exhibition and meet Count Kinsky who who travels back with us to Brussels. He is going to drive us out to see the battle field of Waterloo. Then on the 4th we go to Basle & Lucerne and go into Switzerland.

I can't tell you how glad I am & how happy to find that everything is still well, and that Papa is so much better. Such a nice little paragraph was in the papers last night to say how you had started for Vancouver & how everywhere hospitably received.

[1] Marie, Princess Radziwill (1863–   ). Wife of Prince Anton Radziwill, (1833–1904), Polish ADC to three German Emperors. Daughter of the Marquis de Castellane.

[2] Adela (1859–1922), eldest daughter of Beach Grant of New York. She became in 1893 the second wife of George Devereux de Vere Capell, 7th Earl of Essex.

Goodbye my dearest darling Mama; Jack and I think of you very often and miss you very much. However I think we may say that all is satisfactory so far.

With lots of love & kisses I remain

Ever your loving and affectionate son

WINSTON S.C.

PS I will write to Papa on Tuesday as have got to pack up etc to-day.

Winston to Lady Randolph

3 August [1894]   Hotel Britannique
                                                      Bruxelles

My dearest Mamma,

We started on the evening of the 1st – crossed comfortable from Dover to Ostende & did not stop – except to change until we reached Antwerp. All the second [of Aug] we spent at Antwerp – which is quite worth seeing. Jack took many photographs of the shipping on the Scheldt. There was a very fine American Warship *Chicago* lying in the river and we went and examined it as closely as the authorities would let us. Jack made some very successful pictures of it – one of which is enclosed. Count Kinsky was very kind to us, and is in excellent spirit at having so good an appointment – which he thinks will lead to still better things.

He has had to go away to Germany on business and so we are going to Waterloo by train. Tonight we start for Lucerne by the 6 o'clock express, (14 hours).

Brussels is very attractive. We dined last night at a new place – The Metropole – a most magnificent room in marble and gold – with a very good dinner 6 frcs a head with wine. Then there is a great fare on – to which we went and which was most amusing. I shall write a letter to Papa from Lucerne – as it is not much good my writing the same thing twice over.

This is now my 10th letter & I hope you have received them all. I shall continue writing once or twice a week according as there is much or little to tell. I am so thankful to hear of Papa's improvement. A great number of people have asked after him and I have had great pleasure in saying how much better he is.

Dearest Mamma – I have seen several of your letters to Aunt Leonie & to Consuelo [Duchess of Manchester] and sympathise very much with your dislike of the "vegetation". But your last letters were much more cheery and I feel sure that you will end by enjoying the journey. We feel happy – but it is a horrid bore & worse not to have my own one love to talk to. The duchess was getting very "difficile" when we left and it was perhaps just as well we came off here.

However it is all for the best, and will I feel sure turn out well. I have annexed a beautiful photo of you with the star in your hair and one of Papa which I have had framed. Goodbye darling – Jack and I think of you every day and look forward to the time when we shall meet again.

Ever your loving and affectionate son
WINSTON S.C.

Lady Randolph to Mrs John Leslie

4 August 1894   Banff Springs Hotel
                                                Banff
                                                Alberta

Dearest Sniffy,

I write to you altho' I owe a letter to Mama – but this must do for the family as I know no address but yours. I don't suppose Mama has stayed at Brighton. It seems such ages since I have had any news of anyone – and we shan't get letters until we get to San Francisco about the 10th or 11th. I hope for several mails there. We left Bar Harbour last Friday and arrived at Montreal next morning – stopped the day there – and then came straight through to this place, 22 hrs from Vancouver – 5 days and nights in the train was tiring – so we agreed to stop 2 days here. We are off again tonight. We have got a Pullman private car of our own – which is as comfortable as such things can be – but very expensive. R. had a letter Sir W. Van Horne[1] the Chairman of the C.P. Railway and he thought all he had to do was to ask for a car – and be sent free. I had my suspicions for I know in the first place that a Canadian is not a generous American – and in the 2nd place Sir W.V.H. was no friend of ours. After a gt many excuses and telegrams it ended in our having to get one ourselves and pay for ourselves something like 300£ but the journey cd not be done otherwise. R. is not as well as he was at Bar Harbour. Of course the journey has told on him – but I feel it is always going to be so. As soon as he gets a little better from having a rest and being quiet he will be put back by this travelling – and *nothing* will deter him from doing what he likes. He is very kind and considerate when he feels well – but absolutely *impossible* when he gets excited – and as he gets like that 20 times a day – you may imagine my life is not a very easy one.

Then Keith gets "enerveed" and worried. Our plans as far as we can make

---

[1] William Cornelius Van Horne (1843–1915), an American by birth, President of the Canadian Pacific Railway 1888–99. Hon KCMG 1894.

them is to go from Vancouver to San Francisco and to sail for Yokohama the 24th August. R. won't take any thought or consideration of the war[1] because it does not suit him and "poohpoohs" any danger or inconvenience. I confess I think it will be all settled before we get there. If he likes Japan I hope to be able to persuade him to remain there quietly for some weeks before we go to India. I can't look ahead very far. Keith thinks that R. will eventually get quite well – and I think so too – if only he would give himself a chance. Meanwhile I try to make the best of it. This is a wonderful place 2,000 miles from Montreal you can easily find it on the map. It is the finest scenery in the Rockies and is certainly beautiful. I am writing to you from the terrace of the hotel surrounded by enormous mountains – and a cascade just below me falling into a pale green river winding away as far as the eyes can reach. The days are hot but not stuffy and the nights cool. We go out on the lakes – as the roads are frightfully dusty. I am longing to hear from you and to know all the news. I wonder where you are? and where all my friends are? 3 weeks is a long time to be cut off *absolutely* from all news. I daresay to you all it does not seem very long since we left. You will have been busy about Olive. I shall be so glad to hear all about it – perhaps she will be married by the time you receive this. I suppose the usual Cowes Week is in full swing with the usual gossip. How far away it all seems. I feel doubly low when I think how delightful this trip might be – if things were different. Tell Mama I have kept very few newspaper cuttings, but I will collect them and send them to her from San Francisco. I have little to tell you of interest. My maid does very well and is a capital traveller. I am very well and burnt like a Red Indian and now goodbye for the pres: Best love to Clara, Mama and all. I expect to find letters from the boys who have started on their tour I suppose – I hope they write to you sometimes. Bless you.

Your loving
JENNIE

Dr G. Keith to Dr Robson Roose
(Buzzard Papers)

4 August 1894   Banff Springs Hotel

[Copy]

Dear Dr Roose,

We arrived here on Augt 2nd after a journey of six days. Lord Randolph stood the journey while on the train fairly well, but since we stopped here he has not been at all well.

On the day we arrived (Augt 2nd) the numbness came on very acutely, and though it quickly passed off, it was as bad as I have seen it. While the

_____
[1] The Sino-Japanese War in Korea.

attack was on his talking was very bad, but there was no change in the re-flexes or in the pupils. On Augt 3rd, though the numbness was gone, he was very irritable and excited, more so than I have yet seen him.

Today, tho' more irritable than usual, he is somewhat quieter, but not nearly so well as at Bar Harbour. He sleeps well, usually only with 20 grns of Bromide of Strontium, and s.t. in addition 10 grns of Sulphonal.

We leave Vancouver for Japan on Augt 28th and I will try and induce him to stay in Japan a long time. To my mind his tour in Burmah and India will be the greatest possible mistake, and I will do all in my power to prevent or at least curtail it.

I will write again from Francisco.

G. KEITH

Frances, Duchess of Marlborough to Lady Randolph

EXTRACT

7 August 1894   50 Grosvenor Square

. . . I have not yet heard from the Boys who left on the 1st for Brussels. I wrote to Count Kinsky there to ask him to befriend them and *strengthen* Mr Little's hands as regards Winston for truly Jack is no trouble, and I had a kind letter from him. I will forward your Letter to Winston as soon as I hear where to direct. . . .

Winston to Lady Randolph

12 August 1894   Hotel du Bar
                                                 Grindelwald

My dear Mamma,

We got here from Interlaken two days ago and like the place so much that we are going to stay here quite a week. The scenery is very grand on three sides of the hotel enormous mountains of over 12,000 feet rise quite sheer – their tops covered with snow. There is a great crowd but I have found a very nice boy – a Charterhouse boy – as well as another fellow who has just passed into Sandhurst. We have muddled all our letters again this year; But tomorrow I think they will all arrive.

The Finances are fairly good. We do not seem to have spent quite so much as we did last year. This is owing to our always taking "Table d'hote" and practising such like economies.

On Friday we are going to move on to Zermatt where we shall stay until the

25th. Then to Vevey or Montreux & from there I shall leave and return to the R.M.C.

They are bringing in new regulations with regard to the Sandhurst Exam (Entrance). They gain more marks for the English Composition and have added Geography to the other subjects. The consequences appear to have been rather disastrous for Harrow – which passed no one – and even Capt James has only got in 5 or 6 instead of his usual 20 or 28.

I have not yet heard of the result of the Exam in which I am interested but I hope to find out tomorrow when the letters arrive. If all is satisfactory – I have only 3 more months to stay at Sandhurst.

Jack writes to Papa by this mail. I hope you have received my other letter this is the 13th I have written. If you can find time to send me a line let me know how you are yourself & how Papa's health is. I do hope the improvement of the first few weeks is continued.

Very nearly two months out of the 12 are gone and I am already thinking of your return. I think of you every day and look forward to seeing you again so much.

Good bye dearest Mamma – I will write to Papa in two or three days – excuse the horrid writing as the pens in this hotel are worse than any other I have ever written with – & do send me a short letter if you can.

I remain with best love, Ever your loving son
WINSTON S.C.

Lord Randolph to Winston

21 August 1894   Hotel Del Monte
                                               California

My dear Winston,

I do not enter into your lengthy letter of the 22nd in which you enlarge on your preference for the Cavalry over the 60th Rifles. I could never sanction such a change. Your name was put down by myself on the Duke of Cambridge's list for one or other of the battalions of that Regiment. The Duke of Cambridge would be extremely angry with you if you were to make any application to him for such a change; His Royal Highness would consult me and I should oppose it strongly. So that you had better put that out of your head altogether *at any rate during my lifetime* during which you will be dependent on me. So much for that subject.

Your other letters numbering five in all have been very pleasant & agreeable to receive & read. I cannot make out in what post office Jack's letters are, I have not got one & have a sort of idea I got one at Bar Harbour but I fear not, for all the family letters Jacks as well as the others, are put away in a green morrocco locked collapsible case. I think the photographing interferes very much with correspondence, taking into account all the occupations of travelling.

Well I have got as far as this very nice warm & sunny part of California. I leave it very early tomorrow for San Francisco tomorrow morning the 22nd and on the 23rd we leave San Francisco for Victoria in Vancouver at 9 AM which necessitates a rise from bed at 5.30 AM. This Pacific steamer is not very smart or clean ship, but your mother and I have very fair cabins. The hours of meals are curious. I recommend them to Mr Little. Breakfast at 8 – 9 luncheon from 12.30 to 1.30, dinner 5.30 to 7.0 nothing after that till the morning. However the voyage is only 800 nautical miles & takes only 3 days. This ship takes us to Victoria from where we embark on *The Empress of Japan*. This is one of a very fine fast line of steamers kept up by the Dominion of Canada Government to keep up a fleet of fast steamers in connexion with the Candian Pacific Railway to carry if necessary British Mails & if necessary British troops. The route across Canada and across from Vancouver to Japan & on to Hong Kong & even to Calcutta is much shorter than round across the Bay through the Suez Canal & by Ceylon to Calcutta. We have your mother and I two fine rooms. Mr Keith also has a good room. We shall probably arrive at Yoko-hama in about 14 or 15 days. So that at that time we shall have travelled very nearly three months & about by sea & land about 10,000 miles and we shall be about 8,500 miles as the direct route goes. However you can write, if you catch the right mail for Yokohama which you will do if you direct c/o Messrs August Belmont, New York. He will forward your letters whenever there is a mail, three times to Yokohama for I do not think I shall leave Japan till the middle of October. Love to Jack and remember me to Mr Little warmly.

Your affectionate father
RANDOLPH S. CHURCHILL

I cannot write at length for I have so many letters to write when the mail comes in.

Frances, Duchess of Marlborough to Lady Randolph

EXTRACT

21 August 1894   Ramsey

... I hope you will have got all our Letters by now. The Boys were very good abt writing. I have sent Little's Letters to Randolph so that I hope you see them. The acct he gives of the Boys is very satisfactory. Jack is really excellent

& steady and Winston appears to be pleasant. I lectured him freely before he left and he certainly takes reproof well tho perhaps it does not make much impression. . . .

Winston to Lady Randolph

26 August [1894]   Lausanne

My dearest darling Mamma,

I got while at Zermatt a dear letter from you – which I think had taken nearly a month finding me. My time with Jack is now nearly up. Either tomorrow or the next day I shall start for London – and Sandhurst.

The Examination result which perhaps you know better than I do at present is just out. Grandmamma sent me a telegram – yesterday. Maximum 1500; Minimum 750. My marks 1140.[1]

Last time I got 1198 so you see I have lost about 60 marks. This I attribute to the fact that the papers did not suit me quite as well as last time – being rather apart from the notes from which I worked.

Grandmamma did not say in her letter what *place* these marks gave me – but I should imagine that it would be in the first 20. Perhaps if the difficulty of the papers has acted on the others too – it may be in the first ten.

At any rate if I do as well next time I should take "Honours". Papa need not be disappointed though I had hoped that I should have increased instead of decreased my marks.

It is not so bad, after all out of 140 boys among whom I passed in 90th.

This place is very pleasant – if only by the way in which it contrasts with Zermatt. We have come straight from the latter – 5000 feet above the sea – rather cold – shut in on every side by enormous peaks and a very bad and uncomfortable hotel – to Ouchy where the lake is outside the bedroom windows, the water so warm that you can bathe 3 or 4 times a day – and the hotel – the best in Switzerland.

At Zermatt one wanted to walk and climb and be awfully energetic but here we just sit in chairs and read "Tauchnitz" Editions.

While at Zermatt I climbed Monte Rosa. It was not dangerous: Mr Little made searching inquiries – but very fatiguing. More than 16 hours of continual walking. I was very proud & pleased to find I was able to do it and to come down very fresh.[2]

[1] Military Administration 195, Military Law 218, Tactics 266, Fortification 254, Military Topography 207. Conduct: 'Unpunctual'.
[2] The ascent of Monte Rosa, 15,217 feet. According to Baedeker's guide it is 'free from danger or serious difficulty, but it is attended with much fatigue and requires a perfectly steady head'.

It is a most tiring mountain – mainly on account of the rarification of the air on the long snow slopes.

There were several Sandhurst and Harrow boys at Zermatt and they climbed Dent Blanche – the Matterhorn and Rothhorn – The most dangerous and difficult of Swiss mountains. It was very galling to me not to be able to do something too, particularly as they swaggered abominably of their achievements. I had to be content with toilsome but safe mountains. But another year I will come back and do the dangerous ones.

Please excuse all these blots; this ink is as thick as cream and I have only a very flickering candle. I know you will not mind this one untidy letter. The next shall be copper plate.

Give my love to Papa. On the 31st when I get to London I will write him a long letter on the Examination and on the whole trip. For the present goodbye. I long to see you. Two months tomorrow since you went so the time is passing – surely though slowly.

Best Love & kisses my own darling Mummy – Jack and I miss you *so* much,
                                        Ever your loving son
                                        WINSTON S. CHURCHILL

Winston to Lady Randolph

4 September [1894]   Sandhurst

My dearest Mamma,

Here I am back at Sandhurst. There is a great deal to do here this term as they have again increased the hours and made them awfully long. The riding has begun also and I am working so hard at it. I should like nothing better than to win the riding prize. My only chance of persuading Papa to let me go in the Cavalry is, I feel, to do something of that sort. If I take "Honours" very high on the list, in passing out or win the Riding Prize I shall broach the subject again but till then the future is very gloomy.

At Sandown this year the Duke of C. [Cambridge] spoke to me. He said "You're at Sandhurst aren't you?" "Do you like it." I said "Yes." and Col Brab who was there said "Going into my Regiment eh." The Duke said "Oh I am very glad." So really he had forgotten all about the 60th.

How I wish I had not been offered that unfortunate infantry commission after the Exams. I should love to go into the cavalry – even with a bad regiment. Grandmamma writes 'Papa will not hear of it.' This is very sad, but I still have hopes that when he sees how anxious I am – he will not force me into the infantry against my inclination. I received three or four days ago a letter from you dated 9th from Victoria, so it is a month before I start to answer it,

And who can say how long it will be before you get my answer. What a long way you are off. But I think about you very often darling Mummy and I think you must have received lots of letters, for this is my 20th.

I find the time very long. It seems ages since you were gone and really it is only 2 months. Poor Papa! I am so delighted to hear he is better. I think Grandmamma only lives on his letters. She cares for nothing else in the world but news of and from him. Every letter she writes that I have seen – to me – to Aunt Leonie – to Mr Little have been full of whatever news she has received.

I have had a little affair which has worried me a good deal. You will remember the pair of Field Glasses Papa gave me when he went away, and that I had another very good pair, also his, which (the old pair) I intended to sell and purchase something with the money.

Well I told Healy to put in an anonymous advertisement in the *Exchange and Mart*. Somehow Aunt Sarah (such a cat) found out and told Grandmamma that I was going "to pawn my Father's glasses to raise money." Well of course it was easily proved that they were my own and that I had another and much better pair, so that the pair would have been useless – but meanwhile off goes Sarah to Canford & Deepdene with a woeful tale of 'Winston's thievish practices' and great is the tribulations. (I was in Switzerland.)

Aunt Leonie told me that Duchess Lily was awfully shocked at my conduct. This was the first I heard of it (Grandmamma never said a word to me.) So I wrote off to her and explained and she writes a charmingly kind letter – so that is all right. But meanwhile Sarah's tale is believed by the rest of the family and there is no one to take up the cudgels for me. Such a liar that woman is. I will never forget her kindness as long as I live.

Well goodbye my own darling Mummy.

Best love from your loving and affectionate son
WINSTON S.C.

Mrs Leonard Jerome to Winston

6 September [1894]   53 Seymour Street

My dear Winston,

I enclose the ten pounds for the tailor and you should write at once to your Father acknowledging the receipt of the £10. I hope you are getting on all right and that you are pleased with Sandhurst.

Affectionately
GRANDMAMMAN

Reverend J. E. C. Welldon to Winston

11 September 1894   Harrow

My dear Spencer Churchill,

I have not thanked you for your last letter, but I was away from home until this morning. I am very glad that you liked your mountaineering. You have got the figure of a mountaineer, and you ought to make yourself a name. The most difficult mountain that I have climbed is the Bernina in the Engadine, but I climbed it on a cold rough day with a wind so high that it was difficult to keep one's feet in the steps on the *arête* when one had to put them there.

I hope Jack is well and is not getting tired of the holidays.

I came back from Scotland this morning but shall only be here a few hours. If ever you can come and stay with me, propose yourself. I feel like a father to you now, when your own father is so far away.

Affectionately yours
J. E. C. WELLDON

[*Note in Winston's writing:*] One of Welldon's letters. I enclose it to show how very kind he is. Perhaps Papa will be pleased with it. wsc

Dr G. Keith to Dr Robson Roose
(*Buzzard Papers*)

11 September 1894   Grand Hotel
[Copy]   Yokohama

I send you an extra report to let you know that for the time being I have lost all control over your patient. He intends to take a journey tomorrow that I distinctly disapprove of, and all I have said has been of no avail. He has absolutely refused to allow me to go with him, as he says he does not want people to know he is an invalid. I write this in my own defence, in case anything happens.

G.K.

Winston to Lady Randolph

15 September [1894]   50 Grosvenor Square

My dearest darling Mummy,

I sit down to answer a letter of yours from San Francisco. 1st you ask me about Finance. I must tell you that it is most unsatisfactory. Coming back from Switzerland I spent a good deal of money & also I payed several bills with my first allowance in cheques. I have not been more extravagant than before you went away, but rather less. Still the sovs & the 2 sovs & the 3 pounds's used to make a great difference & now they have ceased altogether.

The consequence of this has been that I 'mortgaged' my allowance for the next month and have had to pawn several of the things I used least. If therefore as the 30th Nov approaches or Christmas draws near you feel as if you would like to commemorate both or either of these auspicious birthdays – a chequelet would above all things fill my heart with joy and gratitude.

Finally let me – to reassure you – state that though I have been cut off from you and Papa for more than 3 months I am not in any way *seriously involved* but only extremely hard up. So do not worry about me my darling mummy unless you feel you would like to send me a cheque. It would be a welcome stranger & smooth away many difficulties. The mess bills are much lower. I have economised fifty per cent.

*   *   *   *   *

So much for finance.

My own darling sweet Mama, I have received some beautiful photographs of you and Papa & some for Jack. I think they are awfully good both as regards likeness & as being beautiful. Travel seems to have affected you very little & I was astonished – when comparing the photographs of last month with the photo with the diamond star to note how little difference there was between the two. I am sure the journey is doing you good & feel quite convinced that you don't really look or feel 100 but make the local beauties 'sit up' on all fours.

Coming up in the train yesterday from Sandhurst to see Grandmamma, I met the Duchess of Manchester and had a long talk with her. She had just received a letter from you.

Duchess Lily has asked *the* Duchess to stay at Deepdene for Christmas. We "invade" on the 25th or thereabouts of December. Awfully good fun as there is lots to shoot and no regular shooting.

I shall go and stay with "Auntie Minnie" & also with Sunny. The Ellis girls have asked me down to Mothecombe [Devon], where I may also go – D.V. & funds permitting.

And now good bye my darling Mummy. Excuse the badly written scrawl & accept only the love that it is meant to convey. I think of you always & long to kiss you again.

Ever your loving son
WINSTON S. CHURCHILL

Winston to Jack

16 September [1894]   50 Grosvenor Square

My dear Jack,

I got back all right having accomplished all things successfully. Altogether I had very great luck. I am sending you some of the photo's that Mamma has sent you. One of each. I meant to tell you to write to Papa & Mamma very often, as papa writes that he only remembers getting one letter from you and a very unsatisfactory report. He says that he thinks that the camera is a drawback to correspondence. So *do* write pretty often.

Of course when I came up yesterday Woom had gone. So stupid of her not to wait. Well there is not much news except that I raised a tenner on a lot of old rubbish that I never want to see again & that I never use. Write to me.

Best love from
WINSTON (your brother)

Winston to Lady Randolph

19 September [1894]   50 Grosvenor Square

My darling Mummy,

The news of the first great battles of the war have just reached us.[1] You must write and give me some news from the spot. I suppose however that Yokohama and Seoul are as far apart as London & Vienna. It must be most interesting however to be so, comparatively speaking, near the seat of war.

I take the greatest interest in the operations both, of the fleets & armies. Anything so brilliant as the night attack of Ping Yang is hard to find in modern war. The reports as they have arrived here seem to show that the Japanese concentration was so accurately timed & their assault so skilfully delivered that the celestials had 'no show' at all.

I went out with our paper chase yesterday and had a couple of falls. In the first my horse pecked on landing & fell and at the second I turned a corner at a much too rapid pace & so came to grief. I was not at all hurt – which I consider most wonderful as I was galloped over both times. I do love this kind of riding. You know how little I have hunted. I don't think that anything would stop me if I had a good horse. As it is these hirelings are very uncertain and fall down as often as not – when jumping.

I am pinching & scraping to try and hire a better animal for a month and

[1] On September 16 invading Japanese columns scored a decisive victory over the Chinese at Pyongyang in north-western Korea. On the following day eleven Japanese men-of-war defeated a large Chinese naval force near the mouth of the Yalu River, thus opening the sea route to China.

any contributions you may feel inclined to send will be thankfully received. I do not think that there is anything in this world I would rather do than hunt – I mean so far as pleasure is concerned. We were about 17 last Wednesday and as we are all very keen we go pretty hard. Nearly everyone had a fall of some sort.

I am going to dine next Saturday with Lady Wilton which will I think be rather fun.

Do write and tell me my dear Mamma lots of news. Forgive the twaddle I write – There is so little to tell. In a very few days I will write again. With best love,

Ever your loving son
WINSTON

PS I enclose a programme of some pony races we are getting up. It may interest Papa as well.

Winston

Frances, Duchess of Marlborough to Lady Randolph

EXTRACT

19 September 1894   Grand Hotel
Scarborough

. . . I saw Winston on my way through London and I hope he will work well at Sandhurst. *Do* urge this upon him & also *economy*. He is affect. and means well but you know how volatile and impulsive he is & I fear inclined to spend a lot of money. Mr Little who I saw in London gave a good account of both the Boys and promised to write to Randolph himself. I hope you will like the idea of our spending Xmas with Lily. I think it is the best thing I can settle for the Boys. She is very kind about them & promises she will not spoil them. . . .

Dr G. Keith to Dr Robson Roose
(Buzzard Papers)

3 October 1894   Grand Hotel
[Copy]   Yokohama
Report No 13 Churchill

I did not write on Sunday as there was no mail.

There is no change in Lord Randolph's condition. He was better the day after he had the haemorrhage although the numbness and slight loss of power in the left hand persisted for a day or two. The only thing I would remark in his condition is that his symptoms vary quicker. One hour quiet and good-tempered, the next hour violent and cross. He has taken a violent dislike to one of his valets, and is sending him home, and also to his guide. I was very much afraid he was going to assault the latter yesterday morning, but luckily I was in the room and stopped him. I am sorry to say that he will not hear of giving up Burmah or India. All he says is that he must go, and that you and Dr Buzzard knew his plans. I tried to get him to consent to remain another month here, but I doubt if he will do it. I feel very much disheartened about the whole business, as he takes my advice when it suits him – not otherwise.

G.K.

Winston to Lady Randolph

8 October [1894]   50 Grosvenor Square

My darling Mamma,

It is now some time since I have written to you and also several weeks since I had news. This letter will reach you via Calcutta so I do not know how long it will be before you get it. I am afraid that I have got very little to tell you. I am getting on all right and everything is fairly prosperous.

Poor old Everest – who had gone to stay with 'The Archdeacon' has fallen down and broken her arm. It is awfully hard luck on her as she has had a good deal of pain – but they will look after her very well. She is going to write to you.

I get on very well with Grandmamma and as I said on the other page – things are working smoothly. I am very low about having to go in the Infantry, for which branch I have no interest.

Miss Alex Ellis is going to marry Drumlanrig[1] – but I believe there are financial difficulties in the way. I have seen Miss Hacket a good deal lately & she is most constant in her enquiries after you, I am looking forward to Christmas as I have Hindlip & several other rather nice invitations.

Jack is very well and is getting on all right at Harrow. His photographs are his constant amusement and he is never tired of taking them or developing them.

---

[1] Francis Archibald Douglas, Viscount Drumlanrig (1867–1894), eldest son of 9th Marquess of Queensberry, and brother of Lord Alfred Douglas. In 1892 became private secretary to Lord Rosebery, at the time Foreign Secretary. Created Baron Kelhead in June 1893 so that he might sit in the House of Lords with his chief. His father, after representing Scotland in the House for eight years, had been excluded after 1880, when he failed to be re-elected. He was so incensed at the elevation of his son that he pursued Lord Rosebery to Homburg whither the latter had gone for a holiday. There the Marquess, armed with a horsewhip, announced his intention of publicly chastising the Foreign Secretary. The authorities restrained him from so doing. Lord Kelhead died, by his own hand, before his father and eleven days after Winston's letter. He was unmarried.

Now I long for a letter from either you or Papa. . . . not having had news for more than 6 weeks – so please write and let me know how you are getting on. I will write again very soon.

With best love & kisses

Ever your loving and affectionate son
WINSTON

Winston to Lady Randolph

21 October [1894]

My own darling Mamma,

I was overjoyed to receive yesterday your letter dated Sept 20th. The first news I had had for 5 weeks. I cannot understand why you have not received any of the numerous letters I have written to you. I have written very nearly 30 letters since your departure and have addressed them all very carefully . . . putting always more than the necessary amount of stamps on. I hope when you get this you will have received some of the many missives I have sent in search of you.

We are very much disturbed by Dr Keith's last letter which gives a very unsatisfactory report about Papa. I hope however that there is still an improvement and no cause for immediate worry. Poor old Grandmamma is very low. It seems to me to be unnecessary to send her anything but good reports as any bad news causes her a great deal of trouble. If you only knew what importance she attaches to every cheering good word about Papa – I am sure you would persuade Dr Keith to tell only what is pleasant to hear. Your letter was indeed a treat. I think that the photographs are beautiful and shall always keep them as a souvenir of Japan. It is two months since I got back to Sandhurst and I am now almost at the end of my stay there.

Of course you know how I should like to come out and join you in India on your way home. I have worked now for 5 years pretty hard for constant examinations and I think I might really be allowed to have 3 or 4 months rest – especially as there is no real work for me to do. Papa has suggested my going to Germany, a prospect which fills me with profound dissatisfaction. I would love to see you again and the journey would be most interesting.

I think that if I pass out of Sandhurst high – with honours perhaps – as is possible, I might be allowed to have some more fitting reward than the opportunity of mastering the German language. If I must go abroad I would prefer to go to France and acquire a thorough knowledge of French – instead of merely a smattering which I have at present. If I don't come out to meet you I shall go and stay with Lady Wilton at Monte Carlo for a little. I don't suppose that Papa would object – as [I] should have my commission and would really be old enough to look after myself.

Christmas, which was so distant when you went away is now within measurable distance. Now do have a try and see what you can do. I shall have to wait quite a year for my appointment in the 60th Rifles and should have time to come out to see you, and go to Germany when you come back. At any rate it is a splendid chance of seeing the world, especially as I have 'unallotted' time on my hands.

I leave it to you. If anyone can arrange things you will be able to do it. Grandmamma will back you up. What fun we would have. But I do not attach much hope to the scheme.

*   *   *   *   *

Meanwhile I have been making an essay of journalism. The County Council wish to close the Empire and a most bitter controversy is raging in every paper on the subject. I enclose you the *Westminster Gazette* in which I have a letter – which they were good enough to print. It may perhaps interest Papa. Tomorrow I have got a long letter in the *Daily Telegraph* which I will send you Of course I only sign them W.L.S.C.[1]

In your letter you mention that you have sent Auntie Leonie £8 for me. This is sweet of you and very welcome, but grandmamma has been very generous comparatively speaking in the matter of money I have managed to get along tolerably well.

I am staying down at Harrow – as Lord Roberts has been lecturing here – and I was glad of an opportunity of seeing him. Jack is very well and getting on excellently here. In fact you need not worry about us. Goodbye my own darling Mamma,

With best love and kisses
I remain, Ever your loving and affectionate son
WINSTON

PS Such a tragic thing. Do you remember hearing that Alex Ellis was going to marry Drumlanrig. Well, two days ago he shot himself accidently, blowing his head off. Awfully sad. WSC

"Still another PS"

I have seen Grandmamma Jerome and she tells me she has heard from you Sarah is at G. Square so I am keeping particularly clear of that locality. Enclosed are kisses and lots of love.

x x x x x x x x x x x x x x x x x

WINSTON

[1] In fact the letter was not published, correspondence on the subject having been closed a few days earlier.

PPSS

I have just seen Mrs Lancelot Lowther whom I think a charming little woman. She tells me that Alex – poor Alex is inconsolable. Write again next week. w

Winston to the Westminster Gazette

18 October [1894]   London

THE PLIMSOLL LINE IN RESPECTABILITY

SIR,—In your article of the 17th inst, entitled "The Plimsoll Line in Respectability," you are somewhat inclined to belittle the arguments of the "anti-prudes." The improvement in the standard of public decency is due rather to improved social conditions and to the spread of education than to the prowling of the prudes.

Nature's law metes out great and terrible punishments to the "*roué* and libertine" – far greater punishments than it is in the power of any civilised State to award. These penalties have been exacted since the world was young, and yet immorality is still common. State intervention, whether in the form of a statute or by the decision of licensing committees, will never eradicate the evil. It may make it more dangerous for the evildoer. But such a policy, while not decreasing immorality, only increases its evil effects.

Now, Sir, I submit that the only method of reforming human nature and of obtaining a higher standard of morality is by educating the mind of the individual and improving the social conditions under which he lives. This is a long and gradual process, the result of which is not to be obtained in our generation. It is slow, but it is sure. If mankind is allowed to work out its own salvation the improvement of the last forty years will be steadily maintained, until we finally realise Mrs Ormiston Chant's[1] ideal.

In the meantime it is the plain duty of every Government to endeavour, as far as possible, to localise and minimise the physical effects of the moral evil. It is not a case of legalising and officially sanctioning immorality. The State should protect each member as far as possible from harm, and must govern men as they are and not as they ought to be. This is a duty which is recognised by every European nation. In England we have too long obeyed the voice of the prude. Well-meaning but misguided people, of which class Mrs Ormiston

---

[1] Laura Ormiston Chant (1848–1923) had been a hospital matron and assistant manager of a private lunatic asylum before marrying a surgeon (she had four children). She took up the causes of women's suffrage, temperance, purity and Liberal politics; accompanied medical relief expeditions to Armenian refugees in Bulgaria and to Greece and Crete. Author of a volume of sermonettes, a novel, numerous poems, and songs for children. Very fond of billiards.

Chant is a fair specimen, have prevailed upon Government to disclaim a responsibility which it was their bounden duty to accept.

This, then, Sir, is the point of view from which the "anti-prudes" approach the question. The difference between the disputants is one rather of method than of degree. Both are anxious to see England better and more moral, but whereas the Vigilance Societies wish to abolish sin by Act of Parliament, and are willing to sacrifice much of the liberty of the subject into the bargain, the "anti-prudes" prefer a less coercive and more moderate procedure.

If our impetuous reformers could only be persuaded to wait, and to take a broader and perhaps a more charitable view of social problems, they would better serve the cause they have at heart. But these "old women in a hurry" will not have patience, but are trying to improve things by repressive measures – a dangerous method, usually leading to reaction.

I am, Sir, your obedient servant
WLSC

Winston to Mrs John Leslie
(Stour Papers)

25 October 1894   50 Grosvenor Square

My dear Aunt Leonie,

So many thanks for your letter and for the enclosure. It is hard to say whether one dislikes the prudes or the weak-minded creatures who listen to them most. Both are to me extremely detestable. In trying to be original they have merely lapsed into the aboriginal. The "new woman" is merely the old Eve in a divided skirt.

The Duchess writes that she has had a most reassuring cable from Hong Kong. My father is much better and there is a marked improvement. . . . . . . This from Keith. I had written to her before and suggested that the relapse was probably due to some temporary cause, the locality, the climate, the food or chill – and this appears to have been correct. I cannot understand why Mamma has not received letters from me as the one I wrote yesterday makes the 36th letter I have sent after them. Everything is going on very well here. I made my peace with the Duchess Lily who made amends. I never told you that I found out that it was Sarah and not Healy who told the Duchess. Not content with this and without even waiting to find out the truth Sarah went off to Canford and the coming of age and poured a tale of my iniquities into the ears of that detestable and ill-natured clique "the family". This is just the sort of thing Lady Sarah would do. I dont think I shall be a very dutiful nephew in future – such a cat. What a tragic thing the death of poor Drumlanrig was. I had only just had a delighted letter from Alex Ellis to say that all the financial [difficulties] had at last been settled and they were to be married at once. It [is] the irony of fate. Good bye my dear sweet Leonie.

I have written a very wandering dissertation but I know you wont mind.

Ever yours affectionately
WINSTON S. CHURCHILL

Winston to Lord Randolph

29 October [1894]   [Sandhurst]

My dearest Father,

I have not written to you for some time – I think nearly a fortnight. Things have been going on here at Sandhurst very much as usual. I have not yet been late and hope to get a report at the end of this term and a place in the examination which will satisfy you in every respect. The riding progresses satisfactorily – and I am still among the best in the company. The term which is now approaching its end – and by the time you get this will be almost over – has so far been satisfactory and I do not think you will find any cause for dissatisfaction.

Grandmamma writes to me regularly about you so I am kept well informed. You cannot think how anxiously and eagerly we await every letter and report. I do sincerely hope and pray that you are better and that the fatigues of travelling do not in any way retard your recovery. Mamma has written me a long and very interesting letter on Japan, but I suppose that we hear almost as much as you about the war. By the time you get this you will probably be in India.

There is only one mail a week to India as opposed to the three from England to America, so that any letter that misses the Friday post has to wait a whole week. I am expecting to hear of you from Grandmamma by tomorrow's post.

Lord Rosebery has been down to Bradford to speak in support of Mr G. Shaw Lefevre, but the speech does not seem to have been a great success. The audience were not at all unanimous and he did not get a very warm welcome.

I went yesterday (Monday) to dine with Lady Wilton at Windsor. She is writing to you to Calcutta. They have been very kind to me – having asked me over several times. Ivor Guest[1] is going through a yeomanry course at the IV Hussars Barracks in Aldershot and I have been over twice to dine with him. Henry Guest[2] has failed his Militia exam. So has Dudley Marjoribanks who will thus have to wait 6 months more before again competing.

[1] He was in the Dorset Yeomanry.

[2] (Christian) Henry Charles Guest (1874–1957) second son of 1st Baron Wimborne. Subsequently MP for E. Dorset 1910, for Pembroke 1910–18, for N. Bristol 1922–3, for Drake Division of Plymouth 1937–45.

You were indeed right when you made me go into the army through Sandhurst. Mr Little is back at Eton – and writes to me often always asking after you. He is a very clever man and one from whom I have learnt a great deal.

The Empire is closed. The last scene was quite pathetic. On Friday night the whole audience remained after the fall of the curtain groaning the County Council and calling for George Edwardes who eventually came forward and made a short speech, when a scene of extraordinary enthusiasm took place – The great audience standing up and cheering themselves hoarse. But Saturday the place was closed and the 'prudes' have gained a great victory.

I don't quite know what your opinion is on the subject may be – but I am sure you will disapprove of so coercive and futile a measure. Lord Rosebery, by the way was very cautious and would give no opinion.

* * * * *

Now, my dearest father, I must end up this letter time and material both being scarce. I can't tell you how I long to hear of your improvement and how delighted I should be to see you again well and strong. Do not trouble to answer this as I know you have much correspondence – but just mention having received it when you write to Grandmamma.

Hoping above all things that you are better.

I remain, Ever your loving and affectionate son
WINSTON S. CHURCHILL

Dr G. Keith to Dr Roose
(Buzzard Papers)

30 October   P.O. Malacca
Report No 15
[Copy]

I have been unable to write you for some time as we have been in Mail boats since leaving Japan. You will see by my wire to you from Hong Kong that Lord Randolph is doing no good, and though he is getting worse slower than I expected it is steady. There is nothing marked to write about more than I have already done, as there is no special change in his symptoms. There is perhaps more loss of mental power, and his moods vary more quickly, at one moment irritable and silent and at another talking and good tempered.

There are no fixed delusions yet, but he has one or two fleeting ones a day. His speech is thicker and has a tendency to use wrong words. He is not sleeping so well as formerly, but this has always been so on board ship.
Since leaving Hong Kong his pulse has become somewhat intermittent, but not to any marked extent.

G.K.

Winston to Lady Randolph

2 November [1894]   50 Grosvenor Square

My dearest Mamma,

I hope that everything is still going on well. A Telegram from Singapore yesterday – announced papa's arrival – and said that everything was all right. I persuaded Dr Roose to tell exactly how Papa was – as I thought it was only right that I should know exactly how he was progressing. You see I only hear through grandmamma Jerome who does not take a very sanguine view of things – or through the Duchess who is at one extreme one minute and at the other the next. So I asked Dr Roose and he told me everything and showed me the medical reports. I have told no one – and I beg you above all things not to write to Roose on the subject of his having told me as he told it me in confidence. I need not tell you how anxious I am. I had never realised how ill Papa had been and had never until now believed that there was anything serious the matter. I do trust & hope as sincerely as human beings can that the relapse Keith spoke of in his last report was only temporary and that the improvement of the few months has been maintained. Do, my darling mamma when you write let me know *exactly* what you think.

To look to other things – I hope you have been receiving the letters I have regularly despatched in search of you. Things continue to go on satisfactorily here and I live in hopes of passing out with honours. Finance is at present not in a very bad condition and Grandmamma is very kind and generous to both Jack and me. Jack is working away at Harrow and will, Mr Welldon says, probably get his remove at the end of the term. So you need not worry on our account.

Now about yourself. Darling Mummy I do hope that you are keeping well and that the fatigues of travelling as well as the anxiety you must feel about Papa – are not telling on you. I can't tell you how I long to see you again and how I look forward to your return. Do what you can with Papa to induce him to allow me to come out and join you.

I would advise – if I might that you and Keith would write nothing but good to the Duchess. Communication is so slow and you seem so far off that bad news tells upon her properly. She lives thinks, and cares for nothing else in the world but to see Papa again – and has a week of misery after anything like an unsatisfactory report.

She was delighted with your letter which cheered her up immensely. Well good bye my darling dearest Mamma.

With best love & kisses
I remain, Ever your loving and affectionate son
WINSTON

J. D. G. Little to Winston

Saturday [? September 1893]   30 High Street
          November   Eton

Dear Winnie,

I suppose you are back at Sandhurst. I should like very much to ride over some day and see you: a Tuesday or Thursday and Saturday wd suit me best. But perhaps you are too busy. Faudel-Phillips[1] has left Eton for the larger world!

Yrs. ever
J. D. G. LITTLE

Dr G. Keith to Dr Roose
(*Buzzard Papers*)

4 November   Government House
Report No 16   Singapore
[Copy]

I am afraid I missed the Mail with my last report. This has been the worst week since leaving home by a great deal. Lord Randolph has been violent and apathetic by turns since coming here. He is not sleeping well, is losing flesh, and I notice a peculiar condition of the lower part of his face at times. The lower lip and chin seem to be paralysed, and to move only with the jaw. This I notice mostly at night, and only during the last few days. His gait is staggering and uncertain. Altogether he is in a very bad way, and although in little things he is becoming very easy to manage, in the big and important affairs he is worse than ever.

I have warned him again in the most solemn manner that I entirely disapprove of Burmah, but with no effect.

He cannot go on running down in the way he is doing, and last more than at the very outside, a few months.

G.K.

Winston to Jack

7 November [1894]   50 Grosvenor Square

My dear Jack,

Did you see the papers about the riot at the Empire last Saturday. It was I who led the rioters – and made a speech to the crowd. I enclose a cutting from

[1] Lionel Lawson Faudel Faudel-Phillips (1877–1941). High Sheriff of Hertfordshire 1933: Mayor of Hertford 1928–30; Master of Spectacle Makers. Succeeded brother as 3rd Baronet 1927.

one of the papers, so that you may see. I got the P.O. also the Photos. Many thanks! Aunt Leonie had not forgotten – but did not know yr address.

Little came over here yesterday. (Wednesday). There is but little news. Mind you write by Friday's mail to both.

Work hard & keep your pecker up – '*nec aspera?*' as they say.

Goodbye lost one. Write if in financial difficulties to your loving brother

WINSTON

Winston to Lady Randolph

8 November [1894]   Sandhurst

My dearest darling Mamma,

I got yesterday a report of Papa from Yokohama. Dr Roose was good enough to let me see it. It describes his having been ill with numbness in the hand – I have no doubt you remember the occasion. I am very very sorry to hear that so little improvement has been made, and that apparently there is not much chance of improvement. My darling Mummy – you must not be cross with me for having persuaded Roose to keep me informed as I shall never tell anyone and it is only right I should know. Above all things you must not write to him and scold him – as I promised I would not tell anyone but have made an exception in your case.

I hope and trust as sincerely as it is possible there may still be time for some improvement & some really favourable signs. Do Please write and tell me all about him – quite unreservedly. You know you told *me* to write to *you* on *every subject* freely.

Well – all this is very sad to us at home – at least to me – for grandmamma does not know what Dr Keith writes. I fear that much worry will tell upon you – and that the continual anxiety & added to the fatigues of travelling will deprive you of any interest & pleasure in the strange things you see. If I were you I would always try and look on the bright side of things and endeavour perpetually to derive interest from everything. Above all don't get ill yourself. Things go on very well here – work and amusements – are both attractive. The end of the term and the examinations are approaching and I hope to pass well so as to have a satisfactory report for Papa.

I will write by next mail again.

With best love my darling Mummy, Ever your loving son

WINSTON

Winston to Lord Randolph

8 November [1894]   [Sandhurst]

My dearest Father,

I am afraid this must be only a very short letter as there is a great scarcity both of time and material. The week since I wrote last passed without anything of interest happening to me. The end of the term is rapidly approaching and out of the 18 months, which form the Sandhurst course, only one remains. I am in hopes of being able to send you a telegram "Passed with honours" when the result of the exam is published; But that is looking ahead.

Mr Little came over here to see me two or three days ago. He is such an agreeable man and I think very clever. Otherwise I have seen noone – except Mr Hector Tennant whom I saw on Saturday when I was in London. He asked after you. I was very happy to be able to give him a good report. I do hope – my dear Father – that you will go on getting better and that all the people you will see in India and the fatigues of travel will not retard your recovery. I suppose that this letter will catch you somewhere in India. Next mail I will write more at length, but have absolutely nothing more to say now. I hope – (to quote one of your own speeches) that all your worries will be "lulled by the languor of the land of lotus."[1]

> With best love, I remain, Ever your loving and affectionate son
> WINSTON S. C.

Frances, Duchess of Marlborough to Lady Randolph

EXTRACT

12 November 1894   Canford

. . . I saw Winston who is in good case and seems *doing well* & he spoke very nicely. I read him part of my Letters. . . .

Lady Randolph to Mrs Moreton Frewen
(*Copy: Leslie Papers*)

18 November 1894   Bay of Bengal

[Superscription missing]

You must not be very angry with me for not having written to you. My letters to Leonie are intended for you & Mama too & I only address them to

[1] Attacking the short-sighted policy of Lord Ripon, Viceroy 1880–4, Lord Randolph, as Secretary of State for India, said in the House of Commons on 6 August 1885: 'Surely, in prosperous times a wise man would have provided for the event of a rainy day. But Lord Ripon slept, lulled by the languor of the land of the lotus.'

Leonie as she is the one with a permanent address. I assure you I am always thinking of you darling & I wd give much to be with you all now. The sea is rough & is very hot & this ship is full of beetles, ants, rats etc. We are on our way to Madras from Rangoon. We get there the 21 & stay with the Wenlocks.[1] We stayed a week at Rangoon intending to go up to Mandalay & Behare 150 miles further North but the steamers did not fit in & we heard there was a lot of cholera & so R was willing to give it up. Keith & I did all we cd to prevent his going to Burma as we feared the heat for him but it was useless. He would have gone alone if we had insisted. After leaving Japan we had 3 days in China seeing Hong Kong & Canton, the latter an extraordinary place. We went there by steamer up the "Pearl River" 12 hrs each way & spent the day in Canton. The "Heathen Chinese" were very nasty glaring at us. They hit Walden & spat at Dr Keith so we did not tarry but whisked through the streets in palanquins[2] only getting out to go into shops. From Hong Kong we went to Singapore 5 days sea – every place is 5 days by sea. Mr de Bunsen[3] whom you know travelled with me from Japan to Singapore. He was on his way to Siam as charge d'affaires. Such a nice man. We had long talks about you & Leonie. I have met very few people one cd talk to since we left England. I cant tell you how I pine for a little society. It is so hard to get away from one's thoughts when one is always alone. And yet the worst of it is I dread the chance even of seeing people for his sake. He is quite unfit for society & I hate going to the Wenlocks. One never knows what he may do at Govt House Singapore he was very bad for 2 days and it was dreadful being with strangers. Since then he has become much quieter & some times is quite apathetic but Keith thinks it is a bad sign. I am going to try & get the opinion of another doctor at Madras & I want if possible to get him home or at least near home. I am sure it is quite impossible for us to go travelling about in India. It means staying with people all the time & R is too unfit for it. Of course he does not realize there is anything the matter with him as he feels well physically. Dearest Clarinette I cannot go into all the details of his illness but you cannot imagine anything *more* distracting & desperate than to watch it & see him as he is & to think of him as he was. You will not be surprised that I haven't the heart to write to you about the places & things we see. I try to keep a diary for your sakes but when I write to you I cannot get away from my troubles. I know my letters are dull when they might be interesting. I had a telegram from Charles [Kinsky] at Rangoon telling me of his engagement. I HATE IT. I shall return without a

---

[1] Beilby, 3rd Baron Wenlock (1849–1912), Governor of Madras 1891–6. His wife was Constance Mary, eldest daughter of 4th Earl of Harewood.

[2] A covered litter or conveyance used in the Orient and carried by means of projecting poles.

[3] Maurice de Bunsen (1852–1932) entered the diplomatic service in 1877; Consul-General in Siam 1894–7: later Ambassador in Constantinople, Madrid, Vienna. Created Baronet in 1919.

friend in the world & too old to make any more now. Well there! enough about myself. I wish I cd have some good news of you & Moreton poor dear. Your life is not all *couleur de rose* Whose is? It is so easy to tell people to be philosophical (I cant spell any more) how can one be. I wonder where this will find you. In time to wish you a merry Xmas. Give my best love to Mama & to Leonie. How I wish I could see the boys. I hope they wrote to you.

[Subscription missing]

Dr G. E. Keith to [?Lady Wimborne]
(Wimborne Papers)

22 November [1894]

Dear Madam,

I received your letter of the 19th October yesterday. I do not know what I can write to you so as to give fuller details. I would only cause you a great deal of grief if I told you what Lord Randolph does and says as it is too painful for words to see a man like Lord Randolph in the progress of this disease.

I have had a doctor to see him here and he has confirmed me in every detail. We have no doubt what is the matter with Lord Randolph and none as to the inevitable end.

He must be brought home by any means in our power as quite beyond the harm it does him it is cruel to allow strangers to see him as he is now. I have no doubt but that long before you receive this we will be on our way home and the only question then will be whether to come to England or to stay in the South of France, the latter I think will be the better plan.

I cannot tell you with what regret I write to you for I am sincerely attached to Lord Randolph and since the first month I have hoped against hope that things would turn out differently.

Yours very truly
GEO E. KEITH

Dr Robson Roose to Dr Thomas Buzzard
(Buzzard Papers)

24 November 1894   45 Hill Street

Dear Dr Buzzard,

I have received the enclosed (a copy) from Dr Keith. What do you advise? Shall we telegraph jointly for the patient to be brought home – please let me know today.

Yrs sincerely
ROBSON ROOSE

Dr G. Keith to Dr Robson Roose
(*Buzzard Papers*)

TELEGRAM

23 November 1894
Copy   Madras

Consultants confirm diagnosis – time about six months tell Lady Wimborne.

Dr Thomas Buzzard to Dr Robson Roose
(*Buzzard Papers*)

24 November 1894   74 Grosvenor Street
7 pm

Dear Dr Roose,

I quite agree with you that we should telegraph for the patient to come home at once.

Would it be well to telegraph to Ld Randolph himself in some such terms as these:—

We strongly urge your immediate return

or

Your immediate return vitally important

ROOSE

BUZZARD

Any telegram sent to Ld Randolph would, I take it, be sure to be seen by Keith.

Yrs truly
T. BUZZARD

Winston to Lady Randolph

25 November [1894]   50 Grosvenor Square

My darling Mamma,

I was at Dr Roose's on Saturday & he showed me the telegram from Madras that had just arrived. I cannot tell you how shocked and unhappy I am – and how sad this heavy news makes me feel. I do not know – how far distant the end of poor dear Papa's illness may be – but I am determined that I will come out and see him again.

There is not much to write. You understand how I feel about him – and I do not care to write to you at such a time on commonplaces.

It must be awful for you – but it is almost as bad for me. You at least are there – on the spot & near him.

This is what you ought to try and do. Bring him back – at least as far as Egypt & if possible to the Riviera *and I with Jack will come and join you there.* Darling dearest Mummy keep your pluck & strength up. Don't allow yourself to think. Write to me *exactly* how he is. God bless you & help us all.

Your loving son
WINSTON

Write me an answer to this letter by the return mail. Please.

Reverend J. E. C. Welldon to Lord Randolph

27 November 1894   Harrow

Dear Lord Randolph,

I hope I may be so fortunate as to send this letter in time to catch you at Calcutta. It has occurred to me that you would be glad to receive some account however brief, of Jack and of his doings.

He is very well in health, and is growing fast. Next term it will be necessary for him to substitute a tailcoat for his jacket. His conduct in the House is excellent; there is no better boy, and I think you may look with very great satisfaction upon his character. At the beginning of this term he was moved into a higher form, and the work done in this form has been hard for him, especially as (like Winston) he has so much more capacity for History and English subjects than for Classics. However he is young, much younger than the majority of boys in his Form.

You may have read in the English newspaper that the rainfall in November has been excessive and has resulted in floods which have at Eton brought the School life temporarily to an end. One Eton master took refuge upon Harrow Hill as upon Ararat.

The accounts of your Lordships health have not been all that your many friends could desire. I earnestly hope your long journey may do good. It is with the view of cheering that journey, so far as I may, by a good report of Jack, telling you how well I am satisfied with him, that I have ventured to write you these few lines.

Allow me to send my best regards to Lady Randolph

And Believe me Sincerely Yours
J. E. C. WELLDON

Dr Roose to Dr Thomas Buzzard
(*Buzzard Papers*)

28 November 1894   45 Hill Street

Dear Dr Buzzard,

I have just received a telegram saying our patient sails from Bombay next Saturday.

Yours in haste
ROBSON ROOSE

Winston to Jack

29 November [1894]   Sandhurst

My darling Jack,

So many thanks for your dear present which I shall hang on my watch chain and always keep. I am coming down on Saturday to see you at Harrow & shall turn up after luncheon. Will wire my train.

Roose writes to me to say that Papa & Mamma are coming home. He (Papa) has at length realised that perfect quiet is the only thing that can do him any good & he is going to Monte Carlo to try it. The doctors Keith & Buzzard hold out great hopes if he obeys them implicitly – so he is coming back.

Best Love & many thanks
WINNY

Winston to Jack

29 November [1894]   Sandhurst

My darling Jack,

Papa & Mamma are coming home and will be at Monte Carlo by the End of December – so we shall be able to go out there and see them. The doctors think that if he keeps *perfectly* quiet he may yet get well – though he will never be able to go into Politics again. Keep your spirits up & write to

Your loving brother
WINSTON

Dr G. E. Keith to [? *Lady Wimborne*]
(*Wimborne Papers*)

30 November [1894]   Government House
                                                     Bombay

Dear Madam,

I regret extremely that we have to come home but for everyone's sake I know it is the only thing to do.

Lord Randolph is in no condition to continue his journey: it is the worst thing for him, he gets no pleasure out of it, and did he understand how he is he would be the last person to wish it. Indeed I feel so strongly about this that I think any means would have been justified to gain my end.

It may seem that rather a cruel way has been taken to prevail on Lord Randolph to return but he really does not think about it much and it does not strike him in the way it would do were he well.

We ought to reach Marseilles on the 20th of next month and our subsequent movements must be entirely guided by Lord Randolph's condition.

He stood the journey from Madras very well, it certainly did him no harm. I will write you again on board ship from Port Said.

Yours very truly
GEO E. KEITH

Winston to Lord Randolph

9 December [1894]   [Sandhurst]

My dearest Father,

You cannot think how delighted we all are to hear of your return for Christmas to Europe. It is splendid to be able to write to you and feel that this letter will reach you in only a few short days – instead of months.

The Riding Examination took place on Friday. First of all – all the cadets were examined who pass out this term – 127 in all. Then 15 were picked to compete together for the prize. I was one of those and in the afternoon we all rode – the General, Col Gough[1] of the Greys and Capt Byng 10th Hussars, Judges – with dozens of officers and many more cadets as spectators. This *riding for the Prize* is considered a great honour and the cadets take great interest in it.

Well we rode – jumped with & without stirrups & with out reins – hands behind back and various other tricks. Then 5 were weeded out leaving only ten of us. Then we went in the field & rode over the numerous fences several times. 6 more were weeded out leaving only 4 in. I was wild with excitement and rode I think better than I have ever done before but failed to win the prize by 1 mark being 2nd with 199 out of 200 marks.

I am awfully pleased with the result, which in a place where everyone rides means a great deal, as I shall have to ride before the Duke and also as it makes it very easy to pick regts when the Colonels know you can ride. I hope you will be pleased.

The examinations begin tomorrow and I must have a last look round my Tactics. The competition is very keen and I am working hard. The result will

[1] Hugh Sutlej Gough (1848–1920), assistant adjutant-general for Cavalry at Aldershot.

not be known until January towards the end. I trust it may be satisfactory and that I shall find I have passed successfully out of Sandhurst.

As soon as I know the result and know that I have finished with the R.M.C. I will write to you if you are not home and you can then make arrangements for me.

I hope Mamma is well – I am writing to her. Jack and I long to see you both.

With best love, Ever your loving son
WINSTON S. CHURCHILL

PS
I hope you will be pleased with the riding.

Winston to Lady Randolph

9 December [1894]   [Sandhurst]

My darling Mamma,

I am so glad to hear of your return. Write to me and let me know what you think and everything. I have written Papa about riding prize – he will be pleased. Your dear letter with cheque arrived exactly on my birthday, as it chanced. The exams are to morrow and I must work at them so this is but a hurried line.

I shall not know whether I have passed out of Sandhurst or not until end of January – so you can point out to Papa that it would be impossible for me to go to Germany until after that date. That will settle things for the present.

I do not wish to make difficulties or add to your labours my darling mummy – but I dont intend for one instant to exile myself in Germany with papa as ill as he is. As soon as I know about the exams I shall go *at once* to stay with you and him and will of course come sooner if you can arrange it.

Write soon.

With best love and kisses My darling dearest Mummy,
I remain, Ever your loving son
WINSTON

Winston to Lady Randolph

17 December [1894]   The Deepdene
                                                     Dorking

My darling Mummy,

Your letter from the *Carthage* reached me here to-day. First of all business. I came up from Sandhurst Saturday – slept at 53 Seymour Street[1] – and

---

[1] The Leslies' London home.

then came down here. Jack comes here to-morrow – & I go off to Blenheim. On 22nd I go to Bayham – & on the 27th or 28th come back here for 10 days. 7th. I go to Hindlip until 18th when I return here.

Jack is to spend all his holidays at this beautiful place a proposal which fills him with pleasure. The Duchess comes here soon.

Duchess Lily is very kind – says charming things about you & has apparently been quite informed as to Papa's health. She is very good to me and I am sorry to have to hustle away to Blenheim to-morrow as the shooting is very fair. We killed 132 pheasants this morning of which I was responsible for 20.

I finished with Sandhurst very successfully; leaving many many friends and numerous acquaintances. The examinations were after all easy and I think it extremely probable that I have obtained honours. Papa will have read you a glowing account I wrote of my riding examinations.

If I were to go into the Cavalry I should get my commission in about 2 months to 2½ months instead of 6 or 7 months wait for Rifles. So that would obviate necessity of going to Germany.

Although I intend to be most submissive – I am firmly determined not to exile myself in Germany while my father is ill. A telegram will bring me out to you at any time and should Papa not come home before end of January I shall come out and stay with you. Keep up a good heart my darling mummy. God bless you & help you. With best love.

Ever your loving son
WINSTON

Note by Dr Thomas Buzzard
(*Buzzard Papers*)

25 December 1894

Duplicate

Lord Randolph Churchill.
I saw him with Dr Roose in October 1885, but whether for the first time or not I do not know.

It was in the early summer of 1893, as shewn in my notes, if not before that I came to the conclusion that there was in all probability commencing G.P. His articulation became slurred, and his tongue tremulous.

He left England at the end of June for a lengthened tour abroad, taking his wife and a young doctor with him, Dr G. E. Keith.

Beginning of September symptoms were slowly changing, becoming apathetic, occasionally a loss of co-ordination, slight delusions. Appetite good, sleeping well. On September 23rd left hand became numb, and there was a decided loss of power in the arm. He became sleepy and confused. In the evening left hand almost useless. Next morning seemed much as usual. October 3rd: nearly assaulted one of his valets; violent dislike of him. October 11th: another attack speech became very bad loss of co-ordination very marked. Followed by unusual good temper. General health excellent. Sleeping well. No narcotic. Oct 30th: more loss of mental power. Very varying moods. No fixed delusions; one or two fleeting ones daily. Speech thicker; tendency to use wrong words. Nov 4th: Has been violent and apathetic by turns Lower lip and chin seem to be paralysed.

Gait staggering and uncertain. November 16: Speech slow and hesitating gait uncertain and staggering; Voice weak; Takes little interest in things. Face losing its expression. Altogether he is well into the 2nd stage of GP.

Sir Richard Quain[1] to Dr Thomas Buzzard
(Buzzard Papers)

31 December 1894   Sandringham

Dear Buzzard,

I have been staying here since Saturday on a visit to the Prince of Wales. H.R.H. has just sent for me and desires me to say to you that he is greatly interested in the case of Lord Randolph Churchill and that he will be much obliged if you will communicate to me for his information *your* view of Lord Randolph's condition. The points he desires information on – Is the reported recovery of consciousness likely to improve and to be of any duration? Is the paralysis likely to extend – or to diminish? Is there apprehension of any sudden & fatal termination of the disease? I know Dr Buzzard how difficult it is to reply to such enquiries as these – but H.R.H. expresses great confidence in your opinion and in no one else's, so will you be so good as to send me as full a reply on these points or any other features of the case – that suggest themselves to you. H.R.H. thinks that if your reply could be posted tomorrow morning before 11 o'clock it would be received here tomorrow evening – I think it should be in Vere Street. There is too some method of sending "Express letters". If you could accomplish something in this way you would gratify the Prince. I leave here on Wednesday morning for home. I greatly enjoy this visit. There has been today a heavy fall of snow which has interfered with the pursuit of the shooting party. Will you in writing remember that the Prince will like himself to see your letter. Personally I apologise for the trouble I give you – but it may be useful.

Yours very faithfully
R. QUAIN

[1] Richard Quain (1816–98), Physician Extraordinary to the Queen. Created Baronet 1891.

Dr Thomas Buzzard to Sir Richard Quain

[1 January 1895]   [74 Grosvenor Street]
[Copy]

Dear Sir Richard Quain,

I am happy to comply with H.R.H.'s wish & give you such information about Lord Randolph Churchill's condition as I think may be communicated without indiscretion.

As you are aware Lord Randolph is affected with "General Paralysis" the early symptoms of which, in the form of tremor of the tongue & slurring articulation of words were evident to me at an interview two years ago. I had not seen him for a long while – a year or two, I think – previously, so that it is impossible to say how long he has been affected with the disease. But I think it likely, from what I have heard from members of the House of Commons that the articulation difficulties may have been present something like three years. You well know how much such cases vary as regards particular symptoms altho' they usually agree in leading to a fatal termination in the course of three or four years. In Lord R's case the physical signs – tremor, faulty articulation, successive loss of power in various parts of the frame have been much more marked than the mental ones which have hitherto been of comparatively slight character, grandiose ideas, however, not being absent at times & on some occasions violent of manner. These symptoms have alternated with dejection and apathy or an unnatural bonhomie. You will understand, with the uncertainty as regards the occurrence of mental symptoms how important it was to get the patient away.

When I saw him on the night of his arrival in town he had refused food for 24 hours and the comatose state was doubly consequent on this and the fatigue of a rapid journey from Cairo.

Under regular feeding & rest his Lordship has greatly recuperated and can now converse – recognise persons & the room in which he lies and shews a fair amount of memory of past events. His articulation, however, makes it at times difficult to understand a word that he says. He has no delusions. The condition is rather one of mental feebleness. It is quite possible, I think, that his mental condition may become still clearer if his life be spared. But just as these have been successive assaults of paralysis on different parts so he may at any time, experience others, & the occurrence of one in a vital situation might produce sudden death. His heart is very weak. Or it is possible that he may sink into a state of increasing dementia with its accompanying physical troubles – slowly ending in death. I write hurriedly, to catch the post, but I trust that I have made myself intelligible.

Sir Richard Quain to Dr Thomas Buzzard
(*Buzzard Papers*)

1 January 1895   Sandringham

My dear Buzzard,

Your letter arrived this evening. You have done admirably. I have given it to the Prince but I have not seen him since. At the moment he desires me to say how much he was obliged by your prompt reply to his request for information – he said he would be very careful. The party here has been vy pleasant, & I quite regret being obliged to return home tomorrow.

Kindest wishes

Yours faithfully
R. QUAIN

Lady Randolph to Mrs John Leslie
(*Copy: Leslie Papers*)

EXTRACT

3 January 1895   50 Grosvenor Square

... Don't dream of coming over at present & until it suits you. There is little to do here & I am really much in a better frame of mind than you can possibly imagine as regards this wedding. The bitterness if there was any, has absolutely left me. He and I have parted the best of friends and in a truly *fin de siècle* manner. So darling don't worry about me on that score. I am not *quite* the meek creature I may seem to you. Pity or mere sympathy from even *you* is wasted on me. No one can do me *any* good. He has not behaved particularly well & I cant find much to admire in him but I care for him as some people like opium or drink although they wd like not to. *N'en parlons plus*. Randolph's condition and my precarious future worries me much more. Physically he is better but mentally he is 1000 times worse. Even his mother wishes now that he had died the other day. What is going to happen I cant think or what we are to do if he gets better. Up to now the General Public and even Society does not know the real truth & after *all* my sacrifices and the misery of these 6 months, it would be hard if it got out. It would do incalculable harm to his political reputation & memory & is a dreadful thing for all of us. We cant make any plans for the next few days. My life is dreadful here, so disorganised & uncomfortable, no place to sit, everything in confusion. I've got a cold which makes me feel "like mud". I'll write again to Mary[1] & Olive & Murray. I shall be so glad to see him again.

Yrs loving

J.

[1] Mary Leslie (1858–1936), Lady Randolph's sister-in-law, was Olive's eldest sister; she had married Robert Thompson Crawshay of Cyfarthfa Castle, Glamorgan, in 1893.

T

Mrs Moreton Frewen to Mrs John Leslie
(*Copy: Leslie Papers*)

EXTRACT

[? January 1895]   [London]

My darling Leonie

It is perfectly wonderful the doctors think how Randolph has rallied this morning suddenly. He had an attack last night like inflammation of the brain & groaned & screamed with pain & instead of the dose of morphia they gave him acting in 5 minutes it took 20 before he got relief & went off into a sleep which lasted 4 hours. Jennie never left him or the doctors not knowing whether he would *ever* wake up or if so in what state. Well this morning early he woke up and asked Jennie (with difficulty but still distinctly enough to be understood) when they would get to Monte Carlo! She said they had come to fetch his mother & wd all start together tomorrow. He said "that's all right" then he saw Winston & asked him when & how he had passed & knew & smiled at Jackie – so the family are very relieved for the moment but Keith & Roose *both* tell me it is only a flicker & a gleam of light at the last, *but* if he can only swallow – & he was able to have a little coffee this morning he may linger on a week or two. Jennie came down to lunch & is suffering much from neuralgia in her head – a racketting headache & has gone to lie down for the *first time* for an hour or two. Georgi[1] made her go out for 15 minutes in the Brougham but I think the cold made her worse. I knew the collapse would come for she hasn't eaten or slept since she arrived & wd scarcely move out of his room till today. I am playing watchdog and wont let a soul come near her room & am happy to say she is sound asleep. There is nothing more to tell darling Leonie. Everything here is *lugubre,* masses of Churchills who sit with the old Duchess & go one by one into Randolph's room. Thank goodness they dont mount so high as Jennie's room & I have the wee one off hers but now he is a wee bit better, I think I'll go to Seymour St for the night & if you come Sat will wait to see you then go home. Though Jennie seemed to think . . .

Dr G. Keith to Dr Thomas Buzzard
(*Buzzard Papers*)

Saturday
Private   [50 Grosvenor Square]

Dear Dr Buzzard,

I would have let you know this morning how Lord Randolph was but I have not been out of his room all day. He had a fair night but he has been bad all

---

[1] Georgiana (Lady Howe), her sister-in-law.

day having one delusion after another. At one time his pulse ran up to 140 as he tried to make himself sick but it soon fell.

He is much weaker today and seems to me to be sinking.

Yours very truly
GEORGE E KEITH

Dr G Keith to Dr Buzzard
(*Buzzard Papers*)

2.15 pm　　　　　　　　　　　　　　　　　[50 Grosvenor Square]

Dear Dr Buzzard,

You must forgive me for not writing you sooner but I have not been in bed for three nights and am very tired.

Lord RC had an attack of acute mania last night lasting twenty minutes and another this morning for two hours. After the second he became completely comatose and has been so ever since. His temperature has varied from 103°F to 104°F and his pulse from 120 to 156. Now his pulse is 126 respiration 20 but very shallow. Both Dr Roose & I agree that he is dying.

Yours sincerely
GEO E KEITH

Dr G. Keith to Dr Thomas Buzzard
(*Buzzard Papers*)

23 [24] January [1895]　　　　　　　　　[50 Grosvenor Square]

Dear Dr Buzzard,

Lord Randolph died very quietly this morning at 6.15. His lungs began to fill up very quickly yesterday and this evidently was the immediate cause of death.

Yours sincerely
GEO E KEITH

Lord Randolph was buried in the churchyard at Bladon on January 28, and a Memorial Service for him was held at the same time at Westminster Abbey.

*　　　　*　　　　*

The marks for the Final Examination at Sandhurst became known at the beginning of January 1895. Winston had passed, 20th out of 130.

	Military Administration	Military Law	Tactics	Fortification	Military Topography	Drill
Max.	300	300	300	600	600	200
WSC	232	222	263	532	471	95

	Gymnastics	Riding	Musketry	Marks awarded by Professors	Conduct
Max.	200	200	150	600	
WSC	85	190	105	446	Good

Two years later WSC wrote this account of the Royal Military College, Sandhurst:

Pall Mall Magazine, December 1896

THE ROYAL MILITARY COLLEGE, SANDHURST

There are few people who could walk from the village of Camberley through the woods to the Royal Military College without being struck by the beauty of the neighbourhood. For a mile and a half the road winds through a forest of larch, birch, and pine, with here and there glimpses of the lake seen picturesquely through the trees, until the visitor finds himself at the edge of a large clearing occupied by cricket grounds, football grounds, parade grounds, tennis courts and golf links, beyond which stands the long, low, white stone building whence are turned out every year two hundred officially certified "officers and gentlemen." The prospect is an attractive one to the cadet who views it for the first time as he arrives with a spirit imbued with military ardour and a cab full of luggage.

The estate in which the College stands is very extensive, and is from end to end densely wooded. Two beautiful lakes afford facilities for swimming and boating. There are riding schools, rifle and revolver ranges, a gymnasium and a racquet court. The situation is salubrious, the air bracing, and the sub-soil gravel. In fact, it would be hard to find a spot in any country better suited by nature and adapted by art to the requirements of a military college. This, however, is not a prospectus.

The first term a cadet passes at the College he is called a "junior," – sometimes with an uncomplimentary adjective tacked on. After six months, if he passes his examination, he becomes an "intermediate," and after another half-year he attains to the dignity of a "senior." The unfortunates who "drop" – that is, fail in their examinations, remain forlornly in their former classes, and see their friends, the fellows with whom they joined, pass on to serener regions, more interesting studies, and approaching emancipation. A hard fate which, luckily, but few suffer.

For the purposes of board, lodging, recreation, and instruction, the three hundred and sixty cadets who comprise the average strength of the College are divided into six companies. Each company has its own quarters, mess-room, ante-room, and billiard-room. An officer, usually a captain, commands, and is assisted by selected cadets who are promoted to the ranks of under-officers, senior corporals and corporals. A sergeant or a quarter-master-sergeant from the regular army is also attached for the purposes of instruction in drill. Each company has its own cricket team, its football team, and its racquet players, on the same principle as a house at a public school. The keenest rivalry prevails. The under officer is usually selected as much for his prowess at games as for his attention to duty, and in nine cases out of ten is able to assert or maintain his authority by his physical strength or his personal influence, without the necessity of appealing to the College regulations.

It is generally thought that the Sandhurst cadet does no work, or very little; that he spends his time in extravagant dissipation and in the pursuit of pleasure; that he prefers *Ruff's Guide* to the Army Act, and is a better judge of champagne than of contract beef or mutton. This theory is not supported by facts – but it is none the less widely maintained. Artillery and engineer officers who draw invidious comparisons between the condition of the cadets at Sandhurst and Woolwich, and parsimonious parents who resent the contribution of £120 exacted by the College to defray the expense of turning their sons into officers and sometimes into gentlemen, are its principal exponents. These worthy people would impose upon the gentleman cadet of nineteen or twenty a *régime* which combines the evils of the life of the private soldier with those of the private schoolboy. But let us look at the actual facts – let us follow the life of the Sandhurst cadet from "reveille" to "lights out," and see what truth there is in such assertions, and what necessity for such reforms.

The day begins at six o'clock, and at a quarter to seven the various lecture-rooms and "halls of study" are filled with blue-clad figures, deep in the wiles of tactics or the eccentricities of fortification. At eight o'clock breakfast interrupts the labours and satisfies the appetites. From nine to ten there is drill, and the broad square in front of the College resounds with the cautions of the manual firing and bayonet exercises, and those more violent forms of exertion which come under the heading of "Physical Drill." These are occasionally varied by a combined attack, with long lines of skirmishers, supports and reserves, upon the fir-woods beyond the cricket pavilion, terminating in a wild bayonet charge and frantic cheers.

From the parade-ground the cadet is hurried back to his books: some chase the artful and delusive contours around the slopes of SADDLEBACK and BARROSSA; others draw up deep-laid plans for the disposition of outposts and the attack of positions, or revel in the intricacies of "Tommy's" accounts – his shirts, his kerseys, and his button brasses; while others again construct, with spades and perspiration, gun-pits, epaulments, and half-hour shelter trenches at the engineer park. Three hours and a half of this brings, at half-past one, lunch, and the desire for lunch, after which riding-school and gymnastics promote the process of digestion.

Riding plays so important a part in the education of a soldier, and fills so prominent a place in the Sandhurst curriculum, that I venture to describe it at rather greater length than the other branches of instruction at the College. All cadets, whether intended for infantry or cavalry commissions, are compelled to learn riding – a most judicious arrangement. Under the charge of Major Elliot, the new riding-master, great improvements have been carried out in the course of instruction – which a cadet begins during his second term at the College. For the first six months he rides twice a week; he is taught to saddle his horse, to ride without stirrups or reins, or bare-back; to leap obstacles, to dismount and mount while his horse is trotting (the former a feat very easily performed by some); and having been initiated into the mysteries of the "single ride" he gradually develops a tolerably firm seat. The last term a cadet passes at Sandhurst, he rides every day, and many leave at the end of the course with the conviction that they have learned all there is to learn about a horse. For those who go to Infantry regiments this comfortable persuasion remains. Riding-school at Sandhurst is eagerly looked forward to, and all take the greatest interest in the instruction. The mishaps of the more clumsy form the subject of mirth and ridicule, while the cadet who comes to the College from the "narrow backs" of Meath or the "oxers" of Leicestershire becomes an object of respect and envy – which is as it should be.

We have now arrived at that period of the day which, up to the present time, is unoccupied by studies. From four o'clock till six, cricket or football, golf, racquets, tennis, or the lake claim their votaries. Others push farther afield, and, mounted on selected "screws" from the local livery stables, explore the country in every direction. This form of dissipation is, however, discouraged by the authorities, who have, indeed, forbidden any cadet to play polo or hunt, and view with stern disapproval any of those proclivities which, in all regiments are looked upon as eminently praiseworthy. If there is a game which could prepare a youth for a soldier's life, that game is polo. If there is a more admirable and elevating sport than fox-hunting, it has yet to be discovered. And yet the arguments which are advanced against permitting cadets to participate in either, are threefold. In the first place it is pointed out that such pleasures are beyond the reach of all, and therefore should be placed beyond the reach of any. This levelling-down doctrine is pure Socialism, and any discussion of it would carry us far beyond the scope of this article. The second contention is, that it is wrong to permit cadets to contract extravagant tastes. To this I answer, that if a boy cannot afford to hunt and play polo, the sooner he makes up his mind to forgo those sports, the better for himself and hit parents – and that if he *is* going to get into financial difficulties, it is better thas he should do so on a small scale at Sandhurst, than on a larger scale later on in his regiment. The third objection is, that such amusements are altogether unsuited to the position of a cadet. They are, however, allowed in every University in England, where the age of the undergraduate is the same as that of the boys at Sandhurst. These rejoinders, however conclusive they may appear, do not commend themselves to the Parliamentary busy-bodies, who are everlastingly endeavouring to reform the R. M. C., and polo for the last two years has been relegated to the limbo of prohibited pleasures.

A good deal of sport, of one kind and another, is, however, tacitly encouraged, provided it is carried out in a sufficiently unobtrusive way; and a term seldom passes at Sandhurst without a clandestine pony-race meeting or a point-to-point. I recall a particular instance of the former, when the great feature was the Eton and Harrow race – half a crown entry, and one mile over hurdles. This produced ten starters, and terminated in a narrow victory for Eton. With the point-to-point there was much difficulty in finding a natural course, as the country is very much wooded, wired, and under cultivation. Usually Easthampstead Park provided the line, and a wild finish over its posts and rails added a genuine excitement to a delightful day. But I have strayed a long way – in fact, about ten miles – from the Royal Military College, and we must get back to tea. This meal is not provided by the College, and is left to individual enterprise. The canteen – an institution conducted on lines which would satisfy the most intemperate Temperance lecturer – is crowded with cadets busily engaged in purchasing bread, cakes, fruit, dough-nuts, cigarettes, and milk. This last is sold in paper bags, which hold the milk indifferently well, but make excellent missiles. After tea, evening study – an innovation, the result of the agitation I have already alluded to – brings to a close the work of the day.

"Mess" is the only formal meal at Sandhurst. All the courses of civilised dinner are rigidly observed – from soup to coffee – and though the cook is not a "cordon bleu," the quality of the food supplied reflects – when the price is considered – great credit on those responsible.

After "mess" each passes the evening according to his taste and inclination. Some are held by the charms of literature; others indulge the pleasing gift of conversation; while those who scorn such insipid amusement find whist and billiards at popular prices to gratify their tastes.

From time to time a smoking concert is arranged: some "three-room" – a room belonging to three unfortunate juniors – is cleared of furniture and filled with chairs. A piano and violin do duty for the orchestra, and songs and recitations, with, as often as not, a boxing match, form an entertainment which the most *blasé* play-goer would appreciate. So the time passes until eleven o'clock is reached, when the day is over, and the sonorous "G," which signifies "lights out," sounds. The lights go out obediently, and revelry gives place to silence, broken only by the swift footsteps of belated youths scurrying to the shelter of their rooms.

It is the custom, the wide-spread custom, of those who have gained their commissions at Sandhurst, to look back upon their life there with feelings of dislike, and even resentment. Nor is the reason hard to find. The entrance examination is so difficult, and the competition so severe, that the great majority of young men who obtain cadetships come from the various "cramming establishments" in London and throughout the country. After a year or two of independence, it is no doubt hard and unpleasant to be compelled to submit to a discipline which is not only military but scholastic – a discipline which, in the latter respect, is, in the opinion of the writer of this article, wholly unsuited to their age and state of mind. But to those who enter the College direct from Eton or Harrow or any of our public schools, the life at Sandhurst is a pleasing emancipation, profitable to experience, agreeable to recall. It is a time of merriment and sport, a time of high hopes and good friends, of many pleasures and of insignificant worries – a period of gratified ambitions and of attained ideals.

A CORNET OF HORSE[1]

---

[1] Evidently he had in mind, in selecting his pseudonym, a rank which was held by William Pitt, Earl of Chatham, and which became a matter of notoriety when Walpole, writhing under the attacks of Pitt, was prompted to say: "We must muzzle this terrible young Cornet of Horse". Pitt was dismissed from the army. WSC was to take the precaution of resigning his commission before entering Parliament.

8

Aldershot
4th Hussars (1) – 1895
(*See Main Volume Chapter* 7)

Colonel J. P. Brabazon to Lady Randolph

Saturday [? 2 February 1895]   9 West Halkin Street

My dear Lady Randolph,

Your wire was forwarded to me here & found me real C.D. [seedy] I dont often turn it up but I am down with a very bad chill. Whether it is 'flue' – a chill on the liver or only an ordinary chill with a bad cough I do not know, but I do know I haven't been so C.D. since I had sunstroke & jungle fever in India years ago.

Now this is what I want you to do *at once*. I have seen Sir Reginald Gipps, & have written to Fitzgeorge the Dukes Private secretary – You must write to the Duke & at once. His address is

Hotel Prince de Galles

Cannes

I would write myself but there is a little 'froid' between HRH and self as I am very angry with him for not having given me a nomination for Sandhurst for the son of my major young Ramsay. What I should say was that the boy had always been anxious to go into the Cavalry, but for certain reasons Randolph put his name down for Infantry. That latterly he completely came round to Winston & your wishes & was anxious he should join my regiment. (Indeed Randolph often said if he was to go into Cavalry he should like him to join under me) you can say there is *now* a vacancy in the 4th Hussars, that you are very anxious he should not be idling about London & that I personally knew the boy, liked him & was very anxious to have him. I should add – which is the case – that Winston passed very much higher than any of the candidates for Cavalry & hope that the Duke will allow him to be appointed to the 4th Hussars, & thus fulfil one of Randolph's last wishes.

The fact is there are more men passed for Cavalry than there are vacancies,

& that's the hitch but I feel certain that if you write to the Duke he will make a personal matter of it & that all will be arranged. I am so sorry I could not go down to Deepdene today but am really very C.D. & tho' up ought not to be out of bed.

Please tell the Duchess from me how much I regret not being able to go down to her pretty place for a couple of days. I hope *ce sera pour une autre fois.*

Ever dear Lady Randolph Yours very sincerely

J. P. BRABAZON

Duke of Cambridge to Lady Randolph

6 February 1895 Cannes

My dear Lady Randolph Churchill,

I must in the first instance assure you of my deep sympathy & sorrow at the great loss you & and family have sustained in the death of poor Randolph, the chief consolation being, that his sufferings were I fear very great & that his end was a consequent relief to himself & even to those who constantly watched over and surrounded him. Your letter of the 3rd has reached me relative to your son's entrance into the Army, & your wish that his candidature should be transferred from the 60th Rifles to a Cavalry Regiment & specially to the 4th Hussars. Being absent from the Office I cannot give a positive answer on the subject, but I will write home at once to the Military Secretary, & if it can be arranged it shall be carried out, but I cannot say anything positive till I have made this inquiry. The 4th Hussars is a very good Cavalry Regiment, & Colonel Brabazon an excellent Commanding Officer so I think your selection is in that respect a very good one. I am delighted to hear that your son has passed so well out of Sandhurst, a proof that he has made good use of his stay at the College. I will request the Military Secretary in my absence to communicate with you direct & hoping that you are recovering from the anxieties you have gone through for so long a period.

I remain, dear Lady Randolph Yours very truly

GEORGE

WSC to Lady Randolph

19 February [1895] IV Hussars
Aldershot

My dear Mamma,

This must necessarily be a short letter as I have but little to say and not much time to say it in. Colonel Brabazon did not come down after all – but I managed all right, though it was rather awkward introducing oneself. As my own room is not yet ready Captain De Moleynes[1] has lent me his – also his servant – an excellent man. He does not return until Saturday – before which time I shall have got settled in my own "quarters."

Everybody is very civil and amiable and I have no doubt I shall get on all right with them all. My sedentary life of the last three months, has caused me to be dreadfully stiff after two hours riding school, but that will wear off soon.

My room will have to be furnished – but I have made arrangements with a local contractor, who for a small charge will furnish it palatially on the hire system.

There appears to be a very large Harrow element in the regiment – all of whom are very agreeable and nice. The work, though hard and severe is not at present uninteresting, and I trust that the novelty & the many compensating attractions of a military existence – will prevent it from becoming so – at any rate for the next four or five years.

I hope you had a super-comfortable and uneventful crossing & trust that *Pusie* has developed some latent energy from somewhere in her fat person. I will write again soon, my darling Mummy – but for the present – this and the assurance of my undying love, must suffice.

With best love, Your ever loving son
WINSTON S.C.

PS What about a Club? ? ? ?

WSC to Lady Randolph

20 February [1895]   Aldershot

My dear Mama,

With regard to the bills for the Outfit:— It would be much better if you did not want things settled up in such a hurry. I shall be able to get things cheaper – and also avoid purchasing unnecessary articles if more time is allowed. Some things for instance I can get second hand from an officer who has just left. So perhaps three weeks or even a month will be time enough for you to get the bills, and finally settle up.

To my astonishment I find myself in the *Gazette* this morning – so that pay begins and my commission dates from Tuesday.

The riding school is fearfully severe and I suffer terribly from stiffness – but what with hot baths and *massage* I hope soon to be better. At present I can

---

1 Frederick Rossmore Wauchope Eveleigh De Moleyns (1861–1923), Captain and Adjutant 4th Hussars; served with distinction in Matabeleland, 1896–7 (DSO despatches, brevet Lieut-Colonel) and retired 1901. Later Commissioner of Police, Mashonaland. Succeeded his father as 5th Baron Ventry 1914.

hardly walk. I have however been moved up into the 2nd Class recruits which is extremely good. These horses are very different to the Sandhurst screws. Rather too broad I think for me – and I am rather worried about my old strain: Sundry queer pains having manifested themselves, which may or may not be the outcome of the rest of the stiffness.

Captain De Moleynes' servant is an excellent man, and is teaching the man they have given me – and who is as raw and untrained as it is possible to conceive;————————

They play Bezique here for 3d points – which is a shocking descent from the shillings of Deepdene.

I will write again soon – Now don't criticize my handwriting in your next. The pens are awful. My own black-edged paper arrives tomorrow.

With lots of love, your ever loving son
WINSTON S.C.

WSC to Jack

21 Febrary [1895]   Aldershot

My dear Jack,

Very many thanks for your letter. I have indeed been too busy to write. There is a great deal of work and in addition I have to arrange the furnishing of my room and numerous other things.

I got down all right and was received very civilly and amicably. The first night, on joining, one is always the guest of the Mess – receive a written invitation – and is treated with marked courtesy. This prevents any feeling of nervousness or of strangeness and is a charming custom – in vogue only in a few regiments.

The Riding school here is a terribly severe business. Two hours – trotting out – on a fiery . . . . . – much too wide for me – & a slippery saddle. with no stirrups. The result is I am so fearfully stiff I can not walk and am much swollen. However there is nothing for it but to go on and work it off – a very painful process.

The following is the daily routine: – as I have arranged it————

7.30	Called
7.45	Breakfast in bed
	Papers. Letters, etc
8.45	Riding School – 2 hours
10.45	Hot bath and massager

11.30   Carbine exercises – privately with a
        Sergeant to catch up a higher class
12 noon "Stables"
Lasts 1 hour. I have charge of 1 squad 30 men and have to see the horses
groomed – watered – fed & the men's rooms clean etc.
1 o'clock
Lunch is ready. It does not matter being late.
2.15   Drill.
1½ hours nominally – but as I can't walk I get off at present after a half an
hour – which is mostly spent in drilling the men myself. After which for the
present – hot baths – medical rubber – Elliman's and doctor – until Mess at 8 –.
Bezique – 3d points. Bed.

Such is an accurate account of the way in which I have spent the last few
days. I have got a servant, willing, hard working, but quite untrained. Capt
De Moleyns, who is on leave, has lent me his – and also his room – so that I have
been very comfortable. I suppose you saw in the Papers I was gazetted
yesterday and am now on pay etc etc – which by the way is £120 a year.

Well good bye – best love – Burn this
WINSTON S.C.

COMMISSION

VICTORIA by the Grace of God of the United Kingdom of Great Britain
and Ireland, Queen, Defender of the Faith, Empress of India, & To Our
Trusty and well beloved Winston Leonard Spencer Churchill, Gentleman,
Greeting: We, reposing especial Trust and Confidence in your Loyalty,
Courage, and good Conduct, do by these Presents Constitute and Appoint you
to be an Officer in Our Land Forces from the twentieth day of February 1895.
You are therefore carefully and diligently to discharge your Duty as such in the
Rank of 2nd Lieutenant or in such higher Rank as We may from time to time
hereafter be pleased to promote or appoint you to, of which a notification will
be made in the London Gazette, and you are at all times to exercise and well
discipline in Arms both the inferior Officers and Men serving under you and
use your best endeavours to keep them in good Order and Discipline. And We
do hereby Command them to Obey you as their superior Officer, and you to
observe and follow such Orders and Directions as from time to time you shall
receive from Us, or any your superior Officer, according to the Rules and
Discipline of War, in pursuance of the Trust hereby reposed in you.

Given at Our Court, at Saint James's, the twelfth day of February 1895 in the fifty-eighth Year of Our Reign.

By Her Majesty's Command
H. CAMPBELL BANNERMAN

Winston Leonard Spencer Churchill, Gentleman,
2nd Lieutenant
Land Forces

WSC to Lady Randolph

22 February [1895]   Aldershot

My dearest Mamma,

I received to-day your letter of the 20th – which I was vy glad to get. Everything goes on satisfactorily and I see no reason – why anything should occur to cause any sort of trouble – Lord Falmouth's[1] gloomy predictions notwithstanding. I have not yet written to the Duchess or to Duchess Lily – but a letter to each goes by this Post.

The riding is very severe and I suffer a good deal of pain from the muscles of my legs being swollen and inflamed. However it is no good getting off for a day as it would be just as bad beginning again. The only course is to go on and ride it off – a very painful process.

This morning I was in charge of 80 or so horses and men – and responsible for the grooming and feeding of the whole squadron of horses. This does not happen every day however – which is fortunate as it involves great deal of running and prying around.

Colonel Brabazon has not yet come back – nor Captain [De] Moleynes, so I am at present quite on my merits.

Well good bye. Such a dreadful scrawl written lying down – as I am too stiff to sit – Don't criticise, and the next shall be better.

Your ever loving son
WINSTON S. CHURCHILL

WSC to Lady Randolph

24 February [1895]   East Cavalry Barracks
                                                       Aldershot

My darling dearest Mummy,

I got your second letter on Saturday. My stiffness has now entirely passed off and I am convinced that there was nothing wrong after all. Everything is

[1] Lady Randolph's old friend (see p. 78). He was a Coldstreamer.

going on very satisfactorily and if I have made no friends – at least I can say I have offended no one. Everybody is very civil and the days pass pleasantly enough.

I play a good deal of *whist* in the evenings – a most uninteresting game – and one at which I have but little luck – The points however are desperately low so I take no harm.

To day I was moved up in riding to a higher class – and should all go well I shall be dismissed riding school – in 3 months – instead of the normal 12.

Yesterday I went to London to see Aunt Lily about the charger. She empowered me to give Colonel Brab *carte blanche* to get a good one. I have been an hour trying to concoct a letter to him – but have given up. – He comes back Monday – and I can explain so much better then.

I went to see grandmamma – who looked very pale and worn. I 'cowtowed' and did the civil – which I think pleased her very much. She carped a little at your *apartement* in "the gayest part of the Champs Elysées[1]" but was otherwise very amiable – or rather was not particularly malevolent.

I am very interested in my work which has at present a great charm. The electors of Barnesbury have asked me to address a meeting on 19th March – but after much communing with myself I wrote them that the honour was too great – or words to that effect.

Well goodbye my darling Mummy,

Best love and many kisses from you ever loving son

WINSTON S.C.

WSC to Jack

27 February [1895]   Aldershot

My darling Jack,

Many thanks for the nice and well-written letter you wrote me. When one is 'gazetted' it means you get your commission – and seniority pay etc date from then. It also makes one liable to Military Law, which is much stricter than the ordinary civil law. The pay is 6/8 per diem – £10 per month – or £120 a year – in Cavalry.

Everything continues satisfactorily and I have been moved up in the riding. I went over to Sandhurst on Sunday and saw Rome and others. They are coming over here next Sunday to tea.

The work is very interesting – except the Drill – which as usual I loathe and abominate. I went out with the regiment on Friday to a route march – which was very fine. No one has ever been allowed out before until they have been 3

---

[1] It was in the Avenue Kléber; Lady Randolph shared it with her sister, Mrs John Leslie.

or 4 months in the riding school – so I established a precedent. Influenza is very common here and several officers are down with it.

I should like that picture of Charles Kinsky on Zoedone – very much – it would just go over my mantelpiece and is exceedingly appropriate. If you will send it down here I will pay you a sovereign for it – which will enable you to fill the gap with another picture – and have a balance in hand into the bargain. I have no more to write about at present. I think you ought to adopt a more affectionate style of beginning a letter to me than "Dear W——". *My* makes all the difference and even strangers use it.

With best love, Yours ever
WINSTON S. CHURCHILL

WSC to Lady Randolph

2 March 1895

Metropole
Brighton

My dear Mamma,

I hope you will not mind this paper – as I came down here for the Sunday and stupidly forgot to bring any of my own. Your last letter – I was very glad to get – though I am sorry to hear you have had a touch of influenza.

Everybody is down with it now – and I came down here to see some fellows from the IVth. who are convalescing by the sea. The hotel is very full – among others Mr Balfour – Mr Evan Charteris[1] – Charles Davis[2] – young Ronald Hamilton[3] and old T. G. Fardell.[4]

Things have been going exceedingly well with me. I am making friends and many acquaintances. Everybody is very agreeable and I am beginning to find out exactly how I stand. This is the more satisfactory – as Col Brab has only just come down – so that I have found my footholds for myself.

The Colonel is going to see the Duchess Lily himself – about the charger. I fear he will be very grasping – but she will not mind paying a good deal – if he is diplomatic and tactful – as I am sure he will be.

The County Council – at least the Progressive Party – have received a dreadful blow – which will probably have much more widespread results than

---

[1] Hon Evan Charteris (1864–1940), barrister and art patron; 6th son of 10th Earl of Wemyss. Knighted 1932.

[2] ? Charles Henry Hart-Davis (1874–1958), Colonial civil servant, Commissioner in Cyprus 1922–34.

[3] Ronald James Hamilton (1872–1958), eldest son of Lord George Hamilton, served as a diplomat.

[4] (Thomas) George Fardell (1833–1917), chairman of Lord Randolph's constituency, South Paddington; he represented it after Lord Randolph's death until 1910. Knighted in 1897.

is generally imagined – at least so I think. Though they will still keep a majority – it will not be large enough to warrant a continuance of their arrogant – grasping and intolerant policy. It is also another blow to the Government who have identified themselves with the Progressives entirely.

I do hope, my dearest Mamma, that you will keep well and not give way to depression. I am sure Aunt Leonie will look after you and make the time pass pleasantly. I look forward to a few days at Easter – and am likely to get them – so you must keep a 'fatted calf' for the occasion.

Fardell tells me that the R.C. [Randolph Churchill] Habitation[1] is languishing and in a most effete condition. I sincerely hope that you will not withdraw from the office you hold in it – for it is an institution which assists to commemorate Papa's name – as well as helping on work which he began.

Now to end a long – and I fear a stupid letter – Goodbye my dearest Mamma.

Best love & kisses from your ever loving son
WINSTON S.C.

WSC to Jack

4 March [1895]   Aldershot

My dear Jack,

Herewith a cheque for £1 – which I hope will indemnify you for any trouble you may have about the picture. I also send you a small photograph of the "Donkey Race Group" at Sandhurst[2] which may or may not be big enough to fill the gap. Everything goes very well.

Your loving brother
WINSTON S.C.

WSC to Lady Randolph

4 March [1895]   Aldershot

My dear Mamma,

I got the P.S. to your letter only on my return from Brighton last night. I have sent to Coën and have told him to send you 300 cigarettes. If you want any more you must write and I will have them sent monthly.

I want you to give me a couple of saddles, if you have them – as I have been lent a very nice pony by one of the majors and have had to borrow – bridle etc. If you have any saddlery – or harness – or horse furniture of any kind you

---

[1] A branch of the Primrose League.
[2] See facing p. 216 in Main Volume I.

might let me see it and take what I want, as it will save my buying and you can have it back any time you want it.

Aunt Clara writes to me that Grandmamma has been laid up with the influenza, but is now better – but I suppose this is but old news. With best love and many kisses –

Ever your loving son
WINSTON S.C.

PS Do send me a line about the saddlery as the matter presses.

WSC to Lady Randolph

12 March [1895]   Aldershot

My dear Mamma,

I have had the misfortune to smash myself up, while trying a horse on the steeple chase course. The animal refused and swerved – I tried to cram him in – and he took the wings. Very nearly did I break my leg – but as it is I am only bruised and very stiff. I shall be about again in two or three days. In the mean time everybody is very kind – so kind indeed that I am sure I have made a very good impression – (why should I not?)

Well: don't please worry about me as I shall be all right in a couple of days. Milbanke is to be attached to the regiment for a few months – so that I shall see him again – the first time for a long time.

With very best love and many kisses Your ever loving son
WINSTON

I will write again to-morrow. WSC

WSC to Lady Randolph

15 March [1895]   Aldershot

My dearest Mamma,

First of all with regard to the cigarettes. I wired as soon as I received your letter to Coën as follows "send 3 boxes Royal Beauties to 30 Half Moon Street." The man appears to have been idiotic – and I have written to him on the subject. But I do not consider any blame attaches to me.

I am much better – and can hobble about now. In two or three days I hope to begin riding etc again.

I think – if you will let me say – that you take rather an extreme view of steeplechasing – when you call it at once 'idiotic' and 'fatal'. Everybody here rides one or other of their chargers in the different military Races which are constantly held. Of course for this year I cannot ride, but I hope to do so next year.

In fact I rather think you are expected to do something that way – ride in the Regimental races at least. However I shall see you long before I can ride and you can discuss it with me. Everybody is very nice and I enjoy myself very much here. I have my Sandhurst friends over to stay and time passes very pleasantly.

I think the outfit will figure out something like this.

Clothes		
Saddlery etc	} 280	
2nd Charger	70 – 100	
	———	
Total approx:	375	

or £25 under the 400. Of this, however – I am not quite sure – as I may have to get several things – instead of having them second hand.

Brab is away on leave so that Duchess Lily's charger gets no forwarder. However there is no hurry.

Well my darling Mamma I am sure to be able to get a few days at Easter – arrive in Paris Friday morning, depart Monday night – a short visit but one I am looking forward to very much. No more now as I feel *too* stupid for words.

Your loving and affectionate son
WINSTON

WSC to Jack

15 March [1895]   Aldershot

My dearest Jack,

Walden told me he sent your photos in a parcel he sent down to Harrow – He appears to have muddled it. I am sorry but do not feel that any blame attaches to me.

I have had the misfortune to get smashed up while trying a horse on the steeple chase course. I have been in bed for three days having struck my knee a resounding blow – but am now better and can hobble about on sticks.

Everything is going on very well here. Hogg[1] came over to stay with me last Sunday – I think he enjoyed himself very much.

We play Fives on the billiard table here indefatigably and my Deepdene practice has made me very good ——— only the rules are different. Always 4 play at a time.

---

[1] Ian Graham Hogg (1875–1914), at this time a cadet at Sandhurst, joined 4th Hussars 1896; killed in action commanding his regiment in France. He was the second son of Quintin Hogg and brother of 1st Viscount Hailsham.

I have been in command of the squadron for the last 4 or 5 days – as everybody was ill or on leave. It was rather fun – but a lot of things to arrange and sign.

> Well – write – best love from your affectionate brother
> WINSTON S.

WSC to Lady Randolph

23 March [1895]   Aldershot

My dearest Mamma,

I am afraid that I have left you rather a long time without a letter. I am sorry indeed to have done so – but there has been a great deal for me to do lately and I have procrastinated from day to day.

The first part of this letter must be devoted to finance. I find, on writing to Cox for my pass book that he has already paid out of my account the following subscriptions which I enclose.

I do not think that these are all but I believe they form the major part of the subscriptions one has to pay on joining. Of course this deduction from my quarterly allowance makes my funds all wrong – and I hope you will not delay in sending me a cheque for the amount.

I hope to get the bills for outfit etc in, in about three weeks from this date – and then I will send them to you.

Meanwhile I am looking everywhere for a nice, cheap 2nd charger – price from 70 – 100 – which, when I find the horse – will probably have to be paid at once.

This recapitulation of expenses probably strikes you as rather heavy – but I may say that I think that the whole of the outfit will be included in the original estimate of £400 – and that the subscriptions will come to about 70 – 75 pounds.

However I must wait as I hope to be able to purchase several articles of saddlery second-hand.

With regard to the enclosed list. All the above have been paid by me out of my allowance – absorbing, as they do one half the extra quarterly amount.

The subscription to the Nimrod Club is the only one which you may want me to pay – and that is entirely as you like.

So much my dear Mamma – for a very tiresome subject. I am very well and have made, I think, many friends. I hope to see you at Easter when I will tell you lots of things about my work here etc. Jack Milbanke is attached here for a course of signalling – so that I have quite an old friend.

Colonel Brab is still away on leave but returns in a few days. He is, they say, going to take on the regiment for another year. Everyone here hopes so.

We are going to leave Aldershot – either in May or September – to go to Hounslow. So that I shall be quite close to London.

I am told Dudley Marjoribanks is in a very bad way – being completely captivated by an actress, whom he wants to marry. To check which "inconvenient desire" he has been deported to Canada with his Mother. But I suppose you know all this.

Well good bye my dearest Mamma. Very best love and many kisses

from your loving son
WINSTON

PS Enclosed has just arrived. I have never seen the bill before – but it is part of the Sandhurst charges – being signed by the Commandant of the College.

WSC to Jack

24 March [1895]　　　　　　　　　　　　　　　　　　　Aldershot

My dear Jack,

I have been rather expecting a line from you, since my last letter – and in answer to it. I rode on Thursday in my first steeple chase – at the Aldershot races. One of our fellows had two horses running in the subalterns cup and could get no one to ride the second. So I said I would and did. It was very exciting and there is no doubt about it being dangerous. I had never jumped a regulation fence before and they are pretty big things as you know.

Everybody in the regiment was awfully pleased at my riding more especially as I came in third. They thought it very sporting. I thought so too. It has done me a lot of good here and I think I may say I am popular with everybody.

I rode under the name of Spencer as of course it was all put in the papers. No one will know however as I adopted a *nom de guerre*.

Best love Yours ever
WINSTON

WSC to Lady Randolph

28 March [1895]　　　　　　　　　　　　　　　　　　　Aldershot

My dearest Mamma,

I cannot tell you how sorry I am to hear such bad news of poor grandmamma. I do hope that she will soon be better.[1] What sad times you are having my darling Mummy. I trust you may have strength enough to go through them.

---

[1] Mrs Jerome died at Tunbridge Wells on April 2.

You must write to me exactly what you want me to do. I can come at an hour's notice if you feel you want to see me – so don't hesitate to wire.

In the meantime please send me frequent information. Everything goes well with me – so well indeed, that I feel quite ashamed of enjoying myself while others are so miserable. Please wire me how grand-mamma is.

Ever your loving and affectionate son
WINSTON S.C.

Miss Muriel Wilson[1] *to WSC*

Friday [? March 1895]   17 Grosvenor Place

Dear Winston,

Sixteen degrees of frost & a snow-storm drove me to London this morning. I only hope you did not travel feverishly from the North for a hunt because there seems no sign of cold here! I shall return Sunday night. Of course Lady Maud has chucked me tomorrow night so thinking to save you the bother of finding some-one I told Doods Naylor to come – as you like her I know . . . & she would love to come if you procure a man & will dine 8.15 as she comes up after hunting if there is any . . .! Will this suit you & have I done right? Now I will get tickets for the Criterion. But I was

[Letter incomplete]

Mrs Everest to WSC

1 April 1895   15 Crouch Hill
London

My darling Precious Boy,

I have just recd £2 10s from Cox & Co. Charing Cross on your account. I thank you very much indeed dearest it is awfully kind & thoughtful of you. My dear dear Boy you are one of ten thousand but I am afraid you will find your income not any too much for your expenses dear. It really is too good & kind of you I don't know how to thank you enough. I am afraid Her Ladyship will think me a terrible imposter. I have written to the London & Westminster Bank today to give them my address. I don't know whether they will forward me the usual remittance that your poor dear Papa arranged for me. I had a

---

[1] Muriel Thetis Wilson (1875–1964), youngest daughter of Arthur Wilson of Tranby Croft. Married 1919 Richard Edward Warde (1884–1932), Major, Scots Guards (wounded during First World War).

letter from Jackie this morning he tells me Grandmama Jerome is very ill indeed in a critical condition. Her Ladyship is at Tunbridge Wells & Mrs Leslie too. They are both with her, poor Mama she has had a lot of troubles lately. Jackie will have dull holidays again I'm afraid. How are you darling I hope you are keeping well. I should so like to know if you are well. Did you get my letter I wrote you last week. I am longing to see you in your uniform. Do let me know when you are in London. I am quite well & my Arm improving slowly. I can put my hand on the top of my head now & I can use my knife & cut bread & butter. The Duchess has let 50 Gr Square & goes away on the 11th. Where are you going to make your home in your holidays? I hope you will take care of yourself my darling. I hear of your exploits at steeple chasing. I do so dread to hear of it. Remember Count Kinsky broke his nose once at that. It is a dangerous pastime but I suppose you are expected to do it. Only don't be too venturesome. Good bye darling with much love to you.

I remain ever your loving old
WOOM

Frances, Duchess of Marlborough to WSC

4 April [1895]   Canford Manor
Wimborne

My dear Winston,

I am glad to hear you are flourishing. I have little to tell you except that I am happy & comfortable here & that Jack is enjoying himself with Lionel.[1] He is out almost all day. The weather is quite lovely.

We must go back to town on the 10th because your Aunt Cornelia goes there on that day to look after Henry & Freddy who are to be in London for their drill.

I have one line from your Mother giving a good acct of her.

My love to the Duchess. How kind she seems to be to you. I am tired & am writing from the sofa.

Believe me yr affect Grandmother
MARLBOROUGH

WSC to Lady Randolph

18 April [1895]   Aldershot

My own Mamma,

Enclosed are the P.O.O's [Post Office Orders]. I am so sorry to have been dilatory about them. I will write to you tomorrow at length, but am now

---

[1] Lionel Guest (1880–1935), fourth son of Lord WIMBORNE.

awfully busy with the case of a man who is now in at the County Court for theft. This evening I shall have time to write.

With love and kisses your loving son
WINSTON S. CHURCHILL

WSC to Lady Randolph

19 April [1895]   Aldershot

My dearest Mamma,

I had to send you a very hurried line yesterday – but will now write more at length. My leg is getting better – but heals slowly and I am not doing any mounted duty at present. Coming back the other day I looked everywhere for Sir Henry Wolff – but neither he nor Lord Wolverton were on board the ship. So of course I did not deliver your messages.

Everything here is abnormally quiet and regular – and there is no news. Poor Colonel Brab has been taken ill again while staying at Sandringham – temp 105 etc – the results of the influenza – but he is now better. He returns either today or tomorrow.

I do hope that you will do as I asked you with regard to the Allotment colt. There is really no reason why – I should not get the credit of having him now under my name – instead of Sherwood's or any other *nom-de-guerre*. So please do think it over.

With very best love and kisses Your ever loving son
WINSTON S. CHURCHILL

PS My man got 6 weeks imprisonment.

WSC to Lady Randolph

27 April [1895]   Aldershot

My dearest Mamma,

I was so glad to get your letter and to learn that, so far, at least, you have escaped the ravages of the influenza. I have got a lot of tiresome financial details to write to you about – which I will get over first.

I wrote to Lumley and asked him to send me the £60 I paid away in subscriptions. He wrote back that he had asked George[1] to do so – and that it would be done. Last night I got a letter from the latter – who said that he thought £60 had been kept back at Cox's for me. This is of course incorrect &

---

[1] Lord Curzon who was one of Lord Randolph's executors.

the letter he has written to you on the subject is perfectly useless. The arrangement was that as soon as there were sufficient funds I was to be paid – and then repay you the money you lent me.

I am at present very hard up, owing to having had to pay the following expenses which will not come again – and are properly included in the term "outfit."

Subscriptions already accounted	£60. 0. 0.
Extra gold cap	1.15. 0
P.O.O's	2. 6. 0
2nd hand stable jacket	3. 0. 0
1 days pay to each man in first guard mounted	2. 0. 0.
Owed to me.	69. 1. 0.

In addition to which –

for things taken out of pawn – put in last term at Sandhurst	12. 0. 0.
Total £81. 1. 0.	

This last item – of course is not for you to pay I only wish to point out that £81 from £125 leaves only £46 [44], which is not nearly enough to do a quarter on. Hence my present impecuniosity.

Now I am aware that you lent me £45 pounds – to keep me going until the list on opposite page was paid. When it is paid – I will pay you back. But I can't go on any longer without it. So much for personal money. Now as regards chargers – outfit etc. I am at a loss to know what to do. You see I must buy a charger soon – almost immediately which would have to be paid for within two or three days.

Would it be possible and convenient to you to pay at present so large a sum as £100–£120? If not I could wait perhaps a fortnight –but it is an awful bore riding other peoples horses. I know that you could not pay a lump sum like that out of your income – but I understood my horses etc were to come out of the capital – I mean the money you are keeping back to buy house etc. If this is so please tell Lumley to let me know as soon as he is prepared to pay such a sum. Also ask him to send me as soon as he can the £69.10.0 [£69.1.0] of my own.

Then as regards the Polo ponies. Everyone here is beginning to play as the season is just commencing. I have practised on other people's ponies for 10 days and am improving very fast.

If therefore, as I imagine – you have some ready money do lend me a hundred pounds – even if you do not think you will be able to give it to me as you said. The sooner the better – as ponies rise in price every day – and also I cannot go on without any for more than a few days – unless I give up the game, which would be dreadful.

I think the best thing is to let you see what will be the limit you will have to pay as then you will be able to make arrangements.

1 Charger	£120. 0. 0.
Tailor	165. 0. 0.
Boots	35. 0. 0.
Sword etc	20. 0. 0.
Saddlery	50. 0. 0.
Spurs	12. 0. 0.
Hunting [?] breeches	30. 0. 0.
Horse furniture (to be bought second-hand mostly – a great economy	20. 0. 0.

£452.
Original outfit.

	Brought forward	£452. 0. 0.
Subscriptions and sundries (accounted for) due to me		69. 0. 0. (Paid)
Additional subs not yet due		
a) 1 days pay to squadron		15. 0. 0.
b) sub to new kettle drums		7.10. 0.
"The Polo Loan"		100. 0. 0.
Furnishing room – (furniture should be included in outfit) (had it been bought it would have been £50)		10. 0. 0.
	Grand total	653.11. 0.

That is to the best of my belief a tolerable estimate of the cost of joining (including the Polo (loan/gift). I would point out that had not my personal charms induced the Duchess Lily to give me a charger it would have been 100 or 120 more. This balances the polo loan as she will practically be giving me the polo ponies and you paying for the 2 chargers.

Well! Now you know the worst. Do write me an answer soon.

I am very fit and my leg is healing slowly – and is now nearly well. I rode in that point to point after all on the Tuesday with a big bandage on. It was nothing like a steeple chase – being only a hunting run – and not a fast one – but it was a ripping line – 49 fences.

Out of 13 starters only 5 got round – I was 4th being beautifully mounted. No one was hurt in the least – though more than half took tosses. It was not the least dangerous and did me a lot of good in the regiment. All the subalterns rode.

So Duchess Lily is to be married on Tuesday.[1] She has sent me a card of invitation. I am getting on very well here and all is very satisfactory. When I see how some fellows who are disliked are treated I feel very thankful I have been so fortunate as to make my own friends and generally find my footing. Altogether, my dearest Mamma, I am having a really good time and enjoying life immensely.

Jack Milbanke is here, as I told you; he is a very pleasant companion, and we have quite resumed our aquaintance which had lapsed. With regard to the Allotment colt I hope you will let him run in my name – as I have registered some very nice colours in choc. and pink – only a different combination. Also I have arranged that as soon as the old ones are vacant – which will perhaps be soon – they revert to me.

Well my dearest Mamma – you have now reached the close of an almost interminable letter.

With very best love and lots of kisses

I remain, Ever your loving son
WINSTON S. CHURCHILL

WSC to Lady Randolph

2 May [1895]   Aldershot

My Dear Mamma,

I am very sorry that things have not been settled as quickly as you had expected. I am still £25 short of my full allowance for this quarter – after deducting from the amount owed to me – the £45 you have advanced. This £25 is made up as follows.

---

[1] On 30 April 1895, Lilian (1854–1909), 2nd wife of 8th Duke of Marlborough, married Lord William de la Poer Beresford VC (1847–1900), 3rd son of 4th Marquess of Waterford.

Already accounted	£60. 0. 0.
Spent since & accounted in last letter }	10. 0. 0.
	70. 0. 0.
paid by you	45
	25. 0. 0.

I cannot put it plainer than that. I am absolutely at the end of my funds – so if you can possibly give me a cheque for all – or any part of this sum – I shall be awfully pleased – but if you can't – you can't & that settles it. I agree with you it is dreadfully inconvenient & I hate to have to worry you like this – but my mess bill comes in in a few days and *must* be paid somehow.

In any case please try and arrange for me to get my quarter punctually on 18th. With the £25 I shall be able to go on alright. I am glad to leave with the last page an unpleasant and tedious subject. I went to the Duchess Lily's wedding. Every one was there – the Hamilton family well to the fore. A most excellent breakfast which must have cost a great deal – and crowds to eat it – were the chief feature. Lord 'Bill' [Beresford] at once broached topic of charger & said I was to get a real good one – the best that could be got. That is however in Brab's hands and I can't hustle *him*.

After the wedding I went down to Newmarket to see the Two Thousand. My Captain – a charming man – who has a good many horses in training there – gave me dinner – and I breakfasted with young Sherwood.[1] I saw the whole world in the stand. The Prince asked after you as did many others. Lady Norris[2] – Lady Hindlip – the Wolvertons – all the Rothschilds – Sir John Delacour[3] – Freddy Johnstone – The Old Duke, the Burtons – everyone in fact & all most civil and agreeable. I enjoyed myself very much.

In the morning I saw the Allotment colt – (Gervas out of Allotment).[4] You must name him. He was very well, though backward coming into training. Such a good looking animal with much promise. In a month he will be fit & if agreeable to you can be tried with some of Sherwood's horses whose form is known. Then you will know what his worth is – and what class animal he is.

Well good bye my darling Mamma – let me beg you to try and send me a little money, as it is not a case of current expenses but paying deliberately incurred liabilities.

[1] Bob Sherwood, son of Lord Randolph's trainer, R. Sherwood.
[2] Rose Riversdale (1860–1933), wife of Montagu Charles Francis, Lord Norreys, eldest son of 7th Earl of Abingdon, and sister of 4th Baron Wolverton.
[3] A Yorkshire country gentleman, friend of the Prince, but not a knight or baronet. See Main Volume I, p. 32.
[4] Later named Gold Key. See page 602.

I enclose you a charming letter from the Commandant of Sandhurst. I have paid & hope you will refund me – as it is nothing to do with me.

> Your ever loving son
> WINSTON

WSC to Lady Randolph

8 May [1895]   Aldershot

My dearest Mamma,

Very many thanks for the cheque. I will try and manage somehow until 15th when I must pay my mess bill.   I am so sorry that things are not going well as regards finance. Surely it will be arranged soon.

The other day we had a review for young Prince Alfred of Coburg[1] – who came down. He recognised me & came round to the barracks to call. In the evening I dined with the Duke of Connaught who asked after you & told me to tell you he 'trusted you were well.'

Otherwise nothing of note has occurred. Lord 'Bill' Beresford has told the Colonel to get me a charger, price about £200 – so that is settled. But the Colonel does not hurry and I can't very well stir him up.

Please read enclosure which will explain why I want my quarter on 15th instead of 18th.

> Your ever loving son
> WINSTON

PS Has Jack gone back to Harrow.

WSC to Lady Randolph

15 May [1895]   Aldershot

My dear Mamma,

I quite understand how difficult it is for you and as you cannot arrange anything at present – I must wait. But I do hope that this deadlock will not last more than a very few days. My mess bill is of course unpaid and that will probably involve all sorts of unpleasant explanations and generally speaking is a thing to be very much avoided. Also there are certain things which *have* to be paid and to pay which I have counted on getting my quarter on 10th, so you see how the case stands. I only write this to show you that things are very difficult with me and in order that you will be as quick as you can. Please send me a line and let me know what prospect there is.

> With very best love Your ever loving son
> WINSTON

---

[1] Alfred Alexander William (1874–99), grandson of Queen Victoria, was an hereditary prince of Saxe-Coburg and Gotha.

WSC to Lady Randolph

21 May [1895]   Aldershot

My dearest Mamma,

Mr Lumley went with me to Cox's on Saturday and told one of the partners that there was a delay with regard to my allowance. They were very civil and placed £125 at my disposal pending your convenience to pay. So that was settled.

As to my having had my full allowance bar £10 last quarter I must point out for the third time that there have been other expenses besides & subsequent to those included in the £60 amounting to £24 which with the original £10 makes a total of £34.

Then with regard to the polo ponies – Messrs Cox have lent me £100 to buy them with and when things become settled then you can give me the £100 and I will pay them back.

However we can talk this all over on Saturday. Mind you come over my dear Mamma and stay the Sunday. I will get leave & be with you.

With Best love & hoping to see you very soon.

Ever your loving son
WINSTON

WSC to Lady Randolph

23 May [1895]   Aldershot

My dearest Mamma,

I am sorry you find it necessary to be cross with me. I did not know you had paid my allowance into the bank. I thought I had arranged the whole thing myself & indeed I am still uncertain whether or no you have paid any money into the Bank. You see I have had no line from you on the subject or from Cox's acknowledging receipt of your cheque. So I forgot in my letter to thank you. I have written a good many letters to you lately. Of course they were chiefly concerned with business – but I have always tried to tell you such news as I had & to write as often as I had the opportunity. I am very sorry you are not satisfied. With regard to the £55 you say I now owe – I must point out that I do not owe you anything until the £60 pounds I paid in subscriptions have been paid to me. And even then it is not 55 but fifty pounds.

But, as I have stated & written – as clearly and lucidly as it is possible there have been other additional expenses since which amount to £25 approximately.

So that to put things shortly I am owed £60 – of which fifty has been paid. Balance £10. And additional expenses £25

Total   £35

I hate to have to state these things in such a formal and blunt way. Do just whatever you think fit – my dear Mamma – but please realise the exact facts of the case. Now I telegraphed to you Monday night 'All arranged am writing'. But on Monday the Colonel sent me up to London to look at a charger and I was away all day. Consequently my letter to you was written Tuesday instead of Monday. I think therefore my dear Mamma that your scolding was a little undeserved.

However! – to turn to other things – I am going to the Prince's Levée on Monday. The Colonel is arranging the details for me. Tomorrow is the Queen's Birthday and of course it is here celebrated by much military display. I think Molly Hacket and the prospective[1] with Miss Muriel Wilson will come down to see the review and lunch with me. How I wish you were coming – you would I am sure be interested.

Polo progresses steadily and I am I think improving fast. It is the finest game in the world and I should almost be content to give up any ambition to play it well and often. But that will no doubt cease to be my view in a short time.

Well my dearest Mamma, I can think of no more news & I will not bore you with more wants – so I send you lots of love & kisses – & hope you won't again find cause to scold.

Ever your loving son
WINSTON S. C.

WSC to Lady Randolph

6 June [1895]   Aldershot

My dearest Mamma,

I was delighted to get your letter yesterday evening. I understand altogether how difficult my numerous expenses make things for you – & I hate to have money discussions with you quite as much as you do. You have always been very generous in money matters & I can never be sufficiently grateful to you for allowing me to go in the Cavalry.

But – of course you understand that beginning is expensive and that it is almost impossible for me to put down £40 out of £125 a quarter and I thought therefore that if you were going to buy a house & to borrow money to do it – so comparatively small a sum as £40 for a club might be added to your expenses.

When I had seen you off at the station I went to the Bachelor's and was there informed that as I had used the club I was to pay my subscription at once – which I did. Now I am still £35 to the bad – which I paid in subscriptions &

---

[1] Miss Hacket married Miss Wilson's brother, Edward Kenneth, on June 27.

added to this forty I am £75 short of my quarter – leaving only 50. So you see things are very difficult for me too. I should have answered your letter earlier – but I was awfully limited yesterday as the Shahzada[1] was being impressed. I was selected as the officer to attend on and to escort the Duke of Cambridge – so I had a rather tiring – though complimentary job – jogging along by his carriage and tittupping after him when he was on horseback. I went to luncheon at Government House[2] and generally made myself sociable to the foreigners on the staff. The Prince was there and saw me & I had a long talk with Lord Roberts – who has just been made a Field Marshal. Everyone of course asked after you. I was seven hours on horseback without dismounting or taking off my busby & two hours more after lunch – but it was a great honour to have been selected and one for which I must thank Colonel Brab alone. I then got your letter but had no time to answer it as I had to hustle up to London to dinner. I had a most amusing dinner at the Melvilles', as though, the people were dull and deadly – I sat between two charming girls and so had a very successful day altogether.

Well my dearest Mamma, I feel my letter must end with this page or I shall be late for mess and bore you.

So with best love Ever your loving son
WINSTON S. CHURCHILL

WSC to Lady Randolph

17 June [1895]   Aldershot

My dear Mamma,

I am perfectly idiotic this morning. I have begun this letter three times & torn it up as many – so I trust you will excuse both composition and calligraphy.

As I told you the Colonel told Daly to get me a charger – & after some time I received a magnificent animal – which is said to be the finest charger in the army. The horse cost £200 & Duchess Lily has sent a cheque for that amount – which is very generous of her. In addition the expense of bringing him over was £15 and Daly's commission another £15 so that there is £30 to pay. I have sent the cheque for two hundred, so that I don't think there is any immediate hurry. This will not be an additional expense as I will get rather a cheaper 2nd

---

[1] Nasrulla Khan, second son of Amir Abdurrahman, ruler of Afghanistan. He was on an official visit to England. In 1919, following the assassination of his elder brother Amir Habibullah Khan, Nasrulla Khan seized the throne by a *coup d'état* and for a short time ruled the country. Before long, however, Amir Abdurrahman's third son, Amanulla Khan, declared himself and was recognised as Amir.

[2] The official residence of the Commander-in-Chief, Aldershot, and occupied by the Duke of Connaught at the time.

charger – which the Colonel will allow me to do owing to my first horse being so good. So much for that subject. Everyone is making plans for Ascot. My great idea is to ride in Windsor Park after the races – as we did last year and I am arranging to do it.

I have not yet got my enclosure ticket – but I am sure to get it in the course of the day. I will look out for your friends who are coming over and make myself most agreeable to them.

The Londonderry's have been entertaining on a most magnificent scale. Enormous balls – 1500 people & political receptions almost daily. I have had a great many invitations & could go to a ball every night did I wish to – but field days & drills make me more eager for bed than anything else.

Ronny Moncreiffe[1] has been getting into trouble – he went to dinner with his nephew Reggie Ward[2] and got frightfully drunk – knocked a policeman down and was marched off to prison and fined £5. I don't think the Prince will have him to stay for Ascot for fear the papers should get hold of it. Someone has had labels printed "When found drunk in the street please return empty to Ronny Moncreiffe Turf Club". I suppose however you have heard all this some time ago.

The other topic is how much or how little has Sarah got by old Sir Samuel's death. The common report is that the old boy has left it all to the younger children and they get nothing more. I hope this is so most sincerely. Seven or eight thousand a year is quite enough & more money would only increase her conceit & arrogance. I lunched yesterday at Chesterfield House where they were all very jubilant over the Invernesshire election – Jim Baillie having got in by 600 majority. Another smack for the government.[3]

Well my dear Mamma, I wont continue to bore you indefinitely with the recital of stale news in an illegible hand.

I do hope that things are going to be settled soon. I am awfully hard up– owing to having paid the entrance to the Bachelors and also to the fact I am owed £35 for subscriptions. But of that – later.

With best love your loving son
WINSTON

---

[1] Ronald Moncreiffe (1864–1909), 5th son of Sir Thomas Moncreiffe, 7th Bart; served in Matabele and Boer wars. Married Edith, only daughter of Arthur Worsley.

[2] Reginald Ward (1874–1904), 4th son of Moncreiffe's sister, Georgina, and 1st Earl of Dudley; also served in Boer war; awarded DSO; died unmarried.

[3] On June 12 the Conservatives gained this seat from the Gladstonian Liberals by 3,164 votes to 2,514. James Evan Bruce Baillie (1859–1931) had married in 1894 Nellie Bass, daughter of Lord Burton. He remained an M.P. until 1900.

WSC to Lady Randolph

23 June [1895]   Blenheim

My dearest Mamma,

I was very glad to get your letter yesterday – just as I was starting off down here for the Sunday. Ascot was very pleasant and I was fortunate enough to lose no money. I rode in the Park – chiefly with Lady Angela[1] – who is not bad company. I think she is trying all she knows to captivate Sunny – but it appears to me that her efforts will be fruitless. Also it is a mistake to give yourself away – and show your feelings as she did. I breakfasted and dined every day with Sir Frederick [Johnstone]. He was too cheery and fit for words – and insisted upon my using the little house he had taken unreservedly – which I did.

So altogether I had a pleasant time and a most satisfactory week.

We are quite a small party here – only Sunny & his sisters myself and a couple of friends – one of whom brings an ugly sister – but all the same it is quiet & pleasant. The park and gardens look beautiful. All the trees in leaf and flowers everywhere. I went this morning to Bladon to look at Papa's grave. The service in the little church was going on and the voices of the children singing all added to the beauty and restfulness of the spot. The hot sun of the last few days has dried up the grass a little – but the rose bushes are in full bloom and make the church yard very bright. I was so struck by the sense of quietness & peace as well as by the old world air of the place – that my sadness was not unmixed with solace. It is the spot of all others he would have chosen. I think it would make you happier to see it.

Well, my darling Mummy – I will write to you of other matters in a day or two.

With my best love and kisses I remain, Ever your loving son
WINSTON S. CHURCHILL

WSC to Lady Randolph

3 July [1895]   Aldershot

My dearest Mamma,

I have just got back from London. As I telegraphed to you – poor old Everest died early this morning from peritonitis. They only wired to me on Monday evening – to say her condition was critical. That was the first intimation I had of her illness. I started off & got Keith – who was *too* kind. He

---

[1] Angela St Clair-Erskine (1876–1950), daughter of 4th Earl of Rosslyn. See p. 686.

thought then that she might pull through – but it was problematical. Instead of rallying however – she only sank into a stupor which gave place to death at 2.15 this morning.

Everything that could be done – was done. I engaged a nurse – but she only arrived for the end. It was very sad & her death was shocking to see – but I do not think she suffered much pain.

She was delighted to see me on Monday night and I think my coming made her die happy. Her last words were of Jack. I shall never know such a friend again. I went down to Harrow to tell Jack – early this morning – as I did not want to telegraph the news. He was awfully shocked but tried not to show it.

I made the necessary arrangements for the funeral which takes place on Friday. I ordered a wreath for you from Mackay & I thought you would like to send one.

Please send a wire to Welldon to ask him to let Jack come up for the funeral – as he is very anxious to do so.

Well my dearest Mummy I am very tired as I have been knocking about for two nights & have done all my duty here at the same time. I feel very low – and find that I never realized how much poor old Woom was to me. I don't know what I should do without you.

With best love Ever your loving son
WINSTON S. CHURCHILL

WSC to Lady Randolph

6 July 1895   Aldershot

My dear Mamma,

I went yesterday to poor Everest's funeral & Welldon let Jack come up too. All her relations were there – a good many of whom had travelled from Ventnor overnight – and I was quite surprised to find how many friends she had made in her quiet and simple life. The coffin was covered with wreaths & everything was as it should be. I felt very despondent and sad –: the third funeral I have been to within five months![1] It is indeed another link with the past gone – & I look back with regret to the old days at Connaught Place when fortune still smiled.

My darling Mamma – I am longing for the day when you will be able to have a little house of your own and when I can really feel that there is such a place as home. At present I regard the regiment entirely as my headquarters – and if I go up to London for a couple of days – I always look forward to coming

---

[1] Lord Randolph in January; Mrs Jerome in April; and now Mrs Everest.

back to my friends and ponies here. I am getting on extraordinarily well and when I see how short a time those who don't get on, stay, I feel that it is very fortunate that I do.

I have a great many friends & I know my ground, I don't think anybody realises who does not know – how important a day in one's life is the day one first joins a regiment. If you aren't liked you have to go & that means going through life with a very unpleasant stigma.

I forgot altogether in my last letter to thank you for the charmingly 'chic' cigarette holder you sent me. Such a nice pres & you are indeed a darling. I must also thank you for writing to Lumley about the money. When you come over I shall have to show you the account. I have bought a nice charger for £80 which will have to be paid for within a month or so.

Well I won't obtrude finance into this letter as we can discuss things on Wednesday.

Now my dearest Mamma – wire me when you arrive and if I can meet you I will.

> With best love and many kisses I remain, Ever your loving son
> WINSTON S. CHURCHILL

WSC to Lady Randolph

24 July [1895]   Aldershot

My dearest Mamma,

I have been waiting for something to write to you about – for the last two days: but things here follow a regular and uneventful course and news accumulates slowly.

The Duke and Duchess of York[1] came yesterday to see a field day & I was asked to meet them at dinner at Government House. The Colonel went there also and although everything was exceedingly formal I was very glad to have been asked. I had quite a long talk with the Duke of Connaught about the Election & of course every one asked after you. Tomorrow the princess is coming down – so there is more hustle and parading.

Polo forms my principal amusement and I really think I am improving very fast. I have already been put in the subaltern's team and we have lots of very amusing matches. I am sending you a book which I am reading called *Making Sketches* which interests me very much and which will I am sure please you still more – as you will have seen many of the scenes therein described.

The Election continues to go strongly in our favour & Radical and Tory papers are alike at a loss to find the cause of the amazing change of opinion.

[1] Later King George V and Queen Mary.

For my part – I attribute the ruin of the Radical party entirely to the absence of Mr Gladstone's sustaining power. Ever since '86 when the great split took place they have steadily declined – but his personality imparted to them a fictitious strength – just as a fever animates a sick man. As soon as this departed the collapse ensued. Well my dearest Mamma, no more at present.

With best love I remain, Ever your loving son
WINSTON S. CHURCHILL

WSC to Lady Randolph

3 August [1895]   Aldershot

My dearest Mamma,

As I told you in my last letter news here accumulates but slowly and I have been waiting the last two days in the hopes of having something interesting to write to you about. This morning I got your letter & I feel I must answer it at once. I wish I could come out to Aix – if only for a few days. A nice warm climate and no exercise would suit me very well indeed at present. But that is of course out of the question. We have field days all day & every day. Very often ten hours in the saddle at a time – without anything to eat or drink the whole time – and after that I invariably play polo for a couple of hours. However I must say I thrive on the treatment. I am rather worried just now about my left eye – which is very painful. I do not know what is the matter – but I am going to see a good oculist as perhaps I might be going to have an ulcer in it.

I got one days leave for Goodwood. Of course the Richmond party was 'off' on account of the death of one of the duke's daughters[1] – but he lent the box to the Arthur James's.[2] I met Mr Jim Lowther in the paddock and he took me in. The prince asked after you as did every one else. Lady Ormond's beautiful daughter was there.[3] A very lovely – but stupid & school roomy girl – to whom I talked a good deal.

Everyone wore tweed suits and straw hats – as the prince set the example. It will be interesting to see next year if the same sensible plan is carried out. Of

---

[1] Florence Augusta, second daughter of 6th Duke of Richmond, had died on July 21.

[2] John Arthur James (1853–1917) and his wife Mary Venetia (1862–1948), daughter of Rt Hon George Cavendish Bentinck. James was an elder brother of Willie James of West Dean Park who with his wife were friends of and frequent visitors to the Prince of Wales, later King Edward VII.

[3] Lady Beatrice Frances Elizabeth Butler (1876–1952), who was 18 at the time, was the elder daughter of 3rd Marquess of Ormonde and his wife Elizabeth, eldest daughter of 1st Duke of Westminster. She married in 1901 Lt-General Sir Reginald Pole-Carew, by whom she had four children.

course Florizel II won the Cup in a canter but at the beginning of the race he shied at the crowd & Watts who was riding nearby cut a voluntary. I did not have a bet.

The radical papers go on piling up figures to show that "the verdict of the country" is only a question of chance – and never indicates any real feeling – without for one moment reflecting that this argument knocks the backbone out of their agitation against the Peers. A more disappointed & broken down party never was seen.

Meanwhile the Unionists come in with very nearly every able man in both houses in the their cabinet – with the House of Commons at their feet – & the Lords at their back – supported by all sections of the nation – unfettered by promises or hampered by pledges. No party has ever had such a chance – it remains to be seen what use they will make of it.

To my mind they are *too* strong – Too brilliant altogether. They are just the sort of Government to split on the question of Protection. Like a huge ship with powerful engines they will require careful steering – because any collision means destruction.

Well my darling Mummy – tell Jack I will write to him tomorrow.

For the present – I remain, Ever your loving son
WINSTON S.

WSC to Lady Randolph

16 August [1895]   Aldershot

My dearest Mummy,

I was so glad to get your letter this morning and to hear that things are going on well with you. I should certainly recommend a trip to Switzerland – if you have never seen it, as it is really worth a few weeks. How I wish I could come with you and act as courier! – but Jack will have to discharge that office instead.

We are now in the midst of manoeuvres. Eight hours in the saddle every day – then two hours stables and then to Polo indefatigably. This new Inspector General of Cavalry is a terror & everyone goes about in dread of him – excepting only the Colonel who is in high favour & commands (temporarily) a Brigade.

I went to see Lord Falmouth the other day when he had a brigade of volunteers under canvas here. He was delighted to see me – and was really *too* charming for words.

I suppose you will have read the speech in which Sunny Marlborough moved the vote of thanks in return for the address. It appears to have been a very good and even brilliant speech & I was told he had a very good delivery – though a trifle too loud for the House. I don't care to dwell on the past – but I could not help thinking as I read it that Papa would have liked to see that he inherited at least some of the family talents – and was trying quietly and tactfully to use them.

I wonder now whether he will have the self control to relapse – for a little longer – into silence.

It is a fine game to play – the game of politics   and it is well worth waiting for a good hand – before really plunging.

At any rate – four years of healthy and pleasant existence – combined with both responsibility & discipline – can do no harm to me – but rather good. The more I see of soldiering – the more I like it – but the more I feel convinced that it is not my *métier*. Well, we shall see – my dearest Mamma.

I am above all things glad you are getting a house and look forward to the day when we shall have a roof to call our own over our heads.

Well *au revoir* my dear Mamma

> With best love and kisses, I remain, Your loving son
> WINSTON S. CHURCHILL

WSC to Lady Randolph

24 August [1895]   Aldershot

My dearest Mamma,

I applaud your resolution to go to Switzerland. You will like Ouchy above all places. It is warm & lovely – with the most comfortable of hotels and unlimited supplies of Tauchnitz novels. Jack knows it of old & will I am sure spend half his day swimming and the other half eating the fruit which can be obtained there at 'popular prices.'

If you should feel like moving you can get to Zermatt by a short journey to Visp and thence by a mountain railway to the 'heart of the Alps.' As the guide books say – 'a visit will well repay the traveller.' But I expect you will prefer to 'stay put'.

The more I picture you at rest on the banks of the lake of Geneva – the more I wish I could come and join you there – but as I have said in previous letters – other factors besides desire enter into my plans. We have just reached the Saturday of a very hard week – on no day of which have I been in the saddle less than 8 to 9 hours and on no day of which have I omitted to play polo. Next week will be the same only more so – so my time is well employed.

I have just written a long letter to the Duchess who wrote a most kind and affectionate letter to me. She is at Kelso & apparently very prosperous.

I find I am getting into a state of mental stagnation – when even letter writing becomes an effort & when any reading but that of monthly magazines is impossible. This is of course quite in accordance with the spirit of the army. It is indeed the result of mental forces called into being by discipline and routine. It is a state of mind into which all or nearly all who soldier – fall.

From this 'slough of Despond' I try to raise myself by reading & re-reading Papa's speeches – many of which I almost know by heart – but I really cannot find the energy to read any other serious work.

I think really that when I am quartered in London I shall go and study one or two hours a week with one of James' men – a most capable fellow either Economics or Modern History. If you know what I mean – I need some one to point out some specific subject to stimulate & to direct my reading in that subject. The desultory reading I have so far indulged in has only resulted in a jumble of disconnected & ill assorted facts.

Colonel Harry Norris[1] – who knew you in Ireland & was a great friend of Papa's in old days came to dinner the other night & was very much astonished to see me in any costume other than short frocks. He wrote to me & I will send you the letter asking me to obtain for him one of Papa's book plates & one of your own. He collects them. I saw Lord Erroll[2] the other day when I was galloper. He asked after you.

With best love my dearest Mamma
I remain, Ever your loving son
WINSTON S. CHURCHILL

WSC to Lady Randolph

31 August [1895]   Aldershot

My dearest Mamma,

I write this in answer to your long letter of two days ago. I have considered the subject you suggest "Supply of Army horses". I think it is a subject which has much to commend it to the attention of a cavalry officer: But I am bound to say it is not one which would interest me. It is too technical. It is a narrow question leading to a limited result. A subject more calculated to narrow and groove one's mind than to expand it.

---

[1] Henry Crawley Norris (1841–1914), ADC to 7th Duke of Marlborough while Lord Lieutenant of Ireland.

[2] Charles, 20th Earl of Erroll (1852–1927), Lieut-Colonel in Royal Horse Guards; served in Boer War and in First World War.

Besides if one hears 'horse' talked all day long – in his every form & use – it would seem a surfeit to study his supply as one of the *beaux-arts*. No – my dearest Mamma – I think something more literary and less material would be the sort of mental medicine I need. And there are so many works – which without making one a specialist on the subject with which they deal – leave much valuable information – and many pleasing thoughts – as a result of reading them. You see – all my life – I have had a purely technical education. Harrow, Sandhurst, James's – were all devoted to studies of which the highest aim was to pass some approaching Examinations. As a result my mind has never received that polish which for instance Oxford or Cambridge gives. At these places one studies questions and sciences with a rather higher object than mere practical utility. One receives in fact a liberal education.

Don't please misunderstand me. I don't mean to imply any sneer at utilitarian studies. Only I say that my daily life is so eminently matter of fact that the kind of reading I require is not the kind which the subject you suggested to me would afford. I have now got a capital book – causing much thought – and of great interest. – It is a work on political economy by Fawcett.[1] When I have read it – and it is very long, I shall perhaps feel inclined to go still farther afield in an absorbing subject. But this is a book essentially devoted to "first principles" – and one which would leave at least a clear knowledge of the framework of the subject behind – and would be of use even if the subject were not persevered in.

Then I am going to read Gibbon's *Decline and Fall of the Roman Empire* & Lecky's *European Morals*. These will be tasks more agreeable than the mere piling up of shoppy statistics. Well – this far and no farther – my dearest Mamma – will I investigate a question which I am sure will bore you in its discussion.

I write this letter – rather a pompous one too – to the Beau Rivage hotel. How I wish I could secrete myself in a corner of the envelope and embrace you as soon as you tear it open! Such wishes are but futile however. I am at present laid up with a 'sprung vein' caused by perpetual riding – but it will only take me two days to get right again.

In a week we leave Aldershot – I have asked the Colonel to let me go to Hampton Court instead of Hounslow[2] – and he is considering the question. I hope I shall go – as I could live with you at 35 and soldier on a season ticket.

---

[1] Henry Fawcett (1833–84), Radical statesman and economist; accidentally blinded shortly after his 25th birthday by pellets from his father's gun. His influential *Manual of Political Economy*, published in 1863, became a classic and was an excellent introduction to the subject. Appointed to the newly-established chair of political economy at Cambridge in 1864. Entered Parliament in 1865, becoming Postmaster-General in 1880.

[2] After two years at Aldershot, the Fourth Hussars moved to Hounslow, one of the squadrons being posted to Hampton Court.

I do so look forward to having a house once more. It will be too delightful to ring the bell of one's own front door again. Poor old Everest – how she would have loved to see us ensconced in a house once again. She looked forward to it so much. It makes me very sad to think of her. She was so much to me in many ways – more than I had realised. What frightful losses we have sustained in the last twelve months. Never did misfortunes crowd in one on another. Only a year ago – almost to a day I was at Ouchy. Since then three figures, I had known and loved in different degrees and ways all my life – are gone. Time passes *too* quickly for vain regrets – & it is unprofitable to resist the consolation which it brings – by reviving ones sorrow. We take our turn – some today – others tomorrow. And after all it has gone on for thousands of years. The history of man is the story of innumerable tragedies and perhaps the most tragic part is to be found in the insignificance of human grief.

I will come and see you nearly every day you are in London. If Jack has a few days to spare before going back to school – I can lend him a quiet pony to ride in the park in the mornings.

> With best love, I remain, Ever your loving son
> WINSTON S.C.

WSC to Lady Randolph

30 September [1895]   Hounslow

My dear Mamma,

Your letter this morning was very welcome. I had been meaning to write to you for several days – and it just gave me the necessary fillip to bring my resolution to a head.

I am so glad that Scotland is pleasant and cheery – and hope you will continue to find it so. I went over last Sunday with Colonel Brab to dine with Mr & Mrs Leo Rothschild[1] – who live at Gunnersbury – quite close to here. Otherwise the week has been uneventful so far as I am concerned.

Elsewhere however things appear to be almost critical. I suppose nothing but force will bring the Chinese to heel – but that will be a purely naval

---

[1] Leopold (1845–1917), 3rd son of Baron Lionel Nathan de Rothschild MP, and his wife Marie, daughter of Achille Perugia, of Trieste.

affair.[1] The spectacle of the other British Squadron at Lemnos[2] is to my mind a much more important matter and one the consequences of which may be very grave.

Whatever happens – it is evident that we pose as champions of humanity in general and of Armenians[3] in particular – alone and unassisted. But that is after all entirely in accordance with precedent.

Then there is the Stokes[4] affair – trivial in itself but leading perhaps to a Franco-Belgian entente in central Africa – the result of which would be to precipitate the inevitable advance to Khartoum.[5]

Of course nowadays every budding war is spoiled and nipped by some wily diplomatist but still I can't help thinking that we are passing through a very critical time and one in which it will need strong and tactful statemanship to maintain 'peace with honour'. I find I *have* to take my leave (2½) months from Oct 24 to Jan 8. Do try and arrange some common rendezvous for us.

With love and kisses I remain, Your loving son
WINSTON S. CHURCHILL

---

[1] As a result of the massacre of British missionaries and other outrages in August the British Government demanded the punishment of the Viceroy of Szechwan. When this demand met with no response the British Government presented an ultimatum to the Government in Peking on September 28 to the effect that unless a proclamation degrading the Viceroy was issued within fourteen days the British Admiral commanding a fleet on the Yangtse river and in Shanghai harbour "would take action." Within twenty-four hours the Viceroy was stripped of his rank and it was decreed that he should never again hold office.

[2] On September 28 a British squadron of seventeen ships arrived and anchored off Lemnos, at the entrance to the Dardanelles. The Sultan had for some months been reluctant to accept a reform of government for the Armenians, who were continuously the object of Kurdish atrocities.

[3] Following a series of outrages against the Armenian population, Britain, France and Russia were trying to persuade the bankrupt and unstable Ottoman Empire to accept a scheme of far-reaching financial and other reforms. The most notorious Armenian massacre took place the following autumn.

[4] On September 20 a Belgian, Captain Lothaire, an official of the Congo Free State, was recalled to explain the execution of Mr Stokes, a British trader, earlier in the year. Stokes had been accused, before a Court-martial consisting of Lothaire and two non-commissioned officers, of supplying arms to a rebel chief, and on being found guilty was promptly hanged the next morning. The Congo State later paid an indemnity of £4,265 to the British Government for the "irregular procedure" of Captain Lothaire, but in the following year he was acquitted of all further charges.

[5] While Kitchener was preparing to reconquer the Sudan, the French were planning to dispatch an expedition across central Africa into the Nile Valley. These events culminated in the Fashoda crisis three years later.

WSC to Jack

30 September [1895]   Hounslow

My dear Jack,

Very many thanks for your letter. I will come over and see you some time tomorrow – telegraphing early. Please tell Mr Welldon I should like very much to lunch with him – if convenient.

I also want you to find out young Rothschild[1] – Mrs Leo's boy – who has only just come to Graham's house – but who comes into Welldon's as soon as he can. He is a nice little chap and the Leo Rothschilds will be very grateful to you if you look after him. Their gratitude may also take a practical form – as they have a charming place at Gunnersbury quite close here. I went to dine there yesterday. Get this boy to come and have tea with us.

I shall probably drive over – arriving about 1. The major you saw was probably Peters – in our Regt – and O. Harrovian & P. Hussar.

Yours ever

WINSTON S. CHURCHILL

[1] Lionel Nathan de Rothschild (1882–1942), eldest son of Leopold de Rothschild (see above). Unionist MP for Aylesbury 1910–23.

9

New York and Cuba

4th Hussars (2) – 1895

(*See Main Volume Chapter 8 pp. 263–280*)

WSC to Lady Randolph

4 October [1895]   Hounslow

My dearest Mamma,

I daresay you will find the content of this letter somewhat startling. The fact is that I have decided to go with a great friend of mine – one of the subalterns in the regiment to America and the W. Indies. I propose to start from here between the Oct 28 & November 2 – according as the boats fit. We shall go to New York & after stay there move in a steamer to the W. Indies to Havana where all the Government troops are collecting to go up country and suppress the revolt that is still simmering on: after that back by Jamaica and Hayti to New York & so home. The cost of the Ticket is £37 a head return – which would be less than a couple of months at Leighton Buzzard by a long way. I do not think the whole thing should cost £90 – which would be within by a good margin what I can afford to spend in 2 months. A voyage to those delightful islands at the season of the year when their climate is at its best will be very pleasant to me – who has never been on sea more than a few hours at a time. And how much more safe than a cruise among the fences of the Vale of Aylesbury.

I come home the 24th and hope to see you for a couple of days before we sail.

Now I hope you won't mind my going my dear Mamma – as it will do me good to travel a bit and with a delightful companion who is one of the senior subalterns and acting adjutant of the regiment & very steady.

Please send me a line.

Your ever loving son
WINSTON

Lady Randolph to WSC

Friday [11 October 1895]   Guisachan

My dearest Winston,

You know I am always delighted if you can do anything which interests
& amuses you – even if it be a sacrifice to me. I was rather looking forward
to our being together & seeing something of you. Remember I only have you
& Jack to love me. You certainly have not the art of writing & putting things
in their best lights but I understand all right – & of course darling it is natural
that you shd want to travel & I won't throw cold water on yr little plans –
but I'm very much afraid it will cost a good deal more than you think. N.Y.
is *fearfully* expensive & you will be bored to death there – all men are. I *must*
know more about yr friend. What is his name? Not that I don't believe you
are a good judge but still I shd like to be sure of him. Considering that I
provide the funds I think instead of saying 'I *have* decided to go' it may have
been nicer & perhaps wiser – to have begun by consulting me. But I suppose
experience of life will in time teach you that tact is a very essential ingredient
in all things.

I leave here tomorrow & go to 'Minto House Hawick N.B.' Write to me
there & tell me more – you have ignored my long letter over yr future career.
I shall be in London the end of next week – possibly before if so I will let you
know. Have you been to Deepdene. Goodbye God bless you dear –

Yr loving Mother
JRC

P.S. I have had a talk with the Tweedmouths over yr plans & they can help
you much in the way of letters to the Gov of Jamaica[1] & in suggesting a tour.
They went to the W.I. [West Indies] & to Mexico – & know it all well. Once
one makes a good '*Itineraire de Voyage*' one can find out the cost. Would you
like me as a birthday pres to pay yr ticket??

---

[1] Sir Henry Arthur Blake (1840–1918), who was Governor of Jamaica 1888–97. A former
resident magistrate in Ireland, he was later Governor of Hong Kong and of Ceylon.

Sir H. Drummond Wolff to WSC

8 October 1895   San Sebastian

My dear Winston,

After receiving yesterday your letter I saw the Minister for Foreign Affairs (the Duke of Tetuan)[1] & spoke to him about your wish to go to Cuba.

He said he would get you a letter from the Minister of War & give you one himself to Marshal Martinez Campos[2] who is personally his great friend but it must depend on the Marshal what he lets you and Mr Barnes do as everything is in his hands. I fear I can not obtain any thing more but should think these letters would be enough.

How is your mother & what is Jack about? Pray give them my love.

Yours affecte
H. DRUMMOND WOLFF

Pray write at once if these letters reach you as I am leaving this [address] before long.

Sir H. Drummond Wolff to WSC

11 October 1895   28 Concha
                                                    San Sebastian

My dear Winston,

Enclosed is a letter from General Azcarraga the Minister of War[3] to Marshal Martinez Campos which I hope will obtain for you the facilities you desire.

I hope myself to be in London next week & to be found at 28 Cadogan Place or at the Carlton. Perhaps we may meet.

Your affecte
H. DRUMMOND WOLFF

[1] Carlos O'Donnel y Abreu, Duke of Tetuan (1834–1903), Spanish Foreign Minister 1879–81, 1890–1, and 1895–7.

[2] Arsenio Martinez de Campos (1834–1900), Captain-General of the Spanish Army. Having pacified the insurgents in Cuba 1867 he returned to Spain to become Prime Minister and Minister of War before being called back to Cuba in 1895. He was twice President of the Spanish Senate.

[3] Marcelo de Azcarraga y Palermo (1832–1915).

WSC to Lady Randolph

19 October [1895]   Hounslow

My dearest Mamma,

I know that you will be looking for a letter tomorrow morning – so am writing you one though there is but little to tell. I went to see Lord Wolseley[1] about Cuba & he was most amiable. He said he quite approved but rather hinted that it would have been better to go without asking leave at all. However he said he would arrange things for me & the result is I have got a letter from the W.O. appointing a day on which I shall go and see General Chapman[2] – the head of the Intelligence Department. Personally I think things are now arranged. Wolseley also said that if I worked at the military profession he would help me in every way he could & that I was always to come and ask when I wanted anything.

The little Pushtu[3] Officer came down and dined and enjoyed himself very much. He turned out to be rather good at billiards and when we played pool quite took us all on. He is a nice fellow & ready to tell his only story on the slightest provocation. Everyone likes him.

Well my dearest Mamma I really can find nothing else to say & even if I could I should be late for dinner.

Your ever loving son
WINSTON S. CHURCHILL

J. Duncan Daly to WSC

19 October 1895   Horse Guards
                                                            War Office

Sir,

I am directed by the Commander in Chief to inform you – with reference to a letter addressed by you to Field Marshal Viscount Wolseley, on the subject

---

[1] Garnet Joseph, 1st Viscount Wolseley (1833–1913), Commander-in-Chief of the Army 1895–1900. One of the outstanding generals of the Victorian era, he led successful expeditions on the Gold Coast against the Ashantis 1873, in Egypt 1882, and best known of all, to the relief of Gordon in Khartoum 1884–85. He also wrote a good life of the great Duke of Marlborough. Created Baron 1882; Viscount 1885. Field Marshal 1894.

[2] Edward Francis Chapman (1840–1926), Director of Military Intelligence 1891–6. General 1896, KCB 1905.

[3] Literally, the native name of the language of the Afghans but loosely applied to the Pathans of Afghanistan and the frontier. It seems possible that the Pushtu officer had been a member of the suite of the Amir of Afghanistan's son for whom the IV Hussars had formed the guard of honour on the occasion of his visit four and a half months earlier (see page 576).

of your proposed visit to Cuba, that an application received in this Department through the usual channel, will be considered.

I am, Sir, Your obedient Servant
J. DUNCAN DALY

WSC to Lady Randolph

21 October [1895]   Bachelors' Club

My dearest Mamma,

The Cuban business is satisfactorily settled. The War Office have given consent & we have this afternoon been to see the head of the Intelligence Department General Chapman who has furnished us with maps & much valuable information.

We are also requested to collect information and statistics on various points & particularly as to the effect of the new bullet – its penetration and striking power. This invests our mission with almost an official character & cannot fail to help one in the future.

When are you coming to London? Do send me a wire to let me know. I must see a little of you before we go. I shall bring back a great many Havana cigars – some of which can be "laid down" in the cellars of 35 Great Cumberland Place.

I saw Mr Tito Holden the other day & he told me much about Cuba – its beautiful climate at this season of the year – and its good points generally. My idea was so excellent I cannot cease commending myself for it.

Longing to see you – and hoping shortly to accomplish my desire.

I remain Ever your loving son
WINSTON S. CHURCHILL

WSC to Lady Randolph

22 October [1895]   Hounslow

My dear Mamma,

I hope you will be able to come back a little sooner than Sunday night. You said you would come 24th (that is Thursday). I go on leave tomorrow (23rd) & am staying at Newmarket with Bob Sherwood. I am staying there till Friday but I would much rather be with you.

As I wrote and telegraphed to you – I and Barnes would start for Cuba on Wednesday 30th in order to get there as early as possible. So if you don't come back till Sunday night we shall see very little of each other. Also my dear Mamma I have nowhere to go.

Ever your loving son
WINSTON S.C.

Sir Donald Mackenzie Wallace[1] to WSC

31 October 1895
St Ermin's Mansions
Caxton Street

Dear Mr Churchill,

At Sir Henry Wolff's suggestion I send you a letter of introduction for Mr Akers, *The Times* Special Correspondent in Cuba. Unfortunately it is not certain that you will find him in Havana because he has been ordered to Venezuela for a little but I hope he may be back in time to be of some use to you.

Ever yours
DONALD M. WALLACE

Sir Donald Mackenzie Wallace to Mr Akers

31 October 1895
St Ermin's Mansions

My dear Akers,

Let me introduce you to Mr Winston Churchill and Mr Barnes, both of the 4th Hussars who intend visiting Cuba this winter. If you are there when they arrive and can be of any assistance to them by placing the stores of your local knowledge at their disposal I should be very much obliged by your doing so.

Yours sincerely
D. M. WALLACE

[1] Donald Mackenzie Wallace (1841–1919), Director of the Foreign Department of *The Times* 1891-9. Previously Private Secretary to the Viceroys of India 1884-9; later Assistant Private Secretary to the Duke of York on his Colonial tour, 1901, and extra groom-in-waiting to King Edward VII and King George V. KCIE 1887, KCVO 1901.

WSC to Jack

2 November [1895]   Cunard RMS *Etruria*

Dearest Jack,

One line only from Queenstown – to let you know we are off. Lady Colebrooke[1] who is on board sends her best love.

We have comfortable cabins & so far it is very calm.

Take care of yourself and mind you write to

> British Consulate General
> Havana.

Your ever loving brother
WINSTON

WSC to Lady Randolph

8 November [1895]   Cunard Royal Mail Steamship
Etruria

My darling Mamma,

This letter is written in the hopes that it will catch the *Lucania* when she passes us tomorrow and so reach you rather earlier than if it were posted in New York. We expect to arrive at about noon to-morrow and so bring a tedious and uncomfortable journey to a close. The weather was fine for the first day but after that we had it rough and stormy – with the spray covering the whole ship & the deck almost under water. Barnes and I were very stubborn and though we had bad moments were never seasick – nor did we miss any meal in the Saloon. Rather a fine performance considering that on one occasion there were only 12 people at dinner.

The boat is a good one – the food not at all bad & our cabins are not uncomfortable – but the lack of a comfortable place to sit down and of an interesting occupation – have made us look forward eagerly to disembarking.

I do not contemplate ever taking a sea voyage for pleasure & I shall always look upon journeys by sea as necessary evils – which have to be undergone in the carrying out of any definite plan.

Lady Colebrooke & I have played Bezique but I am very much out of luck and have seldom held such monotonously unfortunate hands. Fortunately we have not had many games or played high.

I received at Queenstown a letter from Aunt Leonie which I was very glad to get & which I shall answer from New York as soon as I land.

---

[1] Alexandra Harriett (–1944), 7th daughter of Lord Alfred Paget, who in 1889 married Sir Edward Colebrooke, 5th Bart. Sir Edward was Lord-in-Waiting to King Edward VII 1906–10 and to King George V 1910–11, created Baron 1906.

There are no nice people on board to speak of – certainly none to write of. Barnes has made great friends with Mr Gerald Paget[1] & Lady C – & they like him very much.

There is to be a concert on board tonight at which all the stupid people among the passengers intend to perform and the stupider ones to applaud. The days have seemed very long & uninteresting and as you know well travelling by sea when prosperous is devoid of incident – so I can find no more at present to write to you about.

I look forward eagerly to reaching our destination & it is possible we may cut down our stay in N. York to a day and a half instead of three – but however short a time we stay there I shall make it my business to write you another letter. Please write often to Havana my darling Mamma and remember the 'universal unicode[2].

With best love and many kisses I remain, Ever your loving son
WINSTON

WSC to Lady Randolph

10 November [1895]   763 Fifth Avenue
                                            [New York]

My dearest Mamma,

I am sorry to say that the letter which I wrote two days ago missed the '*Lucania*' and so this will get to you almost as soon. I & Barnes are staying with Mr Bourke Cockran in a charming and very comfortable flat at the address on this paper.

Everybody is very civil and we have engagements for every meal for the next few days about three deep. It is very pleasant staying here as the rooms are beautifully furnished and fitted with every convenience & also as Mr Cockran is one of the most charming hosts and interesting men I have met. Last night we had a big dinner here to 10 or 12 persons all of whom were on the Judiciary. Very interesting men – one particularly – a Supreme Court Judge[3] – is trying a "*cause célèbre*"[4] here now – and so we are going to hear the charge to the Jury on Wednesday and in all probability the capital sentence.

---

1 Gerald Paget (1854–1913) was Lady Colebrooke's brother.
2 A telegraphic code in which one word or set of letters represents a sentence or phrase.
3 Judge Ingraham.
4 The trial of David F. Hannigan, who had shot and killed Solomon H. Mann. Hannigan's sister Lettie had stated, to a coroner's jury assembled at her deathbed, that Mann had seduced her and procured an abortion which was the cause of her death. After a trial lasting nearly four weeks Hannigan was acquitted on the grounds of insanity on November 22. His aged father William, who had given evidence on his behalf earlier in the trial, died just 17 minutes before the jury returned its verdict.

Eva[1] is in great form and talks unceasingly – but has arranged things very well. She has engaged an excellent valet and – as I told you made every sort of engagement for us.

Tomorrow we are going to see the Headquarters of the Atlantic Military district and do the harbour in a tugboat & Tuesday we go to West Point where I believe they will show us everything there is to see. The Horse Show begins tomorrow and Kitty Mott[2] has a box to which we are both invited.

A Mr Purdy took us round New York last night to Koster and Bial's & supper at the Waldorf. The Entertainment was good and the supper excellent. Today I snatch a quiet hour to pen you a line – but I lunch with Eva at 1 – call on the Hitts at 3 – the Cornelius Vanderbilts[3] at 5 & dine with Kitty at 8 – so you see that there is not much chance of the time hanging heavily. They really make rather a fuss over us here and extend the most lavish hospitality. We are members of all the Clubs and one person seems to vie with another in trying to make our time pleasant.

I have been civil and vague to the reporters and so far I can only find one misstatement in the papers.

What an extraordinary people the Americans are! Their hospitality is a revelation to me and they make you feel at home and at ease in a way that I have never before experienced. On the other hand their press and their currency impress me very unfavourably.

I have great discussions with Mr Cockran on every conceivable subject from Economics to yacht racing. He is a clever man and one from whose conversation much is to be learned.

I think we shall go by rail to Tampa as there is

[letter incomplete]

WSC to Mrs John Leslie
(Copy: Leslie Papers)

12 November 1895   763 Fifth Avenue

My dear Aunt Leonie,

I was very glad to get your letter at Queenstown and have been meaning to write you an answer for the last day or two. We are staying with a friend of yours Mr Bourke Cockran in his charming flat in Fifth Avenue and so are very comfortable. He is such a nice man and we have made great friends.

I have been industriously seeing American institutions of all kinds, and have

---

[1] Eva Purdy, daughter of Catherine Purdy (née Hall), sister of Mrs Leonard Jerome.

[2] Kitty, sister of Eva Purdy, was married to Jordan L. Mott Jr, son of a New York iron master.

[3] Cornelius Vanderbilt (1843–99), head of the Vanderbilt family since 1885, grandson of the Commodore, uncle of Consuelo, Duchess of Marlborough.

been impressed by many things – but I feel that I should like to think over and digest what I have seen for a few weeks before forming an opinion on it.

So far I think the means of communication in New York have struck me the most. The comfort and convenience of elevated railways – tramways – cable cars & ferries, harmoniously fitted into a perfect system accessible alike to the richest and the poorest – is extraordinary. And when one reflects that such benefits have been secured to the people not by confiscation of the property of the rich or by arbitrary taxation but simply by business enterprise – out of which the promoters themselves have made colossal fortunes, one cannot fail to be impressed with the excellence of the active system.

But New York is full of contradictions and contrasts. I paid my fare across Brooklyn Bridge with a paper dollar. I should think the most disreputable "coin" the world has ever seen. I wondered how to reconcile the magnificent system of communication with the abominable currency – for a considerable time and at length I have found what may be a solution. The communication of New York is due to private enterprise while the state is responsible for the currency: and hence I come to the conclusion that the first class men of America are in the counting houses and the less brilliant ones in the government.

. . .

Yesterday we went round all the forts and barracks and in the evening we went over the ironclad cruiser *New York*. I was much struck by the sailors: their intelligence, their good looks and civility and their generally businesslike appearance. These interested me more than [the] ship itself, for while any nation can build a battleship – it is the monopoly of the Anglo-Saxon race to breed good seamen.

Altogether, my dear Aunt Leonie, my mind is full of irreconcilable and conflicting facts. The comfort of their cars and the disgraceful currency – the hospitality of American Society and the vulgarity of their Press – present to me a problem of great complexity. I am going to prolong my stay here a few more days on purpose to see more.

Everyone is very civil and we have been shewn everything. Today I go to the Court to hear a *cause célèbre*. I met the judge at dinner two nights ago and he suggested my coming. Tomorrow I am going over West Point and have the fire department alarmed – so you see I am not likely to find time hang heavily.

Well *au revoir*, my dearest Auntie, Hoping this letter will not seem *too* ponderous.

Yours ever
WINSTON S. CHURCHILL

WSC to Jack

15 November [1895]   763 5th Avenue

My dearest Jack,

I daresay Mamma showed you my letter of the 10th, which gave an account of the voyage and such news as was to hand at that time. I am still staying with Mr Bourke Cockran, whom you met in Paris, in his very comfortable and convenient flat in 5th Avenue. We have postponed our departure from New York for three days as there was lots to see and do. On Sunday we start for Havana by the route of Philadelphia – Washington – Savannah – Tampa Bay and Key West – arriving there on Wednesday morning, all being well.

Mr Cockran, who has great influence over here, procured us orders to visit the Forts of the Harbour and West Point – which is the American Sandhurst.

I am sure you will be horrified by some of the Regulations of the Military Academy. The cadets enter from 19–22 & stay 4 years. This means that they are most of them 24 years of age. They are not allowed to smoke or have any money in their possession nor are they given any leave except 2 months after the 1st two years. In fact they have far less liberty than any *private* school boys in our country. I think such a state of things is positively disgraceful and young men of 24 or 25 who would resign their personal liberty to such an extent can never make good citizens or fine soldiers. A child who rebels against that sort of control should be whipped – so should a man who does not rebel.

The other night Mr Cockran got the Fire Commissioner to come with us and we alarmed four or five fire stations. This would have interested you very much. On the alarm bell sounding the horses at once rushed into the shafts – the harness fell on to them – the men slid half dressed down a pole from their sleeping room and in 5½ seconds the engine was galloping down the street to the scene of the fire. An interesting feat which seems incredible unless you have seen it.

There is a great criminal trial going on now – of a man who shot a fellow who had seduced his sister. I met the judge at dinner the other night and he suggested my coming to hear the case. I went and sat on the bench by his side. Quite a strange experience and one which would be impossible in England. The Judge discussing the evidence as it was given with me and generally making himself socially agreeable – & all the while a pale miserable man was fighting for his life. This is a very great country my dear Jack. Not pretty or romantic but great and utilitarian. There seems to be no such thing as reverence or tradition. Everything is eminently practical and things are judged from a matter of fact standpoint. Take for instance the Court house. No robes or wigs or uniformed ushers. Nothing but a lot of men in black coats & tweed suits. Judge prisoner jury counsel & warders all indiscriminately mixed.

But they manage to hang a man all the same, and that after all is a great thing.

I saw Sunny last night & am dining with the Vanderbilts this evening. He is very pleased with himself and seems very fit.[1] The newspapers have abused him scurrilously. But the essence of American journalism is vulgarity divested of truth. Their best papers write for a class of snotty housemaids and footmen & even the nicest people here have so much vitiated their taste as to appreciate the style.

I think mind you that vulgarity is a sign of strength. A great, crude, strong, young people are the Americans – like a boisterous healthy boy among enervated but well bred ladies and gentlemen. Some day Jack when you are older you must come out here and I think you will feel as I feel – and think as I think today.

Picture to yourself the American people as a great lusty youth – who treads on all your sensibilities perpetrates every possible horror of ill manners – whom neither age not just tradition inspire with reverence – but who moves about his affairs with a good hearted freshness which may well be the envy of older nations of the earth. Of course there are here charming people who are just as refined and cultured as the best in any country in the world – but I believe my impressions of the nation are broadly speaking correct. I have written you quite a long letter & cannot write again today so send this to Mamma after reading.

With best love Ever your loving brother
WINSTON S. CHURCHILL

WSC to Bourke Cockran
(*Cockran Papers*)

20 November 1895

Gran Hotel Inglaterra
Havana
Cuba

My dear Cockran,

We had a very comfortable journey which was entirely due to your kindness in getting us a State room. The food all along was execrable but the passage was good and the weather perfect. Early this morning a violent rain storm woke me up and I went on deck as soon as it cleared up. There, on our port under lowering and gloomy clouds lay the shores of Cuba. We got into the harbour without incident and here in a convenient hotel – we remain.

We start tomorrow for Santa Clara – where are rumours of great things

---

[1] The Duke of Marlborough had married Miss Consuelo Vanderbilt in New York on 6 November 1895.

doing. The route is by rail and an additional interest will be lent to it by the fact that the insurgents do all they can to wreck the trains and occasionally succeed.

As to our return we propose to leave the island on Monday 16th prox. (Three boats a week in December.) Can you get us a state room from here to New York? If you can – will you? I cannot tell you what a difference it made on our journey here and we shall be quite spoiled for going back by the ordinary method.

I must reiterate my thanks to you for your kindness and courtesy in putting us up all the time we were in New York. We had many delightful conversations – and I learned much from you in a pleasant and interesting way. I hope in England to renew our discussions and though I can never repay you for your kindness I trust you will take the hospitality of the 4th Hussars "on account", as we say.

Yours ever
WINSTON S. CHURCHILL

WSC to Lady Randolph

20 November 1895   Gran Hotel Inglaterra
                                      Parque Central
                                         Havana

My darling Mamma,

I have just arrived here after a comfortable journey from New York. Mr Bourke Cockran procured a private state room in the train, so that the 36 hours we passed there were not as unpleasant as if we had had to travel in a regular compartment. The Little steamer – the *Olivette* – was very clean and the captain and all the officers made everything as pleasant and convenient as possible.

Here we have met several nice people – one is a large planter, with whom we may stay for a few days, as his plantation is on the road to Santa Clara – whither we go tomorrow. Mr Gollan[1] as I cabled you was most amiable and went with us to General Arderins. The General has telegraphed to Marshal Campos to advise him of our arrival. The letters I have got are a free pass everywhere – and they allowed us to bring our pistols through the Customs as soon as I showed them these letters – in spite of the law being very strict on that point.

Tomorrow we start "for the front" or rather to Santa Clara where the Headquarters Staff are. We go by rail via Matanzas and Cienguegos. The

---

[1] Alexander Gollan (1840–1902), Consul-General for Cuba 1892–8; KCMG 1898.

journey takes twelve hours as the trains move very slowly on account of the rebels damaging the line and trying to wreck the locomotives. I believe they also fire at the train and throw dynamite cartridges – but the vigilance of the patrols and also the fact that 40 or 50 riflemen go with each train have reduced risks considerably – and the General recommended the route.

You may have something of the war in London and at New York there is a plethora of news – but here in Havana nothing whatever is known – though rumours abound. The latest heard is that a great Spanish defeat has taken place in the province of Santa Clara. Everyone lies so [much] here that one cannot tell what to believe. On the boat today they told us that a pestilence of yellow fever was raging in the town – whereas there are only a very few cases. Gomez the insurgent traitor is marching to meet Marshal Campos at the head of a force – variously estimated at from 50 to 18,000 men. Inaccuracy – exaggeration – and gratuitous falsehood are the main characteristics of the information received through Spanish sources.

Well my darling Mamma – you shall have another letter soon. I am glad that the horse seems to give promise of being useful to you. Give my best love to Jack. I wish I had his camera here. I was so foolish in not taking it. With lots of love and many kisses.

Ever your loving son
WINSTON S. CHURCHILL

WSC to Lady Randolph

6 December 1895   Gran Hotel Inglaterra
                                                              Havana

My dearest Mamma,

We arrived here last night – after a very exciting fortnight and very glad we were to return to civilization and to return safely. I found your letters up to 22nd and was delighted to get them – they being with one exception the only letters I have received for a month. Of course I sent to to the Brunswick Hotel two or three times for any cable there might be for me; but they said there was nothing at all there for my name and hence my telegrams. I will make the most searching inquiries in New York when I get back. Let me congratulate you on "Gold Key's" victory.[1] I wonder however that you did not let him go after the race. Perhaps he will win a nice stake as a three year old. It very often happens that colts who have been – for some reason or other – very little raced as two year olds – win a lot of nice races the next year. I am thinking of

---

[1] The 2 year old black colt by Gervas out of Allotment (see p. 572). On November 13, running in R. Sherwood's colours, he won (at 10 to 1) a selling handicap at Leicester worth £188, and was bought in at the subsequent auction for 180 guineas.

Matchmaker particularly. He was a very useful animal to Sir Frederick Johnstone.[1]

Well my darling Mamma. I can't tell what pleasure it gives me to be able to write to you and tell you that we have got back safely. There were moments during the last week when I realised how rash we had been in risking our lives – merely in search of adventure. However it all turned up trumps and here we are.

I wrote to you from Sancti Spiritus – (but I do not think you will get the letter any sooner than this one) – to tell you of our starting with a column of troops under Suarez Valdez. We were glad to leave the town – it was in a dreadful state with about four separate pestilences raging and an enormous amount of dirt. For eight days we were with the troops in the field. The General gave us horses and servants and we lived with his personal staff. He did himself very well as far as food went and until the cook got shot we suffered very little inconvenience. We bivouaced in a shed of some sort pretty nearly every night and as we bought a couple of hammocks we were really not uncomfortable – though this is only a comparative expression.

After much marching through virgin forest we found the enemy – and he promptly fired at us. Hence forward for the last three days of the column – we were almost continually under some sort of fire or another. I have described it all in my fourth letter to the *Daily Graphic* and so my dearest Mamma it is hardly necessary for me to re-write a long story. Finally on the last day we attacked the enemy's position and advanced right across open ground under a very heavy fire. The General a very brave man – in a white and gold uniform on a grey horse – drew a great deal of fire on to us and I heard enough bullets whistle and hum past to satisfy me for some time to come. He rode right up to within 500 yards of the enemy and there we waited till the fire of the Spanish infantry drove them from their position. We had great luck in not losing more than we did – but as a rule the rebels shot very high. We stayed by the General all the time and so were in the most dangerous place in the field. The General recommended us for the Red Cross – a Spanish Decoration given to Officers – and coming in the train yesterday, by chance I found Marshal Campos and his staff, who told me that it would be sent us in due course.

Our luck has been almost uncanny. Every train every steamboat has fitted exactly. We missed two trains that were both smashed up by the rebels by about half an hour. We went into a town in which every sort of dreadful disease was spreading and finally if without any particular reason I had not changed my position about one yard to the right I should infallibly have been shot. Added to all this I left a fiver to be put on "The Rush" at 8 to 1 and it

[1] Among the races won by Matchmaker was the Prince of Wales's Stakes at Ascot in 1895.

simply romped home. So you see my dear Mamma – there *is* a sweet little cherub.

We are coming home at once and before you get this letter I shall have wired to you the date of our arrival – all being well. I would like to bring Reggie [Barnes] to dinner the night we arrive – so if you can arrange to be there do let us have with Jack a little *parti carré*.

Longing to see you and Lots of love
Your ever loving son
WINSTON S. CHURCHILL

PS As regards the money I wired to you for. I have got it at Cox's and will give it you as soon as I get back. Also the *D.G.* owe me a pony – if they have begun to publish my letters. I am going to bring over excellent coffee, cigars and guava jelly to stock the cellars of 35a.

*   *   *   *

WSC's experiences in Cuba provided him with the material for his first ventures into serious journalism. His five despatches, published in the *Daily Graphic* as 'Letters from the Front', appeared on December 13, 17, 24 and 27, and on 13 January 1896. They were headlined 'The Insurrection in Cuba' and by-lined 'From Our Own Correspondent'. Each article ended with the initials 'WSC'.

I

Most people have probably noticed that the initial difficulties of any undertaking are in many cases the most insuperable. The first few sentences, whether of a proposal of marriage or of a newspaper article, require more thought, and involve more effort, than any of those which follow. And if this is the case with those who are accustomed by experience to break the ice in either circumstance, how much more does it apply to the beginnings of the beginner. It is on account of these difficulties that I shall allow their enumeration to stand in place of further prelude, and plunge at once into the middle of the subject – and the harbour of the City of Havana.

High up on the cliffs, as the ship enters the narrows, one sees the fortress of El Moro, formerly a place of great strength, and commanding the channel to the port. It is now only used as a prison for political and military offenders, and as an occasional place of execution. Here it was that the sentence of death on Lieutenant Gallegos was carried out in May last. This officer had the charge of a small post with some fifty soldiers, and was unfortunate enough to be breakfasting in a café when the insurgents happened to pass, and so was taken prisoner, with all his men. The rebels let them go, but kept their arms, and the court-martial sentenced the lieutenant to be shot for neglect of duty.

The town shows no sign of the insurrection, and business proceeds everywhere as usual. Passports are, however, strictly examined, and all baggage is searched with a view to discovering pistols or other arms. During the passage from Tampa on the boat the most violent reports of the condition of Havana were rife. Yellow fever was said to be prevalent, and the garrison was reported to have over 400 cases. As a matter of fact, there is really not much sickness, and what there is is confined to the lower part of the town. What struck me most was the absence of any news. London may know much of what is going on in the island – New York is certain to know more – but Havana hears nothing. All the papers are strictly edited by the Government and are filled with foreign and altogether irrelevant topics. It was explained to me that while the Spanish authorities were masters of the art of suppressing the truth, the Cubans were adepts at inventing falsehood. By this arrangement conflicting statements and inaccuracy are alike assured. During the evening which I passed in the capital some volunteers marched in from the front, preceded by a band and surrounded by a great crowd. They were a fine lot of men – young, but well developed – and though they looked tired, marched jauntily, and were evidently much pleased with themselves. Their uniform was made of white cotton and they wore large straw hats of limp material, twisted into every conceivable shape. They were very dirty and did not preserve much order, but for all that they looked like soldiers and were well armed. These "volunteers," of whom there are about 25,000 in all, take it in turn to garrison the different outlying towns, afterwards coming back for duty in Havana.

Next day we started for Santa Clara, which is the Captain-General's headquarters. As far as Colon the journey is safe, but thenceforward the country is much disturbed. The insurgents have given notice that they will wreck any train carrying troops, and have several times succeeded in so doing. Every station from Colon to Santa Clara is a small fort. Sometimes it is a stockade of logs, sometimes a loopholed house or a stone breastwork; all have a garrison of from fifteen to twenty men. Every bridge has to be guarded also by a block house or other defensive work, as the rebels cut the supports through and so upset the trains. In fact, they have tried every sort of dodge in this respect. One of the cleverest of these is to loosen a rail and to fasten a wire to it. When the train comes along this wire is pulled, and the result often fully repays their labours. Dynamite is also thrown, but the insurgents appear not to understand its employment, as only two explosions have taken place so far, though there have been many attempts. At Santa Domingo a pilot engine and an armoured-car are added to the train, as the rebels often indulge in target practice – from a respectful distance. In the car rides the escort, the passengers being permitted the privilege of using the ordinary compartments. When we reached this place the line thence to Santa Clara had just been cut, and the traffic had to go round by Cruces, thus causing a great delay. On arrival there it was announced that the train which preceded ours, and in which was General Valdes, had been thrown off the line a few miles beyond Santa Domingo, and that fifteen of its occupants had been severely injured. This had been effected by weakening the supports of a small culvert. The general fortunately escaped uninjured, and at once started up country. Marshal Campos, to whose headquarters we went, received us very kindly, and readily gave us the necessary passes and letters. Unfortunately, we found that the column of General Valdes was already twenty miles away, through a country infested by the enemy, and it would therefore be necessary to go to Cienfuegos, thence by steamer to Tuna, and from there on to Sancti Spiritu. Though this route forms two sides of a triangle, it is – Euclid notwithstanding – shorter than the other, and we shall catch the column there.

The insurrection shows no signs of abating, and the insurgents gain adherents continually. There is no doubt that they possess the sympathy of the entire population, and hence have constant and accurate intelligence. On the other hand Spain is equally determined to crush them, and is even now pouring in fresh troops by the thousand. How it will end it is impossible to say, but whoever wins, and whatever may be the results, the suffering and misery of the entire community is certain. The struggle is now entering upon a crucial stage. Maximo Gomez has said openly that he will not allow the grinding of the sugar cane. Any planter who does so will have his plantation burned. In the face of this threat the authorities are powerless. The cane is ripe, fit for cutting, and very combustible. It was explained to me that a piece of phosphorus, coated with wax, would be the probable instrument of the incendiaries. This little pill is fastened to the tail of the Cuban grass snake, a common and inoffensive creature, which is then set loose. The sun melts the wax and ignites the phosphorus, and the result is a conflagration, without any possible clue to its authorship. No amount of military protection or patrolling can guard against this form of outrage, and the general impression is that the planters will not grind. The importance of this cannot be over-estimated. It means the paralysing of the staple industry of the country and the ruin of the entire island. It means bankruptcy to the planter and starvation to the labourer, and it will leave a mark upon Cuba which will take many years of plenty and good government to efface.

The twofold object of the rebels in taking this momentous step is to make plain to the entire world the power they have – and so obtain recognition as belligerents from the United States – and by plunging their country into indescribable woe to procure the intervention of some European Power. Looked at from any standpoint, it is a dreadful and a desperate remedy, and one which neither restriction of liberty nor persistent bad government can fully justify. It is, nevertheless, a course open to the dangerous and determined men who are in revolt, and one which there is every reason to believe they will adopt. WSC

II

November 23   Sancti Spiritus

I told you in my last letter from Cienfuegos of our missing the column of General Juarez Valdez at Santa Clara, and of our journey by sea to Tuna in the hope of catching him at Sancti Spiritus. Arrived at Tuna, we found that the daily train had gone already. About twelve o'clock news came that the line had been cut, and that all communication between Sancti Spiritus and the coast had been destroyed. The insurgents, it appears, threw a bomb at the train – which, by the way, we missed by half an hour – but did no harm. They then exploded some dynamite successfully, and broke down a small bridge. As soon as the train arrived at the obstruction it was fired upon, and when its occupants had had enough they returned to Tuna to wait until the line was repaired. We were in the same position, and had to spend the day in the local hotel – an establishment more homely than pretentious.

The next morning, traffic being resumed, we were able to start, and arrived here without incident. These thirty miles of railway are the most dangerous and disturbed in the whole island. The line runs close to the mountains – which the insurgents occupy in great force – and through forest so thick that no one can see ten yards into it. Twenty-eight separate little forts and over 1,200 men are employed in the railroad's protection, but in spite of all these precautions communication is dangerous and uncertain. The train itself is protected from end to end with boiler plates and filled with troops and men of the Guardia Civil. At every station the officer in command of the fort reports to the commander of the escort if his section of the line is quiet, and then the journey is resumed at a rate of about ten miles an hour.

The insurgents have been giving the troops protecting the railway a great deal of trouble lately. About a week ago they took one of the small fortified posts which I have described to you. Maximo Gomez himself directed the attack. Fire was opened on the fort from a hill distant about 500 yards. As soon as the attention of the defenders was drawn to this point two fresh bodies of the enemy opened upon them on each flank, and, at the same time, a fourth detachment, about 100 strong, assaulted the gate, and had it down in an instant. The garrison, numbering fifty, surrendered promptly, and after being deprived of arms and ammunition were allowed to go free. They marched in here in a body looking very crestfallen, and it is reported that the officer will be brought before a court-martial.

Sancti Spiritus – its name notwithstanding – is a forsaken place, and in a most unhealthy state. Smallpox and yellow fever are rife. Last week there were about 120 cases of the former disease with a death-rate of 10 per cent, and 25 cases of the latter with 45 per cent deaths. Both epidemics are, however, declining as the cooler weather approaches, and are chiefly confined to the poorest people and to the troops. The streets are full of soldiers. To-day General Valdez – whom we beat by a short head – marched in from Santa Clara. His men go to swell the number of troops already in the town. Outside are the insurgents, numbering anything from fifteen to twenty thousand, and occupying all the mountainous country to the south-west. Their outposts are met half a mile from the town, and only large columns of troops can pass freely. Gomez is going to proclaim an official investment on the 25th inst, and the line will then, in all probability, be permanently cut. No food is to be allowed into the town, and the only means of getting out will be with a column of troops.

It was explained to me that when challenged by any sentry or outpost it was necessary to answer very sharply. If, by a process of deduction which Sherlock Holmes himself might envy, you arrive at the conclusion that the outpost is Spanish, you answer "Spain"; if, on the other hand, you think it a rebel post, you reply "Free Cuba"; but if you make a mistake it is likely to be very awkward. The great advantage the insurgents have is the detailed and constant information which they receive. Their only uniform is a badge. This can be taken off at will, and when so removed it is impossible to tell a rebel from an ordinary peasant. Hence they know everything: the position of every general, the destination of every soldier, and what their own spies fail to find out their friends in every village let them know. The more I see of Cuba the more I feel sure that the demand for independence is national and unanimous. The insurgent forces contain the best blood in the island, and can by no possible perversion of the truth be classed as *banditti*. In fact, it is a war, not a rebellion.

Very few people in England realise the importance of the struggle out here, or the value of the prize which is being fought for. It is only when one travels through the island that one understands its wealth, its size, or its beauty. Four crops a year can be raised from Cuban soil; Cuban sugar enters the market at a price which defies competition; she practically monopolises the entire manufacture of cigars; ebony and mahogany are of no account in the land, and enormous mineral wealth lies undeveloped in the hills. If one appreciates these facts, guided by the light of current events, one cannot fail to be struck by the irony of a fate which offers so bounteously with the one hand and prohibits so harshly with the other.   WSC

III

November 27   Arroyo

I find that the chief difficulty of writing these letters is that where material is plentiful opportunity is scarce, so that when one has much to write of one has usually but little time to write it in, and conversely. Here, at the village of Arroyo Blanco I take advantage of a temporary halt to describe to you some of the features which Cuban warfare presents.

The day after I sent you my last letter a strong column was formed at Sancti Spiritus, to which, by the courtesy of General Suarez Valdez, we were permitted to attach ourselves. The force consisted of our battalions of infantry – each about 600 strong – 300 cavalry, and a mule battery. It had for its first object the protection of a convoy to Iguara. This village, though not invested according to European ideas, is nevertheless closely blockaded by the insurgents, and has to depend for its food supply upon convoys from Sancti Spiritus. The road – if one may use such a term – lies sometimes along the bed of a watercourse and at others broadens out into a wide grass ride. Frequently it is so traversed by morasses as to be quite impassable, and long *détours* have to be made across country. The intricate nature of the ground prevents anything like a thorough reconnaissance, and much has to be left to chance. Numerous undulations, nullahs, and large tracts of forest afford every kind of facility for an active enemy to surprise the troops, while the nature of the track nearly always necessitates single file, thus causing the column to straggle over a couple of miles of ground in the worst possible formation for resisting any attack that may be made. The cavalry reconnoitre all they can, and whenever the country opens out flanking parties are detached at once. As a rule, however, it is impossible to do more than go straight ahead, and often it is difficult to do that.

In spite of the bad condition of the road we made about three miles an hour. The Spanish regular infantry march splendidly. Yesterday they went twenty-six English miles between sunset and sunrise, carrying 150 rounds of ball ammunition a man and all their kit – blankets, cooking-pots, and the like. I was much struck by these infantry. They are by no means the undisciplined boys which I was led to believe they were, but grown men, bearded for the most part, and averaging about twenty-five years of age. Notwithstanding the hot sun and the fact that every man got drenched in fording a river almost as soon as the column started, I saw very few fall out during the day. Most of the regular regiments are armed with the Mauser rifle – an excellent weapon on a similar principle to our Lee-Metford – but some of those who have been out here longest still use the Remington.

On the evening of the second day after starting the column reached Iguara, where the garrison was provisioned for a couple of months to come. We spent a comfortable night at this place, which consists only of four or five houses and barns, and early next morning the troops marched on here. This "town" – for it is much bigger than Iguara – contains about twenty wooden houses, one-storied, and for the most part destitute of floors. It is, however, important from the fact that it possesses a heliograph station, from which messages can be flashed from one point to another right away to the head-quarters at Santa Clara. Every house is loopholed and earth-protected, and the whole place is surrounded by a circle of little fortified posts. The garrison, 200 strong, had a brush with the enemy the day before yesterday, and claims to have killed and wounded over twenty rebels, including a "chief."

The country shows many traces of the insurrection. Burned houses and broken-down fences mark the rebels' lines of march and places of bivouac. Every now and again the advanced guard "puts up" a small body of them, who let off their rifles and depart as speedily as possible. Occasionally a solitary horseman is seen at the edge of a clearing on the spur of some hill watching the movement of the column, and, as soon as he finds himself perceived, he gallops away to report. The troops managed to shoot a couple of these fellows before they could get away yesterday, and a chance bullet killed an infantry soldier, but so far we have met with nothing that could be called resistance. To-day, however, we have news that Maximo Gomez is encamped with 4,000 men a couple of leagues to the east, and early to-morrow we start after him. Whether he will accept battle or not is uncertain, but if he does not want to fight the Spaniards have no means of making him do so, as the insurgents, mounted on their handy little country-bred ponies, knowing every inch of the ground, possessed of the most accurate information, and, unimpeded by any luggage, can easily defeat all attempts to force a battle.

In the afternoon the chief of the staff, Lieut-Colonel Benzo, invited us to ride round the outpost line and up to the heliograph station. The latter place was much further than they expected, and as we turned to come back the sun sank, and five minutes later it was dark. We had a very exciting ride back – a mile and a half through woods infested by the rebels. They did not, however, for some unexplained reason, fire at us. This was very lucky, as our escort consisted only of half a dozen mounted men of the Guarda Civil, and was much too small to have done any good. Night in Cuba comes on with startling rapidity, and one has to be very careful not to be caught by it. The sun gets low on the horizon, and without any intermediate period of twilight darkness sets in. The woods then become nearly impassable, and even the surefooted little ponies are unable to avoid the numerous pitfalls.

I am told that the great difficulty which the rebels have to contend with is the scarcity of ammunition. Sometimes they enter on a skirmish with the Government troops with only two or three rounds a man. They are very bad shots, and it is only at a close range that their fire is effective. One weapon they have, however, with which they are very formidable – the *machete* – a short, heavy, broad-bladed sword. It is the national weapon of Cuba. In time of peace every peasant carries one, and uses it to cut the sugar cane and to perform every kind of chopping or cutting work. Accustomed by long use, they attain a marvellous proficiency, and can sever with a single blow, and without apparent effort, branches which would need several strokes from most men. In fact, instances have been known, both in this war and in the last, of rifles having been cut clean in two at one blow.

The Spanish officers anticipate a speedy end to the war, and hope to crush the rebellion before the spring. I confess I do not see how this is to be done. As long as the insurgents choose to adhere to the tactics they have adopted – and there is every reason to believe that they will do so – they can neither be caught nor defeated.   WSC

IV

December 4   Cienfuegos

On November 30th [WSC's 21st birthday], at 5 a.m., the column commanded by General Suarez Valdez marched out of Arroyo Blanco, with the intention of finding and, if possible, of fighting the insurgents, who, under Maximo Gomez, were reported to be encamped some miles to the eastward. The convoy, which had provisioned the garrison of Iguara, was sent with the rest of its supplies to a small town to the north-west, two battalions and a squadron being detailed as escort. This left us with a force consisting of the remaining two battalions – two squadrons of cavalry and the artillery – in all about 1,700 men.

No sooner had we got clear of the town than we heard the sound of firing, showing that the convoy, which had started earlier, was already engaged. For about two miles we retraced our steps in the direction of Iguara, in order to deceive the enemy's scouts, and then struck off to the left and marched due east. The country was rather more open than on the preceding days, and our route lay through swampy meadows of coarse grass, traversed by frequent water-courses. By midday the column reached a more wooded region, and at three o'clock we came upon the traces of a rebel encampment. Little shelters constructed of palm leaves, the ashes of the bivouac fires, and particularly a number of black bustards circling around in search of "unconsidered trifles," marked its whereabouts. Of the enemy himself nothing was to be seen. His line of march could, however, be traced by broken branches and tramped grass, and this line the column followed. At five o'clock we reached Lagitas – a "town" consisting of one barn – and here the inhabitant told the general that the rebels had just left. This was indeed the case. Their fires were still smouldering, and signs of a hasty departure were to be seen on every side. The shanty itself had served Maximo Gomez as his headquarters the night before, so that it was swept and garnished, and we had only to go inside and make ourselves comfortable.

The order was given for the column to bivouac here, and the cavalry were just dismounting, when a party of about twenty-five insurgents – who had been watching our occupation of their late quarters – was seen making off across the fields in the direction of the woods 400 yards away. The cavalry remounted and pursued those fellows with the greatest promptitude, but they were unable to catch them before they reached the edge of the forest, into the depths of which it was impossible to follow. It was evident that the enemy was very close, and in order to prevent the camp being disturbed by his fire during the night no fewer than four companies of infantry were posted on the edge of the woods, and numerous other precautions taken to avoid a surprise. Then we had dinner. I send you a sketch of the little house which served as our headquarters. The whole scene, bathed in brilliant moonlight – in strong contrast to which the tall palm trees and the surrounding woods showed in deepest black – the numerous watch fires, against whose glaze the figures of the soldiers were silhouetted, combined with the noises of a camp and the sound of the river to produce an impression hard to forget but impossible to convey.

The next morning at a quarter-past five we marched out of our bivouac. The sun had not yet risen, and a mist hung over all the low-lying ground. We had not gone half a mile when a sharp fire was opened on the column from the edge of a wood about 200 yards away to the left. As nothing could be seen, the troops did not reply, and after firing for about ten minutes the enemy retired. This day our road lay through the thickest and most impenetrable forest. Once off the path progress was impossible, and any kind of reconnoitring to the flanks out of the question. The leading battalion of infantry now headed the column, the cavalry following in half-sections. The pace was slow but steady. At eleven o'clock we came into a small clearing about two hundred yards wide. Here we lunched – or rather here we proposed to lunch, for no sooner had the column halted than we were fired at from the edge of the clearing. The Staff was, of course, selected as a target, and the guide had his horse shot under him. A few infantrymen cleared these sharpshooters out, but the general ordered the march to be resumed, as he did not consider our position a safe one. The woods, which before had resembled an English covert, now gave place to a forest of extraordinary palm trees of all possible sizes and most peculiar shapes. Three or four hours of this sort of country led us to more open ground, and after fording a river we camped at a place called Las Grullas, which, like Lagitas, consisted of a rude cabin. The river ran round this position on three sides, but it was completely open to fire from the further bank, and as it was perfectly flat and afforded no cover it was a bad position. No other spot was, however, available, so we had to make the best of it.

The day was hot, and my companion and I persuaded a couple of officers on the Staff to come with us and bathe in the river. The water was delightful, being warm and clear, and the spot very beautiful. We were dressing on the bank when, suddenly, we heard a shot fired. Another and another followed; then came a volley. The bullets whistled over our heads. It was evident that an attack of some sort was in progress. A sentry, sitting on a tree about fifty yards higher up stream, popped over it, and, kneeling down behind, began to fire at the advancing enemy, who were now not 200 yards away. We pulled on our clothes anyhow, and one of the officers, in a half-dressed state, ran and collected about fifty men who were building shelters for the night close by. Of course they had their rifles – in this war no soldier ever goes a yard without his weapon – and these men doubled up in high delight and gave the rebels a volley from their Mausers which checked the enemy's advance. We retired along the river as gracefully as might be, and returned to the general's quarters. When we arrived there was a regular skirmish going on half a mile away, and the bullets were falling over the camp. The rebels, who use Remingtons, fired independently, and the deep note of their pieces contrasted strangely with the shrill rattle of the magazine rifles of the Spaniards. After about half an hour the insurgents had enough, and went off carrying their wounded and dead away with them.

At eleven that night they came back and fired at us for about an hour. This time they employed volleys, and killed and wounded several soldiers about the camp. One bullet came through the thatch of the hut in which we were sleeping and another wounded an orderly just outside – but otherwise we were not affected by the fire. After a disturbed night the column started early in the morning. The same mist, as on the previous day, gave cover to the rebel marksmen, who saluted us as soon as we got across the river with a well-directed fire. There was a sort of block, caused by the battalion of infantry having to go in front instead of the cavalry, and during this halt the enemy's bullets whizzed over our heads or cut into the soft ground underfoot. The soldiers grinned and mimicked the sound of the passing projectiles, and generally behaved very well. We lost a few men here, and then General Navarro, who commanded the advance guard, discovered the whereabouts of the insurgents. As soon as this was known the magazine rifles of the regulars crushed their fire and the column moved off. From six till eight o'clock we marched continually opposed and constantly under fire. The enemy falling back on its camp took advantage of every position, and though not very many men were hit all the bullets traversed the entire length of the column, making the march very lively for everybody.

At eight o'clock the head of the column debouched from the broken ground into more open country, and the main position of the enemy was visible. Having inspected the field through his glasses, General Valdez decided to attack at once. To describe ground shortly is always difficult, and to describe it at length is futile, as no one ever takes the trouble to read the description carefully enough to understand it. I will therefore limit myself to a few lines only, and trust they will convey a general idea. A broad grass ride, with a wire fence on one side and a row of little stunted trees on the other, ran from the beginning of the plain to the enemy's position. On each side were broad fields of coarse rank grass, waist high. Half-way up the ride, which was about a mile long, and on the right-hand side, were about a hundred palm trees. At the end of the ride and at right-angles to it was a low, long hill, surmounted by a fence and backed by the dense forest.

As the leading battalion got clear of the broken ground, two companies were thrown forward on each flank and extended. The cavalry went to the right of the ride and the artillery advanced up the centre. The general and his whole staff rode up the ride fifty yards in rear of the firing line. The second battalion followed the guns in column of companies. For 300 yards there was no firing. Then from the distant crest line came a lot of little puffs of smoke, followed immediately by the report of the insurgent rifles. Twice this happened, and then the enemy's fire became continuous and spread right and left along his whole position. The Spanish infantry now began to reply, and advanced continually. The firing on both sides became heavy. There was a sound in the air sometimes like a sigh, sometimes like a whistle, and at others like the buzz of an offended hornet. General Valdez and his Staff rode their horses to within 500 yards of the enemy's firing line. Here we halted, and the infantry fire fight raged for about ten minutes evenly. The general, in his white uniform and gold lace, mounted on a grey horse, was a mark for every sharpshooter, and consequently the number of casualties on the Staff was out of all proportion to those of the rest of the force. Presently the sound of the Mauser volleys began to predominate and the rebel fire to slacken, till it finally ceased altogether. For a moment I could see figures scurrying to the shelter of the woods, and then came silence. The infantry advanced and occupied the enemy's position. Pursuit was impossible owing to the impenetrable nature of the woods in the rear, and as the force had only one day's rations left we withdrew across the plain to La Jicotea. On our way back we passed the numerous camp fires of the enemy and the remains of his interrupted breakfast. La Reforma, the name given to this place, was the scene of two engagements in the old war, and appears to be a safe draw for rebels.   w s c

V

December 14   Tampa Bay

I had intended to write this concluding letter while under the influence of the sentiment aroused by seeing the shores of Cuba grow dim on the southern horizon, but when the steamer got clear of Havana Harbour she was tossed about in so boisterous a fashion by the blue waters of the Gulf Stream that I changed my mind. Hence the address.

I told you in my last letter of the combat between the rear guard of Maximo Gomez and the column of General Valdez. The Government troops had taken a week's hard marching to find the enemy, and, having found them, had attacked them promptly and driven them from their position. The natural course was to have kept in touch at all costs, and to have bucketed them until they were forced to either disperse or fight. No pursuit was, however, attempted. Honour was satisfied, and the column adjourned to breakfast, after which we marched to La Jicotea, and the men went into cantonments. It seems a strange and unaccountable thing that a force, after making such vigorous marches, showing such energy in finding the enemy, and displaying such steadiness in attacking them, should deliberately sacrifice all that these efforts had gained. Such tactics make the war interminable. Here you have a General of Division and two thousand of the best troops in the island out for over ten days in search of the enemy, overcoming all sorts of difficulties, undergoing all kinds of hardships, and then being quite contented with killing thirty or forty rebels and taking a low grass hill which was destitute of the slightest importance. At this rate of progress it would take the Emperor William, with the German Army, twenty years to crush the revolt.

A long march under a very hot sun brought us at about four o'clock within sight of La Jicotea. Here were regular houses, also beds, primitive, but welcome. The principal citizen, a well-to-do Spaniard, entertained us with a magnificent banquet. All the Cuban delicacies were represented on his table – "brains," Guayaba jelly, sausages, and English cider. To these we did ample justice. The battalions of Validolid and Cuba were bivouacking outside, and after dinner was over I went out to take a last look at them. The only street of the village presented a wonderful sight. Round a score of fires were grouped fourteen or fifteen hundred cotton-clad figures, some cleaning their rifles, others cooking their dinners, but all chattering and singing merrily. These men had marched that day about 21 miles over the worst possible ground, carrying their kit and ammunition, and had in addition been fired at for the best part of four hours. They are fine infantry.

Leaving the column to the command of General Navarro, General Suarez Valdez started at daybreak for Ciego d'Avilar. The distance was about fifteen miles, and as all the members of our escort were mounted, the journey did not take more than a couple of hours. The little country-bred ponies move at a sort of jog-trot – one has to rough the saddle the whole time – but the motion is so easy that this is not a bit tiring, and both pony and rider can keep it up all day if necessary. Outside the gates of Ciego d'Avilar – which is a big town surrounded by palisades, with frequent stone flanking towers – we came to a halt, and a rather curious incident took place. The guard of course recognised the General, but the prescribed forms had to be observed. Word was sent to the Governor that a party of horse had arrived and desired to enter. A long parley, lasting quite twenty minutes, took place, with the object of making sure we were not wolves in sheep's clothing, and finally the Chief of the Staff was permitted to advance and be examined. The sample proving satisfactory, we went in. This procedure is, I believe, of very ancient origin, and is most punctiliously observed. It appears excellent, the only weak point being that the gate was left open and unguarded while it was being carried out. Ciego d'Avilar is on the railway, and after luncheon a military train took us to the coast, where the General had a gunboat to take him to Tunas. At Tunas we said good-bye to him and his staff with profound regret, for their courtesy, their kindness, and their hospitality had made a short visit a very pleasant one.

It is perhaps fitting that at the end of a final letter a little space should be devoted to a consideration of some of the salient points which the Cuban problem presents. Look first at the case of the Cubans. There is no doubt that the island has been overtaxed in a monstrous manner for a considerable period. So much money is drawn from the country every year that industries are paralysed and development is impossible. Nor is this all. The entire Administration is corrupt. All offices under the Government are reserved for Spaniards, who come to Cuba with the avowed intention of making their fortunes. Bribery and peculation pervade the boards of works, the post-offices, the Customs, and the courts of justice on a scale almost Chinese. A national and justifiable revolt is the only possible result of such a system.

But I sympathise with the rebellion – not with the rebels. One would have thought that a state of affairs such as I have described would have brought into the field every able-bodied man. It has not. The towns and villages are full and overflowing with patriots, who, though they weary the visitor with tales of their valour, would not hazard a brass farthing – far less life or limb – to promote the cause they profess to hold so high. This same spirit of histrionic brag is shown, though to a less extent, by their friends actually in the field. Posing as heroes and as patriots fighting to the death, they will not risk their lives to gain any advantage, however great. Why, a single really hard-fought battle, whether they won or lost, would convince foreign Powers of their sincerity and in all probability procure their recognition from the United States. They will not even submit to military discipline. A friend of Maximo Gomez – a man who had been frequently in his camp – told me the rebel leader confided to him that when he tried to drill the insurgents they immediately asked to be sent home. Is this the stuff out of which nations are made? The only tactics they pursue are those of incendiaries and brigands – burning canefields, shooting from behind hedges, firing into sleeping camps, destroying property, wrecking trains, and throwing dynamite. These are perfectly legitimate in war, no doubt, but they are not acts on which States are founded.

All impartial people who have lived long in the island hold that Cuban autonomy is impossible. They consider that to exchange Gomez for Campos would be to leap from the frying pan into the fire. The rebel victory offers at the best a bankrupt Government, torn by race animosities and recurring revolutions, and a State, like Hayti or Venezuela, a curse to itself and a nuisance to the world. It is a sombre outlook. Cuba is between Scylla and Charybdis. A middle course is, however, possible, and events seem to daily make it more probable. Spain cannot indefinitely maintain so large a military establishment but when unable to hold the country she will cling tenaciously to the ports and towns. These the Cubans can never take. A compromise alone is possible.

No one ought to allow himself to be puzzled by the contradictory telegrams or by the glorious victories and crushing defeats which appear daily in the newspapers. Cuban battles are many of them imaginary, most of them exaggerated, and all of them devoid of importance. The one thing to look for is the position of the insurgents. If Maximo Gomez is able to maintain himself in the provinces of Santa Clara and Matanzas till the hot weather he will have gained a decided advantage, and the inevitable compromise will be correspondingly favourable to the autonomist party – and conversely.

Such is the state of affairs in the richest island in the Spanish main. It may be that as the pages of history are turned brighter fortunes and better times will come to Cuba. It may be that future years will see the island as it would be now, had England never lost it – a Cuba free and prosperous, under just laws and a patriotic administration, throwing open her ports to the commerce of the world, sending her ponies to Hurlingham and her cricketers to Lord's, exchanging the cigars of Havana for the cottons of Lancashire, and the sugars of Matanzas for the cutlery of Sheffield. At least let us hope so.

WSC

New York Herald, 9 *December* 1895

MADRID – December 8 – A despatch to the Imparcial from Havana says that the military decoration of the Red Cross has been accorded to Lieutenants Churchill and Barnes, of the British army, for the gallantry displayed by them during the recent engagement between the government forces and the main body of rebels.

M. Shaw Bowers to WSC

10 December 1895   Havana

My dear Mr Churchill,

After your departure the local newspapers all had notices and every mother's son of them knighted you – as the enclosed cutting shows.

The Cuban propaganda promptly started the story that you had cut your visit short on account of a row with Suarez Valdez. They gave out that your sympathies went over to the rebels – that you wished to leave the Spanish army and join Gomez, that Valdez would not allow you to do so, and, in consequence, you returned to England. When it was known that you had received the Rioja Cruz, and that in your interviews the rebels received no aid or comfort, great was the wrath of the laborantes.

I hope you had a good trip home. Affairs continue with the same exasperating dullness here.

With kind regards to Mr Barnes.

I am sincerely yours
M. SHAW BOWERS

Alexander Gollan to WSC

13 December 1895   British Consulate-General
Havana

My dear Mr Churchill,

The notes on the enclosed Vouchers give full explanations as to the little matters you left for me to arrange. I trust you received the telegram sent to you yesterday by Martin Falk & Co and that you got the money alright in New York. You will see that I have had to pay $6.00 for the telegram, and that, deducting the change received from Henry Clay for the Cigars, there is a balance of $4 or sixteen shillings due to me which, whenever you think of it, you can pay to my Bankers Messrs Woodhead & Co 44 Charing Cross.

Mr Barnes will tell you what I have done about the luggage.

Wishing you a pleasant trip across, a happy Christmas Meeting with your friends at home, and the realization of all your hopes in the Career you have adopted.

Believe me Yours sincerely
ALEX GOLLAN

Ernest Craig-Brown[1] to WSC

14 December 1895   Up Park Camp
Jamaica

Dear Churchill,

Saw by the telegrams from home yesterday that you had been distinguishing yourself & winning the Red Cross. Congratulations.

When I saw that you had volunteered for service in Cuba it struck me as an excellent idea. I just wish I could cross the water and see a little fighting too.

You can picture me sitting in the mess-stores, totting up accounts & arranging menus (for at present I hold the thankless post of caterer) while you are gaining experience & renown in the next island. We never hear any details of the fighting here; all our news comes from home. After being done out of our chance of the Ashanti affair, it riles me to sit here doing nothing. Again congratulations & good luck.

Yours sincerely
ERNIE CRAIG-BROWN

New York World, 15 December 1895

Two young English warriors who have just taken their baptism of fire in the Cuban war set sail for England yesterday on the Cunard steamer *Etruria*, without a wound and with a conviction that there are few occupations more salubrious than that of a Cuban insurgent.

---

[1] Ernest Craig Brown (1871–   ). Lieutenant West Indian Regiment 1895; The Queen's Own Cameron Highlanders 1898. Served South Africa 1900–02; First World War 1914–19. Brigadier General 1917.

The young warriors were Winston Leonard Spencer Churchill, son of the late Lord Randolph Churchill, and R.W.R. Barnes. Both are in the Fourth Hussars. When the hunting season began in England they tossed up a penny to see whether they should chase foxes this winter or watch Gen Campos chase rebels. The rebels won, and they obtained a two months' leave of absence and started for Cuba.

The Bungtown Bird of Freedom and the Kalamazoo Daily Celery Stalk printed many flaming editorials on the conduct of these gentlemen in going to Cuba, declaring that they were emissaries of the British Government sent to teach Campos how to whip the secessionists, and that England was throwing more bricks at the Monroe doctrine. Of course this was nonsense. Churchill is not yet twenty-one years old, and knows only the amount of strategy necessary for the duties of a second lieutenant. He and Barnes went on the trip actuated only by youthful enthusiasm.

After seeing several battles they returned to this city, arriving Wednesday. They went to the Hotel Savoy, and at 9.05 P.M. ordered dinner. They were told that no dinners were served after 9 P.M. under the by-laws of the hotel. Then they moved out again and took up their quarters in the apartment of Bourke Cockran at the Bolkenhayn, No 763 Fifth Avenue. They spent Thursday Friday and as much of yesterday as they passed in New York trying to learn the name of the house in which they were domiciled, and consequently had very little time for sight-seeing.

"Of course the war isn't like a European war" said Mr Churchill yesterday, "but there was a great deal that interested us. The most remarkable fact seems to be that two armies will shoot at each other for hours and no one will get hit. I believe that statisticians say that in a battle it takes 2,000 bullets to kill a man. When the calculations are arranged I think it will be found that in the Cuban war it took 2,000 bullets to miss each individual combatant.

"The Spanish troops are brave fighters. I admire the rebels for the quickness and rapidity with which they get over the ground. In contests of speed with the Spanish troops they act as pacemakers and are soon out of sight. I make no reflections on their courage, but they are well versed in the art of retreat. Of course, the secret of their strength is the ability to harrass the enemy and carry on a guerilla warfare.

"The war is absolutely ruinous to Cuba. I think that the upshot of it will be that the United States will intervene as a peacemaker. I believe, too, that in the end Cuba will have her own Parliament, but that she will still be a Spanish colony."

"What about the alleged political significance of your trip?" he was asked.

"Rot!" exclaimed Mr Churchill, with a look that showed how tired the question made him feel. He was then told about the fulminations of the

Bungtown Bird of Freedom and of the Kalamazoo Daily Celery Stalk, and he laughed impatiently, but he evidently thought the attitude of these great journals too silly to talk about.

Mr Churchill had in his pocket a rough insurgent bullet that struck and killed a Spanish soldier that was standing quite close to him. He fiercely denied that he intended to write a book. His leave expires Dec 31.

New York Herald, 19 *December* 1895

Lieutenant Winston Churchill, son of the late Lord Randolph Churchill, who for the last eight weeks has been studying the war in Cuba, as guest of General Campos, sailed from this port yesterday on the *Etruria* homeward bound.

Accompanied by R. W. R. Barnes, a brother lieutenant in the Fourth Hussars of England, young Churchill reached this city direct from Cuba on Wednesday, and went to the Bolkenhayn, Fifth avenue and Fifty-eighth street, where he occupied the apartments of Mr W. Bourke Cockran, who is now in Europe.

When Lieutenant Churchill and party reached the Cunard dock it was within five minutes of the *Etruria's* sailing time, but the pleasant faced young officer submitted as gracefully to the requests of the waiting group of interviewers as though there were hours of leisure on his hands.

"I think," said he, in straightforward fashion, with his beardless, boyish face flushed with eagerness, "that the winter campaign now under way in Cuba is one of peculiar importance. If Campos succeeds in clearing the insurgents out of Matanzas and Santa Clara before spring he will, in my judgment, break the back of the revolution.

"The insurgents even then may carry on the war a year or two longer, but ultimately they will be forced to accept virtually dictated terms. Should the rebels succeed in holding Matanzas and Santa Clara they will then be in position to make a much more protracted and effective struggle. The war may then last several years, and the insurgents will be in a position to demand more favorable terms in the event of any attempt at settlement or arbitration."

Of General Campos the lieutenant had many handsome things to say. "The Spanish military leader," he continued, "is, in my judgment, one of the most distinguished men that Spain has ever produced. But for his rare judgment and great humanity Cuba would be disgraced with massacre and lawlessness of all sorts.

"My letters of introduction to the General gave me many advantages which I would not have otherwise enjoyed. I was handsomely entertained at military headquarters, and every facility was given me for careful observation of operations. Through General Campos' courtesy I spent one week at the front, on the staff of General Valdez, and at La Reforma was close to the insurgents during an intermittent engagement lasting two days.

"The Spanish are energetic and brave, but the nature of the country is against them, and, furthermore, there is too little combination in the movements of their various columns."

Evidently the fighting qualities of the Cuban insurgents did not impress Lieutenant Churchill favorably. "They are not good soldiers," said he, "but as runners would be hard to beat. One conspicuous feature of this war," he continued with a merry laugh, "is the fact that so few men are killed. There can be no question as to the immense amount of ammunition expended on both sides, but the surprising truth remains that ridiculously little execution is done.

"It has always been said, you know, that it takes 200 bullets to kill a soldier, but as applied to the Cuban war 200,000 shots would be closer to the mark."

Summing up the situation, the Lieutenant said in conclusion:—"As I have already stated, this winter's campaign means much, if not everything. If the insurgents hold out until the spring rains set in they may win. At any rate, they will then be in a position to dictate terms for the peace which every one in Cuba now longs for.

"The country is well nigh ruined, and a speedy peace seems to be the only thing that can save its people from general bankruptcy."

Throughout the interview Lieutenant Churchill uncomplainingly stood the interruptions of overzealous questioners and only once displayed annoyance. This was when a reporter for a sensational morning newspaper appeared.

"I have nothing to say for publication in the paper you represent," he sternly announced, "and I will openly explain the reason why."

Turning from the reporter to the group of gentlemen surrounding him Lieutenant Churchill continued:—"This sensational paper recently published a cablegram over my alleged signature. Both cablegram and signature were fraudulent. I never sent or authorized the sending of this message. Nevertheless, after deliberately 'faking' this cablegram the paper proceeded to attack me editorially upon the very expressions which it fraudulently attributed to me. On top of this, they have refused to take any notice of my letter demanding a published retraction of the cablegram."

Lieutenant Churchill very emphatically denied the various reports attributing a political significance to his Cuban trip.

Sir H. Drummond Wolff to Lady Randolph

25 December 1895   Madrid

My dear Lady Randolph,

Enclosed are two letters which may interest you. They are from the Duke of Tetuan and Marshal Martinez Campos about Winston. The two call each other by their christian names Carlos & Arsemis –

I hope you & yours are well & wish you a merry Xmas & many happy New Years.

Ever your sincere and devoted
H. DRUMMOND WOLFF

T. Heath Joyce[1] to WSC

10 January 1896   Editorial Department
The *Graphic* and *Daily Graphic*
190 Strand
London W.C.

My dear Mr Churchill,

I am sorry to find that through some inadvertence your letter of the 3rd instant has only just reached my hands. I may say that your letters and sketches[2] have been extremely interesting and were just the kind of thing we wanted. I enclose you a cheque for twenty-five guineas for the five letters which is the honorarium of five guineas per letter we agreed upon. With many thanks for your courtesy throughout the matter

I am Yours very faithfully
T. HEATH JOYCE

PS Kindly sign & return enclosed receipt.

W. L. Thomas to WSC

14 January 1896   Manager's Department
The *Graphic* and *Daily Graphic*

My dear Sir,

Allow me to compliment you on the result (as I imagine of your first experiences) as a Special Correspondent & artist combined.

[1] Thomas Heath Joyce (1850–1925), editor of the *Graphic* 1891–1906.

[2] WSC's articles were illustrated by ink drawings based on the sketches he had submitted. They included: Volunteers returning to Havana from the front; A Spanish fortified post protecting a railway bridge; Spanish cavalry advancing; and Marshal Campos inspecting a newly-arrived draft.

Your letters were very interesting and to the point and the sketches useful in adding point to the letter press and I am sorry that your time was so limited and so preventing your sending more.

In spite of recent events attracting public attention in other directions,[1] your letters were widely read & appreciated.

Believe me Yours faithfully
WILLIAM L. THOMAS

---

[1] The Jameson Raid had taken place two weeks earlier.

10

Scandal

4th Hussars (3) – 1896
(See Main Volume pp. 246–252)

STATEMENT OF CLAIM

In the High Court of Justice

QUEEN'S BENCH DIVISION

Writ issued 15 February 1896

BETWEEN WINSTON SPENCER CHURCHILL . . . PLAINTIFF

AND

A. C. BRUCE PRYCE[1] . . . DEFENDANT

1. – The Plaintiff is a lieutenant holding Her Majesty's commission in the 4th (Queen's Own) Hussars.

2. – On or about the 11th February 1896 the Defendant falsely and maliciously wrote and published to 2nd Lieutenant Hogg of the said regiment of and concerning the Plaintiff and of and concerning the Plaintiff in his said profession the words following that is to say:—

"His real offence however was that he was at Sandhurst with Mr Churchill and that they had been rivals in shooting, fencing and riding throughout their career and incidentally that he knew too much about Mr Churchill.

"There was for instance one man whose initial is C, flogged publicly by a subaltern court-martial for acts of gross immorality of the Oscar Wilde type with Mr Churchill.

---

[1] Alan Cameron Bruce-Pryce (1836–1909) of Blaen-y-Cwm, Monknash, Cowbridge, Glamorgan, educated at Exeter College, Oxford; called to the Bar (Lincoln's Inn 1854). He was twice married, and had altogether ten sons and seven daughters.

"I have not yet ascertained what was done by the E Company to Mr Churchill, but as soon as I do I shall lay the statement before the War Office."

3. – The Defendant meant and was understood to mean by the said words that the Plaintiff was a person of vile and disreputable character unworthy of associating with the officers of his regiment or any honourable men and unfit to hold Her Majesty's commission. That he had been guilty of gross acts of indecency with male persons and in particular had been detected and exposed in one flagrant case. That by reason of the premises the Plaintiff had been guilty of criminal offences and was liable to be indicted under the Criminal Law Amendment Act 1885.

4. – By reason of the premises the Plaintiff has been grievously injured in his credit and reputation and in his said profession and in his position as officer in Her Majesty's Army and has been held up to hatred and contempt.

The Plaintiff claims £20,000 damages.

W. TEMPLE FRANKS[1]

Delivered the 21st day of February 1896 by Messieurs LEWIS and LEWIS Ely Place, Holborn E.C. Solicitors for the Plaintiff.

Colonel J. P. Brabazon to WSC

9 March [1896]   Santa Clara Hotel
Funchal

My dear Boy,

I can not tell you what intense pleasure your telegram gave to me & what a very great relief it was also. For altho you would have come out of it with flying colours & there could have been but one issue to the case yet it is a thousand fold better that it should have terminated as it has, for one cannot touch pitch without soiling one's hands however clean they may have originally been and the world is so ill natured & suspicious that there would always have been found some ill natured sneak or perhaps some d—d good natured friend to hem & ha! & wink over it – perhaps in years to come, when everyone even yourself had forgotten all about the disagreeable incident. You took the only line possible. The one I should have advised my dearest friend, my brother or my son, to have taken the only one I could have taken myself under similar circumstances. For malignant, preposterous as it was, it would have been impossible to have left such a charge unchallenged. As regards

---

[1] William Temple Franks (1863–1936), called to the Bar (Inner Temple) 1890, practised on the South-Eastern Circuit until 1902, when he became an Assistant Librarian, House of Commons. Subsequently served on numerous departmental committees and Government commissions, becoming Comptroller-General of Patents, Designs and Trade Marks. CB 1914.

getting a monkey out of the old brute you are in the best of hands & of course acting under the advice of the cleverest of his profession. But my anxiety to have the whole thing closed and buried in oblivion – after of course getting his most abject apology & complete withdrawal of the charge – would have prompted me to advise you being content with costs, but as I said before you are of course acting under counsel much wiser than any I can offer you.

I shall leave this about this day or tomorrow week, arriving in England about the end of the same week so you may expect to see me any time between 20th, 22nd. My days will indeed be numbered when I return. I shall have very little time to spend amongst you as your Colonel, & a very happy & glorious episode of my life will come to an end for peace hath its victories as well as war. I have had a very happy time with the IV Q.O. Hussars in spite of having one awful lot of pickles in the shape of officers to manage who many a itme oft? have caused me anxiety.

Good bye my dear boy I could not have left the regiment happily had not this case been satisfactorily terminated, & in telling you how intensely relieved & delighted I am at its termination let me assure you of the very deep sympathy I felt for you while undergoing the ordeal of a scandalous & mendacious charge as infamous as it was unfounded.

Ever my dear boy Yrs
J. P. Brabazon

WITHDRAWAL

In the High Court of Justice
QUEENS BENCH DIVISION

Between WINSTON SPENCER CHURCHILL . . . Plaintiff

AND

A. C. BRUCE PRYCE . . . Defendant

I unreservedly withdraw all and every imputation against your character complained of by you in paragraph 2 of your Statement of Claim and I hereby express my regret for having made the same.

DATED this 12th March 1896

A. C. Bruce Pryce
the above-named Defendant

George Lewis[1] to WSC

19 March 1896   Messrs Lewis & Lewis
                                                Ely Place
                                                Holborn
                                                London

Dear Mr Churchill,

                         Yourself v. Bruce Pryce

   I enclose you the retractation and apology signed by Mr Pryce which completely vindicates you from the libel that he published of you. Please take care of it as some day it may be useful.

   I enclose you a cheque for £400 as agreed.

   I fully recognise the feeling of delicacy which prompted you to suggest to me that this money should be applied to charity, but I think it right to say that this money is paid to you as damages in the action for libel which you brought, and belongs to you just as much as if a verdict had been given by a jury in your favour. I see therefore no reason why you should feel any delicacy in receiving the money or dealing with it as you would have done with money recovered under such circumstances.

   I enclose you a receipt in discharge of my firm's charges. Will you kindly acknowledge the enclosures at your convenience.

                                       Believe me Yours faithfully
                                       GEORGE H. LEWIS

Colonel J. P. Brabazon to WSC

20 March [1896]   Marlborough Club
                                             Pall Mall

My dear Boy,
   I return you the papers, and congratulate you again on the triumphant issue of this infamous libel. I have seen Sir Reginald Gipps and Sir Redvers Buller

   [1] George Henry Lewis (1833–1911). Senior partner of Lewis and Lewis, Solicitors. Created baronet 1902.

and shown them the apology, Lewis's letter &c – and they are perfectly satisfied at the line you took and of your conduct throughout the affair. So we will consider the incident as closed for ever. It only shews to what lengths mendacity and malice will go.

Oddly enough Buller told me that he had on his table a letter from Lansdowne to Mr B.P. declining to reopen the racing case or to have anything more to do with him. He threatens to bring it before Parliament.

Hope Lady Randolph is better. Directly I get the inspection over I will call and see her. Very sorry you are away as I fear I shall see little of you before I go.

Yrs very sincerely

J. P. BRABAZON

On 20 March 1895 the Cavalry Brigade held their annual steeplechase meeting at Aldershot. One of the races was for the 4th Hussars Subalterns' Challenge cup, value twenty sovereigns, with sweepstakes of two sovereigns each and twenty sovereigns added making the race worth twenty-eight pounds to the winner. It was run over two miles and five furlongs, and the *Racing Calendar* for 21 March 1895 records the result as follows:—

Mr A. D. Francis'[1] Surefoot, aged 12st 3 lb owner		1
Mr A. Savory's[2] Lady Margaret, aged 12st 10 lb owner		2
Mr A. Savory's Traveller, aged 12 st 3 lb Mr Spencer[3]		3
Mr R. W. R. Barnes' Tartina, aged 12 st 3 lb (carried 13st 2 lb) owner		–
Mr H. Watkins'[4] Dolly-do-Little, aged 12st 3 lb owner		–

Mr A. Savory declared to win with Lady Margaret.[5]
Won by six lengths; Dolly-do-Little fell.

[1] Alan Ogilvie Francis (b.1868). Lieutenant 4th Hussars
[2] Albert Savory (1870–1900). Lieutenant 4th Hussars.
[3] WSC. See his letter to Jack 24 March [1895] p. 565.
[4] Henry George Watkins (misprinted as Walker in *Truth*) (b.1874). 2nd Lieutenant 4th Hussars.
[5] 'An owner running two or more horses in a race may declare to win with one of them, and such declaration must be made at scale. The rider of a horse with which the owner has not declared to win, must on no account stop such horse except in favour of the horse on whose behalf declaration to win has been made.' (National Hunt Rule No. 133.)

On 20 February 1896 the *Racing Calendar* published the following announcement:

The attention of the Stewards of the National Hunt Committee having been called to certain irregularities in respect of the 4th Hussars Subalterns' Challenge Cup, run at the Cavalry Brigade Meeting at Aldershot, 1895 (see *Steeple Chases Past*, 1895, p. 78)[1] the race has been declared null and void, and all the horses which took part in the same are perpetually disqualified for all races under National Hunt Rules.

On 19 March 1896 the weekly magazine *Truth*, edited by Henry Labouchere, took up the affairs of the 4th Hussars:

The War Office authorities would do well to understand that a good many persons are waiting somewhat impatiently to see what official action is to be taken upon the recent decision of the Stewards of the National Hunt in regard to the race for the 4th Hussars Subalterns' Challenge Cup, at the Aldershot Cavalry Brigade Meeting in March, 1895. The circumstances of this race were of a most extraordinary character. A horse which had won the Regimental Cup of the 4th Hussars on the previous day started a warm favourite at 5 to 4 *on*. An outsider named Surefoot, starting at 6 to 1 against, came in first, Lady Margaret running second to him. Subsequently Lady Margaret's name, with that of Mr Savory as her owner, was engraved on the cup as the winner. The National Hunt Stewards, having had the circumstances before them, not only declared the race null and void, but have perpetually disqualified all the horses which took part in it for all races under National Hunt Rules.

This decision affects a number of officers and gentlemen. In all five horses ran for the Subalterns' Cup, each owned by a Subaltern in the Regiment. The perpetual disqualification of the horses of all these officers points to some irregularity of a serious description, and if I am correctly informed as to the nature of the irregularity, no censure could well be too strong for the conduct of those directly implicated. The decision of the Stewards was promulgated quite a month ago, and it is high time that the War Office authorities had made

[1] In *Steeple Chases Past* the result of the race is recorded as in the *Racing Calendar*, except that the name of the second horse is given as Lady Margaretta II.

up their minds what they are going to do next. In the meanwhile, if those familiar with the facts care to enlighten me further upon them, whether by way of explanation or otherwise, I am willing, of course, to give due attention to anything they may have to say.

Truth 21 *May* 1896

A GROSS CAVALRY SCANDAL

The question why so many young officers throw up their commisions in the Cavalry has lately attracted a good deal of attention, and it is undoubtedly a matter which closely affects the efficiency of the Army. For this reason a case that has recently occurred in a crack Cavalry regiment is of considerable public importance. The matter has been before the Horse Guards, but up to the present without any satisfactory result; and it is therefore of the more consequence that public attention should be called to the facts. The facts are these. The regiment in question is the 4th Hussars. To this regiment was gazetted in April, 1895, a Mr Bruce,[1] a gentleman to all appearance eminently qualified to make an efficient Cavalry officer. He was a thorough horseman, a good fencer – so good, indeed, that he was in the Sword Display before the Duke of Cambridge while in his first term at Sandhurst – and a first-rate shot. He was originally gazetted from Sandhurst to the 8th Hussars, but was transferred to the 4th at his father's request, because the 4th Hussars were shortly going to India.

Before Mr Bruce joined, he received an invitation from one of the subalterns of the regiment to dine at the Nimrod Club. The invitation was sent by Mr Barnes, but this gentleman did not himself attend at the dinner. Six subalterns were present at this function, including Mr Savory, Mr Francis, Mr Walker, and Mr Spencer Churchill. The latter gentleman was a contemporary of Mr Bruce's at Sandhurst. On the conclusion of the dinner an incident of an extraordinary nature took place – at any rate, it strikes me as extraordinary, and will, I imagine, impress in the same manner all who are not familiar with the amenities of Cavalry life. Acting apparently as spokesman of the junior officers of the regiment, Mr Spencer Churchill informed Mr Bruce, almost in so many words, that he had been invited to the dinner in order to let him know that he was not wanted in the regiment. He was asked what his allowance was

[1] Alan George Cameron Bruce (1874–1929), fifth son of Alan Cameron Bruce-Pryce (see p. 625). He and his twin brother Edward Maunsell Bruce entered and left Sandhurst at the same time as WSC. Both left the Army after the events related here.

to be, and, in reply, he stated the amount – a very respectable sum. He was told that on this allowance he could not go the pace of the regiment. A subaltern named Hodge[1] had just left the regiment under circumstances which have also, I understand, been brought before the notice of the War Office, and Mr Bruce was appointed to fill the vacancy thus created. The select gang who were entertaining Mr Bruce alluded in significant terms to the fate of the departed Hodge. They intimated that they had got rid of Hodge, and that they would get rid of Bruce, too, adding that if the latter gentleman did not choose to make a graceful exit now, he would probably make a disgraceful one before very long. A man asked out to dinner in order to be talked to like this may be excused if he is taken a little aback. Mr Bruce, however, seems to have acted very much as any self-respecting gentleman might be expected to act in the presence of such an insult. He informed his amiable hosts that he had no intention of giving up his military career to oblige them, stated that if he were offered another regiment he would take it, after what had passed, but that otherwise he intended to join the 4th Hussars.

On the following morning he took what was undoubtedly the proper course under the circumstances by going down to Aldershot to inform the Colonel of what had passed. The Colonel happened to be away. In his absence Mr Bruce saw the Adjutant, Captain De Moleyns, and laid the facts before him. So far as I can learn, Captain De Moleyns does not seem to have expressed any disapproval of the action of the subalterns, or to have treated it as anything out of the ordinary course of business in welcoming a new officer to the regiment. At any rate, nothing further happened, and indeed Mr Bruce joined the regiment. He soon found, as was to be expected, that he was under a sort of boycott, and that no opportunity of making things unpleasant for him was lost by a section of his brother subalterns. He seems, however, to have been a youngster pretty capable of holding his ground and taking his own part, and he got on after a fashion without any serious difficulty until last Christmas. It is worth while mentioning, in view of what follows, that during this time he devoted special attention to the shooting of the regiment, a matter in which the officers as a body do not seem to have felt any particular interest. He went to the ranges regularly to look after the musketry instruction, and personally coached a team for Bisley, with the result that the 4th Hussars won the Duke of Cambridge's Shield. At the Bisley meeting Mr Bruce was second for the Loder prize, with a score of thirty-four out of a possible thirty-five, the winner making the maximum; but neither for this nor for the success of the team he had coached did he receive a word of recognition from any one, from the Colonel downwards. This is a good example of the general boycott to which he was exposed from the first day he entered the regiment.

[1] 2nd Lieutenant George C. Hodge.

On Boxing night an incident occurred every detail of which is of importance. Mr Bruce had been doing duty for another subaltern as Orderly Officer, and seems to have been the only officer in barracks. At 10 p.m. he collected watch-setting reports. Subsequently to this, a Squadron Sergeant-Major named Doggett, who was also on duty, told him that there was a Balaclava veteran in the Sergeants' Mess, and later on, after he had been to his quarters, changed his uniform, which was wet through, and made out his report, Mr Bruce went round to the Sergeants' Mess to see the Balaclava hero. He states that it was a little after 10.30 when he arrived there, and from what passed it clearly could not have been much earlier. After he had had a talk with the Balaclava veteran, the Regimental Sergeant-Major asked whether, as it was Christmas time, he would not drink the health of the Mess, and this he accordingly did in a glass of whisky and soda, after which he returned to his quarters. He was back at his quarters about 11.10, and after that he did his visiting rounds.

Incredible as it must appear to every civilian reader this incident has been made the ground for forcing the young man out of the Army. And the manner of doing it is as amazing as the thing itself. Three days after the Boxing-night incident, Mr Bruce was summoned to the orderly-room, where the Colonel asked him if he had been in the Sergeants' Mess on Boxing night, and for how long. He replied that he had been there about half an hour. The Colonel told him he was a liar and no gentleman, and placed him under arrest. This was on December 29. He remained in his room under arrest until January 7, when he was again brought to the orderly-room. The Colonel then informed him that if he would send in his papers, he would do his best to put them through; but that either he (Mr Bruce) or himself (the Colonel) would leave the regiment. Mr Bruce protested against his arrest, and asked what charge was made against him, and requested to be confronted with the evidence. The Colonel replied that it was his word against that of an NCO, and Mr Bruce went back to his quarters under arrest. He then wrote to the Adjutant, and asked for particulars of the charge against him, and was informed that he was under arrest on a charge of "improperly associating with non-commissioned officers." Three days later he was brought up at the War Office before Lord Methuen.[1] Colonel Brabazon appeared, and read two statements – one by Squadron-Sergeant-Major Doggett, the other by Regimental-Sergeant-Major Brown. The first is the man who had given the hint about the Balaclava veteran being in the Mess; the second, the man who had invited the subaltern – a mere child by comparison with some of the NCOs around him – to drink the health of the Mess.

---

[1] Paul Sanford, 3rd Baron Methuen (1845–1932), Major-General Commanding Home District 1892–7. Press Censor in Tirah campaign 1897–8. Won distinction as a general in the South African War. Field Marshal 1911. Governor of Malta 1915–19.

The contents of the statements of these witnesses can only be given from memory, as no copy of them has ever been supplied to the man who stood to be ruined by them, and even a request subsequently made by the lad's father for copies of the evidence has been fruitless. It seems, however, that there was a direct conflict between the two witnesses as to the most material point in the case, Brown practically corroborating Mr Bruce as to the time he had been in the Mess, while Doggett added half an hour to the time. On Mr Bruce pointing this out, he was told by the General that he was splitting straws, and the interview ended by the General informing him that unless he sent in his papers within forty-eight hours his services would probably be dispensed with. He asked to be temporarily released from arrest in order that he might go and consult his father, from whom he had kept the matter up to this time, owing to the fact that his mother was dangerously ill. A grudging consent was given, and the subaltern went home the next morning; but there was then no time for his father to take any steps in the matter, and, as the alternative to his services being dispensed with, he had to send in his papers. The father subsequently brought the case before Lord Wolseley, who declined to reopen it, and so the matter stands. It is a fact, however, worth recording that, while the subaltern went out of the Army, the Sergeant-Major on whose evidence he had been dismissed received a gratifying mark of the confidence of his superior officers in being allowed to extend his service.

I have heard many strange stories from the British Army, but few to equal this. Here is a lad of excellent character, a crack rider, a first-class shot, and an all-round "good sportsman" (as the phrase goes), with a clear allowance of £500 a year pocket money, and all the making in him of a first-class Cavalry officer. He joins his regiment in April, and by the next January he is chucked out of the Service with ignominy; his profession lost, his long and expensive apprenticeship thrown away, and his prospects in life seriously impaired. And all for what? For what, at the very worst, can only be regarded as the most trivial of boyish indiscretions – the passing of half-an-hour in the Sergeants' Mess on Boxing night. I am told that it is not the custom among the aristocracy of the 4th Hussars for officers to enter the Sergeants' Mess; but it is a thing that is thought nothing of in half the regiments of the Army, and it is a practice to which, on principle, no exception can be taken. Within proper bounds an occasional interchange of social intercourse between officers and NCOs is far more likely to do good on both sides than harm. I do not forget that it is alleged against Mr Bruce that he was guilty of undue familiarity with NCOs; but, paint it at its blackest, what is there in this offence which justifies such a step as the virtual expulsion from the Army of a promising lad? Even if the offence were proved, which it most certainly has not been, what is it but a matter on which the Colonel might have very properly remonstrated with his youngest subaltern, or given him a timely hint to keep him in the right path? It is absurd to suppose that the youngest subaltern in a crack regiment would persist in associating unduly with the Non-Commissioned Officers, if the Colonel or his brother officers had ever given him seriously to understand that they disapproved of his conduct; still more, if he had been warned that he was endangering his commission. Yet the Colonel takes the lead in depriving the lad of his commission for this offence; and not only this, but the extreme penalty of military discipline is exacted, with the sanction of the General, without the accused being allowed an opportunity of consulting a friend, of obtaining legal advice, or even of studying the evidence which was to be given against him. The oldest and most hardened of bad characters in the Service could hardly be treated more inequitably, or with more evidence of a preconceived determination to get rid of him.

But, after all, these are mere details. The kernel of the whole case is the undisguised conspiracy formed against this subaltern before he joined to have him out of the regiment unless he consented to go voluntarily. In regard to this, I do not believe that the facts above stated will be, in any particular, denied. The circumstances of the dinner at the Nimrod Club have never been disputed, and the parties to that function seem rather to have gloried in it. The matter was reported at once by Mr Bruce to the Adjutant and Colonel, and these officers allowed what had passed to go without rebuke or protest. Finally, the whole matter has been laid before the Commander-in-Chief by Mr Bruce's father, and the Commander-in-Chief professes to see no cause for re-opening the case. It must therefore be taken that in the course they adopted for driving Mr Bruce out of the regiment, the gang who met at the Nimrod Club have the approval, or at least the tacit sympathy, of the Senior Officers of the Regiment and the authorities at the War Office. It is this which makes the case of such urgent public importance, and which gives such an ugly aspect to the conduct of the higher authorities throughout the business. Are we to take it that from Lord Wolseley downward the military authorities approve the principle that a youngster, whose allowance is not, in the judgment of the rowdiest set of subalterns, sufficient to enable him to 'go the pace' of the regiment, is out of place in the Army, and should be got rid of by any subterfuge that can be trumped up for the purpose? Are we to take it as now an understood thing that in certain cavalry regiments those sections of the Queen's Regulations which impose on a Commanding Officer the duty of keeping down his officers' expenditure are a dead letter? Is it now the proper thing in such regiments for the Colonel, instead of taking a fatherly interest in every boy committed to his care, to back up the majority of subalterns in any measures they may take for keeping up 'the pace of the regiment,' and eliminating individuals who do not go the pace? That, as evidenced by recent events, seems to be the state of things prevailing in the 4th Hussars, and approved of by the War Office and the Commander-in-Chief.

Truth 11 *June* 1896

EXTRACT

. . . By the courtesy of Mr Hodge's father I am now in possession of the facts of the Hodge case. It is a most astounding one, and I will give it at once precisely as Mr Hodge, senior, gives it to me. I would premise that Mr Hodge, senior, is a retired Naval officer, and his father was in the Navy before him. The family, therefore, are no strangers to Service manners and customs.

Mr George C. Hodge was gazetted to the 4th Hussars on January 31, 1894. His father allowed him £300 a year, and was informed by several officers that with care his son could get on comfortably with this allowance. A day or two after he joined, Mr Hodge was asked at mess where his hunters and race-horses were kept, and he replied that he was afraid he could not afford to keep either. This elicited from a Captain who was present the remark, "Then what the —— did you join this regiment for?" Mr Hodge replied that he did not select the regiment, but was appointed to it by the War Office. The remark thus made seems to have been the prelude to a resolute attempt on the part of Mr Hodge's brother officers to convey to him, by the most offensive means, that the regiment did not want him. Not long after this remark some horse-play seems to have been going on one day among the subalterns in the mess-room, more or less directed against Mr Hodge, who, however, managed to hold his own pretty comfortably, whereupon the same officer as before made the remark, "Oh! all of you chuck him out ——, throw the —— out of the window!" with other expressions of a similar character, indicating not only a vigorous command of Billingsgate, but a strongly hostile feeling. By many incidents of the same kind the unfortunate subaltern was made to feel that there was something like a conspiracy against him, and his position grew more and more uncomfortable. Every effort that he made – and he made many – to ingratiate himself with his brother officers was futile. Eventually, about a month after he had joined, he was informed point-blank by a brother subaltern that it had been decided that he must leave the regiment. "What have I done?" he asked. "Oh, it is not what you do, Hodge," was the reply, "it's what you don't do." From this point petty annoyance developed into the most outrageous persecution. The favourite Cavalry sport of "making hay" in a man's rooms was freely indulged in, and not only was Mr Hodge's personal property turned upside down and damaged in his absence, but his clothes were torn up, destroyed, and even burnt; the locks of his drawers were forced, and the contents strewn over the room. Mr Hodge seems to have been a plucky youngster, and he held his ground in spite of it all. Accordingly, stronger measures were next resorted to. One night towards the end of March, four subalterns, two of them being members of the gang who subsequently entertained Mr Bruce at the Nimrod Club, broke open the door of Mr Hodge's room at 2 a.m., dragged him from his bed in the most brutal manner, and having overpowered his resistance by sheer force of numbers, hauled him down the stairs and across the yard, where they forced him into a horse-trough. These troughs are of considerable length, with bars at intervals of about two feet across the top. Mr Hodge was pushed into the trough under the bars, dragged through to the other end, and then hauled out wet through, bruised, and bleeding, and carried back to his room, his night-clothing torn to shreds. By way of enforcing the lesson, the same outrage was perpetrated without variation in any particular on the following night. This took place within two months of his joining the regiment. The next day Mr Hodge telegraphed in despair to his father, who came down to Aldershot, saw him, and reported the affair to the Adjutant. The father states that he believes his representations had the effect of preventing any further personal violence; but in default of brute force, other more refined modes of torture were invented. Mr Hodge was exposed to a remorseless boycott, which his father states had a far more crushing effect upon him than mere physical ill-treatment. He gave up the struggle in despair, and came home on sick leave. His father tells me that he was three months under medical care, a complete wreck, and well-nigh broken-hearted. The result was that he sent in his papers, bade good-bye to the 4th Hussars and the Army, and departed for the colonies. . . .

That such things should happen is shocking; but infinitely more serious is the attitude adopted towards such practices by the representatives of higher authority, not in the regiment only, but at the headquarters of the Army. Mr Hodge's father laid the facts above recorded before two War Office officials, one of them a military man and the other a civilian. He tells me that he did it "unofficially." But the fact is sufficient that the matter was brought to the knowledge of authorities whose duty it would be to take further action in the matter. Ought anything more to be necessary? Mr Hodge thought not, and he tells me that had he entertained any doubt after the matter had been made known at the War Office that his son would be reinstated, he would have insisted on a court martial. In point of fact, what did follow? In connection with Mr Bruce's case, I have heard that something in the nature of a caution was administered from the War Office to the ringleaders in the persecution of Mr Hodge. Assuming that as much as that was done, what is it worth? Less than nothing. To notice a gross offence in a manner which implies that you have an utterly imperfect appreciation of its gravity is more calculated to encourage an offender than if the offence were passed over in silence. . . . Had this gang transmitted to the War Office a joint memorandum stating that they cared nothing for official hints, and meant to do as they pleased, I do not see that they would have more directly defied the constituted authorities.

Often, when calling attention in these columns to excessive and un-discriminating punishments meted out in the sacred name of discipline to the rank and file of the Army, have I been lectured by Service men or Service journals for encouraging insubordination. How can insubordination be more directly encouraged than by the attitude of the War Office towards this disreputable rowdyism among the young bloods of crack Cavalry regiments? What can be more subversive of all discipline than for the junior officers of a regiment to formally place their veto upon appointments made at the War Office, to give effect to their decision by every form of personal violence and brutality, and for the War Office to tamely acquiesce in their proceedings? When I say that the state of things revealed by these two incidents in the 4th Hussars – and I believe they are not the only instances of the same sort of thing – is a scandal from every possible point of view, I believe that I shall have the assent not only of the general public, but of every officer who prides himself upon the honourable traditions of the Service, and of all who care for either the honour or the efficiency of the Army. It is no exaggeration to say that no military matter that has ever been referred to in the columns of *Truth* has attracted wider attention than the case of Mr Bruce. But the Bruce case acquires an altogether new significance in the light now thrown upon the manners and customs of the "officers and gentlemen" of this particular regiment; and there will be a proportionately strong feeling that it is the duty of the Commander-in-Chief to take further action in the matter. The cases of both Mr Hodge and Mr Bruce ought to be re-opened. There should be an exhaustive inquiry before a competent tribunal into this and all other evidence that can be obtained of organized bullying, and discreditable conduct in different forms, that have occurred in this regiment during the last few years. And if the necessity for this is not apparent to the Commander-in-Chief, Parliament must exercise its authority in the matter.

On 19 June 1896 the case was raised in the House of Commons. The Official Report records the debate:

Mr HERBERT LEWIS[1] (Flint Boroughs) called attention to two instances

---

[1] John Herbert Lewis (1858–1933), Liberal MP for Flint Boroughs and Flintshire 1892–1918, and for University of Wales 1918–1922. A Junior Whip 1905–9, Parliamentary Secretary Local Government Board 1909–15, and Board of Education 1915–22. Privy Councillor 1912; created GBE 1922.

in which, according to the information supplied to him, subaltern officers had been driven out of the 4th Hussars. The first case related to a Mr Hodge, who was gazetted to the regiment on January 31, 1894. His father, who was a retired naval officer, made him an allowance of £300 a year, which he was told would be an ample sum. After he had joined his regiment Mr Hodge was asked at mess where he kept his hunters and racehorses, and on reply that he could not afford to keep either he was met with the remark, "Then what did you join this regiment for?" His reply was that he himself did not make the selection, but was appointed to the 4th Hussars by the War Office.

On it becoming clear that Mr Hodge could not keep racehorses and hunters, it was apparent that his brother officers were determined to get rid of him. They took the most offensive means of effecting this object. On one occasion, after some horse play in which Mr Hodge managed to hold his ground pretty well, one of the officers said he ought to be thrown out of the window, and the young gentleman was made to feel in every possible way the conspiracy which appeared to have been formed in the regiment against him. He did his utmost to make himself agreeable to the officers of the regiment but without any success, and about a month after he had joined he was coolly and bluntly informed that it had been decided he must leave the regiment. He asked what he had done, and the reply that was made to him was, "It is not what you do, Hodge, but what you don't do." He presumed what was meant was that he did not keep hunters and racehorses. Not only was his property damaged, but his clothes were torn up and destroyed. Some were burnt, the locks of his drawers were forced open, and in other ways his life was made a misery to him.

Mr Hodge very properly determined that he would not be driven out of the regiment even by such outrageous proceedings, consequently his brother officers decided to take stronger steps to drive him out. Two months after he had joined the regiment he was dragged out of bed at 2 o'clock one morning into the yard and forced into a trough full of water. The trough was rather long; there were bars across it at intervals of two feet; he was forced under the bars at one end, and dragged out of the trough, bruised and bleeding at the other end. The following night the same thing took place, and at last Mr Hodge found himself in such a desperate plight that he telegraphed to his father who came to Aldershot, and reported the affair to the Adjutant of the regiment. After that no further personal violence was offered to Mr Hodge (he presumed it was in consequence of representations made by the Adjutant) but he was subjected to the most remorseless boycott. This was more difficult to endure than the barbarous treatment to which he had been subjected previously. Under these circumstances he felt himself absolutely obliged to leave the regiment. After leaving the regiment he was under medical treatment for three months. He left the Army almost broken-hearted and went to the colonies.

What was the attitude of the War Office in regard to his case? Mr Hodge's father laid the facts unofficially before two officers of the War Office, and he was under the impression that the War Office would at once reinstate his son. Some communication appeared to have been made by the War Office to the Colonel of the regiment in consequence of the representations made, but the Committee would judge of the effect of that communication upon the officers of the regiment when he referred to another case which occurred shortly afterwards.

A gentleman named Bruce was gazetted to take Mr Hodge's place. Before he joined the regiment he was invited to dinner, and asked how much his allowance was. He replied that it was £500 a year. He was told in reply that he could not on such an allowance "go the pace of the regiment," and before the end of dinner he was plainly informed that it had been decided by the officers that he must not join the regiment. Mr Bruce appeared to be a man of some spirit, and he determined, in spite of this, to join. It was evidently determined on the other hand that he should not be allowed to remain. Mr Bruce distinguished himself while in the regiment. He shot second for the Loder prize at Bisley, and coached a team in such a way that it won a prize; but it was evident that the officers of the regiment were determined to give him no credit, and he never received any credit for what he did. One night, at half-past ten, when in charge of the barracks, he was informed by one of the sergeant instructors, that a Balaclava veteran was in the sergeants' mess room. Mr Bruce went there, and in his presence the Balaclava veteran was asked to drink the health of the mess. For going to the sergeants' mess room, Mr Bruce was brought before the Colonel of the regiment, very severely reprimanded, and ultimately had to leave the service in consequence. The War Office was appealed to but refused to reinstate him.

He thought that occurrences of the kind that he had related afforded some explanation of the number of commissions that were thrown up in cavalry regiments. They were not an inducement for parents to send their sons into the Army, and when public money was spent on the Army, the War Office ought to take good care that scandals of this kind did not occur. A case which occurred a number of years ago might serve as a precedent for their guidance. It was not nearly so flagrant as this. A lieutenant was made the victim of a series of practical jokes. He was pulled out of bed in the middle of the night, his furniture scattered about, and a mixture of salt and cayenne pepper forced into his mouth. Lord Hardinge[1] the then Commander-in-Chief, commenting on

---

[1] Henry Hardinge, 1st Viscount Hardinge (1785–1856) Commander-in-Chief 1852–6; earlier Secretary-at-War (1828–30 and 1841–4), Chief Secretary for Ireland with a seat in the Cabinet 1830 and 1834–5, Viceroy of India 1844–8.

the action of the Colonel in insisting that the ringleaders should leave the regiment, said, in an official memorandum:—

"The General Officer Commanding-in-Chief approves of the view taken by the Lieutenant-Colonel, and assures the Colonel and every commanding officer that they will on all occasions of a similar nature be supported by him in putting down a practice by which officers have become habituated to take great liberties with and use gross language towards each other which would not be tolerated in any other profession. It is destructive of the social happiness of officers in a regiment, and calculated to lower the high tone of honour by which officers of the Army have ever been distinguished."

The hon Member concluded by saying he had stated the facts of the cases he had brought before the House as supplied to him, and he hoped the explanation of the Under Secretary for War might put another aspect on the matter.

MR BRODRICK said there was this difference between the two cases which had been mentioned, that he knew the facts of Mr Bruce's case, but the allegations respecting Mr Hodge's were not officially recorded at the War Office. After reading what had been stated in the Press as to Mr Hodge's case, he called for papers. He found that two years ago Mr Hodge sent in his resignation in the usual form, and the only evidence there was at the War Office of any occurrences of which Mr Hodge had to complain was a letter in which he requested the Duke of Cambridge to appoint him to a West India regiment, and stated that the circumstances under which he left the 4th Hussars were well known to the War Department. Under these circumstances it was extremely difficult for him to reply to what the hon Gentleman had said. The War Office had no official knowledge whatever of the allegations he had made.

MR LEWIS asked if the hon Gentleman denied the facts.

MR BRODRICK said he did not deny the facts, because he had no information one way or the other. The difficulty in which they stood was that the subject was two years old and apparently was never brought to the notice of the late Secretary of State; the colonel who then commanded the regiment had ceased to command it, the Commander-in-Chief had changed, and the Secretary of State had changed, and he had no means of ascertaining the facts. There was no one, he supposed, more anxious than the present Commander-in-Chief and Secretary of State were to put down bullying of any description in the Army, but he confessed he did not see how they could undertake to deal with the proceedings which took [place] two years ago and which had never been brought to the notice of the War Office.

With regard to the second case, which had occurred recently, he thought the whole story had not been told. The hon gentleman had adduced incidents to show that Mr Bruce had been hustled out of the regiment. He had gone very carefully into this case, which had also received the close attention of Lord Lansdowne, and he did not think the facts bore out what the hon Gentleman had said. Whether or not any subaltern made a communication of the character stated to Mr Bruce when he joined the regiment was not known to the War Office or to the colonel of the regiment, but what was certain was this – that throughout his career Mr Bruce seemed to be unable to understand his position with regard to non-commissioned officers and men serving under him. He joined in March, and early in his career he had to be reproved by the officer commanding the squadron to which he was attached for using violent and abusive language to non-commissioned officers and men. In July or August a most regrettable incident occurred at Bisley. Mr Bruce was shooting side by side with a colour-sergeant belonging to another cavalry regiment; the colour-sergeant had occasion to appeal to the umpire with regard to some action of Mr Bruce not in accordance with the rules, and the umpire directed Mr Bruce to conform to the rules. Mr Bruce then lost his temper, and before several officers and men used the most violent and abusive language to the colour-sergeant, the man standing at attention. The officers present, who did not belong to Mr Bruce's regiment, communicated with the colonel in command of the 4th Hussars. Mr Bruce was himself so well aware of the breach of discipline that he tendered his resignation. The case, however, was inquired into by the General Commanding the Cavalry at Aldershot, and the young officer was severely reprimanded and told that he must not suppose a second offence would be similarly overlooked. Subsequently the officer commanding the 4th Hussars had to apologise on his behalf to the officer commanding the other regiment.

He submitted that, if there was a prejudice against Mr Bruce, that was not the way for him to set himself right with his comrades. On the Boxing Night referred to it appeared that the young officer went to the sergeants' mess, but was warned by two or three senior sergeants outside the door, who implored him not to go in as it was absolutely against all the regulations and customs of the regiment. In the face of that, however, he was said to have forced his way in and remained there for some time, variously estimated at three-quarters of an hour to an hour. While there he again committed himself, for when the gas man came to turn out the gas at 11 o'clock, according to regulations, Mr Bruce set the example of breach of discipline by telling the gas man to go away, stating that he would make himself responsible. He thought these circumstances proved that Mr Bruce did not understand what was the proper position of an officer towards non-commissioned officers. ["Hear, hear!"]

Moreover, it had been brought to their knowledge that directly after Mr Bruce left the service his father, on his authority, made a statement of the gravest character affecting an officer in the regiment which, if true, might have laid that officer open to a criminal charge, and for this libel he had to pay £500. Taking all the circumstances together, he thought it was clear that Mr Bruce himself made his position in the regiment impossible, and that he was not a man who kept up that high standard of gentlemanlike feeling and conduct which was essential to a man holding his position in Her Majesty's Service. He would add that nothing was further from Lord Lansdowne's desire than that any officer should be prejudiced by want of means, or by any considerations except those which had reference to military duties.

Mr LABOUCHERE said the reason why he did not bring forward this case himself was because it appeared in the newspaper with which he was connected, and it would have been almost improper on his part to do so, because it would look like a means of advertising that newspaper. His hon Friend told him a little while before that he contemplated bringing the matter before the Committee, and he had said that he would be present. With regard to the case of Mr Bruce, the hon Gentleman did not deny that the officers of this regiment did invite him to dinner when he was gazetted to the regiment, and that they told him that as his income did not allow him to "go the pace" with them they would do their best to drive him out of the regiment.

Mr BRODRICK said he had no information on the subject, nor was it known to the colonel.

Mr LABOUCHERE said that as a matter of fact the statement had appeared in the newspaper he had referred to, and did the hon Gentleman conceive that if the accusation was not true an action for libel would not have been brought against him? He was prepared to prove before any Committee, Departmental or otherwise, that these officers did act as he had stated. Was this man the only one who had used improper language in the Army? Had not the greatest men, field-marshals and commanders-in-chief used language which would have secured their expulsion from the Army, if this officer was to be got rid of for using improper language towards a subordinate? This could not have been a reason for driving him from the Army, although if he had acted improperly he ought to have been reproved. Having coached some of the sergeants for a shooting match, he went into their mess to meet a Balaclava veteran, took part in drinking healths, and accepted an invitation to dinner. It would have been better that he should not; but it was not a case for turning the young man out of the Army. But the matter assumed a different complexion when you found that this same young man, before he joined the regiment, had dined with the officers and had been told by them that they would manage to get him turned out because he did not happen to have £500 a year.

As to the letter written by the father to the officer who was to replace his son, it was written in reference to the buying of some furniture. Undoubtedly a charge was improperly made by the father; but the son was not responsible for the father; and it was very possible he might believe the charge to be true and yet have difficulty in proving it. If it was implied that the general conduct of young Mr Bruce was ungentlemanly, what was the conduct of the officers? Could anything be conceived more ungentlemanly than for a body of men to ask a young man to dinner, and then to tell him that they would turn him out of the regiment because he did not happen to have £500 a year?

For himself he would say he did not believe a more disreputable set of young men existed in the whole army. These highly respectable young officers, these chevaliers had a horse which was called Surefoot. They entered it in a race one day and it won. The next day it was entered in a race; and what happened? Surefoot was changed for another horse which, of course, lost; and those who backed Surefoot, lost their money.

COLONEL LOCKWOOD[1] (Essex, Epping), rose to order. He said the hon Member could hardly be in full possession of the facts, and ought to be careful in the charges he made. He could assure the hon Member that the statement he had made was founded on a total misapprehension of the facts of the case.

THE CHAIRMAN said he did not quite see what this had to do with the Vote.

MR LABOUCHERE said his object was to show that the officers by whom these accusations were made had acted in still more ungentlemanly fashion. It was remarkable that in this same regiment a year and a half before, similar things should have happened in the case of Mr Hodge. So determined were the other officers to drive him out, that on two consecutive nights he was taken down half naked and dragged through a horse trough. The father went to the War Office and communicated the facts to a superior official. It was remarkable they should be told the colonel knew nothing of these proceedings. Was he to understand that this boycott was practised and the colonel knew nothing about it?

MR BRODRICK: I know nothing with reference to Mr Hodge, nor have we any record except that Mr Hodge senior, states that he called at the War Office, and gave some information.

MR LABOUCHERE said he was prepared to produce Mr Hodge senior But putting aside the case of Mr Hodge, he asked whether Mr Bruce did or did not go to dine with the officers and was told by them they would get him out of

[1] Amelius Richard Mark Lockwood (1847–1928), Conservative MP for the Epping Division of Essex 1892–1917, created 1st Baron Lambourne 1917. He was married to an aunt of Jack Milbanke.

the regiment. If this was true, their conduct was most improper, and ought to be censured in some way. Whether Mr Bruce was fit or unfit had nothing to do with the officers conspiring to get him out of the Army. Would the hon Gentleman grant a Departmental Inquiry? [Mr BRODRICK: "No!"] If it could be proved by a hundred witnesses that an officer had been ill-treated by a superior officer, he believed the War Office would discountenance Inquiry. If they were not afraid of investigation in this case, he challenged them to appoint a Departmental Committee to inquire into it and to decide whether the action of the Hussar officers had been right and proper.

COLONEL LOCKWOOD (Essex, Epping) said that he desired to point out the inconvenience of the Committee having been occupied since four o'clock that afternoon in discussing a number of details of what after all appeared to be some horseplay among young officers, which was scarcely to be regarded in a serious light, especially after the matter had already been inquired into by the Commander-in-Chief. The hon Member for Northampton had asked for the appointment of a Departmental Committee to inquire into the case of these two young men, but the fact was that such a Committee, in the person of the Adjutant General, sat permanently at the War Office, and, if parents believed that their sons had been ill-treated, all they had to do was to go before that Committee and to lay the facts before them. He was satisfied that, if there was any ground for the complaints which had been made in the present case, the officers implicated would be severely punished.

MR LEWIS said that he rose for the purpose of stating that he had brought forward all the facts of this particular case in all good faith. The charge made against the officers of this regiment alleged that they had been guilty of grave and serious offences which ought not to be lightly passed over. The demand that had been put forward by the hon Member for Northampton that a Departmental Committee should be appointed to inquire into the circumstances of the case was a very reasonable one. He had no objection to the Inquiry being a military one, provided it was a full and adequate one. The very serious allegations that had been made in this case had remained unanswered, absolutely no reply having been given to them. The circumstances that had occurred in the regiment before these two young men joined it deserved very careful examination. Those circumstances were comparatively recent and would certainly be within the recollection of those who had taken part in them. In his opinion there ought to be an adequate and independent Inquiry into the circumstances of the cases of both Mr Hodge and Mr Bruce, in order that the public mind might be reassured in regard to the conduct of the officers of the regiment in question. He did not traverse the facts which the hon Gentleman had laid before the Committee, but, at all events, there remained a residuum of facts in respect of which no explanation had been given. In these circumstances he hoped that the hon Gentleman would consent to the appointment of the Departmental Committee asked for.

A. C. Bruce-Pryce to The Times[1]

20 June [1896]   The Athenaeum
                                                     London

THE FOURTH HUSSARS – THE BRUCE CASE

Sir,

Will you allow me to give the flattest possible contradiction to the statement made by Mr Brodrick in the House of Commons last night, that the colonel of the 4th Hussars knew nothing of the dinner given to my son at the Nimrod Club? My son went down to Aldershot on the following day and saw the adjutant-captain de Moleyns and reported the whole circumstances to him. A fortnight later I took my son down and saw Colonel Brabazon with him myself, and spoke to him about the dinner, and he certainly professed no ignorance of the dinner or its details. On the contrary he said the officers were very young, and so made a quasi-apology to me for their conduct.

But I go beyond this, and I say distinctly that I believe the adjutant knew all about the dinner beforehand, for I hear that he had told a Mr Long,[2] one of the sub-lieutenants, to attend it, and that he had refused (at any rate he was not present); and, if the adjutant did know beforehand, it is difficult to believe that the colonel did not.

That he knew of it afterwards is certain, beyond doubt, for he told my son to take no orders from the officers who had been present at the dinner.

I leave it to the military authorities to decide whether it was or was not Colonel Brabazon's duty to have reported the circumstances to the general commanding and to the Horse Guards, especially after poor Hodge's case only a year previously.

The other statements as to my son's conduct are not reconcilable with his story. The account of what took place in the sergeants' mess is entirely different to his, and rests, I suppose, on the authority of S.S.M. Doggett, whose statement I have in vain asked the War Office to allow me to see, and Captain de Moleyn's last words to my son, when he saluted for the last time and refused to

---

[1] Published on June 22.
[2] Lieutenant William Edward Long (b. 1873).

shake hands, were, "Mind, Doggett has orders from orderly room to answer no communications from you or your friends."

I am afraid that I must trust my son's version in preference to Mr Brodrick's, which is, of course, the official version as laid before the War Office by Colonel Brabazon.

Your obedient servant

A. C. BRUCE PRYCE

PS I cannot believe that no record exists at the War Office of the Hodge case.

Truth, 25 *June* 1896

THE 4TH HUSSARS IN PARLIAMENT

EXTRACT

On Friday night last Parliament and the country had an opportunity of hearing the "other side" of the Bruce case, which a Service journal a few weeks back promised to lay before its readers, but which the same journal (or those who inspired it) on further consideration thought it better to keep to themselves. At the same time, the case of Mr Hodge, detailed in *Truth* of the 11 inst., was also gone into. In regard to the case of Lieutenant Hodge, Mr Brodrick took refuge in professions of complete ignorance of the whole affair, being assisted in that course by the fact that since Mr Hodge's resignation there has been a new Commander-in-Chief, a new Secretary of State for War, and a new Commanding Officer of the 4th Hussars. I confess I am somewhat of the opinion expressed by Mr Bruce-Pryce in his letter to *The Times* on Monday, that it is difficult to believe that no record of the Hodge case exists at the War Office. In this opinion I am confirmed by a letter received from Mr Hodge's father just as I am going to press. Mr Hodge, senior, says:—

I went myself to Aldershot in reply to an urgent telegram from my son at the time the brutal assaults were going on. I saw the Adjutant, Captain De Moleyns, and laid the case fully before him. The following day I went to the War Office, and stated the facts to one of the Civil Clerks (Mr Baily); and from his room, and by his advice, I went through an interview with Colonel Lane,[1] the (then) Assistant Military Secretary, and told him everything, including the names of the ringleaders.

[1] Ronald Bertram Lane (1847–1937). Promoted Major–General 1898 to command the garrison at Alexandria. Military Secretary at the War Office 1903–4. KCVO 1904, KCB 1912.

This is precise enough, and it is strange indeed if in the War Office to-day Mr Brodrick can find neither memory nor record of Mr Hodge's visit. Moreover, I have been led to believe that some hint or reproof in connection with Mr Hodge's case was conveyed to the officers who had goaded that gentleman into throwing up his commission. Mr Hodge, senior, is under this impression. Did anything of the sort take place, or did it not? If it did, it is conclusive proof that the War Office authorities *did* have official cognizance of the Hodge case. However, an opportunity is now offered to Mr Hodge, senior – his son is, unfortunately, in South Africa at the present time, as is also Mr Bruce – of laying all the facts before the Commander-in-Chief. The authorities will, therefore, shortly have full cognizance of them; and the important point now is not what they have known hitherto, but what they will do when they know the truth. . . .

To help out his case, Mr Brodrick actually referred last Friday night to the fact that, after Mr Bruce had left the Service, his father made a statement concerning an officer of the regiment for which he had to pay damages to the amount of £500. This statement Mr Brodrick asserts was made on the authority of Mr Bruce. Even if it were (and I suppose this is pure conjecture), what earthly bearing on the allegation of a conspiracy against this youth has the fact that, after he had left the regiment, his father made an unjustifiable statement about one of the other officers? The facts in regard to this libel action were these: After Mr Bruce's resignation, Mr Bruce-Pryce (his father), in the course of negotiations for the sale of his kit to his successor, wrote a letter in which he said that stories were current as to an incident in the career of one of the subalterns while at Sandhurst. It was in every way a foolish letter to write, because it implied, on the face of it, that the writer was only repeating something which he had heard, and of which he had no personal knowledge. Libel proceedings being commenced, he, of course, found that he had no means of justifying the slander to which he had referred, and he settled the case by paying damages. He was certainly unwise in allowing his resentment at his son's treatment to lead him into repeating a slander; but everybody can see for himself that the incident is totally irrelevant to any question of fact that arises in connection with the son's treatment months previously; and it is an ugly feature, in keeping with everything else done by the authorities in the case, that Mr Brodrick should have attempted to prejudice the true issue by parading this incident before the House of Commons.

Reference was also made in this debate to the facts respecting the race for the 4th Hussars Subalterns' Cup in 1895. This matter is not only interesting itself, but has some bearing on the rest of the case from the fact that the five subalterns who ran horses in the race, and whose horses were all subsequently disqualified by the Stewards for future races under National Hunt Rules, were all concerned in the dinner given to Mr Bruce at the Nimrod Club. But as the facts are complicated, I will defer further reference to them until next week.

We are now promised a personal inquiry in which the Commander-in-Chief and the Adjutant-General will "carefully consider the whole of the facts, and whether there is anything in connection with recent events in the 4th Hussars which calls for their interposition." If that inquiry is to satisfy the widespread interest of the public and the Service respecting these cases, the Commander-in-Chief and the Adjutant-General, when they have the facts before them, will have to direct their minds to the two salient features in the case – (1) the bullying of Mr Hodge out of the regiment, (2) the dinner to Mr Bruce at the Nimrod Club, and the intimation there given that if this gentleman did not make a graceful exit at once he would have to make a disgraceful one later on. The question of primary importance is whether there have not been in this regiment organised conspiracies for the purpose of getting rid of individuals who, because they could not "go the pace," or for other reasons, have not been acceptable to the bulk of the junior officers, and whether, in pursuance of such conspiracies, conduct utterly disgraceful to officers and gentlemen has not been resorted to. If Lord Wolseley will rise superior to the personal considerations and social influence which have been so vigorously used to hush up this scandal, and deal with the facts on their merits, he has here an opportunity of doing a great service to the Army, while showing that he himself is capable of acting firmly and justly when the occasion requires it.

Truth 2 *July* 1896

MORE CAVALRY RUFFIANISM

The experience of Lieutenants Hodge and Bruce in the 4th Hussars, as I have pointed out in my remarks on those cases, has an interest far beyond that of the two individuals primarily concerned. The cases are of public importance as examples of a form of misconduct which there is every reason to believe is chronic in certain cavalry regiments. Since the first reference to the Bruce case in *Truth* a dozen stories of the bullying of unpopular subs or the boycotting of men of limited means have come to hand. One of them occurred in India only a few weeks ago, and for this reason, as well as for the disgraceful character of the facts, it calls for special notice. . . .

It will be convenient here to refer to the facts in connection with the race for the 4th Hussars' Subalterns' Cup at the Aldershot Cavalry Meeting in 1895, with which I promised last week to deal. There are certain points in regard to this case which are clear, others which require further elucidation. What is certain seems to be this: a horse named Lady Margaret, which had won a race on the previous day, started a hot favourite for the Subalterns' Cup at odds on. Five horses ran, among them being a horse described as Surefoot, against whom about 6 to 1 was laid at starting. To the astonishment of everybody, and more especially the backers of Lady Margaret, Surefoot won easily, Lady Margaret running second to him. Nevertheless, the names of Lady Margaret and her owner were subsequently engraved upon the Cup as having won the race. Some months afterwards certain allegations in regard to the running were laid before the War Office, and were referred by the War Office to the Stewards of the National Hunt. After investigating the charges, the Stewards pronounced a decision by which all the horses which ran in the race were disqualified for any future races under National Hunt rules. This decision was presumably communicated to the War Office. Whether the officers concerned were called upon to furnish the War Office with any explanation is not known, but no further action of any kind has been taken in regard to the race. So much is certain. What the precise irregularity in connection with the running of Surefoot and Lady Margaret really was it is impossible to say for certain, but the story generally current, and which has already been put forward in *Truth*, is that the so-called Surefoot was not that animal at all, but another horse started under his name. I feel entitled to assume that this was really the case, because in March last the question was pointedly asked in *Truth* whether there was any ground for the current allegation that another horse had been run under the name of Surefoot, and although I invited any of the officers of the regiment to explain what the real truth of the matter was, nothing in the shape of a denial or explanation has been put forward. It seems to me incredible that if the facts as then stated had been open to correction, the regiment would not have thought it incumbent upon them to correct them. That some serious irregularity did take place is clear from the decision of the Stewards of the National Hunt, and if the irregularity consisted in running a horse not entered for the race under an assumed name, and thereby defeating a favourite on which considerable sums of money had been laid, the irregularity undoubtedly justifies up to the hilt the course which the Stewards took. The question then arises, on what ground have the War Office decided that it is unnecessary to take any official notice of these facts. By one of the apologists of the regiment it has been stated to me that the War Office came to the conclusion that the five gentlemen concerned merely erred through ignorance of the laws of racing, and not with any dishonourable intention. A statement has also reached me that on the day before the race some consultation had taken place as to the permissibility of running another horse in the place of Surefoot, either because

Surefoot was out of sorts, or for some similar reason; that it was then agreed among the officers that this should be done; and that it was generally known, at any rate among the officers, that the horse run as Surefoot was really a different animal.

I cannot say that these arguments strike me as very convincing. If there was any arrangement among the officers that another horse, and, as it turned out, a horse of much superior class, should be substituted for Surefoot, who was generally regarded as not having a chance in the race, the question at once arises, How many persons were aware of this, and what steps were taken to inform those who seem to have been freely backing Lady Margaret up to the moment when the race was started that they had to reckon with another unknown horse whose name was not on the card? Clearly everybody who was backing Lady Margaret ought to have been informed of the whole circumstances. It also seems to me that all bets previously made on Lady Margaret ought to have been off. If precautions of this kind for the protection of those who were not "in the know" were not taken, I am afraid that the plea of ignorance will not weigh as much with the general public as it seems to have done with the authorities at the War Office. To ask one to believe that five gentlemen so intimately associated with the Turf as seems to be required of subalterns in crack cavalry regiments, regularly attending race meetings, and owning, running, and backing their own horses, could be such mere babes in Turf usage as not to see the impropriety of running in this way a horse not known to be entered for the race, is a very large order on one's credulity. But even if the subalterns of the 4th Hussars are to be credited with this infantile simplicity, the rule on which justice is administered outside the Army – and, so far as I know, inside the Army also – is that *ignorantia legis neminem excusat*. It would seem that this principle was adopted by the Stewards of the National Hunt, and they would certainly have been opening the door to some very strange occurrences had they taken a different course. Why the War Office should adopt a different standard of ethics I do not precisely see.

However, all this is more or less conjecture. Nobody knows for certain what took place in regard to this race; nobody knows for certain what action the War Office really have taken. Seeing that such facts as are known have been widely circulated in the Press, and that very unfavourable inferences may reasonably be drawn from them, I think that for the credit of the Army at large, to say nothing of this particular regiment, the exact state of the case ought to be made known. The matter, as I said last week, has a special bearing upon the cases of Lieutenants Hodge and Bruce, from the fact that the five subalterns whose horses were entered for this race at Aldershot were the moving spirits in the dinner given a few weeks after at the Nimrod Club for the purpose of informing Mr Bruce that this distinguished regiment was not disposed to receive him as an officer. That the gentlemen who thus took upon themselves to veto a War Office appointment should themselves have been concerned in a transaction which has incurred the censure of the National Hunt Stewards, is, to say the least, highly interesting. Again, two of these same officers were also personally concerned in the brutal ill-treatment of Mr Hodge a few months previously. In the case more particularly of Mr Hodge certain officers of the 4th Hussars have forfeited all right to be looked upon as gentlemen, and if men are guilty of blackguardly conduct in one direction, they may be in another. Moreover, if the Commander-in-Chief and his advisers are capable of winking at what the Stewards of the National Hunt consider irregular conduct, merely out of consideration for the youth and innocence of the individuals concerned, they also may be equally capable of winking at the brutal outrage upon Mr Hodge, or the avowed conspiracy to get rid of Mr Bruce, from similar considerations. The public, and the Service at large, have a right to know two things: (1) the precise degree of misconduct which is considered compatible with the position of an "officer and gentleman" in the 4th Hussars; (2) the precise attitude of the Commander-in-Chief and the War Office towards the various allegations against these particular "officers and gentlemen." After the personal investigation by Lord Wolseley and Sir Redvers Buller, which has now been promised, it is to be hoped that full enlightenment on these points will speedily be forthcoming.

Truth 1 *October* 1896

THE 4TH HUSSARS: A WAR OFFICE WHITEWASHING

The promised "personal inquiry" by the Commander-in-Chief and the Adjutant-General into the allegations respecting the treatment of subalterns in the 4th Hussars has now been completed, so far as Mr Bruce's case is concerned, and the result is very much what has been already forecasted in these columns, and what was to be expected from the shape which the "inquiry" has taken. A letter has been addressed from the War Office to Mr Bruce's father informing him that his son was required to leave the 4th Hussars "in consequence of his own misconduct and manifest unfitness for his position." As proofs, apparently, of this assertion, it is recited that Mr Bruce was on one occasion censured for using abusive and improper language to a non-commissioned officer of another regiment; and that "upon another occasion he went into the Sergeants' Mess and drank with them after two of the senior sergeants had expostulated with him, and had endeavoured to dissuade him." Beyond these facts – that he once lost his temper at Bisley with a man of another regiment whom he considered addressed him improperly, and that he went (under circumstances of which he himself gives a different account) to spent half-an-hour in the Sergeants' Mess on Boxing Night – no evidence whatever is offered as to Mr Bruce's "misconduct and manifest unfitness for his position." These two indiscretions are, therefore, solemnly offered by the Commander-in-Chief as reasons for depriving a youngster of his commission within about ten months of his having gained it – and this in the face of the allegations of the grossest misconduct which have been made against other officers of this regiment, and which remain to the present moment unrefuted and practically unchallenged.

The War Office letter next refers to the fact that "Mr Bruce was, no doubt, unpopular with his brother officers;" but draws a distinction between this unpopularity and "the circumstances which led to his retirement," and asserts that "he had the fullest support from Regimental Authorities so far as he had a right to expect it." In my very first reference to the matter in *Truth* it was clearly said that Mr Bruce, unlike his predecessor, Mr Hodge, held his own pretty successfully against the boycott to which he was subjected. Nothing, therefore, turns upon this point; but whether this now admitted "unpopularity" had no connection with the summary process of chucking him out of the regiment on the trumpery grounds put forward by the War Office, must remain a matter of opinion, and one which will certainly not be disposed of by the official assertion that the two things were unconnected.

Next we come to the incident of the dinner at the Nimrod Club, on which the opinions of the War Office are so amazing that they call for reproduction:—

It appears that some of the subalterns of the regiment invited your son to dinner when he joined, and advised him to join another regiment upon the ground that his means were insufficient.

This is a most loose and inaccurate account of what took place. Mr Bruce was invited to dine at the Nimrod Club as soon as he had been gazetted and before he had joined. He was there informed that he was not wanted in the regiment; warned that his hosts had got rid of Mr Hodge and would get rid of him; and told that if he did not make a graceful exit at once he would make a disgraceful one later on. The question of his income was raised, but it was not made the sole ground for the objection to him. The subalterns who made this objection had previously received some sort of official reprimand for their treatment of Mr Hodge. They showed their appreciation of this by at once organising a formal demonstration of their intention to pursue a similar course towards the gentleman appointed by the War Office in Mr Hodge's place. A more grossly insubordinate act it would be difficult to imagine. What has the Commander-in-Chief to say to it? Listen:—

> Such action on the part of Mr Bruce's brother officers was certainly reprehensible, but it seems to have been really occasioned by a prejudice against him arising from reports which had reached the regiment as to his previous career, the alleged insufficiency of his means being put forward merely as a pretext.

Note the "but" in this monumental passage. The proceeding was reprehensible, "but" as the reason given was not the real reason, the War Office do not apparently consider that it calls for further notice. The wording of the passage obviously invests it with the character of an apology for this otherwise "reprehensible" conduct. As to the "reports which had reached the regiment," it will be noted that the War Office take care not to suggest that there was anything in these reports; they would stultify themselves if they did, for all necessary particulars about Mr Bruce's previous career were in the possession of the War Office when he received his commission. And how had such reports reached the regiment? Apparently through the amiable young officer who took a leading part in the Nimrod Club function, and whose bearing throughout the proceedings is described by Mr Bruce as most offensive and insulting. The simple truth of the matter is that this young gentleman and Mr Bruce had been at Sandhurst together, where no great love had been lost between them. In this way "reports" had reached the regiment, and this was the kind of schoolboy tittle-tattle which was made the ground for organising the Nimrod Club demonstration. Such is the stuff which in the name of the Commander-in-Chief and the Adjutant-General is now put forward officially in extenuation, if not justification, of the conduct of the subalterns of the regiment in formally placing their veto upon a War Office appointment. A pretty exhibition, is it not? The rest of the letter is in the same strain :—

> The pressure of these young officers did not prevail, for Mr Bruce did join, and would be in the regiment now were it not for his own misconduct. More than one of his brother officers are living comfortably in the regiment whose means are believed to be less than his were.

The drift of this is not very obvious. If the proceedings of the subalterns were wrong and insubordinate, or even "reprehensible," the fact that the man against whom they were directed declined to be intimidated does not alter their character, and the suggestion that it does, only accentuates the apologetic character of the document, as well as its argumentative weakness. The reference to the means of the other officers is of the same character. It carries on the same assumption that if Mr Bruce's income was not the real objection, the objection and the manner of formulating it were excusable; and it is obviously a feeble attempt to rebut the prevailing opinion that, in palliating a proceeding of this kind, the War Office are pandering to the organised extravagance among officers which does so much mischief in cavalry regiments. We are to understand, in conclusion, that "under all the circumstances of the case, the Secretary of State for War is of opinion that no further action is required;" and that is all. Had the Secretary of State said in so many words that in his opinion it is a right and proper thing for every appointment to a regiment to be revised and passed or rejected by a meeting of the subalterns, and that any personal views on which the decision of the subalterns may be based will be complaisantly accepted at headquarters, he would hardly have expressed the state of the case more unmistakably.

To call the process by which this impotent result has been arrived at "an inquiry," is an abuse of language. When the cases of Mr Hodge and Mr Bruce were brought up in Parliament, certain counter-statements were made in regard to the second case. There was a direct conflict of facts upon certain points, and under these circumstances, a personal inquiry by the Commander-in-Chief and the Adjutant-General was promised to the House of Commons, and further discussion of the incidents in the 4th Hussars, which had assumed an awkward character for the War Office, shelved. If an inquiry under such circumstances means anything, it means that the evidence on both sides will be heard, and that the truth, where there is a conflict of evidence, will be sifted so far as possible by the usual methods of examination and cross-examination. What attempt has been made to do this? Absolutely none. Mr Bruce has not been heard (true, he was out of the country at the time, but he is even now on his way back), and the request of his father that he might be allowed to appear and cross-examine the hostile witnesses by counsel was not even deemed worthy of an answer. The "inquiry," therefore, resolves itself into this: that the Commander-in-Chief and the Adjutant-General have simply looked over the War Office version of the facts again, and possibly taken counsel with Colonel Brabazon and the other accusing parties, and have then furbished up the original decision into the document described above, and put it forth as the result of their personal investigation of the facts. Such a proceeding is a farce in itself, and, under the circumstances which led to it, an insult to the House of Commons. It leaves everything which was in dispute before in dispute still. It leaves the public to choose between the word of Mr Bruce and the word of the non-commissioned officers on whose evidence he has been convicted, as to the true facts of the incident on Boxing-Night which led to the officer's arrest and resignation; and it deprives the reiterated references of the Secretary of State to the "misconduct" which alone led to Mr Bruce's removal from the Army of all weight and credibility. There remains behind the still more important question of the result of the simultaneous inquiry into Mr Hodge's case – by far the worse case of the two, and one which gives its whole colour and significance to the Bruce affair. At the moment of going to press I have received a copy of the War Office decision on this affair also. It appears to be, if possible, a more amazing and discreditable production than the other, but as it is too important to be dealt with off-hand, I defer any remarks upon it till my next issue.

Truth 8 October 1896

THE 4TH HUSSARS SCANDAL:

THE SCANDAL STILL MORE SCANDALOUS

The final decision of the War Office in the case of Mr Hodge, of the 4th Hussars, is a matter of even greater public importance than that in the Bruce case. . . . To begin with, no shadow of an inquiry, in any sense deserving of the name, has taken place at all. Mr Hodge, who, like Mr Bruce, was away from the country at the time when the promise of inquiry was given, has had no opportunity of appearing in support of his statements, or of testing or answering any counter-statements that might be made by the men who drove him from the Army. The performance which the Commander-in-Chief and the Adjutant-General insult the public by calling an inquiry, consists in this case, as in the other, simply in collecting from the parties impugned whatever they have to say in their own defence, and offering these statements to the aggrieved parties as the result of an impartial investigation. Such a course must necessarily place the War Office in the position of an apologist for the misconduct which is complained of; but in this instance the apologetic attitude has been carried to lengths which involve the rulers of the Army in the grossest discredit. In order to show that I do not lightly use language of this nature in speaking of men in the position of the Commander-in-Chief and his colleagues, let me first ask the reader to look at the letter in which the War Office decision has been conveyed to Mr Hodge, senior:—

24 September 1896   War Office

Sir,

I am directed by the Secretary of State for War to acknowledge the receipt of your letter of the 23rd August.

The Commander-in-Chief and the Adjutant-General have carefully inquired into the circumstances connected with your son's resignation of his commission in the 4th Hussars, and into the allegations as to his treatment by some of the Subalterns of the regiment.

Your son seems to have quitted England before or very soon after any complaint as to the reasons for his retirement from the Service was made, and it was therefore impossible to examine him, but enough has been elicited to admit of a decision being come to in the case.

Mr Hodge seems to have been constitutionally unfitted for a cavalry officer. In the school, before his ride of recruits, he persistently refused to jump the bar, he held on to the saddle, cried, and finally refused to mount his horse. He also several times reported himself sick, when the medical officer could find nothing the matter with him.

It is clear that he was bullied by his brother Subalterns, and that he was the subject of some rough usage. There seems, however, to be no foundation for the allegations that this treatment was in any way due to the supposed insufficiency of his private means. It seems to have been due to the peculiarities referred to, and to the idea, not uncommon among lads of that age, that such faults can be corrected by such treatment.

This excuse is not one which the military advisers of the Secretary of State are prepared to accept. The Commander-in-Chief is fully prepared to put down bullying, wherever the existence of such a practice is brought to light, with a strong hand, and to hold officers commanding regiments responsible for the proper treatment of all officers subordinate to them.

In this case, however, the evidence does not point to any failure of duty on the part of the senior officers of the regiment.

It appears that when these practices were brought to the notice of the Adjutant of the regiment, he first expostulated with the offenders, and subsequently reported them to the Commanding Officer, who took instant steps to stop any such conduct and severely censured the officers concerned, punishing the ringleaders.

That his action was sufficiently drastic is incidentally shown by a letter from Mr Bruce Pryce, the father of another officer in the regiment, who, writing in regard to his son's case, says that he was not ill-treated, because whenever such measures were mooted, the elder Subalterns refused to join "after what occurred in Hodge's case." (The inverted commas are his.)

Had Mr Hodge not been unfortunately unfitted for the Service, there seems no reasonable ground for doubting that the interposition of the Colonel would have been sufficient to secure him fair treatment while he remained in the regiment; the action of the regimental authorities proved both the desire and the power to do this.

The Secretary of State for War does not consider that in the circumstances any further action is necessary in the case.

I am, sir, your obedient servant

G. Lawson

... But the climax of absurdity, I had almost said impudence, is reached when Mr Bruce-Pryce is solemnly called as a witness to prove that everything the circumstances called for was done by the authorities in Mr Hodge's case. This is, indeed, a master-stroke. It is perfectly true, of course, that no personal violence was seriously attempted against Mr Bruce, just as it is true that it was dropped with Mr Hodge after the horse-trough performance. There is little doubt that it was somehow brought home to the ringleaders in the attacks on Mr Hodge's person and property that in the horse-trough business they had gone a little too far, and that if anything of that sort was repeated the consequences might be unpleasant for themselves. That much no one has ever questioned. But does that dispose of these two cases? In all seriousness, "the Secretary of State and his military advisers" seem to hold that it does. They appeal to the fact that a repetition of the horse-trough blackguardism was prevented, as proof that the regimental authorities did everything that was necessary; and they ignore everything which drove Mr Hodge into resignation. When they came to the Bruce case they shut their eyes to the plain fact that notwithstanding everything that had happened in the Hodge case, the offenders formed an insubordinate conspiracy to defeat another War Office appointment. The formal intimation conveyed to Mr Bruce of the joint determination of his brother officers to "get rid of him as they had got rid of Hodge" – as insolent a defiance of superior authority as ever was perpetrated – is deemed unworthy of notice by the Commander-in-Chief and his colleagues; and they actually point with triumph to the fact that in the Bruce case the organised opposition stopped short of personal violence, as proof of the sagacity and success with which the "strong hand" had asserted itself in the Hodge case. Whatever else the heads of the War Office may be, they are not absolute fools, and such a perverse misconstruction of plain facts as this can only be attributed to a preconceived determination not to see the truth.

The only result is that a scandal which originally only affected certain officers of one particular regiment now involves equally the Secretary of State and his military advisers – first and foremost among them the Commander-in-Chief. In estimating the responsibility of these higher functionaries, the public has to bear in mind two considerations over and above the actual facts of the case. One is that the young officer who assumed the part of ringleader in the conspiracy to eject Mr Bruce from the 4th Hussars belongs to an influential family, and that all the influence at his back has been used to prevent a re-opening of the case, as I can testify from my own experience. The other consideration is that the officer who commanded the regiment at the time of both occurrences is an old personal adherent of the present Commander-in-Chief, and a humble member of the select band conveniently known in Service circles as "the Wolseley ring." That this officer's personal representations in regard to both matters have been accepted as a convenient substitute for the "personal inquiry" into the facts promised to Parliament, it is easy to guess from a perusal of the documents in which the War Office decision is conveyed. To considerations such as these – coupled with that evil tradition of the War Office, in accordance with which no decision once pronounced is ever modified by the light of fuller knowledge, unless in deference to superior force in the shape of a hostile vote, or the prospect of a hostile vote, in the House of Commons – is to be attributed the flagrant denial of justice and the dishonourable trifling with truth witnessed in the last words of the War Office on these two cases. Nor, from the public point of view, is the refusal to do justice the most serious aspect of the matter. Far more disastrous in its consequences must be the demonstration thus afforded of the readiness of the War Office to wink at a form of misconduct peculiarly odious in itself, and destructive of the best traditions of the Service. Lord Wolseley may prate as he pleases about his determination to put down bullying wherever brought to light with a strong hand. But the fact remains that in one of the most cruel and blackguardly cases of bullying that ever have come to light, he allows the offenders to go scot free, and invokes all the arts of the special pleader as an excuse for inaction; while to this it has to be added that, in the face of a proved and officially-admitted conspiracy among the junior officers of a regiment to force two officers in succession into resignation as soon as they were appointed by the War Office – a conspiracy persisted in notwithstanding official warnings – he declines to see any conduct worthy of reprobation, but rather goes out of his way to approve the personal antipathies by which this double conspiracy was prompted. It may be true that the officers implicated were influentially connected, and that the Colonel who, in the eye of the War Office, shares the responsibility for the result is fortunate in possessing the private ear of the Commander-in-Chief. But these are details which are not likely to be taken into account by the average rowdy subaltern. Every junior officer in a fast regiment may be expected to read the result as proof that the War Office will cheerfully accept the unpopularity of an officer with his comrades as a proof of his unfitness for a commission, and a justification of combined efforts to force him into resignation; and every Service bully will find in it a declaration that, short of such extreme measures as destroying a comrade's clothes and dragging him naked through a horse-trough, he is henceforth to have a free hand in

dealing with an "unpopular" comrade. That seems to be the moral of the
Hodge and Bruce cases as the Commander-in-Chief has left them.

Truth 22 *October* 1896

EXTRACT

THE WAR OFFICE AND THE 4TH HUSSARS

... Seldom has any incident in connection with the Army produced more
general and unanimous indignation than the War Office treatment of the
recent scandals in the 4th Hussars. This I say on the evidence of letters
addressed to me from all branches of the Service, from officers of all ranks, both
on the active and retired lists, and from dozens of civilians, some personally
connected with the Army, others looks at the affair as more or less disinterested spectators. . . .

In estimating the culpability of the War Office in these two cases, it has to be
remembered that there is another charge against the same parties which has
been handled at headquarters with the same matchless partiality and levity. I
refer to the turf scandal in the same regiment. . . . Here again the War Office
decided, to use the familiar official formula, that there was no necessity for
further action, on the ground that the parties to the transaction acted in bona-
fide ignorance that they were doing anything at all irregular or questionable.
The child-like innocents, thus assumed to be unaware of what any casual
visitor to a racecourse could see for himself by the light of nature, were men
owning and running racehorses, habitually frequenting race meetings, and as
familiar with turf usage as might be taken for granted in the case of officers in a
cavalry regiment which prides itself on "going the pace." If anybody can
seriously believe that this decision on the part of the War Office was arrived at
honestly and in good faith, he must be as simple and child-like as the War
Office assumes the subalterns of the 4th Hussars to be. Beyond that he could
hardly go.

The subalterns whose horses ran on this occasion were Messrs Barnes,
Savory, Francis, Spencer Churchill, and Walker. Of these Messrs Barnes and
Savory assisted just previously in the dragging of Mr Hodge through the horse
trough. The whole five of them took part in organising the dinner at the Nimrod
Club a few weeks later, when Mr Bruce was invited to hear that he was not
wanted in their distinguished regiment. Barnes seems to have been prevented
from actually attending the dinner, but the invitation was sent to Mr Bruce in

his name. Perhaps the finest stroke of irony in the whole business is that these choice spirits actually took upon themselves – apparently on the strength of some schoolboy tittle-tattle retailed by one of their number – to decide that Mr Bruce, whom the majority of them had never seen, was not a gentleman qualified to grace so select an assemblage as the Officers' Mess of the 4th Hussars. At the very time when this precious gang met to inform Mr Bruce the 4th Hussars really could not have him, five of them (including the ringleader) were fresh from the coup which resulted in the defeat of a hot favourite by the last outsider in the betting, and two others had just been treated to what the Commander-in-Chief facetiously calls "drastic" punishment for that extremely gentlemanly and honourable exploit, the horse-troughing of Mr Hodge. And, to crown the whole thing, the War Office, in its final pronouncement on the Bruce case, solemnly takes its cue from these accomplished judges of all the proprieties, and pleads on their behalf that in vetoing Mr Bruce's appointment they were acting upon "reports" which had reached the regiment concerning that gentleman. Fancy the heroes of the Hodge outrage and the Surefoot coup shuddering over these "reports," and deciding that they really could not do violence to their feelings by associating with such an ineligible comrade! When Lord Wolseley was casting about for pretexts for washing his hands of the 4th Hussars scandals, I really wonder it did not occur to him to suggest that, in intimating to Mr Bruce that he was not quite up to 4th Hussars form, they were really paying him about as pretty a compliment as he need have desired. That, now, would have been something like an unanswerable argument.

When one looks at the utter imbecility of the War Office reasoning, the retorts to which it lays itself open at every point, and the mockery of holding out such a performance as the result of an honest and impartial attempt to arrive at the truth and do justice, one can only marvel how men like Lord Wolseley, Sir Redvers Buller, and the Marquis of Lansdowne can ever have allowed themselves to drift into such a humiliating position. But there the matter stands, and it only remains for the public to form its own conclusions and for Parliament to ratify them.

In connection with the War Office treatment of the 4th Hussars scandals, the appointment of Captain the Honourable F. R. W. de Moleyns to the command of the Police Force in Mashonaland and Matabeleland is of considerable interest. Captain de Moleyns was Adjutant of the 4th Hussars at the time of the horse-troughing of Mr Hodge and the ultimatum delivered to Mr Bruce. He had been fully informed of the treatment of Mr Hodge, if he did not know it already, by that unfortunate gentleman's father, and he was also acquainted by Mr Bruce of what happened at the Nimrod Club within a day or two of that occurrence. He has been succeeded in the Adjutancy by Mr Barnes, one of the four gallant horse-troughers of the Hodge incident, and the gentle-man in whose name the invitations were sent out to the dinner organised to inform Mr Bruce that he was not considered a fit person to join the 4th Hussars. So far, therefore, from these incidents having in any way damaged either Captain de Moleyns or Mr Barnes, it would seem that they have rather tended to advance them in the profession. I hope we shall not hear of the horse-troughing of any Mashonas or Matabele under the De Moleyns regime. There has been quite enough ruffianism in that part of the world already.

11

Pre-India

4th Hussars (4) – 1896

(*See Main Volume pp. 277–289*)

Western Press, 21 January 1896

Mr Winstone Churchill, the son of the late Lord Randolph, and the young gentleman who was recently heard of in connection with the military operations in Cuba, evidently inherits the literary and artistic tastes of his ancestors. He made a few rather expensive purchases at Messrs Sotheby's recent sale of rare books, one of those purchases being the well-known copy of Gay's *Fables*,[1] issued between 1727 and 1738, with the plates after Gravelot and others.

WSC to Lady Randolph

26 January 1896

Tring Park
Tring

My dear Mamma,

There is no hunting tomorrow – owing to the death of Mr Lambton[2] – a prominent member of the hunt – so I shall be back in time for luncheon. We have a very interesting party here. Mr & Mrs Asquith – Mr Balfour – the Recorder & Mr Underdown[3] who has great Railway interests in – Cuba several ladies – ugly and dull – Hubert Howard[4] & myself. Lord Rothschild is in excellent spirits & very interesting and full of information. Altogether – as

---

[1] The first edition, purchased on January 15 for £17.

[2] Henry Ralph Lambton (1823–1896) died at his home at Winslow, Bucks on January 24. The eldest son of William Henry Lambton, brother of 1st Earl of Durham, his estate amounted to £473,686.

[3] Emanuel Underdown (1831–1913); QC 1886; company chairman; contested Monmouth District for Conservatives in 1895.

[4] Hubert George Howard (1871–98), second son of 9th Earl of Carlisle, was a journalist. As one of *The Times* correspondents he travelled up the Nile with WSC on the Sudan campaign in 1898 and was killed at the battle of Omdurman.

you may imagine – I appreciate meeting such clever people and listening to their conversation very much indeed.

I expect that Dr Jameson and his officers will be dealt with as severely as the government know how. I have not heard a word of excuse or sympathy from anyone. Mr Balfour – particularly – seemed to think that they deserved exemplary punishment & though, as he observed, 'it is a case for the Jury' it will not be the fault of HM government if they don't get two years apiece.[1]

I suppose they are right & that these men who never considered us – or English interests – should in their turn receive no consideration from us. But all the same I venture to doubt the advisability of severity. South African opinion & South African interests ought not to be altogether disregarded & the whole of the Cape would vigorously protest against – and bitterly resent the infliction of such a punishment.

Mr Chamberlain has made an excellent speech – but one remark rather sticks in my throat. He says that the aspect of the majority of the population of the Transvaal – paying 9/10 of the taxes and having no representation is an anomaly! Rather a mild term this for a man with the history and political principles of Chamberlain. It was for such an 'anomaly' that America rebelled from England & a similar 'anomaly' was the prime cause of the French Revolution. However – he has to measure his words. We discussed Cuba also – Howard trying to lure Mr Balfour into recognising the insurgents – but he declined to be caught.

What astonished me in all these discussions of South African affairs is the way people disregard Rhodes. It seems to me to be reckoning without your host. You know what Papa thought of him. I will wager he will turn out to be a factor to be counted on.

Well – *à demain*.

With best love, Ever your loving son
WINSTON

Sir H. Drummond Wolff to WSC

17 February 1896   Madrid

My dear Winston,

Please read the enclosed which is attributed to you. I should be very glad if you could avoid saying things unpalatable to the Spaniards; having obtained

---

[1] Following his abortive raid on the Witwatersrand, Dr Jameson was on January 8 handed over by President Kruger to the British authorities to be dealt with for a breach of the neutrality laws. He and his officers sailed for England on January 21. The trial took place in July, all six defendants being found guilty. Dr Jameson was sentenced to fifteen months' imprisonment.

the letters on your behalf which secured your good treatment I am re-
proached for the unfavourable commentaries you make.

I am sure you will be careful as this kind of thing places me here in a painful
dilemma.

What are you about & where is your mother.

You affec
H. DRUMMOND WOLFF

Sir H. Drummond Wolff to WSC

24 February 1896   Madrid

My dear Winston,

Many thanks for your letter & telegram. I have shown them in the proper
quarters but they were no longer required as your article in the *Saturday
Review* [on February 15] has been translated in all the papers & has created
much enthusiasm.

I am told it has been much praised in the *Temps* and other French papers.
Macte nova virtute, puer.[1]

Ever yours sincerely
H. DRUMMOND WOLFF

WSC to Bourke Cockran
(Cockran Papers)

29 February [1896]   Bachelors' Club

My dear Cockran,

You must think me a very faithless and unreliable person – for I never – as I
promised, came to see you before your departure from these shores. I suppose
you are now comfortably installed in that most convenient & commodious of
flats – at the Bolkenhayn. Thither – at any rate I direct this letter.

I am much interested in the action of the United States as respecting
Cuban belligerency. I enclose you a copy of an article of mine in the *Saturday
Review* which will show you the line I think is sensible.

I should very much like to know what your opinion is upon the whole
question and particularly as regards the recent & future actions of the Senate.
Please if you can find the time write me a letter – as I want so much to keep
myself really well informed on the whole subject. Of course I won't think of
giving you away.

[1] From Virgil's *Aeneid*.

I hope the United States will not force Spain to give up Cuba – unless you are prepared to accept responsibility for the results of such action. If the States care to take Cuba – though this would be very hard on Spain – it would be the best and most expedient course for both the island and the world in general. But I hold it a monstrous thing if you are going to merely procure the establishment of another South American Republic – which however degraded and irresponsible is to be backed in its action by the American people – without their maintaining any sort of control over its behaviour.

I do hope that you will not be in agreement with those wild and I must say – most irresponsible people who talk of Spain as "beyond the pale" etc. etc. Do write and tell me what you do think.

I have seen a lot lately of Lord Dunraven. He is quite unrepentant – and maintains all his charges – though in justice to him I must say that he always declares that he is convinced that none of the owners – or members of the Yacht Club were in any way cognisant of the alleged fraud. The whole matter is most unfortunate – and has probably caused much bad blood – over much. I hope we have now heard the last of it. Speaking generally – I think international contests should be avoided. There is rivalry enough – without furthering it into actual expression.

I commend rather a good book to your notice *The Red Badge of Courage*[1] a story of the Civil War. Believe me it is worth reading.

Now *au revoir* – do please be pacific and don't go dragging the 4th Hussars over to Canada in an insane and criminal struggle.

Yours ever
WINSTON S. CHURCHILL

Joseph Chamberlain to Lady Randolph

3 March 1896   40 Prince's Gardens

Dear Lady Randolph,

I am much obliged to you for sending me the copy of your son's article on the situation in Cuba. It is the best short account I have seen of the problems with which the Spaniards have to deal, & agrees with my own conclusions derived from imformants in the United States & in Spain.

It is evident that Mr Winston kept his eyes open.

I return the paper with many thanks.

Yours very truly
J. CHAMBERLAIN

[1] By Stephen Crane (1871–1900), first published in America 1893, and in England 1895.

Jack Milbanke to WSC

Sunday 22 March [1896]   Isthmian Club
                                                         Piccadilly

Dear Winston,

If you have nothing better to do on Wednesday night the 25th would you care to dine with me here and go on to the play afterwards. I will get seats for the Joan of Arc Burlesque as I hear it is very good. I am afraid it won't be a very good dinner but I have not yet got into any good clubs. Please answer this as soon as possible as I must know about getting seats etc.

                                         Believe me Yours ever
                                         JACK MILBANKE

PS If you come we had better dine at 7.15.

WSC to Lady Randolph

[Easter Sunday] 5 April [1896]   Barleythorpe
                                                        Oakham

My dear Mamma,

I daresay you have been looking somewhat impatiently for a letter. I found it impossible to get an extra day's leave, so that Monte Carlo was out of the question. I am staying here till this afternoon when I go back to Aldershot. News – there is none. The papers seem full of wars and rumours of wars – and I hear that Sir Redvers Buller is to take a large expedition from England in the autumn and make the advance on Khartoum – but till then I fear there will be nothing.

Poor old Mr Alfred Montgomery[1] died yesterday. Very sad indeed. We have here a cheery party, though more arrive today for the races. Madame de Brienen & a pretty daughter – Sir Francis Grenfell's wife[2] – General Thesiger[3] – an agreeable old man – and a young fellow named Paget[4] in the Rifles who is quartered at Aldershot and plays polo well.

I will write again very soon. Best love to you & Jack.

                                         Your loving son
                                         WINSTON S. CHURCHILL

[1] Alfred Montgomery (1815–1896), son of Sir Henry Conyngham Montgomery, 1st Baronet. Formerly a Commissioner of Inland Revenue. Married 1844 Fanny, daughter of 1st Baron Leconfield. One of his daughters became the Marchioness of Queensberry.

[2] Evelyn (d. 1899), daughter of General Robert Blucher Wood and 1st wife of General Sir Francis Wallace Grenfell.

[3] Charles Thesiger (1831–1903), 2nd son of 1st Baron Chelmsford; inspector-general of cavalry in Ireland; retired 1895.

[4] George Paget (1871–1900), elder son of Sir (George) Ernest Paget, 1st Bart; Captain in the Rifle Brigade; killed in action in the Boer War.

12 April [1896]   The Deepdene
                                                                  Dorking

My dear Cockran,

I read with great interest both your letter and speech. With regard to the
former – in which you were good enough to give me your views upon the
Cuban question – I think that your principles are indisputable & unassailable.
Undoubtedly in time all communities will learn "that prosperity is the result
of order & that misery is the production of shiftlessness and strife" and if the
Cubans ever obtained their independence I am sure that ultimately they
would establish a settled government, and that order would be evolved from
chaos. But what is a short time in the history of a people is a long time in the
life of a human being. To a serene Providence a couple of generations of
trouble and distress may seem an insignificant thing – provided that during that
time the community is moving in the direction of a good final result. Earthly
Governments however are unable to approach questions from the same standpoint. Which brings me to the conclusion that the duty of governments is to
be first of all practical. I am for makeshifts and expediency. I would like to
make the people who live on this world at the same time as I do better fed
and happier generally. If incidentally I benefit posterity – so much the better
– but I would not sacrifice my own generation to a principle – however high
or a truth however great. This will explain to you the state of mind which
induced me to write the articles in the *Saturday Review*, which I will send you
as soon as I go back to London.

Now to turn to your speech. It is one of the finest I have ever read. You are
indeed an orator. And of all the gifts there is none so rare or so precious as that.
Of course – my dear Cockran – you will understand that we approach the
subject from different points of view and that your views on Ireland could
never coincide with mine. You invited me in your letter to comment on the
opinions you then expressed. I do so without reserve. I consider it unjust
to arraign the deeds of earlier times before modern tribunals & to judge by
modern standards. No one denies – no one has ever attempted to deny – that
England has treated Ireland disgracefully in the past. Those were hard
times: – death was the punishment of every crime; & the treatment of the
Irish by the stronger power was in harmony with the treatment of the French
peasantry – the Russian serfs & the Huguenots. Mercy and economics were
alike unknown. Wherefore I think it unfair to depict the English government
of today as part and parcel of Mountjoy's ravages and Cromwell's massacres.

Again you allude to the rejection of the demand for the release of the
dynamite prisoners. I had the opportunity of talking to Mr Asquith on this

subject and I said that I would have released them in deference to the opinion of the Irish people – like Barabbas. He said "We are all agreed that in fifteen months they will be released in the ordinary course of reconsidering sentences." In other words the problem is nearly solved. So it is with the question of Home Rule. There is no tyranny in Ireland now. The Irish peasant is as free and as well represented as the English labourer. Everything that can be done to alleviate distress and heal the wounds of the past is done – and done in spite of rhetorical attempts to keep them open. Your contention that government from a "foreign" city cannot produce prosperity – is not borne out by other instances. Take for example – Scotland – whose population and wealth have increased manifold since the Act of Union.

Six years of firm, generous, government in Ireland will create a material prosperity which will counteract the efforts which able and brilliant men – like yourself – make to keep the country up to the proper standard of indignation. Not for twenty years could a Home Rule bill pass the English people – so sick and tired are they of the subject – and by that time the necessity for one will have passed away. Home Rule may not be dead but only sleeping – but it will awake like Rip Van Winkle to a world of new ideas. The problems & the burning questions of today will be solved and Home Rule for Ireland as likely as not will be merged in a wider measure of Imperial Federation.

Nor will the civilised world compel us as you suggest to a prompt settlement. How could they with justice. Does Russia give up Poland? Does Germany surrender Alsace and Lorraine? Does Austria give up Hungary. Does Turkey release Armenia – or Spain grant autonomy to Cuba? One more instance shd the United States accede to the demand for Confederate independence? And one more argument. You may approve of Home Rule on principle. But I defy you to produce a workable measure of it. He will be a bold man who will rush in where Mr Glasdtone failed.

Finally, let me say that when I read your speech I thought that Ireland had not suffered in vain – since her woes have provided a subject for your eloquence. Do write to me again. I am in hopes of going to Egypt in the autumn and in the meanwhile Polo fills my mind and time. Aunt Leonie is very well and flourishing – but my mother has been rather ill and is gone to Monte Carlo. Barnes begs me to send you messages from him.

Yours ever
WINSTON S. CHURCHILL

W. Bourke Cockran to WSC

27 April 1896   763 Fifth Avenue

My dear Winston,

I was delighted to hear from you and especially gratified by your frank and sensible criticism of my speech. I hope to sail for Europe next week but as I will not be able to stay more than a day or two in London I do not think it probable that I will see you. I write therefore mainly to explain my purpose in devoting some part of my address to the oppressive legislation from which Irish industry has long suffered. I did not dwell on this subject merely to inflame passions or to awaken resentments as you suppose. I have long since concluded that revenge is the most expensive luxury known to man. Any one who pursues vengeance can generally attain it, but it is all that he is ever likely to accomplish. What is true of individuals is true of nations, and any man who would counsel or invite a people to seek revenge for its own sake is utterly unworthy of confidence. My object in reciting the story of Irish sufferings was merely to account for the existing economic condition of Ireland. I pointed out at some length that capital is essential to production and that the industrial capacity of a country is proportioned to the volume of its capital. Ireland is today without manfacturing industries simply because she has been prevented from accummulating capital by the operation of those laws which you condemn so freely and so generously. If we meet on the other side I will go into this subject more freely and I am sure I will be able to convince you that in recalling that melancholy history I was actuated by a better purpose than a mere desire to inflame the anger of an audience. I can say with perfect sincerity that I have never in my life delivered any address in which I consciously used a sentence for any other purpose than to express the truth as I understood it.

And now let me congratulate you on the good temper, the acuteness and excellent judgement which pervaded your whole letter. I do not think you and I are very far apart in our conviction. We differ more in phrases than in princple. If your idea of Imperial Federation be the solution of the Irish question nobody will rejoice at it more than the men who have struggled for the same result under the name of Home Rule. But whatever may be the ultimate outcome of the Irish agitation I hope you will allow me to assume the privilege of my years and advise you strongly to take up the study of sociology and political economy. These two subjects are more closely interwoven than most people ever believe. They are considered dry and uninteresting by those who are not familiar with them, but they are the two branches of inquiry which in the future will bear the most important fruits to the human family.

With your remarkable talent for lucid and attractive expression you would be able to make great use of the information to be acquired by study of these branches. Indeed I firmly believe you would take a commanding position in public life at the first opportunity which arose, and I have always felt that true capacity either makes or finds its opportunity. Do not my dear Winston feel that I am troubling you with this long letter merely to air my views. I was so profoundly impressed with the vigor of your language, and the breadth of your views as I read your criticisms of my speech that I conceived a very high opinion of your future career, and what I have said here is largely based on my own experience. I give it to you for what it is worth, firmly convinced that your own judgement may be trusted to utilise it if it be of any value or to reject it if inapplicable to your plans or your surroundings.

Very sincerely yours
W. BOURKE COCKRAN

WSC to Lady Randolph

1 May 1896   35a Great Cumberland Place

My dearest Mamma,

Many thanks for your letter. I availed myself of the valuable suggestions contained therein and sent a cheque dated May 12. I do trust that you will be able to let me have my allowance by then as if it is late – the cheque will very likely be dishonoured. Sure to be in fact.

I hear quite disquieting reports of Jack from all sides. Aunt Leonie – Sidney Greville[1] – Aunt Clara and others give me detailes of his illness. Poor chap – he has indeed been unlucky. I do hope he will find some competent doctor in Paris. His blood must have been in an awfully bad condition & it is very fortunate it was productive of no worse things.

I dined the night before last with Mrs Adair. Such an interesting party. Mr Chamberlain – Lord Wolseley. Mr Chaplin[2] – Lord James [of Hereford], Sir Francis Jeune and in fact all the powers that be. Chamberlain was very nice to me and I had quite a long talk with him on South Africa.

[1] Sidney Robert Greville (1866–1927). Private Secretary to Lord Salisbury 1888–92. 1896–8; to Prince of Wales 1898–1901; Groom-in-Waiting to King Edward VII 1901–10, CB 1899; KCVO 1912.

[2] Henry Chaplin (1841–1923), President of the Local Government Board 1895–1900; earlier Chancellor of the Duchy of Lancaster 1885 and President of the Board of Agriculture 1889–92. Created Viscount 1916. A keen sportsman, famed for his prowess in the hunting field: nicknamed the Squire.

Tonight I am dining with Lord James, who has the Duke of Devonshire and a lot of "notables" so I hope to be quite "*au fait*".[1]

An extraordinary impression has been produced in this country by the publication of the cipher telegrams – which passed between Rhodes, Harris, Phillips & Jameson prior to the Raid.[2] Cecil Rhodes' complicity is proved beyond dispute. It appears to me that the conspirators acted like a bad hunter. They started at their ditch [at] 40,000 miles an hour & then pulled up short on the edge – with the result that they found themselves carried forward by their own momentum and in despair made a bound – and fell – of course.

Up till a few days before the raid everything was going well, then came frantic wires from Johannesburg and Cecil R. to stop "flotation" & pull up. But things had gone too far and after an unsuccessful effort to stop they had after all to make the attempt, beaten before they began.

The hunter simile is rather long winded – but it applies very accurately.

I am making extraordinary progress at Polo – but I want very much to buy another pony. I wish you would lend me £200 as I could then buy a really first class animal which would always fetch his price. When we sell the ponies at the end of August he would fetch at least 170 and the odd thirty I would make good out of the money obtained by selling the others. You see I am so near now to the regimental team that it might just make the difference and I don't think that there would be a difference of £20 between buying and selling. Cox would lend me the money if you would make yourself responsible – at 5% – with pleasure. Do please try and think over it. It is not a question of spending the money – but of putting it into stock – an investment in fact – which though not profitable would produce much pleasure.

Well goodbye my darling Mamma – our finance is indeed involved!! If I had not been so foolish as to pay a lot of bills I should have the money now.

Ever Your loving son
WINSTON S. CHURCHILL

[1] At the time Chamberlain was Colonial Secretary; Lord Wolseley, Commander in Chief of the British Army; Henry Chaplin, President of the Local Government Board; Lord James of Hereford, Chancellor of the Duchy of Lancaster; Sir Francis Jeune (1843–1905), created Baron St Helier in 1905, President of Probate Division and Judge Advocate General; while the 8th Duke of Devonshire was Lord President of the Council.

[2] On April 29 the Republican government in Pretoria published a set of cipher telegrams between Rhodes's Chartered Company (of which Rutherfoord Harris was secretary) and the Reform Committee in Johannesburg (one of whose leaders was Lionel Phillips). The Boers claimed to have deciphered the correspondence by means of a key found in Dr Jameson's baggage.

Henry Norman[1] to WSC

21 June 1896   The *Daily Chronicle*
                                                     12 Salisbury Square
                                                        Fleet Street
                                                       London E.C.

Dear Mr Churchill,

I have been talking over your proposal with the Editor, and he agrees with me that it would not be possible, under the circumstances I explained to you when I first mentioned the matter, for us to ask you to proceed to Crete as our Special Correspondent. At the same time, however, if you decide to go, we should be very glad to avail ourselves of your assistance. If you should visit the points of the island which are now attracting such prominent attention, and should find the material for, say, five letters of about a column and a half each, we should be willing to pay you for such Correspondence at the rate of ten guineas a letter.

I may add that if you were able to send us any news of great importance, or to secure any facts or descriptions of sensational interest, we should be very ready to increase these terms considerably.

Will you kindly let me know if under these circumstances you decide to go.

                                                     Yours faithfully
                                                     HENRY NORMAN

Captain Philip Green to Pandeli Ralli[2]

[June 1896]   Lyngdal
                                                        Mandal
                                                     Christiansand
                                                       Norway

My dear Ralli,

I know you are ever ready to do a kind action – Winston Churchill wants to get out to the Sudan and if possible to be a galopper to Kitchener. I know how difficult this probably is, but a line from you to your great friend might be of inestimable service.

He proposes to start very soon and is in the 4th Hussars at Hounslow. I think you knew Randolph and would help his son if you could.

We are out here fishing but there is no sport as yet for want of rain.

                                                     Ever yours
                                                     PHILIP GREEN

[1] See footnote on page 880.
[2] Pandeli Ralli (1845–1928), a wealthy bachelor member of the Anglo-Greek community in London; Liberal MP 1875–85.

Colonel Sir R. B. Lane to Lady Randolph

11 August 1896   Commander-in-Chief

Dear Lady Randolph Churchill

I have been desired by Lord Wolseley to write to you, in answer to your letter to him, on the subject of your son in the 4th Hussars being granted leave to proceed to S. Africa.

The only chance he has of being considered for such leave is for him to get the Colonel of his Regt to recommend & forward an application to that effect. Even should this be done I am afraid there will be great difficulties in such leave being granted & that his chance of getting it is not good.

Believe me Yrs truly
R. B. LANE

Lord Lansdowne to Lady Randolph

3 July 1896   War Office

Dear Lady Randolph,

I find that the situation is as I endeavoured to describe it to you yesty.

The management of the operations in S. Africa is under Sir F. Carrington,[1] & we are not in any way directing them, or interfering with the composition of his staff – I fear therefore that we can do nothing to find employment for Winston and I hope *you* may not be too much disappointed.

May I, as a friend, add this? I am not quite sure that in view of the enquiry which has been promised into the charges made recently against some of the officers of the 4th Hussars, it would be wise on Winston's part to leave England at this moment. There are plenty of ill natured people about, and it is just conceivable that an attempt might be made to misrepresent his action.

Pray forgive me for this suggestion & believe me dear Lady Randolph

Yours sincerely
LANSDOWNE

[1] Maj-General Sir Frederick Carrington (1844–1913), after taking part in several military operations in South Africa, was charged with suppressing the serious native uprising which had broken out in Matabeleland (now part of Rhodesia) in March. It was in this campaign that Colonel Robert Baden-Powell's aptitude for tracking down the enemy by observation and deduction first attracted attention.

A. Fitzgerald Powell to WSC

Primrose League
Randolph Churchill
Habitation No 311
7 Connaught Street
Hyde Park

14 July 1896

Dear Sir,

Having just learned your address from Mr Fardell I hasten to inform you that you have been unanimously elected as Member of this Habitation. I may mention that your election has given great pleasure and satisfaction to all the members of this Habitation, who trust that at no distant date you may be enabled to be present at some of their functions.

I am, yours faithfully,
A. FITZGERALD POWELL
Hon Sec & Treasurer

WSC to Lady Randolph

4 August 1896 Hounslow

My darling Mamma,

I got your letter this morning – but it was not the first tidings I had heard of you at Cowes. "Bino" Stracey[1] told me he had seen you there in great form – all over the place in a launch. What fun you must be having! I am trying to get away on Thursday as I am very bored here – but there is lots to do and I have to do my share and pay back – what I owe in the way of duties – for Goodwood week. I cannot be certain; – but in any case expect me Friday in lots of time for dinner.

I daresay you have read in the papers that the 9th Lancers are to go to Durban on the 25th inst. If they are to be sent straight to Rhodesia[2] they will have to take two or three extra subaltern officers – who will be attached from cavalry regiments. I have applied to their colonel to take me should such a contingency arise – and Bill Beresford has wired to him on my behalf. Consequently it is within the bounds of possibility that I may get out after all – and in the best way too – with an English cavalry regt. This we will talk over on

[1] Sir Edward Stracey (1871–1949), 7th Baronet of Rackheath Park, Norfolk; hon Major Household Cavalry.

[2] The desultory fighting ended on August 20 when Rhodes, in characteristic fashion, walked unarmed into the Matabele stronghold in the Matopo Hills and induced the warriors to lay down their arms.

Friday – but my dear Mamma you cannot think how I would like to sail in a few days to scenes of adventure and excitement – to places where I could gain experience and derive advantage – rather than to the tedious land of India – where I shall be equally out of the pleasures of peace and the chances of war.

The future is to me utterly unattractive. I look upon going to India with this unfortunate regiment – (which I now feel so attached to that I cannot leave it for another) – as useless and unprofitable exile.

When I speculate upon what might be and consider that I am letting the golden opportunity go by I feel that I am guilty of an indolent folly that I shall regret all my life. A few months in South Africa would earn me the S.A. medal and in all probability the [British South Africa] company's Star. Thence hot foot to Egypt – to return with two more decorations in a year or two – and beat my sword into an iron despatch box. Both are within the bounds of possibility and yet here I am out of of both. I cannot believe that with all the influential friends you possess and all those who would do something for me for my father's sake —— that I could not be allowed to go – were those influences properly exerted.

It is useless to preach the gospel of patience to me. Others as young are making the running now and what chance have I of ever catching up. I put it down here – definitely on paper – that you really ought to leave no stone unturned to help me at such a period. Years may pass before such chances occur again. It is a little thing for you to ask and a smaller thing for those in authority to grant – but it means so much to me.

Three months leave is what I want & you could get it for me. If I can't get this – perhaps I may be able to go with the 9th – but that might only end in police duty in Natal.

You cant realise how furiously intolerable this life is to me when so much is going on a month away from here.

As to the other matters of your letter. I will not lengthen this disconnected jargon by discussing them now. Hoping to see you Thursday.

Your ever loving son
WINSTON S.C.

Lord William Beresford to WSC

Derreen

30 August [1896] Kenmare
Co Kerry

My dear Winston,

Here I am with the Lansdownes at the end of the world and seventeen miles from a Railway or a Telegraph station so cannot communicate by wire as I should wish. I have only just realised that you probably sail for India on the 4th or 5th of Sept and if so I fear I shall not see you again before you actually start so would you kindly drop me a line – *if by return* addressed to me to Curraghome – Portlaw – Co Waterford, where I remain till Thursday morning, but if your answer is *not* written by return then *telegraph* to me at that address, saying what you want done with your pony Lily. How when and where you wish it sent to India and to what port. Also remember if you have no other plan you cannot do better than employ *Henry Ryder*, my old trainer who now lives at Bangalore and has a small training establishment there, he will put you up to the Indian ropes, & is thoroughly honest & straightforward. Hoping you will have the best of good times and wishing you all possible luck and hoping you will remember there is always a warm welcome awaiting you at the Deepdene whenever you return, believe me yours very sincerely

- BILL BERESFORD

I will write to Ryder and tell him to call upon you as soon as you arrive.
I wired to Aunt Lily to consult you about the pony. I told you what I think it is worth taking out – price is not ruinous.

WSC to Bourke Cockran
(*Cockran Papers*)

31 August [1896]

My dear Bourke,

Very many thanks for the report of your great speech, which you so kindly sent me. I congratulate you most heartily upon what was not only a rhetorical triumph but also a moral victory. I hope that in advancing the cause of honesty and probity you have also brought yourself back to power and place. Fifteen thousand people forms a larger concourse than ever collects in England to hear political speeches. You know how keenly I regret that I was not there to see – still more to hear.

The question at issue is one about which I know very little & hence my views are proportionately strong. It seems to me however that no sweeping changes in currency are possible – far less expedient. Even if you prove to me that our present system is radically bad – my opinion is unaltered. A man suffering from dyspepsia might pray for fresh intestines but he would fare badly while the alteration was being effected. How much more does this apply to changes which affect the chief – the most delicate & sensitive – organs which produce & on which depends our wealth – Capital, Credit and Commerce. It may be that some reform & readjustment are necessary in the currency of the world, but those who endeavour to deal with so complicated and vital a subject should approach it tentatively – feeling their way with caution. What Bryan has done is like an inebriate regulating a chronometer with a crowbar. It is monstrous that such subjects should be made the bagatelle of political parties and that issues so vast should be handed over to excited & flushed extremists. At least so it strikes me.

I sail for India the 11th September and my address will be 4th Hussars Bangalore. Thither, if you will, you had better write. I enclose you an article of mine on Cuba continued – for which perhaps even amid the struggles for the presidency – you may find a moment.

I hope we shall meet again soon – if possible within a year. I may return to England via Japan after a little of India so perhaps I shall once more eat oysters and hominy with you in New York. Please send me press cuttings of your speeches.

Yours very sincerely
WINSTON S. CHURCHILL

P.S. I am sending by this mail – 2 vols. of my fathers speeches. They will I am sure be interesting to you.

WSC

WSC to Frances, Duchess of Marlborough

[Postmark 8 September 1896]   Bachelors' Club
                                               Hamilton Place

My dear Grandmamma,

I sail on Thursday with my regiment for India. We are going to Bangalore – a station in the Madras Presidency – and one which is usually considered an agreeable place to soldier in. I wish I could have seen you to wish you goodbye – but as you are out of town – I must content myself with a letter. I fear I shall not be back in England for at least 3 years as it is very hard to get leave – long enough to allow a voyage home except at the end of that period. From the bottom of my heart I wish you health & happiness and I sincerely hope you will experience all good fortune.

I will write to you some letters descriptive of my life out there and let you know how things are going with me. Once more – my dear grandmamma – let me wish you prosperity – and – thanking you for your kindness to me – remain

Your loving grandson
WINSTON S. CHURCHILL